ANTONIO LATINI'S "THE MODERN STEWARD, OR THE ART OF PREPARING BANQUETS WELL"

Portrait of Antonio Latini, from Volume I
of *Lo Scalco alla Moderna* (Naples, 1692).

FOUNDATIONS

This series responds to the pressing need for new primary texts on the premodern world. The series fits Arc's academic mission to work with scholars of the past in expanding our collective horizons. This source of accessible new texts will refresh research resources, engage students, and support the use of innovative approaches to teaching. The series takes a flexible, case-by-case approach to publishing. The works may be original language editions, facing-page (with English translation) editions, or translations. Each edition includes a contextual introduction and explanatory notes to help the reader situate the text.

Advisory Board
Robert E. Bjork, *Arizona State University*
Alessandra Bucossi, *Università Ca' Foscari, Venezia*
Chris Jones, *University of Canterbury / Te Whare Wānanga o Waitaha*
Sharon Kinoshita, *University of California, Santa Cruz*
Matthew Cheung Salisbury, *University of Oxford*

ANTONIO LATINI'S
"THE MODERN STEWARD, OR THE ART OF PREPARING BANQUETS WELL"

A COMPLETE ENGLISH TRANSLATION

Edited and translated by
TOMMASO ASTARITA

British Library Cataloguing in Publication Data

A catalogue record for this book is available from the British Library.

© 2019, Arc Humanities Press, Leeds

ISBN (print): 9781641893343
e-ISBN (PDF): 9781641893350

www.arc-humanities.org

Printed and bound by CPI Group (UK) Ltd, Croydon, CR0 4YY

CONTENTS

THE MODERN STEWARD, OR THE ART
OF PREPARING BANQUETS WELL
PART THE FIRST

PART THE SECOND

LIST OF ILLUSTRATIONS

All images are from the original edition of *Lo Scalco alla Moderna*,
courtesy of the Biblioteca della Società Napoletana di Storia Patria.

ACKNOWLEDGEMENTS

I AM INDEBTED to Georgetown University for a sabbatical semester during which I completed much of this project. I am very grateful to Simon Forde and Anna Henderson, and to Arc Humanities Press, for their kind and effective support for and assistance with this project. I am grateful to Ken Albala for advice and support.

The late John Marino supported my initial work on Latini with his usual cheerful encouragement, as well as with wise advice and practical suggestions. I miss John, and will always remember him and feel grateful that I knew him.

My deep gratitude goes to Gillian Riley and Ivan Day, for making me feel welcome in the community of food mavens and historians, and for cheerfully—and enlighteningly—answering my many queries about both translation and cooking issues. I hope we get to meet soon, and to share a good meal.

Finally, my heartfelt thanks to Lawrence Hyman, who by now has lived with Latini for many years, always patiently, and indeed without ever slacking in his encouragement.

INTRODUCTION

IN 2014, I published a book containing translated excerpts from an Italian text titled *Lo scalco alla moderna* (*The Modern Steward*), first published in two quarto volumes in Naples in 1692–1694.[1] This 2014 book contains about one quarter of *Lo Scalco's* text, accompanied by my own commentary, context, and notes. The present volume offers the first complete translation of *Lo Scalco* into English (or any other language). I refer interested readers to my earlier book for more extensive discussion of some of the topics covered in this introduction.

Lo Scalco's author, Antonio Latini (1642–1696), was an experienced cook, steward, and banquet manager who worked in Rome and central Italy, and then served some of the leading families and individuals in Naples, at the time Italy's largest city and the capital of its largest state. His book is, in large part, what we may call a cookbook, but in fact includes much more (and something less) than we would expect to find today in a cookbook. Its title, in its full Baroque richness, is *The Modern Steward, or the Art of Preparing Banquets Well, with the Choicest Rules of Stewardship, Taught and Applied to Benefit Professionals, and Other Scholars* (*Lo scalco alla moderna, overo l'arte di ben disporre li conviti, con le regole più scelte di scalcheria, insegnate e poste in prattica a beneficio de' professori, ed altri studiosi*). It has never been published or translated since its original appearance in 1692–1694, except for two modern facsimile Italian limited editions.[2]

Latini's work has long been known to historians of cooking primarily because it is the first publication to include recipes that use tomatoes.[3] But the book has a broader claim

---

1 Tommaso Astarita, *The Italian Baroque Table: Cooking and Entertaining from the Golden Age of Naples* (Tempe: Arizona Center for Medieval and Renaissance Studies, 2014).

2 The facsimile editions are Antonio Latini, *Lo scalco alla moderna*, 2 vols. (facsimile, Lodi: Bibliotheca Culinaria, and Milan: Appunti di Gastronomia, 1993); and Latini, *Lo scalco alla moderna*, 2 vols. plus a volume of commentary (facsimile, Florence: Polistampa, 2004); a collection of a few of Latini's recipes appears in Claudio Novelli, ed., *Né pomodoro né pasta* (Naples: Grimaldi, 2003).

3 See for instance Rudolf Grewe, "The Arrival of the Tomato in Spain and Italy: Early Recipes," *The Journal of Gastronomy* 3 (1987): 67–82; Alan Davidson, "Europeans' Wary Encounters with Tomatoes, Potatoes, and Other New World Foods," in *Chilies to Chocolate: Food the Americas Gave the World*, ed. Nelson Foster and Linda S. Cordell (Tucson: University of Arizona Press, 1992), 1–14; Silvano Serventi and Françoise Sabban, *La pasta, storia e cultura di un cibo universale* (Bari: Laterza, 2000), 337; the entries for "Latini" and "tomato" in Gillian Riley, *The Oxford Companion to Italian Food* (Oxford: Oxford University Press, 2007); and David Gentilcore, *Pomodoro! A History of the Tomato in Italy* (New York: Columbia University Press, 2010), 50–52, and "The Impact of New World Plants, 1500–1800: The Americas in Italy," in *The New World in Early Modern Italy, 1492–1750*, ed. Elizabeth Horodowich and Lia Markey (Cambridge: Cambridge University Press, 2017), 190–206; the first Spanish book to include recipes with tomatoes appeared in 1745, though there is evidence that tomatoes were eaten in Spain as early as the early seventeenth century (see Juan Altamiras, *New Art of Cookery. A Spanish Friar's Kitchen Notebook*, ed. Vicky Hayward (London: Rowman and Littlefield, 2017), especially 126–27). Tomatoes were originally regarded as ornamental plants and they entered cooking, especially elite cooking, only slowly: in his 1560s compendium of vegetables, Costanzo Felici describes the tomato as "more beautiful than good" (*Scritti naturalistici: Dell'insalata* (Urbino: Quattroventi, 1986), 90); see also Astarita, *Italian Baroque Table*, 127–32,

on our attention. Latini's work can help us see the transition from the earlier courtly Italian cooking style to the new French style that came to dominate European cooking during the eighteenth century as a less sudden and absolute revolution than historians sometimes present. Beginning in the mid-seventeenth century, French cookbooks offered a new approach: they emphasized the main ingredient of each dish, as opposed to variety and even confusion of flavours; relied on butter and herbs and sauces more than on sugar and spices; divided savoury and sweet flavours more clearly, restructuring also the order of the meal—all this in the name of rationality, refinement, and subtlety. Though Latini's cooking style is still by and large the more varied and lavish one of his predecessors, many features of his approach also point in the direction of the more local and national cuisines that developed, even without direct French influence, in the new era of French-dominated high cuisine. Some of the more extravagant elements of Latini's overall approach to cooking (such as the use of the rarest ingredients, like musk or ambergris, or his passion for decorating tables with sculptures in sugar retouched in gold) might seem quite exotic, though they have in fact experienced somewhat of a resurrection in our own times. Other elements of his work speak more directly to modern concerns. His interest in local ingredients and local practices, his attempt to join local styles with the international traditions he inherited, and his comments on the harmful effect of cruel methods of raising animals parallel some of today's trends towards both fusion cuisine and the use of local and organic ingredients. His attention to the connections between diet and health, however wrong-headed his science, may also speak to modern concerns about nutrition.

Latini's text is massive: almost nine hundred pages, divided into two volumes published two years apart. The first, larger volume covers all issues and dishes pertaining to ordinary cooking and entertaining, which at the time meant meat-centred cooking. Meat—with its great variety, high cost, and long association with hunting—was traditionally the food of the elites. This was what in Latini's time was called "fat" eating. The second, appropriately slimmer volume deals with "lean" cooking, necessary for Lent and all other times when Catholic tradition required abstinence from meat, but when the kinds of people who employed stewards still expected to be able to enjoy lavish meals, and to offer impressive feasts to their guests. This distinction was, in the sixteenth and seventeenth centuries, a standard way to organize books about cooking matters.

One of the major themes running through Latini's text is his desire to glorify the role of stewards, which he does explicitly by praising their skill and knowledge of elite life and its protocol, and implicitly by displaying, often rather heavy-handedly, his own erudition and medical knowledge. Stewards were officials working for elite families and charged with organizing and supervising all the eating and entertainment that went on in the households of great lords or prelates in the pre-modern age. The Italian term *scalco* came from the German and originally referred to those charged with the preparation of meat.[4] In medieval courts the "seneschal," or "senior scalco," was a noble official

---

and Carolyn A. Nadeau, *Food Matters: Alonso Quijano's Diet and the Discourse on Food in Early Modern Spain* (Toronto: University of Toronto Press, 2016), 87–95.

4 Ken Albala, in *The Banquet. Dining in the Great Courts of Late Renaissance Europe* (Urbana-

charged with the management of the ruler's household. Latini's pride in his profession draws in part from these noble origins. The responsibilities of stewards included the supervision of all cooking, but extended considerably farther. Latini therefore intended his work to guide stewards not only in how to prepare all types of dishes, but also in how to arrange meals and banquets, how to set the table, how to supervise the kitchen and household staff, and how to ensure the success of their noble employers in the competitive arena of social life.

Latini's Life

Antonio Latini was born in Collamato, near Fabriano in the central Marches, a region on Italy's north-central Adriatic coast, on May 26, 1642. He came from a humble family and was orphaned at a young age. The editor of his autobiography acknowledged only that Latini "did not come from the first and oldest families of our town," but Latini himself averred that as children he and his brother wandered around their town "asking for bits of bread from door to door." He entered the service of local families in his birth region, where he learned to cook, read, and write, but already in 1658, at sixteen, he left the Marches to try his fortune in Rome. Between 1658 and 1682 he came and went between Rome and various small towns in north-central Italy. He worked in the households of various secular lords and prominent prelates both in Rome and elsewhere, starting with Cardinal Antonio Barberini. Outside Rome, Latini's most important posts were in Macerata, in his native Marches, a town that hosted numerous prominent guests on their way to Rome or to the important Marian sanctuary in nearby Loreto. These visits afforded Latini opportunities to shine and form useful connections. In 1670–1673 he served at Mirandola, a small duchy in Emilia where he "began to be well known in stewardship." Latini was thus part of a movable population of skilled servants who easily crossed political boundaries to find ever better conditions of employment. His first jobs in Rome were lowly, and in his autobiography Latini admits to youthful restlessness, laziness, and vague vices; he might have chosen to go back to a quieter provincial life until he felt ready to handle the pressures and competitiveness of Rome. Throughout his career, he relied on a network of fellow men from the Marches for contacts, support, and advice.[5]

Champaign: University of Illinois Press, 2007), translates *scalco* as "banquet manager," a term which he himself notes offers an incomplete idea of this official's responsibilities; in *Cooking in Europe, 1250–1650* (Westport: Greenwood Press, 2006), 18, Albala calls the steward the "head waiter" but "not a menial servant." Other authors—e.g. Roy Strong, *Feast: A History of Grand Eating* (New York: Harcourt, 2003), 134–35, and Terence Scully, in his translation of Bartolomeo Scappi, *The Opera (1570)* (Toronto: University of Toronto Press, 2008), have preferred "steward." Throughout this work, I have italicized Italian words (and explained them) only at the first use; the glossary includes all such terms.

5 The quotes are from Latini's autobiography, which he wrote around 1690–1692 and sent to the cleric Francesco Maria Nicolini, who also hailed from Collamato and was putting together a history of their town, which remained unpublished. The section of this manuscript containing Latini's autobiography was published much later as Latini, *Autobiografia (1642–1696), La vita di uno scalco*, ed. Furio Luccichenti (Rome: LEBERIT, 1992), quotes on 12, 16, and 34–35.

On the frontispiece of *The Modern Steward* Latini proudly wrote of himself that he was "practised in the service of numerous prelates and great lords." In 1682, through various contacts, Latini moved to and soon settled in Naples, where he rose to service at the pinnacle of the city's social scale. He worked as steward for Don Stefano Carrillo y Salcedo, who had a long and distinguished career in the administration of Naples from 1648 until his death fifty years later, and who was, at the time of Latini's arrival, the dean (or most senior member) of the Collateral Council, then the highest political and administrative body in the kingdom of Naples, and a very influential member of the kingdom's government elite; his palace above the Chiaia bridge was famous for its terrace overlooking the bay and for his collection of statues, ancient marbles, and works by Luca Giordano and other leading artists of the time.[6] In his book, Latini describes banquets and feasts he organized, and they include events in Naples, at various vacation spots near Naples, in Rome, in Loreto, and in other courtly settings in central Italy. His masters and their guests at these occasions show the breadth of Latini's contacts: princes and cardinals, the viceroy of Naples, countless noblemen and noblewomen, and officials at the top of the Neapolitan state's administrative hierarchy.

When he wrote his book, Latini could thus look back on a life of satisfaction, success, and prosperity. The oval portrait engraving that graces the first volume shows a self-confident man, in a slightly rigid pose, with a fashionable wig and elegant clothes. Shortly after the first volume appeared, in October 1693, Latini received a Roman knightly title. Latini may have been personally known to Pope Innocent XII (ruled 1691–1700), who was born Antonio Pignatelli and had served as archbishop of Naples in 1686–1691. The inscription surrounding Latini's portrait in his second volume labels him "knight of the golden spur and count of the sacred apostolic Lateran palace." Here Latini looks somewhat older (the two portraits depict him at forty-five and fifty respectively) and maybe stouter, but the clothes and wig are even more impressive, and on his left sleeve, prominently visible, is the cross of knighthood. Moreover, he is holding a copy of his own book. The humble kitchen hand from Collamato had probably succeeded beyond his wildest hopes. Latini died in Naples two years after publishing his second volume, on January 12, 1696. He seems to have had no family, and bequeathed his estate to the church of Fatebenefratelli (now della Pace), where he was buried.[7]

---

6 See Emilio Ricciardi, "Il 'Poggio delle Mortelle' nella storia dell'architettura napoletana" (unpublished PhD dissertation, University of Naples, 2005), and Diana Carrió-Invernizzi, *El gobierno de las imágenes: Ceremonial y mecenazgo en la Italia española de la segunda mitad del siglo XVII* (Madrid: IberoAmericana, 2008), 364–67.

7 Claudio Benporat, *Storia della gastronomia italiana* (Milan: Mursia, 1990), 211 for Latini's burial; Kate H. Hanson, "Visualizing Culinary Culture at the Medici and Farnese Courts" (unpublished PhD dissertation, University of Southern California, 2010), 114–15 on authors' portraits in cooking books. The Pace church today is fairly dilapidated, and displays no obvious trace of its late seventeenth-century tombs.

Latini's Naples

Antonio Latini lived in Naples at the end of the long period of Spanish rule in Naples, Sicily, and all of southern Italy. In 1503, during the Italian Wars (1494–1559) that pitted France against Spain in a struggle for control of the Italian peninsula and for European hegemony, Spanish forces conquered the kingdom of Naples (which included the entire continental South of Italy). Naples was thus added to the Italian domains of the Spanish Crown, which already included Sicily and Sardinia, and which would soon also include the duchy of Milan and a few smaller territories. Spain's dominion and hegemony were largely undisputed until the early eighteenth century, when a succession crisis of the Spanish monarchy led to a Europe-wide war and in 1707 to the Austrian takeover of the southern Italian kingdoms. From 1503, a series of Spanish viceroys exercised and embodied royal authority in southern Italy and presided over its administration and defence.[8]

The city of Naples prospered under Spanish rule. The city, already—with about one hundred thousand inhabitants—quite large at the turn of the sixteenth century, grew dramatically and possibly reached as many as three hundred thousand inhabitants around 1600, and over four hundred thousand by 1650. Naples was then by far the largest city in all of Italy, one of the three largest in Europe (with Paris and London), and indeed the largest city ruled by the Spanish kings in their global empire that spanned from Mexico to the Philippines. The population growth reflected the poverty of the Neapolitan kingdom, as masses of the rural poor sought a better life in the capital city. There they found work opportunities, and also fiscal and legal advantages, as well as—usually—guaranteed bread and basic food provisions at controlled prices.

Not only the poor flocked to Naples, though. Spanish officials, administrators, soldiers, and businessmen came to govern, defend, and profit from the city and kingdom. More and more members of the southern Italian nobility—a powerful class of largely feudal landowners—lived or spent much time in Naples, where they quickly joined ranks with the city's old elite. In Naples, nobles found access to royal law courts; enjoyed the pomp, social connections, and cultural offerings of city life; and gained lucrative and prestigious opportunities to serve the Spanish king as diplomats, administrators, or soldiers across his world dominions. Both noblemen and leading commoners occupied the vast number of offices required by the Spanish government, and large numbers of lawyers served the needs and interests of the city's litigious population—in the process often acquiring significant wealth and status. Foreign merchants and diplomats from all over northern Italy and the rest of Europe—Florentines, Genoese, Venetians, French, German, Flemish, Portuguese, English, and others—also added to Naples' growth: they established communities, founded churches, and many developed local roots. Naples, as a city writer put it in the 1630s, was "the whole world."[9]

---

8 For essays on all aspects of Spanish Naples see Astarita, ed., *A Companion to Early Modern Naples* (Leiden: Brill, 2013).

9 Giulio Cesare Capaccio, *Il Forastiero* (Naples: Roncagliolo, 1634), 940.

In Latini's time, Naples housed the only university of the continental South and hundreds of students came there from all the kingdom's provinces to study and begin their careers. Naples also had the largest port in southern Italy and was the capital of the largest Italian state. Finally, the city was home to a huge number of clerics: by the end of the sixteenth century, it already included thirty-seven parish churches, and housed about one hundred monastic houses, plus scores of chapels, charitable institutions, confraternities, hospitals, and other pious entities (and these numbers increased during the seventeenth century). The clergy probably formed about three percent of the city's population, or several thousand men and women, ranging from aristocratic nuns in the city's elite convents to ignorant and poor deacons and other minor clerics.

The city government was largely controlled by the families that belonged to the city's five noble districts, membership in which was carefully monitored by the royal government. Nobles enjoyed fiscal and other privileges, and they formed the city's—and the kingdom's—wealthiest and most powerful group. The rest of the city's population formed the so-called *Popolo* (People), a conglomeration of all other non-clerical citizens. An elite of lawyers, judges, merchants, financiers, and other professionals dominated the Popolo and occupied prominent positions in the kingdom's government organs. In the course of the seventeenth century, families from this group began to intermarry and integrate with both the city's old nobility and the kingdom's feudal aristocracy to form a single elite.

Much of the rest of the city's working population was organized in guilds, or trade associations, which guaranteed their members a set status in the city's social and cultural hierarchy and offered various forms of corporate solidarity and protection. Below them, street peddlers, domestic servants, unskilled day labourers, beggars, criminals, prostitutes, vagrants, and a mass of recent and indigent immigrants formed what writers usually called the "plebs," a potentially frightening population that had to be handled with cheap bread, rituals, and the threat of force. In 1585 a bloody urban riot, due to shortage and a subsequent spike in the price of bread, featured extreme mob violence and severe repression that echoed across Europe.

This rich, lively, large, and at times dangerous city became by the turn of the seventeenth century a major centre of Italian art and architecture, and in the course of the seventeenth century literature and music also flourished. Naples rivaled Rome as a centre of Italian Baroque art, and magnificent church buildings, aristocratic palaces, and a few royal projects dotted the city. The city's level of artistic production remained high in quality and quantity through the eighteenth century, and music life in particular expanded even more in the later century.

Naples, however, suffered some major blows during the seventeenth century, both natural and man-made. In 1631 the worst eruption of Vesuvius since the one that had destroyed Pompeii in 79 AD brought death, damage, and terror. It also greatly enhanced the worship of San Gennaro, one of the city's numerous patron saints and after 1631 its most deeply venerated protector. In 1647–1648 a major revolution shook the city and the kingdom: peasants attacked feudal estates, mobs killed noblemen in the capital, and everywhere tax collection ceased. It took the Spanish government nine months and significant reinforcements from Spain to restore order. Finally, and most devastatingly in terms of human losses, in 1656 a major epidemic of plague killed probably more than half of the city's population, and thousands across the kingdom. Though Naples remained by far the largest city in both its kingdom and Italy as a whole, the city's population would not return to the pre-plague level of over four hundred thousand until the late eighteenth century.

The Naples in which Latini worked in the 1680s and 1690s was therefore somewhat diminished compared to the city of two or three generations before. Nevertheless, the city remained large and vibrant, and was still home to a diverse and wealthy elite, a numerous clergy, and an international population. Indeed the late decades of the seventeenth century also witnessed a rebirth of intellectual activities in Naples. Scientists and philosophers began to publish original works, and to read those of other European scholars. With resurgent interest in the natural sciences across western Europe came also more interest in the natural phenomena for which the South was famous. By the late seventeenth century, Naples and the South began to attract visitors who came not for trade, pilgrimage, diplomacy, or other practical purposes, but to see the ancient ruins and the volcanic sites in which the Naples neighbourhood was so rich even before the discoveries at Pompeii and Herculaneum in the 1730s and 1740s.

Latini thus found in Naples plenty of opportunities for contacts with the highest levels of the Italian social hierarchy. There he served patrons whose wealth allowed them to support large establishments and the lavish entertainments Latini knew how to provide so ably. The city also contained a large and skilled working population, and it guaranteed abundant supplies of all sorts of food provisions. Naples was surrounded by reasonably rich farmland, the product of which flowed into the city, and provisions were also shipped from more distant provinces as well as at times from other countries. In the sixteenth century, the city relied for its food provisions largely on nearby farms and orchards, especially in fertile volcanic lands immediately to the city's east that enjoyed good water and abundantly produced both winter and summer crops. There were even several orchards and gardens within the city walls. As the city grew dramatically during the Spanish centuries, many of these farm areas were lost to building or simply became insufficient for the city's needs, and provisioning Naples became ever more challenging. In famine years the government had to balance the city's food needs with the Madrid government's demands for grain shipments from southern Italy to Spain itself.[10] Latini must have often entered the food market himself, and he indeed maintained a suspicious attitude towards all providers, be they farmers in the country or city vendors, and included in his book advice on how to guard against the "malice" of fishermen, peasants, and shopkeepers. Still, even with these challenges, overall Naples proved a fertile ground for Latini's imagination and creativity, and a worthy theatre for his gastronomical triumphs.

---

10 In these pages I draw from Astarita, *Between Salt Water and Holy Water: A History of Southern Italy* (New York: W. W. Norton, 2005), and from Giovanni Muto, "Le tante città di una capitale: Napoli nella prima età moderna," *Storia urbana* 32, 123 (April–June 2009): 19–54.

The Context of Latini's Book

Latini's *The Modern Steward* occupies an important place in the history of books about cooking in Italy and in Europe at large, as it appeared at a time of transition from the elaborate standards and tastes of the Renaissance and Baroque periods to a new focus on relative simplicity and natural flavours.[11] Written works on culinary matters generally reflect established patterns and practices, and thus usually offer a somewhat traditional view of what people in any given period were cooking and eating. Great originality was neither expected nor especially appreciated in early modern technical books, and thus these works usually include large amounts of materials drawn more or less directly from earlier works. As Pamela Smith has argued, in the fifteenth through seventeenth centuries "all writing was viewed as wholly or partially an act of compilation and incorporation ... how-to books did not emerge from single authors, but from knowledge made, held, and shared collectively."[12] Moreover, most of our knowledge of cooking and eating pertains to what the European elites expected, preferred, and sought. The importance or even existence of foods customarily eaten by the poor, but considered vulgar or inappropriate by the elites, may thus be hidden to us in printed texts about cooking, though information about the eating habits of the poor may at times be gleaned from other texts.

Elite European cooking in the late Middle Ages was lavish and cosmopolitan, with little attention to regional traditions or ingredients.[13] The emphasis was on the mixture of what to our taste might be discordant flavours, and spices were liberally applied, because their high cost made their use a sign of status and prestige and they were often deemed to have medicinal value. The aim of medieval cooks was to impress their masters and patrons by their concoctions: the eaters should be surprised, even mystified, by the clever and rare flavours they encountered, and the aim of great cooks was to transform the natural flavour and appearance of ingredients through their skill. In Mediterranean Europe, the influence of Arabic tradition was also fairly strong, as seen in the popularity of perfumes and scented waters, almond milk and lemons, spices and dried fruits, though most of these could be found to various extents also in northern Europe.

With the blossoming of the Renaissance, Italy and its Humanist movement influenced the rest of Europe in culinary matters, just as they did in art and political ideas. Around 1470 Bartolomeo Platina, an Italian Humanist who became the first papal librarian, wrote

---

11 For concise overviews of the historiography on medieval and early modern food in Europe see Paul Freedman, "Food Histories of the Middle Ages," in *Writing Food History: A Global Perspective*, ed. Kyri W. Claflin and Peter Scholliers (London: Berg, 2012), 24–37, and Claflin, "Food Among the Historians: Early Modern Europe," in *Writing Food History*, 38–58.

12 Pamela H. Smith, "Why Write a Book? From Lived Experience to the Written Word in Early Modern Europe," *Bulletin of the German Historical Institute* 47 (fall 2010): 25–50 at 39; on cookbooks as a genre, including on issues of originality, see recently Henry Notaker, *A History of Cookbooks: From Kitchen to Page over Seven Centuries* (Berkeley: University of California Press, 2017).

13 A discussion of early texts is in *Cuoco Napoletano. The Neapolitan Recipe Collection*, ed. and trans. Terence Scully (Ann Arbor: University of Michigan Press, 2000); see also Bruno Laurioux, *Une histoire culinaire du Moyen Age* (Paris: Champion, 2005), and Ken Albala, "Introduction," in *A Cultural History of Food in the Renaissance*, ed. Ken Albala (London: Berg, 2012), 1–28.

a Latin treatise entitled *On Right Pleasure and Good Health* (*De honesta voluptate et vale-tudine*), which drew heavily on the Italian work of Maestro Martino, a cook and author of the greatest Italian culinary work of its time.[14] While continuing the lavish preparations of late medieval cooking, Platina's book also emphasized the medical and moral aspects of cooking and eating and offered at least some examples of simpler cooking. Its success spread Italian ideas about cooking and eating across Europe. In the sixteenth and seventeenth centuries other Italian authors published influential works that offered advice for lavish banquets and menus, and Italy remained at the vanguard of culinary theory and gastronomical virtuosity. The major features of late Renaissance and early Baroque cooking for the elites were still, by and large, an extravagant variety and profusion of ingredients and flavours; a continuing focus on spices and the mixture of sweet and savoury; and impressive, awe-inspiring presentation. But, from Platina on, delicacy, refinement, and clarity also joined these earlier features as prized values in cooking.

In the second half of the seventeenth century, however, change accelerated. France rose as Europe's strongest power, and French culture gradually came to gain influence over most of Europe. French writers defined new standards for theatre, literature, painting, music, and so on, which came to be recognized across much of Europe. Numerous books were published in France that also attempted to define the proper, rational ways of cooking, serving food, and eating. A new focus on refinement and elegant restraint, on simplicity and rationality, and on nature, resulted in a new emphasis on enhancing the flavour of the main ingredient in any given dish. Flavours had to be appreciated in a reasonable manner, following notions of "good taste," rather than succumbing to the assault on the senses represented by the older approach. French cuisine thus began to define a new, clearer way to structure the meal, and to embrace local and regional ingredients and flavours instead of cosmopolitan and expensive spices. Into the eighteenth century and beyond, many French texts would be translated into Italian and other languages, and these innovations would make French cuisine the most influential across Europe.[15]

Latini's work came at the cusp of these developments. His book was the last of the great Italian culinary books published since the Renaissance, and has been described as the "most comprehensive" and "most ambitious in scope," as well as "a joy to read."[16] Latini's recipes and methods were in many ways still steeped in the earlier Italian traditions. At the same time, Latini was more interested than previous Italian authors in the regional context of his work: the vegetables, herbs, seafood, and even language of

---

14 Both books are available in English: Bartolomeo Platina, *On Right Pleasure and Good Health: A Critical Edition and Translation of De Honesta Voluptate and Valetudine*, trans. Mary Ella Milham (Tempe: Arizona Center for Medieval and Renaissance Studies, 1998); Maestro Martino, *The Art of Cooking: The First Modern Cookery Book*, ed. Luigi Ballerini, trans. Jeremy Parzen (Berkeley: University of California Press, 2005).

15 On these changes see for instance Susan Pinkard, *A Revolution in Taste: The Rise of French Cuisine, 1650–1800* (Cambridge: Cambridge University Press, 2008).

16 Elizabeth David, *Harvest of the Cold Months: The Social History of Ice and Ices* (New York: Viking, 1995), 142–43, and Riley, *The Oxford Companion*, 273. On Latini's place within the history of texts about cooking, see also Agnese Portincasa, *Scrivere di gusto: Una storia della cucina italiana attraverso i ricettari* (Bologna: Pendragon, 2016).

Naples mattered a good deal to him and he found ways to stress their qualities and advantages. Latini's banquets, in true Baroque fashion, were perhaps even more stunning visually and more formal in protocol than those arranged by his predecessors, but at the same time the food eaten was somewhat simpler, and dishes and courses were fewer and more streamlined than in the previous century. Latini was also the last Italian author about culinary matters before the spread of the French style; thus, his approach reflected both cosmopolitan sources (especially Spanish, given Naples' ties with Spain at the time) and his specific regional focus. Later Neapolitan writers, particularly Vincenzo Corrado in the late eighteenth and Ippolito Cavalcanti in the early nineteenth century, would struggle under the competing influences of French cuisine and their own regional methods and traditions.[17]

Latini's life and book embody also another, somewhat parallel, transition. He wrote when the kind of lavish service for private, elite patrons in which he excelled was beginning to diminish in prominence. As the European population overall—and that of Europe's cities in particular—grew in the eighteenth century, and as commercialization affected ever more areas of Europeans' lives, public commercial cooking establishments and eating venues began to increase in importance. Courtly cooking and lavish aristocratic entertainment continued for a long time but they no longer represented the necessary apex of a career in the field of cuisine and entertaining. Naples lagged somewhat behind from this point of view, but eighteenth-century Paris or London housed great public cooks, and an increasing number of public places where gentlemen could eat well and impressively entertain their friends. In a sense, as Sara Pennell has argued, books like Latini's, though they certainly enhanced the professional status of their authors, also provide us with evidence of the increasing commercialization of expert knowledge about cooking and entertaining: no longer a craftsman's secret of limited interest beyond the household of his master, such knowledge itself became a commodity available through the book market. Thus Latini's book offers us a window into significant changes not only in the European approach to cooking, but also in the social world in which that cooking took place.[18]

---

17 Thus Latini offers much more than a tired repetition of old information, as claimed by John Dickie in *Delizia! The Epic History of the Italians and Their Food* (New York: The Free Press, 2008), who, in a brief chapter on Naples that includes several factual errors, flippantly dismisses Latini with "there is nothing modern about *The Modern Steward*" (163). Henry Notaker also slips when he badmouths Latini: in stating that Latini was "superficial and uninformed" in his knowledge of philosophy (which is correct, though not exactly surprising), Notaker describes him as "chief steward at the court in Naples" (*History of Cookbooks*, 278; the same claim also on p. 265), whereas Latini never worked at the viceroy's court. See also Katherine McIver, *Cooking and Eating in Renaissance Italy: From Kitchen to Table* (London: Rowman and Littlefield, 2015), chap. 6, for the transition from Renaissance to Baroque.

18 Sara Pennell, "Professional Cooking, Kitchens, and Service Work: *Accomplisht* Cookery," in *A Cultural History of Food in the Early Modern Age*, ed. Beat Kümin (London: Berg, 2012), 103–21; see also Kümin, "Eating Out in Early Modern Europe," in *A Cultural History of Food*, 87–101.

The Role of the Steward

The steward was the leader among the "officials of the mouth," who handled all matters related to food acquisition, preparation, and presentation. The other household official with a traditional claim to elevated status was the carver, the man in charge of serving most dishes, especially meat dishes, to the master and his guests. The carver performed the delicate and elegant task of slicing meat and other foods for distribution to each guest. This task was originally performed by the steward, and indeed the Italian verb *scalcare* refers to preparing cooked meat for serving. By the Renaissance the carver's work had become prominent in all Italian courts and his job had expanded to the slicing of all sorts of foods besides meat. Carving evolved into quite a spectacular art by the turn of the seventeenth century. By Latini's time the carver was subordinate to the steward, and Latini indeed insisted that a steward worth his salt should also be a skilled carver.

The steward was locked into an uneasy relationship with the cook, that is, the man in charge of the actual food preparation, along with his own team of assistants. Though many writers celebrated the importance of the cook, his job remained too manual a craft, and his appearance was too likely to be stained and inelegant, for him to acquire great status in the very hierarchical social structure of these centuries. Most cooks remained confined to the kitchen and subordinate to the steward. Bartolomeo Scappi, the greatest sixteenth-century Italian cook, celebrated the greatness of what he called in his title the "art and craft of a master cook," but even he recognized that "it will always be more honourable for the cook to know how to serve as Steward than for the Steward to know how to serve as cook." The steward Cesare Evitascandalo, writing in the 1570s, warned that "the steward who leaves everything to the cook will be in a very bad situation." A century later the cook Bartolomeo Stefani also reluctantly allowed that cooks owed obedience to stewards "in what concerns the serving of dishes."[19]

Other subordinates of the steward included the man in charge of acquiring provisions (*spenditore* or purchaser); the man in charge of storing and keeping provisions (*dispensiero* or stock manager); and the man in charge of all glasses and beverages (*bottigliero* or wine steward). One more official, the *credenziero*, requires a bit more explanation. This officer took his name from the position at which he worked, the *credenza*, which was—and is—a piece of furniture: a sideboard, buffet, or bureau. In other contexts the credenziero was simply an accountant, named presumably after the credenza in which he kept his accounts.[20] In the kitchen context, the credenziero also kept accounts, but his credenza was the stage for far more varied activities.

Credenze typically decorated dining halls and came to play important functions in early modern banqueting. Their name (related to the verb *credere*, to believe) may derive

---

19 Scappi, *Opera*, 382; Cesare Evitascandalo, *Libro dello scalco* (Rome: Vullietti, 1609), 1; Bartolomeo Stefani, *L'arte di ben cucinare* (1662; repr. Bologna: Forni, 2000), 9. Sean Takats, *The Expert Cook in Enlightenment France* (Baltimore: Johns Hopkins University Press, 2011) discusses the rising status of cooks in eighteenth-century France, while acknowledging their continuing inferiority to *maîtres d'hôtel* (who held a role similar to that of Italian stewards).

20 John A. Marino, *Pastoral Economics in the Kingdom of Naples* (Baltimore: Johns Hopkins University Press, 1988), 171–72.

from the medieval practice of testing the food for poison once it was brought to the dining hall: a dependent, often the steward, would use a little bread to taste each dish, to assure the master and his guests that there was no danger in it. The steward Domenico Romoli implies that this test had become a ceremonial formality by the 1550s.[21] The credenza—large and visible to all diners—was the stage for this test, and remained the stage for the formal presentation of many dishes, which would be displayed there before being served to the diners at their tables. Over time, as the splendour of dining increased, several credenze developed: one was called *da mostra* or for show, and it displayed the silver, gold, and crystal vases and plates that demonstrated to the guests the wealth and sophistication of their host: at the 1600 banquet in Florence celebrating the marriage of Marie de' Medici with Henry IV of France, two thousand pieces of gold, silver, and gilt plate were displayed. Ottaviano Rabasco, like many other writers, blamed Spanish influence for such excesses: "today in Italy, and even more in Spain, we follow the practice of having a lot of silver displayed on the credenze, not for use in the banquet, but to show greatness and magnificence."[22] Another credenza might be used to hold all beverages that would be served during the meal. The main credenza remained where much food would first be presented.

By the late Middle Ages, banquet service also differentiated between types of foods, and an elegant banquet consisted of distinct "services" or courses, each consisting of numerous dishes. These services came to be divided into "kitchen" services, namely hot foods brought from the kitchen just ahead of being served, and "credenza" services, which usually began and ended the meal and consisted of cold dishes, fruits, salads, and sweets. The credenziero was the man in charge of preparing all these dishes, and he became also responsible for keeping and displaying all linen, plates, and silver, most of which were kept in credenze. This separation would continue even after the rise of the French style: French cooking always maintained a clear separation between the products of the *cuisine* (kitchen) and those of the *office* (office, or the credenziero's kitchen, where for instance all sweets were prepared).[23]

The status of the credenziero evolved over time, especially vis-à-vis the cook. Though in 1560 Romoli mentions the credenziero as one of the steward's principal dependents, the great cook Scappi—writing a few years later—barely mentions this figure, and indeed implies that the steward was himself directly responsible for the credenza dishes. Perhaps professional rivalry was at work here, because the credenziero became in effect a parallel to the cook. Giovan Battista Rossetti in 1584 and Antonio Frugoli in 1631 again listed the credenziero as one of the top officials supervised by the steward. The credenziero usually had a subordinate staff—as well as a kitchen—of his own. The

---

21 Domenico Romoli, *La singolare dottrina* (1560) as quoted in Emilio Faccioli, ed., *L'arte della cucina in Italia* (Turin: Einaudi, 1987), 362.

22 Strong, *Feast*, 165, on Henry IV's wedding; Ottaviano Rabasco, *Il convito* (Florence: Giunti, 1615), 231.

23 I will leave the term credenziero in Italian, as no apt term exists in modern English. Latini uses the term interchangeably with *ripostiero*, which came from the Spanish and was not used generally by Italian authors not working in Naples.

credenziero's specific work, however, remained relatively neglected in many books from these centuries, perhaps because much of his work did not require actual cooking. In any case, no Italian credenziero published a book about his craft, and the first book devoted exclusively to it only appeared in Naples in 1778, by which point French cuisine and habits were the rage across Europe.[24]

These officials shared one characteristic: they were all men. Apparently, neither Latini nor any other Italian culinary author ever considered that women could serve in these capacities. Women of course cooked, in the great majority of households, but not usually in grander ones. The steward Cristoforo Messisbugo dismissively mentioned that he would not "spend time or effort to describe various vegetable or legume soups, or to teach how to fry a tench or grill a pike, or similar things, which any humble little woman will know how to do perfectly well."[25]

Clear evidence of the superior prestige of stewards over all other professionals involved with food comes in the number of texts authored by Italian stewards in the sixteenth and seventeenth centuries. After the invention of printing in the 1450s, the relative status of a profession could almost be measured by the number of authors among its practitioners and by the number of books devoted to explicating its role and practices. Books by cooks were rare: Scappi was the most famous cook to publish a book about his craft in the sixteenth century, Stefani the only one in the seventeenth. On the other hand, there was a profusion of books written by Italian stewards, and their books typically do not only cover the steward's own responsibilities, but also discuss most matters pertaining to cooking.

Latini's precursors included Messisbugo (1549), Romoli known as Panunto (1560), Rossetti (1584), Evitascandalo (1609, but written in the 1570s), Vittorio Lancellotti (1627), Frugoli (1631), Giovan Francesco Vasselli (1647), Giacomo Colorsi (1658), and Venanzio Mattei (1669).[26] All of these authors, including Latini, hailed from central Italy (Emilia, the Marches, Tuscany, and Latium). Many princely and sovereign courts in this region offered employment to stewards. The region also of course included the papal court of Rome, the most splendid Italian court and the one that long dictated the standard protocol for all of Europe's rulers and lords. The papal court was itself surrounded by the wealthy establishments of cardinals, Roman aristocrats, and foreign ambassadors to the papacy, traditionally the top position in any ambassadorial career. Most of the authors just listed in fact worked in Rome for at least part of their career.

---

24 See Romoli in Faccioli, *L'arte*, 366–67; Scappi, *Opera*, 131, 382, and 625–26; Giovan Battista Rossetti, *Dello scalco* (1584; repr., Bologna: Forni, 1991), 28; Antonio Frugoli, *Pratica e scalcaria* (1638; repr., Bologna: Forni, 2005), 5–6; the 1778 book is Vincenzo Corrado, *Il credenziere di buon gusto* (1778; repr., Bologna: Forni, 1991). See also Benporat, *Storia*, and Notaker, *A History of Cookbooks*, chap. 2.

25 Cristoforo di Messisbugo, *Libro novo* (1557; repr., Bologna: Forni, 1980), 39v; Takats, *Expert Cook*, chap. 1, on women cooks.

26 I give here the dates of the first editions of their works on stewardship; on reprints, see June di Schino and Furio Luccichenti, *Il cuoco segreto dei papi, Bartolomeo Scappi e la confraternita dei cuochi e dei pasticcieri* (Rome: Gangemi, 2008), 61.

One somewhat different book, which might nonetheless be relevant to Latini's work, was Giovanni Battista Crisci's 1634 *Lucerna de corteggiani* (*Lantern for Courtiers*), published in Naples, which contains a dialogue about courts, a discussion of court officials, and then an enormous set of menus for meals and banquets for every day and season of the year. It is not clear whether the rather obscure Crisci was a steward (the main speaker in the dialogue is, but Crisci belonged to a literary academy and also authored a historical "tragicomedy," so his own professional identity is unclear); what is most interesting about his book is that he often includes the regional or local origins of the ingredients he includes in his lists, and that these origins are predominantly from the Italian South and Sicily. In this way, Crisci anticipates Latini's more local focus, in a perhaps conscious distancing from the predominant central and northern Italian tradition of earlier decades.

The topics and organization of these books by stewards (and a few cooks) display substantial similarities. Often, a first section describes and celebrates the role of the steward, and explains how to arrange banquets. There are then two main sections to all of these books: first, the authors offer detailed discussions of various categories of ingredients or preparations. This is most often where we find most of the recipes these books usually contain; as the intended audience consisted of experienced professionals, the recipes are rarely the main focus of these books (though they may occupy the most pages), nor are they very detailed: cooking times, heat levels, and precise measurements are rarely included, and ingredients and preparations are often described in shorthand language.[27] The final regular element in these books is a series of menus of banquets and other meals arranged by or otherwise known to the author. The authors include not only rich lists of dishes served, but also descriptions of room and table decorations, of musical or other entertainments that accompanied the meal, and of elaborate serving etiquette. These banquet descriptions may appear at the start of the book (as in Messisbugo), as the central section (fairly short as in Romoli or very long as in Rossetti), or as a final substantial section (as in Frugoli); they may also be interspersed throughout (as in Vasselli) or indeed they may form virtually the entirety of the book (as in Lancellotti, Colorsi, and Mattei). These two elements—the discussion of various types of foods and the description of banquets—also form the core of works by cooks, such as Scappi and Stefani.

Latini's work was the largest of the lot, and it was the only one published as two separate volumes; its separation of "fat" and "lean" dishes was thus more absolute than in prior texts. It includes all the elements mentioned here, and several more, such as discussions of regional ingredients and wines, and a diet for convalescents. To serve his intellectual and social ambitions, Latini appears to have made a conscious effort to show off his familiarity with important books generally, in terms not simply of content, but also of his book's appearance: compared to those published by most of his Spanish and Italian peers, Latini's volumes are more clearly organized and structured, richer in illus-

---

27 The modern standard in recipes of separating a clear list of ingredients from a description of how to prepare them only began in the late eighteenth century, see Notaker, *A History of Cookbooks*, chap. 7.

trations (though he did not match Scappi's famous and numerous engravings of kitchens and utensils), and include fulsome dedications, poems in praise of the author, and other accompanying material that was customary in Renaissance and Baroque high-end publications. Latini also deployed more erudition than any of his predecessors (except perhaps the highly born Rossetti a century earlier), again in his aim to elevate the status of the steward. Finally, Latini was the only one of these Italian authors to have worked for much of his career outside of central Italy, and his text reflects his interest in and affection for his adopted home in the kingdom of Naples.

Concepts of Food and Health

Like his predecessors, Latini saw all foods as fitting within the dominant understanding of the human body and the natural world. Since antiquity, an understanding had prevailed in Europe and the larger Mediterranean world that human health was based on the proper balance of four humours (blood, phlegm, choler, and bile). These humours were defined by their qualities: they were hot or cold, moist or dry, in different combinations, and they shaped individual personalities and temperaments. These qualities were also present in all foods. Food thus helped maintain—or could disrupt—the proper balance of the humours in the body, and therefore it could cause illness or aid in the recovery of good health. One ought to eat in moderation and with careful consideration of the food's own qualities. Thus writers on food indicated the hotness or coldness and dryness or moistness of each ingredient. Each food possessed these qualities to varying degrees: the first and second degree had relatively modest effects in most cases. The third degree indicated actual therapeutic power. Any quality in the fourth degree, the highest, could prove fatal if consumed without correctives or by someone of the wrong temperament, bodily balance, or lifestyle.

Animals, in addition to having these qualities, were traditionally associated with various traits, which should also be taken into account by those planning to cook or eat them: wild animals might be better than domestic ones for some eaters, timid animals would influence those who ate of them in that emotional direction, and each animal's own diet may shape the effects of eating that animal's meat. The individual nature of each person—her or his humoural temperament—had to be taken into account to determine which foods he or she should eat or avoid. The purpose of cooking, from a medical point of view, was thus to counter the potentially negative qualities of each food, to enhance the positive ones, and to facilitate digestion and nourishment for each individual eater.

This approach was based not only on the humoural theory, but also on the prevailing understanding of what happened during the digestive process. The stomach was conceived almost as an oven: it took the food in, it cooked or "concocted" it, and thus it made possible both the absorption of nutrients into the body, and the passage of waste through—and out of—the body. Different foods were more or less harmful in as much as they aided or slowed down this necessary process, and this could also vary by the individual's age, sex, rank, lifestyle, astrological sign, temperament, or other characteristics. Part of the appeal of spices in late medieval and Renaissance cooking was indeed based on the belief that they greatly facilitated the digestive process. In this overall conception, all foods were, in a sense, also medicines, as they fundamentally affected humoural balance and bodily well-being.[28]

On this point too, Latini straddles an older approach and a new era. His understanding of the healthiness of foods was steeped in the old humoural theory which by his time was increasingly disputed across western Europe by both doctors and cooks. New chemical and physical approaches to medicine were spreading in the late seventeenth century and affecting medical views of the process of digestion, and thus of the role of food in the maintenance of health. Some physicians stressed chemical notions, seeing digestion as the decomposition of food through chemical processes, whereas others emphasized physical and mechanical processes, such as grinding and pressure.[29] In fact Giovanni Alfonso Borelli, one of the main exponents of this new mechanical understanding of digestion, which challenged some of the tenets of the old theory, was a Neapolitan near-contemporary of Latini's, though he mostly lived in Sicily and Rome. There is no evidence in Latini's book that he knew or understood these new ideas.

On the other hand, Latini's views on the overall need for moderation and on the individual context of any diet echoed notions that became quite popular during the eighteenth century, and that resonate also with modern concepts. In the early eighteenth century many doctors and dieticians, whatever their views of digestion, not only proposed a general moderation in eating, but argued against the eating of heavy meats, fatty foods, and spices, and for more consumption of vegetables, fruits, and foods prepared in simple ways, all suggestions that can be found also in Latini's approach. Aesthetic, medical, and culinary factors came together in this transition that, in Jean-Louis Flandrin's words, emancipated gastronomy from medicine. The long-term trend in medicine, as Ken Albala has written, was toward the "shift from prevention to therapy" and thus toward a smaller role for diet and nutrition in medical theory and practice. Ultimately, therefore, cooking and medicine separated, and the medical understanding that had sustained cooking when Latini learned his craft faded away; but these developments were quite slow, and Latini's work offers us also a sense of the underlying continuities that link his approach to our own.[30]

---

28 See e.g. Nancy Siraisi, *Medieval and Early Renaissance Medicine: An Introduction to Knowledge and Practice* (Chicago: University of Chicago Press, 1990), chap. 5; David Gentilcore, *Food and Health in Early Modern Europe: Diet, Medicine, and Society, 1450–1800* (London: Bloomsbury, 2016); on spices see Paul Freedman, *Out of the East: Spices and the Medieval Imagination* (New Haven: Yale University Press, 2008), chap. 2.

29 For the chemical understanding of digestion see Allen G. Debus, *The Chemical Philosophy: Paracelsian Science and Medicine in the Sixteenth and Seventeenth Centuries*, 2 vols. (New York: Science History Publications, 1977), 2:368–71, 529–30; see also David Gentilcore, "Body and Soul, or Living Physically in the Kitchen," in *A Cultural History of Food*, 143–63.

30 See Pinkard, *A Revolution in Taste*, 64–71 and 165–71; Maurizio Sentieri, "Un'indagine sulle ragioni della persistenza della dietetica galenica lungo l'età preindustriale," in *Alimentazione e nutrizione secoli XIII–XVIII*, Acts of the 28th Settimana di Studi dell'Istituto Francesco Datini di Prato, ed. Simonetta Cavaciocchi (Florence: Le Monnier, 1996), 787–95; Jean-Louis Flandrin, "Diététique et gastronomie, XIV–XVIII siècles," in *Voeding en geeneskunde/Alimentation et médecine*, ed. Ria Jansen-Sieben and Frank Daelemans (Brussels: Archives et Bibliothèques de Belgique, 1993), 177–92; J. Estes, "Food as Medicine," in *The Cambridge World History of Food*, ed.

Banquets and Protocol

The organization of Latini's two volumes was, as mentioned above, not unusual: after preliminary matters such as the status of the steward and management of the household, meat always came first, and then came discussions of various ways to prepare food (roasting, boiling, and so on, roughly in a progression of complexity). In these sections, Latini did not offer precise recipes, but simply outlined for his readers—who were experienced in the kitchen or at least advanced in training—the characteristics, challenges, and effects of each preparation. These sections were followed by descriptions of table decorations, and then elaborate descriptions of banquets and other fancy events. The second volume followed the same organization, though it included some other matters as well.

Banquets – and indeed most dining occasions for the elites – followed a standard protocol and structure. At the start of the meal, guests were offered water to wash their hands, and then usually helped themselves from the cold dishes set on the table. After this service was removed, the first of possibly several kitchen—or hot—services was brought in under the careful direction of the steward. Service could be "at two [or three, or more] plates," which indicated how many plates of each dish were served together (usually, one plate would serve four to six guests). Serving plates were displayed on the table, and the carver often prepared individual portions for the guests. Little plates of sauces and condiments were also available, usually set in neat geometric patterns on the table around the larger serving plates. Table cloths were removed after each service, and often new napkins provided to the guests, who still did much of their eating with their fingers.

Guests did not usually have individual glasses in front of them: when they wished to drink, they signalled a servant, who brought them wine, water, and a glass (guests usually watered their wine), and these were then quickly taken away again: bottles and glasses did not appear as regular fixture of the table until the late eighteenth century. The final service was always a credenza service of salads, fruits, and other cold dishes. This was followed by the ritual of hand-washing, when each guest would be offered a basin, water, and probably yet another napkin. Finally, candied delicacies and other sweets—and toothpicks—were set on the table. The properly run banquet thus took care of all the guests' needs, and indeed Evitascandalo suggested that the steward also "order that in rooms [nearby] urinals and beds be prepared, so that, if guests need rest or other necessities, nothing should be lacking."[31]

Kenneth F. Kiple and Kriemhild Coneè Ornelas, 2 vols. (Cambridge: Cambridge University Press, 2000), 2:1534–53; Ken Albala, "Insensible Perspiration and Oily Humor: An Eighteenth-Century Controversy over Vegetarianism," *Gastronomica* 2, 3 (summer 2002): 29–36 at 30; Sydney Watts, "Enlightened Fasting: Religious Conviction, Scientific Inquiry, and Medical Knowledge in Early Modern France," in *Food and Faith in Christian Culture*, ed. Ken Albala and Trudy Eden (New York: Columbia University Press, 2011), 105–23; and J. Trémolières, "A History of Dietetics," *Progress in Food and Nutrition Science* 1, 2 (February 1975): 65–114 at 83 and 95.

31 Evitascandalo, *Libro dello scalco*, 19; the exhibition catalogue Marina Cogotti and June di Schino, eds., *Magnificenze a tavola: Le arti del banchetto rinascimentale* (Rome: De Luca, 2012) includes essays on several of these topics.

Definitions and Translation Issues

Latini used several terms that require a bit of context and explanation. I will here outline some prominent categories and how I have approached them in this translation (Latini's own use of these terms is not always consistent, so I have tried also to be guided by context).

1. The words *minestra* and *zuppa* can be confusing, as their meaning in Italian today varies by region. Some reference works translate minestra as simply "dish" (which is today a northern Italian usage of the term); others translate it as "pottage," to indicate a chunky soup; others use "sops" for most zuppe to indicate their usual foundation in soaked bread. In Latini's usage, minestra tends to be thick and chunky; I will call these dishes "stews." Zuppa almost always includes bread, and I will use "soup" for these dishes (indeed, in several cases, zuppa is simply bread soaked in broth topped with one or two particular ingredients). Latini uses *brodo* (broth) for thinner preparations he usually defines as "nourishing and healthy." There are also various *brodetti* (literally, little broths), which may refer either to a particularly thin and light broth, or to a liquid preparation used to moisten or thicken the ingredients used inside a pie. I have used "thin broth" and "little broth" for these two uses of this term. Finally, Latini describes some other thick soup- or stew-like dishes as *pottaggi*, which I have rendered simply as "pottages."

2. There are several terms used for pies and tarts. *Pasticci* are savoury or sweet pies (or both), usually enclosed in a hard crust all around, and baked. Often, broth or juice is added in the last phase of baking by removing and then replacing the pie cover, which often was not eaten. *Crostata* today in Italian indicates an uncovered tart, generally sweet and often fruit-based, but Latini used this term for covered tarts, as fully enclosed as his pasticci: the difference lies rather in the dough, which is more solid for pasticci, while flaky and multi-layered—and more clearly meant to be eaten—in crostate. Generally more of Latini's crostate are sweet and fruit-based, but we also find some with vegetables or meats as the main ingredient.[32] Finally, Latini tended to use *torta* for uncovered tarts, and *pizza* more broadly for any kind of tart (the modern version of pizza is a later development in Neapolitan cuisine).

3. Terms to describe various types of pasta varied depending on shape or on time period and region.[33] In the sixteenth century dry pasta was produced, in Sicily, for instance, and traded; it was consumed generally by the poor, or by sailors on ships. But

---

32 Latini's crostate therefore do not fit the distinction as articulated by Albala (in *Banquet*, 93–94) and by Alberto Capatti and Massimo Montanari (*Italian Cuisine, A Cultural History* (New York: Columbia University Press, 2003), chap. 2), who state that a crostata is a shallow, uncovered tart; on these terms, and also on minestra and zuppa as they are used in Italy today, see also Fabio Parasecoli, *Food Culture in Italy* (Westport: Greenwood Press, 2004), 27 and 52. On our modern notion of the pizza, which did not appear until the nineteenth century, see for instance Antonio Mattozzi, *Inventing the Pizzeria: A History of Pizza Making in Naples* (London: Bloomsbury Academic, 2015).

33 For this and what follows see especially Emilio Sereni, "Note di storia dell'alimentazione nel Mezzogiorno: i napoletani da 'mangiafoglia' a 'mangiamaccheroni'," in Emilio Sereni, *Terra nuova e buoi rossi* (Turin: Einaudi, 1981), 292–371 (originally published in the journal *Cronache meridionali* in 1958); Lejla Mancusi Sorrentino, *Maccheronea: Storia, aneddoti, proverbi, letteratura, e tante ricette* (Naples: Grimaldi, 2000); and Serventi and Sabban, *La pasta*.

the rich ate fresh pasta: stuffed, as with ravioli; as an ingredient in stews and many other dishes; or as part of the stuffing for pies of all sorts— but rarely as a dish in itself. Fresh pasta was almost invariably served with sugar (a practice echoed in the modern meaning of the English term "macaroon"). By 1546 Naples had a guild of pasta-makers (specifically, *vermicellari*); other Italian cities soon followed suit. In the early seventeenth century pasta (now generally called maccheroni) spread as a common food in Naples, and many literary texts mention it as an increasingly typical Neapolitan food, but it remained fairly expensive. By mid-century, however, economic trends and technological innovations led to the great popularization of pasta consumption. Suburban orchards became rarer and insufficient to the growing city's needs, so that the transport of vegetables to the city became more expensive. New types of presses both made the production of dry pasta cheaper and allowed for a larger variety of forms. Naples' relatively warm and dry climate made it a perfect location for this production, which required a quick and easy drying process. The result over time was that dry pasta became the standard food of the Naples poor and a significant local industry. But in Latini's circles dry pasta remained a lowly food. Fresh pasta appeared in many of his dishes, under numerous terms, but virtually always as a subsidiary ingredient, and often with a sweetened flavour.

4. Various things, but especially fruits, could be preserved to be used when needed by being either cooked in a sugar syrup or candied. This was ordinarily the responsibility of the credenziero, and the process could be long and time-consuming. *Sciroppare* was the term for gentle and repeated cooking in a sugar syrup, which resulted in soft, sweet, and dense fruits that could be used at short notice, often to decorate dishes; I have simply referred to this as "cooking in syrup," or "fruits [or other things] in syrup," or "syruped," depending on the context. When Latini used the term *candito* to refer to candied foods, he was referring to a related process, by which fruits (or other foods), after being at least partially cooked in syrup, would be dried out at a low temperature, and then likely plunged into hot sugar syrup, resulting in a thin candy coating; I have referred to these foods as "candied." Finally, Latini uses the term *confetture* for preserves, usually served at the end of meals, though the term also included thick fruit pastes that could be moulded and used to decorate tables or particular dishes (confections); *confetti* (as a noun) were aromatic seeds or spices coated with layers of sugar, whereas Latini often used confetti (as an adjective) to refer to other foods that had undergone this process (again, mostly to be used as decorations); I have used "comfits" for the former, and "confected" for the latter.[34]

In translating Latini's work, I have aimed to simplify his difficult and at times obscure sentence structure; I have also occasionally toned down his extravagant vocabulary. At the same time, I have sought to maintain a flavour of the Baroque prose and of the high literary style to which Latini clearly aspired as part of his program of celebrating the status and learning of stewards. Though likely unschooled in the traditional sense, Latini had acquired some learning, and one of his aims was to accentuate the intellectual standing of stewards. Many previous writers debated whether experience or learning was more valuable to a steward, but Latini usually emphasized both his practical experi-

---

34 I am deeply grateful to Ivan Day for his help in understanding these terms and processes.

ence and his erudition. He did not so much argue that culinary knowledge was in fact knowledge rather than mere competence, but that to be truly competent in the kitchen one also had to have outside knowledge of a traditional learned type.[35]

Latini's particular interest in the language level and tone of the book is evident from its first pages, especially in his explanation, in the address to the reader, of why he chose to adjust his language to the regional terms and forms of Naples, rather than adhering closely to the Tuscan standards that had long before his time become the norm for elegant Italian writing. On this point Latini's commitment to the regional context of his work trumped his obvious desire to write in a recognizably elevated manner. Around the time he wrote, intellectuals and literary writers in Naples were in fact just beginning to devote more attention to the local dialect, a process which would lead in the early eighteenth century to the flourishing of dialect theatre and opera, and perhaps Latini consciously reflected these trends.[36]

On the other hand, I must note that Latini's text as a whole can be quite frustrating to understand. In his description of banquets or when discussing other elevated topics, he obviously aimed to impress with his learning and elegant style. Many parts of the text, though, especially in the second volume, are sloppy and careless, with typographical errors, repetitions, and the most irritatingly unclear use of punctuation it has ever been my fate to encounter, to the point that in some passages it is difficult to understand what precisely is being described, or what is being done with (or to) what ingredients. I suspect Latini might have dictated some parts of the book, particularly in the rush to publish the second volume (which unlike the first one lacks an errata page at the end). Latini could also be quite inconsistent in his use of technical terms, a few of his terms appear virtually nowhere else in seventeenth-century Italian texts, and his use of pronouns can be rather casual, all of which also can obscure his meaning. I have tried nonetheless to stay as close as possible to his words, and to the visual appearance of the original text, to convey both Latini's content and his tone.

---

35 I take this formulation of knowledge versus competence from Sara Pennell, "'Pots and Pans History': The Material Culture of the Kitchen in Early Modern England," *Journal of Design History* 11 (1998): 201–16, where she develops it in terms of gender roles.

36 See Barbara Ann Naddeo, "Urban Arcadia: Representations of the 'Dialect' of Naples in Linguistic Theory and Comic Theater, 1696–1780," *Eighteenth-Century Studies* 35 (2001): 41–65.

THE MODERN
STEWARD,

Or
the Art of Preparing Banquets Well,
with the Choicest Rules of Stewardship, Taught and
Applied to Benefit Professionals, and Other Scholars,

BY ANTONIO LATINI
FROM COLLE AMATO,

experienced in the service of various prelates
and great princes.
In which we teach the easy and noble manner of carving, and of preparing roasts,
boiled dishes, stews, many elegant dishes, royal soups, delicate little dishes,
nourishing broths, appetizing fried dishes, all sorts of pies,
with their dosages fit for as many guests as one has,
different composite dishes, tarts or royal pizze,
with their dosages, sauces, and
condiments of various sorts,

WE TEACH ALSO AN EASY MANNER OF PREPARING PERFUMES,
in various ways, fragrant and healthful vinegars, how to preserve fruits
throughout the year, how to prepare noble and beautiful
table decorations, how to set tables properly,
and how to know the qualities
of all edible animals,
additionally, we discuss the first discoverers of how to eat various animals,
both land ones and birds, and of how to prepare various dishes from them.

With a note of the territories of this Kingdom, from which come fruits,
wines, and other similar things, for use in banquets.

PART THE FIRST,

in which we discuss non-Lenten cooking.
In Naples, at the new press of the partners
Domenico Antonio Parrino and Michele Luigi Mutii, 1692.
With licence and privilege of the authorities.

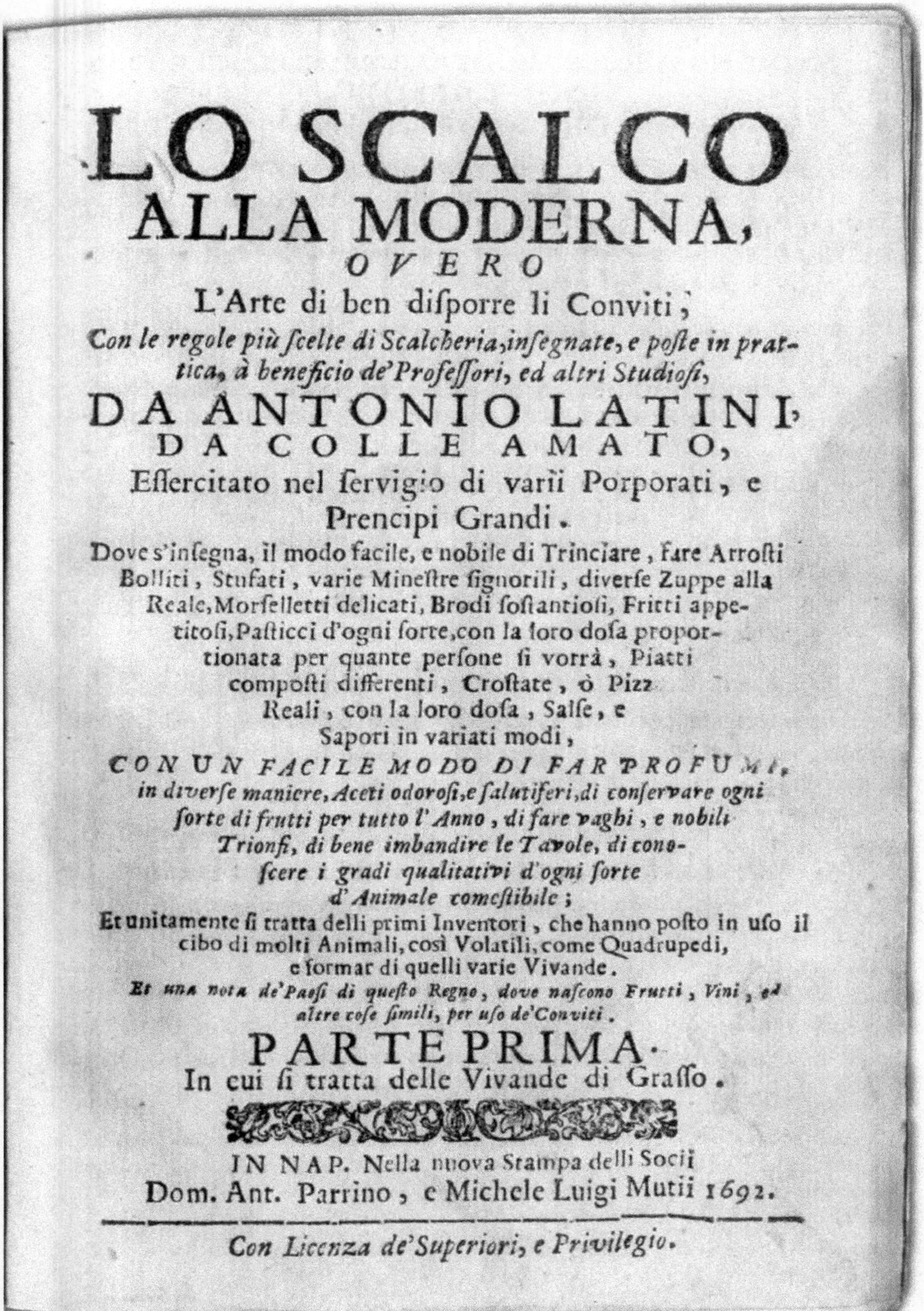

LO SCALCO
ALLA MODERNA,
OVERO

L'Arte di ben disporre li Conviti,

Con le regole più scelte di Scalcheria, insegnate, e poste in prattica, à beneficio de' Professori, ed altri Studiosi,

DA ANTONIO LATINI, DA COLLE AMATO,

Essercitato nel servigio di varii Porporati, e Prencipi Grandi.

Dove s'insegna, il modo facile, e nobile di Trinciare, fare Arrosti Bolliti, Stufati, varie Minestre signorili, diverse Zuppe alla Reale, Morselletti delicati, Brodi sostantiosi, Fritti appetitosi, Pasticci d'ogni sorte, con la loro dosa proportionata per quante persone si vorrà, Piatti composti differenti, Crostate, ò Pizz Reali, con la loro dosa, Salse, e Sapori in variati modi,

CON UN FACILE MODO DI FAR PROFUMI, in diverse maniere, Aceti odorosi, e salutiferi, di conservare ogni sorte di frutti per tutto l'Anno, di fare vaghi, e nobili Trionfi, di bene imbandire le Tavole, di conoscere i gradi qualitativi d'ogni sorte d'Animale comestibile;

Et unitamente si tratta delli primi Inventori, che hanno posto in uso il cibo di molti Animali, così Volatili, come Quadrupedi, e formar di quelli varie Vivande.

Et una nota de' Paesi di questo Regno, dove nascono Frutti, Vini, ed altre cose simili, per uso de' Conviti.

PARTE PRIMA.

In cui si tratta delle Vivande di Grasso.

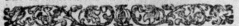

IN NAP. Nella nuova Stampa delli Socii Dom. Ant. Parrino, e Michele Luigi Mutii 1692.

Con Licenza de' Superiori, e Privilegio.

Figure 1. Cover page of Volume I of *Lo Scalco alla Moderna*.

TO THE MOST ILLUSTRIOUS AND EXCELLENT LORD
DON CARLO
DE CARDENAS,

LORD OF THE HOUSE OF CARDENAS, PRINCE OF THE HOLY ROMAN EMPIRE, FIRST MARQUIS OF LAINO, OF THE KINGDOM OF NAPLES, COUNT OF LA CERRA [ACERRA], PALATINE COUNT, LIFETIME MAYOR OF THE CITY OF PLUTIA IN THE KINGDOM OF SICILY, AND PREFECT OF THE MILITIA OF HEAVY ARMOUR.[1]

I dedicate this book of mine to sobriety and temperance, though at first sight the book may seem a school for luxury and intemperance. I devotedly offer it to the most sober prince of this kingdom who used to partake always in the Platonic banquets of wisdom, and to detest the Epicureans' tables, will deign sponsor my convivial teachings which, though they may seem stimuli to luxury and gluttony, are in fact the norms for an exquisite frugality. Here I do not teach to live in order to eat, but rather to eat in order to live; not to eat much, but to eat well; not to Epicureanize, but to Platonize, in the joys of a frugal table. This volume of mine implores the patronage of a virtuous and authoritative prince, in order to be defended against all censure which it may receive from the Momi and the Aristarchi of whom the world today abounds.[2] I entrust this book reverently to the valuable protection of Your Excellency, who is supremely venerated both in Spain and in this Kingdom, not only for your great talents and singular qualities, but also because of your glorious ancestors, of whose heroic virtues I could offer a long catalogue; what was remarkable in Your Excellency's ancestors, you practise and is admired in you; you never leave the orbit of justice and the right path of equity, you never shun your duty and that propriety that promotes all forms of piety, you never, in any matter, offend the ideals of leadership, and you satisfy all the requisites of the most just leader. In your government responsibilities, you do not impose punishments without having preceded them with warnings, as you know that heaven does not cast its thunders without first alerting us with lightning. You are endowed with that generous nature which begets the greatest actions, and which lives only in the noblest of breasts; which satisfies all the qualities of civil life; prudence is the guide of all your deeds, as is necessary to those who wish to govern well. May Your Excellency enjoy this book, which is your own, because it is the fruit of your generosity; please deign accept gladly this proof of my veneration, however small it may be, mindful that the sea does not refuse the tribute of

---

1 Cardenas (1652–1694) came from one of the many Spanish families of officials that had settled in the kingdom of Naples and gained prominent offices and titles of nobility there; by the late seventeenth century, the Cardenas were counts of Acerra and had formed family relations with the Carafa and Caracciolo, probably the two highest aristocratic clans of the kingdom.

2 Momus (the Greek god of mockery) and Aristarchus (a Hellenistic scholar known for his severe criticisms) are common erudite references in Baroque prefaces. Latini here, as through his references to Epicurus and Plato, is showing off his learning and laying claim to being a serious "professional" and "scholar," the terms he uses in his title to describe stewards. Epicurus and Epicurean were at the time routinely used as terms of abuse, implying shameful devotion to pleasure for its own sake.

rivulets, nor does the sun refuse to be attended by shadows. With which, in confirming my undying obligations to you, I kiss your hands most reverently.

Naples, April 6, 1692.

Of Your Excellency,

the most humble, devoted, and grateful servant,

Antonio Latini.

Benevolent reader:

If in this book you will not find (O courteous reader) that pure language and that propriety of terms and words, which the perfect Tuscan language requires, I beg you to deign take pity on me, because, since I wrote in Naples, I thought it best to use the terms familiar to this country, rather than foreign ones, here not understood.[3] Besides, I profess myself especially fond of this land, for the many advantages that I have always drawn from it, and much more for its own rare qualities. When one considers these qualities, one cannot help admitting that Nature went to much effort to endow this land with all the things which everyone admires in it. In the other works which I am preparing for publication I will endeavour (God willing) to improve my style, in as much as the weakness of my talent may allow it, and to approximate more accurately the common style. I advise you to consider that in this volume I do not propose rules to reason well, but to season well;[4] thus my only pretension is to render easier for beginners and others unskilled in this office the ways to organize banquets, prepare dishes, clarify the table service, and, at small or modest expense, satisfy the taste of those in command, and on the occasions that may present themselves. To someone perhaps little instructed in such affairs and in the customs in such things the practice of the specific matter contained in this book, and of a few extravagant dishes, may appear odd, expensive, or difficult; once however he will have considered them carefully he will find that they can all be done with all easiness, and that they will succeed to full satisfaction for whoever will try them. My life consumed in the courts of prelates and princes, my long practice of this office, and the advice of my amiable fellow professionals, who have aimed at the common benefit of those who will wish to enter in this craft, have moved me to publish this work, which has been approved by those same men. Appreciate then, O reader, my desire, which will always aim to the service of others, and while I prepare myself to give birth to other works, which will be useful to the practice of this exercise, I beg you to forgive my errors, and to maintain your health.[5]

---

3 It was common in Italy in this era to label as "foreign" everything from a state or even city other than one's own.

4 I am adapting Latini's pun: "*ben dire/ben condire*" (speak well/season well).

5 Latini uses a variety of terms to refer to activities, and I have tried to be consistent in rendering them: *arte* (craft), *esercizio* (exercise), *professione* (profession), and *officio* or *ufficio* (charge or position).

[After these two addresses, the volume contains several sonnets and other verses and anagrams in praise of the author, in both Latin and Italian, typical of erudite books of the time, which we can without regret omit here. The one perhaps most worthy of note is a "madrigal" authored by Silvestro Panicali, identified as "steward of the Most Excellent Lord The Count of Santo Stefano, Viceroy of Naples," which (rendered, I am afraid, in far too plain prose) reads: "Latini, your knowledge has no equal; you give laws to banquets, norms to tables, and food to the mind; you surpass, in stewardship, all marks and goals; in your book, I learn all that is new and rare in stewardship."[6]

These prefatory matters conclude with the permissions granted by the ecclesiastic and secular censors, attesting that the work contains nothing offensive to orthodox doctrine, good morals, or royal authority.]

ON THE DIGNITY
OF THE STEWARD,

And the qualities of his officials and assistants,
PART THE FIRST,
PUBLISHED
BY ANTONIO LATINI,
FROM COLLE AMATO.

So that everyone should have sufficient notice of the dignity and prerogatives of the steward, and of the excellence of this charge, I have deemed it appropriate to sketch them here, before I explain the qualities needed in the steward and demonstrate with how much good reason princes and grandees regard this charge with that particular esteem which compensates the merit of those who can fill it with the necessary decorum. Everyone agrees that the charge of the steward is to be considered among the greatest offices of any court, an opinion strengthened by many reasons, the most prominent of which is that to the trustworthiness and will of the steward are entrusted the life and honour of the master; thus the steward is bound to the greatest faithfulness.

The honour of the charge is verified by the second chapter of the Gospel of Saint John, in which the steward is called *Archytriclinus*, a word that indicates mastery and prominence, as it signifies the master of banquets, the person commanding all those who attend to food services.[7] No historian reports who truly invented the office, but it is certain to be very ancient, because I could not believe that the dinners of Lucullus, the banquets of Elagabalus, or the meals of Cyrus took place without a director.[8] In any case, it is certain that our Lord Jesus Christ, when he joined the marriage at Cana, was

---

6 On these kinds of texts in published cookbooks, see also Notaker, *A History of Cookbooks*, chap. 8.

7 John 2:8–9 (the marriage at Cana); the King James version translates the word Latini refers to as "governor of the feast" and "ruler of the feast."

8 Lucullus was a first-century BC Roman leader, famous for his rich table, Elagabalus was a notoriously lavish emperor (ruled 218–222), and Cyrus was a wise and all-powerful Persian emperor of the sixth century BC. Latini peppers his pages with evidence of his erudition: starting with scriptural and classical references was standard practice for any learned text in this era.

attended by such a minister, referred to in the Gospels as mentioned above. In the papal court the steward is greatly esteemed and so remarkable that, when there are banquets for royal ambassadors or other great personages, the principal knights of the Roman court follow the steward, and in the service of the papal table they are dependent upon the steward's orders. When the pontiff appears in a riding procession or other functions, two important prelates surround the steward, who thus attends to that sovereign monarch. On the occasion of conclaves the steward also enjoys very favourable treatment, among the cardinals; on this occasion he represents the very person of the master himself: in carrying the meals the court's gentlemen go first, forming a procession, and after them comes the mace before the steward, who occupies precisely the place of a cardinal, and he is followed by those bearing the dishes, and thus they all proceed up to the wheels of the conclave.[9] Once the new pontiff is elected, the steward obtains a privilege by papal bull, and is declared a palatine count, and he is authorized to wear the Cross of Christ on his chest and to hold any office in all cities in the papal domains. He is also exempted from all fiscal burdens, and has the right to transfer pensions and benefices; if a steward is made a bishop, as has happened several times, he only pays half the cost of the appointment bulls.

In the court of the Most August [Holy Roman] Emperor and of the Unvanquished Catholic Monarch [of Spain] this charge is reserved for the most important lords. The Spanish grandees are chosen for the service of their king for the royal table, and since there are many each of them is assigned a specific time, not to exceed a week. It is true, however, that, since it would not be decorous for such princes to enter the kitchen, they are in this charge assisted by others who take care of the kitchen and of all that is necessary, according to the commands of these lords; the lords, at the proper eating hour, go with their pages to take the dishes and accompany them to the royal table, where the dishes are then distributed according to the norms of each place, with each lord succeeding another, week by week.[10] In the court of the Most Christian King [of France] there also are many noble lords who exercise this charge, and the noblest and worthiest knights exercise it in the courts of many European princes, always with subordinate officials who actually oversee the kitchen, so that it be well ordered; the nobles simply attend the table of their sovereigns, with four substitutes, and rotate [in this role] each week.

The steward, in order to succeed, needs a quick and lively mind and must be courteous in manner and candid in approach; he must be clean in his dress, a friend of virtue and enemy of vice, and well organized in his actions. The fear of God must be the guiding light of his life, and he must faithfully ensure the health of his master, by giving him good food, proper to each season. He must spend liberally when needed, for his own glory and the dignity of his master; he must make clear the zeal he puts in serving his master with all care; he must be affable with all the members and dependents of the noble household and in particular with his own subordinates. He will command them agreeably, if he

---

9 The cardinals were enclosed for the election, and thus their meals were served through wheels rotating through walls or closed doors.

10 Here Latini reluctantly acknowledges that any remnant of the steward's tasks performed by actual noblemen represented largely a façade and involved no real service.

wishes to be served with apt precision, remembering that harsh commands produce hatred and ruin. Since in many courts the steward also serves as majordomo, I wish to offer advice also for the discharging of that office, one which the steward should hesitate in accepting, given that much work is needed already to be a good steward. Were he obliged to accept it, he must assume the care of all servants,[11] and in particular of the pages, providing them with good instructors, teaching them to be clean, how to go about hatless and gloveless, prohibiting them from sitting in his presence, reminding them often that, in serving at the table, they must not lean on, nor get too close to, any chair, and be careful in all their tasks. The steward should moreover visit, at different hours, and especially during the night, the pages' rooms to see whether they miss their hours, and whether they gamble, which must be prohibited, as gambling is often the reason of many excesses, and those most greedy for money never follow proper conduct.

The steward must attend to the care of the pages' rooms and beds, and when they need something, he should alert those responsible, and if the latter delay, the stewars should report them to his master, with such consideration that the latter will not be too angry. The steward must guard and protect the pages as if they were his children, and to regulate their shifts and days of work, he will prepare a written order and will display it in their rooms, so that they may use it as a guide to go eat before the master sits down to his table, and the steward will ensure that the pages be punctual in all their functions.

The steward must command the chamber assistants and pages to bring water bowls and towels, arranged above the bowls or on separate plates, and if the bowls were too heavy so that a page may not handle them by himself, he will order one of the gentlemen to help the page, since the steward himself must at all times stay near the master, or near the individual at the table who enjoys the highest respect, and to that person he must reverently and most precisely attend, even more than to the master himself.[12]

Once the guests are seated, the steward must appoint a gentleman for each guest, who will be constantly near him, and assist and serve him in all necessities of the table; no man should ever leave his assigned guest, unless asked to fetch his drink, in which case he will leave, take the cup tray, and bring it to the guest; should there be royal personages in attendance, or sovereign princes, at night time the steward himself, in between two torches or candle-holders, must offer them to drink with a deep curtsey, and then he will have one of his assistants bring the cup tray back to the drink station. Then another gentleman, [carrying] a gilded silver cup on a cup tray, covered with a white napkin, in between two round plates, will present this napkin to the guest after the guest has taken his drink, and then with a curtsey take it back. If there are royal personages, the steward may also change the napkins, as needed, during the meal.

---

11 Latini's term here is *famiglia* (family), which draws from the Latin term for the household staff, and links to traditional notions of the household as an extended family that includes all servants. The whole paragraph expresses Latini's paternalistic concept of the steward's role.

12 Latini refers to these attendants as *Gentil Huomini* (gentlemen), though they are clearly members of the serving staff. Besides Latini's constant desire to ennoble his craft, this usage reflects also the old tradition of employing young nobles as pages to great lords; this would have been extremely rare in Latini's time and circle.

The steward must warn the pages and other helpers not to show gluttony at the table, since it is highly indecent that, when the dishes are taken away, the servants should taste the food, and create embarrassment with the credenziero, as this produces many troubles.

The steward will make sure to ask the cook if the food is ready at the allotted hour, and to note when the table and credenza are ready and set with all that is needed. After ascertaining all this, he will go to his master and, approaching him discreetly, he will whisper to him that the table is ready. Having received the master's order to start the service, the pages and other assistants, or the other stewards, will have the dishes brought to the kitchen by a footman, who will take them from the credenziero.

The steward also, once he knows the character of the pages, ought to give them work appropriate to their mind and status, keeping them from laziness, which engenders all evil. If any of them were desirous of studying, the steward will ask the chaplain to teach them, and if another should wish to learn the exercise of arms, the steward will provide an apt master; if another is interested in riding, the steward will ask the guardian of the horses, or his assistant, to deign instruct him; it will be good to teach them to dance before they learn to ride, because through dancing they become slimmer and more dexterous in riding; and so in all activities, which will always result in glory for the master and in praise for the steward. In instructing the pages, it will be wise to inquire into the will and desires of their parents.

Since I have for twenty-five years organized sumptuous banquets for great personages, I deem myself able to offer some advice to those who wish to embark in such a noble charge. The steward must remember that the life and honour of his master are in his hands, and must therefore by all means acquire the benevolence of his master, and meet his taste in food. A steward would be worthy of blame if he wholly trusted the cooks, from whom one cannot always expect diligence, punctuality, and exactitude.

He deserves the name of true and perfect steward who knows how to order all sorts of soups, sour and sweet, and who has served with praise and good reputation at many splendid and royal banquets.

The steward must provide the court with four able officials, informing the majordomo of his choices and seeking [to make] advantageous appointments. The steward must appoint a cook, a credenziero, a purchaser, and a stock manager.

Of the qualities needed in the cook.

It is above all necessary that the cook be an honest, loyal man, and that he know how to do his job well, with diligence and punctuality; that he not be a lover of wine, because a cook who is guilty of this vice often ruins the steward's reputation, by cooking without the necessary condiments. He must be sure to serve very carefully, and to be clean in cooking dishes, never permitting, as much as possible, that his assistants be too involved in it. He must not waste any of the provisions given to him for the kitchen's needs, remembering that he must account most strictly for them to the steward. He should be watchful that assistants and servants not cause his loyalty to become suspect. He should divide clearly all provisions to be used in cooking, and he must order his most experienced assistant to do the same; he should also well instruct some of his assistants in his profession, so that, should the cook be ill, there will be someone able to step in. He should not allow in the kitchen any traffic of people from the household or from outside, because such traffic always ends up being harmful and deplorable. He should in all things abide closely by the orders he will receive every day from the steward. The latter, in choosing the cook, should make sure that he be neither too young nor too old, lest limited experience, or excessive fatigue, make him incapable of his task. Therefore it would be a good idea, before receiving a cook into one's service, to try him out in the preparation of some dishes, in the working of some pastry dough, and in the cooking of both regular and lean dishes.

If faithfulness is required in the cook, how much more it is needed in the credenziero, whom one must know very well, because he is the guardian of the silver, the linen, and other things necessary to the master's service, including all cold dishes.

He must make sure to clean the silver, to keep the sideboard neat, to guard the linen, which must be folded in various ways, especially the napkins, in the shape of birds or other animals. He must be experienced in preparing cold dishes, in garnishing them, and in placing them on the table properly, all under the watchful eye of the steward. The same official should also be experienced in preparing royal salads, cold waters, and similar things, for use at the sideboard, such as to ice fruits, and other things that may be needed.

The purchaser should be young, experienced in shopping, and faithful, as proved by his actions, because he will hold the money needed to provision the house and buy all that is needed for the kitchen. He must be able to read and write, because when travelling it is up to him to note the daily expenses. He ought always to buy the best available foods, and not to be duped by sellers, who almost all tend to cheat. He must obey the steward more than anyone else in the court, and follow the steward's shopping list. He should bring to the storage places everything that he purchases. He should not overpay for anything, nor be too close to the stock manager, who must counter-sign all lists of purchases; the steward will also check all lists and, if he finds any untruthful ones, will correct them. Therefore lists should be always examined carefully, especially by the steward, whose responsibility this task is. If the steward should suspect any flaws in the lists, he should mention it to the majordomo.

I conclude by saying that, since this charge may be the object of much jealousy, it is necessary that the purchaser raise no shadow of suspicion, by either licentious conversation, or frequent gambling, or clothes overly sumptuous and unsuited to his condition.

Instructions for the stock manager.

Since this official cares for all foods and other things he must be known as a reliable man, of clear conscience; should he give any sign of licentiousness or carelessness he would produce a most deplorable impression.

He must mark every day in his books every small thing that is purchased or given, noting who gives it, and its quantity, weight, or number. He also must mark every day what leaves the stocks for the service of the master and household.

What he has in storage he must keep in good condition, and provide the steward with a full list, so that the latter, in forming the shopping lists, knows what cured meats, birds, cheese, wine, and other things are in stock. The steward must frequently inspect the stock manager's books, so as to be always truly informed of everything. The stock manager should maintain all necessary tools to measure and weigh what is given to the servants, with all precision, and when he gives to others he should not appear greedy for himself, since this would create a bad opinion of him.

The steward must also warn the credenzieri to keep the silver and linen clean and safe, the knives well sharpened, and the tableware in good condition; to prepare tasty salads, and to do well all that they are responsible for. The steward must know how to arrange any dish perfectly; he may take one for himself when the dishes are removed from the table, as he wishes, though this only applies to a married steward, or if he eats by himself, because, if he eats with the other gentlemen, then he does not enjoy this privilege.

The stock manager must dispose of anything that is worn or no longer good, with the steward's consent, who will select such things as his prudence suggests.

Instructions for the wine steward.

The wine steward must be very proficient in making prepared waters, with sugar in the right proportions; he must be clean in his service; and choose the wines for the master's table, even though in some courts this responsibility goes to the cup bearer.

The wine steward must not allow anyone to drink from the same glasses as the master; he must keep the sideboard provided with waters and wines, refreshing the glasses, of which he will need many, including some whimsical ones for when there are outside guests.[13] He must also keep his office well furnished in carafes and barrels, and above all he must always take care of the master's magnificence and reputation. When travelling, he will bring with him a small cellar of good wines, and guard it carefully; also, a small basket with the cup tray, glasses, small carafes, and other necessary things.

The lists that the steward must prepare for his subordinates.

When the master wants to hold a banquet, the steward will receive from the master, or his officials, the necessary orders, and his preferences as to the style of the banquet, and how many services are called for; all this the steward must notify to the credenziero, purchaser, and cook, so that they all know clearly what they need to do.

The steward must be careful to save as much as possible when shopping, trying to limit expenses; however he must not be so keen on saving that the result be indecorous, or a mark of sordidness for himself or his master, whose glory and fame are in the steward's care.

---

13 *Foresteria* implies guests who stay for a time in the household, not simply dinner guests; the term literally means a space for foreigners, but it is not actually required that the guests be foreigners.

List for a banquet for six people, to be shown to the master, so that he may increase or decrease it as he prefers.

First cold credenza service, which may be put on the table to be seen.

A pie decorated with the coats of arms of the guests, filled with bits of veal, chicken, ham slices, udder slices, thin slices of cured back fat, slices of *soppressata*, the usual spices, and other suitable ingredients.[14]

A turkey, seasoned with salt and pepper, larded with slices of candied pumpkin, the plate garnished with pulled ham mixed with lemon slices and variously coloured aniseeds.

A royal salad, placed in the middle of the table.

A covered tart with fruits cooked in syrup, glazed on top like marble.

A light soup for each guest with a tender pigeon boiled with liver bits, small lettuce stems, breads slices underneath, with a light broth of egg yolks and lemon juice, and cinnamon on top.

First kitchen service.

A mixed fried dish, with brains, veal sweetbreads, slices of veal liver, whole chicken livers, quartered artichokes, all fried in good lard, the plate garnished with Genoese-style small pastries mixed with lemon slices.[15]

A boiled capon, surrounded by beef slices, the dish garnished with slices of salted meat, with herbs and salt on top.

A French-style pottage with bits of pigeons, veal chops, whole chicken livers, ham slices, St. George's mushrooms, pine nuts, the usual spices, truffle slices, and other suitable ingredients.

A little pie for each guest, made with short crust pastry and filled with a ground mixture of veal, sweetbreads, cockscomb and chicken testicles, pistachios, pine nuts, the usual spices, and the usual little broth of egg yolks and lemon juice.[16]

Roasted veal fillet garnished with various puff pastries, surrounded by lemon slices.

You will also serve some pizza or covered tart, which will already be on the table.

Place on the table all the fruits you can find.

Parmesan cheese.

---

14 Soppressata is a kind of dry salami, which in Italy today is available in many regional varieties, cured or uncured. Latini never specified what "the usual spices" were to him; the Spanish cook Francisco Martínez Montiño in his *Arte de cocina, pasteleria, vizcocheria, y conserveria* (Barcelona: Maria Angela Martí, 1763; 1st ed. 1611) explained that, when he said to use "all spices" he meant "pepper, cloves, nutmeg, ginger, and saffron" (83); Latini however mentions all of these individually (ginger only rarely).

15 The small pastries here are *bocconotti*; Latini often uses this term (which is related to the Italian word *boccone*, meaning a bite, a mouthful), and also *offelle*, for small pastries (the ingredients of offelle are usually sweeter than those of bocconotti).

16 Shortcrust pastry is Latini's *pasta frolla*, a sweet crust used today in Italy primarily for desserts, though in Naples still also used with savoury fillings of pasta, meat, or vegetables; see Riley, *The Oxford Companion*, 380–81.

Having thus noted how to prepare the dishes for the banquet, you need to show the master the list, and he will increase or reduce it as he wishes, and then you will give the shopping list to the purchaser.

Shopping list from the above menu for the first cold dish.

Five pounds of flour.[17]
One pound of lard.
Six ounces of sugar.
Four eggs.
One cockerel.
One pigeon.
One pound of veal.
Four ounces of ham.
Two ounces of cured back fat.
Three ounces of soppressata.

Shopping list for the second cold dish.

One turkey.
Six ounces of candied pumpkin.
Four ounces of pulled ham.

Shopping list for the third cold dish.

Salad, one *baiocco*.[18]
Twelve *taralli*.[19]
Raisins, pine nuts, olives, capers, five baiocchi.
One pomegranate.
Six ounces of grapes.
One pound of candied pumpkin and citron.
Two hard boiled eggs.
Two ounces of ground meat, and other ingredients at the steward's discretion.

Shopping list for the fourth cold dish.

One and a half pounds of flour.
Five ounces of lard.
Two *rotoli* of pears.
Two pounds of sugar to make the syrup for the pears.
Two ounces of sugar.
One-eighth of one ounce of cinnamon.

---

17 The Naples pound in Latini's time was about 320 grams (i.e., a tad under three-fourths of a modern US pound, which is 453.5 grams); see details on all measurements in the Appendix.

18 A baiocco is a fairly low-value coin.

19 Taralli are circular, braided, or twisted breads, today usually hard and savoury (the most popular version in Naples today is called "lard and pepper").

Shopping list for the light soup.

> Six pigeons.
> Six fresh eggs.
> The livers of the said chickens [thus in the text; I presume Latini meant the pigeons].
> One lemon.
> Two bread loaves to make slices.

Shopping list for the first hot dish.

> Two pairs of sweetbreads.
> One pair of brains.
> One pound of liver.
> Six chicken livers.
> Four artichokes.
> Two pounds of lard for frying.
> One pound of flour.
> Four eggs.
> Eight ounces of flour for the small pastries.
> Half a pound of sugar.
> One thigh bone.
> Six ounces of candied pumpkin and citron.
> Four eggs.
> One lemon.

Shopping list for the second hot dish.

> One capon.
> Two pounds of beef.
> Six ounces of soppressata.

Shopping list for the third hot dish.

> Two pigeons.
> One pound of veal.
> Six chicken livers.
> Three ounces of ham.
> One quarter pound of St. George's mushrooms.
> Two ounces of pine nuts and pistachios.
> Four ounces of truffles.

Shopping list for the fourth hot dish.

> One *rotolo*[20] of flour.
> Eight ounces of butter.
> Eight eggs.

---

20 A rotolo was almost 0.9 kilos.

Two pounds of veal.
One pair of veal sweetbreads (twelve if one uses kid sweetbreads).
Four ounces of pistachios and pine nuts.
Four eggs for the little broth.
One lemon.
One pound of sugar.

Shopping list for the fifth dish.

Two rotoli of veal fillet.
One pound of flour for the pastry.
Six ounces of sugar for the same.
Four eggs.

For this entire meal, one can use the following spices.

One and a half ounces of cinnamon.
Two ounces of pepper.
One ounce of cloves.
Two nutmegs.
Two pounds of salt.
One rotolo of cured back fat to season these dishes.
Two rotoli of beef to make broth.
Eight lemons and sour oranges, and aromatic herbs.

The steward, having drafted a list like the one above, will add up all the totals, for instance, all the veal adds up to X pounds, or the flour to X pounds, and so for all the ingredients for all the dishes, so as to give it to the purchaser; and if the master should wish to know the cost of the entire meal, the steward will give him a thorough account, according to the prices current wherever they are, though this happens rarely.

Having prepared these shopping lists, the steward has to prepare lists for each seller: for instance, in the list for the druggist or spice-seller, the steward will note all the spices, sugars, and other goods sold by them; the butcher's list will include all the meats, that is, veal, beef, udder, and the like; the list of the poulterer will include all the chickens and birds; and each seller with whom the household does business will have his separate list, which the purchaser will give to the steward, leaving always a copy with each seller, so that they can be later compared.

Having prepared the list of everything needed for the kitchen, the steward will prepare another one to give to the cook, in which he will describe how all the things that have been bought should be cooked; the steward should not neglect to visit the kitchen every now and then, to check that things proceed well and in good order, and to ensure that all kitchen helpers practise their tasks, for instance he should tell the person in charge of pottages how many dishes the latter must prepare, or the person who makes the pies how many are needed, so that everybody in the kitchen will act with order and avoid confusion.

The credenziero should receive the list of all cold dishes, which he will check, and he will make sure that all the plates are retouched in silver or gold, and to decorate all the triumphs that are to be placed on the table;[21] if the banquet room should be small, the nearest and most contiguous room should be used to prepare the table decorations, and in managing these decorations the credenziero will do only as he is ordered to by the steward; the same credenziero should be practised in the folding of napkins and table cloths.

How to set the dishes on the table.

The under-steward, who stays in the kitchen, will diligently take care that all the dishes that will be served at the table be set up in the order prescribed by the steward; as the cold appetizers are already on the table when the guests sit down, the steward will have the hot appetizers carried first, and then the main and hot dishes, as set for the kitchen services; if the guests are served with two dishes, then each food will be carried in two dishes at the same time, and the same with three or four dishes, always in the same order.

When the servings have arrived in the banquet room, the steward will place them on the table, without allowing anyone else to do so. They will be handed to the carver, to divide them into portions; one must never remove servings from the table until the next ones have arrived from the kitchen, so that there always are at least two full hot dishes on the table, or more, as called for by the specific order of service.

The steward also must care for every need of the table, such as bread or wine or anything else, so that nothing ever be wanting. One must never take away the hot small plates from the guests, unless the proper time has come, so as not to trouble their enjoyment; one must wait discreetly that they finish their food, and delay the change to the cold service and the fruit service; one must pay special attention not to violate the rules of an apt service.

Here are important warnings for the steward
for his advantage with any house guests.

The steward must diligently inform himself of how many sets of guests there will be, and of those who eat at the prince's table, which he can ask either of the herald who comes in advance, or of the gentlemen who meet the guests by coach, or of other neighbours who have lodged the same guests.

The prince's first table, with six personages, can be served at one royal plate; one dish for each guest up to the number expected; one can give them a light soup made with various ingredients, and other appetizers, in small plates that are not counted among the dishes; then the dishes will be a fried one, a roast, an English-style pie, a composite dish, and others like these, at discretion.

The second table, of main officials, who will eat after the prince, will sit ten people, to be served at two royal plates, with the same order as the first table, and if there should

---

21 Triumphs (*trionfi*) were elaborate table decorations, in the most remarkable shapes and materials; see sections below for details and descriptions; retouched is a literal translation of Latini's *ritocco*, which suggests some form of embellishment.

be no carver, then the guests can be served at a single royal plate, but well provided. By royal plates I mean composite dishes, all of the same quality, and, so that these guests be well treated, they should be offered five or six servings.

A table of titled gentlemen who eat at the same time as the prince may sit twelve guests; they should be served at two royal plates, and in the same order as above.

The table of lower officials, with fourteen people, should be served at two royal plates, and five hot servings.

The table for low servants and other common people, which accompany the others, will have thirty guests, and will be served at four royal plates, in the same order as above. Those chosen to serve these common people must be forewarned to treat them well, because this sort of men always have the trumpet ready at their mouth, and if they are treated less than well they love to ruin their hosts' reputation.

The burden of this service must be given to capable people, who will bring honour to the host, and two apt people will be better at this than several inapt ones, because a multitude brings confusion, and the proverb is true that says that where many roosters sing, daylight never comes, and I speak from experience, because in many circumstances when masters gave this task to several incompetent people, things did not go well, with little honour for the master or the steward.

When managing wedding banquets, one must know how many gentlemen will be at the first table, and whether any more people are expected, and one should arrange the lists as described above. If there will be thirty people at the table, they can be served with four royal dishes, well provided, filled with varied and perfect compositions and with the best condiments. The steward must have good broths ready, and meat juices, and the juice of a wether roast, making sure that everything is cooked properly, in the right proportions, and with the right amounts of spices and aromatic herbs for each dish.[22] Once the meat is cooked, and all the ingredients, one must compose the dishes with order, with their soups underneath, as preferred, and with a few flavourful condiments; I deem it much better to prepare fewer good dishes, than many that taste badly.

Every grand banquet can be offered with twelve hot dishes, well arranged and brought to the table with order; I beliebe those err who fill the table with fifty dishes, because that causes a great expense and gives poor satisfaction to the guests, who will far more enjoy ten good hot dishes than fifty poorly seasoned, insipid, or tasteless ones.

The steward must have the tables properly set, with their triumphs and cold dishes in the right places, and in apt locations, according to the season, because if a banquet is held in summer, it will be better to hold it in a fresh and airy place, near some garden, so that the eyes may enjoy a pleasant and pretty view.

The steward must provide the court with good officials, subject to him, such as cooks, credenzieri, purchasers, and stock managers, choosing such that will meet with both his and the master's approval, and he must devote much attention to this, because it is these officials who make the steward's reputation.

The steward must make sure that everything that will be served for banquets can be seen by everybody, and that the food and wine credenze be properly set.

---

22 The wether is a castrated ram; it was quite common in cooking in Latini's time.

It will rebound to great reputation for the steward if at times the master will demonstrate publicly some sign of his confidence, for instance by whispering in the steward's ear, or performing some other such act of trust, as happened to me a few times with the Lord Cardinals Rossetti and Antonio Barberini, glories of the holy college and of the Vatican, who many times called me aside pretending to have something important to tell me, and instead it was some trivial thing, but important for me, since it gave those present evidence of their esteem for me. Cardinal Rossetti many times, both in Rome and in his diocese of Faenza, honoured me by asking me to offer him my arm, and to accompany him thus to his coach, and this seems very proper, that a lord should display some courtesy to someone who has in his hands the master's life, reputation, and good bodily management, all of which rest on food.[23]

Although I here speak of eating well, and of seasoning food well, I would not want any Aristarchus or censor to accuse me of being a glutton, or a lover of excess, because even though I praise good eating, I do not approve of parasitical eating, or of excess or immoderate gluttony; indeed I detest those men given to avid voraciousness, as we read of Ulatislao Iacello, Artidamus of Miletus, and a certain Albinus, of whom we read, not without disgust, that in one meal he ate five hundred figs, one hundred peaches, ten melons, a large basket of grapes, one hundred warblers, as many oysters, and ten capons. I detest gluttony, as a capital sin, and I praise a neat, sober, and proper eating, because it contributes to our life and preservation.[24]

I must warn that in summer one must have at the ready marinated pigeons, cockerels, wild doves, veal tongue, and veal feet, to be used in various dishes and fried plates. These things must be boiled and cooked, and then boiled vinegar, cloves, and cinnamon must be sprinkled over them for a marinade or *scapece*.[25] When these things must be served at the table, first they must be floured, then fried with lard, and over them a royal sauce of vinegar, sugar, and cinnamon; this sauce can also be used in fish-based dishes of all sorts.[26]

---

23 These episodes and suggestions reflect Latini's grand view of the steward. They also suggest the performance aspects of Baroque social life, in which even domestic actions were public, and pretending was the rule of the game for everyone. Crisci, in a long list of the steward's qualities, includes that he ought to be "expert in conversation, civil with all," *Lucerna de corteggiani* (Naples: Roncagliolo, 1634), 58. Carlo Rossetti (1614–1681), cardinal in 1643, was bishop of his native Faenza since 1643; in his autobiography Latini claims to have initially resisted entering Rossetti's employment, as the prelate had the reputation of being "fastidious, difficult, and impossible to please," but he later declares himself very pleased with his experience in this employment (Latini, *Autobiografia*, 43). Antonio Barberini (1607–1671), nephew of Pope Urban VIII (ruled 1623–1644), became a cardinal in 1627.

24 Here again Latini seeks to impress the reader with his erudite references: the first man mentioned might be Ladislaus III Jagiellon, a fifteenth-century king of Poland accused by some opponents of excessive indulgence; Albinus is Emperor Clodius Albinus (one of several claimants to imperial power after the murder of Commodus in 192), and Latini's source for his gluttony is the *Life of Albinus* in the *Historia Augusta* (11.2–3); I have not identified Artidamus.

25 Scapece was popular in Spanish cuisine too (*escabeche*) and is still a popular Neapolitan preparation: fried food marinated in boiled vinegar and served at room temperature with herbs, today done in particular with zucchini.

26 "Royal" preparations were of course elaborate ones, and the dishes thus labelled varied in

Similarly, chickens seasoned with salt and pepper must first be boiled, and then seasoned, and they are eaten cold; the same is done with capons, hens, and pullets; if you wish to eat these hot, you should put them back in the griddle, broken into pieces, with bread crumbs and pepper on top, with malmsey wine or lemon juice, as you prefer, in the dish.

Soused fish must first be fried and then seasoned with salt, pepper, lemon or sour orange juice, or another sauce as you prefer; this fish is usually eaten cold, and it is tasty, though it is not a lean dish, and I will speak of this in its own chapter; it too can be heated in the griddle, with crustless bread on top.

To season trout, you first fry it, then spray it with vinegar with a little brush or a rosemary twig, sprinkle various spices on it, and underneath it put myrtle or bay leaves, as is convenient; usually it is served cold, garnished with myrtle or bay leaves, and if you wish to serve it hot you should not put it in a griddle, but in a well-tinned pan, garnishing the side of the dish with lemon slices, or with whichever fried pastries you prefer.[27]

There are different varieties of trout, white or of other colours; the white ones are the true and best ones. Perfect ones are found here in the Kingdom of Naples, and in other places, dotted with small red dots, or others slightly olive-coloured, known as *carpioni*; the duke of Sora has these latter ones in an estate of his known as La Pesca [Fishing].

You will always be able to use salami of any sort, soppressata from Nola [near Naples] or other places, Bologna or Florence *mortadella* [a pork salami], if you boil them in water and wine, cut along their long side, and held in a cloth, with myrtle and bay leaves; similarly good hams, if served whole, are usually served by the credenziero raw, sliced, in small plates.

Larger salami can be served hot or cold, as you prefer, noting that, if one is serving meals to the same guests over a number of days, they should be served hot on the first day, with herbs around them or other garnishes; the next day they should be placed cold on the table, atop folded napkins, with laurel or myrtle branches around them; the carver usually slices them or cuts them into small corners, and they are served in small plates.

When guests will be served stews, the carver must first serve them the appetizers, that is, salami, hams, sausages, or other salted things; then the boiled dish must be served, if there are no other appetizers. Cold pies can be served instead of boiled dishes; afterwards, one serves the roast, and if there are no other appetizers aside from the salted things, such as sweetbreads, livers, brains, testicles, or fried chicken livers, you may serve, as a second appetizer, warblers, larks, thrushes, or other small birds, surrounded with sausages.

---

different authors; "royal sauce" usually included sugar, cinnamon, vinegar, citron, and spices (today, the term is used often for a sauce with carrots, parsley, flour, milk, onion, and crustless bread).

27 Latini often uses *foglie di lauro* in cooking; he also often uses *frondi di lauro*, occasionally in cooking, but more often for decorative purposes, or placed on a plate under cold foods (rarely does he refer to *frondi di alloro*, the two names often referring to the same tree); I have translated the former as bay leaves and the latter as laurel branches, trying also to suit the context.

If the first appetizer does not include ham or salami, in the second one you may use birds or liver; after the roast you may serve a pottage or stew, or meatballs, composite dishes, or small pies.

Midway through a meal, especially a lean one, in the morning, when you bring out the fruit, you must also serve olives, or small spinach salads, with their *tondini*[28] garnished at your whim, a condiment of quinces or plums, pizze or covered tarts, peaches or sour cherries in syrup, which things the credenziero must place on the table at the end of the fruit service; you can also serve little soups of St. George's mushrooms or truffles, and in Naples we also serve sea food; once the fruit is removed, the confections follow [*confettura*].[29]

If you wish to follow Spanish-style service, once you have set the table, with all the cold dishes, you can prepare bowls of good broth, with slices of toasted bread in it, covered, and give one to each guest; then you will serve the roast, veal or pullets or pigeon or any sort of chicken; then you will serve the appetizers in small round plates, placed in front of the table settings. On lean days, you will serve salted tuna belly, caviar, anchovies, dried tuna salami, gurnard, and other sauces as you wish; on non-lean days, you may serve sweetbreads, livers, or other such things; then you will serve a composite dish or a pie or a stew and then another roast. You may also serve a stew or salad, and at the end a sweet dish, and this is the true order of Spanish service. One must note that all the composite dishes must be spicy; at the end fruit and the confections as usual.

Service in the French, English, or German style can be arranged following Italian practice. Service in the Venetian style must always have the dishes full on the table, and they are brought all together, well covered and six in number; you uncover them and arrange them in order, three per side, each pair facing each other; when the guests sit down, the dishes are carved one by one and placed back in their place; if the plate is emptied, as often happens, you will cover it and place a small round plate on top, and you will return it to its place, and you will do this until the end of the meal. Do the same with the fruit once you place it on the table; then the sweet things. Generally, follow Italian practice, which is the best service of all, always following your master's taste, and the pleasure of those who command you.

Here I show how the master should act with his officials, and the officials, and the entire household, with the master.

As many times it happens that in the courts of great lords the officials do not receive that good treatment which is apt to animate each man to serve with due faithfulness, it seems useful to discuss a few specifics; I urge all to divest themselves of vehement

---

28 Here, and in several other places, Latini mentions *tondini* (small round plates; he also uses *piattini*, which simply means small plates); later, in his descriptions of banquets, he uses the term tondini also to indicate a whole category of small side dishes.

29 Confetture today primarily means jams, but in Latini's time the term could also refer to more heavily manipulated fruits (see introduction): in describing actual banquets, Latini usually used the term in conjunction with candied things and the context indicates something one could eat with one's fingers (thus, probably "confections").

passions, which sometimes clutter our spirit, which is only too credulous toward the malicious reports of envious tongues. Thus a prudent master should never lend his ear to those who try to arouse his suspicions against the steward or other officials, as this is a way for him to lose the respect of those who must serve him; if these should see the ease with which the master believes all that he hears they may no longer execute the steward's orders; they may even become so obstinate that they despise or deride the steward, as someone deprived of the credit and good graces of his master. Thus the only result of all of this is bad service for the master, and bad reputation for the steward or other officials, who become wholly incapable because they do not get their due respect. Therefore, if the master suspects any of his officials, he should try to gather information about his habits, qualities, and life from people outside the household; if he finds him to be guilty of some fault, he can remove him from service, but in such a way that the domestics and those who dislike the accused not think that this is the effect of their malice. It is a proven fact that in any court there is always someone who hates the steward or any other official who enjoys some power. The steward must always pay attention to punctual service and to his master's budget; if each official tried solely to satisfy the greedy spirit of the servants it is certain that he would cause the ruin of his master. In many courts the steward is also the majordomo, so that the whole household is subject to him; if he should find any servant lacking in honesty or faithfulness, he must warn him in a fraternal spirit, but if the servant should fail to correct himself the steward must alert the master; the master, if he is sure of the integrity of the official, must trust him, since experience teaches that many servants seem the image of goodness in the presence of their master, but in his absence they have nothing in them but the finest and most deceitful guile. Therefore the master must esnure the quality of all his servants, and not trust appearances; if the master is sure of their good qualities, he will tell the steward, the cook is a man of all goodness, the purchaser is honest, the credenziero is loyal in his service and has been in the household for a long time, therefore it is good that you should treat them with courtesy and with all sweetness; thus the steward will find himself forced not to use that rigour that he may otherwise employ. He should carefully perform his service, and let everyone perform theirs and follow the master's interests, lest they bring detriment to the steward.

The steward, and majordomo, must never be deprived of authority over the cook, stock manager, purchaser, credenziero, and others in the household; without the authority of the steward, everyone would do what he pleases. Those officials who do not regulate the government and economy of the household are useless; and some masters find satisfaction in challenging the steward or the majordomo or other household officials, in front of everyone, and this ruins the officials' standing. If the master finds that he has to scold some official he should do it in secret, in the same manner employed by a master worthy of eternal praise, who, whenever any household official entered his chamber to discuss household business, asked everyone else to leave, even his confidants, and the result in his court was a marvellous order and the greatest peace.

The master should therefore consider it true munificence to obtain above all the advancement of his faithful servants, because this is a way to acquire praise and eternal veneration, both from the domestics and from outsiders, as we can see in the acts of many generous lords who achieved the advancement of their faithful ministers. A prime example of this is the splendour of Pope Clement X [ruled 1670–1676] who, recognizing all the virtues of an honest life in his steward, Monsignor Gentile of Camerino, made him so rich that today he lives with all dignity in the city of Rome, where he has built palaces and many other conveniences. Many other princes are still remembered for their generosity; once, when Emperor Charles V [also king of Spain, ruled 1516/19–1556] brought the Imperial Eagle to the kingdom of Naples [in 1535–1536], he was received with all munificence by the prince of Bisignano, the most illustrious lord of that kingdom; since the prince's steward had, with the highest skill, organized the emperor's meals during his entire stay in the kingdom, as a reward he was invested by the emperor of some fiefdoms in the kingdom, which his descendants still enjoy, having added to them extraordinary titles and riches.[30]

It is true that to attain such things he who serves in any court is bound to every diligence, because that is the ladder by which one acquires the benevolence of one's master, from which emanate all other good fortunes which serve as the basis to one's aggrandizement. Attempt therefore above all things to please the temperament of your prince, from whom you will then obtain all the benefits you desire for yourself and your descendants.

Useful instructions for the carver.

Although in Naples often these two offices and names, of steward and carver, are confused, and the same man exercises both, in Rome and other Italian courts they are different charges and the one does not meddle in the tasks of the other.

The carver should be young, because old men's hands tremble and so they cannot easily keep things up in the air on the point of their long forks.

He must dress well and be neat, with his sword, where it is customary, even when he is carving at the table in a country habit.

He must be elegantly placed at the table of his master, especially in the presence of guests, who are apt to criticize every small flaw.

The carver should wear a beautiful ring on the little finger of the left hand, so that when he carves in the air it may be more visible to the guests; he must avoid facial gestures or frowns; rather he has to do everything with gravity and grace. He should not touch anything with his hands, but everything with the point of his knife or long fork, and he should not raise too high the arm with which he holds the long fork, so that the fat should not drip onto his hand.

He should not be too close to the carving table, but at a distance of two *palmi* [about 20 inches], and he should never leave the carving station until the fruit service is finished.

If he should have need to blow his nose, clear his throat, or spit, he should skillfully leave his station and immediately return, pretending that he had left to fetch something needed for his task. He should not speak unless questioned, and when he replies he

---

30 Here are Latini's wildest dreams, of stewards acquiring princely riches, titles, and fiefdoms, joining thus the very elevated social group in whose service Latini spent his entire life.

should be courteous and speak well, as Pythagoras says that a man who speaks moderately makes clear both what he knows and what he does.[31]

If he has occasion to laugh, he must do so with his mouth only half-opened. When he carves in silver plates, he should watch out not to dent the plates. When he carves in the air, he should not show any fear; fear weakens all actions. He must avoid any chance to provoke the master to publically scold him.

He must make sure to offer dishes proper to the quality of each guest; he should take into consideration the age, the corpulence, the temperament, and the condition of the teeth of each guest.

TREATISE I: *On the Art and Craft of Carving*

Though other authors have taught the way to carve, I esteemed it a merit in my work to add a few notions, rather to give lustre to this profession than for the needs of these professionals. I know full well that this office is learned more with practice and exercise than with study and reading; nonetheless it will be nothing but profitable to give its rules and study its prescriptions.

Once the guests are seated, the carver should approach the table, and go to the carving station, greeting all the guests with a humble and modest bow, beginning with the master and extending his bow around the whole table. Since cardinals cede precedence to nobody, except a few great ladies, it will be good for the carver to bow to everybody, but with his head somewhat lower when facing the highest-ranking guests. Having come near the table, he will always face his master, and be careful not to get confused, and to remember fully which guests have received their plate and which have not; if the carver's memory is not too sharp, it will be good that he always have in front of himself as many plates as there are guests, and that they be served in good style, without confusion, trying to avoid those fights that tend to happen among pages eager to remove the plates quickly from the table, which can cause indecency and scorn, not without demerit of the carver or steward.

When the carver starts carving, he will hold his long fork and raise what he needs to carve slightly above the plate; if there is no space on the master's table, he must arrange for a knife station nearby, making sure that it be in front of the master, so that the carver can more carefully perform his work. It is however always better to carve at the table at which the master is seated.

In the courts of great lords the carver, after having given each guest his portion, usually also takes a plate for himself of whatever he prefers; I believe it is better to prepare this plate in advance, before the dishes of the various foods are all mixed together. A good carver, I believe, will always carve in the presence of the master, and at his table, or at a nearby table. A carver should have civility, urbanity, a handsome appearance, good speech, modesty, and sagaciousness.

---

31 Crisci noted that the carver should not "speak, laugh, or spit," and that he should be "deaf, and not repeat what he hears at the table," *Lucerna*, 56–57.

A good carver must be well versed in carving all birds and quadrupeds, both whole and in pieces, with two knives, and all this meat he must know how to grind; this carving has to be done with the long fork held high, with that dexterity and agility that are the marks of good professionals. I declare that what I write here I address to practised professionals, not to inept and inexperienced ones.

Of how to carve domestic and wild birds.

The carver who has reached a reasonable level of expertise and ease in his profession must be able with his long fork to take any food presented to him; once he has well skewered the bird, or any other animal, he will carve with ease and grace, cutting where needed in the bird's joints, always mindful to garnish the plate properly.

In carving a cockerel, he must skewer it with the tip of his knife in the breast, raise it somewhat in the air, and turn it so that the bird's breast face one of the plates placed on the left of the knife station; then he will take it with the long fork in the back, and will cut the joints in two places, at the neck and the torso, on both sides, so as to drop the bird's neck onto the plate. Then he will cut the tip of the right wing, making sure the tip of the knife always come outward. Having cut the right wing, he must cut the right thigh in three places, between the thigh and the torso, under the thigh on the side of the *coderone*, and at the thigh joint itself, separating it, if he can, from the upper thigh.[32] Similarly, he must cut the right shoulder, above the joint to the wing, making sure not to detach it completely, which he should do also with the other joints of birds. Turn the cockerel so that the neck faces to the right, and cut the tip of the left wing, as you did the right wing; cut carefully at the shoulders, thighs, and upper thighs; then give two cuts to the coderone, one to the left and one to the right, always turning the bird with the head towards yourself: in turning any bird, the head of the bird should face the carver's chest, because it would be uncivil the other way, with the coderone towards the chest, as I have seen done at times by people with little practice.[33]

The same carving must be used with all other birds to be shared between the master and the guests, that is, hens, young turkeys, and capons, and other larger birds, because they cannot be placed whole in front of the guests, but have to be carved.

How to carve hens, capons, and young turkeys.

How to carve depends on how you skewer the animal, and thus for these birds there are three methods: one, to pick it up by the breast, and, having lifted it somewhat, to skewer it through the neck, at the joint with the torso, so that the long fork goes through the middle of the neck, and you push the fork through to the breast bones; then, holding the bird always with its feet upwards, you start cutting the neck, and on through the whole body.

The second method is to take the bird with a knife in the breast, lift it, and skewer it from the coderone, which you will place between the two tips of the long fork; push the

---

32 Coderone is the fleshy part of any bird closest to the tail, considered a special delicacy; an Italian proverb still says that "a chicken's ass is a cardinal's morsel."

33 In this passage, as elsewhere, Latini alternates between the third and second person when speaking of the carver.

fork through to the breast bones; the bird's head should stay always upwards, and then you cut with grace.

The third method is to lift it with the knife and to skewer it through the back, so that the tips of the long fork reach the ribcage, near the wing tips, and thus the breast remains upwards, and cutting it is convenient; this method is more apt for smaller chicken and similar birds.

Some authors also teach a fourth method, namely, to skewer it through the ribcage above the plate, and push the fork's tips through the back, then, lifting it, start cutting, beginning with the tip of the left wing; then three cuts to the thigh, and the other body parts, keeping the neck for last, which, having detached it, one will place above the plate; then cut the front of the breast, and thus place the plate in front of the guests. This method is little used, and I have practised it only rarely.

The first two methods are necessary to carve large birds, the third for small ones, including pigeons and cockerels, and all those birds that are presented whole to the guests; I believe I have said enough about skewering, so here I shall speak of how to divide up the three above-mentioned birds, that is, the capon, hen, and young turkey, which will be about the same size.

The carver should make six parts of these birds, and of the young turkey perhaps more, if it is large, and depending on the number of guests.

Common practice calls for two capons for six guests. Therefore, the plate where they are served should be such that the carver can easily take hold of one and lift it; he should start carving it from the neck, which, detached from the torso, he will let fall onto the plate; then he will cut the tip of the right wing; then three cuts to the right thigh, which he will also let fall onto the plate; turning the capon, with the coderone to the carver's left, he will make the same cuts to the left wing and thigh, using the tip of the knife to let it fall onto the plate; then he will cut the coderone twice on the left; if the bird be stuffed, then the carver should place it with the tip of the knife onto a separate plate, in order to use that to garnish the plates that he will serve.

Then he shall start with the first plate, cutting the right wing at the shoulder joint; letting it fall with the knife's tip onto the plate, together with a bit of the breast meat, he will salt it appropriately, and add the stuffing if there is any, and then present the plate to the proper person; he will continue with the left wing and some of the breast meat, garnishing the plate with the apt salt, and he will serve this plate as well. He will then cut the front of the breast with some of the breast meat and one of the bones of the coderone, which will be given to whoever is due it; then, removing all the meat from the ribcage, he will place it with a knife onto a plate, together with the coderone and its bone, and garnish with apt condiments, and place it in front of the guests; he will then skewer the right thigh with the tip of his knife and will place it in another plate, and will do the same with the left one, and proceed to the customary distribution; finally he will skewer the remaining skeleton, cleared of all meat, by placing the knife atop its back and keeping the tip of the long fork turned towards the plate.

A good carver should always follow this method, and fairly divide up these birds, because I do not believe it is decent to give one guest just the thigh and another just the breast, especially since the breast is usually the most exquisite part of the bird; the carver should therefore aim to divide up the breast into as many parts as possible, and to divide the thigh from the upper thigh, so that in this manner everybody may enjoy the better and less good parts of the chicken. This is my general advice to the carver, who will above all in any case consider the greater or lesser merit of the guests.

Boiled chicken must be carved in the plate, setting the fork in its breast; you will cut it up appropriately, garnishing the plates with aromatic herbs and other apt garnishes. If the boiled chicken is not too cooked, and thus may be lifted, the carver should carve it while lifting it, because it will be easier than doing it on the plate, as in the latter case the carver's agility cannot properly shine.

You will carve any other birds the same way.

With small birds, like thrushes or others, one can carve three or four at one time, by skewering all of them carefully together, but this style is not easy, and only to be practised by those most experienced in this profession.

The grey partridge can be carved in two ways; the first is the same one used with pigeons, but with a few differences. The carver, after placing the plate with the partridges in front of him, will take his third long fork and with its companion knife pierce the bird through the front of the breast; having lifted it, he will place it breast first onto one of the plates and skewer it through its back, pushing the tips of his fork through the ribcage or the breast bone; lifting it again, he will use the knife to start cutting from the neck, which he will let fall onto the plate. He will then cut the right thigh three times, and after cutting the joint of the shoulder with the right wing he will also cut the breast meat all along, up to the bottom of that wing. He will use the same style for the left side; after cutting the coderone twice, he will unskewer the bird and place it on the plate, as before, making all his cuts with the greatest agility.

The second method is used when one wants to grind the breast meat; in this case, the carver will carve the partridge as I described for the hen and capon, dividing up the two thighs at the neck and at the coderone, and letting them fall with order onto a plate; at this point the breast will still be on the fork, with all its meat, which he will grind; he should make sure to let all parts of the bird fall at the edges of the plate, so that he can then let the ground breast fall in the middle of it, after removing the skin, and slicing it thinly. Having completed the carving, he will unsekwer the skeleton and place it on the same plate, so that, should any meat remain on it, the guests may enjoy it.

This plate will be served with a thin sauce, and will be garnished with pastries, salt, and slices of sour oranges.

Partridges and woodcocks are carved the same way as grey partridges.

How to carve any roasted animal thigh.[34]

Before teaching how to carve thighs or any other roasted animal parts, the carver must know how to carve boiled meat: this has to be carved on the plate, and I have never seen a good carver carve it in the air, and whenever I have had to carve boiled meat I have always done it on the plate, and so I opine that all good carvers should do.

---

34 Latini uses the term *quadrupedi*, i.e., four-legged (or land) animals.

The roasted thighs of any animal should all be skewered the same way, that is, with the large fork and from the greater side, so that the bone remain in the middle of the fork's tip, pushing up to the leg bone, which should also remain between the tips; always keep the bottom facing upwards, and then with the mid-size knife start slicing, cutting four or six of them to place on a plate, garnished with salt, lemons, and other garnishes around them, and offering it in the right order.

If the carver wants to grind some of the roast, he should place two or three slices in each plate, and then let fall the ground meat in the middle, and serve the plate with various sauces on top and a bit of salt on the side.

It often happens that attached to roast thighs there may be some of the loin; in this case, similarly one should skewer the meat with the large fork, above the loin, and push the tips inside the roast; then you start carving from the loin, and you will grind part of the meat and slice the rest thinly, always serving each plate with the necessary sauces, salt, and other condiments.

Since I am writing about this, it is not inappropriate for me to correct some errors that I have seen many times committed by those with little practice, namely to carve part of the roast and to put it on a plate, then to leave the roast on the large serving plate, in order to arrange each plate more conveniently; this seems to me to be a considerable error, from which to warn and correct carvers, because the agility of a good carver in arranging each plate must be seen in serving it with its garnishes without ever leaving the roast, which the carver should continue throughout to hold in the air with his left hand, above the serving plate, so that no fat should drop on the table cloth; the carver must hold the roast up no higher than his own chest, and after arranging the first plate he will start on the second one, and then all the others until the end of the carving, setting aside the skeleton with any left over meat until the steward has placed on the table the next dishes; the carver should also not let anyone else handle the plate, but he must do it himself, handing it to the pages or assistants responsible for the table service.

How to carve the loin or fillet of suckling calves or any other animal.

There are two ways to skewer these, but one is more common. The carver should use the mid-size fork, skewering so that one of its tips should remain in the middle canal of the back bone, and the other penetrate the meat of the fillet; once this is done, the carver should use the companion knife to start cutting in the air, slicing thinly or grinding; having cut the entire fillet, he will divide up the ribs, cutting them carefully, and then letting them fall on the plate and preparing the portions for each plate, garnished with salt, lemon slices, and other garnishes, to be served to the guests.

If he wants to prepare slices that include some of the bone, he will do as I just mentioned for the ribs; in this case, he may set the fillet on the serving plate to slice it as needed, then dispose the slices on each plate, cut each two or three times, garnish the plate, and serve it in order to each guest. It is permitted to set the fillet on the serving plate, because it is a large piece and thus difficult to hold in the air and to cut it with that agility which a good carver should ordinarily display.

The other way, which I have often practised and thus I endorse it, is to skewer with the fork from the tip of the fillet and to push it through up to the back bone; then on the serving plate to carve appropriately. No doubt this carving could also be done in the air, but as it is difficult and not to be attempted except by the most experienced in this office, I suggest this only to those most practised.

How to carve the front quarts of various small and tender animals.

It often happens in banquets that the carver is faced with the front quarts of various small animals, so I decided not to leave them unmentioned, even though whoever can carve the hind quarts will have no difficulty carving the front ones. Both should be skewered from the larger side, always making sure that the bone should remain between the fork's tips, and that the tip of the foot should face upwards. The carver will start carving from the shoulder, cutting it into two or three parts, and continue as convenient. As these animals are tender and soft, I recommend they be carved on the plate, since their tenderness does not allow them to be carved in the air.

How to carve the hind quarts of the hare, together.

Having taught thus far how to carve various thighs, I deem it useful to teach how to carve the hind quarts of the hare, attached to each other, as this is among the most difficult carving tasks.

They can be skewered in two ways: one, by placing one of the fork's tips in the middle of the back and the other in the meat of the fillet, and lifting it; two, you do the same thing, but make sure that the back bone end up in between the paws, pushing the tips in until the upper thighs. The carver will thus skewer the hare by one of these methods with whichever fork he prefers, and start carving from the leg joints, which he will let fall onto the serving plate; then he will cut the cutlets, and let them fall similarly; then, to prepare the first plate, he will cut as many slices as he wishes and place them on a plate to which he will add ground loin and one of the kidneys, garnishing the plate with salt, lemon slices, and other apt garnishes, and then passing it on to the pages or assistants to serve it to one of the guests; the same he will do with the second plate and the second kidney, and then four more plates or more, as needed, always with prudence; if the loins are not enough to grind meat for all the plates, he may use some of the meat from the back, where there always is a bit of extra meat; then, removing the fork, he will place the hares on the serving plate, as one would do with the quarts of a kid or another tender animal.

Kid loins, however, as they are very soft, one cannot grind.

How to carve the head of the suckling calf.

The head of the suckling calf, if boiled, is difficult to skewer and carve in the air, because it is so tender that it would break into many pieces; therefore, you must place it on the plate, turn it with the tip of the fork, and cut it in half along the top of the head, opening up the skin, so that one can remove the top bone and the rest of the top skull, which should be placed on a plate and immediately removed, as it would be a disagreeable sight at the table. The carver, having uncovered the brains, will divide them up onto various plates; he will then cut the right ear, separating it from the skin that surrounds it, and will place it on a plate and cut it into two or three bits. He will also cut the right eye all around and having extracted it he will place it on the same plate where he placed the ears, also cutting it a bit, and garnishing the plate with various sauces, salt, and other apt garnishes, ready to serve as appropriate. He will prepare a second plate with ears, eyes, a bit of brain, and apt garnishes. From the rest of the meat he will serve various plates, as many as needed, putting in each a bit of brains, salt, garnishes, and apt sauces. I believe it is far easier to carve this in the plate than in the air, as in the latter one cannot so neatly make the necessary portions. Use the same method for the heads of all other land animals, except for animals caught in the hunt, which always have rotten brains, and if one wanted to carve such heads in the air, one would need to skewer them from the bottom and hold them well high, following the order I described above.

How to carve veal tongue, stewed or roasted.

Often veal tongue is stewed, and if so it has to be carved in the plate, carving round slices in the plate itself which will also hold the condiments and various fruits, to be apportioned in different plates as the carver will deem proper.

If the tongue is roasted, then it can be carved, skewering it a bit above the tip, with the fork's tips pushed to the sweetbreads, and this can be carved on the plate, as one prefers. However you carve it, the slices should be round, and placed on the plates divided so that every guest may taste all their parts.

How to carve hams, salami, and mortadella.

It is common practice to place on the table hams cooked in wine and water, or in milk, and then placed inside an uncovered stand pie, with glazed sugar and confected *cannelloni*;[35] the carver should remove the glazed sugar and cannelloni with the tip of his knife, and it will not be unsuitable to drop some of them onto the individual plates, because many enjoy a sweet taste; he will then skewer the ham as I described for the lamb roast, raise it, and slice it as he wishes, to prepare the individual plates, which he will serve without adding salt or anything else. He will then place the ham back in its stand pie; if there are salami or mortadelle, even though the latter are usually sliced at the credenza, should they come to the table whole, cooked in wine, and cut up half-way, the carver will skewer some part of it, with the fork he prefers, raise it, and let slices of it fall onto the individual plates to be served, keeping the blade of the knife always towards his chest.

How to carve a suckling pig.

Since the meat of the suckling pig is very tender, I believe it should only be carved on the plate, even if roasted. Therefore the carver should turn the pig's head towards himself and skewer it with the fork in the middle of its belly. Then, with the large knife, he will cut the neck and separate the head, which, if the master wishes that it be served to some of the guests, he will carve as I described above for the head of the calf, but without dividing it. Having cut the head, the carver will cut all along the belly and remove the stuffing with his knife, if it is stuffed, and then with his spoon he will divide it up

---

35 Cannelloni today are pasta tubes, usually stuffed with sauce or meat or cheese; I'm not sure what these sweet versions here are, though presumably they too are tube-shaped.

between the various individual plates. He will then cut the right shoulder, place it on a plate with the stuffing, garnish it with salt and lemon slices, and serve it to whom he prefers. Then he will cut the right thigh and do the same; then the same with the left thigh; he will then cut all along the back, until he reaches the loins, and, placing the knife between the ribs, he will detach the right side, placing it onto a fourth plate, with the same garnishes and condiments; the fifth plate he will prepare with the left side, the sixth one with the left shoulder; and all plates will be served as preferred. If he wishes to carve this animal in the air, he will skewer it by the neck, pushing the fork all the way to the upper thigh bone, and having raised it he will cut off the head and let it fall onto a plate; having put down the animal, he will cut the head into two halves, skewering it with another fork through the nostrils; then he will raise it again, and cut and separate the various parts onto various plates. Eventually, he will unskewer what is left of the animal on the main plate. A good carver will follow this method for any small land animal placed whole on the table.

How to carve any pie, or impanata, in the Naples style.[36]

Pies, called in Naples impanate, must be carved with great agility. The carver will need a fork and cut around the pie, on the side or on its top, so that it be open; he will then place it onto another plate and he will carve in very small pieces the meat that is in the pie; he will then take this meat with the spoon and place it on the individual plates; then he will cut the pie's bottom crust and serve that in the individual plates as well, adding some of the meat as well as a piece of the pie's top crust; the aim is that each individual serving will look like a pie. If the pie has ground meat inside, then it should be cut as one would cut any tart, without removing the top dough, and so the carver will distribute the portions, without placing the knife underneath each serving or the fork above it, to place them onto the individual plates.

Often one does not serve the pie dough at all, placing in the individual plates only the meat and other ingredients of the pie. I leave this to the choice of the carver, who should always act according to the commands of his prudence.

How to apportion composite dishes.

All composite dishes, either of small birds or of other animal meat, the carver should divide into portions only with his large spoon, preparing all the individual plates he needs; this sort of dishes have to be well cooked, and so they cannot be carved, given their great softness. If these dishes include pigeons or cockerels, the carver will simply mark the cuts, without actually cutting them, and will serve them with condiments and garnishes.

How to carve covered and uncovered tarts.

Even though the way to carve crostata and torte is easy and known to almost all, I thought of including it, because the carver needs to divide them as appropriate to the number of

---

36 Latini's use of the synonym *impanata* shows of course a Spanish influence.

portions to be prepared. Having cut a slice, he will take it with the knife underneath and the fork above it and place it on the plate to be served aptly, and he will do the same for all portions. If the tarts include milky cheeses, he will use the big spoon, and make the necessary portions.

How to carve all sorts of fish.

I have sufficiently discussed how to carve birds and land animals, both whole and in parts, so now it is reasonable to teach how to carve all sorts of fish, so that this volume should not deprive the student of any desirable training. Larger fish, such as sturgeon, tuna, and others, when stewed, the carver will slice and place in the same serving dish, having removed all the bones; he will form the plates with the slices, adding condiments and juice with his large spoon, and slices of sour oranges around the plate, and then distribute the plates following the order of the table. If these fish are roasted, they can be carved in the same plate, slicing them into three or four slices, at the carver's discretion, making sure the slices suffice for all the plates, which he can then serve with royal sauce, lemon slices, and sufficient salt. If a carver wants to show off his openness and agility, he will skewer the fish by the side and slice it in the air, with the knife's blade turned towards his chest, and then he will ground some of the fish, and add it to all the plates, with convenient garnishes.

How to carve sole and similar fish.

This fish, if cooked with the due diligence, will always please, and it is always desired and appreciated at the tables of the nobility. Once it is placed on the table, the carver will turn its head towards his left hand, with the back inside the plate; take the best suited fork, depending on how large the sole is, and apply it to the fish, placing the fishbone between the fork's points; then cut from the head to the tail, right along the middle of the fish, and another cut on the back side to remove the bones; do the same on the stomach side; having made these three cuts, also cut under the head and near the tail, and uncover and remove the central fishbone; place it next to the fish, and also use the knife to remove it smoothly. Then prepare the plates with the usual garnishes and condiments; all fish of the same flat form should be carved this same way.

How to carve sea bass, grey mullet, and other sea fish, both large and small.

To carve these fish, both roasted or boiled, the carver will place the right fork and skewer near the head, so that the central fishbone is between the fork's points; then he will cut with the knife along the back from head to tail; then, with the knife's side he will detach the flesh to uncover the central fishbone; then he will cut under the head and near the tail, completely to uncover the fishbone with the fork, with which he can then remove it. He can then make the portions, though if the fish is small each will serve for one plate, garnished always with salt and lemon slices and other condiments, already placed on the fish; this is the true way to carve all fish, small or large, of salt water or fresh water, as long as their bone is in the middle of their body; among them are also tench, pike, trout, red mullet, and others like them.

How to carve eel and similar fish.

Lamprey, eel, and similar fish are usually brought to the table already cooked and divided into pieces; thus the carver should remove the fishbone, make apt portions, and serve two or three pieces to each guest, with the usual garnishes.

Here I want to mention also how to carve fish pies, both hot and cold.

With hot pies, the carver should remove the lid, as with meat pies; that done, if inside there is a large fish, the carver should first remove its fishbone and then make the portions he deems suitable to serve all guests, adding the condiment or broth of the pie with his large silver spoon, and placing on the plates various parts of the pie; if the fish inside the pie are small, he can serve one on each plate without removing their fishbone, and add some of the pie crust, so that the guests will know that this is a pie and not a simple fish dish.

If the pie is cold, he will serve it the same way, but with no broth, because the broth is not good for cold pies.

If the pies are small, the carver will serve one to each guest, if the ingredients are ground, with the lid over it, otherwise with the usual garnishes, and simply cutting the lid, without removing it.

On seafood.

Although seafood is always brought to the table after having been already cut at the credenza, nonetheless, in order to pay my debt in full and not to defraud the carver of due advice, I state here that among the most esteemed seafood is lobster, which, after having been cooked, should be placed back in its shell, divided into parts, and with the usual condiments. For six people, usually one serves two lobsters, if they are large, so the carver should be careful to make the portions correctly; he may choose to cut them into small bits, and serve all plates accordingly, always with condiments and salt.

Spider crab is served the same way, usually at six per serving, so the carver will serve one in each plate, with salt and sliced sour oranges.

Rarely does one place turtles on the table cooked and served in their shells; but if they are served in their shells, then they should be served like other seafood. If they are stewed, they should be served in plates with the large silver spoon, with condiments on top and salt on the edge of the plate.

Oysters are usually served two or three in each half-shell; the carver should serve them carefully, according to the number of guests, with sour orange juice in the shells and salt around the plate; if they are stewed they should be distributed with the large spoon, garnished with the usual condiments.

Crab and fresh water crayfish are served in plates with pepper, vinegar, and salt on the side. From these instructions, the good carver will know how to carve and serve all sorts of fish.

How to carve any land fruit.[37]

I have always believed that a good carver cannot carve well for more than six guests; and yet I have often seen in this city of Naples a carver carve for eighteen people, which greatly surprised me, since it is most true that any carver, however skilled he may be in this exercise, will never be able to prepare portions aptly for so many people, and consequently he will not be praised as he may deserve, as it is indubitable that such numerous guests could not be served in good time, nor will the carver be able to fulfill his task with due diligence. He should avoid such a challenge, therefore, and if he has to face it, he should request at least one partner, to avoid blame and accusations of negligence or incompetence.

It will bring great praise to the carver to know how to carve fruit elegantly and rapidly.

Figs are usually brought to the table in a large plate, over leaves, and covered with ice, carved already at the credenza or in the office, so that the carver only needs to take and hold them from the tip with his fork, then pinning them with the knife he will place in the plate as many as he deems fit.

If they should be brought to the table with their peel, on a plate and over leaves, the carver should skewer them from the tip, cross-cut the stem, and remove the peel with all possible dexterity, leaving it attached to the tip side, which he should also cut.

These fashions, though they were practised in the past, are now out of usage, and today both in the court of Rome and in any other court of great princes figs are simply brought to the table already carved, in small dishes, garnished with ice and over green leaves; and as this seems to me a very decorous and apt style I have mentioned it here, so that the carver may follow it, and set aside other styles, now rarely used, and not worthy of much praise.

Melons are also placed in plates at the credenza, often already carved into small bits, or sliced; if they are in small bits, the carver should serve them on plates with his knife.

If they are sliced, he will take three or four, at his discretion, place them on the plates, and cut each slice four or five ways, and serve them aptly as needed, and it will not be out of place to drop a bit of ice on each plate. Sometimes, one or more whole melons are brought to the table, cold, and in such cases the carver should skewer them from the tip, a bit askew, lift them and cut them at the tip and the stem; he will then cut and slice as he sees fit, skewering each slice with the fork by the peel.

Since there are many varieties of pears, I chose to discuss them separately. I warn the reader that when they are very small they should not be carved but simply placed in the plates as deemed suitable. If they are larger, they should be carved in "little-hat" style: skewer each through the middle with the right fork, leaving the tip in the middle of the fork's points, lift it with the fork to straighten it well, then with the knife's tip cut the middle of the pear up to the stem, very gently, and then peel it all around, in the shape of a little hood, and let the peel fall onto the plate; the carver will then cut the peel all around, posing his thumb on it to have a clearer cut. Having made these cuts, he will

---

37 Latini probably specifies "land" fruit because the Italian for seafood is *frutti di mare*, literally sea fruits.

skewer it again with the knife's tip from the stem, and will take it with the fork and turn it in the air with the tip above, and cut through the middle without completely separating the parts; he will then place the pear with the tip down, and cut four ways, making four parts, with the core and seeds as the fifth part. Having done all this, he will take with the tip of his knife that little hood he had placed on the plate, cover the pear with it, and serve to whom he wishes; this is called "little-hood" carving.

To carve pears in a single long thread, he must skewer the pear as above and start cutting from the stem, make the slice as thin as possible, place his thumb on the peel, and continue until he has passed the middle of the pear, then he will skewer it again on the other side, and continue slicing up to the tip, which he will cut but not completely; then he will place the pear in the plate and cut it aptly, leaving around it the long single thread, and so he will have it served.[38]

To carve pears in the shape of a rose.

They must be taken and skewered the same way as other pears; then the carver will make his cuts all along from the stem to the tip; he then will skewer it with the knife's tip in the middle and skewer it again in the stem, always keeping it in between the tips; then he will cut the tip, without completely dividing it, and will place the pear in the plate making the five cuts, or maybe up to eight cuts, leaving the core as the ninth part, and so he will have it served. It will be pleasing to the guests to see a fruit converted into a flower simply by the dexterity of a good carver, who will know how to leave the peel around with the greatest grace; since these methods have been mentioned also by other artists and professionals, I decided not to write more. If the carver wants to carve a pear so that it will not be recognized as such, and leave its entire peel on it, so that it should appear untouched, he will take a needle and white silk and thread all around the pear (this can also be done with an apple) putting the needle near the stem, passing the silk lightly under the peel and as close as possible to the tip, and then back to the stem, and up again five or six times, always the same way.

Having thus threaded the pear with the silk, he will take all the ends of the thread near the stem and pull from the top thus removing the silk; this way, the pear peel will remain wholly separated inside from the pear itself, even though the pear appears whole and nobody could tell that it has been carved. The carver should not perform this operation at the table, but in a place where he cannot be seen, a little before the guests sit at the table, since if people see how this is done the effect will be spoiled.

The carver will make sure to place such pears or apples in front of the guests whole, without touching them, so that each guest, when he will start peeling it, will find it already carved, which will result in great praise for the carver.[39]

Apples are carved in the same style as pears. When they are carved in little-hood style, it's however called little-basket, because what falls onto the plate is placed on the

---

38 I confess that I am somewhat baffled by this carving method and its goal: Latini calls it *fettuccia*, which seems to suggest a single long thread, but I am not positive of the intended result of this complex operation.

39 It is hard to imagine a more Baroque moment than this illusionistic trick.

apple with its concave part upwards, and in it one can serve bits of parmesan cheese or other things at pleasure.

Parmesan, when it is brought to the table in a large block, must be skewered with the fork atop the rind, then sliced with the knife, as needed, and served in the plates. If the blocks are small, one should place them on a napkin with one's left hand, take them with the knife, and slice them, as is done with Florentine *marzolino* [another cheese]; if he wishes to carve it another way, the carver can skewer it askew, since it is customary to place it on the table cut into two parts; he should use the same manner with any cheese.

Peaches are usually served in plates atop greens; they should be skewered with the three-prong fork, then peeled and sliced in the same plate, so that the pit remain clean; then one places them in the plates with wine and sugar on top.

If artichokes are brought whole to the table, they must be skewered from the stem, placing it in the middle of the fork; then one cuts the tip, letting the points of its leaves fall onto the plate. Once you have reached the tender part, you skewer it in the middle with the knife's tip, from the top, and you start to clean the stem; then you put them in the plate, with a cross cut on the stem, and serve them with pepper and salt on the edge of the plate; it is customary to leave a few tender leaves on the top.

Fennel is usually served clean from the credenza; the carver must however finish cleaning it at the table. He will skewer it in the stem, holding on the plate with the knife, then lift it, cut the outer leaf, detach it, and let it fall onto the plate, and the same with the other leaves, until he has uncovered the tender leaves at the top. Then he will start with the knife's tip and his thumb to clean the peel, pulling it down to the stem, and letting it fall onto the plate; he will then serve it with salt.

Cardoons and celery are usually brought to the table already arranged by the credenziero, so that the carver will simply have to clean them with the tip of his knife and place them on the plates with salt and pepper around them. If by chance they are brought to the table still whole, he will skewer them by the stem and clean them as he cleans fennel, and then distribute them aptly.

Peas and similar legumes are brought to the table cleaned and without their pods, so the carver just needs to serve them with salt on the side. If they come to the table whole, he will skewer them by the stem and cut the side all along, so that the beans can be separated and served.

Boxes of candied quinces are placed on the table on plates, over white napkins, so the carver should take the napkin and place it on his left hand, then take one of the boxes, place it on his left hand, and cut the small wooden circle around it as quickly as he can with a cut across from the top of the box, leaving in his hand just the bottom of the box with the quinces, and he will detach the quinces with his knife from the bottom and will place it on the plate, with a cross-cut on it; he will serve it with white aniseeds, which he will take with a large silver spoon. If there are glass cans with various fruit preserves, he will make a single cut in the middle of the preserves, place it this way onto the plate, and serve it as due.

I have written this essay to benefit professionals, and if some ingrate will censure it unjustly he will show himself deprived of those pious sentiments which should be abundant in all those who have a sincere heart. I have little fear of censors because I said what I have to say and treated those matters that others have treated, in a manner proper and suitable for this profession. I have made an effort to compensate for the bitterness of my style with the sweetness of those condiments which I have been taught and which the craft itself has suggested to me; if I have committed any error, I hope it will be met with compassion, because I have done everything to the greater advantage and benefit of professionals.

Here are a few warnings to arrange banquets well.

I must here warn that when the carver settles at his station, he should not keep the carving instruments in front of him, but to his left, and to his right the serving plates, and in the middle the main plate on which he will carve, so as to have everything convenient.

The carver should be sure never to lack for serving plates.

No carver can succeed in carving or serving effectively at a banquet for more than six guests; if he will need to serve a larger number, he should be careful to do it well and proportionately: the rush to serve everybody may result in serving indecently and without praise.

The steward must always place the plates in front of the carver, and not elsehwere, to avoid confusion; the plates must always be brought in a timely fashion, and hot.

The carver should never remove any plate until the next one comes from the kitchen; if the plate should become empty, as often happens, he should put a small plate on top of it, and then remove it himself. The steward should make sure that bread is never lacking at the table.

Every grand banquet can be done with twelve hot dishes, and as many cold ones, and this is left to the splendour of the masters.

Once fruit and confections are finished, the carver should remove his instruments, with a graceful reverence to the guests.

Preserves should not be placed on the table until the fruit has been removed.

The table should be well set with cold dishes and triumphs, to produce a pleasing sight.

Good and varied wines should be on the table.

When in the presence of the guests, the carver should stay in a good posture, and show himself to advantage; he should not fold his hands, hold an unpleasant attitude, or make any bad gestures with his eyes or mouth, all of which would render him ridiculous to those present.

The carver should keep his knives clean and ready, and carve only at the table of his master, and use his own plate for himself.

The steward, not the carver, should taste the dishes.

The carver should not carve any dishes other than what the steward places in front of him; if the carver must check something for suspicion of poison, he must run the tip of the knife on the side where the suspicious food is, and then dip a bit of bread and give it to eat to whom he chooses.

I have here in several places referred equally to meals and banquets, and I leave the difference between them to the right and intelligent judgement of professionals and readers.

The steward must know not only stewardship but also the art of carving well, because these two offices have between them a great connection. So the steward should know how to organize the dishes, make them into portions and carve them properly, and distribute them with order. It will in many circumstances be useful for the steward to know how to perform both offices, from which he will gain praise and effectiveness.

A drawing of all the knives and forks for the carving station, according to the modern usage of Rome and other parts of Italy.

Even though these images may not serve for every case, they could be augmented or diminished as needed; I have simply sketched here a model that can be increased or reduced at the discretion of professionals. The knives must be made by good craftsmen who know how to make the tips of knives properly, so that they can resist the hardness of bones; if they were to bend like hooks, this would result in confusion and disorder.[40]

TREATISE II: *Of the Suckling Calf and its Condiments, by Parts.*[41]

Dishes made with veal have the first place among the most exquisite, healthy, and nutritious dishes that one may taste at the most splendid tables, and there is no part of it that cannot be seasoned. This meat offers such substantial and profitable nourishment that Avicenna, followed in this by other physicians, gives the calf primacy among all quadrupeds. This meat can be altered with varied ingredients; its essence aided by human industry can render admirable to both taste and sight this most delicate of animals, when it is well seasoned by art. The Egyptians, had they known the health-giving qualities of this tastiest of animals, would not have foolishly adored onions and crocodiles in their superstitious rites, but, with more reason, would have transferred their worship to a less detestable idolatry, namely to the cult of calf meat, more precious than the Golden Calf built by the Hebrews with such temerity. Let us therefore devise how to prepare this meat, and, to keep to the standard way, let us begin with the head.[42]

---

40 Between pages 78 and 79 of the first volume is a print of various knives and other carving instruments.

41 Latini refers to calves of both sexes: I will call them all "calf" without using also the term "heifer." Latini thought so highly of the suckling calf that he devoted almost forty pages to it.

42 Avicenna (Ibn Sina, 980–1037) was a great Muslim philosopher and doctor, whose works exercised a strong influence on western medical ideas. In this one paragraph Latini manages to show off his knowledge of antiquity, medieval philosophy, and the Bible. The suckling calf of the Naples area was celebrated widely: Ortensio Lando, in his 1548 survey of Italian regions, wrote that its meat "melts in the mouth producing even more delight than sugar does" (cited in Montanari, *Nuovo convivio: Storia e cultura dei piaceri della tavola nell'età moderna* (Bari: Laterza, 1991), 44).

Here we teach in how many ways one can prepare the head of the suckling calf (also known as Sorrento calf).

The calf head can be boiled, wrapped in a white cloth, with ham slices inside; once it is cooked, serve it hot with herbs on top, borage flowers around the plate, surrounded with tartelettes filled with green sauce.

The head, carefully deboned, can be stuffed with a paste made with pounded veal, bits of sweetbreads, thin slices of ham, thin sausages, chicken livers, egg yolks, grated cheese, as desired, bits of mozzarella or *provatura* [a pulled cheese similar to mozzarella], cream tops as you see fit, bits of calf tongue, the eyes and brains of the calf, first boiled and cut into pieces, bits of pounded calf kidney fat, slices of truffles, pine nuts, ground candied citron (if you wish to make this dish spicy, the citron is not necessary), the usual spices, ground *mostaccioli*, marjoram, and perfumed water as you prefer.[43] Once prepared with these ingredients, you will return the head to its prior shape and, with a needle and white thread, sew up its openings. Then you will place it in a pot or other vessel, with slices of thin cured back fat and ham and a bit of good broth; turn it frequently, so that it be well stewed, and when it will be past the half-cooking point, put it in an oven, but not too hot. Once cooked, remove it from the oven and cover it with cream tops; then take sugar, lemon juice, and fresh egg whites and make a glaze to top it with. You can also make a baked custard with milk, cream tops, sugar, and fresh eggs, with a pastry twist around the plate filled with candied things in syrup, and I think this could serve well in any great banquet. You can increase or decrease the doses; remember that once the head is cooked and placed on the plate, you need to remove the thread with which you sewed it.[44]

You can also braise it, having buttered it well, with the same stuffing, whole or cut into parts, as you prefer; one can make a condiment for it with almonds, pine nuts, beaten egg yolks, sour orange juice, and lemons, and you will serve it hot with the condiments on top.[45]

The same head, after boiling it, can be sliced, dredged in bread crumbs, salt, and pepper, and grilled, or, as people say, coaled, with a bit of malmsey wine.

One can also wrap it in bread, sugar, and cinnamon, with a royal sauce on top, and then fried in a pan.

One can also fry it, after boiling it; cut it into pieces, dip it in egg and dredge it in flour, with a mostacciolo sauce on top, or juice of lemons or sour oranges.

---

43 Cream tops is Scully's translation of Scappi's (and Latini's) *capi di latte*, i.e., what rises to the top of slowly heated milk; Riley (*The Oxford Companion*, 147) renders this as "clotted cream." Mostaccioli are hard, sweet, spiced cookies that still exist in several Italian regional varieties; they were common ingredients—usually ground—in sixteenth- and seventeenth-century cooking; Latini later includes a recipe for them.

44 The twist was a common element of these elaborate dishes: it could be eaten but also served a decorative function. A French writer observed already in 1560 that "calves' heads decorate the splendid tables in great houses," cited in Sarah T. Peterson, *Acquired Taste: The French Origins of Modern Cooking* (Ithaca: Cornell University Press, 1994), 93.

45 Here as well I follow the editor of Scappi, *Opera*, in using "braise" for "*sottestare*," which refers to cooking in an earthenware lidded vessel (a *testo/a*), in an oven or in embers.

From this head, one can also take little bits of milk or light fat deposits, which with the eyes of the same calf can be used to stuff little pies, with other usual ingredients.

The same head, deboned and boiled, can be spit-roasted, whole, and stuffed with hard egg yolks, various fresh or dried fruits, first cut into pieces and sautéed, bits of candied citron, sour cherries, pears, and other fruits as you prefer, with bits of sweetbreads and chicken livers, with the usual spices; you will wrap it in paper or in caul, with a sauce of lemon juice or verjuice.[46]

The same, deboned and stuffed as above, and with other noble ingredients as you prefer, can be stewed in good white or malmsey wine, with the usual spices and various candied fruits and fruits cooked in syrup. Once it is cooked, you will place it in a royal plate, with sour grapes in syrup on top, sliced truffles, candied *moscarole* pears, plums, pine nuts, and lemon or sour orange juice, with the usual spices and a fat broth; you will serve this hot, and this dish may be served in any sumptuous banquet; it can be done in various ways, as I will indicate in the chapter on dishes.[47]

This head, deboned, as above, can be stuffed with various fruits, like pears cut into bits, thinly sliced truffles, raisins, pine nuts, plums, dried sour cherries, and others, as I will discuss in a later chapter, unripe grapes, lemon or sour orange juice, and the usual spices; do not add wine to this, as it would become too viscous; stew it in a good fat broth, from capon or other broth, and serve it hot, garnished with the same fruits on top, and unripe grapes in syrup.

The same head, after cooking it in plain water, can be halved and deboned, then dredged in mostacciolo crumbs, dipped in egg and good lard; you can serve it hot, with sugar and cinnamon on top, and lemon slices around the plate.

It can also be prepared this way: boiled, cut in half, deboned, as above, then dredged in flour and fried in good lard; serve it hot, with a *frittata* on top made with calf brains; before cooking the brains, grind them minutely and mix them with eggs, sugar, and cinnamon, aromatic herbs, good grated cheese; the sugar and cinnamon you will spread on top of this frittata, with a bit of lemon or sour orange juice, and you will garnish the plate with lemon slices mixed with unripe grapes in syrup. On top you will use varied aromatic herbs and marinades, as discussed in a chapter below.[48]

This head, deboned and boiled, can also be placed whole on the table, and may be served cold. You can serve it inside a stand pie surrounded by sliced cured back fat and enough spices; if you wish to serve it hot, you will add to the pie cardoon and artichoke

---

46 Caul (*rete* in Italian) is a "lacy layer of membrane marbled with fat enclosing the intestines of an animal" which was used to keep ingredients together during cooking and for basting, Riley, *The Oxford Companion*, 107. Verjuice is the juice of unripe grapes (*agresta*), a very common ingredient in late medieval and Renaissance cooking and still quite common in Italian cooking of Latini's time. I am using "sautéing" for Latini's *soffriggere*; by this he usually means a quicker, lighter frying than *friggere*, and sautéing seems to me preferable to stirfrying in this context.

47 Moscarole are "musk-pears." Latini also uses, more often, *moscarelle* pears, a sweet variety, so possibly here he means the latter as well.

48 What Latini means by frittata seems to be a flat, unrolled omelet, to be used as a cover (or at times bottom level, or even as both) for various dishes, a bit like a big pancake at least in shape and consistency. I will use the term myself when he does, for lack of a better one.

bits, first boiled, sliced ham, marrow, and spices at your discretion; if you wish to serve it as a sliced pie, you will put in the pie all the ingredients mentioned above, plus a little broth made with egg yolks, a bit of good broth, and verjuice or sour orange juice; beat everything together and put it in the pie; bake it, and serve it hot, with a glaze on top made of lemon juice, sugar, and fresh egg whites, as you prefer.

The same head can be fried another way: boil and cook it, debone it, and dredge it in flour, whole or sliced as you prefer. Fry it in good lard and serve it with salt, pepper, and aromatic herbs; on top put an imperial frittata made with egg whites, cream tops, and sugar; on top of the frittata, put sliced Genoa pumpkin, having first boiled it, and garnish the sides of the plate with little cookies or *mostaccere* or royal cookies; it will be a welcome and noble dish.[49]

This head, boiled and cooked as above, can also be deboned, and with it you can form plates in the French style, with a fat broth; add three or four small meatballs to each plate, made with veal, or small chops as you prefer, the calf's brains cut into bits or dipped in egg, raisins and pine nuts or candied pistachios; if in season, you may also add asparagus tips, artichoke bits, first boiled in water, and the usual spices; it will be a tasty dish. With the same head one can also make another dish with aromatic herbs and all sorts of fruits, as I will discuss in a later chapter.

Of the brains of the suckling calf.

The brains, boiled and cooked, can be served hot, sliced, with salt, pepper, parsley, and lemon or sour orange juice.

They can be dredged in flour and fried in good lard or butter, and served hot, with lemon juice, pepper, and a bit of salt, or a mostacciolo sauce, as one prefers.

Once cooked and finely ground, they can be used to make a little condiment, mixing them with hard egg yolks, candied citron, candied quince, powdered mostaccioli, and lemon juice; this condiment is cooked in a pan, and will be very nourishing.

These brains, in whatever dish they are used, must first be cooked in water, vinegar, and salt, or purified water, as one prefers, and the longer they boil the harder they become. Therefore, before boiling them, they must be washed and cleaned of blood and skin, and they must be skimmed before the water boils, lest they turn black.

These brains, once cooked and finely pounded, can be used in a frittata with finely ground aromatic herbs, good cheese, sugar, and cinnamon on top, and lemon or sour orange juice.

These brains can also be pounded in a mortar, adding egg yolks, a pinch of salt, bread crumbs, good cheese, aromatic herbs, pepper, and a bit of cinnamon; once you have pounded everything together into a paste, you will use it to form small dumplings [*gnocchetti*] and will cook them in a good fat capon broth; with this you can make a very tasty and noble dish which can be served to any great lord.[50]

---

49 Here and elsewhere Latini mentions mostaccere as a type of cookie, elsewhere specifying that they were rough equivalents of Savoy cookies (today, ladyfingers); this term is no longer used in Naples.

50 This is an example of the fluid use of the term gnocchi in Latini's time: almost any combination

These brains, after cooking them, can be pounded in the mortar with aromatic herbs and good grated cheese, eggs, sugar, the usual spices, and diluted with good malmsey or white wine; with this you can make fritters, dredge them in good flour, and fry them in good lard or butter; serve them hot with sugar and cinnamon on top, and lemon or sour orange juice; if you make the dough harder, they can be dipped in egg and fried, and they can serve as a garnish for many dishes.

These brains, once cooked and pounded in the mortar, can also be mixed with cream tops, beaten eggs, sugar, and cinnamon, and with them you can make a very tasty tart, mixing them with good butter, which can also be used for the short crust pastry cover.

These brains, once cooked in a meat broth, can be taken out of the broth and, before they cool, placed in a vessel with good broth and white or malmsey wine, so as to cover up to one finger's width above the brains. Add the usual spices, with sour orange juice or verjuice. Close the vessel well and boil everything until it reduces by half; take it off the fire, and slice the brains thinly, as with naked ravioli, and place them in a bowl or another vessel, with fat capon broth, or another you like, with marrow cut into bits, almond milk, beaten egg yolks, a little bit of sour orange juice or verjuice; blend everything together on a low flame; serve them hot, with sugar and cinnamon on top; if you wish to serve them with good grated cheese on top, then do not add the milk, but only the eggs and the verjuice, with the other ingredients, and it will be a tasty dish.

These brains, once cooked, can be sliced and dredged in good grated cheese and egg yolks, then fried in good butter; they will be tasty, and you may serve them as fritters, or use them as garnishes for other dishes.

These brains, once cooked, may also be used in another frittata, thus: pound the brains finely with aromatic herbs, beaten eggs, good grated cheese, the usual spices, cream tops, and a bit of fresh milk, then fry them in good butter or lard, and serve them hot with sugar and cinnamon on top.

You may also book these brains on a low fire, with almond milk or fresh butter, egg yolks, cinnamon, and perfumed water, and you can use them for a hot stew, with lots of sugar, and cinnamon on top.

You can also make another frittata with these brains, once cooked: grind them with good aromatic herbs, and pound them in the mortar with beaten eggs, grated cheese, sugar, and a bit of cinnamon; dilute them with some good malmsey or other white wine, and make them into a paste, softer than the one mentioned above for fritters, because it has to spread by itself in the pan; once cooked, serve the frittata hot, with sugar and cinnamon on top.

These brains, once cooked, can be cut into small bits, wrapped in wether or pig caul, adding sugar, cinnamon, pepper, and a bit of salt; fry them in good lard or fresh butter; serve them hot with sugar on top, and lemon or sour orange juice, and they will be most tasty.

---

of ingredients that could be mixed together into a paste, made into small shapes, and cooked quickly in water or broth could be defined as gnocchi (today in Italy the term refers primarily to potato dumplings).

These brains, once cooked can be used to make many tarts; grind them minutely with aromatic herbs, and pound them in the mortar, adding ricotta, fresh mozzarella or provatura, as you prefer, enough spices, sugar, grated cheese, beaten eggs. Pound everything together, and dilute it with good white or malmsey wine and good fat capon broth, or another broth as you prefer. Make a paste of this, quite soft, and place it in the pan with flaky pastry sheets, as discussed in the chapter on tarts, and serve them hot or cold, as you prefer, with sugar and cinnamon on top.

With these cooked brains you can also make tartelettes: pound them in the mortar with pine nuts, sugar, and cinnamon, fresh egg yolks, cream tops, butter, and a bit of perfumed water; cook them in the oven as you wish, and they will be quite exquisite.

They can be used in other dishes: after cooking them, pound them in the mortar with aromatic herbs, grated cheese, fresh egg yolks, sugar, cinnamon, pepper, and cloves, but not many, and mix in a bit of lemon juice or verjuice; make all this into a paste, divide it into small bits, as large as *ambrosine* almonds; cook them in a good fat broth, coloured with saffron, and with aromatic herbs and bits of parmesan cheese.[51]

These brains, once cooked, can be ground minutely with candied citron, sugar, cinnamon, and marrow; use this to fill flaky pastries and fry them in good fresh butter; they will be excellent, as I will discuss in a later chapter.

These brains, cooked and pounded in the mortar with pine nuts, hard egg yolks, candied pumpkin and citron, and various other candied things as you like, can be served thus: pound everything together, as just mentioned, and use it to stuff all sorts of flaky pastries or others, as needed, and you may use them to garnish dishes.

Once cooked, these brains can be pounded in the mortar with ox marrow, marzipan paste, aromatic herbs, grated cheese, and beaten egg yolks with half of their whites, and then you may serve these as convenient.

Of the tongue of the suckling calf.

The tongue, served in a small box of short crust pastry, cleaned and after one has diligently removed its thin skin, can be halved and boiled in broth or water; once it is half cooked, remove it from the fire and let it cool; have an apt pot prepared on the fire, with good fresh butter or lard, sauté it for a bit, add the tongue, half a glass of good white or malmsey wine, a bit of salt, two garlic cloves (first boiled in another broth), pepper, cinnamon, ground nutmeg; after all this has boiled for a bit add candied sour orange peel, bits of candied citron, all finely pounded with a knife, bunches of sweet small fennel, about ten whole cloves, and mostacciolo crumbs; serve it hot, with grated cheese and cinnamon on top; it will be a very tasty dish, and can be served to any great lord.

After preparing the small boxes of short crust pastry, and after baking them in the oven, put the halved tongue in them, arranging it diligently, and apportion on top this preparation [just described] and form with it a royal dish, which you can serve at any banquet; you can also use these small boxes with the tongue inside to garnish many royal dishes, as you prefer.

---

51 Ambrosine almonds were the most prized variety and appear in several Italian cookbooks since early in the Renaissance.

The same tongue, cooked and cleaned of its skin, can be cooked in a lard broth, and served hot with spices, as will be said in the chapter on dishes.[52]

After cleaning it, you can slice the tongue thinly, dredge it in flour and dip it in egg; fry it and serve it hot with sugar on top, and lemon juice at your pleasure.

After cleaning it as above, you can also wrap it in pork or wether caul and surround it with cloves, slices of cured back fat, and bits of cinnamon; spit-roast it and serve it hot with a royal sauce on top, at your pleasure.

After cleaning it, you can stew the whole tongue with salted pork throat, with peas and artichokes (first heated), with thin slices of apple, pear, quince, and other varied fresh or dried fruits, such as plums, sour cherries, dried apricots, or other fruits as you prefer, with raisins and pine nuts, a good fat broth, unripe grapes, a glass of malmsey or other white wine, and if you don't have the grapes you can use a bit of lemon or sour orange juice, with the usual spices; serve it hot with this preparation.

After cleaning it, you can roast the tongue on a grill, wrapped in paper, as in a stand pie, with inside the thinly sliced tongue, with bits of butter, aromatic herbs, and the usual spices; serve it hot with lemon or sour orange juice on top.

After cleaning it, you can slice the tongue thinly, dredge it in good flour, and fry it in good lard, and serve it with pepper and sour orange juice on top.

After cleaning it, you can halve the tongue, grease it with good lard, dredge it in bread crumbs, pepper, and salt, and grill it; serve it hot with sour orange or lemon juice and with slices of the same fruits on top.

This tongue can be prepared in a pie;[53] after cooking and cleaning it, put the whole tongue in the stand pie, and add slices of pork throat, the usual spices, various fresh fruits, peas, artichoke stems (first boiled), and whatever else you like; once it is cooked, remove the pie from the oven and add to it a bit of capon broth and a bit of lemon juice or verjuice, as you prefer, and serve it hot, as will be said in the chapter on dishes.

After cleaning and browning it, you can braise the tongue in an apt pot in the oven, thinly sliced, and add minced onions, aromatic herbs, pepper, cinnamon, and sliced sour orange with its peel, and good fresh butter; once cooked, serve it hot, it will be very tasty.

After cleaning and browning it, you can serve the tongue in another pie; place it in the stand pie, made with short crust pastry, riddling the tongue with cloves, cinnamon sticks, and small slices of cured back fat, surrounding it with slices of pork throat, and spraying pepper and a bit of salt on top; serve the pie hot or cold, as you prefer.

After cleaning it, one can cut the tongue into bits or cubes and sauté it in a pan with good lard, salt, crushed pepper, aromatic herbs, minced small onions, a sliced sour orange with its peel; serve it hot, and it will bring honour to the table.

---

52 Lard broth is perhaps an unappetizing-sounding rendition of *brodo lardiero*, which was a common dish with various versions: usually, it was prepared by boiling meat (first cleaned with water and wine) together with diced cured back fat, breadcrumbs, aromatic herbs, spices, and possibly eggs.

53 Latini here says that the tongue can be *impasticciata*; this term clearly refers to pies (*pasticci*); in this and other cases Latini explicitly mentions a pie or a stand pie, but in many he does not; still, I assume the term always refers to the preparation of pie fillings.

Another stew for the tongue; after browning it stuff it with veal or other meat, finely pounded, and add raisins, pine nuts, unripe grapes without their seeds, cow marrow, finely ground candied citron, boiled egg yolks, the usual spices, and thin slices of pork throat and ham; stew it, as mentioned above, and serve it hot, with a royal sauce on top, or whatever else you prefer.

Another pie with the tongue, after cleaning and browning it, as above, place it in a stand pie and add pork throat, pine nuts, raisins, bits of cardoons or artichokes (first boiled), thin slices of ham, cow marrow, the usual spices, and other ingredients as you prefer; add also small birds, whole or halved, or pigeons first browned in a pan with a bit of cured back fat or lard, sliced or whole as you prefer, and add also a little broth made with egg yolks, lemon juice, and a good meat or other broth; cook it in the oven, and then make a glaze for it with sugar, egg whites, and lemon juice; serve it hot, and it will be exquisite; note that this tongue can be placed in the box whole, stuffed, or in bits, as you prefer.

Of the neck of the suckling or Sorrento calf.

This neck can be cooked in many ways, for instance in a lard broth with a good fat broth, the usual aromatic herbs, bits of cured back fat or pork belly or throat, with the usual spices and various fruits in it.

The neck can be braised in the oven with a bit of malmsey wine, thin slices of ham, sliced pork throat, the usual spices, lemon juice, unripe grapes or verjuice, aromatic herbs, and a good fat broth; add fresh or dried fruits as you prefer.

The neck can be stewed, whole or in bits, with the same ingredients.

The neck can be used for a pie, whole or in bits as you prefer, in a suitable pan or pot, in a box of short crust pastry, and inside also bits of chicken or whole small birds, the usual spices, pork belly and sliced pork throat, various fruits, fresh or in syrup or dried, as you wish, and other noble and tasty ingredients, as will be said in the chapter on dishes; serve it hot, with a glaze on top made with sugar, egg whites, and lemon juice, and inside also a little broth of eggs, lemon juice, and good fat broth.

The neck can be boiled, with various salty ingredients, and aromatic herbs.

Of the lower neck of the suckling or Sorrento calf.

The lower neck of this calf, after cleaning it of all the blood, can be stewed whole or in bits, with plums and dried sour cherries, raisins, pine nuts, the usual spices, and other noble ingredients as you prefer.

The lower neck can be cooked in a pie, whole or in bits, with also slices of pork belly, bone marrow, the usual spices, and other suitable ingredients.

It can be cooked in a lard broth with thin slices of cured back fat, the usual herbs and spices, and other noble ingredients.

It can be braised in the oven with its sauce and many noble ingredients, as will be said in the proper place.

Of the belly or flank of the suckling or Sorrento calf.

The flank or belly can be stuffed with eggs, grated cheese, pine nuts, raisins, thyme, bread crumbs, pitted sour cherries, a bit of saffron, the usual spices, and other noble ingredients; it can be served hot or cold, whole or sliced; the flank, after stuffing it with the usual ingredients and cooked in broth, can be put into a press, under a weight.

The flank, stuffed and boiled in good broth, can be heated on a grill, to give it a crust with salt, pepper, bread crumbs, and mostacciolo crumbs, and served with lemon juice, as you prefer; slice it and it will be very good, also good for various soups.

This flank, after cooking and stuffing it, can be sliced thinly, and placed over a vegetable dish with thin slices of salty ingredients, and it will be very tasty and worthy of the table of any great lord.

After cooking it, this flank can also be stuffed with stuffing cooked in syrup, with various ground meats, as will be said in the proper place; it can be placed in a pie, whole or sliced, with many ingredients and condiments.

This flank, stuffed with various small birds, candied fruits, bits of pigeon, cow marrow, sliced ham, boiled egg yolks, and other ingredients as you prefer, with the usual spices, can be stewed; serve it hot with sour cherries or syruped unripe grapes on top; it will be a worthy and noble dish; it can be sliced, and one can add to it other Naples-style stews.

This flank, stuffed, can be spit-roasted, wrapped in pork or wether caul, larded with thin slices of cured back fat, and riddled with cloves and cinnamon sticks, covered in mostacciolo and bread crumbs; serve it hot with lemon or sour orange juice on top, as you prefer.

Once cooked and stuffed as usual, this flank can be thinkly sliced along the long side, and used to garnish many dishes.

These slices can also be dredged in good flour, dipped in egg, and fried, and served hot with a mostacciolo sauce on top, or a royal sauce, according to taste.

This flank can also be done in other ways, as will be said at the proper place.

Of the back or shoulder of the suckling or Sorrento calf.

This shoulder or back can be done as chops, to garnish many dishes.

This back can be spit-roasted, covered in cloves and cinnamon sticks and larded with thin slices of cured back fat, wrapped in the caul of this same calf, with a garlic flavour, and it will be tasty; serve it hot, with lemon or sour orange slices on top.

It can also be boiled and served hot with pepper and herbs on top.

The same, cold and minced, can serve for salads and various ground dishes, with a fat broth and a bit of nutmeg.[54]

Of the breast of the suckling or Sorrento calf.

This breast, stuffed with ground meat of the same calf or another animal, bits of ox marrow, the usual spices, candied citron and pumpkin, cut into small bits, chicken livers first cooked on embers and then finely ground, slices of various salami, syruped unripe grapes, and other noble ingredients, can be spit-roasted, wrapped in pork or calf caul;

---

54 Ground dish is *piccatiglio*, a preparation of Spanish origins (as its name also suggests) that consists of ground meat mixed with ground vegetables, and usually then with broth and eggs.

serve it hot with mostacciolo sauce on top, either spicy or vinegary as you prefer, as will be said in the chapter on sauces.

This breast, once cooked in broth, can be grilled, with a crust of salt, pepper, and bread crumbs, without stuffing it; serve it hot, with sugar and cinnamon on top, sour orange juice or malmsey wine; you may call this "coal" breast ["*incarbonato*"].

This breast can be stewed in a pan with the usual spices, and covered with small gnocchi, first boiled in good broth, with cut sausages and other noble ingredients.

This breast can be cooked in salted water or in a simple broth, and can be served cold, sliced, with salt and pepper on top, and borage flowers, with a bit of Roman mint on top, finely minced, and lemon slices around the plate.

It can be served in a pie, in a pan, with the usual spices, surrounded with strips of pork throat and pork belly or ham, and with syruped unripe grapes inside or syruped sour cherries; serve it hot with other fresh or unripe fruits, as you prefer.

The tip of this breast can be boiled and served hot, with herbs on top or without, as you wish.

This tip, once cooked, can be sliced thinly, dredged in good flour, and fried in good lard; serve them hot, with sour orange juice on top.

It can be stewed, with a bit of malmsey wine, adding various candied things; it can be stuffed with good grated cheese, or with mostacciolo, ground salami, aromatic herbs, a bit of pounded cured back fat, pine nuts, raisins, pepper, cloves, nutmeg, fresh eggs, a bit of salt, and the usual spices; you should sew it with thread and set it to boil in a fat broth; once it is boiled, you should remove the thread, flour it well with sponge cake crumbs, and fry it in butter; serve it hot with royal sauce.[55]

It can also be spit-roasted, stuffed as above, larding it with cured back fat, and then served with a bread crust on top and sliced lemons; it can be served cold, and it will be very good.

This breast can also be cooked in a good broth, cut into bits, sautéed in a pan with pepper, cinnamon, lemon juice, and unripe grapes, and served hot; it will be a tasty dish, with a thin broth of egg yolks.

It can be cooked in a lard broth, with ham bits, slices of pork belly, aromatic herbs, the usual spices, and other ingredients.

This breast can be braised in the oven, stuffed or not, with the usual spices, aromatic herbs, salt, pepper, and other noble ingredients.

Of the thigh of the suckling or Sorrento calf.

The thigh of the suckling calf can be boiled and served hot or cold, with pepper, salt, and sour orange juice on top, sliced or whole, as you prefer.

This thigh, once cooked and left to cool, can be made *in saltrida*, Spanish-style: grind the cold meat finely with minced onions, and add a bit of salt, pepper, cinnamon, Roman mint finely ground, and lemon or sour orange juice.[56]

---

55 In many recipes Latini includes *pan di Spagna* (literally Spanish bread), a light sponge cake that is today an ingredient in many Italian desserts; in Latini's times it was quite popular for both savoury and sweet dishes; when cooked twice it would become hard, like a biscuit.

56 The words *in saltrida* sound Spanish, but I am not sure of their exact meaning; Latini's description however gives a good idea of this preparation.

This thigh can be finely pounded, then add minced candied citron, bits of truffles, cow marrow, candied pitted plums, also finely minced, candied pine nuts or pistachios, pitted black olives, good grated cheese, beaten eggs, the usual spices, and salt; wrap everything in pork or wether caul, and with this you can make a French-style dish, very noble and tasty; it can be spit-roasted in bits, making sure not to waste the juice dripping from the roast, but rather to collect it in a pan; you will later use this juice to dress the roast as a condiment; serve it hot with this juice and other noble ingredients, as will be said in its proper place.[57]

This thigh can be stewed with various ingredients, the usual spices, and other condiments, cooked in a good broth and with malmsey or other strong white wine; serve it hot with garnishes of fruits on top, as you prefer.

This thigh can be stuffed with various small birds, with their heads sticking out, and other noble ingredients, and then spit-roasted, as will be said in its place.

This thigh can be cooked in a lard broth, with aromatic herbs, pepper, cinnamon, and salt, bits of ham, slices of pork belly, and other noble ingredients, whole or in bits.

This thigh can be braised in the oven with good white wine, slices of cured back fat, ham, lemon juice, and unripe grapes, with the usual spices and other noble ingredients, as you prefer.

This thigh can be cooked in a pie, putting it in a suitable pot, with pepper, cinnamon, sufficient slices of pork throat, covering it well, so that no smoke comes out; cook it in the oven, at a low fire, and serve it hot with syruped unripe grapes on top, or other condiments as you prefer.

This thigh can be cooked in a pie of short crust pastry; serve it with the same garnishes used for chops of the same thigh, cold or hot as you wish.

Chops can be made of this thigh, marinated and fried, and served with a bastard sauce or other condiments, as you prefer.[58]

Cut into large bits, this thigh can also be boiled in a good broth with a bit of salt and pepper, and it will provide a gentle nourishment.

This thigh, once boiled and spit-roasted, can be used to make cold or hot dishes, ground or not, in various ways, as you prefer, and depending on the occasion; it can be used to make small meatballs, accompanied by veal chops, with artichoke stems, marrow, good broth, nutmeg, a bit of pepper, lemon juice, and other suitable ingredients, with which you can make a French-style dish, and garnish it with slices of kidney fat, fried bread, and sugar on top.

With chops made from this thigh you can stuff fine or flaky pastries, either to fry them in butter or to bake them.

You can also use it to stuff flaky tubes, and adapt them to many things; you can use them to make tortellini, in boiled dough, which you can then dress with ox fat and mostacciolo crumbs.[59]

---

57 The pan for the dripping juice is a *liccarda*, a Neapolitan term etymologically linked to licking (the presumably intensely flavourful pan); I'll use dripping pan in later occurrences.

58 In Italian cuisine today bastard sauce is made with butter, flour, water, and egg yolks.

59 Latini writes (here and a bit later) *cannoncini* (literally, small cannons), so a tube shape seems

This thigh, once pounded, can be made into a paste together with small bits of candied citron or pumpkin, ox marrow, the usual spices, and other noble ingredients, as will be said in its place; with this, you can form balls as large as an egg yolk, more or less, as you like; braise it in the oven, or in a pan, with good fat broth, on a low fire; you can add fruits to it as you wish, and serve it hot, with other good ingredients, and you can thicken it with eggs.

With the same paste you can make a meatloaf with various candied things inside, and you can use it in various composite dishes and condiments; you can bake it in the oven, with low fire above and under it, and it will turn out better, and serve it hot, with the usual ingredients.

With this pounded meat, accompanied by boiled pumpkin, placed in a plate with rich ricotta, milk cream, a bit of salt, egg yolks, sponge cake crumbs, pepper, and cinnamon, all mixed, you can make a dish which, greased with butter and sprinkled with cinnamon, will be very tasty.

This meat can be ground finely, cooked in good fat broth (roasting it is even better), and then add cinnamon, cloves, bits of bone marrow, boiled egg yolks, candied pumpkin and citron cut into bits, raisins and pine nuts; serve it hot with cinnamon on top and lemon juice as you prefer; you may also add unripe grapes, or good white wine, as you like.

This same ground meat can be used to stuff pies of all sizes; first brown it in a pan; it can also be done in bits or stuffed, with various fresh or dried fruits, or syruped fruits, the usual spices, bits of pork throat, and other noble ingredients.

The same thigh one can use to stuff thin frittatas made with one egg, to be used as garnishes for a dish, shaped like tubes; it can be served with fat ox broth, and sugar on top.

This thigh, sliced very thinly, can be marinated in a perfumed vinegar for a couple of hours; then remove it, dry it well, and dredge it in good flour, and fry it in good lard; once half-cooked, remove it from the pan and place it on a silver plate or a pan, as you prefer; simmer it with a royal sauce on a low fire; serve it hot and it will be quite tasty.

From this thigh one can make chops, and marinate them in strong vinegar for two hours, if you have the time, then place them in a pan with fresh butter, with a bit of nutmeg, pepper, salt, and cinnamon, making sure the pan is well lidded; let it cook on a low fire for one hour, and it will be a tasty dish.

From this thigh you can take a haunch which can be roasted, stuffed with varied things, as you prefer, and served hot with verjuice on top, but a bit sweeter than sour, or with another condiment as you prefer.

This haunch can be stuffed, stewed, or braised in the oven, with varied ingredients and condiments, fresh or dried fruits; serve it hot, with the usual ingredients, as will be said in its place; it can be cooked the same way also if it is not stuffed, and served as above.

This haunch, together with the rest of the thigh, can be spit-roasted, and the juice from the roasting can be used as a condiment for any dish; this juice, with cream tops,

---

to be intended.

sugar, a bit of condiment as you prefer, every thing dissolved together, with one fresh egg yolk and lemon juice can be used to stuff various pastries; you then heat them in the oven, and they will be tasty; it will seem like eating meat without eating meat; this juice can be used in many other ways, as will be said in its place.

This haunch can be stuffed with various ingredients; remove the inside meat from it, and mix it with eggs, or without, or with pounded boiled eggs, as you prefer; spit-roast it, or stew it in a pan, with various ingredients, and pitted sour cherries and aromatic herbs.

Of the sweetbreads of the suckling or Sorrento calf.

Ordinarily these sweetbreads, cleaned, are dredged in flour and fried in good lard, with lemon juice, surrounded with slices of bread dipped in egg and fried, and lemon slices.

The suckling calf's sweetbreads can be cut into bits, larded with pork throat, salt, pepper, and cinnamon; wrap them in paper greased with lard or butter, and spit-roast them; serve them hot, with or without the paper, and a mostacciolo sauce on top.

You can use them in pies, with bits of marrow, truffles, pine nuts, and suitable spices; place them in the plates cut in small bits, with artichoke stems and cardoons, and other noble ingredients, first boiled and then fried in butter.

After cooking them in broth, let them cool, slice them thinly, dredge them in good flour, and fry them in good lard; serve them hot with pepper, lemon juice, salt, or a sauce, as you prefer; after frying them, they can be dressed with various sauces, as will be said in its place.

After frying them, as above, you can mix them in a thin broth made with lemon juice, beaten fresh eggs, sugar, and cinnamon, and serve them as a stew, as you prefer.

After cleaning them and browning them in a pan with good lard, you can use them in small pies, also with truffle slices, bits of cow marrow, bits of cardoons and artichokes, first boiled, pine nuts, the usual spices, and other noble ingredients; serve them hot with sugar on top of the pie crust.

These sweetbreads can be cooked in a pan or pot with the usual spices, pine nuts, and pistachios; thicken them with a little broth of egg yolks, and serve them hot, with the above condiments or other ingredients on top.

These fried sweetbreads can serve as garnishes for various dishes and in various dishes, as will be said in its place.

These sweetbreads, after cleaning them, can be wrapped in paper with salt, pepper, and slices of cured back fat; tie them with thread or string; spit-roast them and serve them in the paper with lemon slices; they can also be roasted or cooked in other ways, with a royal sauce on top.

They can be braised in the oven or simmered in a pan with various condiments and ingredients, as will be said in its place.

These sweetbreads are good in any form and preparation, and they ennoble any meat pie; they can be suitable everywhere, and can be used in many light stews.

Of the liver of the suckling or Sorrento calf.

The liver of the suckling or Sorrento calf can be sliced, placed in fresh water, changing the water several times, so that it will come out perfectly; dry it well, dredge it in good flour, fry it in lard or good oil; serve it hot with salt, pepper, and lemon juice as you prefer.

This liver, cut into bits, as one does with pork liver, you can dust with salt, pepper, and bread crumbs, and wrap in pork or wether caul; spit-roast it, mixed with bay leaves; serve it hot with sour orange juice on top, or another sauce you prefer.

This liver can be spit-roasted, whole or in bits, and larded French-style; serve it hot, with a royal sauce on top; it can be spit-roasted, after removing its thin skin, whole or in bits; you can cover it in bread crumbs, salt, pepper, sweet fennel, in a paper greased with lard; serve it hot inside the paper or caul, with a sauce on top as you like best with lemon or sour orange juice.

With this liver one can make various mortadelle, in pork guts, with good spices.

This liver can be prepared German-style, sliced in the shape of *vermicelli*, cooked in fat broth, with eggs, cheese, and aromatic herbs; it can also be used in various mixtures, to stuff pumpkins and other things.[60]

This liver can be thinly sliced, which you marinate for eight hours, more or less, as you prefer, in good milk, enough to cover the slices, with sugar; after the marinate, remove them, dredge them in mostacciolo or sponge cake crumbs and fry them in good lard; serve them hot with sugar and lemon juice on top; they will be very tasty.

This liver can be prepared Lombard-style, cut to a length of half a palmo (more will be even better), and thin like vermicelli; boil them in good fat broth with aromatic herbs, a bit of pepper, cinnamon, and beaten eggs; serve it hot with sugar on top.

This liver, whole or in bits, cleaned ot its thin skin, can be used in pies, dusted with cinnamon, and with cow marrow, larded with thin slices of soppressata from Nola, thin slices of ham, and other salami, and also thin slices of pork throat, the whole riddled with pine nuts and bits of the peel of candied citron; cook it in the oven, and serve it hot or cold as you prefer.

This liver, besides many dishes or roasts, can also be used in various stuffings, with pumpkin or fried bread, or other ingredients, as will be said in its place.

Of the kidney of the suckling calf.

This kidney, after spit-roasting it or cooking it in broth, can be pounded and sliced thinly, then add slices of pork throat, soppressata from Nola, and ham or other salami, bits of cow marrow, raisins and pine nuts, and other noble ingredients, with sugar, pepper, cinnamon, and bits of butter, mixing everything together also with beaten eggs; put this in a pan on a sheet of pastry, and make it into a pizza or tart or covered tart; serve it hot with sugar on top; with the same mixture you can stuff loaves of white bread, and you can also use it as an ingredient for many pies, minutely minced, or sliced, with beaten eggs; as will be said in its place.

The whole kidney can be spit-roasted, riddled with cloves and cinnamon sticks, wrapped in caul; serve it hot with sour orange juice or a mostacciolo sauce on top.

---

60 Vermicelli in Italy today are roughly the same shape as, but somewhat thicker than, spaghetti.

The whole kidney can be stewed with its own fat and the usual spices, aromatic herbs, and various other ingredients; serve it hot with sour orange juice and unripe grapes on top.

This kidney, after cooking it in broth or spit-roasting it, with its fat, can serve, as I said above, finely minced or sliced, to accompany many dishes and pies, as will be said in its place.

The kidney can also be spit-roasted in another way, rolling it first in bread or mostacciolo crumbs, salt, and pepper, in caul or in paper greased with lard; serve it hot, with the paper or without, or with the caul, with a royal sauce on top or on the side in a separate plate, as you prefer.

Of the tripe of the suckling or Sorrento cow.

This tripe, after cleaning it and washing it repeatedly in fresh water, so that it be white and without its bad smell, can be cooked in unsalted water, skimming it well; let it boil for a couple of hours, then remove it and place it in new cold water, so that its fat not drip; then you can cut it into bits of various sizes, according to what you need it for, and you can use it in many dishes, as will be said in its place; note though that in any dish in which you will use this tripe you should avoid sugar, because the result would be bad and have a bad flavour, since sweetness does not go with it.

This tripe can be stewed with salt, pepper, cloves, and nutmeg, and other noble ingredients as you prefer, and served with bread dipped in egg and fried and halved sour oranges.

This tripe, first boiled, and having removed the fatter parts, can be used in more liquid pies, accompanied by veal flesh and meatballs.[61]

This tripe can be cooked together with kid feet, with aromatic herbs and the usual spices, ham bits, white chickpeas, whole garlic heads, and a bit of chili pepper, and it will be quite tasty.[62]

This tripe can be boiled in a good fat broth, together with slices of ham or other salami, grated cheese, the usual aromatic herbs, pepper, and cinnamon; you can use this for soups and stews, with bread slices underneath and above, mixed with the same tripe; cover the dish with grated provatura, pepper, and cinnamon, and it will be very tasty; it can be stewed with a bit of its own fat broth, or another, as you prefer, as will be said in its place.

After cooking it, you can cut the harder part of this tripe into bits, and garnish them with ham slices, with pepper, a bit of salt, and mostacciolo crumbs; wrap it in paper greased with lard, spit-roast it and serve it hot; it can also be used to garnish various dishes, and to accompany various fried meats, as will be said in its place.

If you wish to use the guts, called in Naples *padiata*, you need to clean it first, then stuff it with veal or another meat, finely pounded, adding raisins, pine nuts, and egg

---

61 Flesh here and in many other places across the work is *polpa*, which I believe indicates the meat cleared of bones, fat, and nerves.

62 *Peparolo* is Latini's Neapolitan word for the chili pepper.

yolks; make a paste of this, with a bit of grated cheese, aromatic herbs, the usual spices, and a bit of salt; then cut it into bits, and serve it as you prefer, cooked in a good broth.[63]

This gut can be stuffed with the same pounded tripe, bits of minced pork belly, egg yolks, good grated cheese, aromatic herbs and the usual spices; cook it in a good fat broth with a bit of saffron, as you prefer, and serve it hot, sliced.

One can make meatballs from this, mixing it with eggs and other ingredients, and they will be tasty.

Of the feet of the suckling calf.

The best feet are the front ones because they are fleshier and fuller than the back ones, as is true in beef as well. Clean them well, first in hot and then in cold water, and cook them in water with a little salt, skimming them well, so that they be white; halve them, debone them, cut them into pieces, dredge them in good flour, dip them in egg, and fry them in good lard; serve them hot with a royal sauce on top.

These feet, once they are cooked and deboned, or also with the bones, can be floured and fried in good lard, and served hot or cold, with salt and pepper and sour orange juice, or anything else, depending on the taste of the diners.

These feet, after cooking, can be halved and grilled; make a crust for them with bread crumbs, salt, and pepper, and serve them hot with any sauce or sour orange juice, as you prefer.

Once cooked in water or broth they can also be served hot or cold with salt, pepper, and parsley, or with a condiment of sugar, cinnamon, cloves, perfumed vinegar, and mostacciolo crumbs, or other things, as will be said in its place.

Once the feet are cleaned, they can be made into jellies of various colours as you prefer; cook them in good white wine and vinegar, with the usual spices wrapped tightly in a little cloth so that the broth only take their smell; cook them as long as one usually does with jellies; you can give them colour with saffron, or almond milk, or an herb sauce, or ground cinnamon, as you prefer.

Once cooked in water, these feet can also serve for pies, or be spit-roasted, wrapped in paper or caul, with or without the bones; but first you need to marinate them; then serve them with the usual ingredients.

---

63 In addition to giving the Neapolitan word for this, Latini calls it the *budello gentile* (literally, the "gentle gut"), which refers to the end part of the intestine.

TREATISE III: *Of the ordinary or country calf; its qualities and cooking.*[64]

The country calf is very good, when it is fed with good grass and in gentle air; it should be young, so it will give more sustenance and benefit. Though the meat of this calf is not as good as that of the suckling or Sorrento calf, it is still quite good, but its meat is not apt for convalescents, since it is of more difficult digestion and of less sustenance than the suckling calf. It is cold in the first degree and dry in the second; its best season is in May, but it is good throughout the year.

Of the head of the country calf.

The calf's head, cleaned, cut, and deboned, can be boiled, with salted things inside, and is served with herbs on top, and it is exquisite.

One can make stews with it, with varied fruits inside, which is also a tasty preparation; after boiling it, if you cut it into pieces, dredge it in good flour, and fry it, it will be very good.

Once boiled, let cool, and cut into slices, you can serve it with salt, pepper, and a bit of vinegar, and it is of great quality.

Of the brains of this calf.

The brains, cleaned and skinned, can be boiled with a bit of vinegar and salt; let them cool, cut them into pieces, flour them, and fry them.

Cook them as above, and serve them cold, with parsley, pepper, and lemon juice on top.

Boil them, cut them into pieces, dip them in egg, and fry them; serve them hot with a royal sauce on top.

Cook them as above, and make them into dumplings with hard egg yolks, mostacciolo crumbs, and other noble ingredients.

With these brains you can make pies and tarts with the usual spices and other noble ingredients; serve them hot, with sugar on top.

You can make other dishes with these brains, also to accompany other dishes; refer also to what I wrote about the suckling calf.

Of the tongue of this calf.

Once cleaned and skinned, cook the tongue in salted water, and serve it hot or cold, with pepper and lemon juice on top.

Cook it as above and slice it thinly; dredge it in flour and fry it (you may also dip it in egg), serve it hot, with a royal sauce on top; it can also be used as garnish for other dishes; before you cut and fry it, you can also stuff it, as you prefer.

Boil it as above, stuffed or not, and then you can spit-roast it, finely larded and wrapped in caul or paper; serve it hot with a mostacciolo sauce.

---

64 The title that follows the number of this treatise refers only to its first segment; it covers in fact all other quadrupeds (in 54 pages).

Boil it and let it cool, slice it thinly, and you may use it for salads, with salt, pepper, and a bit of vinegar.

Boiled as above, you can cut into pieces and stew it in a good fat broth, with the usual spices and other ingredients.

You can cook it in a pot with a sauce of toasted almonds and other ingredients, as I will mention in its proper place.[65]

Of the thigh of this calf.

The thigh can be boiled, with or without salted things, and served hot or cold, sliced, with salt and pepper on top, and borage flowers, or other aromatic herbs.

You can make chops from it, with lean meat, and serve them in various ways, after cooking and preparing them.

You can use it for ground dishes, or in Spanish- or Genoese-style gigots, dressing it with its own juice or another fat broth, with apt ingredients.[66]

You can make meatballs or meatloaf with it, encrusted with pine nuts and with strips of candied things, and these can be stewed and served with noble ingredients.

The meatloaf can be sliced into thick slices, dipped in egg, and fried; serve them hot, with a royal sauce; these slices can also garnish other dishes.

You can use the meatballs as garnishes for pies, or you can stew them with chops and other noble ingredients.

With this thigh, you can make various pies, garnished and surrounded with meatballs or chops made with the same thigh, quarts or bits of chicken or other small birds, and other noble ingredients; you can ground them or not, as you prefer.

You can use it in large bits for pies, with sliced salted things inside, with their ingredients; serve them hot or cold as you like.

The thigh can be stewed, first cut into pieces, large or small, and mixed with pounded cured back fat, the usual spices, dried or fresh fruits, and other noble ingredients.

You can braise it in the oven, with varied noble ingredients.

You can use it for ground dishes or English-style pies, with apt ingredients, as I will say in its proper place.

Pounded, this thigh can serve to stuff any dish, for instance lettuce, cucumbers, pumpkins, cabbages, and similar things.

I conclude by saying that, when this thigh is small and white, you can use it as with the suckling calf, because if it is well pounded, and with the right ingredients, there is not much difference between them.

---

65 *Mandorle atterrate* (today usually *attorrate*) today refers to almonds cooked with water and sugar and then toasted, a recipe that exists in various regional varieties and today is exclusively a sweet snack or dessert.

66 Gigot is here *scigotto*, a term Latini uses fairly often, and which today would refer to a cooked leg (e.g. of lamb); he seems to use it for preparations in which meat (often ground) is used to form more complex dishes, and at times it refers more to a shape (as in a large pie) than to specific ingredients.

Of the haunch of this calf.

The haunch can be stuffed with ground meat, bone marrow, bits of candied things, St. George's mushrooms, and pine nuts, the proper spices, and other noble ingredients; you can also spit-roast it, larded, and serve hot or cold as you like it.

Once roasted and finely pounded, you can use it for tarts, with various candied things, cream tops, and other noble ingredients, the usual spices, mostacciolo crumbs, and sugar, binding everything together with beaten egg yolks, and served hot with cinnamon on top.

You can use it for meatloaf, with or without stuffing, or roast it, wrapped in caul, and served hot, with any sauce you like.

Of the breast or flank of this calf.

You can boil it, with or without stuffing, with herbs on top, or a green sauce.

After boiling it, you can cover it with fennel bunches, which you first cook in a good fat broth.

After boiling and stuffing it, you can press it; then slice it thinly and you can serve these slices under an herb stew together with other salted things, which you first cook well.

These slices can serve to garnish various dishes, or they can be fried (dipped first in egg, or not), and served with royal sauce on top, mixing the dishes with various fried things and small pies.

These slices can be used in pies, by themselves, or mixed with salami and mozzarella or *provola* slices, and other noble ingredients, and with the usual spices and a little broth; serve it hot, with sugar on top.[67]

The flank can be used for pies, with the usual spices and other noble ingredients.

It can also be stewed, whole or in pieces, stuffed or not, and served hot with the usual garnishes on top.

Once boiled, you can cook this on a grill on coals, with bread crumbs, salt, pepper, mostacciolo crumbs, and good malmsey wine.

Of the liver of this calf.

Once skinned, the liver can be sliced, floured, fried, and served hot with salt and pepper on top.

You can cut it into pieces, dredge them in bread crumbs, salt, and pepper, wrap them in pig or calf caul, then spit-roast them, with bay leaves between the pieces.

You can mix the fried slices with other fried meats, or use them for meat towers with various sauces on top, as I will discuss in its proper place.[68]

You can boil and cook the liver, ground it, and mix it with pounded cured back fat; then you can use it to make rolls, together with bits of ham, candied citron and pumpkin (ground or in small bits), cow marrow, mostacciolo crumbs, apt spices, and other noble

---

67 Provola is smoked mozzarella, still very common in the Naples region.

68 Latini says *torresi*, which suggests a pile, a tower, but I have found no clear meaning for this.

ingredients; roll everything together in caul, then spit-roast it, mixed with bay leaves, and serve it hot, with lemon or sour orange juice, as you prefer.

You can also roast the liver, whole, having first skinned it; dust it with bread crumbs, salt, pepper, wrap it in caul or paper, and spit-roast it, as I said above; serve it hot, with the condiments you prefer.

You can prepare it in Genoese style: slice it, fry it in good oil or lard, and put it on a plate with a sauce on top; make the sauce with a piece of the same liver, first roasted and boiled in water, then ground and thoroughly mixed with good vinegar, ground garlic cloves, mint leaves, salt, pepper, and a bit of pounded cured back fat or lard; after a quick boil, pour the hot sauce on top of the fried liver slices, and serve them hot; it will be most tasty.

Of the feet of this calf.

Clean them well, and boil them in water with a bit of salt; serve them cold, in a salad, cut into small bits, with salt, pepper, aromatic vinegar, and ground mint.

You can also flour and fry them and serve them with royal sauce.

You can use them to make jellies of various colours, and they will be best than in any other preparation; this is however a coarse food, which you serve only to people of low status; you may also prepare them in many other ways, as you prefer.

Of the ox, the cow, and their quality and cooking.

The ox is very nutritious and benefits especially men who perform strenuous work all the time, as it produces abundance of blood; it diminishes the choleric humour. It must be young, fat, and well exercised in plowing or other work. The cow shares the same quality; both are cold in the first degree and dry in the second; the cow however, if pregnant and near giving birth, is moist in the first or second degree.

Prometheus was the first to eat ox meat; before, there was a law severely prohibiting the killing of this animal, as it was a servant of Ceres and a companion to man in the exercise of agriculture. Bovine meat is divided into four categories: calves, bullocks, adult oxen, and old ones. The untamed ox can be tamed by tying it with a woollen rope; from its cadaver are born bees, mothers of honey, as Virgil attests.[69]

Of the head of the ox or cow.

Clean and skin it, and cook it in water with salt, or in broth, first deboned; you can cut into pieces and stew it with salami, various fruits, fat broth, and other noble ingredients, with the usual spices and aromatic herbs.

You can use this head in various dishes, for instance in a lard broth, and in various ways; note that, however you prepare it, it will always be better after aging.[70]

---

69 Ceres was the Roman goddess of agriculture; Virgil speaks of the miraculous birth of bees from dead oxen in his *Georgics*, 4.281–314, 554–58. For many of his food items, Latini gives a mythical "inventor," or someone whom he credits with first eating (or cooking) the particular item (or animal); like many other writers about such things, he took most of this information from a popular 1548 treatise by Ortensio Lando.

70 *Frolla* is Latini's word here, i.e., meat that has been hanged to drain it of blood.

Of the tongue of the ox or cow.

Clean and skin the tongue, and you can stuff it with various noble ingredients, and then cook it in broth, or as you prefer, and serve it hot or cold, whole or sliced, with the condiments and garnishes you prefer.

Once cleaned, skinned, and cooked, you can use it in pies, stuffed or not, sliced or cut into pieces, with also bits of salami and dried fruits, with the usual spices and other noble ingredients; serve it hot or cold, as you prefer, with sour orange juice.

Once cleaned as above, you can stew it, sliced or in small pieces, with the usual spices, fat broth, ham slices, aromatic herbs, raisins, pine nuts, sour cherries, dried plums, and other noble ingredients, with a bit of white or cooked wine; if you wish to mix it with eggs, then the wine is not needed; this tongue will work out better for monks or friars in monasteries, because it is easy to share it and make dishes from it.

You can braise it, whole, in the oven, stuffed or not, with the usual spices, sour grapes, lemon juice, various fresh fruits, and other ingredients, with a bit of cooked wine or fat broth; serve it hot, with the same fruits on top.

You can cook it in a lard broth, with the usual aromatic herbs, slices of pork throat, apt spices, and other noble ingredients.

Once cleaned as above, you can lard it with cloves and thin strips, roast it in caul, wrapped in paper; grease it with liquefied lard, and add a crust on top made with grated crustless bread, salt, and pepper; serve it hot with a sauce or lemon juice on top; you can roast it stuffed or not, and serve it hot or cold as you prefer with the usual condiments.

You can also salt it or smoke it, and then use it in various dishes, or as garnishes, as I will say in its proper place.

Of the brains of the ox or cow.

Clean them, skin them, and remove all the blood from within them, and boil them in water, vinegar, and salt; skim them before the water starts boiling, so that they come out white; when they are well cooked, you can use them in many dishes, as will be said later, as we said of the calf's brains.

After cooking them as above, can be served hot or cold, with ground parsley, pepper, and lemon juice on top.

After cooking them, you can use them to make a thin stew with fat broth, tinted with saffron, and with aromatic herbs and the usual spices; they can be mixed with eggs and bits of good parmesan cheese; or served with grated provatura on top, sugar, cinnamon, and a bit of lemon juice, as you prefer.

After parboiling them and grinding them in the mortar, you can use them for a stew, with mostacciolo crumbs, hard egg yolks, beaten fresh eggs, diluting the mixture with the same eggs; make a paste with this, and form small dumplings; cook them in a good fat broth, with bits of marrow and candied pumpkin, with the usual spices, aromatic herbs, thinly ground ham, syruped sour grapes or lemon juice, small bits of parmesan cheese, grated mozzarella or provola, cinnamon, and other ingredients.

After cooking them in water, you can ground the brains in the mortar with good grated cheese, aromatic herbs, sugar, cinnamon, marrow, mostacciolo crumbs, and other noble ingredients; make a paste with it, diluted with beaten eggs and a bit of perfumed water and good broth; mix it with sliced candied pumpkin and citron, and other noble ingredients, and various milky cheeses, such as mozzarella or provatura; with this, you can make a pizza or covered tart, over a layer of short crust pastry; serve it hot with sugar and cinnamon on top, or with strips of pastry, as you prefer.

You can dilute the mixture above with good white wine and some more fresh beaten eggs, and then make it into a frittata, to be served with lemon juice, sugar, and cinnamon on top, or something else as you prefer.

The same mixture you can dilute with goat milk and mix with pine nuts or pistachios; then use it for fritters dredged in sponge cake crumbs, mostacciolo crumbs, and good flour; fry them in good butter or lard, and serve them hot with a mostacciolo sauce on top, or another condiment as you prefer.

You can dilute the same mixture with fresh ricotta, and then use it to make ravioli; dredge them in good flour, cook them in water, and as soon as they boil add sugar and cinnamon.

These brains, cooked as above, can be used to stuff various meats and birds, and in various dishes, as we said of the brains of the suckling calf.

Of the neck and lower neck of the ox or cow.

The neck can be cooked on a medium fire, and served hot or cold, with sour orange juice and borage flowers on top.

You can cook it in a lard broth, cut into pieces, with bits of pork belly and other salami, the usual spices, aromatic herbs, and other ingredients, with good fat broth and fresh fruits.

You can stew it, in bits, in a good fat broth, aromatic herbs, and spices, various fresh or dried fruits, raisins, pine nuts, and other noble ingredients.

You can braise it in the oven with the same ingredients, with a bit of good white wine, sour grapes or lemon juice, and a good fat broth; serve it hot.

You can use this neck in various dishes, except pies, as I will discuss in the chapter on dishes.

Of the breast of the ox or cow.

After cooking it in broth, you can slice this breast and serve it in vegetable soups.

After cooking it as above, you can cut it into small bits, or shred it, and serve it Spanish-style.

After cooking and boiling it, you can serve it cold, sliced, with lemon juice on top, and ground parsley, borage flowers, lemon slices, or other condiments, as you prefer.

You can stuff this breast with various ingredients, and serve it hot or cold, whole or sliced, as you prefer.

After cooking it, stuffed or not, you can slice it, dip the slices in eggs or not, and fry them in good broth; serve them hot, with or without a condiment on top.

You can use it in pies, cut into small or large pieces, with slices of pork throat and ham and other salami, the usual spices, and varied fruits, first browned in a pan, and other noble ingredients; make a little broth for inside the pie, and serve it with a glaze on top and sugar, as you prefer; make sure the breast has been aged, because often it comes out a bit hard.

You can stew this breast, or braise it in the oven in a lard broth, with various ingredients and fresh or dried fruits inside, with the usual spices and other noble ingredients; you can prepare it in various other ways, as you wish.

Of the flank of the ox or cow.

This flank can be stuffed with beaten eggs, grated cheese, ham bits, and pork throat, the usual spices, aromatic herbs, raisins, pine nuts, and other noble ingredients, and then cooked in broth; after cooking it, you can press it, so that it will appear flat and not swollen; then cook it again on the grill, with a crust made of bread crumbs, pepper, and salt; first, though, you need to grease it as you prefer; serve it hot with a mostacciolo sauce or another condiment.

After stuffing, cooking, and pressing it as above, you can slice it thinly and use it under any vegetable stew, together with sliced salami, first cooked in broth.

You can also dredge these same slices in good flour or mostacciolo or sponge cake crumbs, dip them in eggs, and fry them, even without dipping them in eggs, and then use them as garnishes for many dishes; they will also be good on their own, with a bastard sauce or another condiment on top.

After stuffing it and cooking, you can spit-roast this flank, larding it with hot cured back fat, and making a crust for it with bread crumbs, salt, and pepper; serve it hot with various condiments.

You can cook it in a lard broth with a good fat broth, the usual spices, aromatic herbs, various fresh fruits, and other noble ingredients.

This flank can be used in many preparations, as I wrote of the flank of the suckling calf.

Of the ribs or fillet of the ox or cow.

The ribs or fillet of ox or cow, after boiling them, are served cold, sliced thinly, with salt and pepper on top, and with borage flowers.

They can also be stewed, with a bit of wine and the usual spices; be careful not to remove them before they are cooked, and let them stew with their own juice in a covered pot, well sealed, together with various fresh and dried fruits, a bit of lemon juice or verjuice, and they will be very good.

You can grill the ribs, and they will be very tasty, with fennel flowers, or coriander, and salt, sprinkled with verjuice.

You can use them in pies, with the usual spices, slices of various salami, beef chops, with artichoke bits, cardoon stems (first cooked), bits of marrow, and other noble ingredients, with a good broth.

These same chops you can use for ground dishes, and can be served with various condiments, as will be said in its proper place.

Of the inner fillet of the ox or cow.

Here in Naples we often use the inner fillet of beef, and it is generally of great quality and goodness. We marinate it in oregano, crushed garlic cloves, finely chopped chili pepper, and salt as needed; stew it with a bit of aromatic vinegar, after leaving it to marinate for five or six hours, or from evening to morning. You can also spit-roast it. Then cut it in thin slices; it is fit for anyone's table, and it is very tasty.[71]

You can stew this fillet, in large chunks or small pieces, with various sliced salami, marrow, varied fresh and dried fruits, as you prefer, and a bit of the marinate described above, with the usual spices; serve it hot.

You can make chops from this fillet and cook them in various ways; slice them thinly and pound them with the back of a knife, grease them with beaten cured back fat, sprinkle with salt, pepper, cloves, cinnamon, and ground sweet fennel; wrap them like saveloy sausages, and spit-roast them mixed with slices of cured back fat, sage leaves, or dried bay leaves.[72]

You can roast these chops on the grill, without wrapping them; set them aside, on top of each other, and grease them with the dripping juice from the pan, sprinkle them with aromatic vinegar, and serve them with a royal sauce on top, as you wish.

You can stew these chops with good lard, and sour grapes or lemon juice.

You can ground this fillet thinly and make it into meatballs or meatloaf, in various ways, with the usual ingredients, with grated cheese, beaten eggs, the usual spices, and a bit of bread crumbs; to make them more tender, add fat from the same cow and marrow, everything together, with raisins, pine nuts, ground aromatic herbs, bits of candied citron or pumpkin; you can make a paste with the entire mixture, with other ingredients.

Of the thigh and haunch of the ox or cow.

The meat of this thigh, cut into large pieces of about six pounds each, can be spit-roasted; once perfectly cooked, remove it from the spit and press it; you can use the juice for those who have a weak stomach, and also give it to those who have trouble digesting; it is of very good quality.

This juice can also be placed in a pot, and let cool; as it cools it forms a layer of fat on top; remove this layer carefully, put the juice on a low fire, and cook it with apt spices, salt, and lemon juice.

This juice can also be served in composite dishes, gigots, ground dishes, and they will all be very good.

You can prepare this juice also another way: cut the meat into chops, not too thin; cook them on the grill, without burning them; once perfectly cooked, press them, one piece atop the other, and the juice will be of very good quality.

Some physicians say that the best juice is the one that comes out of roasts, when they are sliced in the plates at the table.

---

71 This is one of the many points where Latini emphasizes local usages; today the oregano and garlic would still be typical Neapolitan touches; Latini was the first to publish recipes that employ the chili pepper, a New World ingredient that probably had arrived to Naples from Spain, though it does not appear in Spanish cookbooks until after Latini's time, see Riley, *The Oxford Companion*, entry for "Latini."

72 Saveloy sausage (*cervellata*) was a dried sausage usually made from brains.

I, however, when I want to prepare composite dishes, gigots, or ground dishes, of any meat, use beef juice: cut the cow or ox meat into pieces weighing six or seven ounces, neither too fatty nor too lean, place them in a pan or other apt pot, clean them neatly with a cloth, and stew them well; add the usual spices, ham slices, and thin slices of cured back fat, without salt, and cook everything on a low fire; once this is perfectly cooked, remove the meat, and you can use the juice for any pie or other dish, and it will be very tasty.

All these juices can be thickened in the Roman style, with fresh egg yolks and lemon juice; some are very healthy and are given to convalescents.

With this meat you can also make another tasty and nutritious broth: take a piece of this meat weighing about two pounds, according to the number of people for whom you need it; boil it until it is more than half-cooked, then add a wild dove, the thigh or breast of a capon, half a dozen wings of any chicken, and a bit of cured back fat (note that if you need this for ill people, you should use very little cured back fat), half a soppressata from Nola, a chunk of ham or Giugliano fillet, and boil everything until it is perfectly cooked. Add parsley roots and apt spices; add hot water to fill the pot, and let the broth cook until it reduces by half, adding finely chopped aromatic herbs, as you prefer; you can thicken this broth with fresh egg yolks or without, as you prefer; in the Spanish style, one serves this broth in fayence bowls, with slices of toasted bread in it.[73]

You can boil the meat of this thigh, lean or fatty, and serve it hot with a garlic sauce or another condiment, as you prefer.

After cooking it, you can serve it cold, thinly sliced, with salt, pepper, ground parsley, borage flowers, and lemon slices on top, as you prefer.

Lean meat from this thigh, finely pounded, can be used to stuff various other meats, pumpkins, or other things.

You can make chops from it, thinly sliced, and pounded with the back of the knife; grease them with good beaten cured back fat, dust them with salt, the usual spices, ground sweet fennel, a bit of garlic, without sugar; you can stew this meat in a pan, with a bit of cured back fat, without broth, with or without sour grapes, as you prefer.

You can use these chops in pies, together with pounded meat, raisins, pine nuts, the usual spices, bits of marrow, bits of artichokes, cabbages, and cardoons (first parboiled), and other noble ingredients; serve this hot.

You can stew these chops as above, with a bit of fat broth, a bit of cooked wine, the usual spices, aromatic herbs, other noble ingredients, and slices of various salami; this can be served with the same garnishes and ingredients as above.

These chops, stuffed with ground meat, ham bits, and other noble ingredients, can be spit-roasted, mixed with slices of cured back fat and bay leaves, and served with the condiments you prefer.

These chops can be used to stuff bread loaves, with other noble ingredients, and birds, as I will say in its proper place.

---

73 Nola and Giugliano are both near Naples, again reflecting Latini's interest in local ingredients.

Fatty or lean meat, like the haunch, can be used in pies, whole or in small pieces, with various fresh or dried fruits, slices of various salami, marrow, the usual spices, and other noble ingredients.

The lean meat, like the haunch can be stuffed, after cooking it, with various ingredients, and it can also be stewed whole, with the same ingredients; serve it hot.

This same meat can be stewed, without stuffing, riddled with cloves and cinnamon sticks, with slices of pork throat and a bit of malmsey wine; serve it cold or hot, as you prefer; note that, when you use this haunch in pies, cooked whole, or in another way, you first need to pound it with a pin, or brown it in broth, so that it will cook quickly and come out tender.

This lean meat, cleaned of its nerves, can be finely pounded, and mixed with fat from the same animal, beaten eggs, good grated cheese, marrow, bits of candied things, the usual spices, finely chopped aromatic herbs, raisins, pine nuts, and other noble ingredients, and bread crumbs; make a paste of all this, with which you can make meatballs or meatloaf, shaped like flowers or in any way, at your whim, then braise them in the oven with varied ingredients and the usual spices. You can stew the meatballs in a pan, with chops of the same haunch and candied things, or without; you can mix them with beaten eggs and lemon juice, as you prefer.

This mean, lean or fatty, can be used in many ways, for instance ground, or in pies, tarts, covered tarts, and pizze, with the usual ingredients; you can also stew it in pieces, in a lard broth, and use it in other dishes; do the same as with veal.

Of the cow's udder.

The cow's udder, after tying up the nipples, must first be cooked in broth or water, and then it can be used for various dishes.

Once it is cooked and has cooled, you can cut it into thin slices, dredge it in flour, dip it in egg, fry it, and serve it with any sauce.

You can also cut it and stew it, with aromatic herbs and the usual spices, a bit of fat broth, and other noble ingredients; it will also be good if you add eggs.

It can also be braised whole in the oven, with a bit of white wine, the usual spices, unripe grapes or lemon juice, fresh fruit, raisins, pine nuts, ham slices, and other noble ingredients.

Once cooked as above, you can lard it with slices of ham fat and cloves, wrapped in caul, and spit-roast it; serve it with a royal sauce or another condiment you prefer.

You can use it in pies with the same ingredients as when you braise it, with a bit of cooked wine.

You can cook it as above, slice it, and wrap it in short crust pastry, with the usual spices, ham slices, and other salted things, marrow, and other noble ingredients; serve it hot or cold, with a little broth inside or without, as you like it, and sugar on top.

You can serve it in other ways, stuffed with various ingredients, or fried with or without dipping it first in egg, or cooked in the caul; sliced, it may serve as garnish for many dishes or to accompany various soups, as I will discuss in a later chapter.

Of the tripe of the ox or cow.

Clean the tripe and wash it several times in cold water, then cook it in water without salt; you can serve it in all the following ways; note that you should never add sugar to it, because it would not smell good; after cooking it in water, you can cook it in a good fat broth and serve it with Roman mint; tripe is cooked especially well in Rome, more than anywhere else, so much so that Romans at times buy it from tavern-keepers, because they prepare it very well.[74]

After parboiling it, you can use it for soups, cut in thick slices, mixed with bread slices, good grated cheese, and cinnamon; let it stew in a silver plate or pan, with a good fat broth; serve it hot with the said grated cheese and cinnamon on top.

You can use it for stews, cut in small bits, with unripe grapes, a good fat broth, but not salty, with raisins and pine nuts, aromatic herbs, a bit of Roman mint, the usual spices, and other noble ingredients, mixed with beaten eggs and good grated cheese; you can give the broth colour with some saffron, if you wish.

You can cook it as above and cut it in large pieces, and put it in a stand pie made of short crust pastry, mixed with slices of mozzarella or provatura, slices of ham or pork belly, grated cheese, cinnamon, aromatic herbs, and other ingredients, with a little broth of egg yolks and fat broth; serve it hot without sugar, as mentioned above.

After cooking it as above you can pound it minutely with ham and marrow; mix everything with the usual spices, raisins, pine nuts, and other noble ingredients; make meatballs with this, and cook them in a good broth, mixed also with eggs, and with good parmesan cheese on top.

The best tripe is the one of the suckling or Sorrento calf, and it can be used in all the ways and dishes in which you use that calf.

Of the liver of the ox or cow.

Clean and skin the liver, and place it in cold water; then slice it thinly, dredge it in flour, and fry it in good lard or oil; serve it hot, with salt and pepper on top, and lemon juice, or with a sauce made with vinegar and the usual ingredients.

Slice it, dredge it in flour or not, and fry it in good oil, and serve it with a condiment made with liquefied cured back fat, vinegar, and Roman mint; give the sauce a boil and then throw everything in a pan on top of the fried liver, and sprinkle it with pepper (called here in Naples *acetello*).[75]

After frying it in good lard and sprinkling it with salt and pepper, the liver can be served with slices of fried bread above and below it, and with various other fried things, as I will say in its proper place.

Clean and skin the liver and cut it into pieces, as one does with pork liver, and dredge it in bread crumbs, pepper, and salt, and put it in the caul of a pig or wether; spit-roast

---

74 Tripe is still a Rome specialty; Latini's mention of buying food from tavern-keepers hints at what would be a major development in eighteenth-century food consumption patterns.

75 It is not clear syntactically if acetello refers to a type of pepper, or to this sauce, which actually (because of the vinegar and mint) looks rather like a scapece.

these pieces with bay leaves and serve them hot, with lemon or sour orange juice, or another condiment as you wish.

You can prepare this liver in many of the same ways as the liver of the suckling calf, and although it is not as perfect and tender, nonetheless it can can serve in all the ways which I described for the suckling calf.

Of the kidney of the ox or cow.

Cook the kidney in broth or something else, and pound it minutely, with candied citron and pumpkin and other ingredients; you can use it as garnish for pies and to stuff all sorts of meats.

With this kidney, pounded, you can make a stew, with bits of cow fat, ham slices, marrow, raisins, pine nuts, chopped onions, aromatic herbs, the usual spices, and other noble ingredients; sauté everything together, with good beaten cured back fat, a bit of fat broth, and lemon juice, salt, and pepper on top.

Prepare the kidney as above and wrap it in caul or paper greased with lard, and spit-roast it; serve it hot with lemon juice and pepper on top, or royal sauce, as you prefer; however, it will likely be a bit hard.

With this same preparation, adding beaten eggs, grated cheese, sugar, and cinnamon, you can make *crostini*, with slices of grilled bread; heat them and serve them hot, with lemon juice on top; these crostini can serve also as garnishes for various dishes.[76]

You can use this kidney in many of the same ways and dishes as that of the suckling or Sorrento calf.

Of the feet of the ox or cow.

Clean and wash them, cook them in water with a bit of salt, and serve them hot or cold (but first debone them), with salt and pepper on top, or with vinegar flavoured with garlic and finely chopped Roman mint; the forward feet are better, because they are fleshier.

Cooked and deboned as above, you can cut them into bits, dredge them in flour, dip them in eggs, and fry them; serve them with royal sauce and lemon juice, as you prefer.

You can prepare them in all the ways of the feet of the suckling calf.

Of the wether, its quality and cooking.

The best wether is young, aged about one year, and it benefits even the sick. The best, and truly exquisite, are those that feed in mountainous areas, fragrant and rich in good grass. This meat is easily digested, produces good blood, and is very nourishing for people of all ages and complexions. It cheers the melancholy humour, because of its lightness; it maintains a good complexion and balanced temperament, and its broth is also very nourishing.

The wether's quality is temperately hot and moist; it is good at all times, especially in April and June. The best of all are those from the Marches, which is a region of good pastures.

---

76 Latini generally uses crostini (or crostine) to mean simply thin slices of toasted bread; only occasionally, as here, does he indicate anything spread over these (as one would expect in crostini today).

Dremideus was the first to eat this meat, and also sheep meat. According to Pliny the wethers of Puglia are good and healthy, as they feed in good mountain pastures.[77]

Of the head of the wether.

After cleaning and skinning it, you can cook the head in water and salt, or in broth, and use it rather as a remedy [for health issues] than as a food; you can prepare it in various ways, and it is eaten hot.

After parboiling it, you can cut it into pieces and sauté it with chopped small onions, salt, pepper, aromatic herbs, and other ingredients, as you wish.

You can also fry it, cut into pieces and dredged in flour; serve it hot, with pepper and sour orange juice on top.

Of the neck of the wether.

You can cook the neck in water, together with bits of ham and other salami; serve it hot with the same salami and aromatic herbs on top.

You can stew it with slices of cured back fat and a fat broth, the usual spices, and other noble ingredients.

You can cook it in a lard broth, with slices of pork throat and belly, the usual spics, aromatic herbs, and other noble ingredients.

You can cook it in pies, with various fruits, the usual spices, sour grapes or lemon juice, a bit of white wine, and aromatic herbs on top.

You can cut it into pieces and use it for a pie, or roast it together with various pounded meats, with the usual spices and other noble ingredients; serve it hot with a sugar glaze on top.

Of the breast of the wether.

You can boil the breast with noble ingredients and serve it hot with pepper and lemon juice on top.

You can stuff and cook the breast as above, and then press it, so that it will be flat and not swollen; then grill it, and make a crust on top of it with bread crumbs, salt, and pepper; serve it hot with royal sauce or another condiment, as you wish.

After stuffing and cooking it as above, you can slice it thinly, dredge the slices in flour and dip them in egg, and fry them in good lard; serve them hot with the condiment you prefer; they can also be used as garnishes to various dishes.

You can spit-roast the breast, stuffed with noble ingredients, and serve it hot, with or without a crust, and with apt condiments.

You can braise it with the usual spices and other noble ingredients; serve it hot, and it will be tasty.

You can prepare the breast in various ways, following the rules of our craft.

---

77 Pliny (23–79) was a Roman naturalist whose works were popular throughout the Middle Ages and beyond.

Of the flank of the wether.

You can prepare the flank of the wether in all the same ways as its breast.

Of the ribs or fillet of the wether.

The ribs or fillet can be roasted in various ways, and served hot, with apt condiments on top.

You can cook them in broth and serve them hot, with bunches of aromatic herbs on top, first cooked in good broth, and sprinkled with pepper.

You can make chops from them, cook them in various ways, and serve them with apt condiments and a marinade.

You can prepare these ribs and fillet in various dishes, as I will discuss later.

Of the thigh and haunch of the wether.

After spit-roasting this meat, you can press it to draw its juice; you can use it to garnish various composite dishes and other meat dishes, as we said of the thigh and haunch of the ox or cow.

You can cook it in good broth with bits of salami, and serve it hot with the salami, covered with fennel bunches, first cooked in a fat broth.

You can make chops from it and cook them in various ways; they can also serve as garnishes for dishes and pies.

You can ground this meat in various ways; after cooking it in good broth you can garnish it with varied and noble ingredients.

You can use it for meatballs and meatloaf, which can be served also to the convalescent; mix them with various marinades; they will be good with garlic cloves or without, as I will discuss in its proper place.

You can use it for various roasts, larded and served hot, with apt condiments, or even without, as you prefer.

The thigh you can spit-roast, larded with garlic cloves, cloves, and rosemary sticks; serve it hot or cold, depending on the circumstances.

You can use it in stews and soups, in pies, or braised, whole or in pieces, with the usual spices and other noble ingredients, as you do with the thigh of the suckling calf.

You can cook it in a lard broth, with the usual spices, aromatic herbs, and other noble ingredients.

Of the tail of the wether.

After cooking it in water, you can use the tail in various fried dishes, dipped in egg or not, sliced thinly, and served with the condiments you prefer.

After boiling it, you can serve it hot, with a garlic condiment or another one.

After parboiling it you can grill it, moistening it with malmsey wine and sprinkled with aromatic vinegar, with a crust on top made with crustless bread; serve it hot with royal sauce or malmsey wine, as you prefer.

You can use the tail in various tasty dishes, with various garnishes and ingredients.

Of the feet of the wether.

Clean them and cook them in water and salt; then serve them hot or cold, with salt, pepper, and Roman mint, and a bit of vinegar; you can use them to make various jellies.

After cooking and deboning them, you can use them in stews, and garnish these with noble ingredients, as I will say in its place; you can also dredge them in flour and fry them, after boiling them.

Of the liver of the wether.

This can be prepared with all the condiments with which we prepare the livers of other animals.

Of the chamois, its quality and cooking.

The meat of the chamois [a mountain goat-antelope] is not as good as other meats, and one should eat little of it, and only of the young animal, which is better, and the ill should avoid it altogether, as it is not easy to digest.

This animal is dry in the first and second degree; its season is from December through April.

Pliny writes that Marinus Preticus, a military man, was the first to cook and eat chamois; many authors claim that this animal can see both in the day and at night, and that its eyes never move.

Of the head of the chamois.

After cleaning it well, you can cook the head in water and salt, and serve it hot with pepper on top; otherwise, it will not be good. You can also cook it and then grill it on coals, first split in half, as with other heads.

The breast, shoulder, fillet, ribs, flank, and all other parts of the chamois can be cooked in various ways and for various dishes, but first you need to half-cook them on the grill.

They can also be cooked in a lard broth, stewed, or in pies, spit-roasted, or braised, in the same ways and with the same condiments as with kid meat, though it is not as good and perfect as kid meat; if you need to, you can stuff it, as with wether meat; its flesh, cut into bits, you can use for cold pies or ground dishes, mixed with salami and other suitable ingredients; you can also boil this meat, and serve it with a garlic condiment.

The deer, its qualities and cooking.

The best deer is the suckling or castrated one. It is nourishing, but old people who are inactive should avoid it because this meat is difficult to digest; the young and all labourers can eat it, but not too much, lest it burden their stomach.

Deer is hot in the first degree and dry in the second. It can be eaten the whole year, but always moderately, because in large amounts it will always be harmful to all.

Mutio Carbonaro was the first to eat deer meat. Some writers believe that only male deer have horns; however, Euripides writes that does too have horns, and many poets write that the doe defeated by Hercules was horned.[78]

After cleaning, skinning, and gutting the deer, throw away its head and feet, and stuff it with rosemary, whole garlic heads, its own liver (first spit-roasted or roasted on a grill) cut into bits, slices of cured back fat and ham, the usual spices, and other ingredients; thus stuffed, cook it in the oven and serve it hot.

You can spit-roast it with the same stuffing or without, and serve it hot; you can roast it, broken into quarters and well larded, riddled with garlic cloves and cloves.

You can cook it in a lard broth with the usual spices, slices of cured back fat, aromatic herbs, and other noble ingredients.

You can use it in a stew, in good fat broth, with various dried fruits, the usual spices, and other noble ingredients.

Cut into pieces, you can use it in pies, mixed with other meats and other ingredients.

You can boil it, together with other meats, and in other ways, and it will always be agreeable.

Of rabbits and young rabbits.

Large and small rabbits are of the same quality, namely cold in the first degree and dry in the second; those young and fat are more nourishing and easier to digest. They consume excess phlegm, facilitate urination, and are more useful than other animals to all complexions. Their season is winter and part of spring. Their meat must be aged in the open so that it becomes more tender, better, and tastier.

Battavino the Spaniard, citizen of Conca, was the inventor of this food and the first to eat it. Rabbits are fecund, and give birth every month. They like to live in caves and grottoes, as Martial says in these verses:

> The rabbit enjoys living in the caves he has dug;
> he showed the enemy those hidden ways.[79]

Rabbits can be prepared in various tasty ways: you can stuff them with pork liver (first roasted), cut into bits, with mashed garlic cloves, pitted olives, capers, slices of cured back fat, the usual spices, aromatic herbs, and other noble ingredients; you can spit-roast them, stuffed or not, and serve them hot.

They can be cooked on coals, halved or quartered, with good malmsey wine, greased with good liquefied cured back fat, and sprinkled with strong vinegar; serve them hot, with royal sauce on top.

You can prepare them in Portuguese style: grill them briefly, cut into small bits, and sauté them in a pan with chopped small onions, pitted olives, capers, and other ingredients, and the usual spices, and serve them hot.

---

78 In Euripides' *Helen* there is a reference to a golden-horned doe; Hercules, for his third labour, captured the Ceryneian hind, a doe with golden antlers, endowed with supernatural speed and sacred to Artemis.

79 Martial, *Epigrams*, 13.60 (Latini cites the verses in Latin).

The Spanish style: cut them into bits, roast them, and sauté them in good oil, with a bit of good broth and vinegar, and the usual spices; serve them hot.

You can cook them in broth with ham and other salami, and serve them hot with the salami on top, and spices.

You can braise them, or use them in baked pies, stuffed or not, with the usual spices and other noble ingredients; serve them hot.

You can cook them in a lard broth, with slices of cured back fat and other salami, with the usual spices, aromatic herbs, and other noble ingredients.

You can use them in stews, cut into bits or quartered, with dried or fresh fruits, the usual spices, and other noble ingredients; serve them hot, with a fat broth.

They can be used for ground dishes and gigots, and they will all be good.

Of the hare, its qualities and cooking.

Hares caught in the hunt by hounds are the best; one must age them in the open; they are healthy for fat people because they help in losing weight and return natural colour to the face. They are easy to digest when young. Young hares are best.

Hares are cold in the first degree and dry in the second; their season is from November through January.

Attalicus of Cinobica was the first to eat hare meat; hares sleep with their eyes open; they rest during the day and wander about at night. If one takes them to Ithaca, Ulysses' fatherland, they immediately die. They give birth in spring, and it is said that those of the Chersonese have two livers; there is a superstition there that whoever eats hare meat for seven days becomes beautiful.[80]

Hares can be roasted, stuffed, like rabbits; serve them hot, with a caper sauce on top.

They can be used in pies: take their hind quarters, spit-roast them or roast them on the grill, and mix them with salami and other noble ingredients; serve them hot or cold as you prefer.

After spit-roasting them you can use them in ground dishes in the Spanish style, with good spices and other noble ingredients.

They can be cooked in a lard broth with slices of salami and pork throat, raisins, pine nuts, the usual spices, and other noble ingredients.

You can braise them or use them in pies, cooked in a pan, with or without stuffing, with the usual ingredients; serve them hot.

You can use them in stews, with dried fruits, the usual spices, fat broth, a bit of white wine, and other suitable ingredients.

Cut into bits or quartered, you can cook them in the Portuguese style, with pitted olives, capers, chopped small onions, the usual spices, and other suitable ingredients.

---

80 The Chersonese is an ancient name for Crimea. Latini mangles one of these peculiar claims: the notion that whoever ate a hare became beautiful for seven days is mentioned in Martial's *Epigrams* (5.29), Pliny's *Natural History* (28.260), and in the *Life of Alexander Severus* in the *Historia Augusta* (38.1–2).

You can cook them in a Spanish-style light stew: cut them into bits, half-roast them, then sauté them in good lard and then in a fat broth, with aromatic vinegar, the usual spices, and other suitable ingredients.

You can also roast them, larded in the Maltese style, with thin strips with cloves, and serve them with various sauces or condiments, as I will say elsewhere.

Of the porcupine, its qualities and cooking.

The porcupine caught in the hunt and aged in the open becomes very good, and it is beneficial to labourers, since it augments their forces and strengthens weakened nerves. It aids in sleeping and prevents miscarriages in pregnant women. It also benefits those who suffer from kidney stones and it stimulates the appetite.

It is cold in the first degree and its season is December and January, at the coldest of winter.

Aurelius Martial was the first to eat this animal, which is common in some hills, and abounds especially in the Roman Campagna; it is hunted at night.

You must age it well, then grill it, and marinate it, so that it be tastier and of better quality.

You can spit-roast it, quartered, larded or not, whole or in pieces, with the same stuffing as I described for hares; serve it hot with royal sauce on top, and the same marinade as with hares.

You can braise it in the oven, stuffed or not, and serve it hot, with the usual spices and apt ingredients.

You can stew it with a good broth and cooked must, as you like, with the usual spices and apt ingredients.[81]

You can cook it in a lard broth with various sauces, aromatic herbs, the usual spices, and other suitable ingredients.

The hind quarters, after spit-roasting them, you can cook in Portuguese style, as with hares, and with the same ingredients.

You can grill them on coals, with good malmsey wine, sprinkled with good strong vinegar; serve them hot, with lemon juice or another sauce, as you prefer.

You can use them for various stews; the liver, if it is fresh, can be cooked like a kid's liver.

Of the bear, its qualities and cooking.

This animal is just as dangerous after death, in its meat, as it is ferocious and malevolent in life. I have chosen to include it more as a curiosity than to introduce it among the dishes fit for eating.

The bear is caught in all seasons. The Grisons were the first to eat lions, bears, and panthers; many are found in Ethiopia, whose people, Pliny relates, eat this meat.

Bear hind thighs, after marinating for ten or twelve hours in good strong vinegar, salt, crushed garlic cloves, oregano, strong fennel, and ground chili peppers, can be spit-roasted, and are served hot with apt ingredients.

---

81 Cooked must (*mosto cotto*, sometimes also called *sapa*), is the "juice of ripe grapes boiled" down to about a third of the original amount; it was common especially in sweet recipes, Riley, *The Oxford Companion*, 335.

Bear meat can be boiled with a bit of wine and vinegar and sage or bay leaves, and served hot with pepper on top.

If one needs to, it can be used in all dishes made with domestic animals; be fore-warned however to first marinate and age it; one can use it in stews with wine, vinegar, sage or bay leaves, and the usual spices, or in pies with other noble ingredients, and if the pies are small they can be eaten cold; overall, however, I do not praise this meat.

Of the kid, its qualities and cooking.

Kids are hot in temperament up to the second degree; their meat is good and healthy, temperate between moist and dry.

The best kids are the black and red ones, when they are still suckling, no older than six months, and male; if they are nursed by two mothers, they will be even better.

This meat is quite nourishing, easy to digest, healthy and beneficial, also to the sick, the convalescent, scholars, and to all those who do not engage in physical efforts.

It is usually roasted, especially the hind quarters.

They can be roasted whole or quartered, stuffed with various ingredients.

You can sauté kid meat in a pan or pot, with a bit of pounded cured back fat, finely minced onions, aromatic herbs, and apt spices, adding a bit of good broth, raisins and pine nuts, and adding beaten eggs and lemon juice, which serve to thicken it, and this is called a stew.

Feliciano of Thessaly and Terullo were the first to eat kid meat.

You can stew it with a bit of sautéed cured back fat, aromatic herbs, and apt spices; you can make very good dishes with kid innards; with kid guts, well cleaned, you can make tasty and appetizing stews.[82]

Kid head, boiled in water and served with green sauce, is very good.

After boiling the head, halve it, dredge it in flour and eggs, and fry it in good lard.

You can also cover the head with a good frittata, after boiling it; if you fry it, you can then cook it in a good broth, with a bit of pounded cured back fat, pounded aromatic herbs, and a bit of garlic; after frying it, add salt and apt spices; it is also good with a royal sauce or a Portuguese-style condiment.

Skin the whole kid and place it in cold water, on a low fire; once neat and cleaned, you can stuff it with various ingredients, and roast it whole, having re-formed its skin.

Of the lamb, its qualities and cooking.

Lamb is hot in the first degree and moist in the second; the suckling lamb is moist in the third degree and very viscous; but it is less moist when it is one year old.

As soon as it is weaned, it becomes less moist and hotter.

The male born in spring is especially good; when fed with fragrant grass it is nour-ishing and easy to digest, especially if fed on grassy and sweet-smelling pastures.

---

82 "Innards" is here *coratelle*, which usually refers to the heart, lungs, and liver of smaller animals. A few lines above, what Latini says is "called" a stew is *spezzato*, which today refers to a stew.

It benefits those of a melancholy humour, those of hot temperament, and all those who have a choleric and dark complexion; the weaned lamb is easier to digest and more nourishing.

It is commonly eaten in Rome, and its season is from April through June; this food is however not that common on the tables of great lords.

Lamb is often boiled, and improved with cow fat, which in Rome is prepared and preserved for this purpose, and with aromatic herbs. Female ones are far better than the males; in Rome, lamb testicles or glands, once cleaned, are floured and fried in good lard or butter; they are also used in pies, and in various composite dishes; they can be spit-roasted whole, first skinned and larded, or wrapped in paper, with slices of ham and cured back fat.

You can also spit-roast whole lamb thighs, after removing the kidneys, with whole garlic cloves, cinnamon sticks, and whole cloves; they must be cooked thoroughly, moistening them often with cured back fat; serve them cold, sliced, or hot, as you prefer.

They can also be stewed or sautéed, with a bit of cured back fat, in a pan, with a bit of onion, aromatic herbs, and apt spices.

They can be thickened with eggs and prepared as one does with hare, with the usual spices and other ingredients, that is, broth, cooked must, raisins, pine nuts, dried plums, with a bit of mostacciolo crumbs, and testicles and glands.

You can dip in egg and fry lamb brains, and garnish them with lemon juice.

You can use it in pies, stews, ground dishes, all quite tasty.

Eremideo the Egyptian was the first to eat mutton or lamb.

Of the pig, its qualities and cooking.

The pig is a filthy animal, indeed the very symbol of uncleanliness; however, since it feeds from acorns, which were the fruit and food of the golden age, its meat is most tasty, and indeed tastier than all other meats; compared to pork, all other meats seem insipid. It is very common in all kitchens, of both lords and those of middling condition, and if we lacked pork we would miss the most delectable bait for our mouths.

It is hot in the first degree and moist in the high second; the suckling pig is moister, and therefore it is not healthy to eat piglets, as they can be dangerous and are not nourishing.

Galen preferred pork (especially from a castrated pig) to all other meats, and he stated that it is similar in taste to human flesh. In ancient times, when an alliance was formed, it was common to slaughter a pig in the houses of those entering the alliance. The ancient regarded the pig as sacred to Ceres, and Liberio the Egyptian was the first to eat pork.[83]

Pork is best when the pig is male, neither too old nor too young, raised in the country or in the mountains.

---

83 Galen (ca. 130–ca. 200/210) was a Greek physician whose works and ideas exerted enormous influence on European conceptions of health and diet from the Middle Ages through the seventeenth century.

It is nourishing, keeps the body moist, and stimulates urination. Hams and other salted parts excite the appetite and are good for seasoning other meats, to which they add grace.

Pork makes one drink with pleasure, and reduces phlegm.

Pork is good in all dishes and goes well with everything; any dish without pork turns out insipid and of little flavour.

The ribs you can slice thinly and grill with a bit of salt and fennel flower, over bread crostini, and halved sour oranges on top; this will be a dish worthy of any great personage.

The deboned meat of the ham or thigh, cut into chops, can be cooked mixed with other meats, or also stewed with other meats.

Pork fillets are exquisite, roasted, stewed, grilled, and in Portuguese style, with a royal sauce, apt spices, garlic, oregano, salt, and ground chili pepper; you can also roast them after marinating them for four or five hours.

Pig feet, cut in two, pig ears, and pig muscles, can be salted with ground salt, and left on a table until the water produced by the salt drains, for one day and night; then one can put them in a vase, in layers, well arranged and with a weight on top; this way they can be preserved for a long time and used to season dishes.

Of the feet and ears one can also make jellies with apt ingredients, which are appetizing and tasty.

From the pig one makes good cured back fat, to lard any land animal or bird; it can be used in all dishes, and to them all it brings good flavour.

One can make very good hams from pork; those from Abruzzo are especially exquisite, or from other places with good pastures.

Pigs from mountains are the best; from their hams one can make the tastiest sauces, which will be beneficial to those suffering from a weak appetite.

You can also use pork to make soppressata, salami, and saveloy, and from pig blood you can make good *sanguinacci*, as follows.[84]

As soon as the pig is slaughtered, one should carefully collect its blood and drain it in a cloth, so it does not curdle and is cleaned of possible dirt. Then one seasons it with cinnamon, cloves, muscatel, nutmeg, fat cut in pieces, salt, bread crumbs, and a bit of chili pepper to make it spicy; it will also be good to add a bit of milk. Then one puts the whole thing into cleaned guts, adding raisins and pine nuts, a bit of perfumed water, and salt; boil these stuffed guts, and they will be very tasty.

Pork fillet is boiled in water and wine, with bits of cinnamon, cloves, and two bay leaves (which you should remove after a short while, lest it become bitter); once it is cooked, let it cool, and serve it cold and whole, or in pieces; it will be tasty and refreshing.

Of the boar, its qualities and cooking.

The boar is hot in the first degree and temperately moist; it is not as moist as the domestic pig, because of the quality of the air and of the pastures.

The best one is young, caught in the hunt during winter, and well aged.

---

84 Today in Italy sanguinaccio is an ickily sweet dessert, made with chocolate instead of pig blood, and popular around Carnival.

It is nourishing; ordinarily it is roasted; it is easy to digest, and its meat is very similar to that of domestic pigs.

Small ones can be spit-roasted, whole and stuffed with suitable ingredients; they can be used in ground dishes, also stewed in bits, with various sorts of sausages, both the meat and the innards.

The boiled head of the boar, deboned and cleaned, cut in pieces, together with its jaws and feet, can be boiled in a pot, with salt, strong vinegar, cooked must, spices, and a bit of sugar; boil it for seven or eight hours, and place it on the plates, surrounded with bay leaves, and cleaned almonds mixed with pomegranate seeds on top; add these things when the dish is neither too hot nor too cold, but when it is thickening; thus the dish will look good and can be displayed on the table as a cold dish or a jelly.

When boars are fat, you can use their thighs to make hams; sometimes you can salt them, with the fur still on, cut into pieces. You can also use them for chops, skinned and cleaned, washed in white wine with a bit of pounded cured back fat, sour cherries, plums, pine nuts, raisins, cooked must, and a bit of good broth, with bits of citron, mostacciolo crumbs, and apt spices.

You can use them in pies, hot or cold, with apt spices and ingredients.

Of the roe deer, its qualities and cooking.

The roe deer is hot and dry in the second degree. The first to eat this animal and wild goat was Beleustio of Palermo.

Wild goats can be exquisite. Pliny and other authors state that this animal is never without a fever, and that its urine is beneficial to many illnesses.

It is more nourishing than all other game meat; it works against paralysis and colic; it helps fat people lose weight.

You can use this meat in pies.

Skin the roe deer and cut its meat in pieces; wash it with white or red wine, as you prefer, and cook them as you like, with bay leaves and spices.

This meat can be boiled or cooked in pies, with apt spices and aromatic herbs; also prepared in a lard broth, and in other ways.

TREATISE IV: *Of various birds, both domesticated and wild.*[85]

Of the capon, its qualities and cooking.

Everybody praises capons, both those raised in coops and in the country, as long as they are well fed, to give them good substance. Best are the young, as long as they are neither too fat nor too thin. Those raised in the country give more sustenance than those kept in coops, because they can fly around and thus exercise more. I declare in any case that both are very nourishing, and give more sustenance than any other food or animal: they generate the most perfect blood, stimulate the appetite, and aid memory and sight. They are beneficial to people of any age or complexion, since their meat is easy to digest and temperate in quality. They are good throughout the year and can be eaten in any time or season, and they will always be useful and nourishing.[86]

Melantio Sorano was the first to eat capon; one can fatten these birds with honey mixed with millet flour, and then cook them in milk; they can also be fattened with ground wheat flour, in which case they become moderately fatter.

Capon can be boiled in salted water, as the Jesuit Fathers do; you can serve it hot, with pepper and cinnamon on top, or other condiments as you prefer; capon broth can be used in many dishes, soups, and stews, and it is always nourishing.

Boiled as above, you can serve it cold, stuffed or not, with an apt sauce or condiment, or seasoned with salt and pepper.

Capon, deboned or not, can be stuffed with beaten eggs, good grated cheese, bone marrow cut into small pieces, thyme, minced aromatic herbs, thin slices of ham and of pork throat or belly, other salami, bits of mozzarella or provatura, raisins, pine nuts, small veal or other chops, ground veal or a similar meat, and other noble ingredients; thus boiled, serve it with what condiment you prefer on top.

After boiling it as above, you can serve it cold, larded with various candied things, and wholly greased with a sour cherry sauce or condiment, or with another sweet and sour sauce, dusting it with sugar and cinnamon or with mostacciolo crumbs, and syruped sour grapes.

Ordinarily, you can cook capons as above, in salted water, and thus you can bring them on a journey, and eat them cold, with lemon juice.

After boiling it as above, you can debone it and serve it cold, with pepper and lemon juice on top.

As above, you can debone it and pound its meat finely, then cook it in a fat broth (of capon itself, or another broth), with also bits of bone marrow, slices of Giugliano fillet, bits of ham or other salted things, bits of candied citron or pumpkin, and other noble

---

85 At eighty-eight pages, this is the longest section Latini devotes to meat. Birds were traditionally regarded as choice food, in part because of their association with air and elevation, symbols of their high status in nature and indicative of the lightness of their meat.

86 Latini contrasts here "domestic" capons and those "from the country." There were of course no wild capons, and Latini indeed implies that both types were "raised." By "domestic" he presumably meant kept in courtyards and homes in the city; I think "coops" helps clarify the difference Latini intended.

ingredients, the usual spices and aromatic herbs, then adding beaten egg yolks, goat milk, and lemon juice; it can serve as a stew, with sugar and cinnamon on top.

After boiling it as above, you can cut it into small or large bits, as you prefer, dip it in egg and dredge it in flour, and fry it in good lard; you can skip the egg dipping; serve it hot with royal sauce, if dipped in egg, or, if not, with lemon juice and sugar on top, or another condiment.

After boiling it, you can cover it with boiled cardoons, sliced salted things and saveloy, with good parmesan cheese, and other noble ingredients, in the Milan style.

After parboiling it, stuffed or not, you can lard it with cloves and cinnamon sticks, and wrap it in pork or wether caul; spit-roast it and serve it with royal sauce on top; you can also lard it without parboiling it.

After boiling it in water, you can halve it and grill it, greasing it with grease from the dripping pan, and frequently sprinkled with aromatic vinegar; make a crust for it with bread crumbs, salt, cinnamon, mostacciolo crumbs, and sugar, and serve it hot with the sauce you prefer; this is called "coaled."

You can spit-roast it, without parboiling it first; clean it well of its feathers, and stuff it with pitted olives, pine nuts, bits of ham, of pork throat, and of other salami, bits of bone marrow, boiled egg yolks, thin slices of candied citron and pumpkin, chicken livers (first roasted on embers), truffle slices, sour grapes, the usual spices, and other noble ingredients; spit-roast it, larding it with a piece of hot cured back fat, and make a crust for it with bread crumbs; serve it hot with royal sauce on top, or another condiment as you prefer.

You can spit-roast it, again without parboiling it; once it is half-cooked, remove it from the heat and let it cool; then cut it into bits, and make a French fricassée for it, putting it in a pan to sauté, with apt spices and other suitable ingredients, thickening it with egg yolks and lemon juice.[87]

After spit-roasting it as above, you can cut it into small bits and sauté it in a pan with good beaten lard, minced onion, apt spices, pitted olives, capers, pine nuts, a bit of aromatic vinegar, sugar, sour grapes, if in season, and other noble ingredients, as you prefer; this will be very good, and we call this cooked in the Portuguese style.

After spit-roasting it as above, you can remove the breast meat and use it for gigots and ground dishes, pounding it finely, with the usual spices and other suitable ingredients.

You can also stuff a capon, between its skin and its flesh, with ham slices, pitted olives, pitted sour cherries, pine nuts, raisins, small capers, apt spices, and other noble ingredients; then spit-roast it, wrapped in caul or paper, or not, and serve it hot with a bastard sauce on top.

You can make various roasts from capon, and serve them hot or cold, stuffed or not, as you prefer.

You can roast it, together with ham slices and riddled with cloves and cinnamon sticks; then you can dredge it in bread, and serve it with royal sauce on top.

You can half-boil it in water, then remove it from the heat and cut it into pieces (or leave it whole), stuffed or not, and you can finish cooking it in goat milk; serve it hot over

---

87 *Fracassera alla francese* is the term Latini uses here; fricassée today usually means sautéing followed by adding liquid and simmering.

sliced bread sprinkled with sugar and cinnamon; if you prefer to toast the bread first, then sprinkle it with mostacciolo crumbs, or something else you like.

You can spit-roast it, and, when it is half-cooked, cut it into pieces and stew it in the French style, with good broth or butter, small onions, a garlic condiment, bits of pork belly, a bit of malmsey wine or another strong white wine, lemon juice or sour grapes added if in season, the usual spices, and other suitable ingredients.

After aging it, you can use it for a pie, whole or cut into pieces, stuffed or not, with slices of ham and pork belly, bone marrow, raisins, pine nuts, dried plums and sour cherries, bits of artichokes, cardoon stems first parboiled in water, truffle slices, a bit of strong white wine, lemon juice or sour grapes added if in season, the usual spices, and other suitable ingredients; serve it hot with the same ingredients on top.

You can stew it in various other ways, with various noble ingredients, as I will say in its place.

With capon meat you can make several ground dishes or gigots, with the usual apt ingredients, as I will say in its place.

Pound the capon meat finely, and mix it with beaten eggs, bone marrow, good grated cheese, cream tops, bits of candied citron or pumpkin, raisins, pine nuts, aromatic herbs finely minced, the usual spices, and other noble ingredients; make a mixture of all this and form meatballs or meatloaf, in various forms, at your whim; stew it with noble ingredients; note however that before you pound this meat you need to half-boil it in water or spit-roast to a half-cooking, and then you can pound it, as you do with ground dishes or gigots, preparing it the same ingredients in the Spanish style, with lemon juice on top.

This ground dish or gigot, once half-roasted on the spit or half-boiled in water, can also be prepared with other ingredients; pound the meat with a bit of white wine, bits of bone marrow, lemon juice, apt spices, and other suitable ingredients; serve it hot or cold, with sour grapes cooked in syrup, or anything else you like.

You can use capon in a pie, whole, stuffed or not, larded with cloves and strips of candied citron, sprinkled with spices, slices of ham and pork throat, and other noble ingredients as you like; serve it hot or cold, as you wish; if you serve it cold, you do not need to add anything else, but just what I said above, larded and sprinkled with spices and salami slices, with a glaze or sugar on top.

After half-cooking it, you can cut it into bits, and [mix it in a pie] with chicken livers (first roasted on embers and pounded finely), bits of ox bone marrow, raisins, pine nuts, bits of candied citron and pumpkin, bits of mozzarella or provola, beaten boiled egg yolks, sour grapes in syrup, kid sweetbreads, first roasted and sliced or cut into bits, thin slices of cow udder, first boiled in water, truffle slices, first sautéed with pepper and lemon juice, oysters and limpets, also sautéed the same way, razor-shells, first sautéed in good white wine, wedge shells and clams sautéed the same way, ham and other salami sliced or cut into bits, with the usual spices, and other noble ingredients; garnish everything with veal chops or small birds, as you prefer, with a little broth inside made with beaten egg yolks, a bit of fat broth, lemon juice, and sugar; if you want to use chops, then you should use only a bit of sugar; serve it with the lid on it, and sugar.[88]

---

88 Latini never says that this is a pie, but, given the prior preparation and the details of this one, it seems clear that it is a pie.

You can spit-roast it or boil it in water, to half-cooking, then cut it into pieces, and use it for pies made with short crust pastry, mixed with slices of sponge cake, halved *faldicchere* eggs, veal chops, ground veal or another meat, pistachios, pine nuts, chicken livers first roasted on embers, bone marrow, various sliced salami, artichoke pieces, first boiled, bits of cardoon stems, sliced candied citron and pumpkin, the usual spices, and other noble ingredients; cover it with cream tops, with a lid on top with a glaze or sugar; serve it hot, with a little broth inside.[89]

You can use capon in other pies with other ingredients, as I will say in its place.

Capon livers can be roasted on embers and served with pepper and lemon juice, or another condiment, as you prefer, or even with none.

Capon livers can be spit-roasted, wrapped in caul or paper (or not), mixed with thin slices of cured back fat and bay leaves; serve them hot with a crust on top made with toasted bread, ground and passed through a sieve, salt, and pepper, with lemon juice or another sauce as you prefer.

After roasting the livers on embers, you can pound them finely together with the rind of candied citron, beaten ham fat, a bit of the lean part of the ham, raisins, pine nuts, good grated cheese, bits of bone marrow, mostacciolo crumbs, the usual spices, and other ingredients, bound with beaten eggs; then you can use this to make rolls, wrapped in caul, which you can spit-roast mixed with bay leaves; serve them with royal sauce or another condiment.

These rolls, wrapped in caul, can also be stewed in a pot, with a good fat broth, lemon juice, and other suitable ingredients.

The mixture described above, thickened with eggs, you can use to make fritters; dredge them in fine flour; fry them in good lard, and serve them hot, with a bastard sauce on top; they can also be used to garnish many dishes.

You can also dredge the livers in flour, fry them in good lard, and serve them hot, with salt, pepper, and sour orange juice.

You can parboil the livers, dredge them in flour, dip them in egg, and fry them; serve them hot with mostacciolo sauce on top; they can garnish many dishes, both if you dip them in egg and not; you can riddle them with pine nuts (which first you let sit in water for a while).

You cannot use capon liver in any dish, if you have only a bit of it; if you have plenty, then they can be used for shallow tarts, pizze, and other similar dishes.

Capon breast can be used for pies in the Spanish style, finely ground and browned in a pan with a garlic condiment and other suitable ingredients, as I will say in its place.

You can spit-roast capon breast, then grind it finely, and use it for gigots, with milk, cream tops, diluting everything together, with ground candied citron, fresh eggs, sponge cake crumbs, the usual spices; it is a Spanish style dish, very good and noble, as I will say in its place.

With capon flesh you can make small meatballs for those who are sick, with noble and suitable ingredients.

---

89 Faldicchere (at times Latini writes *faldacchere*) eggs are a peculiarly Baroque preparation: they consist of egg yolks mixed with sugar, then re-formed in the shape of eggs, and baked until they acquire some solidity; the name comes from the Spanish *faltriquera*, pocket or pouch, the idea being that one could carry them in one's pocket without breaking them.

Of the young pullet, its qualities and cooking.

The young pullet, if fed as described below, is very nourishing and easy to digest; it is beneficial and healthy to all complexions, because its meat produces no choler or phlegm, but rather good blood. It also excites the appetite and gives much sustenance, it nourishes the human body more than any other food, however delicate or sustaining it may be. Its quality is temperate in all degrees, and its season throughout the year. Best is the young black one, which has not yet laid eggs; it can be fattened with artifice.

How to fatten these young pullets.

Put them in a cage for twenty days, and feed them a mixture made with milk and corn flour, or bread crumbs (as they do in Rome), or oats, or crustless bread, whatever is customary in each area, always mixed with milk; make them drink the milk as well. With these ingredients, when they are very clean, one can make dumplings with corn flour, also mixed with milk and soaked in it, also to be fed to the pullets for eighteen or twenty days, and then one can eat the pullets. If you wait longer they lose some of their exquisite taste. For those eighteen days they have to drink nothing but milk; watch out that they do not eat anything dirty and that the cage is kept clean and neat; the same method can be used with capons, cockerels, or turkey pullets, which thus will all turn out very good, and be worthy of being eaten by any great lord. For the first four or five days you can also feed them lettuce, to cleanse them, but even without the lettuce the feed described above will work fine.[90]

The best preparation for these pullets is to spit-roast them; you can also use them in pies, whole or in pieces, layered with pounded veal, veal chops, small birds, and other noble ingredients.

Of the domestic cockerel, its qualities and cooking.

Domestic cockerels are the best of all, especially those young enough that they have not yet begun to wake us up in the morning with their song, or to impregnate chicken; these will be more tender and fatter, and their testicles are of the greatest nourishment. When the cockerel is fat it is easier to digest, since its meat is temperate; this meat generates perfect blood, excites the appetite, aids the intellect and the sight, because it does not become either choler or phlegm.

Its season is summer and the whole winter, and it can be eaten every month of the year, as it is always very nourishing.

Its quality is temperate in all degrees.

This cockerel can be cooked in milk or broth, or in water, stuffed between skin and flesh or not, deboned or not, stuffed or not, and can be served with condiments and garnishes as you prefer.

---

90 Latini's approach to this process appears reasonably humane when compared to what is often done today; Scappi also objected to force-feeding, which was generally regarded as bad for the bird's healthiness as a food, Scappi, *Opera*, 540 and 551; see also Albala, *Eating Right in the Renaissance* (Berkeley: University of California Press, 2002), chap. 4.

The cockerel can be marinated, after halving it or cutting it into pieces, with salt, pepper, cinnamon, perfumed vinegar, oregano, and crushed garlic; marinate it for three or four hours, then grill it and serve it hot with the marinade on top. First, though, boil the marinade, and then throw it hot on the roast, as is done with all similar dishes.

After cooking it in water as above, halved or cut into pieces, it can be served hot with the marinade described above; it can also be fried in good lard and served hot, with the same marinade.

After cleaning it, you can cut it into pieces and sauté it with good pounded cured back fat, with a little condiment of garlic, oregano, salt, pepper, and other spices, with slices of ham, pork throat, aromatic herbs, sautéing everything together; then add a bit of fat broth with raisins, pine nuts, and lemon juice, and, when in season, sour grapes, and other noble and apt ingredients.

After spit-roasting the cockerel, you can cut it into pieces and sauté it in good pounded cured back fat, a condiment of garlic, fresh sour cherries, bits of candied citron, perfumed vinegar, sour grapes if in season, the usual spices, and sugar, and it will be quite tasty.

You can stew it in another way: brown it first in broth, place it whole or halved in a pan, with a good fat broth, slices of various salami, raisins, pine nuts, bone marrow, brains or halved sausages, truffle slices, artichokes (first boiled in water), various sliced fresh fruits, aromatic herbs, lemon juice or whole sour grapes if in season, the usual spices, and apt ingredients; serve it hot, with the garnishes mentioned above.

You can use the cockerel in pies, whole, and served with the same garnishes.

You can stuff the cockerel, deboned or not, with what good stuffing you like, or roast them with a good marinade, sauce, condiment, and a crust on top made with bread crumbs, salt, and pepper.

You can use it for pies, whole, stuffed or not, deboned or not, as you prefer, with various garnishes inside; serve them hot with a glaze or sugar on top.

You can serve it cold, in a pie, without garnishes, but just larded and with cloves, dusted with the usual spices, with salami slices; serve it cold, as I said, with glaze or sugar on top.

You can cut these cockerels into pieces, and serve them in a pie, with or without cover; brown them first in a good broth, dusted with spices, then put them in the pie mixed with saveloy and other halved sausages (which you cook first), slices of provola or mozzarella, cream tops, bone marrow, slices of ham and other salami, ground veal or other meat, small slices of candied pumpkin or citron, the livers, testicles, and cockscombs of the same cockerels, and other noble ingredients, with the usual little broth; if you make the pie with a cover, then serve it with sugar on top.

You can boil the cockerel in milk and use it for soups, layered with slices of sponge cake, grated mozzarella or provola, cream tops, each layer dusted with sugar and cinnamon; stew all this with a bit of cured back fat; they can serve for various soups.

You can fry these cockerels, first halved, deboned or not, and also stuffed, and they can be used as garnishes for various dishes, or served by themselves with a royal sauce on top; they can also be dipped in egg, but note that before frying them you need to cook them in milk or broth, as convenient.

You can cook them Portuguese-style, cooked or sautéed in a pan, with a sauce of capers, pitted olives, small onions, apt spices, and other suitable ingredients.

With the cockscombs, testicles, and livers you can make soups for convalescent people; with aromatic herbs and few spices they will be very tasty; you can also use them for small pies; the livers can be cooked on embers, pounded in the mortar, and used for many sauces and condiments.

These livers, wrapped in caul, can be spit-roasted, layered with bay leaves, and served hot, with pepper and sour orange juice; they can also serve as garnishes for various dishes.

Though the liver of this cockerel is very small, if needed it can be prepared in all the ways in which you prepare capon liver.

Of the wild cockerel, its qualities and cooking.

The wild cockerel has the same quality as the domestic one; it is good in all seasons, and especially from July to November; it is nourishing, useful, and healthy to people of all complexions; the best is a fat one, neither too small nor too large.

It can be cooked and prepared in all the ways, and with the condiments, described for the domestic one.

It can be cooked in water, or broth, and be served cold or hot, as you wish; you can serve it deboned or not, stuffed or not, at your preference.

If you wish to serve it hot, you can boil it together with sliced salami, with slices of the same salami on top.

If you wish to serve it cold, after cooking it in water, you can dust it with pepper and cinnamon, with borage flowers and parsley on top.

You can grill it, halved, sprinkled with perfumed vinegar, and dusted with bread crumbs, salt, pepper, cinnamon, making a crust on top; serve it hot, with a royal sauce.

You can use it in pies or stews, in various ways, with various ingredients, stuffed, deboned, or not, as you wish.

It can be used in roasts, as one does with pheasants, wrapped in caul, or in other ways.[91]

Whole or cut into pieces, it can be used in many pies or small pies, with or without cover, and served cold or hot, as we said of the domestic cockerel.

These cockerels can be prepared in all the ways and dishes mentioned for the domestic cockerels, and with the same spices and ingredients.

Of the domestic or wild chicks, their quality and cooking.

Chicks, domestic or wild, are very good; since they are small, their meat is more tender; they are not as nourishing as cockerels; they are cold in the first and second degree, and their season is from June through August.

When they are small, chicks can be larded with cloves and cinnamon sticks, wrapped in caul, and spit-roasted, and they can serve as garnishes for many dishes.

---

91 Latini uses the verb *affaggianare* here (literally, to treat like a pheasant), which probably means to roast a bird wrapped in caul or paper.

You can roast the chicks in various ways; the cook should use the same methods as in roasting other small birds.

After roasting them, stuffed or not, one can stew them in various ways, as with the cockerels; since they are so tender, you can stew them in a silver dish or in another elegant pot, without using a pan, and serve them with various apt condiments.

After roasting them and boiling them in milk, you can use them in various soups that use milk, and layer them with other noble ingredients.

You can use them in various thick pottages, garnished with pork throat and belly, ham slices, the usual spices, and other noble ingredients.

I will not expand further on this food, because here in Naples, in Rome, and in other places, chicks are rarely used, and when used they are usually roasted. Domestic or wild, to be good and nourishing, they have to be aptly large; since they are tender they are pleasing to the taste, especially the wild ones.

Of the domestic chicken, its qualities and cooking.

The domestic chicken is very good, helpful to people of all complexions, healthy to those of all ages, nourishing, and easy to digest; if one eats it often, it clears the voice, excites the appetite, and calms the body's humours; the best one is black, young, with a red beak, and a double and straight cockscomb, and before it lays eggs. It is tempered in all degrees of its qualities; its season is winter and part of spring, and, since it is a nourishing food, it can be eaten in all seasons of the year.

Old, thin, or poorly fed chickens are bad and unhealthy.

Formiano of Messina was the first to eat chicken. Albertus Magnus writes that a chicken was discovered in Macedonia that had laid eighteen eggs in one day, and that from each of these eggs two chicks were born; Pliny writes that farm chicken live an orderly and regulated life.[92]

After removing the feathers and innards of the domestic chicken, you can stuff it with beaten eggs, good grated cheese, bits of bone marrow, of candied citron, and of candied pumpkin, bits of soppressata, ham, or other salami, raisins, pine nuts, thyme, ground aromatic herbs, pepper, and the other usual spices and ingredients; cook it in broth or in water and salt, and serve it hot or cold, stuffed or not; you may also debone it before cooking it and stuff it between its flesh and skin, as you like; if you stuff it this way, you should serve it hot; you can garnish it on top with bunches of fresh fennel, cooked in a good fat broth, saveloy or cut sausages, and salami slices, first cooked, or with other garnishes, as you prefer.

You can serve it cold, cooked as above, stuffed or not, covered with aromatic herbs and with the flowers of various herbs, or with various condiments, as you prefer.

This chicken, cooked as above, stuffed or not, can be served cold, seasoned just with salt and pepper.

After cooking it, you can remove its meat and debone it; serve the pulled meat with salt, pepper, cinnamon, and lemon or sour orange juice.

---

92 Albertus Magnus (ca. 1200–1280), a German theologian later declared a saint and a Doctor of the Church, wrote a book on animals, from which this tidbit of information is presumably drawn, probably indirectly.

It is much used by travellers and seafarers who, before setting off on their journeys, make provisions of boiled chicken, and at every stop or beach eat them cold or hot.

With its meat you can make various ground dishes, with the usual ingredients.

You can use it to make small meatballs, which are good, and can be given to the convalescent.

The meat can be used for various gigots.

You can use the chicken for roasts in various ways, if it is tender, larded or not, with or without a crust, on the grill, as one does with pheasants, with a sauce or another marinade, as you prefer.

You can use it in pies or stews, with apt ingredients, stuffed or not, as you prefer.

After roasting it, you can cut it into pieces, small or big, and use it in various dishes, such as in Portuguese or Genoese style, or in other ways.

You can use it in pies, whole or in pieces, stuffed or not, with ground veal, layered with other ingredients; you can serve it hot or cold, with candied things, covered in salami slices, larded, and garnished with apt ingredients.

Without adding more, I state that chicken can be cooked and served in all the ways I mentioned for capon; both can also be given to the convalescent.

Of the wild chicken, its qualities and cooking.

The best wild chickens are the smaller ones; they are nourishing and benefit the convalescent, because their meat does not produce phlegm, and is easy to digest; they are better than domestic ones; their season is December through May; they are temperate in their qualities, and can be eaten throughout the year, and they are always tasty and healthy.

These chickens can be cooked in water and salt, together with bits of pork belly or throat, ham, soppressata, and other salami; serve them hot with the same salami on top, and stuffed, as you like.

One can stuff these chickens with olives, capers, raisins, pine nuts, pepper, cinnamon, salami bits, truffles, whole sour grapes if in season, little bits of Ischia apples or other fruits, fresh or dry sour cherries, dried plums, cherries, or apricots, the chicken's own interiors, and other noble ingredients; one can also braise them, with lemon juice, cooked must, and other garnishes, as you prefer.[93]

Stuffed as above, you can cook them in a lard broth, whole or in pieces, with the same stuffing, in good broth and a bit of strong white wine; serve them hot, with the usual aromatic herbs, and apt spices.

You can roast them, stuffed or not, and serve them hot, with pepper and cinnamon on top, or another apt condiment.

They can be roasted in various ways, with a crust of bread crumbs, salt, and pepper, or wrapped in caul, larded or not, stuffed or not, as I said of the domestic or wild cockerel.

---

93 Latini writes *mele tramontane*, a type of apple typical of the island of Ischia in the Bay of Naples, and reputed to be somewhat insipid (according to old agrarian dictionaries from Naples, at any rate).

Of the domestic rooster, its qualities and cooking.

This rooster has tough meat and is hot in all its qualities. However, its broth, provided it is cooked well and reduced by half, is always good, more as a medicine than as a dish. This broth is given to those who have digestive trouble; it induces somnolence, brings about bowel movements, and stimulates sexual desire.[94] To achieve these effects one should choose older roosters. Sometimes peasants, with their clever malice, remove the cockscombs from old roosters and in a moment turn them into capons. Often those who buy provisions, seeing these large birds offered at a good price, purchase them and take pride in having scored a deal, without noticing that these are roosters dressed up as capons and that they are bringing home medicines rather than dishes. Often also people buy these roosters as gifts for lawyers or others, who will think they have received a good pair of capons, though in the end they will have in their homes two good musicians, castrated by peasant cleverness.

This rooster, if necessary, can be prepared in all the ways and dishes as the capon, if it be young. If it be old, it can only be boiled, used in pies, or sautéed, having deboned it well; but always make sure to hang it well to tenderize it, and that it should be killed before it lives seven years; after that time, it is of very bad quality, and I would urge you, if at all possible, not to eat it in that case.

Albidius of Syracuse was the first to eat a rooster, because before that roosters were never killed, due to the veneration and reverence granted this bird as the messenger of dawn, and because it was an animal dearest to Latona (as authors of romances write), having served her when she gave birth. Myth says that Mars out of anger transformed the rooster into another bird, because it failed to be vigilant in its watch while Mars held Venus in his arms. Lucretius writes that lions are very afraid of the rooster's singing; those who wish to know more about roosters should read Varro's third book, the ninth chapter.

The people of Libari were so given to sloth that they banned roosters from their city, lest their singing disturb the citizens' sleep.[95]

Of the mountain rooster, its qualities and cooking.

These birds can be found in various areas, and especially in the fields around Trent; their meat is hot in the first degree and moderate in all other qualities; their season is from the start of winter through spring; they are as large as an eagle, and usually have

---

94 Latini here writes: "it provokes Venus." I do not believe this is today considered one of the beneficent effects of chicken broth (and it does seem somewhat at odds with inducing somnolence and moving the bowels).

95 Latini here displays more of his classical erudition: Latona was the mother of Apollo and Diana; the writer Aelian (ca. 175–ca. 235) writes in his *On the Nature of Animals* (4.29) that the rooster was her favourite bird. Mars and Venus were discovered by her husband, Vulcan. I suspect the "Libariti" is a mistype for "Sibariti" or Sybarites, the proverbially self-indulgent inhabitants of ancient Sibari, in Calabria. Chickens generally are indeed the topic of Book III, Chapter 9, of the Latin author Varro's (116–27 BC) treatise on agriculture. The lions' fear of roosters is described in *On the Nature of Things* by the poet Lucretius (ca. 99–ca. 55), 4.710–20.

black feathers, at times mixed with white ones; the area around their eyes is red, as with pheasants.

You can boil this rooster, together with ham and other salami, in a bit of strong white wine, and whole corianders; you can serve it hot or cold, stuffed or not, garnishing it on top with cooked salami.

It will also be good roasted, wrapped in slices of cured back fat, and tied on the chest with twine, stuffed or not; serve it hot, with a royal sauce on top, or another apt condiment.

You can use it in pies, larded, with a bit of malmsey wine, the usual spices, and other noble ingredients.

Larded as above, with slices of cured back fat, and candied citron, it can be used for pies, dusting it with spices and other apt ingredients; serve it hot or cold, as you prefer.

If it is young, this rooster can be served in all the same ways and dishes as partridges or wild cockerels, with the same ingredients, though it will never be quite as perfect as partridges.

Of the domestic pigeon, its qualities and cooking.

Domestic pigeons, or raised in a coop or a dovecote, are all quite nourishing, if tender, and beneficial especially to the old, because they produce good blood and augment natural heat. Weak people who eat them often, without eating other meat, at times when epidemics are suspected, will live in good health; they are easy to digest, but should not be given to those who suffer from fevers, because they are hot. The best are raised in coops or dovecotes, so that they fly hither and thither to get their food, because these are fatter and tastier. Both those raised in homes, and those in coops or dovecotes, are hot and moist in the first and second degree; their season is throughout the year, though they are best in winter; they are beneficial in cold times, because in summer, due to their great heat, they can cause nausea.

Gasparone of Velletri, a town near Rome, a perfect musician, was the first to eat tender pigeons, and the first who prepared these pigeons, grey partridges, quails, and other birds in vinegar.

You can boil these pigeons, stuffed or not, with slices of ham, Nola soppressata, and Giugliano fillet, or other salami, and serve them hot, with bunches of fennels on top, first boiled in a fat broth, and with cooked salami slices.

After cooking them as above, they can be used as layers in various soups, and especially in a royal soup, with apt condiments.

You can boil them, stuffed, with beaten eggs, good grated cheese, bits of ham, and cow bone marrow, with raisins, pine nuts, ground aromatic herbs, whole sour grapes when in season, and with ground veal or other meat, the usual spices, and other noble ingredients; serve them hot with good grated cheese and cinnamon on top; you can cook them, stuffed or not, with various apt condiments on top.

Stuffed in various ways, they can be cooked in goat milk, wrapped in caul, surrounded with ham slices, and served hot, above sliced white bread or sponge cake, with sugar and cinnamon on top; make sure you do not oversoak the bread in milk.

After boiling them, without stuffing, you can serve them cold, with parsley and borage flowers on top.

Take off their heads, which are often harmful, and you can use the pigeons in stews, with good fat broth of capon or other meat, with a bit of perfumed vinegar, sour grapes when in season, plums, dried sour cherries, and whole corianders; serve this hot; this can be very good for old people in the worst times of winter.

You can boil them in various ways, stuffed or not, deboned or not, with various covers, with salami, sausages, saveloy, cooked and cut, with various greens, and apt condiments on top.

You can spit-roast them, deboned or not, stuffed with their own livers or those of other poultry, first roasted on embers, cut in bits or whole, with ground veal, raisins, pine nuts, bits of bone marrow and ham, sour grapes, ground aromatic herbs, the usual spices, and other noble ingredients; grease them on the outside with good cured back fat, with a crust on top made of bread crumbs, salt, and pepper, and serve them hot.

You can roast them as above, and serve them hot with the same crust, or roast them wrapped in caul, larded or not, as you wish.

Clean them of their feathers, halve them, and cook them on the grill, greased with butter or fat from the dripping pan, and make a crust on top with bread crumbs, mostacciolo crumbs, and pepper, dust them with cinnamon, and serve them hot with condiments; we call this preparation "coaled," with malmsey wine.

After cooking them in water, you can halve them or cut them into pieces, flour them with good flour or mostacciolo or sponge cake crumbs, dip them in egg, fry them in good lard, and serve them hot, with a royal sauce on top; they can serve to garnish various dishes.

You can use them in pies, with ham slices, pork belly, raisins, pine nuts, dried plums, sour grapes when in season or lemon juice, good malmsey wine, the usual spices and other ingredients, with the same garnishes on top.

You can stew them, just like in pies, but without the wine, just with good fat broth, aromatic herbs, and the other ingredients I mentioned.

They can be prepared in many other ways and garnished with various ingredients.

They can be roasted as above, stuffed between the meat and the skin.

You can fry them without dipping them in egg, or boil them after marinating them and serve them with the marinade.

Whole or in pieces they can be used for pies, with various noble ingredients.

They can garnish many pies, with or without a cover.

They can be used in any type of casserole and *oglia*.[96]

They can also be used in almond tarts and in many other preparations.[97]

Young pigeons, those not yet covered in feathers, can be roasted, wrapped in caul or paper, stuffed or not; for other dishes, they can be used as I said of chicks (though this is unusual).

---

96 Oglia is the Neapolitan version of the Spanish classic *olla podrida*, a rich stew with varied ingredients, named after its pot.

97 Latini says *pizze di bocca di dama*; bocca di dama (literally, a lady's mouth) today refers to almond cookies and cakes, so I am presuming, somewhat uncertainly, an almond tart here.

Of the wild pigeon, its qualities and cooking.

Wild pigeons are called *torchiati* in Naples; the best are the tender ones, which are beneficial to people of all complexions; they give strength to weakened limbs, help digestion, and improve eyesight; one should not feed them to the convalescent, though, because their meat is moist in the first degree and hot in all other qualities; their season is the whole winter and part of spring.

In all ways in which these pigeons are prepared, one must make sure that they be well aged, in proportion with the tenderness of the meat, because their meat is less tender than that of domestic pigeons.

These pigeons can be stuffed, with ground roasted meat, bits of ham (both the fat parts and the rest), pork throat, raisins, pine nuts, aromatic herbs, bits of candied citron, the usual spices, and other noble ingredients; amalgamate this stuffing with beaten eggs; stuff the pigeons, first cooked in water and salt, add bits of salami, and serve them hot.

Cooked in water as above, these pigeons, not stuffed, can serve as layers in various soups, as will be explained in its proper place.

Cooked as above, stuffed or not, they can be served cold, with pepper and cinnamon on top, aromatic herbs, rosemary flowers, and with a sauce apt for wild birds.

One can cook them on coals, roasting them on the grill, first halved, greased with good melted cured back fat, sprinkled with a perfumed vinegar, with a crust on top made with mostacciolo crumbs or sugar, and cinnamon; serve them hot with a bastard sauce or another condiment as you prefer.

You can spit-roast them, larded with candied things and cloves, wrapped in caul or paper, and serve them hot with lemon juice on top, or another condiment or sauce as you prefer.

You can spit-roast them, without removing from their stomachs the acorns that they might have eaten; make a crust with bread crumbs, salt, and pepper, first all greased with butter or good oil; serve them hot, and they will be quite tasty.

After parboiling or roasting them as above, you can halve or quarter them, dredge them in flour, and fry them in good lard; if parboiled, they can also be dipped in egg; they can serve as garnishes for many dishes, or be served by themselves, dipped in egg or not, with a sauce on top made with roasted chicken or cockerel livers ground in the mortar with other condiments or ingredients, as you prefer.

After half-roasting them on the spit, you can quarter them or cut them into pieces and prepare them in Portuguese style, sautéed with good beaten cured back fat or good oil, with a little condiment of garlic, oregano, minced small onions, capers, pitted olives, apt spices, and other suitable ingredients, with perfumed vinegar and sugar.

Stuffed or not, whole or in pieces, these pigeons can be used in stews, with slices of various salami, a strong white wine, cooked must, dried fruits, apt spices, and other suitable ingredients.

You can use them for pies, in the same way as in stews, adding sour grapes or another sour condiment as you prefer.

You can cook them in a lard broth with slices of pork throat and belly, ham slices, aromatic herbs, apt spices, and other suitable ingredients.

They can serve as garnishes for many pies, first boiled or roasted and cut in pieces, or quartered, or halved; they can serve as layers in pies, and they can be served in all the same dishes as domestic pigeons.

Of the wild dove, its qualities and cooking.

Wild doves are of the same quality as wild pigeons; they are good in the same season, and equally nourishing. They often are brought to Naples from Cava [de' Tirreni, near Salerno], and they are tasty and healthy, and easy to digest. They are abundant in the Marches, where those who kill them are condemned to the galleys. They are healthy and can be given to the convalescent.

Novello Oresta was the first to eat doves; they live for thirty years, and if they are sick they can be purged with laurel.

They can be boiled, stuffed or not, and served hot or cold, with on top cut or sliced salami, with or without condiments, or covered with the flowers of various herbs; they will be tatsy and pleasing in all sorts of dishes.

They can be roasted, on the grill or on the spit, and served with a crust or without, or larded with cloves and slices of cured back fat, or wrapped in caul or paper, and garnished with various condiments, as you prefer.

They can be used in pies or stews, with a strong white wine, a bit of cooked must, and sour grapes; they can always be served stuffed, as you prefer, or cut into pieces or quartered.

They can be used in many pottages and served with various sauces and condiments.

Of the pheasant, its qualities and cooking.

The best pheasants are those chased by hunters in forests, in the most horrid winter times, since they grow free in the open fields. Fat and young ones are of very good quality. Once killed, the pheasant must be aged three or four days in the open, facing north, away from the sun. Thus prepared it will benefit all ages and complexions, and, if eaten rarely and sparingly, will be healthy for those suffering from gout; this meat alleviates gout in the feet, but accentuates it in the hands, and is harmful to both if eaten in abundance; thus I advise those who wish to eat it, in order to benefit from it, to give the larger share to the steward.[98] It is a temperate meat in all degrees; it is better than the meat of all other poultry except the capon; it is easy to digest, helps those with a weak stomach, and benefits those with tuberculosis or generally the frail, because it fattens them and reinvigorates all vital forces. It is a royal food, and its season is from fall to spring.

Agamontino of Persia was the first to eat pheasant; the bird takes its name from the river Fasi in Colchis [on the eastern coast of the Black Sea]; these birds, because they eat all sorts of dirty things, would soon die if they did not purge themselves.

The emperor Severus [ruled 193–211] only had them served at the most important tables, and gave them as gifts to great princes; Elagabalus, out of his grandeur, fed them to other animals.

---

98 Here is a rare occurrence of Latini actually being funny, not just trying to be.

The Lord Duke of Mirandola in Lombardy has a beautiful hunting reserve with numerous pheasants, so many that they at times feed with the nearby peasants' capons. I saw this myself when the Lord Duke Alessandro went to Candia with Friar Vincenzo Rospigliosi, nephew of Pope Clement IX [ruled 1667–1669] of blessed memory, and on that occasion the Duke urgently recommended to his wife the Duchess the upkeep of the reserve. Once the Duke had left, the Duchess entertained many great visitors, among them the Dukes of Modena and Parma and other princes her relatives. The Duchess always wished to have pheasants served at the banquets, but, to keep her word to the Duke her husband, she ordered that those of his reserve be spared. When the Duke returned he found his woods depleted of pheasants; they had been stolen by a man from Crevalcore, a village in the papal state; this man was jailed by the Duke and confessed that he caught the pheasants by stealth at night, placed them in sacks, and sold them to many people, including the Duchess when she had guests, for one *zecchino* each. He was freed after two years' imprisonment, by the intercession of the Lord Cardinal of Este.[99]

The pheasant thief used this ingenious trick in His Highness's woods.

He brought along a large pot in which he kept a pestiferous paste; this he burned on a low fire, and with a funnel and a long pipe he pushed the resulting smoke into the trees where the pheasants slept; the bad smell reached the birds' noses, and they, stunned by this pestilential odour, fell dead to the ground; thus the thief filled his sacks; he later paid the price of his nocturnal thefts with long imprisonment.

You can stuff a pheasant with beaten eggs, good grated cheese, bits of mozzarella or provola, bone marrow, slices of various salami, raisins, pine nuts, bits of candied citron and pumpkin, ground aromatic herbs, apt spices, and other suitable ingredients; then cook it in water and salt together with bits of ham, soppressata, sausages or cut saveloy; serve it hot with the same salami on top, and with bunches of greens, first cooked in a good fat broth.

Pheasant, cooked as above, can be served cold with various sauces or condiments on top, or with parsley and the flowers of various aromatic herbs, with lemon or sour orange juice, and stuffed or not as you prefer.

You can serve it seasoned with salt and pepper, after cooking and stuffing it as above, or also without stuffing, and serve it cold, or at times deboned.

You can stuff it with other ingredients, such as beaten hard egg yolks, bits of candied citron and pumpkin, bits of various salami, bone marrow, slices of pork throat or belly, pitted olives, capers, pine nuts, chicken livers (first roasted on embers, whole or in pieces), ground veal or other meat, veal chops or small birds, whole sour grapes, beaten

---

99 Latini here proudly displays his high contacts: Mirandola was a tiny independent state in northern Emilia, ruled from the fourteenth century to 1708 by the Pico family, which acquired the title of dukes in 1619. Alessandro II Pico was duke of Mirandola in 1637–1691; his wife was Anna Beatrice of Este, sister of the Duke of Modena and Reggio (a larger nearby duchy). Pope Clement IX dispatched several galleys, led by his nephew Vincenzo Rospigliosi (1635–1673), a Commander in the Knights of Malta, to aid the Venetians in the last phase of the war of Candia (or Crete, 1645–1669), but in spite of this assistance Venice had to surrender the island to the Ottomans in 1669. Latini had served in Mirandola in 1670–1673, though not directly at the court. The zecchino was a Venetian coin.

aromatic herbs, apt spices, and other suitable ingredients. After stuffing it, you can spit-roast it, larded with slices of cured back fat, riddling the breast with cloves and cinnamon sticks; roast it on a low fire, and serve it hot, with a royal sauce on top.

Stuffed as above, and larded minutely, in the Maltese style, pheasant can be spit-roasted with a royal sauce on top; leave its tail on, and place back the wings as well, so that in the banquet it can be recognized as a pheasant; this dish can serve as a cold display dish [*rifreddo*], to give a good appearance to the table.[100]

You can spit-roast it, without larding it, well greased with melted cured back fat or butter; make a crust on top with roasted bread, ground and passed through a sieve, salt, pepper, and cinnamon, and serve it hot or cold, with lemon or sour orange juice on top.

You can first parboil it, halved or quartered, and then grill it on coals, making sure it does not burn, greased with butter or fat from the dripping pan, sprinkling it often with rose vinegar, and with a crust on top made with sugar and bread crumbs; serve it hot with a juniper condiment, or another as you prefer.

You can roast it in various ways, wrapped in caul or paper, larded with cloves or other spices, stuffed or not, deboned or not, as you prefer.

Cook it in water, cut it into bits or quarter it, dredge it in flour, and fry it in good lard, and serve it hot, with lemon juice on top.

You can also dip it in egg and fry it, and serve it hot with royal sauce on top.

You can roast it, dredge it in mostacciolo or sponge cake crumbs, and fry it, and serve it hot or cold, dusted with sugar and cinnamon, or with on top a mostacciolo sauce, sour grapes cooked in syrup, and bread slices soaked in almond milk and fried in butter.

You can use pheasant in various fried dishes, and use it as a noble garnish for many dishes.

After cooking pheasants in water, you can lard them finely with pine nuts soaked in perfumed water, strips of candied citron and pumpkin, decorated in various ways, all greased with sauces of various colours, in checkboard patterns; put back their wings, head, and tail, and re-dress them with their own skin and feathers, all retouched in gold and silver, and with similar decorations in the tail, wings, and head; they will serve as cold display dishes and will form a sumptuous sight, especially if you can set them up so that they stand, and in various whimsical attitudes.[101]

You can use pheasant in many cold dishes, in various ways, and decorated with various leaves, according to your whim, with many ornaments, as will be discussed in its place.

After cooking it in water or roasting it, and carefully deboning it, you can use pheasant in various ground dishes or gigots, with various noble ingredients, and serve them hot or cold as you prefer.

---

100 These *rifreddi* are cold dishes used to decorate the table (and impress the guests) as they take their seats; rifreddi were often solely decorative, but many could also be eaten, usually as part of the cold appetizer service.

101 This is a nice example of Latini's Baroque taste for display, illusion, and performance. The "similar decorations" are called *tremolanti*, which literally just means things that tremble or shake easily; in clothing, tremolanti were small pieces of decorative metalwork, used in fringes, for instance on headdresses; in this case the term could mean ribbons, cloth strips, or other things that would mimic the effect of feathers; they show up again a few pages after this when turkey is similarly decorated.

Pheasant can also be cooked quickly, with ham slices on top, riddled with cloves, and spit-roasted, and served hot or cold, with a sour cherry sauce on top, or another apt sauce.[102]

You can stuff it, between its meat and skin, with pitted Spanish olives, truffle slices first sautéed, pepper, sour grapes cooked in syrup, thin slices of soppressata and ham, egg yolks, sliced candied sour orange peel, apt spices, and other suitable ingredients; you can then spit-roast it, greased with butter or with the fat from the dripping pan, with or without a crust, wrapped in caul or paper, and serve it hot with a royal sauce on top.

After stuffing it as above, inside or between meat and skin, you can use it in stews, riddling the breast with cloves, with good malmsey wine, cooked must, lemon or sour orange juice, aromatic herbs, apt spices, and other suitable ingredients; serve it hot, with the same garnishes on top.

You can use it in pies, following the procedure as with the stew above, with whole sour grapes.

You can cook it in lard broth, with slices of pork throat and belly, aromatic herbs, a strong white wine, a bit of cooked must, apt spices, and other suitable ingredients; you can cook it whole or in pieces, stuffed or not, as you prefer; keep in mind that in every dish in which you use a whole pheasant you should riddle its breast with cloves and use a slice of cured back fat to cover the breast.

After part-cooking it in water, you can spit-roast the pheasant, and cut it in pieces or quarter it, and use it in a pie, layered with chicken livers, first roasted, bone marrow, truffle slices roasted on embers, St. George's mushrooms, pine nuts, small birds, first roasted and halved, wrapped in pork or wether caul, ground veal or other meat, aromatic herbs, apt spices, and other noble ingredients; serve it with a cover and sugar on top, and the usual little broth inside.

You can use pheasant, whole, stuffed or not, in a pie, first larding it and dusting it with the usual spices, with sliced salami and other apt ingredients, and serve it hot or cold as you prefer.

Pheasants can be used as garnishes for large or small pies, as I will say in its place.

With the flesh of the pheasant you can make meatballs, with apt ingredients, and they will be healthy also for the convalescent.

With the mixture of these meatballs you can make fritters, dredge them in mostacciolo crumbs, and fry them in good lard or butter; after frying them, you can stew them in a silver pan with good butter; serve them hot with sugar and cinnamon on top; they can also serve as noble and delicate garnishes for various dishes.

With the same flesh you can also make various stews, with their apt ingredients, as I will say in its place.

You can roast pheasant in caul or paper.

You can braise it in the oven, with noble and various ingredients, and use it in various dishes, as I will say elsewhere.

---

102 Latini describes this preparation as *abborracciati*, meaning something done quickly and skimpily.

You can spit-roast it, having tied its wings, tail, and head with a wet cloth, so that they do not burn while it cooks; then you can display it as you wish on the table, and it serves as a cold display dish.

Of the young pheasant, its quality and cooking.

Young pheasants are of the same quality as pheasants; their season is the whole summer and part of winter; they have the same health benefits as large pheasants.

They can be used in various preparations and dishes, similarly to what I said of domestic and wild chicks; you can use them in fried dishes, as layers in soups, in pies, as I said of chicks; they are very good spit-roasted, wrapped in caul or paper, and they can also be cooked in all the ways and dishes as pheasants; as they are more tender, they will be more pleasant to the taste, so that they can be served to any great personage; they can be used in cold display dishes, with their wings, tails, and heads; be careful though that neither large nor small pheasants should be cooked with greens or any dough, because they would turn out bad and harmful.[103] Young pheasants should be cooked whole, larding the breast with slices of cured back fat or other salami, and riddling it with cloves, stuffed or not as you wish.

Of the partridge, its quality and cooking.

The best partridges are young and male, called *perniconi* [big partridges]; older ones are less tasty and not as nourishing; their meat is healthy and benefits those who suffer from the French disease [syphilis]; it is beneficial to people of all ages and complexions, easy to digest, and good for the convalescent; anyone who eats partridge liver every day for a whole year will experience great improvement and relief if he suffers from epilepsy. Their quality is warm in the first degree and dry in the second; their season is winter and part of spring.

Liscinio Aurido was the first to eat partridges; these birds are exceedingly lusty, and are sacred to Jupiter and Latona.

Partridges from Paphlagonia have two hearts, Theophrastus writes; there are many types of these birds, and they are all easily domesticated; Elagabalus greatly esteemed their eggs, which Avicenna also celebrated because they soothe the heart and generate good blood. Partridges can be cooked in water with salt, together with a piece of veal; let the broth reduce to half the original quantity, and add roots of aromatic herbs; this can be given to drink to women, to facilitate menstruation.[104]

You can boil them together with salami and ham slices, with cauliflower on top, first boiled in water and sautéed, with good oil, pepper, and other ingredients; once cooked, serve them with a sauce which you shall serve in small round dishes, made Spanish-style, with white wine, sour orange juice, chili peppers, crushed garlic cloves, and a bit

---

103 Latini warns against cooking pheasants with *erbe* or *paste*; the context suggests to me that he intends greens (and not herbs), and any kind of paste or mixture.

104 Paphlagonia is in northern Turkey and Theophrastus (d. 287 BC) is an early Hellenistic writer, most famous for his *Characters*. Latona, Elagabalus, and Avicenna have come up before. "Facilitate menstruation" suggests that this broth was considered an abortifacient.

of oil and pepper; boil everything together, and place it, as I said, in small round dishes, and it will be quite tasty.

Be aware that, when you wish to serve partridges in dishes with vegetables or legumes, they must be half-cooked in water and salt, and then you complete the cooking in fat broth or in the vegetable or legume dish.

You can stuff partridges with beaten eggs, mostacciolo crumbs, bone marrow bits, cured back fat or beaten pork throat, ham bits, first cooked in wine, whole sour grapes, sliced candied sour orange peel, aromatic herbs, apt spices, and other suitable ingredients; then cook them in water, and finish cooking them in a good broth; serve them hot or cold, with flowers on top, or apt sauces; if you serve them hot, sprinkle them with sugar and cinnamon, and cover them with bunches of aromatic herbs, first cooked in a good fat broth, and layered with sausages or saveloys, first cut halfway.

Cook them as above, and grease them with a mostacciolo sauce, and encrust them with white aniseeds; this can serve as a cold display dish.

You can use stuffed partridges, with suitable ingredients, in various roasts, as we said about pheasants, larded or not, and cooked on the grill, and they can be served with the same sauces or condiments.

You can use partridges in various stews and soups, with suitable ingredients.

With the meat and breast of partridges you can make ground dishes, gigots, meatloaf, and meatballs, with the usual ingredients.

You can use them for pies of all sorts, and for garnishes for various dishes. I close by saying that they can be used in all the ways and dishes, and cold display dishes, as pheasants.

Of the young partridge, its quality and cooking.

Young partridges are the offspring of large partridges, abandoned by their mothers; once grown, they are quite nourishing and easy to digest; they are temperate in all degrees; they are usually eaten in summer, when they are better than large partridges.

The best way to cook them is to roast them, finely larded, wrapped in caul or paper, served with royal sauce on top; if you want to use them for other dishes, you can do as one does with wild pigeons, and with the same ingredients.

Both partridges and young partridges, when they are fat, and have been dead for three or four days, can be spit-roasted; after cooking them, they can be prepared with slices of a small, fragrant lemon, and they will be most appetizing.[105]

Of the grey partridge, its quality and cooking.

Many state that if one eats grey partridges for a whole year, and continuously, one is cured of the French disease; but one has to eat nothing else; on this point, I refer to the opinion of physicians, and affirm on my part that the meat of these birds is useful and healthy for people of all complexions, nourishing, and easy to digest, as long as the birds are young, and not old, and that they be aged, in an open place, in the open air, and thus

---

105 This preparation is described as *sgazzariati*: sguazzariati is a Neapolitan term that means shaken in a liquid, but I am not sure what procedure is intended here.

they will be more tender and cleansed; their quality is temperate in all degrees; their season is from December through March.

Diomede Pescennio was the first to eat grey partridge: he was skilled in all the sciences, and was very fond of this food.

When it is young and has been aged, the grey partridge can be prepared in all dishes, well dressed with spices, served with aromatic herbs, cooked in a good fat broth of capon or another meat, and it will be nourishing and healthy for those of all ages.

You can boil it with suitable ingredients, and serve it hot or cold, as you prefer, with various sauces and condiments.

You can use it in various stews, with varied and noble ingredients.

You can use it in roasts, wrapped in caul or paper, on coals, or in other ways, stuffed or not, with a crust, condiment, or sauce, as you prefer.

You can lard it with various candied things, and riddle it with cloves or cinnamon sticks, stuffed or not; you can also braise or stew it or prepare it in other ways, with various garnishes inside, whole or in pieces.

This bird can be cooked in all the same ways as pheasant, with the same garnishes and condiments, although they are not quite as good.

Of the young grey partridge, its quality and cooking.

Young grey partridges are much better than regular grey partridges, more nourishing, and of elevated quality; their season is July through November.

They are very good spit-roasted, served hot, with royal sauce on top.

They can be roasted, stuffed or not, wrapped in caul or paper, or wrapped in grape or laurel branches, finely larded with ham slices inside, and served with various sauces or condiments, placed in small round dishes.

They can be roasted, greased with butter, with a crust on top of bread crumbs, salt, and pepper; serve them hot, with lemon juice or another condiment, as you prefer.

You can use them in fried dishes, first dipped in egg or not, and serve them hot, with a sauce or condiment on top; they can also serve as garnishes for various dishes.

You can cook them in a lard broth, or in a stew, whole or in pieces, stuffed or not, as you prefer.

They can be used in various Portuguese- or French-style dishes; they can be cooked in all the ways one cooks wild or domestic pigeons, with the same condiments and spices, just changing at times their quantities; always make sure they have been aged, as they will be better.

Of the woodcock, called arciera in Naples, its quality and cooking.

Young woodcocks are quite nourishing, and their meat is similar to that of partridges; their qualities are temperate in all degrees; their season is the whole winter; their best part is the thigh; best are those captured in mountains and woods, but not close to the sea coast.

Perione Perioni was the first to eat this bird's meat; it is caught in woods that are not too thick, and in bushes; if they have eaten anything bad, then they are not tasty.

The tastiest and most delicious way to prepare it is spit-roasted, on a low fire, on the same day that it has been caught by hunters, without removing its innards, and letting its grease fall on slices of toasted bread.

Serve it hot, with the same bread greased with the bird's fat, removing the innards after cooking; spread the innards on the greased bread, with lemon juice and pepper; garnish the plate with crostini of the same bread; you can sprinkle the roasted wood-cock with pepper and cinnamon, or garnish it with royal sauce or another condiment as you prefer; you can also garnish the plate all around with crostini with the bird's head, roasted and halved, with pepper, oil, and lemon juice.

You can cook it in water with salami and strong spices, and serve it hot with the salami on top.

You can cook it in a lard broth, with slices of pork throat and belly, aromatic herbs, the usual spices, and other suitable ingredients.

You can lard it finely, and braise it in the oven, stuffed with various ingredients.

You can use it pies and stews, whole or in pieces, stuffed or not, encrusted, especially in the breast, with cloves and slices of cured back fat, the usual spices, and other noble ingredients.

You can use it for covers of many pies.

Quartered or cut into pieces, you can use it in pies, or also whole, larded, stuffed or not, and serve it hot or cold, with various ingredients inside, with a cover on top, and the little broth inside, with verjuice and beaten egg yolks.

You can use it in various fried dishes, served hot, with condiments on top, and various other dishes as you prefer.

Of the turkey, its qualities and cooking.

Turkeys were caught in Africa and brought to Italy as gifts for great lords. They are called Indian chicken not because they come from India, but because they are of the same sus-tenance, flavour, and goodness as Indian chicken.[106] One must age them in the open air, still unplucked, for four or five days. The best ones are raised in the country, and cooked just a few days after they died; their meat is whiter than that of any other poultry, and if aged properly is easy to digest. If it is cooked well, it generates good blood and can be given to convalescents, since it strengthens the weak; turkey is beneficial to all complex-ions, except to the gouty. It is hot and moist in the second degree and its season is from the start of winter through parts of spring. We read that the first to eat this meat was a certain Solpitius the African.

Turkey can be seasoned with salt and pepper, after cooking it in water, and served cold, with salt and pepper on top, stuffed as one does with boiled capon, or also not stuffed, as you prefer; I leave it up to you if you wish to debone it before cooking it.

---

106 Latini writes *galli d'India* and then *polli d'India* (gallo and pollo are largely synonymous); in this period there was at times confusion between turkey and guinea fowl; given Latini's comments about this bird's white meat, I believe he means turkey here; see Riley, *The Oxford Companion*, 242–43 and 535, and Sabine Eiche, *Presenting the Turkey* (Florence: Centro Di, 2004), 16–22.

You can cook it in white wine, with cloves and cinnamon sticks, and serve it hot, dusted with salt and pepper; you can also debone it and serve it cold, sprinkled just with pepper, cinnamon, and lemon juice; if you wish to serve it whole, without deboning it, that is up to your pleasure.

You can cook it in wine as above, then dress it again with its own wings, tail, and head, and thus it can serve as a cold display dish, setting it up in a variety of whimsical poses, to look like an eagle or another animal, decorated in gold and silver, possibly with a crown on its head, with various ribbons, and with whimsical foliage around it, as I will say elsewhere.

After cooking it in water with various salami, sliced or halved, it can be covered with bunches of greens, first cooked in good broth, layered with the salami, sprinkled with pepper, and served hot; if you wish to, you can first debone and stuff it.

Stuff the turkey with ground veal or another meat, first roasted and finely beaten, cow bone marrow, small birds, first spit-roasted, chops of veal or another meat, slices of ham and pork throat, first well cooked, halved sausages or saveloys, St. George's mushrooms, pine nuts, sliced truffles, first sautéed, pepper, capers, pitted olives, dried plums, bits of candied citron and pumpkin, whole sour grapes, apt spices, and other noble ingredients; then lard it minutely on the outside, cook it in the oven, and serve it hot with bastard sauce or another condiment on top.

It can be spit-roasted, stuffed or not, larded Maltese-style or in another way, as you wish, and served hot with royal sauce on top.

After roasting it and more than half-cooking it, you can use it for a French-style fricassée, cutting it into pieces and sautéing it in a pan with the usual spices and other noble ingredients; thicken it with eggs, and serve it hot, with lemon juice and pepper on top.

After roasting it as above, you can cook it in Portuguese style, sautéed, with good beaten cured back fat, minced small onions, capers, pine nuts, pitted olives, a bit of perfumed vinegar, and sugar, with the usual spices, and other noble ingredients.

After cooking it in the oven or spit-roasting it, you can take the flesh and the skin and use them in various ground dishes or gigots, with good fat broth and other noble ingredients, and they will be tasty and appetizing.

Parboil it to more than a half-cooking, then cut it into pieces or quarter it, and roast it on the grill with malmsey wine, greased with good melted cured back fat, and sprinkled with good vinegar; make a crust for it and serve it hot with royal sauce on top, or another condiment as you prefer.

You can make chops from turkey, with the usual ingredients; these can also serve as garnishes for various dishes.

After boiling it, you can remove the flesh and breast and use them as layers in various soups.

You can use it for Genoese-style gigots, with apt ingredients and garnishes, as will be said elsewhere.

With the flesh you can make meatloaf or meatballs, in various ways at your whim, and cook them diligently.

You can cook it in a lard broth, with sliced salami, aromatic herbs, apt spices, and other suitable ingredients.

You can stew it in good fat broth and various fruits in it, aromatic herbs, apt spices, and other suitable ingredients.

You can braise it in the oven, and use it in pies, stuffed or not, with suitable ingredients, and serve it hot.

It can be used for pies, prepared in various ways, for instance in the shape of an eagle, or with other whimsical decorations, and it can serve as a cold display dish.

It can be used in many dishes, or composite preparations, whole or in pieces, stuffed or not, deboned or not, and giving it a whimsical appearance; it can serve for triumphs and cold display dishes, as will be said elsewhere.

Of the young turkey, its quality and cooking.

These turkeys are more tender than regular turkeys, if young and fat; they are highly esteemed at the tables of great people; they are nourishing and easy to digest, and can be given to the convalescent; they are less diuretic than regular turkeys; they are hot in all degrees, and their season is from May through September.

They are quite tasty, if you lard them finely, and spit-roast them or cook them in the oven, or in water; they are tastier and healthier.

Once cooked, you can use them in all the same dishes as with domestic or dovecote pigeons, with the same condiments and sauces.

When they are as big as a domestic hen, you can serve them in all the same ways as regular turkeys, with the same condiments and garnishes.

You can use them for many cold display dishes, as I said about turkeys; use them stuffed or not, and deboned or not, as you prefer.

Their liver can be used in many preparations, in covered tarts or pizze, to form meat rolls, and also in various roasts or fried dishes, with apt sauces and condiments; if you soak the liver in water for three or four hours it will be more exquisite.

Of the peacock, its quality and cooking.

The best of these birds is the one raised in thin air, not heavy air. It benefits hot complexions, and those who constantly exercise; to be good and healthy, it must be young and not old; those who do not labour much physically should abstain from this food; before cooking it, it must be well aged, hanging it by the throat with a weight attached to its feet, in the open air or in a northern wind, for three or four days; it is dry in the first degree and hot in the second, and its season is the whole winter and part of spring.

Ortensio Quintio of Rome, noblest orator, was the first to eat peacock; ordinarily, this bird lives twenty-five years; it is the emblem for envy and vainglory. When Alexander the Great was in India, the first time he saw a peacock he was stunned by its beauty, and ordered that nobody dare kill it; Marco Eusidio was the first to think of fattening peacocks, and drew much profit from this idea. The peacock from Samos is regarded as the most delicate; this bird is very fond of doves.

This bird's meat is not esteemed in banquets, and can be used only for cold display dishes and for triumphs, displaying it with its tail, head, and wings, to form a beautiful and sumptuous appearance.

You can spit-roast it, tying its wings, tail, and head with a wet cloth, so that they not be burned while it cooks; when it is cooked, you can set it on the table as you prefer.

It can be used in all the dishes in which turkey is used, with the same condiments, stuffing, and sauces; be aware though that if you cook it whole, you must make sure all its blood is gone through the opening through which you also will have removed its innards; in that same opening, place burning coals and keep them there long enough to completely dry that moisture and blood; do the same with young peacocks.

Of the young peacock, its quality and cooking.

Since they are small and raised in good air, these are much better than regular peacocks, as they are fatter and more tender. They are apt for those of all complexions, especially the young and middle-aged, whereas they are not beneficial to the elderly and gouty; they are nourishing and easy to digest, especially for those with a hot stomach.

Their quality is hot in the first and second degree, and their season from June through August; they must be aged as I said about peacocks, but only for two days, because, as they are small, they are tender and may easily be ruined.

They can be used in cold display dishes, with their wings, tail, and head, spit-roasted and placed on the table, to produce a nice view.

They can be larded finely, Genoese-style, in different ways, with royal sauce on top.

They can be cooked in the oven, larded, stuffed or not, putting on their breast slices of cured back fat riddled with cloves and cinnamon sticks; cooked in other ways they will not be very good.

If needed, they can be used in all the dishes I mentioned for domestic and wild cockerels; they will however not be as good and perfect as the cockerels.

Of the domestic duck, its quality and cooking.

Best are those raised in the countryside and in running waters; they should be young and fat, not old and thin; if eaten often, duck makes one fat, brings good colour, clears the voice, strengthens the body, and is very useful to those who practice constant physical activity; its liver is nourishing; its quality is hot and moist to the second degree, and its season is summer through winter.

Giliberto of Smyrna was the first to eat duck, or rather only duck breast, since the rest nauseated him; these birds, if ill, are purged with an herb named *federbita*. Ducks from Pontus feed on poison, and their blood protects one against poisoned foods.[107]

You can cook duck in water, and serve it hot with various condiments on top; you can also stuff it, with various aromatic herbs and other ingredients as you wish.

You can stuff duck with beaten eggs, bits of bone marrow, pounded pork throat or belly, bits of candied things, raisins and pine nuts, ground aromatic herbs, apt spices,

---

107 I have found no information on federbita; Mithridates, King of Pontus, was a famous enemy of the Romans who had made himself immune to most poisons by ingesting small quantities of them, which is probably the origin of Latini's story about ducks from the region (on the northern coast of the Black Sea).

and other suitable ingredients; serve it hot with tortellini on top filled with beaten meat, bone marrow, the usual spices, and other apt garnishes.[108]

You can prepare duck as above, and then cover it with vegetables cooked in a good broth, like celery, cardoons or similar ones; serve it hot, stuffed or not as you prefer.

You can cover this duck with various types of pasta, like maccheroni, small gnocchi, *lasagne*, or ravioli, stuffed with noble ingredients, layered with provola, grated cheese, sugar, and cinnamon, and cover it with cream tops, or dust it with sugar, cinnamon, and grated cheese.[109]

You can spit-roast duck, stuffed with its own liver and stomach, first roasted on embers or spit-roasted, pitted olives, slices of pork belly or throat, ham slices, St. George's mushrooms, pine nuts, sliced truffle, first roasted on embers, bone marrow, cardoon stems, artichokes, first boiled in water, dried plums and sour cherries, aromatic herbs, apt spices, and other suitable ingredients; spit-roast it and serve it hot, with condiments on top or in small plates.

You can cook duck in the oven, stuffed or not, finely larded, and serve it hot, with pepper and lemon juice or other condiments as you wish.

Stuff the duck as above, and use it in stews or pies, with various fruits inside, apt spices, and other suitable ingredients; serve it hot, with the same garnishes on top, a good fat broth, and a good strong wine.

You can also cook it in a lard broth, with thin salami slices, the usual aromatic herbs, apt spices, and other suitable ingredients.

You can serve duck in pies, hot or cold, stuffed or without, as you wish, with the usual spices, and other apt ingredients.

You can use it in pieces, in a pie, layered with various ground meats, with the usual spices, with a cover or without.

You can use it in various roast dishes, stuffed or not, with a crust or a marinade, and with various condiments served in small plates.

You can use it for various pottages, with various ingredients, as I will say in its place.

If you want to cook it whole, you should first soak it in water or briefly spit-roast it.

I declare however that these birds, even if served with all skill and mastery, are unworthy of royal banquets and of the tables of great people, as it is a food apt for people of low condition.

Duck liver and stomach are good roasted, first soaked in milk, and they can be cooked in all the ways you use for capon liver.

Duck tongues can be used in many soups, with various ingredients, with the usual spices; you can parboil them and then fry them, and serve them with a sauce of mostacciolo, or lemon juice, or sour orange, and pepper.

---

108 Latini writes *tortelletti*, which I think here refers to a fresh stuffed pasta type.

109 This is Latini's first explicit mention of maccheroni, which refers generally to various types of fresh pasta (Latini never used dry pasta, which in his time was just emerging as a major food for the Naples poor); gnocchi (dumplings), ravioli, and lasagna (thin layers) are types of fresh pasta still widely in use today in Italian cooking.

Of the wild duck, its quality and cooking.

Wild duck is better than the domestic one; it should be young and fat. It should grow up in the fields, and feed on the banks of rivers, and not in swamps. Its quality is hotter than any other bird, and its season is from December through January, according to common opinion; I however believe it to be June through August, because these animals are tastier in warmer times than in cold ones.

Duck meat is very moist and harmful, and therefore it is only eaten by people of low condition, and is unworthy of the tables of the great.[110]

You can roast it, cooking it well, and cutting its neck.

You can boil it and cover it with pasta, celery, and cardoons, with salted things and good cheese.

You can stew it with plums, sour cherries, a bit of wine, aromatic herbs, apt spices, and other suitable ingredients.

You can use it in all dishes as you do domestic duck; its tongue, liver, and stomach can also be used like those of the domestic duck.

Ducklings can be prepared just like wild or domestic ducks; they are quite good spit-roasted, stuffed or not, larded with slices of cured back fat, and riddled with cloves in the breast and other places.

You can also roast them wrapped in caul or paper, larded with various candied things, and served hot, with royal sauce on top.

Of the coot, its quality and cooking.

Coots are of the same quality as wild ducks, though not quite as good; it is better not to eat much of this bird, and rarely, and the convalescent should avoid it entirely. It is food fit for those who hoe the land, and work hard, since it is hard to digest and not nourishing. Before cooking it, you have to age it well. Its season is throughout the year.

Coots can be prepared in various ways, but only for the lower servants.

You can boil it, and serve it hot, with maccheroni or pasta on top.

You can roast it, stuffed or not, and serve it hot, with pepper and sour orange juice on top.

You can stew it, stuffed with fresh or dried fruits, with a fat broth, a bit of wine, whole sour grapes, apt spices, and other suitable ingredients.

You can cook it in a lard broth, with slices of salami, aromatic herbs, spices, and other usual ingredients.

Of the northern lapwing, its quality and cooking.

Northern lapwings are better than coots and are easier to digest, because they are more tender; they are suitable for the young, not the old, and it is best not to eat too much of them. you must age them before cooking them; they are hot and moist to the second degree, and their season is from December through spring. if you want them to be good,

---

110 The duck's "lowness" is associated here especially with its feeding in swamps; it was typical of the medical—and social—approach of the time to draw parallels between an animal's life conditions and its essential character.

you must cook them with a lot of spices, and they are ordinarily not suited for the tables of great people.

After cooking them in water, you can serve them hot or cold with salt, pepper, a bit of cinnamon, and lemon or sour orange juice.

You can use them in various roasts, stuffed or not, with a crust on top, and serve them hot, with sour orange juice on top, or without, as you prefer.

You can roast them wrapped in caul or paper, stuffed or not, finely larded with various candied things, cloves, a slice of cured back fat on the breast, and serve them with royal sauce on top.

You can cook them in a lard broth, with aromatic herbs, apt spices, and other suitable ingredients.

You can use them in pies, stuffed or not, and serve them hot, with spices on top.

You can stew or braise them with different ingredients, quartered or cut into pieces, stuffed or not, as you wish, and serve them hot with the usual garnishes on top.

You can use them as layers in soups, and they can be prepared in all the dishes for which you use wild pigeons.

Of the domestic young goose, its quality and cooking.[111]

Domestic young geese, to be good, must be raised in fresh waters, and not in muddy swamps; they aid those with strong complexions, because it is a heavy food, hard to digest; they are hot in the first and second degree, and moist in the third; their season is from summer through winter; the best parts to eat are their liver and wings.

Siro of Forlì in Romagna was the first to eat this bird; he was also the first to roast crane.

Goose can be stuffed with ground veal, ox bone marrow, raisins, pine nuts, veal brains, first parboiled and finely pounded, aromatic herbs, apt spices, goose liver and stomach, first roasted and finely pounded, candied pumpkin and citron, and other noble ingredients, bound with beaten eggs; then you can cook it in water, and serve it hot with on top grated cheese, pepper, and cinnamon.

Cooked as above, stuffed or not, goose can be covered with lasagne layered with sugar, cinnamon, and good grated cheese.

You can cover it with celery, cardoons, and bunches of fennels, first cooked in a good fat broth, with salami bits or cut sausages, first dusted with grated cheese, pepper, and cinnamon.

You can cover it with small Sicily maccheroni, with the usual grated cheese and spices.

You can cover it with ravioli stuffed in various ways, or made with ricotta, with sugar and cinnamon on top.

You can cover it with small gnocchi, *tagliolini*, large maccheroni, or other pasta or greens, as you wish.[112]

---

111 Latini says *papara* (today usually *papera*), which in formal Italian refers to the young goose, but is also a term that in Naples today can be synonymous with duck; since he has a duck section, I assume he means here the young goose. He later has a section on *oca*, which also means goose, presumably the fully grown one.

112 Tagliolini are long, thin, flat pasta.

You can cover it with small tortellini stuffed with goose liver, roasted and pounded, together with bone marrow, cow or ox marrow, apt spices, and other noble ingredients.

You can stuff goose with pounded veal, cooked veal kidney, goose liver, first roasted and cut into bits, veal or other chops, first browned in a pan, small birds, first spit-roasted wrapped in caul, kid mammary glands and testicles, cut into bits and first sautéed in good liquefied cured back fat, pepper, pitted Spanish large olives, St. George's mushrooms, pine nuts, ground hard egg yolks, dried plums and sour cherries, slices of candied citron, sliced truffles, first sautéed with pepper, whole sour grapes, artichoke and cardoon stems, first cooked in water and sautéed in good oil and pepper, thin slices of Ischia apples and moscarole pears, first browned in a pan, pounded aromatic herbs, the usual spices, and other noble ingredients; grease it on the outside with good pounded cured back fat, and sprinkle it with white salt; then bake it, and serve it hot with the condiments you prefer.

Stuffed as above, you can spit-roast it, larding it with burning cured back fat, and serve it hot, stuffed or not as you wish.

Stuffed as above, you can use it for a pie, shape the pie like an eagle, and serve it hot or cold, as you prefer, with sugar on top; first though you need to half-cook or -roast it; for pies, it will be better to halve or quarter it.

You can roast it on the grill, with good malmsey wine, halved or quartered or cut into pieces, grilling it on a low fire, greased with liquefied cured back fat, sprayed with vinegar, and with a crust on top; serve it with the condiment you prefer.

You can braise it, stuffed or not, and serve it hot, as mentioned above.

Quartered or cut into pieces you can stew it in a good broth, aromatic herbs, apt spices, and other suitable ingredients, and serve it hot.

This bird, like all other fat birds, abounds in flesh; but since it is difficult to digest, and does not provide good nourishment, it is abhorred by noble people, and is only cooked for dependents or labourers; thus I will not go on at length on how to cook it.

The liver, soaked in milk for five or six hours, can be fried and served with salt, pepper, and sour orange juice; it will be quite tasty.

It can also be spit-roasted, wrapped in caul or paper, stuffed with slices of salami and sprinkled with salt and pepper; it is served hot, with lemon juice or anything you like on top.

The same liver, once roasted, can be used for rolls, together with salami, bone marrow, and other apt ingredients.

Goose liver, as it is larger than a capon's, can be cooked in all the ways in which one cooks calf or pig liver, with the same garnishes and condiments.[113]

Of the wild young goose.

These birds can be prepared in all the same ways and dishes as domestic ones, spit-roasted, baked, stewed in bits or quartered, covered with various types of pasta or greens, and are of the same quality as the domestic ones; their season is the same; young

---

113 Similar recipes for goose liver are in Scappi, *Opera*, 214–15; Italian Jews traditionally fattened and ate geese and their organs, as substitutes for pork.

and fat ones can be good and tasty; but it is a rustic and plebeian food, not usually placed on the tables of grand personages.

Of the goose, its quality and cooking.

Younger geese are nourishing, but not old ones, which are hard to digest; they fatten emaciated people; they clear the voice and bring much utility; they should not be served to those afflicted by a fever, because they can be harmful, and if old they are hard to digest.

Younger geese are hot in the first degree and moist in the second; their season is from the start of October through February.

Alessandro Etholo, the poet, was the first to eat goose, which is hot by nature, and thus likes frigid grass and cold water; a goose never touches laurel; goose heart is a good food, as also its liver, and they were served to Alexander Severus, Lampridius, Scipio, Metellus, and others. One of them was the first to fatten goose with milk and cooked must, and also the first to eat goose liver and other innards, cooked in that way.[114]

Goose can be cooked in all the ways as the young goose, and be served with the same condiments; its fat should be preserved to be used in various dishes, and it will be very good in all.

Stuffed like the young goose, it can be boiled in water and served hot, covered with various pasta, greens, or salami, as I said of the domestic young goose.

You can braise it, whole and stuffed, and serve it hot.

You can use it in pies or stew it, cut into pieces or quartered, and serve it hot, with aromatic herbs, apt spices, and other suitable ingredients.

You can roast it, stuffed or not, larded, and serve it hot, with the condiment you prefer.

You can cook it on the grill, with malmsey wine, quartered or cut into pieces, greased with liquefied cured back fat, sprayed with vinegar, with a crust on top, and serve it hot with the sauce or condiment you prefer.

You can use it in a pie, whole, in pieces, or quartered, with the same condiments as the young goose.

Goose liver can be soaked in milk, and then used in various fried dishes or roasts, in all the ways that I mentioned for veal or pig liver.

Of the wild goose, its quality and cooking.

These birds can be prepared and served in all the ways and dishes as young geese; they are of the same quality and are eaten in the same season; like the others, they are not nourishing, hard to digest, and unsuited to noble people; it is an ordinary food, apt for the lower ranks; I shall not expand on how to cook them, since it is just like with young geese; only younger ones should be cooked, as the older ones are unhealthy and of little taste.

---

114 Alexander Severus was the Roman emperor in 222–235 AD; Lampridius probably refers to a biographer of that emperor; Scipio and Metellus could refer to any of several famous members of prominent ancient Roman families.

Of the common snipe, its quality and cooking.

The best snipes are those caught by hunters near lakes; they are quite tasty, but not very healthy for the convalescent and those with a weak complexion; they are hot and moist in all degrees, and their season is from October through March.

We read that the first to eat this bird was a certain Alberto Osorio from Flanders.

After cleaning them and removing their feathers and innards, you can stuff them with small bits of cured back fat and small pitted olives; roast them, layered with slices of cured back fat and bay leaves; make a crust on top with bread crumbs, salt, and pepper, as you like, and serve them hot with sour orange juice on top.

You can cook them with wine, cooked must, and vinegar, with whole cloves and cinnamon sticks, boiling everything together with the bird, and then serve it hot or cold as you wish.

You can cook it in a lard broth, with slices of cured back fat or pork belly, aromatic herbs, apt spices, and other suitable ingredients; serve them hot with suitable garnishes on top.

You can stew them with the usual spices and other noble ingredients.

After roasting them, you can halve them and marinade them; then dredge them in flour and fry them, serve them hot, with sugar and cinnamon on top; it is up to you whether to serve them with their marinade too.

Of the quail, its quality and cooking.

The best quails are those fattened in a coop, if first castrated, as with capons, removing two testicles they have near their tail, or those caught by preying birds; they benefit the melancholy, are nourishing and tasty, and harmful to old people and to the phlegmatic; the good ones are younger and not too fat. It is best to eat them rarely, because eating them frequently causes various ills and infirmities; their quality is hot in the first degree and moist in the second; they have two seasons: first, from July to part of September; second, from February to part of April, when they are better and fatter.

We read that the first to eat quail was a certain Ascanio Perizzone from Savoy.

Ordinarily, they are spit-roasted, with a crust of bread crumbs, salt, and pepper, and they are served hot.

You can also cook them simply, with slices of cured back fat or ham, riddled with cloves, and serve them hot with a royal sauce on top.

After roasting them, wrapped in caul or unwrapped, you can use them to garnish various dishes.

You can use them to garnish various pies; halved or quartered they can be used for stews.

They can be used in other pies, by themselves, with ham slices and other ingredients, and they will be quite tasty.

When they are fat, you can spit-roast them, wrapped in caul, or in leaves of pumpkin, or fig or grape leaves, and serve them hot, and this is the best way to cook them.

You can sauté them with beaten cured back fat, salt, and pepper, cooking them without a broth, and serve them hot with lemon juice, or covered with broccoli tips, first cooked in a good fat broth; you can also use them in various vegetable stews.

You can braise them in the oven and serve them in various ways, as I will say in its place.

They can be roasted in various ways, and for various dishes, with various condiments and ingredients, as will be said elsewhere.

Of the turtledove, its quality and cooking.

Turtledoves are usually raised domestically, like quails, and this way they become fatter and more nourishing. Ordinarily, they are caught when wheat is harvested, and thus fattened they come out very tasty, easy to digest, and nourishing; they fortify the stomach; their quality is hot and dry in the second degree, and their season is from July to part of October.

We read that the first to eat this bird was a certain Onorio Irlando, who used to prepare them in various dishes and ate them often.

Turtledoves can be roasted, wrapped in caul or paper, or unwrapped, and served hot.

You can stew them with the usual spices and other ingredients.

You can also boil them, covered with fennels or with Sicilian small maccheroni, cooked in a good cow broth, and serve them hot.

You can sauté them in a pan or other vessel, halved, with a glass of muscatel wine, aromatic herbs, and the usual spices, and they will be tasty.

They can be used for all the dishes mentioned for quails, with the same condiments and ingredients.

Of the thrush, its quality and cooking.

The meat of this bird is very tasty, and quite nourishing, easy to digest, good also for the convalescent, and for all those with a weakened complexion; they are hot and dry in the first and second degree; their season is from the beginning of September, at the time of grapes, through Carnival; in winter they come from the mountains near Spoleto and Terni [in Umbria], and are quite fat, because in that season they feed from juniper and myrtle seeds; those caught in December and January, when the cold is most horrid, are also quite good.

Sipontillo Calabro was the first to eat thrush; thrushes make their nests at the top of trees; they are slow in movement, hence the proverb "he is slower and less in a rush than a thrush." When this bird has eaten myrtle seeds, if it is roasted it is very beneficial against dysentery. It was greatly esteemed in antiquity, and Martial asserts that in those times the thrush had primacy among birds.[115]

You can roast it, layered with sausages, and serve it hot, with slices of lemon or sour orange, and it will be tasty.

You can spit-roast it, layered with slices of cured back fat and bay leaves, greased with good oil, sprinkled with bread crumbs, salt, and pepper, and serve it hot, and it will be very tasty.

---

115 Martial indeed mentions thrushes as very esteemed birds in at least a dozen of his poems. Literally, the proverb reads "he is slower and deafer (*sordo*) than a thrush (*tordo*)," but I changed it somewhat to preserve its rhyme structure (however feeble this may be as poetry).

You can boil it stuffed with salted things and covered with fennels or lettuce stems, mixed with eggs.

You can use it to garnish dishes, wrapped in caul or leaves, and served hot, with a mostacciolo sauce.

You can half-boil it, then halve it and fry it, and this way it can serve as part of various fried dishes; it would be good also by itself, with sugar, cinnamon, and lemon juice.

Since thrush is tender and tasty, it can be used in all the ways as quail, with the same garnishes and condiments; if it is not fresh, you should remove its innards, and stuff it appropriately.

Of the francolin, its quality and cooking.

Francolins, if young and fat, are nourishing, beneficial to all complexions, and healthy for all ages; their meat is more delicate than partridge and pheasant; many are found in the mountains near Trent; I have never seen any in our area, except in Rome, with feathers mixed of three colours: black, grey, and white; they are hot and moist in all degrees, and their season is January through spring; if they are fat, they will be good at any time of year.

Ulisse Aldrovandi asserts firmly that Caterino da Pisa, a valiant architect, was the first to eat francolin, a bird which, according to Scaliger, can be found not just in Asia and in Rhodes, but also in the kingdom of Valencia in Spain; he also affirms to have seen many in Italy, and especially in Sicily.[116]

You can roast them, with their tails and wings, as I said about pheasant.

You can use them for various dishes, as I said about young pheasants, with the same garnishes, ingredients, sauces, or condiments; the best way to cook them is to roast them, and that way they will be most tasty.

Of the warbler, its quality and cooking.

These are very tasty and delicate little birds, and thus deserve to be served in any banquet, at any table, and to any personage. Their meat is healthy, suitable for all ages, but harmful to the convalescent; they are hot and moist in the first and second degree; their season is at the time when figs are ripe, from the start of August through mid-October.[117]

We read that the first to east warblers was a certain Rodomiro Dodeo of Sicily, who was very fond of them.

They can be spit-roasted, layered with bay leaves and ham slices, on a strong fire, turning them frequently, and putting on top of them crustless bread and salt; serve them hot, and they will be very good.

Roasted as above, they can serve as garnishes for many composite dishes.

---

116 For once, Latini gives us his source for his usual "inventor" reference, and it is a solid one: Aldrovandi (1522–1605) was one of the greatest naturalists of his time; it is probably through his works that Latini also learned of Joseph Justus Scaliger (1540–1609), another one of Europe's greatest scholars.

117 Latini provides two names: *beccafico* (the Italian name for the bird, which literally means "fig-picker") and *ficedola* (the Neapolitan name).

They can also serve as garnishes for various pies.

You can place a warbler inside an onion, having removed the onion's inner part, so that the bird looks as if in prison; then put it in a pot with ham slices both inside and outside the onion, with suitable spices, and cover the pot well; stew it, and serve it hot, and it will be tasty.

You can also cook them in egg shells, with ham, the usual spices, and then cover the egg with pasta, cooked in the oven, with its own fat; this effects the proverb "it cooks with its own grease;" it is a very tasty dish.

You can use these birds in pies, by themselves, with salami, the usual spices, and other tasty noble ingredients.

You can stew them in a lard broth, and in various dishes, served in various ways, and they will always be nourishing and tasty; they can also be used to stuff various meat dishes and larger birds, both domestic and wild.

Of the ortolan, its quality and cooking.

The best ortolans are those fattened in a cage with millet cooked in milk; these will be very good and of great sustenance, but harmful to convalescents; they are hot in all degrees, and their season is from September through part of spring; if raised in a cage they are good in all seasons. They are abundant in Florence, and exquisite ones are often brought to Italy from Cyprus in earthen vases or boxes, covered in flour.

The first to eat ortolans was Ivone Afrodisio of Cyprus, who enjoyed them very much.

They can be cooked like warblers in egg shells, with the same spices, and salami slices inside.

You can roast them layered with bay or sage leaves, with bread crumbs on top, and can serve as garnishes for many dishes and pies, with or without cover.

After spit-roasting them, you can prepare egg whites with sugar and a bit of sour lemon juice, and put it all on a plate to brown in the oven, and they will be very tasty.

As they are delightful and wonderful birds, they can be prepared for the tables of great people, in all the ways and dishes used for warblers; they are worthy of being served at any royal banquet, and however many one eats, one will always hunger for more, as one can never eat enough of them.[118]

Of the young swallow, its quality and cooking.

The best of these are not those taken from nests, but those which, abandoned by their mothers, go on their own to seek food in the country and on mountains; best are the younger ones, they are nourishing and easy to digest, and suitable for people of any complexion; they are hot and moist in the first degree; their season is from March through almost all of August.

Carebo of Marseilles was the first to eat them, and he always found them appetizing.

---

118 The classically decadent way to eat ortolans in recent times is to drown them in Armagnac and then eat them in one bite, bones and all, though today the bird is protected in many countries.

The best way to cook these birds is to roast them, wrapped in caul or paper, or in grape leaves, or unwrapped, and then to serve them hot with a crust on top, made with bread crumbs, salt, and pepper.

In other dishes, they will not be as perfect; if necessary, they can be prepared and served in all the ways and dishes as I mentioned for quail; they need a lot of spices and good condiments, in order to be pleasing to the palate.

Of the lark, here in Naples called cocciarda, its quality and cooking.

To be good, larks should not be too fat, but middling, and they will be nourishing; they strengthen weakened stomachs; they are temperate in all degrees; their season is October through February; hunters in the country near Rome catch many of them.

The first to eat larks was Salvio Nardi of Florence, who liked to cook them in many dishes.

The best way to cook larks is to roast them with sage leaves, larded.

They can also garnish pies and tarts.

You can cook them in a lard broth with salami slices, aromatic herbs, suitable spices, and other noble ingredients.

You can use them in pies with other small birds as garnishes, and apt ingredients.

You can stew them, or fry them, and serve them in various marinades, and thus they can also serve as garnishes for various dishes. If fried, they can be mixed with other fried things; if roasting them, you can layer them with sage and lard them, and garnish various dishes.

Of the small sparrow, its quality and cooking.

The best sparrows are those that have just left the nest; they are not as good and perfect as other birds, and thus should be eaten rarely and in small quantity; they are not common on the tables of great people; they are hot in the first degree and moist in the second, and since they have excess heat, they stimulate to coition; their season is summer and part of fall.

The first to eat small sparrows was Frontone Scheltrio from Germany, who prepared them in an appetizing way, and enjoyed this dish very much.

You can use them in stews or pies, served hot, with sweet spices, because they are naturally hot, and thus should not be served with strong spices, which would increase their heat; this food is harmful to those who suffer from a fever.

You can cook them in a lard broth, with the usual ingredients and few spices.

You can boil them, covered with greens or pasta, with cooked salami slices. You can spit-roast them, sprinkled with bread crumbs and salt.

If you have many of them, you can use them in various dishes, following the same approach as you did with quail, warblers, and similar small birds.

Of the Cyprus and Crete warbler, its quality and cooking.

These birds are imported from Cyprus and Crete to Italy in earthenware vases, and are placed in a marinade of good white vinegar and strong spices; thus they will be exquisite, and will stimulate the appetite of those who suffer from a weak one; they are cold and dry in the second and third degree; they are eaten at any time of the year; they are as healthy when eaten in small quantity as they are harmful if eaten in abundance.

The first to eat these warblers was Asdrubale Cornaro of Crete, who liked cooking them in various dishes and enjoyed this food very much.

For any dish in which you wish to use these birds, you should first soak them in fresh water, and then cook them with other ingredients.

After soaking them in water, and then parboiling them for a bit in water, you can sauté them in a pan and use them for various sauces and dishes, with various vegetables, such as peas and similar ones, with thin slices of salami, aromatic herbs, apt spices, and other suitable ingredients; serve them hot with the usual garnishes.

You can cook them on the grill, with malmsey wine, and serve them hot with a mostacciolo sauce on top, or another condiment as you prefer.

You can dredge them in flour and fry them, serve them hot with lemon juice on top, and other suitable condiments.

They can serve as garnishes for various dishes, pies, and also for various stuffings.

I thought it good to discuss many birds, domestic and wild, and the various ways in which they can be served, in various dishes, with various ingredients and condiments, so that all those expert in this profession, and even those not yet experienced, may know the best ways to prepare these, to their own honour, in good order and without confusion, and with good rules of stewardship. I must warn that all birds must receive their proper condiment, and that birds caught in mountains or woods are always better, tastier, and more helpful to human health than those caught in waters or swamps, which by and large are difficult to digest and unhealthy. The season for all birds is from June through December. Both large and small birds will be more nourishing when they are fat, and the young are better than the old. When figs ripen, every bird feeds from this delicate food, and grows fatter, especially warblers; birds can be used in pies, after cleaning them well; they can be spit-roasted, layered with fat strips and sage, and cooked on a strong fire; they can serve for composite dishes; they can be stewed with sage and aromatic herbs; they can be wrapped in dough and fried, and thus fried they can serve as garnishes for many dishes, and can also be given to the convalescent, because theirs is a temperate and tender meat; you must always cook them so as to preserve some moistness and avoid dryness; one can insert fat strips, or lard them with cured back fat, and they can serve to decorate many dishes; keep in mind that birds must be fresh, and voided of their innards, neat and cleaned, and when used for composite dishes one must also remove their heads and feet. They can also be fried, mixed with other fried things, and wrapped in dough strips, after spit-roasting them; this will suffice in terms of knowledge of this sort of birds.

TREATISE V: *Of boiled meat and its quality.*

Boiled meat is usually easy and light to digest. It must be neither too fat nor too lean, but rather moderate. It will be best to eat boiled meat at lunch and roasted meat at dinner, since it is harder to digest boiled meat at night. When the meat boils one should carefully remove the foam and add a bit of pork, so that it will gain more flavour; a bit of salt as needed should be added before the water starts boiling, because salt always leaves a bit of dirt. Once cooked, place it on the plate with a few herbs, cleared of leaves but not chopped; garnish the plate with green sauce made with parsley or mustard, or a berry essence, or whatever else you like.

You can also garnish the plate with slices of ham, salami, or soppressata, which will add a good flavour, but keep in mind that boiled meat should not be prepared in the evening for the next morning, as this would ruin it, but rather early in the morning, so that it will be well cooked and ready by lunch time. Observe these rules with all boiled dishes, and dress them with aromatic herbs and the usual spices; many of these dishes will be healthy for the sick or convalescent.

Various examples of boiled meat dishes, suitable for any banquet.

Four boiled capons garnished with salami slices all around and aromatic herbs.[119]

Four pounds of boiled veal, with slices of ham mixed with tartelettes filled with green sauce.

A boiled veal head with ham and other salty things, covered with flowers and aromatic greens, mixed with the same salty things.

Six pounds of boiled local veal served with garlic sauce and mixed with cut sausages.

Three pounds of the tenderest boiled veal, thinly sliced, served hot, with pepper on top, and mixed with game meat, also sliced.

Four pounds of wether.

Two boiled kid thighs, mixed with slices of boiled soppressata, the thighs sprinkled with pepper and cinnamon, and with parsley on top.

Three pounds of boiled goat with sliced ham, sprinkled with pepper.

Four pounds of boiled deer meat, mixed with lemon slices and sour grapes in syrup, and sprinkled with cinnamon.

Five pounds of boiled young wild pig, served with a lemon sauce, sugar, and other ingredients.[120]

Six pounds of boiled wild pig, mixed with small birds, first stewed and halved, with lemon slices, sprinkled with pepper and cinnamon.

Five pounds of boiled domestic pig, mixed with halved sour oranges and with garlic sauce on top.

---

119 Each of these examples starts with *un piatto con/di*, a plate with/of, followed by the specific boiled meat.

120 In the earlier chapter on land animals Latini used *cinghiale* for boar, so here by *porco/porchetto selvatico* I assume he means a wild pig instead (he also follows this with domestic pig).

Two boiled hare hind thighs, served with an almond condiment, and with mostacciolo crumbs on top and lemon juice or verjuice.

Four boiled pheasants, sprinkled with good grated cheese, and covered with bunches of aromatic herbs, first cooked in a good broth.

Three boiled mountain roosters, with various condiments on top.

Six domestic chickens, mixed with slices of various salty things, and sprinkled with pepper.

Four wild chicken, boiled, served with grated cheese and pepper, mixed with small pastries stuffed with ham sauce.

Eight boiled cockerels, mixed with sour grapes in syrup and pomegranate seeds.

Ten boiled wild cockerels, with ham bits, mixed with the same ham and sprinkled with pepper.

Twelve boiled pigeons mixed with halved Abruzzo saveloy, and sprinkled with cinnamon.

Ten boiled wild pigeons, mixed with slices of soppressata and cardoon stems, first boiled, and dusted with pepper.

Eight boiled partridges, covered with fennel bunches and slices of salted things, first boiled in broth, dusted with cinnamon.

Ten boiled grey partridges, mixed with cut sausages, and sprinkled with grated cheese, pepper, and cinnamon.

Twelve boiled francolins, mixed with various sauces, and boiled slices of salted things.

Two boiled turkeys, covered with bunches of white fennel and bits of cardoons, first boiled in a good fat broth.

Four boiled turkey pullets, covered with a mostacciolo sauce and pine nuts soaked in a perfumed water.

Six boiled young peacocks, mixed with cut salami, with herbs on top.

Four boiled domestic ducks, covered with small gnocchi, sprinkled with grated cheese and cinnamon.

Two boiled domestic young geese, covered with various vegetables or pasta, with grated cheese, pepper, and cinnamon.

Two boiled wild young geese, mixed with ham and soppressata slices, cooked in wine, sprinkled with pepper.

Four boiled domestic geese covered with ravioli stuffed with ground meat, sprinkled with grated cheese and cinnamon.

Four boiled wild geese, mixed with ravioli made with ricotta, grated provola, and cinnamon on top.

Twenty boiled thrushes, mixed with salami slices and fennel bunches, first boiled in broth, with pepper on top.

Five boiled tongues, mixed with various salted things, and herbs on top and around them.

Four boiled chicken, which you may cover with cardoons or celery, as you wish.

Another dish: take four clean capons, boil them in water and salt, adding some salted things; once cooked, place them in a plate, cover them with white celery, cooked in capon broth, and garnish them with grated parmesan cheese, sausage slices (cut along their length), thin slices of ham, bits of pork belly, and slices of soppressata or salami, with the usual spices; it will be a nourishing and appetizing dish.

Another dish with two wild ducks: clean them and remove their heads and feet; boil them with a piece of beef; cover them with cardoons, or cardoon stems, and garnish them with sliced lemons; manage this dish as you do the one with the capons.

Another dish, of wild pigeons: clean them well, boil them in water and salt with a bit of pork and a bit of beef; once they are cooked, cover them in wild white fennel, first boiled in a good broth. Garnish with good grated cheese, slices of pork belly and soppressata, thin slices of sausage and ham, and the usual spices. Serve hot with a good broth, and it will be a tasty and nourishing dish.

TREATISE VI: *Of some noble stews [minestre]* *which may be served in any banquet;* *here we teach an easy manner of making them very good*[121]

Take two capons, cleaned, and boil them with enough salt, making sure they do not break apart in the boil; take them off the fire, and once they have cooled skin them; have ready a separate pot on embers, with inside it a fat capon broth, boil it, and add to it the capon skins, cut in thin long pieces like vermicelli, and boil them slowly; then add, little by little, ground cooked pine nuts, melon seed, with no sugar, the whole diluted in a thin broth, and weighing four ounces all together; mix continuously with a silver spoon, and you may add two fresh egg yolks, beaten with rosewater; then take a few slices of sponge cake, which you will use to garnish this stew, with sugar on top.[122]

Another stew.

Take the flesh of two capons; ground part of it very well in the mortar, and cut into small pieces the other part; add to the ground part an ounce and a half of fine sugar, mixing everything together, and dilute it in a thin broth; pass it through a sieve, and set it to boil in a pot on a low fire; as soon as it boils, add the cut part of the capon flesh, with a bit of rosewater, an ounce of smashed pistachios, diluted in citron flower water, two fresh egg yolks, a bit of fine cinnamon, and lemon juice; let it boil turning it with a spoon; when you see it close to being cooked, place it in the plates with sponge cake, cut in the same way as you did with the capon skins above, and sugar on top.

---

121 As discussed in the introduction, minestra is a complicated term to translate: Latini mostly (but not consistently) applies it to thick, often chunky, stew-like preparations with all sorts of ingredients, almost always cooked at least partly in "a good broth."

122 The cooked pine nuts are *pignoccata*, which probably refers to pine nuts "stirred with chopped candied peel into a sugar" and then boiled and creamed, Riley, *The Oxford Companion*, 405.

Another stew, of capon flesh.

Take the flesh of boiled capons and chop it finely with a knife. In a pot boil the fat broth of the same capons, and add the chopped meat and half a pound of cream tops, always stirring with a spoon, and let it boil slowly for a bit. Then add an ounce of crushed melon seed, a bit of lemon juice and sugar, and a bit of rosewater. Once it is cooked, add slices of sponge cake, and serve it hot with powdered sugar on top. If you want to give it colour, you may add, while it boils, a bit of ground mostaccioli and cinnamon.

Another stew, of pulled capon flesh.

Pull the capon flesh thinly; prepare the pot with diluted almond milk and thin capon broth, and boil it on embers; depending on the number of guests, add the pulled meat; while stirring with the spoon add cream tops, as needed, with a bit of lemon juice, a bit of fine sugar, and a bit of rosewater; make it boil very slowly, all the while adding sponge cake crumbs, until it thickens; remove it from the fire, and serve it hot over royal cookies, and sugar and cinnamon on top.

Another stew, of wether gigot.

Take a wether gigot, pound it well, and put it on the spit; when it will be half-roasted, without moistening it, run a knife across it and collect the juice in a dripping pan until it is fully cooked. Remove it from the spit, mince the meat finely, and place it in the dripping pan to fry, adding enough cream tops to cover the meat, a bit of mostacciolo crumbs, beaten fresh eggs, with a bit of rosewater; boil it slowly until it thickens; serve it hot, with sugar and cinnamon on top.

Another stew, of grey partridge flesh.

If you want to fill three bowls, take four grey partridges, spit-roast them, without larding them, and grease them with lard; collect their juice; when they are cooked, halve them; divide their meat into two parts, one of which you will pound minutely in the mortar, adding three ounces of cooked pine nuts, an ounce of melon seeds, and half an ounce of mostacciolo crumbs; mince the other part of the flesh finely with a knife, and put it in a pot to sauté with fat capon cured back fat, but not much of it, so that there be more meat than broth; then dilute with capon broth the meat you pounded in the mortar, and add it to the pot, on a slow fire, to boil it slowly; you may add a bit of ground peel of candied citron and two beaten egg yolks, with rosewater; use this to fill the bowls, with slices of sponge cake below and sugar and cinnamon on top.[123]

---

123 This entry is somewhat confusing: Latini once says skins where he clearly means meat; he also uses the term minestra at the start ("if you want to prepare three minestre"), but since this is a single preparation, I have assumed that here he is referring to serving dishes/bowls; the same occurs in a few later entries.

Another royal stew, of pigeons.

To fill two bowls, take two pigeons, boil them, debone them, and skin them; pound the meat finely in the mortar, with an ounce of mostacciolo and three ounces of cooked pine nuts; dilute everything in a broth, not too salty, and boil it slowly on embers in a separate pot, stirring it often with a spoon; add two beaten fresh eggs, a bit of rosewater, and two ounces of crushed pistachios; when it begins to thicken, serve it hot in the bowls, with sugar on top.

Another stew with cockscomb, wattles, and testicles of cockerel.

Take these things and boil them. Cut them in small pieces and boil them in a pot over a slow fire with a good broth; add four ounces of ground pistachios, diluted in almond milk, and an ounce of fine sugar, for each pound of the main ingredient. You may also add a bit of fresh butter, a bit of rosewater, four ounces of cream tops, and a bit of lemon juice; if you wish to give it colour add cinnamon and a bit of sponge cake crumbs. When it will have gained consistency, place it in the plates and serve it hot, with much sugar on top.

Another stew, of capon livers.

Brown the livers in broth; for two bowls, you will need at least six; but first clean them well of their bitter parts; set them to cool; take a pot with a capon broth, neither too fat nor too thin, and boil it on embers; add part of the livers, cut into small pieces; the others you will ground in the mortar with an ounce of mostacciolo and an ounce of marzipan paste, and half an ounce of grated candied citron; dilute everything in the broth in which you cooked the livers, and add it to the other pot; when it begins to boil add two fresh egg yolks, beaten with a bit of rosewater, and lemon juice, and let it boil for a little while; serve it hot, and it will be a most delicate stew, and quite nourishing.

Another stew, of pheasant.

Put the pheasant on the spit, greasing it with a bit of lard; keep the juice it produces as it roasts; when it will be almost cooked, remove it from the spit; cube part of its flesh with a knife, and ground the rest in the mortar with four ounces of melon seeds; you can give it a scent as you prefer, with mostacciolo crumbs, everything diluted in cream tops; pass everything through a sieve, making sure the cream is not too thick; then put it in a pot with broth, and add the cubed meat, with crushed pistachios and fresh egg yolks, fine sugar at your discretion, and minced marrow, with lemon juice; pour this on top of a few small cookies, with ground cinnamon; this stew will be good for those who suffer from a cold stomach, and who lack natural colour.

Another stew.

Take good broth, and add to it sliced lettuce stems; first boil them quickly in water, then add them to the broth; add small meatballs made with veal or capon meat, bits of pork belly and ham, chicken breast meat, asparagus tips, sliced truffles, St. George's and small mushrooms (first soaked in a good thin broth), with apt spices and aromatic herbs; you can also make this into a light broth, Roman-style, with two fresh egg yolks and bread slices, but not much, and lemon juice; serve it with cinnamon on top.

Another stew, of stuffed pigeons.

Take a stuffed pigeon, and add cardoon stems, first boiled, mixed with truffle slices, bits of chicken livers, bits of sweetbreads, also cooked in a good broth, with sliced bread underneath, and cleaned pistachios on top; serve it hot, with apt spices.

Another stew, of sweetbreads.

Take bits of sweetbreads, cooked in a good capon broth, and make a light broth for them, with fresh egg yolks, milk or cream tops, and sliced bread underneath, apt spices, and lemon juice on top.

Another stew, of ducklings.

Take clean ducklings and cook them well, with salted meat, and once they are cooked cover them with cardoon stems and bits, first boiled and then cooked in a good broth; you can also add bits of pork belly, cut quartered sausages, parmesan cheese, the usual spices; it will be a tasty dish.

Another stew, of annolini.[124]

Take annolini stuffed with kid sweetbreads, first sautéed in butter, add bone marrow, ground pine nuts, and a little frittata with eggs and butter, aromatic herbs, and few spices, and boil them in a fat broth, with a light broth of cream tops, with pine nut milk diluted with broth and fresh egg yolks, with grated parmesan cheese on top, and apt spices.

Another stew, of sweetbreads.

Sauté kid sweetbreads with truffles and St. George's mushrooms, and a light broth of fresh egg yolks, with slices of sponge cake underneath, and cinnamon on top.

Another stew, of kid intestines.

Take the intestines of a suckling kid and boil them in a good broth, first cleaning them well in hot water; you can thicken them with beaten fresh eggs and serve them with bread underneath or without, as you prefer; you can also make this without the eggs, with a good broth, aromatic herbs, and sliced bread underneath, adding also parmesan cheese, and it will be tasty.

Another stew.

Take artichokes stems, gooseberry or sour grapes, thin slices of pork belly, sweetbreads bits, aromatic herbs, and thicken everything together with a light broth of fresh eggs and lemon juice, and serve over bread slices; it will be tasty.

---

124 Annolini is a type of stuffed fresh pasta, today typically round in shape.

Another stew.

Take hard-boiled egg yolks, candied citron ground in the mortar, with a bit of sugar and cinnamon, as you prefer; make a fairly hard paste of it, with fresh egg yolks; form the paste into small sticks, as thick as a finger, and cut them into small bits, as large as chick-peas; use them like little gnocchi and cook them in a fat capon broth; when they start to swell they are cooked, and at that point you add bits of sweetbreads, first cooked, thin slices of provatura or mozzarella, mostacciolo crumbs, smashed green pistachios, a bit of rosewater, and serve it with grated provatura on top.

Another stew, so-called "of Paradise" or bain-marie, which may serve four people.

Take some good broth and beat four fresh eggs in it, then add cinnamon, and a bit of salt or salty broth. When the eggs are well beaten, mix them well in the broth and add a bit of sugar, if you wish to make it sweet. Put the preparation in a well-covered clean pot, with a weight on top, and set it to boil at bain-marie in a tin or copper boiler. Let the stew boil until it is well thickened; serve it hot with cinnamon and sugar on top, but not over bread.[125]

Another stew, of thrushes.

Take the clean thrushes, cut their heads, up to the neck, and the feet; cook them in a good broth, and cover them with fennels, cooked in the same broth, and add bits of pork belly, thin slices of ham, bits of saveloy, apt spices, and cheese as you prefer.

Another stew, of small gnocchi.

Take hard-boiled egg yolks, grind them in the mortar with mostacciolo crumbs, a bit of sponge cake crumbs, marzipan paste, and sugar, and a bit of rosewater or another per-fume, as you like. Combine these ingredients into a paste with raw egg yolks, and spread into little sticks. Cut these in the shape of gnocchi, and cook them in a good capon broth, but first bring the broth to a boil: when it boils throw the gnocchi in, together with bone marrow and beaten raw egg yolks, and [serve] with sugar and cinnamon on top.

Another stew.

Take Genoa pumpkins; put water in a copper boiler on the fire and when it boils add the pumpkins, sliced or pulled as you prefer; boil them a short while and when you like, provided they are not fully cooked, move them to a basin with cold water and leave them there for at least a quarter of an hour; then remove them and squeeze them well; in advance prepare a good broth, and now add bone marrow, bits of pork belly, thin slices of ham, Genoa mushrooms, first desalinated and cooked; then add parmesan cheese, both inside to boil with the rest and then on top, and it will be tasty.

---

125 Latini uses several terms for kitchen utensils and containers: *pignatta* is generally a pan or pot (for which he also uses *tegame* and *vaso*, respectively); here he also mentions a choice between a *stagnara* (from the word for tin, *stagno*) and a *polzonetto* (elsewhere also *polsonetto*), which indicates a vessel with a concave bottom, usually of copper (I will use boiler for the latter).

Another stew, of boiled pigeons.

This you prepare with slices of white bread, soaked in a good capon broth, and covered with peas, artichoke stems, sliced truffles, thin slices of cardoons, bits of sweetbreads moistened with good broth, and this way you can also make for it a thin broth in the Roman style or any other way, as you wish.

Another stew, of Bibb lettuce, in the Neapolitan style.[126]

Take a piece of beef, a piece of pork belly, ham, andouille, a piece of soppressata, a piece of Giugliano fillet, and a bit of smashed cured back fat, and when it is all close to being cooked, add the lettuce, well cleaned; boil and cook it well with all those ingredients, the usual aromatic herbs and apt spices, and a bit of saffron; then let it sit on a low fire; you can use it for several dishes, as you wish.

Another stew, Roman-style.

Take all the ingredients above, and then cabbages, with their leaves removed, and boil them in water, bringing them to a boil two or three times; then remove them; many place them then in cold water, but I disapprove of this, because they lose too much flavour; if anyone should wish to, it is enough to boil them quickly and then remove them and let them sit, with the usual spices, cooked in a good broth.

Another stew, made another way.

Take a rotolo of meat, or three pounds if you prefer, depending on the number of diners to serve; boil it, and add a bit of ham, a piece of pork belly, a piece of beaten cured back fat, and it will be better if you have other salted things, all in the right proportion; then add a couple of endive or escarole heads, a couple of kohlrabi, two leaves of Bibb lettuce, a whole onion, and boil everything together with a piece of cheese, adding the usual spices and aromatic herbs, which you add without first heating them; this will be very tasty.

Another stew, made another way.

Take two pounds of meat, clean it, and boil it, then add some smashed cured back fat, a piece of ham, a bit of salted meat; when it has all boiled for three or four hours with apt spices, and when the time of eating if near, add broccoli, which need only a short cooking because of their tenderness; you can then remove the meat from the pot, to prepare the plates, as you prefer.[127]

---

126 The lettuce is *foglia cappuccia*, which I believe is closest to Bibb. Latini here uses *annoglia*, or andouille, a spiced pork sausage.

127 *Broccoli* in Naples today usually refers to rapini (a leaf vegetable); what is called broccoli in the United States today is called *broccoli di Bari* or *cavoli broccoli*; Latini's mention of their tenderness suggests that he here means rapini, but it is hard to know for sure.

Another stew, with leaf vegetables, in the Neapolitan style.

Even though I mention this also among the composite dishes, I think it appropriate to insert this dish among the stews, since it is exquisite and popular.

Take a chicken and set it to boil with beef; do this when the beef is already more than half cooked, so that the chicken remains solid. Add salted boiled pork tongue; salted meat which first you keep in water; soppressata; a piece of fillet; a piece of pork belly; bone marrow; andouilles; a bit of beaten cured back fat, with salt as needed. When all these things are cooked, you will set the broth aside in a pot. Slice all the meats, including the chicken (instead of which you could also use a capon), keeping each thing separate. Add to the broth one third of these sliced meats. Take cabbages, pumpkins, and onions, and fill them with a stuffing you will prepare thus: pounded veal, egg yolks, crustless bread soaked in broth, raisins, pine nuts if available, and sour grapes. Use this stuffing for all the vegetables I mentioned, with the usual spices and aromatic herbs; you may also add lettuce or escarole, also stuffed. You can place the remaining meat in an orderly fashion in a pan or pot, surrounding it with thin slices of beef flank, slices of boiled cow udder, sausages sliced in half and skinned, thin slices of parmesan cheese, boiled Genoa mushrooms, first desalinated and boiled, and bone marrow; make sure the broth is good. This stew will taste good, and will be apt for any gathering, as everybody will like it, if you follow these directions; many times I have had these stews brought to the table in their cooking pot, because that way they look and taste better, and then you can fill the plates [at the table].[128]

Another stew with leaf vegetables, in the Spanish style.

Take three pounds of beef, a capon, and sufficient chickpeas, and put them on the fire at the same time as you boil the beef, then add all sorts of salted things, in the right proportions; add also cabbage, turnips, onions, two whole garlic heads, with saffron, apt spices, and aromatic herbs; when it is all well cooked, prepare the dishes, still hot; but first they need to rest.

Another rice stew, in the Spanish style.

Take the rice, well cleaned and washed with hot water, then dried in the sun or at the fire. Once it is fully dry, sauté it in a pan with a bit of crushed cured back fat; then add broth in the same pan and bring it to a good boil, but without letting it become too mushy. Once the broth has reduced, to the point that the rice is cooked, add the usual spices, two whole garlic heads, and saffron, and place the pan in the oven at moderate heat. Serve it hot and dry, without broth; often one can add to this, before putting it in the oven, wild ducklings or other wild animals, first spit-roasted, then added to the rice in the oven, and served all together at the table.[129]

---

128 Soups and stews were usually served in large plates, sometimes with a pastry crust to prevent spilling: tureens only became popular in the eighteenth century.

129 The "Spanish" style is given here by the rice, garlic, and saffron, which produce a sort of paella.

Another rice stew.

Wash it as above, so that it is clean; then boil it in good broth with parmesan cheese; when it is cooked, you can prepare the plates; serve them with parmesan on top, and crushed pepper.

You can also add beaten egg yolks to the rice, first grinding it, and it will be tasty.

Another stew, of cardoons.

Take the clean cardoons, removing the outer side; boil them for a bit and put them in cold water, and squeeze into them a bit of sour orange juice, so they do not turn black; remove them from the water and put them in a small pot with a bit of pounded cured back fat; sauté them well with apt spices, adding a good broth, and continue to boil them until the perfect point; then you can add bits of sweetbreads and chicken livers; thicken it with egg yolks and lemon juice; you can also not thicken it, if you prefer; it will be tasty.

Another stew, of celery.

Take the celery and boil it in water; after they are well boiled, let them cool, making sure you do not overcook them; then boil them in a good broth with bits of sausages and pork belly, and serve them with parmesan cheese on top and crushed pepper; you can use them to cover wild ducklings, thrushes, or quail, and they will be very good in cold weather.

Another stew, of chicory.

Boil the chicory well, and put it in cold water; then cook it in a good broth; you can give this to the convalescent or those with a fever, as it is a healthy stew.

Another stew, of lettuce.

Remove the outer leaves, and boil the rest; then remove it and drain it, and finish cooking it in a good broth, thickening it with egg yolks and lemon juice, and it will be very good.

Another stew, of lettuce stems.

Take and clean the stems and cut them in thin round slices; boil them and cook them in a good broth, with cockscombs and bits of livers, with a little thickening broth; it will be very good, with cinnamon on top and thin slices of bread underneath.

Another stew, of parsley roots.

Clean them well, scraping away the impurities, and cut them into pieces; boil them in a good wether broth with apt spices and aromatic herbs, and sliced bread underneath.

Another stew, of borage.

Take the borage and clean it well; boil it briefly and do not put it in cold water; then cook it in a good broth; you can thicken it with egg yolks; it will be a healthy stew.

Another stew, of onion.

Take some clean onions and boil them in a good broth; add a bit of ham and saffron, with apt spices; it will be a healthy stew which stimulates the appetite.

Another stew of stuffed onions.

Take pounded veal or chicken, as you prefer, and add crustless bread soaked in broth, eggs, cheese, pine nuts, raisins, aromatic herbs, and the usual spices; stuff the onions, in proportion to the plates you wish to prepare; then make some small meatballs, as large as buttons, and boil them in a good broth, with a bit of saffron for colouring; make sure to first boil the onions a bit, and remove as much from the interior of the onions as needed to stuff them; once cooked, serve them with cheese on top.

Another stew, of wild fennel.

Take the fennels, clean them, and remove more than half the leaves; boil them in a good broth, adding a bit of salted meat; with this stew you can cover boiled wild pigeons, wild doves, thrushes, with salted things inside; it will be most exquisite.

Another stew, of tender peas.

Cook them for the appropriate time in a good broth with bits of pork belly and aromatic herbs; you can thicken it with eggs and lemon juice, or you can skip this, as you wish.

Another stew, the *millefanti*.

Make bread crumbs from white bread. Combine these with fresh egg yolks and apt spices, to make a paste. Using your palms, split the paste into small bits, the size of wheat grains. Cook them in a good broth and serve them with cheese and spices on top.[130]

Another stew, of bread crumbs.

Grate the bread and boil it in a pot, then add spices and beaten egg yolks.

Another stew, of small Sicilian maccheroni.

Cook the maccheroni in a good broth and serve them with cheese on top and a bit of bone marrow in the broth; they will be very good.

Another stew, of lasagne.

You must cook them in a good broth, with cheese on top, and other suitable ingredients.

Another stew, of cooked bread.

Cook it with a good broth, capon flesh, parmesan cheese, and suitable spices.

---

130 This is an old preparation coming from Arabic cooking (it resembles couscous); Scappi offered two recipes for it. It still appeared in nineteenth-century Italian cookbooks; the name came from *mille infanti*, literally "a thousand children."

Another stew, of hops.

Clean them, arrange them in bunches, and boil them in broth with the usual condiments; this dish is very healthy and refreshing.

Another stew, of eggs.

Take as many eggs as you deem necessary for the number of guests; beat them and put them in a pot with the usual apt ingredients; add good ricotta and grated cheese; it will be an exquisite dish, with aromatic herbs and spices.

Another stew.

Take any roasted meat, and it will be good also if it is boiled; grind it finely, then boil it in a good broth, with sliced bread underneath, and two egg yolks, or more or fewer, with apt spices, and sufficient salt.

Another stew, of small veal meatballs.

You prepare this stew with sliced bread underneath, and sour grapes, cockscombs, chicken testicles, aromatic herbs, and apt spices.

Another stew, of pumpkins.

In winter, you clean the pumpkins and cut them into pieces, then boil them, and as soon as they boil, you pound them in the mortar; then pass them through a sieve, and boil them in a good broth, adding eggs, cheese, and apt spices; it is a tasty dish.

Another stew, of artichokes.

Take the artichokes, remove the outer leaves, and clean their stems; quarter them and place them immediately in cold water, lest they turn black; add asparagus tips, first boiled quickly in water; cook everything in a good broth, adding thin slices of truffles, St. George's mushrooms, and small mushrooms, bits of chicken livers, bits of bone marrow, with bread slices underneath, and with aromatic herbs and apt spices.

Another stew, of rice flour.

Take this flour, well ground, and pass it through a sieve; boil it in a good broth, and if you like you may add egg yolks; add diced bits of bread, first toasted, with salt in proportion.

Another stew, of mountain emmer wheat.

Wash the wheat well in hot water, then dry it and boil it in a good broth; this dish will be most helpful to human bodies, with cheese on top and apt spices.

Another stew, of melon.

Take the melon, when in season, and clean it, cut it into bits, and boil it in a good broth, breaking it with the spoon; then add egg yolks, apt spices, and cheese, as you like.

Another stew, of gooseberry.

Take the gooseberry, when in season, and clean it well; boil it in broth, whichever you prefer; this dish is a bit sour; beat eggs in it, with aromatic herbs, apt spices, and sliced bread underneath.

Another stew, of sour grapes.

Take the grapes, slice them, and remove the seeds; cook it in a good broth, with aromatic herbs, thickening it with beaten eggs, and with sliced bread underneath, and apt spices; this dish is popular in Rome, and healthy in hot weather, and refreshing.

Another stew, of turnips.

Take the round turnips and clean and peel them; slice them thinly and boil them in water, without letting them become too mushy, then put them in cold water; then cook them in a good beef broth, with salted things in it and apt spices, aromatic herbs, and cheese on top; it will be tasty.

Another stew, of radishes.

Take and quarter the radishes, boil them well, then put them in cold water, then cook them in a good broth, with salted meat in it, and cheese on top, and the usual spices and aromatic herbs.

Another stew, of woodcock intestines.[131]

Cook the intestines in a pot or pan; first sauté them with a bit of cured back fat; then add a good broth, and bits of capon livers, cockscombs, and chicken testicles, with herbs, sliced bread underneath, and lemon juice; ordinarily, everybody likes this dish.

Another stew, of a Roman-style thin broth.

Take two egg yolks per person, and beat them with lemon juice. Prepare a pot of good broth and when it boils add to it the eggs. Stir continuously, and you will see that they are cooked when they stick to the spoon. Once the stew has thickened, serve it over bread slices with cinnamon on top. This will be tasty and useful, and can be given to the convalescent and to those who suffer from lack of appetite. It is a nourishing dish, and will not harm anyone.[132]

Another stew, of tripe.

Take calf, lamb, or kid tripe, clean it, and cut it into pieces; cook it in a good broth, and thicken it with eggs, herbs, and apt spices; this will be good and tasty.

---

131 The intestines are of *arciere*: the term in Italian refers to archerfish, but Latini mentioned it earlier as a Naples synonym for woodcock (in Italian, *beccaccia*), and therefore I presume that here he means the bird.

132 This "thin" example shows the porous boundaries between minestra, zuppa, and broth; it is similar to *stracciatella*, an egg soup today typical of central Italy.

Another stew, of tripe.

After boiling the tripe, grind it finely, adding a bit of veal, crustless bread, fresh eggs, aromatic herbs, pine nuts, and raisins; make meatballs with this mixture, which you can cook in a good broth; serve them over sliced bread and with apt spices; it will be healthy and appetizing.

Another stew, of tripe.

Cut the tripe in thin strips, like vermicelli, and cook it in a good broth with bits of ham and pork belly, with sliced bread underneath and aromatic herbs; it will be healthy and agreeable.

Another stew, of ravioli.

Take ricotta, eggs, cheese, a bit of pork belly, marjoram, spices, salt; prepare a layer of dough, and stuff it with this mixture; cook it in a good broth, with cheese, sugar, and cinnamon, as you prefer; it will be agreeable and healthy.[133]

Another stew.

Take fine flour and mix it with pine nut milk; spread it into a thin layer of dough and cut it into long strips, like ribbons; cook them in a good capon broth, adding cream tops, egg whites, and lemon juice, with grated cheese on top, and it will be very appetizing.

Another stew.

Take pigeon flesh, cooked in good broth; add gooseberry or sour grapes, when in season; if out of season, use some other sour thing, with peas and aromatic herbs; make a thin broth with fresh egg yolks and lemon juice, and sliced bread underneath.

Another stew, of small veal chops.

Prepare the chops with peas, sliced lettuce stems, chicken livers and testicles, cockscombs, bits of ground soppressata, gooseberry, aromatic herbs, and with a thin broth of fresh eggs and lemon juice.

[Here the volume repeats almost word for word the two examples just mentioned.]

Another stew.

Take tender artichoke stems and add fresh peas, thin slices of ham, kid sweetbreads, first sautéed, aromatic herbs, and cook everything in a good broth; serve it with sliced bread underneath.

---

133 Latini here does not specify that the stuffed dough be made into ravioli; many of these descriptions employ shortcuts (for instance, in the frequent mention of sliced bread as if it were an ingredient in the preparation, as opposed to part of how the dish is to be served).

Another stew.

Take bits of artichokes, first boiled, and add gooseberry, thin slices of pork belly, bits of sweetbreads, spices, and aromatic herbs, cooked in a good broth; you can thicken the whole thing with a thin broth of fresh eggs and lemon juice, and sliced bread underneath.

Another stew.

Take six ounces of shelled pistachios; when they are fully clean soak them in rosewater, adding a bit of musk, and then grind them in the mortar with three ounces of candied citron peel. Pass this mixture through a sieve and then dissolve it in cream tops. Then boil it slowly on the embers with another bit of milk, a fresh egg, one ounce of fine powdered sugar, and add a little bit of ambergris or other perfume. Keep stirring and when it will have thickened so that you can tell it is cooked serve it with sugar and cinnamon on top. It will be a very appetizing and elegant dish.

Another stew, of thrushes.

Take the thrushes, spit-roasted until almost cooked; remove them from the spit and finish cooking them in a good broth with fennel and sausage; garnish them with lettuce, stuffed and cooked in a fat broth, with bits of diced ham, itself first cooked, with apt spices.

Another stew.

Take bits of sweetbreads, bits of capon breast and ham, eggs, cream tops, pigeon livers, ground salami or soppressata; cook everything together, with a thin broth made with lemon juice, apt spices, and aromatic herbs, thickening with egg yolks, with sliced bread underneath.[134]

Another stew.

Take bits of pigeon flesh, meatballs made with capon meat, a bit of marzipan paste, and candied pistachios, thicken it with a thin broth of fresh egg yolks, lemon juice, with sliced bread underneath and apt spices, making sure that this dish is prepared with a good broth, and careful cooking.

Another stew.

Take the breast of a partridge, first roasted and then cooked, with the juice of a wether thigh, and if it is not enough you can add a bit of good broth, adding also cow marrow, kid sweetbreads, first fried in good lard, thin slices of larded soppressata and of pork belly; stew everything together, with sliced bread underneath and apt spices.

Another stew, of white semolina.

For every pound of semolina, you will use half a pound of fine flour; spread this on a table, and mix it well with your palms, and sprinkle it with warm water, tinted with saf-

---

134 The text has the term *ninatte* which I take to be a typographical error for *natte* (cream tops).

fron; you can also sprinkle the flour on it various times until you use all of it; you then make the mixture into grains, as if it were millet; then press these grains through a colander onto another table, and leave them there for two hours; then grease your palms with a common oil and mix these grains lightly, so that they take on a lustre, like millet grains; cook them in the usual pot with small holes, well sealed all around, and put this pot in a larger pot with fat beef and slices of pork belly, two capons, quartered, so that the grains will cook through the smoke of the larger pot; once the meat is cooked, place it in silver plates and keep them warm; serve this dish with slices of cooked pork belly, cut into largish pieces, with hard-boiled egg yolks, and pour the broth on top.

Another stew, of cardoons.

Take thin slices of cardoons, slices of pork belly, bits of larded soppressata, sliced sausages or saveloy, veal meatballs, cauliflower tips, first boiled and then sautéed, and cook everything together in a good capon broth; serve this with fried chicken livers on top and sliced bread underneath, with the usual spices.

Another stew.

Take strips of pasta, shaped like half-lasagne, made with fine flour, mixed with pine nut milk and egg yolks, with a bit of butter, cream tops, and beaten egg yolks, with a good broth, and a bit of parmesan cheese on top.

Another stew.

Take bits of sweetbreads, cooked in a capon broth, first sautéed, and make a thin broth with egg yolks dissolved with lemon juice, lettuce stems cut into round shapes, but first boiled, add cream tops, with sliced bread underneath.

Another similar stew.

Take kid sweetbreads, meatballs of capon meat, and capon skin, and make them into tagliolini; cook them in broth, and add a thin broth of fresh egg yolks and cream tops, diluted with lemon juice, with cow marrow, and sliced bread underneath, with one or two eggs poached in milk; garnish the plate as you wish.

Another stew.

Take tender pigeons, cooked in a good broth, with a juice of veal or wether, the pigeon livers, aromatic herbs, apt spices, thin slices of ham, fried slices of sweetbreads, with a thin broth of fresh egg yolks and lemon juice, with slices of toasted bread underneath and pine nuts on top, first soaked in rosewater.

Another stew.

Take veal brains, first boiled in water, and cleaned of their membrane; cut them into bits and put them in a pan with a fat broth; add sour grapes or gooseberry, depending on the season, bits of pigeon livers, finely minced, fresh egg yolks diluted with lemon juice. When it has all cooked, and the stew has thickened, serve it with cinnamon on top, sliced bread underneath, and apt spices.

Another stew.

Take cockerel testicles, cooked in a meat juice, bits of truffles, first sautéed, bits of cocks-combs and chicken livers, asparagus tips, first boiled and then sautéed, with aromatic herbs, bits of pork belly, and toasted sliced bread underneath, with a thin broth made of fresh egg yolks, or something else, as you prefer.

Another stew, made another way.

Take bits of pigeons, deboned, lettuce stems, tender artichoke leaves, first boiled and then put in cold water, bits of chicken livers, bits of sweetbreads, first sautéed, bits of thinly sliced ham, sour grapes or gooseberry, depending on the season; boil everything in a good broth, aromatic herbs, apt spices, and slices of sponge cake underneath.

Another stew, made another way.

Take veal sweetbreads and lettuce stems, first boiled and then sautéed with a bit of butter; add veal meatballs as large as buttons; little bits of milk-filled udder, already cooked; cow marrow; thin slices of ham, first sautéed in a pan, with a thin broth made with fresh egg yolks, aromatic herbs, and verjuice, over bread slices, and with cinnamon on top.

Another stew, of *cappelletti* in Lombard style.[135]

Take a bit of fine flour and mix it with a bit of warm water; add two eggs to the dough and spread it into a layer as thin as possible; then cut it into long strips and cut them again into squares; then take the paste made for ravioli, and use it to stuff these square pieces of dough; once you have closed the outer dough, give them a hat shape; you can use these for stews and to cover boiled capons, cooked with a good broth, and they can be served with grated cheese and cinnamon on top.

Another stew, of small maccheroni from Cagliari.

This is a very good and noble stew: cook the small maccheroni in a good capon broth, with parmesan cheese on top; a large silver spoonful of it is enough for a large plate; you can serve it with cinnamon and cheese on top.

Another stew, of nunnery tagliolini.

Take a pound of fine flour and mix it with a bit of warm water and a bit of saffron, two egg yolks, and two whole eggs. Spread out the dough as thin as possible, and with a knife cut it into tagliolini, as nuns usually do. When they are well cut, let them rest for a while and then boil them in a good broth; be careful not to overcook them: as they are thin, they need only a short cooking. Immediately serve them, with grated cheese on top.[136]

---

135 As the text soon makes clear, cappelletti are a type of pasta, hat-shaped.

136 In the last sentence, Latini writes *si minestreranno* for "serve them," using the verb *minestrare* in the sense both of administering (distributing) and of making a "minestra" or dish/plate out of them. Many convents specialized in the production of sweets and various types of maccheroni.

Another stew, of cardoons.

Clean them and remove the leaves; cut the tips and wash them well, then cook them in water and put them in cold water; drain them and put them in a good broth with a bit of salted pork, aromatic herbs, and the usual spices; you can thicken this with eggs, if you wish.

Another stew.

Take a piece of veal, from a part fit to be cut into thin, small chops. Place it in a pot with a bit of pounded cured back fat and aromatic herbs. Sauté it, and add a good broth and when it is half-cooked add the fruits you prefer, such as apricots, peaches, clean pears, cut into bits, or similar fruits, also cut. It will be a good, appetizing stew.

Another stew of small ravioli, made with capon flesh.

Take the flesh of a capon and pound it with a knife. Then grind it finely together with three ounces of creamy fresh cheese, one ounce of marzipan paste, a few sprigs of marjoram, pepper, sugar, sponge cake crumbs, and cinnamon, as needed. Combine this mixture into a firm dough, with two fresh egg yolks, and then make it into small ravioli, as large as hazelnuts. Put a tin pot to boil on embers with a good capon broth, neither too rich nor too thin; dissolve in it some marzipan paste, and put the small ravioli to boil in it. Add a few fresh egg yolks dissolved with two ounces of cream tops. Once it is properly cooked, serve it with sugar on top.

Another stew.

Take the eyes and tongue from a kid head, cook them appropriately, and cut them into small pieces; slice the tongue. Add small cubes of ham and bits of sweetbreads, first quickly boiled. Cook everything in a good broth and when it is near cooked add aromatic herbs, sour grapes cut in two, and the usual spices. Once the stew is cooked, serve it over bread slices; it will be healthy and appetizing.

Another stew.

Take cockscombs and chicken testicles and livers, cut into pieces, and first sautéed, with the usual spices and aromatic herbs. Add a good broth, and boil everything for a while, adding gooseberry or sour grapes or another sour juice, depending on the season; when it has cooked, make a thin broth with egg yolks and lemon juice, and serve this dish over bread slices, and with cinnamon on top.

TREATISE VII: *Of various royal soups [zuppe].*

Make a soup with white bread, skin and breast of capon, ground salami, mixed with ham slices, dipped in egg and fried in butter; add some good capon broth, and cover with sliced roasted provatura or mozzarella; then put cream tops on top of the bread; serve it hot, with good parmesan cheese on top.

Another soup, of sponge cake.

Make three layers of the cake, greasing the plate well with butter; on the first layer put cooked pine nuts and pistachios, citron jam, and capon breast, finely ground, and first roasted; on the second layer put strained eggs; on the third, slices of blancmange, dipped in a good broth; cook over the fire, with good cheese on top.[137]

Another soup, made with turkey flesh.

Roast the turkey, larded, and then make the soup, with double-baked bread underneath, dipped in a good broth, and around it bits of fried sweetbreads and chicken livers; garnish the sides of the plate with layered slices of candied pumpkin, with good grated parmesan cheese on top.

Another soup, of cockerels.

Boil the cockerels, cut into pieces, arrange them with a layer of white bread and a layer of pieces of the same cockerels, boiled in a good broth, with apt spices and parmesan cheese on top; serve them hot.

Another soup, of tender pigeons.

Cook them like the cockerels, in a good capon or beef broth, with apt spices, and parmesan cheese on top.

Another soup, of tender pullets.

Stuff the pullets with pounded veal, egg yolks, aromatic herbs, pine nuts or whole pistachios, and bits of candied citron. Once they are cooked, cut them into pieces and surround them with slices of toasted bread, good cheese, slices of fresh mozzarella or provatura, minced soppressata, and apt spices. Keep in mind that it is necessary to let these sorts of soups boil on a slow fire, and to serve them hot, covered with a lid with a small opening, so that they can better stew with heat from below and above.

Another soup, in the Spanish style.

It is customary to make this one with slices of toasted bread; capon breast, first roasted and finely ground; bits of sweetbreads, first fried; bone marrow; and a layer of bread.

---

137 This is a rare case where Latini says *conserva* instead of *confettura* (I am rendering it as jam); the strained eggs are *ova filate* (at times also *misside*), which referred to dropping the eggs into hot sugar in a pan from a hole through the shell; this is the first mention of blancmange, an old preparation described fully in later examples.

All these things should be layered with each other. Then you will make a Roman-style thin broth, with egg yolks, lemon juice, and good broth. Pour this broth on the soup, cover it with a plate, and place it in the oven to settle, but make sure it does not dry out too much. When you serve it, freshen it with a bit of broth and garnish it with sugar and cinnamon on top.

Another soup, in the Roman style.

This one you make with skin and breast of capon, boiled, eyes and ears of kid, cooked marrow, ground soppressata, all with good capon broth; serve it with grated cheese, fresh butter, slices of toasted bread, and apt spices.

Another soup, in the Lombard style.

This one can be made with toasted white bread, good parmesan cheese or provola or *caciocavallo* [a hard cheese similar to aged provolone], with a good capon broth, with poached fresh eggs on top, with order and diligence, and garnishing it with the usual spices.

Another royal soup.

This one you make with biscuits made with white bread, such as Jesuits make, cooked in advance on embers; grease them well with butter, add bone marrow on top, well cooked, and dipped in a good capon broth; add also capon skin and breast, ground, and first boiled; mozzarella slices, first fried in butter; the juice squeezed from a roasted wether thigh; grated parmesan cheese; bits of fried sweetbreads in two layers; and cover it with slices of mozzarella and cream tops.[138]

Another soup.

This one you can make with slices of toasted bread, mixed with slices of boiled udder, bits of kid sweetbreads, first sautéed, ground ham and soppressata, bits of pork belly, cow marrow, grated provola or caciocavallo, mixing everything together with a good broth and apt spices; serve it hot and after boiling it well, in a plate with a lid on top, if needed.

Another soup.

You can make this one in layers with stuffed veal flank, sliced, quartered tender pigeons, bits of sweetbreads, first cooked and well stewed, apt spices, toasted bread, with a good capon broth between each layer, and salted things and cheese on top.

Another soup.

This one can be made with poached eggs cooked in milk, served with slices of sponge cake, cream tops, and lemon juice; everything in very good broth, with parmesan cheese, cinnamon, and pepper on top.

---

138 This description (which I find rather baffling) is a good example of what can make Latini's text challenging: the syntax and punctuation of the original are quite confusing (I assume, for instance, that the wether thigh is roasted, and thus produces its juice, but the word "roasted" is in fact separated from the wether thigh by a semicolon), and Latini writes on the assumption that his reader will understand the shortcuts in his preparation and various implied terms.

Another soup.

This one can be made with skin and breast of capon, boiled, with ground salami, slices of fresh provatura or mozzarella, bread fried in butter, in various layers, with cream tops over it, soaked in good broth, with cheese, pepper, and cinnamon; serve it hot and it will be tasty and healthy.

Another soup.

This one can be made with birds, first roasted, but not fully cooked, placed in a pan with apt spices and slices of cured back fat, with a glass of muscatel wine; when they are well stewed, take their breasts only and cut them into pieces, with slices of pork belly, ground soppressata, dipping the bread in a good broth, and garnishing with parmesan cheese or another cheese; it will be good to add on top the broth that was left over in the pan; it will be a very appetizing soup.[139]

Another soup, in the Spanish style.

Layer capon breasts, first roasted, sliced sweetbreads, first sautéed, marzipan paste; around this soup [place] fat roasted quails and serve it hot.

Another royal soup.

This one you can make with biscuits of white bread, cooked in advance and well basted with butter, with cooked marrow on top, dipped in a good capon broth, with capon breast and skin, boiled, ground salami, slices of provatura, first fried in butter, with the juice of a wether thigh, bits of fried sweetbreads, in two layers, covering the plate with slices of provola and cream tops spread over it; serve this soup hot, and it will be most appetizing.

Another royal soup.

This one you can make with slices of toasted bread, capon skin, boiled, slices of fresh provatura or mozzarella, fried in butter, eyes and ears of kid, boiled, bits of sweetbreads, fried in butter, ground salami, parmesan cheese, and apt spices; serve it hot, covered with cream tops, first browned in the oven.

Another imperial soup.

Take slices of sponge cake, in silver plates well greased with butter, and pour some good broth on them, layer them with capon breast, roasted and finely ground, place over this a layer of slices of provola or mozzarella fried in butter, with cinnamon on top, and pepper, and encrust it with green pistachios.

---

139 The birds are *folgore*, which I have not been able to identify; the context suggests that they are in fact birds.

Another soup.

This one you can make with pieces of boiled chicken, bits of sweetbreads, first sautéed, thin slices of cardoons, first boiled and cooked in a good broth, veal meatballs, cockscombs and chicken testicles, sautéed, apt spices, slices of ham and saveloy; pour on this soup a thin broth made with egg yolks and lemon juice, everything layered, and serve it hot.

Another royal soup.

Take slices of toasted white bread, dipped in a good broth and basted with butter, with cooked marrow spread on top, in several layers, with capon skin and breast, finely cut and first boiled and well cooked, thin slices of fresh provola or mozzarella, fried in butter after dredging them in mostacciolo crumbs and grated parmesan cheese, ground soppressata, sweetbreads fried in butter, covered with cream tops all around; serve it with cinnamon and pepper on top, quite hot.

Another soup.

Take slices of white bread, dipped in a good broth, and turkey breast, first roasted and then ground, with bits of fried sweetbreads, boiled pigeon breast meat, whole pistachios, grated parmesan cheese, slices of provola or mozzarella fried in butter and dipped in broth; serve the plate with slices of fresh provola, fried in butter.

Another soup.

Take two clean capons, boiled in milk, wrapped in thin slices of ham; serve them hot with slices of double-baked bread underneath, covered with milk; garnish the plate with sliced salami, and twelve fresh poached eggs, with sugar and cinnamon on top; make sure the soup is hot.

Another soup.

This one you can make with slices of toasted white bread, with ground roast veal, bits of sweetbreads, cooked and then sautéed, bits of pork belly, and fresh eggs, layering everything with sliced fresh provola or mozzarella, marrow, parmesan cheese, and apt spices, pouring a good broth over everything, and remembering that this soup needs to be cooked in advance, on a slow fire, in a covered dish.

Another soup, in the Maltese style.

Take as many capons as you wish and boil them with ham, cloves, and cinnamon. Once they are cooked, toast some bread slices and place them on the plate; take the capons, debone them, and mix them with the bread slices. Prepare lettuce, escarole, wild fennel, celery, and borage and boil them. Pound the capon breasts together with some veal, cheese, eggs, good spices, St. George's mushrooms and truffles; make a paste of this and use it to stuff the boiled greens. Place them to stew in a pot, together with ham, the broth of the same capons, or butter. Then prepare the soup by layering the stuffed greens, with a thin broth of egg yolks and lemon juice. Finely chop a bunch of wood sorrel and place it on top of this soup, and serve it hot.

TREATISE VIII: *Of various morsels, broths, and extracts, very nourishing, and beneficial also for the convalescent.*[140]

To make a delicate morsel.

Take one or more capons, as needed, neat and clean. Roast them on a spit with all dili-gence. Once cooked, remove the breasts, making sure they are not salty. Clean them of their skins, nerves, and bones, and grind them in a marble mortar. Prepare sugar for the cooking; once the sugar is perfectly cooked, add to it the ground flesh, with ground cinnamon, and pine nuts that must first have been soaked in rosewater. Boil everything together until it reduces; at that point, place it over a stone or plate and immediately make it into small morsels or mostaccioli, so that it not reduce further. This is an elegant and highly nourishing dish, for which you can also use pistachios instead of pine nuts.

To make another morsel, or nourishing medicine, healthy for the convalescent.

Cook a capon, as above, roasted; remove the breast, as above, and grind it in the mortar; keep *ambivera* ready, cooked, and put the capon meat in it, after grinding it well; once the preparation reduces, remove it from the fire, and make it into small pizze and keep them; they will be very nourishing, healthy for the convalescent; if they have lost their appetite, any little bit of this preparation that they will eat will sustain them for many hours; make sure not to use salt.[141]

To make another morsel, for married people with a weak stomach, in this way.

Take three lizards, three drams of cleaned pistachios, four drams of clean pine nuts, half a dram of nettle seed, one dram of *ascola* seed, one dram of basil seed, three grains each of musk and ambergris; cook the sugar in advance, and ground capon breast, as above; make mostaccioli, tasty to eat, which can be served on various occasions.[142]

---

140 These terms indicate dishes extracted from various ingredients through long processes: Scappi's translator uses "morsel" for *morselletto* (which in Latini are small pastry-like concentrated foods); *sorsico* indicates the result of putting the ingredients under a press to extract their juices; Latini calls the final recipe in this section a *consumato* (consumed, or, as we might say today, a *consommé*, which is usually, as also in this case, a clear soup).

141 I have not been able conclusively to identify ambivera; ambergris is what Latini calls *ambra*, and ambivera might be a mixture of ambergris and sugar; on a few occasions, Latini mentions ambivera as an alternative similar to powdered sugar or a perfumed vinegar. I am grateful to Ivan Day for discussions on this point.

142 In this bizarre concoction, the lizards are *stinchi marini*, which are mentioned in a few early modern pharmaceutical and zoological texts as a type of lizard, typical of the Levant, stimulating to coition, and capable of increasing the quantity and quality of semen – which might explain why this preparation is fit for "married people with a weak stomach"! Most of the ingredients here are rather peculiar, even for Latini; I have not been able to identify ascola. A dram is about one-sixteenth of a modern ounce (or about 1.8 grams).

To make another morsel, very nourishing.

Take a pound of clarified sugar, well drained, when it boils and is cooked enough to mix it with other ingredients add pigeon breast, spit-roasted and well ground in the mortar, keeping in mind that one pound of sugar will go with a single breast.

Add two ounces of clean pistachios, two ounces of pine nuts, two ounces of pitted dates, twenty cockerel testicles, pepper, cinnamon, and cloves as you wish; grind everything together and make it into small morsels or mostaccioli, which will be tasty to eat, and highly nourishing.

Another very nourishing liqueur.

Take twelve sparrows, six quail, and forty cockerel testicles. Roast everything, but until less than fully cooked. Grind everything together, adding ten whole grains of pepper, one whole clove, and two grains of musk. Place everything in a flask of malmsey wine for twenty hours, adding one pound of fine ground sugar. Afterwards, take the whole mixture, add wine, and distill it at bain-marie. Once it is distilled, store it. You can give a good spoonful of this in the morning or the evening to whoever may need it, making sure they take it without other food. It will be very nourishing, and will give strength and vigour.

If you want to make it without any cooking, distilling it simply at bain-marie, as above, it will be even more nourishing and will give greater vigour.[143]

To make very nourishing and very delicate broths.

Take a small piece of our local veal, weighing one pound, with four chicken wings, and a breast or half a breast of chicken, depending on the number of guests, a bit of ham, neither too fat nor too lean (unless you need this preparation for a sick person), salt as needed, three or four bits of cinnamon, cloves as you wish, a bit of nutmeg, two herb roots, well cleaned, and a bit of saffron, according to your taste; put everything in a pot without water, to boil, for three or four hours, closing it with a lid, sealed all around, watching that no vapours come out, and without ever touching it; once it is cooked, you can use this broth, which will be most perfect, and you can also give it to the convalescent, and to all those who suffer from a weak stomach; you can thicken it, if you wish, with egg yolks and lemon juice.

Another juice, of wether thigh.

Take the wether thigh and spit-roast it; collect the juice that falls from it. Once it is more than half cooked, remove it from the spit, cut it into big pieces, and place it under a press. Press it, collect its juice, and add it to the juice you gathered during the roasting. Place it in a clear pot, let it cool off a bit, and diligently remove a white layer that the fat usually produces. Then place the pot on the fire and continue cooking it, adding apt spices. You can use this by itself, with sugar and lemon juice, as you prefer. You can use this juice in many composite dishes, soups, maccheroni dishes, and small pies; it can be given to the convalescent; and if you like you can thicken it with egg yolks and lemon juice.

---

143 Latini calls this preparation a *liquore*, which in Italian today does not require the presence of alcohol (it can be any flavourful beverage).

Another very nourishing juice.

Take four pounds of beef and spit-roast it, but not to full cooking; collect the falling juice; when the meat is perfectly cooked, cut it into two or three pieces and place it under the press to extract its juice, making it drop onto a plate; then let it cool off, and remove the surface fat; cook the juice for a little while, with apt spices, sugar, and lemon juice, as you wish; if you like, you can thicken it with egg yolks, in the Roman style; you can use this in composite dishes; it is very beneficial to those who suffer from low strength or a weak stomach.

To make a very nourishing and good broth.

Take half a capon, a piece of beef, well boiled, as much as you need given the number of guests, a couple of wild doves, the wings of various chicken, a piece of Giugliano fillet, a piece of ham, half a soppressata, a bit of cured back fat, one head of garlic or more if you prefer, aromatic herbs, the usual spices, four chickpeas or something else, as you prefer; note that when someone takes this broth, one needs to blow on the bowl or plate to remove the fat that surrounds it, because that could cause nausea, and would be unappealing.

To prepare a ground dish of veal.

Take veal flesh, in the needed quantity for the number of guests, and spit-roast it; once it is cooked, take the whitest part and cut into bits; grind it in the mortar and dilute it in a thin broth from veal or another meat; pass it through a sieve, and for each pound of meat you can add three ounces of sugar; finish cooking it over embers, on a slow fire, or over a boiling water pot.

To prepare another ground dish, of capon flesh.

Take the breast meat, removing all skin, and boil it without salt, to half cooking, removing also the nerves; then grind it in the mortar and add crustless bread, first toasted and soaked in a thin broth, in a pan, in order to diminish the smell of the meat and so that it causes less nausea to the convalescent; add sugar, as you prefer, dilute it in a thin broth, and pass it through a sieve; heat it in warm ashes, or above a boiling pot, stirring it always with a silver spoon; if you do not want to use bread, you can use half an ounce of melon seed, or ambrosine almonds, and, for every breast, two abundant ounces of fine sugar, and four or five clean almonds; to remove the smell of the meat, you can add a bit of marjoram to the broth, wrapped in a small rag, and so it will be better; make sure the breast is roasted lightly over a slow fire, which we entrust to the judgement and diligence of the person turning the spit.

To make a veal consommé.

Take three pounds of lean veal and pound it finely. Place it in a pan, keeping it always tender, with a bit of chicken broth, and heat it from below and above. When it is well cooked, put it in a cloth and extract its juice. You can put the juice back on the fire with the usual spices and with it you can make various thin broths as you prefer, in the Roman style, with fresh egg yolks. You can use the meat at your pleasure to make various stews. Both the stew and the consommé will be very nourishing and tasty.

TREATISE IX: *Of roasts, and how to make them very good.*

All roasts must be cooked slowly and well seasoned; as soon as they have cooked prop-erly, they must be taken out of the fire and brought immediately to the table, with their apt garnishes, since these are the best dishes that give quality to any banquet, as long as they are cooked to the right point. Rightly do Spanish lords prefer these to all other dishes, and they eat these first, since they are rich in substance. The French eat roasts finely larded and slightly undercooked. The English roast on the spit and as the cooking progresses they cut the roast and serve it. In Malta, at the court of the Grand Master, they eat roasts finely larded, with different types of larding, and the roasts are very tasty and of good appearance. Roasts from large animals are hard to digest; whoever wishes to eat good roasts must choose the meat of more tender animals, and chicken are the best. Here in Naples we raise exquisite young pullets, which are eaten roasted, and they are entirely perfect, surrounded with ham slices and other apt garnishes. Messalino of Rome, a very learned man, was the inventor of roasts, and also of the idea of collecting their juice in a dripping pan placed underneath them while they cook. I devote a short essay to roasts not to teach how to make them, but to ease the work of beginners, so that when they prepare menus they may more easily organize them. I know full well that it is easy for anyone to make a roast.[144]

Roast of suckling or Sorrento veal.

Take the veal fillet with its kidney fat, put it on the spit and cook it diligently; surround it with pastries stuffed with blancmange, and slices of small lemons or sour oranges.

Another roast, of larks.

Roast them on the spit diligently, and for the correct time; mix them with sage and gar-nish them with slices of bread dipped in egg, with halved small lemons or sour oranges, and with a little condiment of lemon juice on top.

Another roast, of twelve chicks.

Wrap the chicks in caul and spit-roast them on a low fire, diligently; once they are cooked, mix them with puff pastries, and sliced small lemons or sour oranges.

Another roast, of ortolans.

This bird comes from the kingdom of Cyprus; in its proper time, it is very fat, and many are caught; remove their feathers and preserve them in the best flour; you can keep them in boxes, or also in clay pots; one can find them easily in Venice, Rome, Florence, and the

---

144 Latini offers here an intriguing survey of national approaches to what was a fundamental and cosmopolitan type of dish, which, as he notes, any cook would be quite familiar with. Roasting took time and was probably the most common method of preparing meat in elite kitchens. The court of the Grand Master of the Knights of Malta was famously brilliant and international. Larding consists of inserting strips of fat into a piece of meat, using a specially designed needle, to insure inner moistness.

Romagna. Spit-roast them, mixing them with meat rolls made with veal liver, with their proper ingredients, and garnish them with sliced small lemons and sour oranges.

Another roast, of wrapped cockerels.

Cook them on a moderate fire; once cooked, serve them with a little baked custard made with marzipan paste, filled with *lazzarole* in syrup.[145]

Another roast, of quails.

Cook them on a low fire, larded and mixed with bits of sweetbreads; serve them with slices of toasted bread, with a bastard sauce on top, over slices of bread dipped in egg, and small lemons and sour oranges around them.

Another roast, of pheasants.

Usually they are cooked wrapped in paper, with the usual ingredients, over a moderate fire; then remove the paper and serve them with beignets, sprinkled on top with a royal condiment.[146]

Another roast, of partridges.

Cook them over a moderate fire, and serve them with sauce, as described in its place; garnish the sides of the plate as you wish.

Another roast, of hare.

Cook it over a fairly strong fire, well larded and dressed, and serve it with a vinegary royal sauce, made with rosemary flowers; adorn the plate with roasted fat little birds.

Another roast, of pheasants.

Spit-roast them wrapped in paper, with the necessary ingredients; once cooked, serve them with wings, tails, and necks made of marzipan paste, shaped to look natural.

Another roast, of lamb testicles.

Take a dozen testicles, or more if you prefer. Clean them well, remove their outer skin, and place them on a spit. Cook them on a low fire, always turning the spit slowly until they are half cooked. Baste them with melted butter until they are fully cooked. Garnish

---

145 The custard here is *tartaretta*, which usually indicates a crustless tart or the filling for a tart or pie, usually baked, see Scappi, *Opera*, 476. Lazzarole are an unusual (and today rare) fruit similar to a large cherry or a very small apple; John Ray praised their "pleasant acid taste," *Travels Through the Low-Countries, Germany, Italy, and France* (London: J. Walthoe, 1738; first ed. 1673), 348; Pierluigi Ridolfi, *Rinascimento a tavola: La cucina e il banchetto nelle corti italiane* (Rome: Donzelli, 2015), claims that they are the fruit of the dog rose (235). The cockerels are presumably wrapped in paper or caul.

146 By beignets I am translating Latini's *paste di siringa*, literally pastries made by passing the dough through a pastry bag.

them with sliced ham cooked in a pot or on the grill, with a bit of vinegar; serve them also with slices of small lemons around them, and with salt and crushed pepper.

Another roast, of quartered kid.

Roast the kid quarters on a strong fire, basting them with good olive oil while they turn on the spit, so that they will be more tender and delicate; once cooked, garnish them with a sauce made with a bit of wine, a bit of broth without fat, a ground chili pepper, one garlic clove, a bit of oil and salt, all as you like, with the usual spices, and sour orange juice.

Another roast, of tripe.

Take the tripe and clean it; once it is cooked, wrap it in the caul of a pig or another animal, as one does with livers; mix it with bay leaves; while it cooks, baste it with a bit of fat; mix it with chicken livers, also wrapped in caul, and serve it with small lemons and sour oranges, and the right amount of salt.

Another roast, of birds [folgore].

Clean them well, and remove their innards; wash them in fresh water, and cut their heads and feet; then spit-roast them, turning them until they are almost cooked; then remove them from the spit and put them in a pan or pot with a bit of white wine and a bit of broth, and apt spices; finish the cooking this way, with embers under the pan, or even better in the oven; serve them with halved sour oranges and small lemons; this is however not a dish for gentlemen, but for common people.

Another roast, of small birds.

At times one finds in the kitchen various sorts of small birds; these should be cleaned carefully, without removing their innards, and then roasted on a thin spit, or on little skewers made for this purpose; mix them with bits of cured back fat and sage leaves; if you do not have enough to fill a plate, you may add whole chicken livers and saveloy or sausages, with lemon juice and halved sour oranges.

Another roast, of veal haunch.

Remove the inner meat diligently and pound it finely, adding a bit of cured back fat, pitted sour cherries, candied citron, raisins, pine nuts, marrow, and the usual spices, with a bit of garlic as you prefer. Stuff the haunch, finely larding it, place around it small lemon slices, with on top bread slices soaked in melted ham fat, with little bits of ham on top. It will be a noble and tasty roast.

Another roast, of woodcocks.

This bird, if caught in mountains or woods, is very good; one can roast it without gutting it, because its innards are exquisite; when it is well cooked, with its usual spices, you can baste it with a good broth and lemon or sour orange juice; garnish it with toasted bread crostini.

Another roast, of pork livers.

Take pork livers and cut them into small pieces, adding a bit of fennel flower; wrap them in caul, mixed with bay leaves, and on the spit mix them with sausages or saveloy, and thrushes or other birds; garnish the plate with halved sour oranges.

Another roast, of pork fillet.

Once roasted, you can slice the pork fillet thinly and mix it with roasted small birds, garnishing the plate with halved sour oranges; it is a noble and lordly roast.

Another roast, of wether gigot.

Cook it after larding it finely with cloves, cinnamon bits, and peeled garlic cloves; cook it on a low fire; serve it hot or cold, as you prefer, covered with sauce.

Another roast, of ewe lamb gigot.

Cook it on low fire with its ingredients, and garnish it as I wrote above of the wether gigot.

Another roast, of cockerels.

Stuff them with livers cut into pieces, sour grapes, and aromatic herbs, bits of ham, and proper spices; sauté them in a small pan or pot with a bit of pounded cured back fat; garnish them with fried beignets and slices of small lemons.

Another roast, of pigeons.

Stuff them with bits of ham, bits of sweetbreads, pitted sour cherries, pine nuts, raisins, sliced truffles, aromatic herbs, and apt spices; sauté them as above, and garnish the plate with pomegranate seeds and lemon slices.

Another roast, of turkey.

Clean it well and stuff it with bits of its own liver, small birds, ham slices, pitted olives, bits of candied citron, slices of *appie* apples, raisins and pine nuts, bits of pork belly, dried sour cherries, aromatic herbs, and apt spices; sauté in a pan and garnish with a proper sauce, small pastries filled with blancmange, and slices of small lemons. This will be a most noble roast, worthy of the table of any lord; be sure to hang the turkey in the cold seasons.[147]

Another roast, of capons.

Stuff them with the same stuffing as I wrote for turkey, and the roast will be quite perfect.

---

147 *Mele appie* (or at times *alappie*) are a variety of apples typical of the Naples region; *The Annals of Horticulture* (London: Cox, 1848), 188 and 554, calls this Vesuvius Pippin Apple, and describes them as small, oblong, and with a live red colour on at least half of their exterior. I will use the Italian name.

Another roast, of pheasant chicks.

Spit-roast them wrapped in kid or pig caul, with a royal sauce on top, and garnish the plate with small pies made with ground chicken meat, mixed with sliced small lemons.

Another roast, of warblers.

Spit-roast them mixed with onion slices, first cooked on embers, and apt larding, on a strong fire.

Another roast, also of warblers.

Cook them inside the egg shells, with apt larding and sage leaves mixed with crustless bread.

Another roast, of Cyprus ortolans.

Spit-roast them on a low fire, mixed with sage and larding strips, and garnish the plate with sliced small lemons and sour oranges.

Another roast, of young swallows.

Spit-roast them on a low fire mixed with slices of cured back fat and crostini of fried bread; garnish the plate with halved sour oranges.

Another roast, of Spanish-style veal.

Take a piece of veal, as large as you need it, spit-roast it, mixed with roasted cockerels, pigeons, thrushes, and quail. This roast will be especially useful if the guests include foreigners. Garnish the dish with halved small lemons and sour oranges, and fried pastries.[148]

Another roast, of tender fat pigeons.

Clean them well; wrap them in paper with slices of cured back fat, and spit-roast them; serve them in a plate still in the paper, but unwrap them enough that one can see what they are; mix them with veal sweetbreads, also spit-roasted; garnish the plate with lemon slices and fried pastries, and it will be a noble roast.

Another roast, of turkey chicks.

Spit-roast them on a moderate fire; garnish with fried blancmange and mix with small pies made of ground veal with the usual spices and ingredients, lemon slices, and sugar; these can also be roasted wrapped in paper, with slices of cured back fat inside.

---

148 Latini's word for foreigners is *oltramontani*, literally those from beyond the mountains (the Alps); I am not sure why this dish would specifically suit their taste.

TREATISE X: *Of various fried dishes, to be cooked for various banquets.*

First fried dish.

Use veal sweetbreads; cut them into pieces, dredge them in good flour, first cleaned; fry them in good lard; garnish the plate with short crust pastries, lemon slices around, and salt, pepper, and lemon juice on top.

Another fried dish.

Slice lamb testicles along their long side, and dredge them in good flour; fry them in good lard, and garnish the plate with fried beignets, lemon slices, and salt, pepper, and lemon juice on top.

Another fried dish, of testicles, in another way.

Clean the testicles well, quarter them, and dredge them in good flour; fry them in good lard, and then prepare the plate; make a frittata with bits of ham inside and a bit of water, and cover the fried testicles with it; garnish the plate with lemon slices and pomegranate seeds.

Another fried dish, of kid tongues.

Boil them and then slice them, together with kid brains and eyes, bits of the liver of a suckling calf, sweetbreads, slices of boiled udder, thin slices of bread, first soaked for a bit and then dipped in egg and fried in good lard; add the proper salt on top, and lemon juice, and garnish the plate with sliced small lemons.

Another fried dish, of veal liver.

Slice it and soak it in milk, dredge it in good flour, and serve it with sweetbreads, bits of veal brains, first boiled and then dipped in egg, slices of ham, sautéed in a pan, and mixed with the fried things; garnish the plate with slices of small lemons, and various short crust pastries.

Another fried dish, of artichoke quarters.

First boil them and then dredge them in flour and fry them in good lard, together with asparagus tips, whole chicken livers, sliced lamb testicles, thin slices of udder, first boiled, and thin slices of bread dipped in milk and then egg. Serve with on top whatever sauce you prefer, and garnish the plate with small pies filled with ground veal.

Another fried dish, of veal head.

Boil the head, and let it cool; slice it and fry it in good lard, with its tongue and brains, also sliced, and a sauce on top made with vinegar, sugar, mostacciolo crumbs, and the usual spices.

Another fried dish, of sliced udder.

First boil it, then dredge it in flour, dip it in egg, fry it, and mix it with slices of veal liver, slices of bread first soaked and dipped in egg, asparagus, first boiled, dredged in flour and fried, and royal sauce on top.

Another fried dish, of bits of tender pigeons.

First boil them, then dredge them in flour and fry them, with several chicken livers, lamb brains and testicles, bits of sweetbreads, quartered artichoke, first boiled, and thin slices of ham sautéed in a pan; mix all these things, with a sauce on top made with olives, capers, bits of candied citron, pine nuts, raisins, verjuice, vinegar, sugar, and the usual spices; garnish the plate with Genoese-style pastries.

Another fried dish, of deboned kid heads.

Boil the kid heads. Then cut them in half, dredge them in flour and dip them in egg, and fry them. Mix them with sliced udder and veal tongue, both first boiled and dipped in egg, as above. Garnish the plate with marzipan paste or other puff pastries, mixed with halved sour oranges and sliced small lemons, and add ground pepper on top.

Another fried dish, of quartered cockerels.

First boil them, dredge them in flour, and fry them in good lard, mixed with veal brains, first boiled and dipped in egg, veal liver, whole chicken livers, quartered artichokes, first boiled, then dredged in flour and fried, cauliflower tips, first boiled, then dredged in flour and fried, the same with asparagus tips, and verjuice on top; if you do not have verjuice, use lemon juice.

Another fried dish, of chickens.

Take chicken blood, cockscombs, and livers, quartered artichokes, first boiled and then fried, sliced udder, sliced bread, first soaked in milk, and asparagus tips, first boiled; fry everything in a pan with good lard; after it is all well fried, put everything in a plate neatly, mixing it with various fried pastries and slices of small lemons, with salt and pepper on top.

Another fried dish, of kid heads, in another way.

Take the heads and cook them well in water; then halve them, making sure the brain does not fall out, and place them in a marinade with a bit of perfumed vinegar, oregano, crushed garlic, and ground chili pepper; stir them in the vinegar and in this marinade; then dredge them in flour and dip them in beaten eggs, and fry them in the pan with good lard; once they are cooked, prepare the dishes neatly; add on top a sauce made with pitted olives, capers, a bit of the same vinegar from the marinade, the usual spices, and sugar; it will be a tasty fried dish, and will be beneficial to those who have no appetite.

Another fried dish, of veal tongue, in another way.

Clean the tongue with hot water, then boil it, and once it is cooked, slice it thinly; let it cool and then put it in a marinade with vinegar, oregano, crushed garlic cloves, ground pepper or chili pepper, and salt; dredge the slices in flour, dip them in egg, and fry them in good lard; garnish the plate with various beignets; you can make this dish with all other tongues as well.

Another fried dish, of kid feet.

Clean them well, boil them in water and salt, but do not overcook them, since they are quite tender; after they are cooked, debone them, halve them, and put them in a good marinade.

Fried squid, also called sea sweetbreads.

Clean the squid well, dredge them in flour, and fry them in good lard. Once they are cooked serve them with lemon slices and salt on top. It will be a very tasty dish, and you can use it also on fat days.[149]

Another fried dish, of veal feet.

Clean them well and cook them in water and salt; let them cool and put them in a marinade with a bit of vinegar, oregano, crushed garlic cloves, the usual spices, and, if you wish to make them spicy, you may add ground chili pepper. Turn them well in the marinade; dredge them in flour, and serve them with beaten eggs [dip them in egg?]; prepare the plate with a royal or bastard sauce, as you wish.

Another fried dish.

You can prepare another fried dish with whole chicken livers, bits of cardoon, first boiled and dredged in flour, chicken blood, small birds, first marinated as I wrote of the veal feet, sliced veal liver, kid sweetbreads, bread slices, first soaked in water or a good broth and then dipped in egg, quartered artichokes when in season, first boiled, asparagus tips, also boiled, cauliflower tips; it will be a royal fried dish. Garnish the plate as you wish, with salt and pepper on top, and pomegranate seeds.

---

149 It is unexpected to find the squid here, but the lard (*strutto*) is rendered pork fat, which makes the dish unfit for lean days. Though one may today use vegetable oil for the frying, the dish is still very popular in Naples. The text says *gl'infrangerai* (literally, "you will break or crush them"), but I assume it is a slip for *gl'infarinerai* ("you will dredge them in flour"). The prior recipe is odd, in that Latini does not mention the actual frying, but that is possibly a shortcut in the text, or a slip.

TREATISE XI: *Of how to make pies of all sorts, with or without cover, in which we teach how much flour, sugar, and lard, and how many eggs, should be used.*

To make a pie for six people, take three pounds of meat; four ounces of cured back fat to lard the meat and to use for the stuffing; five ounces of ham or another salted meat; three pounds of fine flour to make the box; four ounces of lard or butter to knead the flour; three eggs, three ounces of sugar, and half an ounce of spices such as cloves, pepper, and cinnamon. Keep in mind however that, if the pie or impanata will be served cold, as part of the first table service, you can make it without sugar or eggs. In this case, you could instead use only two eggs to brown it. On the other hand, if you wish to make pies of short crust pastry, you can mix eight ounces of butter with two pounds of flour, and if you wish to use the pies to garnish the plates you may add three more ounces of sugar and six egg yolks, and this way the dough will be absolutely perfect.

And if you wish to make an English-style pie, for eight people, you can take two pounds of pounded meat for the stuffing, three ounces of cow or bone marrow, four ounces of ham or salami, also pounded, a couple of calf sweetbreads, or ten pairs if you use kid sweetbreads, two tender cut pigeons, eight fat small birds, four ounces of raisins and pine nuts, or sour grapes if they are in season, three ounces of candied citron. To all of this, you can add four pounds of flour to make the box, six ounces of butter to knead it, and eight ounces of sugar for the entire pie, eight eggs for the crust and the stuffing; two pounds of flour for the cover, and eight ounces of butter. Many ingredients may go into these pies, like pine nuts, pistachios, St. George's mushrooms, truffles, artichoke quarters, if in season; thus, I trust the judgement of those who will put them together.[150]

How to make small pies.

Take three ounces of fine flour, three ounces of any raw meat, one egg, three quarters of an ounce of sugar, one ounce of lard, half an ounce of marrow or fat, spices at your discretion, half an ounce of pistachios and pine nuts, three quarters of an ounce of ham or other salami; if you wish to add a little broth, for every six small pies you can use three eggs and lemon juice as needed. Thus you will be able to make pies of any sort, always employing your discretion, which governs all things. Although I have here marked all these things in detail, I did not do it to issue an edict for anyone, but rather to teach beginners about the quantities and qualities of the ingredients. If you use these rules, you will prepare very good dishes. Even though the ways of making pies are infinite, I offer here a compendium of the most frequent and modern styles of our times, as they are followed today in the kitchens of great lords; my desire is always to be brief in every treatise of this work, and so I trust each professional to increase or diminish the dosages and the ingredients, according to his opinions and the customs of his country, and also

---

150 Similar "English" pies appear in many Spanish and Italian cookbooks (e.g. in Martínez Montiño, *Arte*, 196–98). These pies usually had a hard *cassa* (box) with a cover, which was often not intended to be eaten.

depending on available resources. Cucullo of Granopoli invented pies and other pastries filled with ground meat and other apt ingredients, as he was very fond of eating them.[151]

Neapolitan-style pie.

Take flour, eggs, lard, and sugar; after making the box for the pie, put inside it these ingredients: the first layer should be of ground veal, first sautéed or browned, bits of pigeons, bone marrow, sweetbreads, chicken livers, sliced udder, first boiled, sausages cut lengthwise, truffles, pine nuts, soppressata, Genoa mushrooms, first sautéed, bits of ham, razor shells, sliced candied citron, slices of fresh provola, hard egg yolks, pounded veal chops; everything well sautéed; once you have covered the pie, bake it in the oven; once it is cooked, make a little broth for it, with egg yolks, lemon juice, or something else as you prefer; it will be a very tasty pie.

Little Spanish-style spicy pies.

Take capon meat and grind it finely, then sauté it in a pan, and then grind it again and dress it with the usual spices. Add pine nuts or something else as you prefer; thin slices of bone marrow; bits of finely cut soppressata; bits of marrow; small birds, cleaned and their heads removed; chicken livers; sweetbreads; sliced lamb testicles; bits of brains, first boiled; quartered artichokes; veal meatballs as large as a Spanish olive; sliced truffles; St. George's mushrooms, pine nuts, shelled pistachios, varied seafood; tender peas, first boiled and then sautéed; make a little broth for this with meat juice, fresh egg yolks, and lemon juice.

I must alert that all these things should be sautéed, and it would be better to sauté them separately. Once you have made the pies, make their covers, and cook them in the oven. Once cooked, add a little broth made with egg yolks and lemon juice, and put them back in the oven so that the little broth may thicken. Once they are ready, serve them hot, with a sugar glaze, or just plain sugar, on top.[152]

English-style pie.

Make a good crust with lard or butter; once you have built the box, stuff it with finely ground veal, first browned in a pan, then ground again; the usual spices; tender quartered pigeons, first boiled and then sautéed, veal chops, pounded with the back of the knife, thin slices of ham, bits of pork belly; cook it diligently, and serve it hot, with sugar on top.

---

151 Though we may feel that Latini failed in his desire to be brief, this passage sheds light on his intended audience and on the flexibility with which he envisioned that his readers would approach his materials. Discretion (in the sense of attention to context and circumstances) was one of the dominant concepts in many fields of Baroque culture, from ethics to politics, from art to cooking.

152 The pie cover is usually removable (or sometimes has a hole in it), so that a broth or juice may be added towards the end point of the cooking process; see also the Neapolitan pie below.

Royal pie, in the shape of a heart.

Take pieces of veal, each weighing half a pound, and lard them finely with thin strips; mix them with quartered tender cockerels, bits of veal sweetbreads, ham slices, chicken livers, bits of marrow, thin slices of pork belly, pine nuts, dried St. George's mushrooms, first soaked in a good wine and then sautéed.

Put everything in a pot, with apt spices, a bit of saffron, and the right amount of salt; turn everything together, so that it gain flavour from the spices; put everything in the stand pie, and give that the shape you prefer; bake it in the oven carefully, and serve it hot, with a sugar glaze on top.

Little pies with young grey partridges.

Take the birds and clean them, but do not remove their heads and feathers, wrap them carefully, or put the heads and feathers back after cooking them, retouch their beaks in gold and silver, and place a small mushroom in their mouths; for a banquet, prepare the stand pie as needed, and put inside it thin slices of cured back fat, thin slices of ham, bits of veal sweetbreads, bits of bone marrow, the usual spices, and pine nuts; serve them hot, one for each guest.

Barchiglie [boat-shaped pies].[153]

Take as much veal as needed for the guests, and grind it finely, then add apt spices, thin slices of marrow and pine nuts, and use it to fill the pies; prepare a little broth with egg yolks and lemon juice; cook the pies diligently in the oven and serve them hot with sugar on top.

Another pie, of cockerels, in arms.[154]

Take the cockerels, clean them, and remove their necks and feet; cut them into pieces or halve them, as you prefer, and mix them with slices of cured back fat, ham slices, sliced soppressata, veal chops pounded with the back of the knife, St. George's mushrooms or morels depending on the season, pine nuts, and the usual spices; sauté everything in a pan, and give it the shape you desire; once the pies are cooked, serve them with sugar on top, and a glaze as you wish.

Pie or impanata in the Turkish style, shaped like a pillow, with its bows or other touches as you prefer.

Make this pie with three layers, all made with the same dough; fill the first layer with these ingredients: slices of game meat, first marinated; slices of sausage, ham, and cured back fat; whole thrushes or other small birds; clean whole truffles, stuffed with things in syrup; pine nuts, raisins, and the usual spices. Fill the second layer with veal meat-

---

153 Today *barchiglia* refers to a cake, typical of Puglia, made with almonds, pear jam, and a chocolate glaze, but Latini clearly intends here the shape of the pies.

154 Here and in a few other cases Latini calls a dish *in/con arme*, which usually refers to coats of arms as part of the decoration, but often he does not then specify this in the description.

balls, made with the usual ingredients; slices of veal; bits of cardoons, first cooked and sautéed; artichoke quarters; thin slices of soppressata; marrow bits; thin slices of cured back fat; and the usual spices. Fill the third layer with thin slices of udder, first boiled; bits of veal sweetbreads; eyes and brains of kid, first boiled; kid tongue, cut into bits; tender peas, first heated; bits of pork belly; lemon juice, and the usual spices. Make an apt cover, and cook the pie to perfection. Then put a sugar glaze on top, and serve it hot, and keep in mind that this pie has three flavours, which the guests must taste when at the table the pies are cut and each takes his share.

Another pie or impanata, with arms.

Prepare the crust with the usual ingredients, in short crust pastry. Take veal chops, first pounded with the back of the knife, with two or three small larding strips for each chop; bits of tender pigeons, first boiled; bits of tender cockerels, first half-cooked; large bits of veal sweetbreads, thin slices of ham, soppressata, and udder, first boiled, whole chicken livers, dried or fresh St. George's mushrooms, depending on the season, first soaked in wine, pine nuts, razor shells, sliced truffles, the usual spices, a bit of saffron, lemon juice, and salt; stir everything in a pot, so that it mix with the spices; give it the shape you wish, cook it, and serve it with a sugar glaze on top.

Another pie, prepared in a silver dish.

Take a royal silver plate and put on it a layer of short crust pastry; raise its sides to the height of three or four fingers, and fill it with veal, ground and browned in a pot, then ground again; add bits of marrow, thinly sliced ham, bits of pork belly, bits of tender pigeons, bits of sweetbreads, quartered lamb testicles, quartered artichokes, first boiled and then sautéed, small birds, sliced truffles, pine nuts, and the usual spices; make the cover with flaky pastry, greasing it well with butter or lard; cook it in the oven in the same plate, then add a little broth made with egg yolks and lemon juice; put it back in the oven until the little broth thickens, and then serve it hot, with sugar on top.

Small pies, with one tender pigeon in each pie.

Prepare a layer of dough and form the box, and put in each a clean pigeon, with its little bones well crushed, and cut into two or three pieces, with the head and feet removed; add pigeon liver, thin slices of cured back fat, ham, and soppressata, bits of morels if in season, or other small mushrooms, lemon juice, pine nuts, and the usual spices; once they are cooked, put sugar on top, and you can give one pie to each guest.

Roman-style small pies.

Make a box with short crust pastry, and fill it with veal chops, well pounded and larded, ground meat, bits of marrow, finely ground cow fat, bits of sweetbreads, chicken livers, thin slices of cardoons, first boiled and sautéed, sliced pork salted jowl, sliced ham, hard egg yolks, sour grapes if in season, bits of candied citron, the usual spices, and lemon juice; once they are cooked, remove the lid and add a little broth of egg yolks and lemon juice; put them back in the oven, then serve them hot, with sugar on top.

Spanish-style *pichere* [small pies].[155]

Prepare the short crust pastry and form a small pie, of the height of a finger, and fill it with capon meat, well ground and browned in a pot; add bits of marrow, pine nuts, a little garlic condiment; make the cover of flaky pastry, greasing it well with butter or lard; once the pies are cooked, add a little broth made with egg yolks and lemon juice; serve them hot, with sugar on top; you can also use these pies as garnishes for other dishes, or as you wish.

Another pie or impanata.

Prepare the crust with the usual ingredients. Take good quails, remove their heads and feet, halve them, and put them in a pot, with thin slices of cured back fat, ham, soppressata, or salami, a bit of saffron, lemon juice, spices, and salt.

Stir everything so that the flavours mix; form the pie in whatever shape you prefer, greasing it well with butter or lard; bake it in the oven, and once it is cooked add a sugar glaze on top, and serve it hot or cold, as you prefer.

Another pie, of tender rabbits.

Clean the rabbits and remove their heads and feet; cut them into bits. Make the crust with the usual ingredients and add thin slices of cured pork fat and ham, a bit of saffron, lemon juice, pine nuts, spices, and salt. Form the pie in the shape of a rabbit, with its ears and head, and serve it hot, with a sugar glaze on top.

Other small pies, Spanish-style, in another way.

Make the crust and form the small pies, filling them with pounded and browned veal, ground capon breast, pigeon breast finely ground, sliced marrow, St. George's mushrooms, sliced truffles, pistachios, hard egg yolks finely ground, and the usual spices. Make the covers, greased well with butter or lard; cook them well, and once they are ready add a little broth made with egg yolks and lemon juice; serve them hot with sugar on top.

Another pie or impanata, in arms.

Prepare the short crust pastry and form the box, and fill it with bits of veal, bits of cockerels, sliced sausages and ham, thin slices of cured back fat, sliced soppressata, cardoon stems, first boiled and then sautéed, lettuce stems, also boiled and sautéed, sliced truffles, St. George's mushrooms, razor shells, if you have any, a bit of lemon juice, and the usual spices.

Stir everything together well, to amalgamate it, and form the pie in the shape of the sun; serve it hot with a sugar glaze on top.

---

155 I have not been able to identify this word, but it seems to indicate small pies.

Another pie or impanata, English-style, shaped like the imperial eagle.

Prepare short crust pastry, form the box, and fill it with Sorrento veal, ground and browned; when it is well flavoured, grind it again adding chicken livers, bits of sweetbreads and of tender pigeons, pigeon breasts, thin slices of ham, bits of marrow, small birds, thin slices of soppressata, sliced truffles, St. George's mushrooms, clams or wedge shells, razor shells if you have any, testicles and cockscombs of rooster, pine nuts, whole shelled pistachios, lemon juice, and the usual spices; grease it well on top with butter or lard, cook it well, and serve it hot with sugar on top.

Turkey pie or impanata.

Prepare the dough as with the other pies and make it into layers. Take the turkey, after hanging it well, and cut it into pieces, which will be better; if you prefer to use it whole, you need to crush its bones; fill it with thin slices of cured back fat, sliced ham, sliced veal, pounded with the back of the knife, thin slices of soppressata, cardoon stems, first boiled and then sautéed, chicken livers, pine nuts, the usual spices, and lemon juice.

Turn everything together to amalgamate it well, form the pie, in the shape you prefer, bake it well in the oven, and serve it hot, with a sugar glaze on top.

Small pies in the Mazarin style.[156]

Prepare short crust pastry as for the other pies; form the small pies, and fill them with pounded veal, bits of sweetbreads, first sautéed, bits of ham, finely cut and also sautéed, sliced truffles, chicken testicles, bits of chicken livers, first sautéed, bits of marrow, and pine nuts.

Make a cover for them, cook them well in the oven, and serve them hot with sugar on top.

Small pies of short crust pastry, Spanish-style.[157]

Form the pies diligently and fill them with capon meat, ground and browned, then ground again, as I wrote of other pies, and add the usual spices, a bit of garlic, bits of marrow; make covers of flaky pastry, greased well with butter or lard; cook them well and then add a little broth of egg yolks; put them back in the oven and when they are ready serve them hot, with sugar on top.

Pies made with short crust pastry, for "a lady's mouth" [bocca di dama].

Form the small pies as you wish, for instance shaped like boats, and fill them with roasted pigeon breasts, finely ground, a bit of butter, candied citron finely ground, marzipan paste, ground cinnamon, fresh egg yolks, perfumed water; mix everything together and use it to fill the small pies; cook them and serve them hot with sugar on top.

---

156 I am not sure what gives this recipe its "Mazarin" character, but the cardinal's name was used for several elegant and rich versions of various dishes. Today, dishes *à la mazarine* usually include rice, artichokes, and mushrooms.

157 These pies are shaped like *gubbelletti*, the meaning of which I have not been able to find (it's probably the same as *cuppelletti*, another word which occurs a few times which I have not identified, and which likely refers to a shape like little hats).

Other pies, of glory.[158]

Prepare short crust pastry and use it to make pies as you prefer, stuff them with blanc-mange made with capon meat and the other usual ingredients, adding egg yolks, sponge cake crumbs, and bits of ground candied pumpkin; bake them in the oven; once they are cooked, prepare long thin slices of candied citron or pumpkin, to cover the small pies; serve them hot with sugar on top; these pies can also be served without a cover.

Another pie, Hungarian-style.

You make this without dough, in a royal silver plate, with a large frittata on it, the same size as the plate. First grease the plate with butter or lard, and sprinkle sugar and cinnamon over the frittata, garnishing it with thin slices of candied citron and pumpkin. Take ground veal or chicken breasts and place them in a pan or pot to brown; once the meat has gained flavour, grind it again and add bits of marrow, of brain, of veal, first boiled and sautéed, bits of sautéed sweetbreads, pigeon breasts, a bit of ground beef fat, thin slices of pork belly or throat, thinly sliced ham, slices of truffles, St. George's mushrooms (first soaked and sautéed), four fresh egg yolks, grated parmesan cheese, pine nuts, green pistachios (first soaked in rosewater), warblers when in season or other fat little birds, ground boiled egg yolks, lemon juice, bits of fresh butter, and the usual spices.

Then, cover the plate with another frittata like the first one, well greased with butter, making sure this frittata covers the entire filling. Cook everything well in the oven and when it is ready add a shiny glaze, similar to marzipan, made with egg whites and sugar. Put it again in the oven and serve it hot, or with a sugar ambivera.

Other small pies, made with capon meat, first half-roasted, finely ground.

Prepare the small pies as you wish, and fill them with ground capon, bits of marrow, bits of sautéed sweetbreads, thin slices of cardoons, first boiled and sautéed, meatballs made with pounded veal and the usual ingredients (place three or four of these in each pie), bits of ham, ground hard egg yolks, sour grapes or gooseberries if in season, pine nuts, and the usual spices.

Bake everything in the oven and when it is cooked add a little broth made with egg yolks and lemon juice.

If you have house guests, you can make covers for these pies in lattice pattern, and retouched with gold and silver, with sugar on top.

Another pie with eight small grey partridges, shaped like a star with eight rays, and in each ray one of the partridges, with these ingredients.

Take the partridges, and clean them well, then place them in the pie with the following: thin slices of cured back fat and ham, truffles, and the usual spices. Make a shiny glaze like marzipan, and, if there are house guests, retouch it with gold and silver.

---

158 *Di gloria*, I believe, refers to pies suited for some religious holidays and celebrations.

Another pie.

Prepare a short crust pastry, and fill it, for six people, with three pigeons stuffed with apt ingredients, as I will discuss in its proper place; you can brown them in a pot, then halve them and place them in the crust neatly, mixing them with thin slices of ham and garnishing them with thin slices of cured back fat; add bits of sweetbreads, first sautéed, eyes and tongue of kid, cut into pieces and sautéed, sliced truffles, sour grapes if in season, and if you have no sour grapes then a bit of lemon juice, bits of marrow, the usual spices; cook it well, and serve it hot, with sugar on top.

Other small pies.

Take capon meat, grind it finely, and use it to make small meatballs with fresh egg yolks, crustless white bread, first soaked in broth, pine nuts, bits of ground ham, a bit of pounded cured back fat, ground candied citron, grated parmesan cheese, aromatic herbs, spices, and salt; form the meatballs and wrap them in the skin of the capon, adding eyes, ears, and tongue of kid, first sautéed, ground veal, cow marrow, St. George's mushrooms, thin slices of ham, hard egg yolks, and the usual spices.

Form small pies as you wish, and fill them with this mixture; cook them well, then make a little broth with egg yolks and lemon juice; serve them without the cover; when they are brought to the table put on them a cover for them in lattice pattern, made with sugar paste, retouched in gold and silver; they are called the queen's small pies.

Other small pies, made in silver tondini, one per guest.

Prepare the short crust pastry, and fit a layer to each tondino, greasing it well with lard or butter, and fill it with veal, pounded and browned, and chicken livers and cockscombs, thinly sliced truffles and ham, ground hard egg yolks, pine nuts, fresh peas, if in season, first boiled and sautéed, tender quartered artichokes, sour grapes or gooseberries, and the usual spices; cover each pie with its layer, well greased with butter or lard, and cook them; serve them hot, with sugar on top; one tondino for each guest.

Another pie, of wild boar, in arms.

Take slices, weighing six ounces each, from the part that will be most convenient and lean of the boar, sauté them in a pot with slices of cured back fat, then add the usual spices, sliced ham, bits of soppressata, pine nuts, and lemon juice; give it the shape you wish, cook it well in the oven, and serve it hot or cold, as you wish, with a glaze if you wish.

Another pie with deboned turkey, stuffed with maccheroni.

Debone the turkey and stuff it with maccheroni that you have cooked in a good broth, making sure that they are not too soft; layer them with veal chops, first browned in a pot with the usual spices, but they should not be fully cooked; layer them also with pork chops, roasted on the grill, also not fully cooked; then add bits of sausage, cut lengthwise, parmesan cheese, grated provola, a little bit of juice from the roast, mixed together with the maccheroni, and a bit of pepper; form a crust and place the stuffed turkey inside it, and around the turkey slices of cured back fat, thin slices of ham, and the usual spices;

bake the pie carefully, and it will be very good; it is not an apt dish for a noble banquet, but only for an ordinary evening among friends.[159]

Another pie, of roe deer.

Take bits of roe deer thigh, weighing half a pound each, and stuff them with sliced cured back fat, thin slices of soppressata or other salami, raisins, pine nuts, bay leaves in layers, spices, and salt as needed; give the pie the shape of a roe deer thigh, or another if you prefer, and serve it hot; I believe it would be better cold; it will bring you honour in any gathering.

Genoa-style small pies.

Prepare short crust pastry with butter, sugar, and egg yolks; use it to make pastries and stuff them with marrow, ground candied pumpkin, and add fresh egg yolks, cinnamon, a bit of perfumed water; make it into small pies, and fry them in good butter or lard; you can use these as a dish, or as garnishes for other dishes, as you prefer, with on top sugar or ambivera; it will be a noble dish.

Another pie, of cow udder.

Take the udder and tie the nipples with string, so that no milk comes out, and boil it in water and salt, removing the foam, until it is cooked; then take it from the water and let it cool; then slice it and add cured back fat or a fat ham, veal chops, a bit of pepper, cinnamon, cloves, and nutmeg; prepare the dough in advance, as I said of the other pies, add slices of cured back fat and ham, cover the pie with another layer, and grease it well with lard; bake it well in the oven; when it is almost cooked, take it out, make a hole in the cover, and add a bit of meat juice or good broth, and lemon juice; once it is cooked, serve it hot.

Another Neapolitan pie, made another way, which you can use for eight people.

Take five pounds of flour, six ounces of lard to knead, five egg yolks, four ounces of sugar, and having amalgamated everything together make the dough, which you will divide in two parts, one for the layers and one for the box. Place in the box two pounds of pounded meat, first browned in a pan; three ounces of ox marrow cut into bits; four pigeons, cut, after boiling them and sautéing them in a pan, into eight parts; add then six ounces of soppressata, four ounces of sliced provola, four ounces of candied citron cut into pieces, two ounces of raisins and pine nuts, half a pound of tender peas if in season, with the usual spices. Fill the box and cover it with the dough layers and bake it in the oven; once it is cooked, uncover it and add a little broth made with four eggs, good broth, and lemon juice. Cover it again with the same cover, and put it back into the oven. Once it is ready, serve it with two ounces of sugar on top.

---

159 Today we may feel that this particular pie is indeed fit for a "noble banquet" but in Latini's times the prominence of maccheroni (which remained uncommon in elite dining) probably marked this dish as inappropriate for elegant company.

Another pie, of glory, in another way.

Take good flour, butter, fresh egg yolks, and sugar, as you think best, and make the dough, making sure it is well mixed; place it in boat-shaped moulds, or in others as you wish, and fill them with a mixture of blancmange, fresh egg yolks, sponge cake or Savoy cookies crumbs, ground candied citron, fine powdered cinnamon, and perfumed water; mix all these things well, and divide them into the moulds, and bake them; when they are cooked, sprinkle fine sugar on top; make sure not to over-fill them, because they tend to swell; you can also serve them with thin slices of candied pumpkin on top.[160]

TREATISE XII: *In which we teach the way to make composite dishes for all occasions that may arise, to instruct stewards and whoever delights in banquets, in how properly and promptly to arrange a table.*[161]

In order to prepare these dishes with order, the steward should make sure to have good broths, meat juices, and especially roasts ready, as well as everything else needed for the proper preparation of tables and the good seasoning of foods. Everything should be cooked separately, as appropriate, with spices and salt as needed, aromatic herbs when they are suited, and other necessary ingredients, such as pistachios, pine nuts, and other similar things, for the correct preparation of foods. From these, once they are cooked, one can with order compose dishes, with their soups and condiments, as suited. The steward should make sure that each food has its proper condiment and flavour, as this is very important to please diverse palates.[162] Those who neglect this necessity are blameworthy. In summer time, if banquets have to be arranged, the steward must take special care that poultry, sweetbreads, or other easily corruptible ingredients not be killed more than four or five hours before they must be cooked, so that such things not acquire a bad smell and become useless for the table. And if any of these things—veal, poultry, or other—were left over still raw on the day of the banquet, the steward or cook must store them in a cool place or use whatever expedient is necessary to ensure they keep until the next day. In cold seasons, large poultry in particular can be killed up to

---

160 Savoy cookies today are ladyfingers (in Italian called *savoiardi*), but I am not sure whether they were quite the same in Latini's time.

161 Composite dishes, as Latini's introduction makes clear, are dishes formed by putting together other preparations, already cooked and ready in themselves, in a sort of modular approach. Here, Latini uses even more shortcuts than usual, making the specifics of these preparations at times quite difficult to follow; he was, here in particular, primarily addressing experts who would have had a clear sense of his references and methods. It is somewhat odd that this section should appear in between chapters devoted to more specific, and simpler, preparations, but Latini says nothing of his reasons for this organization.

162 I am here using food for *vivanda* and dish for *piatto*; today the words would be nearly synonymous in Italian, but here Latini clearly intends vivande (which are themselves cooked) to come together to form composite piatti. Moreover, in Italian, piatto, like dish in English, means both a prepared food and a plate on which food is served.

three or four days ahead of the banquet, and it will be perfect. Remember that all composite dishes must be prepared in their proper time, and must not be prepared too early, because they might lose their flavour and would not offer pleasure to the palate; I have often seen in various kitchens dishes sit for many hours before the meal, and thus they were not much esteemed.

Crespino Falisco was the inventor of most composite dishes, as he served a long time as cook for the emperor Elagabalus; to honour a great banquet, he was the first to take peacocks from Samos, francolins from Phrygia, cranes from Melos, black kids, parrotfish from Seville, dates from Egypt, acorns from Iberia, which are the best ones, shells from Lucrino, pears from America, moray eels from Tartary, tuna and conchs from Lucrino, turnips from Norcia, Sicilian cheese, and this was practised in those times.[163]

A Roman-style dish.

Take eight pigeons, or more or less as you prefer, clean them well, and spit-roast them until they are half-cooked; then place them in a pan or pot to stew together with slices of cured back fat, a bit of ham, apt spices, lemon juice, chicken livers, and rolls made with veal liver; you may also add small birds, bits of ham, sausages, and other ingredients; you can make meatballs for this, with veal, bits of soppressata, slices of udder, boiled and then sautéed, with bits of veal sweetbreads, St. George's mushrooms, truffles, pine nuts, and shelled pistachios.

Once you have prepared the dish, with a thin soup underneath, with toasted bread and a bit of marrow, you can add juice of roasted wether, and pistachios on top; serve this dish with a big ribbon filled with things in syrup.

Another dish.

Make this with a veal head, cleaned, stuffed with veal flesh, fresh egg yolks, parmesan cheese, truffles, pine nuts, St. George's mushrooms, ground ham, veal brains, bits of pork belly, bits of candied citron, pitted sour cherries, cream tops as needed, bone marrow, lemon juice, aromatic herbs, and salt as needed.

Stew everything in a pot with good lard or butter, stirring often, on a low fire; when the mixture has cooked nicely, add a bit of malmsey wine and mostacciolo crumbs; once it is almost cooked, cover it with cream tops and put it in the oven; when it is ready, you can make a crustless tart for it, in the dish, with milk, eggs, sugar, cinnamon, and ground candied citron; it will be a good royal dish.

Another dish.

Make it with deboned turkey cockerels, stuffed with their own meat, eggs, cheese, ground peels of candied citron, cinnamon, pepper, bone marrow, turkey livers; cook everything in a pan with sliced cured back fat, small veal chops, bits of sweetbreads, thin slices of ham, quartered artichokes, first boiled, small birds with their heads removed,

---

163 Latini took this bizarre list almost word for word from the seventh book of Frugoli, *Pratica*. How he, or Frugoli, could think that Elagabalus' cook had used American pears baffles me, unless the word "America" here somehow refers to some other place.

pine nuts, sliced truffles, with a little sauce made with meat juice; garnish the plate with pears in syrup, encrust it with white aniseeds, and surround it with flaky pastries.

Another dish.

Take domestic ducks and stew them with slices of cured back fat, with a glass of malmsey wine, and other suitable ingredients; garnish the plate with whole garlic heads cooked in broth, bits of candied quince, German dough squeezed through a pastry bag and fried; garnish the sides of the plate with slices of lemons all around.

Another dish, called appetite-sharpener.

Take veal sweetbreads, spit-roasted, and put them in the middle of the plate, with royal sauce on top and around it veal livers mixed with chicken livers, cooked in a pan, divided into two parts, larded, and spit-roasted; surround them with halved lemons and leaves, with bands made of marzipan paste, and jellies of various colours.

Another dish, called the knight's dish.

This dish is made with hare, cut in pieces, spit-roasted and then sautéed in butter. Dress it in a pan with strong vinegar and mostacciolo crumbs, and sugar first boiled on a low flame. Then place it on a plate surrounded by pastries shaped like eaglets, filled with citron jam, sugar, and cinnamon; around the dish place spit-roasted warblers or ortolans and lemon slices.

Another dish, French-style.

Make meatballs with veal, ground candied citron, crushed pistachios, fresh eggs, grated parmesan cheese, and sponge cake crumbs; once they are cooked, garnish the plate with small pies in Mazarin style, filled with blancmange, egg yolks, candied citron, and wether juice.

Surround the meatballs with slices of bread dipped in egg and fried, with various figures.

Another dish, in the Astorga style.[164]

Take a piece of veal as large as you need for the guests, and half-cook it on the spit; finish cooking it in a pan with slices of cured back fat or butter and apt spices and aromatic herbs; cover the veal with bits of sweetbreads, ham, and pork belly, quartered artichokes if in season, peas, sliced truffles, St. George's mushrooms, and bits of cardoons; cook everything separately, arrange it well with apt spices, lemon juice, and other suitable ingredients; garnish the plate with fried German pastries, with sugar on top, mixed with lemon slices.

---

164 The marquis of Astorga was viceroy of Naples in 1672–1675, so the name of this dish probably refers to him.

Another dish, called the bride's dish.

Take deboned pigeons, stuff them with ground veal, chicken breast, egg yolks, pitted sour cherries, bits of candied citron, marrow, cream tops, a bit of veal kidney fat, shelled pistachios, pine nuts, a little gooseberry if in season (otherwise, use halved sour grapes). Once everything is cooked with its usual spices, arrange it nicely with the pigeon necks and heads set prettily on the plate; under it, a little soup with toasted white bread and on it a little sauce made with chicken livers, cooked on embers and then ground in the mortar and diluted in a good broth, and a bit of lemon juice, plus ground pine nuts, pistachios, and ground candied citron.

Boil this sauce in a pan on a low fire, and pour it over the pigeons, together with dry aromatic herbs and lemon juice; garnish the plate with small short crust pastries filled with small veal chops, small veal meatballs, chicken livers, pine nuts, and apt spices, surrounding it also with pomegranate seeds and slices of lemons or sour oranges.

Another dish, Savoy-style.

Roast a whole veal liver, wrapped in paper well greased with butter or lard, and inside it slices of cured back fat and ham, tied with a string; once it is cooked mix it with stewed small birds, with a royal sauce made with strong vinegar, sugar, and bits of cinnamon, whole cloves, a bit of citron or lemon peel, thinly sliced, to add a good smell, pine nuts, bits of candied citron, and other spices as needed.

Once the liver is cooked, add to it the sauce just described, which should be neither too sour nor too sweet, and garnish the plate with bread slices, dipped in egg and fried, bits of quinces in syrup, with cinnamon on top, and white confected aniseeds.

Another dish, English-style.

Take ground veal and use it to make meatloaf, shaped like a star, stuffed with fat brains, marrow, bits of sweetbreads, butter, pine nuts, ham slices, egg yolks, slices of candied citron, crustless bread soaked in a good broth, with pistachios on top; in between the rays of the meatloaf place a deboned stuffed pigeon, and cover it with a sauce of roasted pistachios, diluted with verjuice; serve it with a cover made of dough in lattice pattern.

Another dish, called the peasant's dish.

Make this with six tender pigeons, cooked in good cow broth; once they are cooked, place them in the plate and cover them with white wild fennels, cooked in good broth, sausages, bits of pork belly and ham, with a little soup underneath moistened with good broth, parmesan cheese, or anything else you like.

Another dish, Spanish-style.

Make this dish with rabbits, first roasted but not completely cooked; then you sauté them in a pan, cut into pieces, together with onions, apt spices, and pounded cured back fat, with a sauce on top made in Portuguese style, with capers and pitted olives; garnish the plate with ham slices.

Another dish, made with bread loaves filled with veal.

Grind the veal and make it into a mixture with cream tops, fresh egg yolks, St. George's mushrooms, truffles, pistachios, pine nuts, pitted sour cherries, gooseberries if in season, bits of veal sweetbreads, kid brains, aromatic herbs, grated parmesan cheese, or anything else you like; use this to stuff the bread loaves, and then soak them in a pot of milk for half an hour, so that everything is well soaked; then put the pot, well greased with butter or lard, in the oven to bake, with a bit of good broth, and when it is well cooked you can make for it a crustless tart with milk, eggs, sugar, cinnamon, and rosewater; sprinkle the sides of the plate with sugar and cinnamon.

Another dish, of royal round meatloaves.

Make them with veal, stuffed with sweetbreads, eyes and ears of kid, sautéed kid tongue, cow marrow, bits of butter or good lard, cubed slices of ham, aromatic herbs, and the usual spices.

After making a mixture of all these, form the meatloaves; boil them in a good broth with a bit of white wine, and serve them with carvings on top, all covered in fried bread, as one uses sides of fat, and garnish the sides of the dish with sliced lemons.

Another dish, with a deboned turkey.

Stuff it with small birds, thin slices of ham, truffles, St. George's mushrooms, turkey livers, candied citron, pounded veal, egg yolks both raw and cooked; after spit-roasting it, make a glaze for it with egg whites and sugar, and garnish the plate with asparagus, sliced lemons, and candied citron.

Another dish, of royal lard broth, made with flesh from a goat thigh.

Take the flesh off this thigh and sauté it with slices of fat ham, four bay leaves, for long enough that the meat take their scent, then remove them; stew everything in a pot or pan, with also muscatel wine, good broth, and apt spices; when it is almost cooked, take plums from Marseille cooked in wine and vinegar and ground in the mortar and mostaccioli diluted in the same broth; mix everything together and finish the cooking; serve it over cookies made with white bread, which first you put in the dripping pan, then soak in malmsey wine, and dredge in eggs fried in lard or butter; garnish the plate with small crustless tarts filled with things in syrup.

Another dish of lasagne.

Cook the lasagne in a good fat capon broth, with the skin and breast of the capon, boiling them well above and below, then layer them with slices of fresh provatura, fried in butter, and good grated parmesan cheese; serve them with a sugar cover on top, retouched in gold.

Another dish of English-style pies without dough.

Form pies in royal nefs or silver plates, covered with a large frittata of the same size as the nef. Dust the frittata with sugar and cinnamon, and slices of candied citron, then place on it a mixture of ground veal, brains, sweetbreads, marrow, ground cow fat, deboned pigeons, thin slices of pork belly, cubed ham, truffles, pine nuts, parmesan cheese, egg yolks, lemon juice, and the usual spices. Remember that this mixture must first be quickly browned in a pan with lemon juice; then cover it with another frittata. Once it is cooked, make a sugar glaze for it, like marzipan, with a gilded sugar crown.[165]

Another dish, an oglia in royal plates.

Make this with a turkey pullet, a partridge, eight thrushes, pork ears and snouts, fine sausages, a woodcock, everything boiled, turnips cut as one does with sides of fat, peas, white chickpeas, cardoons, fennel, shelled chestnuts, while truffles, sliced ham or soppressata, a bit of bread soaked in broth, pine nuts, the usual spices, and other noble ingredients, with in the middle a cabbage stuffed with saveloy, pounded veal, egg yolks, and grated cheese; garnish the plate with Genoa-style pastries all around, mixed with roasted fresh mozzarella or provola, and a crust made with mostacciolo crumbs.

Another dish, of grey partridges, thinly larded.

Spit-roast them until they are half-cooked, place them in a pan or pot with good broth, cauliflower, thin slices of ham, bits of artichokes, bits of sweetbreads, small birds of various kinds, small veal meatballs, pine nuts, and apt spices; once everything is cooked separately, arrange it neatly in the plate over sliced bread and lemon juice, and serve them hot.

Another dish, of deboned capon.

Stuff it with its own meat, with beaten eggs, grated cheese, candied citron, also grated, pine nuts, truffles, and apt spices; once it is cooked, in a good broth, garnish the plate with various boiled salted things, mixing them with stuffed lettuces, over sliced bread.

Another dish, of Capirottata.

Make it with capon flesh, mixed with slices of mozzarella or provola, cream tops, mostacciolo crumbs, marrow, quinces in syrup, egg yolks, and cream; boil everything in a fat broth, in a silver plate.[166]

Another dish, of roasted suckling piglets.[167]

Roast the piglet and put it in a plate with bands and other decorations made with lemons; cover it with fat spit-roasted small birds, or as you wish, mixing them with small pastries filled with cream tops, with sliced lemons and a sour orange in the middle.

---

165 The nef (*navicella*) was a decorative vessel, shaped like a ship (hence the name), which in the Middle Ages had served as salt cellar to the banquet's host (as well as an obvious status symbol), or as a container for spices; Latini seems to employ it as a serving plate.

166 This is a very old dish in a new and simpler version: capirottata (or *capirotada*) was an old Iberian dish, often used also in Italy: Scappi included several elaborate examples, with a variety of ingredients. Latini included also a richer version a few pages later. Today the term refers usually to a Mexican bread pudding.

167 *Porchetta* today is the name of a specific stuffed pork preparation, very popular in central Italy, but the context here, and the word suckling, suggest that Latini intends the young pig.

Another dish, of a piece of wild boar.

Cook it in a good lard broth, with pounded cured back fat, dried plums, a bit of white wine, a little onion, and the usual spices; once you have sautéed it, add raisins and pine nuts, a bit of good broth, and when it is near cooked add a bit of cooked must, sugar, mostacciolo crumbs, ground candied citron, verjuice or strong vinegar; make a sweet and sour sauce for it, and mix it with quinces in syrup; garnish the sides of the plate with stuffed roasted larks, first marinated a bit in a royal sauce.

Another dish, of veal head.

Cook it in milk, then surround it with stuffed kid heads decorated with cauliflower, truffles, and capon livers fried in good lard or butter; encrust the plate with pistachios and in the middle, where the heads are, place a sculpture made from parmesan cheese depicting a butcher in the act and posture of skinning the heads.[168]

Another dish, of small cockerels.

Clean them well and stuff them between their flesh and skin with bits of sweetbreads, thin slices of ham, bits of brains, hard egg yolks, pitted sour cherries, bits of candied citron, a bit of lemon juice, spices, and other ingredients as needed; braise them, well greased with butter or lard; add a sauce made with candied sage flowers; place around the plate thrushes stewed in malmsey wine, with inside juniper seeds, marrow, plums, dried sour cherries, and spices.

Another dish, of veal back.

Take the veal back and stud it with cloves and cinnamon; half-cook it on the spit and then put it in a pan with slices of pork belly, roast juice, malmsey wine, and spices; mix this plate with meatballs of veal flesh, and sliced bread, dipped in egg and fried, and St. George's mushrooms, and other noble ingredients.

Another dish, of veal sweetbreads.

Cook them in a pan with sliced ham, truffles, boiled lettuce stems, slices of pork throat, St. George's mushrooms, chicken livers, aromatic herbs, and the usual spices; garnish the plate with sliced udder, first boiled, and lemon slices.

Another dish, of capirottata, made in royal silver plates.

Make this with capon flesh mixed with slices of sponge cake, grated cheese, sliced provola, mostacciolo crumbs, boiled in cream, sugar, and cinnamon as needed, and with ground candied citron; decorate it with the breast of turkey cockerel shaped like a lance, and garnish the sides of the plate with sliced candied quince and small pastries made of marzipan paste filled with candied things and blancmange; add also fried lamb testicles, with sliced lemons on top, and if you wish you can make a glaze for it as well.

---

168 This is an early, and somewhat gruesome, example in Latini of decorative sculptures made of edible materials; many more follow.

Another dish, of boar thigh, in another way.

Pound it well with a pestle and half-cook it in a pan, with cloves, cinnamon, and other noble ingredients; then stew it with good lard or cured back fat, minced onions, aromatic herbs, Marseille plums, sour cherries, slices of candied citron, mostacciolo crumbs, and the usual spices as needed. Make a nice sweet and sour sauce for it to please the palate. Garnish the plate with thrushes stewed in malmsey wine, surrounded by pears stuffed with things in syrup. Braise it in the oven, dust it with cinnamon, and decorate the sides of the plate with an arabesque made of thin dough drawn all around like a ribbon and stuffed with quince jelly.

Another dish, called royal soup, made with six tender pigeons or chicks.

Make a paste [of the pigeon meat], and stuff it with veal flesh, egg yolks, crustless bread, aromatic herbs, pine nuts, and other noble ingredients, with salt as needed; cook it in a pan with good broth; then braise it, cut into pieces; the soup you make with slices of sponge cake mixed with candied peaches, grated parmesan cheese, St. George's mushrooms, truffles, and capon livers; you must moisten everything with good broth and cream tops, squeeze lemon juice on top, and garnish the plate with fresh eggs poached in milk.

Another dish, of meatballs in Roman style.

Make the meatballs with ground veal, egg yolks, crustless white bread, soaked in broth, bits of candied citron, marrow, a bit of cured back fat, a bit of garlic, raisins, pine nuts, aromatic herbs, grated cheese, and the usual spices; cook everything in a good broth, over an apt little soup and sliced bread; on the plate, intersperse small veal chops, braised or cooked in a pan, with pounded cured back fat, or marinated in verjuice or strong vinegar, that should be cooked fairly dry, with only a bit of broth, and apt spices, and on top shelled pistachios, stewed small birds, their heads removed; garnish the sides of the plate with Genoa-style pastries.

Another dish, of veal head cut into pieces.

Stew it in a pan with a bit of lard, thin slices of ham, plums, dried sour cherries, or another type of fresh fruits, when in season, and the usual spices; when you have sautéed it well, add a bit of good broth, without wine, lest it become too sticky, and lemon juice; garnish the plate with veal tongue, first boiled and marinated, sliced, dredged in flour, and fried.

Another dish, of four pounds of veal.

Without washing it, put it in a pot, with slices of cured back fat, a bit of garlic, whole cloves, bits of cinnamon, and a bit of nutmeg; when it has stewed well, on a low fire, add half a glass of wine and a bit of lemon juice, but make sure not to boil it too much after you add the lemon, lest it become bitter; once it is cooked, place it in the plate with a cover of stewed small birds, bits of ham cooked in a pan, bits of sweetbreads, first sautéed, artichoke quarters, first boiled and fried, sliced truffles, cooking everything suitably, with all the appropriate little sauces; this will be a tasty dish, with pistachios and pine nuts on top; garnish it with fried beignets mixed with lemon slices.

Another dish, of pigeons.

Stuff the pigeons with pounded flesh of Sorrento veal, capon breast, egg yolks, pine nuts, truffles, St. George's mushrooms, marrow, and apt spices; cook them in a pan, and then cut them in half, dredge them in flour, and fry them in good lard; place them in the plate with a sauce made of mostacciolo crumbs, vinegar, sugar, cinnamon, and the usual spices, but make sure it does not thicken too much; on the plate, place also sliced udder, first boiled, then dipped in egg and fried; chicken livers cooked in a pan or pot with apt spices, thin slices of ham, first roasted, a little vinegar condiment, asparagus tips, first boiled, dredged in flour and fried, all mixed with lemon slices, and lemon juice on top.

Another dish, called pottage.

Make it with several chicken wings, first boiled in broth and then sautéed in a pan with a bit of minced onion, and a bit of pounded cured back fat; remove the heads, and stuff the necks of the chickens with pounded veal, fresh egg yolks, crustless bread, first soaked in broth, aromatic herbs, raisins, pine nuts, and the usual spices; tie the necks with string and cook them, together with the wings; with the leftover mixture make small meatballs, which you also cook with the wings and necks; when they are almost cooked, add unborn eggs and the usual spices; after everything is cooked, thicken it with a little broth of egg yolks and lemon juice; garnish the plate as you wish.[169]

Another dish, of deboned, stuffed pigeons.

Stuff them with the usual ingredients and sauté them in a pot with the usual spices, lard, and good broth; then cut them in half and braise them, mixed with veal sweetbreads wrapped in caul, apt spices, and salt as needed; grease the pot with butter or lard, and put meat juice inside; place them in the plate and add a little crustless tart which you can use to cover them; garnish the plate with lemon slices and short crust pastry.

Another dish, called the beard-sullier, made another way.

Take a pot and put in it cured back fat or lard, minced onions, and sauté them well; then add bits of tender pigeons, kid sweetbreads, tender peas, thin slices of ham, sliced pork throat, small mushrooms, artichoke quarters, first boiled, aromatic herbs, small lettuce stems, first boiled, and the usual spices; after everything is cooked, thicken it with egg yolks and lemon juice.

Another dish, of small heads of kid.

First boil them and then debone them and sauté them, adding bits of ham, sweetbreads, chicken livers, bits of hind quarter of kid, cardoon stems, first boiled, St. George's mush-

---

169 Unborn eggs (*nonnate*), now exceedingly rare, are the yolks found inside killed hens (and thus unlaid).

rooms and other small mushrooms, thin slices of truffles, asparagus tips, first boiled, aromatic herbs, and the usual spices; once everything is cooked, thicken it with egg yolks and lemon juice, and serve it hot, garnishing the sides of the plate with lemon slices and various pastries.

Another dish, of small cockerels.

Take the cockerels, clean them, remove the necks, and sauté them in a bit of cured back fat or lard, with cockerel livers, small mushrooms if in season, dried St. George's mushrooms, first soaked in good broth, thinly sliced truffles, artichoke quarters, cardoon stems, first boiled, small birds, cooked separately, pine nuts, lemon juice, aromatic herbs, the usual spices, and sliced bread in the plate; serve them hot, garnishing the plate with lemon slices and various flaky pastries.

A dish called casserole, made another way.

Take sweetbreads and sauté them in a pan or pot together with thin slices of ham and apt spices. Once they are cooked, add razor shells, wedge shells, and clams, after cleaning them of their sand. Put the seafood juice in the same pan and cook with the usual spices. In another small pan put cockscombs and chicken testicles and livers, all sautéed, small birds, thin slices of soppressata, the usual apt condiments, and lemon juice; prepare another small pot with veal chops pounded with the back of the knife, thin slices of pork throat, bits of kid tongue, and kid eyes, first boiled, and aromatic herbs. Once everything has cooked separately, take a silver plate and with good order compose these preparations in the same plate; all united they will form a noble and delicate dish, which you may garnish with Genoa-style pastries mixed with lemon slices.

Another royal dish, of wether thigh.

Spit-roast the thigh, but do not cook it fully, all studded with bits of cinnamon and cloves, then place it in a pan, adding white wine, roast juice, capon and pigeon breast, rabbit meat, lamb mammary glands or sweetbreads and testicles, everything cooked separately; garnish the plate with testicles, livers, and cockscombs of chicken, shelled pistachios, and a sauce inside, made with meat juice diluted with ground chicken livers and lemon juice.

Another casserole, made another way.

Make it with veal chops cooked in a pan, with pounded cured back fat, and well sautéed; prepare an apt sauce and place them on the plate with the following ingredients, cooked separately with broth as needed: bits of pigeons, sweetbreads, veal mammary glands, lamb testicles, bits of ham and pork belly, pigeon breast, truffles, St. George's mushrooms, asparagus tips, chicken livers, bits of udder, first boiled and fried, and seafood, with a pistachio sauce also with seafood and lemon juice; garnish the plate with [basket] pastries, and an apt cover on top.[170]

---

170 The pastries here are *pasta di canestrelle*, which I have not been able to identify—it appears

Another oglia dish.

This can be made in good broth, with the following ingredients: three pounds of beef, two pounds of wether back meat, two capons, Giugliano fillets, soppressata, and ham, bits of pork belly; cook these things and then add Bibb lettuce, aromatic herbs, two whole heads of garlic, a touch of saffron, apt spices, and chickpeas inside, cooked in a good broth; once it is cooked, let it rest and serve it hot; you may also serve the broth in bowls, with a soup of toasted bread underneath, and with a pastry twist around the plate.

Another dish, Swiss-style.

Use four pounds of veal, first roasted, then cooked it in a pot, well studded with cinnamon and cloves, with thin slices of cured back fat, garnished with bits of ham, halved cockerels, cooked in a pan, salted tongues, which should soak overnight, with the usual spices; when the meat is almost cooked, add a bit of white wine, as you see fit, and garnish the dish with [basket] pastries mixed with pears in syrup.

Another dish, called Torrese.[171]

Use tender cockerels, first boiled, then halved and marinated in a bit of vinegar, crushed garlic, oregano, and spices; marinate them for an hour or two, then dredge them in flour, dip them in egg, and fry them in good lard; place them on the plate, mixed with bits of sweetbreads wrapped in pork caul, with spit-roasted chicken livers, bits of veal feet, well deboned and boiled, then dipped in egg and fried, thin slices of ham, first sautéed in a pan, with a bit of vinegar, and a sauce made with vinegar, sugar, olives, capers, pine nuts, raisins, bits of candied citron, and the usual spices; garnish the plate with flaky pastries filled with blancmange.

Another dish, of turkey gigot.

Roast the gigot and let it cool; debone it and grind it finely, and put it in a silver plate with apt spices and lemon juice; garnish it with various small birds, roasted and stuffed with roast juice, ham sauce, mixed with roasted sweetbreads, garnished with fried quartered chicken testicles and livers; garnish the sides of the plate with lemon slices and pomegranate seeds.

Another dish, of chicken wings.

Boil the wings to a half-cooking, in broth, then place them in a pan with a bit of minced onion, pounded cured back fat, aromatic herbs, bits of cardoons, first boiled, sautéing everything together; when you bring it to the table, make a little broth with fresh eggs and lemon juice to thicken it, with apt spices and pine nuts, and it will be a tasty dish.

---

again on the next page of Latini's text, again as a garnish. Canestrelle means small baskets, so it may refer to the shape of the pastries.

171 Probably a reference to Torre Annunziata, a town near Naples.

Another dish, a sort of bisque.[172]

Take tender pigeons and half-cook them on the spit, then put them in a pan and add veal chops, veal sweetbreads dredged in bread crumbs and half-roasted on the spit, small birds cooked in a small pan or pot with apt spices; finish cooking all these things, mixed with rolls made with veal livers, artichokes, first boiled and fried, bits of cardoons, first boiled and stewed in good lard, and other noble ingredients; cook everything separately, with good broth and meat juice, and underneath a little soup made with toasted white bread and lemon juice; compose this bisque neatly, and garnish it with small pastries made with pounded veal, pine nuts, garlic, and apt spices; put shelled pistachios on top.

Another dish, of deboned, stuffed capons.

Stuff them carefully with veal flesh, pigeon breasts, sweetbreads, bone marrow, ham, egg yolks, crustless white bread, soaked in broth, St. George's mushrooms, whole pistachios, pitted sour cherries, aromatic herbs, and apt spices; cook everything in a pan on a low fire and then cover it with a sauce made with wedge shells, razor shells, sea urchins, St. George's mushrooms, truffles, lemon juice, and roast juice; garnish the plate with sliced udder, dipped in egg and fried, mixed with lemon slices.

Another dish, of gigot, with its divisions.

Prepare this in a silver plate, divided with a dough made with eggs, sugar, and lard; divide the plate in as many compartments as you would for a royal salad, and in each compartment place a different flavour of ground meat: capon and pigeon breast, cockerel meat, grey partridge and wild pigeon breast, ground veal, and other meats, all roasted; each of these should have its own condiment, separately, with lemon juice and seafood juice, well presented. This will be a dish worthy of any banquet; around the plate you can place a pastry twist in three layers, one filled with blancmange, one with marzipan paste, the third with apples and pears in syrup, with sugar on top.

Another dish, a Neapolitan-style oglia.

This dish is composed of boiled capons; veal breast; a piece of wether; ham slices; salted tongues, first soaked; pork belly; parmesan cheese; Genoa mushrooms; celery stems; cardoons; turnips; Bibb lettuce; escarole; lettuce; stuffed truffles; garlic; chickpeas; parsley roots; slices of udder and of soppressata; Giugliano fillet; aromatic herbs; saffron; and seafood; garnish it with roasted wether on top, and green pistachios. Let it take flavour well. This will be a most delicate dish; I once made a similar one, for an excursion to Posillipo, with several gentlemen, and it came out so perfect that, of the twelve dishes that were on the table, they only ate this one, to great applause for the cook and his master. You can serve it in the same pan in which you put it together; make sure the juice is good and the broth exquisite.[173]

---

172 This recipe is cited in Riley, *The Oxford Companion*, 275–76; I take the translation of *mezza bisca* as "a sort of bisque" from Riley.

173 Posillipo is a hill just west of Naples, filled in Latini's time with aristocratic villas with beautiful

Another dish of impanata, made empty with short crust pastry, and then filled.

Cook an impanata, by itself, and then fill it diligently with maccheroni cooked in good broth, parmesan cheese, provola, and caciocavallo; layer them with veal or pork ribs, quite thin, fine sausages, first cooked in a pan, half cockerels, first roasted, meat juice from a pan, without adding broth, because the juices coming from these ingredients will be sufficient; cover the pie and place it in the oven to gain flavour, and serve it hot.

Another dish, a pie without dough, or a pie in caul.

Take pork caul, or, if that is not available, the caul of veal or kid or another quadruped; spread it on a silver plate and neatly put in it chops pounded with the side of the knife and thin slices of cured back fat on top of the chops; then form the pie, with ground veal thigh, first browned in a pan or pot, with inside ground chicken breast, bits of tender pigeons, marrow, truffles, St. George's mushrooms, pine nuts, gutted small birds, bits of sweetbreads, cubed ham, small veal meatballs, artichoke stems, first boiled and sautéed in good lard, hard egg yolks, sliced udder, first boiled, veal kidneys, also sautéed, bits of cardoons, first boiled and fried, apt spices, aromatic herbs, and other suitable noble ingredients; tie the caul on top and cook it in the oven in a pan greased with butter, to flavour everything well; once it is cooked, make a glaze like marzipan, on top, with lemon juice and sugar; it will be a good pie without dough; garnish the plate with Mazarin-style small pastries filled with things in syrup, mixed with lemon slices.

Another dish, of cream tops gigot, for six people.

Take three carafes of milk, or four *fogliette* in Roman measurements, one pound of cream tops, half a pound of ground candied citron, one pound of Savoy cookies or mostaccere, a roasted capon, deboned and then ground (it will be better if you only use capon breast), six eggs, a quarter ounce of cinnamon; mix everything in the milk, together with half the cookies, ground, while with the other half of the cookies you will form the basis of the dish; first make a pastry twist to use around the plate, and grease the plate with butter; place the mixture on the plate, and put it in the oven, at a high temperature, when it is all thickened and browned serve it hot, and garnish it with strained eggs or short crust pastry; this will be a noble dish, worthy of any personage.

Another dish, of boiled capons.

Cook the capons and put them in a plate, cover them with artichoke stems, first boiled and sautéed, peas, first cooked and sautéed in a pan, thin slices of ham, bits of sweetbreads, the usual spices; layer the plate with slices of provola fried in butter and garnish it as you wish.

---

sea views. Stews in this style were quite popular in the seventeenth and eighteenth centuries: Day describes a French example of "Spanish olio" from 1736 which also included a wide variety of meats, body parts, and vegetables, Day, *Cooking in Europe, 1650–1850* (Westport: Greenwood Press, 2009), 38–39.

Another dish, of deboned pigeon breast.

Cook it in a lard broth, sautéed with cubed ham, bay leaves (left until they give flavour, then removed); stew everything in a pot with muscatel wine, good broth, and the usual spices; make for this a sauce with Marseille plums, cooked in wine, vinegar, mostacciolo crumbs, diluted with the broth from the pigeons; then mix everything together and finish cooking it, and serve it with toasted slices of white bread, soaked in malmsey wine, and also placed in the dripping pan, dredged in eggs, fried in lard, and with green pistachios on top; garnish the sides of the plate with Genoa-style pastries, fried in butter, sprinkled with sugar.

Another dish, of grey partridges.

Take four grey partridges, boil them well, and then cover them with stuffed cabbage stems, stuffed onions, white chickpeas, fresh peas, artichokes, slices of ham and soppressata, while truffles, and fennel; cook everything by itself; cover the pot or pan with a cover made of flaky pastry, in lattice pattern.

Another dish, of stuffed bread loaves.

First scrape off the crusts and remove the inner part of the loaves, then soak them well in milk; then stuff them with roasted and ground pigeon breast, cream tops, ground cooked pine nuts, candied citron, mostacciolo crumbs, candied pistachios, and egg yolks; grease the plate well with butter and put it in the oven, dredging it in ambivera, and make a royal glaze for it; serve it with in the middle the coat of arms of the invited lords; this coat of arms you will make of marzipan paste, and surround it with little sugar boxes and Marseille plums.

Another dish, of stuffed domestic pigeons.

Stuff them between their flesh and skin with pounded veal flesh, egg yolks, cream tops, ground candied citron, mostacciolo crumbs, and apt spices; cook them in the oven, covered with a thin stew made with thin slices of cardoons, stuffed lettuce stems, sliced soppressata, sliced truffles, and St. George's mushrooms, with sliced bread underneath; garnish the plate with small pastries filled with small veal chops, ham slices, veal sweetbreads, and lemon juice.

Another dish, of cockerels.

Take six cockerels and roast them but not until they are fully cooked, then wrap them in veal caul, and when they have taken a good flavour on the spit put them in a pan or pot, greased well with butter or slices of cured back fat; sauté them well, with the usual spices and a bit of good broth, then add slices of fresh fruits, sour grapes or gooseberries, depending on the season, thin slices of ham; make sure they do not end up too watery; when they are cooked, garnish the plate with rolls made with veal liver stuffed with ground fresh provola, fresh egg yolks, grated parmesan cheese, ground candied citron, boen marrow, pine nuts, spices, perfumed water, wrapped in pork caul and placed in a pan greased with butter, and then cooked in the oven.

Another dish, of deboned turkey cockerels, tender and stuffed, made another way.

Clean them well and stuff them with pounded veal, ground candied citron, fresh eggs, a bit of salt, sliced truffles, pine nuts, grated parmesan cheese, the usual spices, a bit of lemon juice, cow marrow, bits of chicken livers; cook them in a pan or pot; once they are cooked, serve them in a plate garnished with pears in syrup, encrusted with white aniseeds, with a soup underneath with toasted bread.

Another dish, of stuffed bread loaves, made another way.

Stuff the loaves with cream tops, cooked pine nuts, strained eggs, roasted pigeon breast, well pounded, candied citron, and mostacciolo crumbs; fill them well from below, greasing the interior with butter; the loaves need to soak a short time in milk first. Cook them in the oven with a sugar glaze on top and serve them with a gilded sugar crown around them and sugar flowers stuck in the middle of each loaf; prepare a baked custard with milk, cream tops, ground candied citron, sugar, and cinnamon, and cook it separately in a dish; you may then place it on top of the loaves, if you wish.

Another dish, a tomato casserole.

Put together bits of pigeons, veal breast, and stuffed chicken necks; stew them well in a good broth with aromatic herbs and appropriate spices, together with cockscombs and chicken testicles. Once it is aptly cooked, take the tomatoes and roast them on embers, then skin them, cut them into four parts, and add them to the rest, but do not overcook them, because they need only a short cooking; then add fresh eggs and a bit of lemon juice to thicken it; finally cover with a lid and cook with fire below and on top.[174]

Another dish, of turkey breast.

Roast it and cook it in a pan, with a good meat juice and broth, and thin slices of roasted veal; you can add to the plate razor shells, St. George's mushrooms, mammary glands, chicken livers and testicles, roast juice, everything by itself, and garnish the plate with little pastries filled with blancmange.

Another dish, of cockerels, made another way, called Moorish-style.

Take cockerels, whole or in pieces, as you wish, and stew them in a pot with inside also bits of veal, ham slices, and apt spices; once you have sautéed them, you can add a bit of good broth or roast juice, to finish the cooking; then take pistachios, mostacciolo crumbs, a bit of toasted bread, four chicken livers, cooked in embers; grind everything in the mortar and dilute it with good broth, and when it is close to being cooked add also the above-mentioned sauce, with a bit of lemon juice, letting it boil for a short time; then serve it with slices of toasted bread, and garnish the plate with crostini of toasted bread, and on top a ground dish of veal kidneys, with lemon slices around it.

---

174 Here, a few sections before his famous recipe for tomato sauce, is Latini's first use of the tomato as a prominent ingredient in a dish; this casserole also appears later, in shortened version, as part of a description of a banquet.

Another dish, of stuffed capons, made another way.

Stuff the capons with pounded veal, sliced ham, mammary glands or sweetbreads, wedge shells, razor shells, egg yolks, lemon juice, and marrow; put them in a pot with butter or slices of cured back fat and cook them well; garnish the plate with stuffed pigeons fried in good lard, stuffed little tarts, and mostacciolo crumbs.

Another dish of grey partridges, made another way.

After half-roasting them, set them to boil in good broth, and cover them with bunches of white fennel, cooked in good broth, bits of pork belly, slices of ham and truffles, first sautéed in a pan, fine sausages, boiled, pork tongue, first boiled and desalinated, with a sauce inside made with chicken livers, first roasted, and the usual spices; boil the sauce in a pan for a short while and then pour it over the partridges, with slices of toasted bread underneath.

Another dish, a casserole made another way.

Take four pigeons, quartered, and sauté them in a pan or pot, with a bit of pounded cured back fat; then add good broth, and when they are cooked add bits of ham, bits of pork belly, sliced stuffed haunch, small eggplants, fat small birds, veal chops and meatballs, cardoons, first boiled and sautéed, truffles, St. George's mushrooms or small mushrooms, lamb testicles cut into pieces and sautéed, sweetbreads, first boiled and then sautéed, peas if in season, quickly boiled, bits of udder, first boiled, a bit of grated parmesan cheese, quartered artichokes, asparagus tips if in season; then take some clams and open them carefully in a pot on the fire, with a bit of fat or oil, and collect all their juice, and make sure there is no sand in it. Put this juice in the casserole a bit before bringing it to the table, and give it a quick boil to incorporate the juice with the rest; then shell the clams and add them too, after washing them two or three times in water, to clean them well of their sand; then add razor shells, clean pistachios, lemon juice, and apt spices; serve the plate with a big ribbon around it made with dough and stuffed with things in syrup or whatever you prefer. This dish can be increased or reduced, as you prefer, depending on the number of guests, making sure to add the ingredients at the proper time; if, where you are located, one cannot find seafood, you can use meat juice; all these things must be sautéed in a pan, by themselves.

Another dish, of capons, first broken and then sautéed.

Take clean capons and sauté them in a pan with butter or cured back fat, minced onions, marrow, truffles, lemon juice, shelled pistachios, and apt spices; once they are cooked, you may cover them with a frittata made with egg whites, and serve with sugar and cinnamon on top.

Another extravagant dish.

Take clean pork feet and cook them, then debone them carefully, and grind them finely, and add the usual spices, raisins, pine nuts, a bit of grated parmesan cheese, fresh eggs as you prefer, fresh provatura, a bit of ground candied citron, a bit of pounded pork belly, and perfumed water; with this mixture form large rolls and wrap them in pork caul; you can set them aside for a while; then braise them or cook them in a pan with butter or lard; you can use them as a dish in themselves or as garnishes for other dishes; it will be tasty; put on top of this sour orange juice.

Another dish, an oglia podrita in the Italian style, shaped like a mountain.

Use these ingredients, and this dish will be appetizing: a boiled slice of fat beef, two large domestic ducks, first boiled, sliced salami, ham, whole garlic heads, stuffed onions, white fennel, sliced turnips, stuffed cabbages, pitted olives, Milan-style sausages, cauliflowers if in season, truffles, oysters, pistachios, roasted hare thighs, slices of marzolino cheese, and veal sweetbreads, first larded and spit-roasted. Everything must be cooked separately with its proper sauce; place everything in the plates neatly with the usual spices; you can serve this oglia in a stand pie.

Another dish, Swiss-style, made another way.

Take a head of veal, well cleaned and deboned; remove its flesh and stuff it with pounded veal, bits of marrow, bits of ham, veal sweetbreads, egg yolks, parmesan cheese, sliced truffles, pine nuts, sour grapes or gooseberries depending on the season, crustless bread soaked in good broth, pitted sour cherries, mostacciolo crumbs, ground nutmeg, a bit of lemon juice, the usual apt spices, and shape it back like a head, in a pot greased well with butter; cook it on a low fire and when it starts to sizzle add a glass of malmsey wine or a strong white wine; set it to sizzle again, stirring it often, and when it has absorbed the flavour of the wine add some good capon or another broth, covering at least half of the head, always stirring it often; when it is almost cooked, take away the broth fat and take eight chicken livers, well cooked on embers, grind them in the mortar with toasted almonds, and then dilute them with meat juice or the same broth and a bit of lemon juice; add this to the pot and boil for a little while; then place the head on a plate surrounded by six wild pigeons or something else as you wish, cooked in wine with sliced ham inside and the usual spices; serve the plate with ham slices all around, and you can garnish the sides of the plate with a pastry twist with things in syrup; it will be a most noble dish.

Another dish that can be made when a gentleman goes to a friendly gathering, to which everyone is bringing a dish.

Take a veal thigh and take off the shin bone; cut it in half and remove the flesh carefully, but not all of it, leaving flesh to a thickness of at least two fingers; grind the flesh finely and mix with these ingredients: the usual spices, salt as needed, aromatic herbs, marjoram, fresh egg yolks, thin slices of ham, bits of pork belly or jowl, bits of sweetbreads, small birds (warblers if in season), mostacciolo crumbs, artichoke quarters if in season (boiled and then sautéed), clean pistachios, eyes and brains of kid or veal, sliced tongue of the same, a bit of white bread soaked in milk, ox marrow, a bit of kidney fat (but very little), pine nuts soaked in rosewater, truffle slices, dry St. George's mushrooms soaked in malmsey wine, wedge shells, clams, and other seafood (first cleaned of their sand), as you prefer. After mixing all these, with good spices, use it to stuff the veal thigh and give it back its old shape; sew it back with a needle and white thread and wrap it in veal or pork caul, so that it stays well wrapped. Spit-roast it and then place it in a pot, with slices of cured back fat or butter; cover the pot and cook it slowly on a low fire; turn it often so it does not burn; once it has gained good flavour, place it in a basin and cover it with the ingredients listed below, each cooked separately; add spices as needed; each little pan should have its different condiment. These are the little pans:

One with small birds, well stewed, with ham and apt spices.

Another with fried sweetbreads of kid, or another animal, cooked a different way, and with another condiment.

Another with oysters, wedge shells, and appropriate juice.

Another with sliced truffles, sour orange juice, and pepper.

Another with cauliflower, fried in fat, pepper, and lemon juice.

Another with cardoon stems, first boiled and cooked with another condiment.

Another with thin ham slices cooked with a bit of vinegar or verjuice, and a bit of sugar.

Another with St. George's mushrooms sautéed with mint, pepper, and sour orange juice.

Another with asparagus bunches, first boiled and then sautéed.

Another with tender peas, if in season, first steamed and then sautéed.

Take a wether gigot, spit-roast it, and collect all its juice; when it is more than half cooked, cut it into pieces; place it under the press and extract all its juice. Cool the juice, until the fat solidifies; then cook it briefly again in a pan, and add to it the veal thigh, after first taking off its fat, so at to avoid displeasure. Then cover the veal thigh with the ingredients described above, and place it in a basin with around it a pastry twist of three layers: one filled with blancmange; one filled with apples and pears in syrup; and the third filled with varied candied things dusted with sugar. This will be a rare dish, unfamiliar to everybody, and worthy of being brought to any gathering. It is true that it is a costly dish; but in such circumstances one should not worry about such things. He who commands in the kitchen may reduce the cost or the dose as he wishes; remind the carver to slice it thinly, and it will be a most delicate thing.[175]

Another similar dish, made another way.

Stuff the thigh of the ingredients listed below [possibly a slip for above, since none are listed below], and after stuffing it stud it with cinnamon sticks and cloves, then wrap it in white paper with inside thin ham slices, slices of cured back fat, and ground salt; then spit-roast it on a spit with three prongs, and cook it on a low fire; when it is more than half cooked, put it in a pot that is not too large for it; remove the paper and finish cooking it, with wether juice and a bit of lemon juice or verjuice; once it is cooked, place it on a plate or basin, garnishing it with various small pastries, flaky pastries stuffed with ground chicken breast, the usual spices, a bit of garlic, as you wish, clean pistachios and pine nuts,

---

175 This extravagant preparation is for a gathering Latini calls a *conversazione*, which implies a relatively informal—and potluck—event; clearly Latini here intended his master to impress, and almost shame, his friends in a competitive display. *Bacile* (basin), when used to serve food, refers to a large serving dish, usually a type of bowl but wider and perhaps shallower than most bowls; there would be a set on the table (e.g., two or four), not one per guest.

and inside lemon juice with its little broth; if you wish, you can finish cooking it on the spit as well, with the same ingredients, and it will also turn out tasty and very good.

Another dish, of deboned young turkeys.

Debone them and stuff them with pounded veal, ox marrow or bone marrow, fresh eggs (some without the whites, some with them), grated parmesan or other cheese, mostacciolo crumbs, pine nuts, gooseberries if in season or sour grapes, bits of sweetbreads, pitted dried sour cherries, whole clean pistachios; place them in a pot to stew and cook in good lard or butter, and when they are sizzling add a bit of good broth; once they are cooked, place them in a plate, cut into quarters or whole; mix them with veal sweetbreads wrapped in caul and spit-roasted, and with a royal sauce; garnish the plate with short crust pastry made with butter, egg yolks, and sugar, and baked in the oven, with sugar and lemon slices on top.

Another dish, of a small box made of short crust pastry, wrapped all around, with arabesques around it, and inside a deboned veal head.

Stuff the deboned head with pounded veal, ox marrow, parmesan cheese, fresh eggs, pine nuts, sliced truffles, crustless bread first soaked in broth, bits of ham and sweetbreads, whole clean pistachios, pitted sour cherries, mostacciolo crumbs, lemon juice, the usual spices, and other noble ingredients; give the head its prior shape and set it to cook in a pot, with a bit of broth; when it sizzles put it in the oven to finish cooking it in the small box mentioned above; then place it in the plate, and around it place other smaller boxes, each filled with a tender stewed pigeon, with malmsey wine, ham slices, pine nuts, sliced truffles, and St. George's mushrooms; cover everything neatly with lettuces stuffed with the same stuffing as the head, pulled ham, fine sausages cut in half, and cut cardoons, first boiled and then sautéed; garnish the sides of the plate with lemon slices.

Another dish, of veal meatloaf.

Form the meatloaf neatly with ground veal, fresh eggs, grated parmesan cheese, thin slices of candied citron, pine nuts soaked in rosewater, sliced truffles, mostacciolo crumbs, lemon juice, marrow, crustless bread soaked in milk or good broth, the usual apt spices; give it the shape you prefer and cook it in a pot or in a silver plate, greased well with butter or lard, with fire above and below it; prepare a few arabesques for it, made with pine nut cores soaked in rosewater, sticking them into the same mixture, and add to the plate also spit-roasted fat thrushes, with a crust made of mostacciolo crumbs; garnish the plate with small pastries of short crust pastry filled with pounded veal, marrow, pine nuts, and a little broth of fresh eggs, interspersed with lemon slices.

Another dish of rolls wrapped in caul, made with capon livers, first cooked in good broth and then minutely ground.

Prepare the rolls carefully with ground candied citron, cooked pine nuts, fresh egg yolks, mostacciolo crumbs, grated parmesan cheese, ox marrow, raisins, pine nuts, a bit of butter, the usual apt spices, all cooked in a pan, and first sautéed with butter; add a bit of good broth; once they have cooked well, place them in a silver plate with a bit of broth;

mix them with cockerels, deboned and stuffed, with their breasts cut open, and then baked in the oven in a pan or earthen pot first greased with butter or lard; then stud the rolls carefully with pine nuts, first soaked in rosewater, mixed with long pumpkins filled with pounded veal, bits of sweetbreads, cream tops, crustless bread first soaked in broth, egg yolks, pine nuts, parmesan cheese, aromatic herbs, and apt usual spices; cook everything by itself, and then thicken it with a little broth made with egg yolks, and garnish the sides of the plate with lemon slices; it will be a most noble dish.

Another dish, of eight small kid heads, made another way.

Stuff the deboned heads with pounded veal, egg yolks, mostacciolo crumbs, bits of sweetbreads, thin slices of ham, kid brains, first boiled, pine nuts, raisins, gooseberries if in season; then place the stuffed heads in a pot, greased well with lard or butter, with the usual spices; sauté them well and when they have gained flavour add a bit of good broth; while it boils, add various fresh fruits, depending on the season, such as thin slices of pears, peaches, appie apples, and plums; when they are well stewed, add pine nuts and sour grapes; then place the heads in a plate and garnish it with slices of quinces in syrup, with white aniseeds on top and lemon slices.

Another dish, Florentine-style.

Take two geese and stuff them with small birds, chicken livers, bits of pork throat, thin slices of ham, green or dried sour cherries, thin slices of appie apples, bits of sweet-breads, hard egg yolks, bits of cardoons, first cooked and sautéed, sliced truffles, aromatic herbs, and the usual spices; sauté everything in an apt pot, then stuff the geese, and sew them back with white thread; stew them in a pot, greased well with butter or lard, with thin slices of ham; once they are sizzling, add a bit of good broth and half a glass of malmsey wine; before adding the broth, add to the pot slices of various fresh fruits, what is in season, or other things; once they are cooked, place them on a plate garnishing it with meat rolls and fine cut saveloy, mixed with lemon slices.

Another dish, of Bolognese-style rabbits.

Take four rabbits, well cleaned, remove their heads and feet, and stuff them with bits of their own innards, bits of ham, whole truffles, not too large, green or dried sour cherries, halved chicken livers, grated parmesan cheese, ox marrow, thinly sliced appie apples, candied citron, and cured back fat, a bit of garlic and salt, and the usual apt spices; sauté these ingredients in a pan with butter or lard; after you stuff the rabbits, sew them back and place them to stew in a pot with slices of cured back fat or butter, a bit of minced onion, and half a glass of malmsey wine; after they start cooking, add a bit of good broth, tender peas if in season, pine nuts, sliced truffles, bits of pork belly, aromatic herbs, and the usual spices; once they are cooked, place them in the plate and cover them with the leftover ingredients from the stuffing; garnish the sides of the plate with pears in syrup covered with white aniseeds mixed with lemon slices.

Another dish, in Dutch style.

Take a whole wheel of Dutch cheese, as large as the number of guests for whom you need it; clean it carefully on the outside, then carve a hole on the top such that you can empty it of the softer cheese within; keep the lid of the hole you carve. Once it is empty, soak it in warm water for one day and one night, then drain it and fill it with these ingredients: Genoa pumpkin, first boiled and then placed in cool water; Genoa mushrooms; bits of ham; thin slices of pork belly; sliced pork tongue, first desalinated; saveloy sausages if in season; capon skin if you wish; bits of marrow; grated cheese (from the cheese you removed); and the usual apt spices. Once it is filled, add capon broth, cover it with its lid, and boil it in a pot in which it fits snugly, with some ox broth and salted meat. After five or six hours of boiling, remove the whole wheel and place it in a silver platter, garnishing the sides and bottom of the platter with quartered capons, first boiled. Thus, when you slice this cheese, as one would do with melon, the broth that comes out of the wheel will mix with the capon broth, and this is how you make the portions, always mixing the cheese and the capons.[176]

Another dish, of veal, which can be made in March or April.

Take as much veal flesh as you need for the guests, grind it, and mix it with egg yolks, mostacciolo crumbs, a bit of bone marrow, raisins, pine nuts, aromatic herbs, a bit of sour orange juice, salt as needed, the usual spices; prepare a dozen morels, washed repeatedly in water, stuff them with this mixture, put them in a pan with a bit of butter or lard, and sauté them with a bit of white wine; then add a bit of good broth, and thin slices of ham, bits of sweetbreads, whole chicken livers, quartered artichokes, first boiled, tender peas, asparagus tips, sliced truffles, St. George's mushrooms, aromatic herbs, and the usual spices; first sauté everything, then arrange it neatly in the plate, and then cover it with the preparations already mentioned; make sure there is not too much broth; you may add sliced bread underneath; garnish the plate with cauliflower tips, first boiled, dredged in flour, dipped in egg, and fried in good lard or butter, and lemon slices.

Another dish, of a gigot in Mazarin style.

Take two pounds of veal thigh, spit-roast it, larded with hot cured back fat; then grind it minutely and put it in a silver plate with the juice of four pounds of roasted wether and a bit of white wine, and let it cook on a low fire; before you add salt and the usual spices, shape it into a small mound in the middle of the plate, and decorate the mound with various types of seafood, namely, razor shells cooked separately with lemon juice, wedge shells, cleaned of their sand, oysters, also cooked separately with sour orange juice; prepare veal sweetbreads, also cooked separately in a pan; then put everything together neatly, interspersing it on the plate with tender pigeons stuffed with the usual

---

176 I am using "wheel" for Latini's *forma*, still the term Italians use today for parmesan cheese, for instance; I am not sure what Dutch cheese Latini intended here; *keshy yena*, a hollowed and stuffed Edam cheese, is still today typical in Dutch Curaçao.

ingredients; you can also use Genoa-style pastries and pomegranate seeds, and it will be a royal dish.

Another dish, Moorish style, made another way.

Take clean young turkeys and remove their innards, necks, and feet, adjust the wings and thighs, and half-cook it on the spit; then put them in a pan to sauté, with bits of veal, good butter or slices of cured back fat and ham; then add malmsey wine as you wish, and let them absorb the flavour, adding also whole cloves and cinnamon; when they are close to being cooked, add a bit of good broth and garlic heads or whole onions, depending on the guests, and mostaccioli ground in the mortar, diluted with a bit of broth, clear verjuice, and sugar; then boil them in a pot and taste them, until the sour flavour is stronger than the sweet one; then arrange them in the plate neatly, mixed with the veal; add an apt sauce on top, and garnish the plate with Genoa [basket] pastries and pomegranate seeds.

Another dish, English-style.

Take eight tender pigeons, well cleaned and sauté them in a pot with a bit of pounded cured back fat or lard, aromatic herbs, salt as needed, and apt spices; then add half a glass of white wine and continue to sauté until they absorb the wine's flavour; then add the whole pigeon livers, also sautéed; once they are cooked, cover them with bits of sweetbreads, cooked separately in a small pan with apt usual spices and lemon juice; another small pan with ham slices sautéed with a bit of vinegar, artichoke quarters, first boiled and then sautéed, sliced truffles, first sautéed by themselves, with a bit of butter, sour orange juice, pepper, thin slices of kid brain, also sautéed separately, cooking everything its proper way and with the proper condiments; place the pigeons in a plate and pour on them all these other things with a bit of wether roast juice or good broth, but not too much, with pistachios, pine nuts soaked in rosewater, and if you wish you can make for this a little broth with egg yolks; if well done, this dish will be very tasty and nourishing; you can garnish it with small flaky pies in the Neapolitan style filled with the usual ingredients, mixed with lemon slices.

Another dish, peregrine.

Take a cow udder, filled with milk, and tie its nipples lest the milk leak. Boil it in a pot, removing the foam. Once it is cooked, cool it and empty it as best you can. Take some of the stuff you have taken out of it and grind it finely together with bits of ground ham, egg yolks, provatura cheese, grated parmesan cheese, a bit of ground candied citron, butter, thin slices of truffles, pine nuts, whole clean pistachios, bits of marrow, dried pitted sour cherries, veal brain (first boiled and then ground), kid sweetbreads cut into bits, sausage paste if in season, cloves, ground cinnamon, as you see fit, nutmeg, pepper, and a bit of perfumed water. Make it all into a paste, kneading it well so that it comes together. Fill the udder with it, and sew it back with a needle, then boil it in a pot or a tin kettle with a good broth and the juice of various roasts; towards the end of cooking, add bits of cinnamon and whole cloves as you prefer, thin slices of ham, and salt as needed. Once it is cooked place it in a plate with a bit of its broth, over toasted bread slices. You can slice it as you prefer; garnish the plate with a pastry twist filled with things in syrup and various decorations and sugar on top; or you can garnish it with many little tarts filled with bastard sauce or sour cherries in syrup mixed with Genoa-style pastries, or strained eggs, and lemon slices. It will be a noble and intriguing dish.[177]

Another dish, French-style.

Spit-roast some veal, and let it cool; remove the exterior layer and slice the rest of it thinly with a knife; place it in a pan with thin ham slices, and turn it five or six times without a sauce; then place it in a silver plate with a sauce, roast juice, or meat extract; prepare this with St. George's mushrooms, truffles, wedge shells or clams, shrimp tails, white wine, and lemon juice, all cooked separately; garnish the plate with kid sweetbreads, dredged in flour and fried, and chicken testicles, and decorate the sides of the plate with short crust pastries and lemon slices.

Another dish, called the stomach-fixer.

Take twelve tender pigeons, well cleaned, and remove their livers; prepare a pan or pot and sauté thin slices of cured back fat and a bit of minced onions, then add the whole pigeons with salt as needed; sauté them for a good quarter of an hour on a moderate fire, with a glass of white wine, then add the usual spices and a bit of good broth or meat juice (the latter might be better), and let them cook, then place them in a plate and cover them with a sauce made of razor shells, morels, wedge shells, clams, or oysters, without their juice, sliced truffles, St. George's mushrooms first soaked in good wine, everything cooked separately; bits of cubed ham, bits of mammary glands or sweetbreads, first sautéed, the pigeons' whole livers, also sautéed or fried in good lard, with pistachios and lemon juice on top, and the usual spices as needed; garnish the plate with lemon slices mixed with small pastries filled with chicken flesh or pounded veal, bits of ham, pistachios, and pine nuts; it will be a most noble dish, worthy of any royal banquet. If you are in a place where you cannot find seafood, you can use small mushrooms or St. George's mushrooms, sliced truffles, cardoon stems, artichoke quarters, bits of veal, first roasted and then sautéed, like a Genoa-style gigot; all the other things you need to boil and then sauté in good lard or butter, with lemon juice and pepper, tender peas when in season, lettuce stems, celery stems, and bits of sweetbreads, also first boiled and then sautéed; I always trust the judgement of whoever commands the kitchen; this dish will be better in cold seasons than in hot ones.

Another dish, called the lawyer's dish.

Take a well cleaned goose or young goose and place it in a pot to boil, with salt as needed; once it is cooked, place it in a large pan with a bit of broth and while it cooks prepare some rice in another pot and sauté it without water, so that it becomes dark and roasted; once it is ready, place it in the same pot as the goose and cover the pot with another plate

---

177 *Pellegrino* in the title of this dish usually means pilgrim, but here, I suspect, it rather means peregrine in the sense of strange (a meaning also present in the Italian word *peregrino*), a sense reinforced by the word *bizzarro* (here, intriguing) Latini uses at the end of the description.

and wrap the whole thing in a white cloth and place it for one and a half hour under a mattress. This way, you will find the rice well puffed and flavoured, since it will have absorbed all the substance from the goose. Serve it with parmesan cheese and pepper, and garnish the plate with boiled slices of beef; it will be a tasty dish.

Another dish, called of Isabella, which can suffice for six people.

Take six clean thrushes, remove their heads, feet, and interiors, and cook them in a pan with a bit of pounded cured back fat or butter; when they are half-cooked, add bits of cardoons, first boiled and then soaked in fresh water, and tender peas; when these have cooked well together with the thrushes, add bits of sweetbreads and ham, thin bits of pork belly, St. George's mushrooms or small mushrooms (the former first soaked in a bit of good wine); before it all cooks fully, add a bit of good broth, salt as needed, and the usual spices; once they have cooked, make a little broth with three or four egg yolks and lemon juice; once it has thickened, put it in the plate, over slices of toasted bread; it will be a very tasty dish; you can garnish it as you please.

Another dish, called of the gossip, which can serve eight people.[178]

Take four clean tender pigeons and half-cook them on the spit, then cut them in half, making eight pieces, and collect the juice that comes out when you cut them; place them with the juice in a pan or pot with a bit of pounded cured back fat or lard, and salt as needed, and sauté them well, adding kid or lamb sweetbreads (or of another animal depending on the season), cubed ham, sliced truffles, St. George's mushrooms, eight small veal chops pounded with the back of the knife, the whole livers of the pigeons; when everything has been sautéed together, with the usual spices, add a bit of good broth and finish cooking them; then take four pounds of wedge shells, open them in a pan, remove the shells, and wash them well in fresh water, then add them to the pan, adding also the juice they produce when you open them, but not all of it, because the last of it might contain sand; finish cooking everything together, and add clean pistachios; place on the plate large slices of toasted bread, as large as a loaf of bread (from two loaves you can make eight large slices), soaked in good broth; on each slice place half a pigeon with its proper share of the ingredients from the pan; it will be a very tasty dish; arrange the plate neatly and garnish it with lemon juice or anything else you like.

Another dish.

Take veal breast and stuff it with pounded veal flesh, pigeon breast, first roasted and ground, cream tops, butter, bits of ham, thin slices of pork belly, crustless bread first soaked in milk, fresh egg yolks, bits of sweetbreads, chicken livers, pitted sour cherries, ground citron, thin slices of truffles, dried St. George's mushrooms, pine nuts, clean pistachios, the usual spices, and other noble ingredients; once stuffed, spit-roast the breast turning it, on a low fire, for a short time; then put it in a pan with slices of cured back fat

---

178 The dish is "for the *commare*," which literally refers to a godmother, but in Naples the term really means a neighbour, usually one who is a bit of a busybody.

and thin slices of ham, a glass of Greco wine, whole cloves, and cinnamon; sauté it and then remove the cured back fat, and add meat juice and good broth; once it is cooked, cover it with a sauce made with razor shells, morels, clams, wedge shells, shrimp tails, sea urchins, cockscombs and chicken testicles, asparagus tips, and other noble ingredients; garnish the plate with short crust pastries mixed with small pies filled with various condiments, lemon slices, and the usual spices.

A separate note of a few royal dishes, distinct from the other dishes, as they pertain to professionals with the most experience and understanding.[179]

FIRST DISH.

1. take roasted sweetbreads of suckling veal, wrapped in kid caul, sprinkled with perfumes and sugar, bits of finely cut candied things, and garnish the sides of the plate with roasted ortolans, meat rolls, flaky pastries, and sliced lemons.

2. take pheasants and mountain roosters, surrounded by partridges and grey partridges, all roasted and finely larded, with raised citron tips in the middle; above them a small hawk made with marzipan paste, its wings fully open and decorated in gold and silver, and its leg raised and holding a grey partridge, as if the hawk were about to eat it. Garnish the plate with strained eggs and little marzipan pies.

3. a French-style pigeon soup, garnished with larded small suckling veal chops and cauliflowers.

4. a small pottage of chicken innards, St. George's mushrooms, truffles, clean pistachios, thickened with a little broth of milk, pistachios, egg yolks, with a lid on top made with marzipan paste, sprinkled with sugar.

5. roasted winter warblers mixed with larks, with Genoa-style little pies and sliced lemons.

6. an oglia podrita made with a whole capon, and pieces of beef, wether, and suckling veal, bits of ham and saveloy, garnished with cabbages and kohlrabi, white fennel, celery, tinted with saffron, and stuffed lettuces all around.

7. a thigh of suckling veal stuffed with capon breasts, marrow, St. George's mushrooms, and truffles, garnished with slices of ham in syrup and flaky pastries.

8. roasted hare with a royal sauce, finely larded, garnished with various marzipan pastries mixed with pears in syrup.

9. ducks cooked in a lard broth, first larded with ham and half-roasted and then stewed, garnished with little boxes filled with various condiments.

10. stuffed bread loaves, arranged on the plate like a pyramid, covered with strained eggs and sprinkled with sugar.

---

179 The final section of this chapter, covering twelve pages, consists of sixty-five short descriptions of elaborate dishes; at the start, the notation "First Dish" appears, though there is no "second" one; these descriptions, in their abbreviated references, are clearly meant for experienced professionals.

11. roasted turkeys garnished with large stuffed pastries and sliced lemons.

12. pigeons marinated in a royal marinade with candied things, sugar, perfumes, or rose vinegar, garnished with bunches of sage, and things in syrup all around.

13. a truffle soup.

14. roasted woodcocks, larded, mixed with thrushes, garnished with flaky pastries and pears in syrup.

15. roasted boar thighs larded and surrounded with crustless tarts with quinces in syrup.

16. suckling veal breast, stuffed, braised, and garnished with stuffed flaky pastries sprinkled with sugar.

17. French-style tarts made with marzipan paste, egg yolks, capon flesh, candied things, cow marrow, all sprinkled with sugar.

18. a jelly in various colours garnished with capon flesh.

19. suckling veal loin, roasted, garnished with *ciambelle*, apples in syrup, and sliced lemons.[180]

20. tarts with pears in syrup sprinkled with sugar.

21. veal sweetbreads, spit-roasted, with a royal sauce on top, and around them veal livers cut in half, larded, and spit-roasted, mixed with cut lemons and leaves around it made of marzipan paste, with jelly.

22. pulled hare sautéed in butter and put in a pan with strong vinegar and sugar, boiled on a low fire, then placed in the middle of a plate, and around it decorations like ribbons shaped like eaglets, filled with a condiment made with citron juice, sugar, and cinnamon, mixed with spit-roasted ortolans and lemon slices.

23. grey partridges wrapped in paper, spit-roasted, garnished with blancmange dipped in egg and fried, and around it tagliolini made of sugar, and crostini with cooked veal kidney.

24. broth-y pies made with chopped capon, veal chops, oysters, and whole truffles, shaped like lions in half-relief, with gilded bay leaves around them.

25. a boar thigh, cooked in a lard broth; in the middle a hunter made of marzipan paste, his rifle ready in his hands, in the pose of attacking the boar to wound it; from this wound, a pomegranate liquor should be made to come out; garnish the sides of the plate with quinces in syrup.

26. roasted larks covered with strained eggs and mixed with capon livers and bits of veal sweetbreads; garnish the plate with lemon slices and fried beignets.

27. whole veal livers larded French-style with cloves inside, mixed with lamb testicles and fine flaky pastries.

28. grey partridges lightly larded, not fully cooked on the spit, then placed in a fat broth with cauliflowers and sliced ham; garnish the plate with truffles and various types of seafood.

---

180 Ciambelle are ring-shaped cookies or breads, today usually sweet.

29. capirottata of capon flesh mixed with slices of fresh rich cheese, mostacciolo crumbs, ox marrow, candied quinces, egg yolks, and cream tops boiled in a fat broth, the plate garnished with short crust pastries.

30. cockerels drowned and cooked in milk, served with a soup underneath, covered with fresh eggs poached in the same milk, with grated parmesan cheese and cinnamon on top, served hot.

31. roasted turtledoves with a crust made of mostacciolo crumbs around them, fried asparagus, mixed with cut lemons.

32. big tender pigeons, spit-roasted then cut into several pieces, fried in a pan, with sour oranges, sliced candied things, a bit of salt, pepper, placed in the middle of the plate and around them roasted fat quails mixed with fine flaky pastries.

33. suckling piglets with bands and decorations made with lemons, covered with fat small birds, spit-roasted, with a crust made of mostacciolo crumbs, the plate garnished with small pies filled with cream tops, and lemon slices.

34. bits of veal liver, larded, spit-roasted, with royal sauce on top, garnished all around with fried blancmange, mixed with fried lamb testicles, and lemon slices.

35. sliced lamb testicles, fried in good lard, then covered with a sauce of ham slices and fifty pairs of chicken testicles, cooked separately in a pan, and above sea limpets, also cooked in a pan with lemon juice; it is a most noble dish.

36. fat tender pigeons wrapped in paper with inside ham slices, the plate garnished with veal sweetbreads mixed with German pastries and sour orange slices.

37. small boxes made with royal dough, the size of a round plate, filled with oysters, cauliflowers, truffles, St. George's mushrooms, kid sweetbreads, and other noble ingredients, covered with marzipan paste in the shape of leaves; these boxes should be scattered in the middle of the plate, with four small towers made of jelly.

38. veal meatloaves filled with eggs, grated parmesan cheese, crustless white bread, first soaked in a good broth, pistachios, thin slices of candied citron, sliced truffles, tips of Roman mint and fennel, with apt spices, and the plate accompanied with roasted turtledoves, with a crust made of mostacciolo crumbs, mixed with small pastries.

39. pheasants larded with candied citron, spit-roasted, with wings, heads, and tails made of marzipan paste, and around them a crown of dates stewed in good malmsey wine, and sugar.

40. large rolls made with veal liver, fresh fennel, minced candied citron, grated rich cheese, egg yolks, cinnamon, sugar, pepper, cloves, marrow, butter; all these things mixed and wrapped in caul, then cooked in a pan in the oven, and placed in the middle of the plate with sugar on top, garnished with quinces in syrup, and various fat little birds.

41. a large under-cup made of dough, with a high stem, with many gilded decorations, placed in the middle of the plate, filled with fat roasted quails mixed with strained eggs, and around them tender cockerels, their breasts opened and the bones taken out, stuffed delicately and cooked in a pan, with butter, sugar, and verjuice, skewered with fennels cleaned in rosewater, mixed with meatloaves made with veal flesh,

eggs, cheese, pistachios, sliced citron, aromatic herbs, pepper, nutmeg, and cinnamon, with a bit of salt, and in the middle should be visible whole veal sweetbreads.

42. a set of roses made with almond paste, divided into compartments, filled with various condiments, some made with veal brains, egg yolks, cream tops, sugar, bits of *damaschine* [purple] plums, and apt perfumes, others with a quince jelly, and others with fennel, basil, mostacciolo crumbs, and sour orange juice, all raised in the middle of the plate, and lilies of marzipan paste all around like ribbons, filled with sturgeon milk, sturgeon liver, oysters, truffles, capers, cooked pine nuts, and apt spices, mixed with figures in jellies of various colours.[181]

43. towers made with almond paste, with their crenellations, armed on top with small cannons made of flaky pastry, filled with strained eggs; around it a bastion of marzipan paste, and various bulwarks. The whole thing gilded, and in each tower a grey partridge, finely larded and roasted; around this more cannons of almond paste, filled with blancmange, and in all the open spaces fat small birds; garnished with lemon pieces, and the bottom of the plate covered with strained eggs.

44. in the middle of the plate a mound of veal mammary glands, larded and spit-roasted, with royal sauce on top; around it turtledoves stewed in good malmsey wine, a bit of pork lard, sugar, and spices, covered with larded chicken livers, and put on the spit, with salt and lightly crushed pepper on top, and around it fried German pastries mixed with blancmange, also fried, but first dredged in cheese and beaten eggs, and in various spots crostini with veal kidney fat, with various decorations in citron.

45. in the middle of the plate grey partridges larded finely, spit-roasted, and decorated with leaves of almond paste wrapped all around, some of them filled with blancmange and some with quince jelly, mixed with little mounds of lamb testicles, fried pastries, and in various spots small larded veal chops cooked in butter, with a bit of lemon juice and apt perfumes, together with decorations in citron.

46. little cages made with almond paste, retouched in gold, arranged around the plate, with inside a fat pigeon in each, cooked in water and covered with cauliflowers and truffles, and the same stuffing in the middle of the plate, the cages mixed with lamb testicles, and whole slices of citron on top.

47. hunters made of almond paste in the middle of the plate, with a hare made of gilded sugar, on their shoulders their hunting gear, and to their sides two hunting dogs also made of almond paste, with a little gold leash, and around them pulled hare sautéed in butter, then boiled with sugar and cinnamon-flavoured vinegar, and around it pieces of spit-roasted hare loin, mixed with lemons and veal sweetbreads, cooked in butter, a bit of verjuice, and sugar.

48. a pullet made of almond paste, with gilded wings and tail, in the middle of the plate, shown as if sitting on its eggs, and around it tender cockerels, spit-roasted, garnished with blancmange in small pieces, mixed with various German pastries, and with decorations in citron.

---

181 The almond paste is *pasta reale*.

49. cockerels in a scapece garnished with small white comfits on top, and pears in syrup on the plate encrusted with white aniseeds.[182]

50. a bisque made with veal chops, small birds, thin slices of ham, asparagus tips, cauliflower tips, first boiled and then fried, rolls made with veal liver, wrapped in pork caul, St. George's mushrooms, truffles, pine nuts, bits of sweetbreads, and other noble ingredients; garnish the plate with short crust pastries mixed with lemon slices.

51. small young turkeys prepared Swiss-style, garnished with quinces in syrup, in small boxes of short crust pastry, with a glaze on top, mixed with lemon slices.

52. a fried dish prepared with veal liver, first soaked in milk, sweetbreads, bits of veal mammary glands, small birds, quartered artichokes, cardoon stems, first boiled, veal brains, sliced udder, first boiled, whole chicken livers, thin slices of ham, sautéed in a pan, the plate garnished with flaky pastries filled with blancmange.

53. stuffed bread loaves, first soaked in milk, and inside them bits of candied citron and pumpkin, marzipan paste, hard egg yolks, whipped butter, pitted sour cherries, candied pears, ground cinnamon, perfumed water, and other suitable ingredients, mixed with a crustless tart made with eggs, sugar, and candied citron.

54. a bisque made with tender pigeons, small birds, small veal chops, sweetbreads, sliced ham, fine saveloy or sausages, chicken livers, rolls made with veal liver, with a pistachio sauce on top, and roast juice, the plate garnished with small queen's pies made with chicken breasts, bone marrow, wedge shells, white truffles, pistachios, egg yolks, with its apt little broth.

55. *agnoline* [a type of fresh pasta] made of ground pork cheek, ricotta, grated parmesan cheese, aromatic herbs, cooked in capon broth, egg yolks, spices, garnished with heated maccheroni, with good grated cheese on top.

56. turkey gigot, first roasted, garnished with kid sweetbreads, with its own roast juice, the sides of the plate garnished with pomegranate seeds and lemon slices.

57. *cresette* [likely a type of fresh pasta] in Genoese style, mixed with capon skin and breast, with good grated cheese.

58. *saporiglia* with ground veal lung, egg yolks, both cooked and raw, mammary glands, wedge shells, bone marrow; garnish the plate with saveloy, brains dipped in egg and fried, and lemon slices.[183]

59. an uncovered tart made with ground turkey, kid sweetbreads, marrow, seafood, truffles, ground candied citron, fresh egg yolks, butter, pistachios, pine nuts, ground cinnamon, and garnished on top with marzipan paste, in the shape of a Maltese cross.

---

182 *Confetti* today are sugared almonds, popular at weddings and other celebrations; here Latini probably meant more generally confected things rather than strictly comfits.

183 Saporiglia can refer basically to any tasty casserole or stew (the term is linked to the word for flavour, and has a Spanish inflection); often, the term is used for dishes that include organ meat, as in this case with the veal lung.

60. young pullets, roasted and mixed with Spanish-style small pies made with short crust pastry, filled with capon and pigeon breast, cockerel testicles, bits of sweetbreads, with a spicy sauce inside.

61. Spanish-style soup prepared with roasted capon breast, sweetbreads, ham, small veal chops, also roasted, seafood, mixed with slices of toasted bread, the plate garnished with udder slices, with a cover on top made with sugar paste, basted with a good broth, and served hot.

62. pies in veal caul, prepared with ground turkey, sweetbreads, seafood, ham, bone marrow, pine nuts, candied pumpkin and citron, and sugar, thickened with egg yolks and lemon juice, and apt spices, the plate garnished with German pastries.

63. cow udder, first boiled, then roasted, with royal sauce on top, garnished with candied citron, slices of bread dipped in egg, and around the plate provatura, also dipped in egg.

64. an *alcaparrato* of rabbits in Portuguese style, the plate garnished of small pies and halved lemons.[184]

65. A dish called *Raù*, veal flank filled with pounded veal flesh, egg yolks, pitted sour cherries, ground ham, marrow, sliced truffles, mostacciolo crumbs, pine nuts, aromatic herbs, the usual spices, and other fine ingredients; braise it, well greased with butter or lard, and with a meat juice; once cooked, cover it with bits of sweetbreads, cauliflower tips, and sautéed asparagus, and garnish the plate as you wish.[185]

TREATISE XIII: Here we teach an easy way to make covered tarts, or royal pizze, with their doses, which will easily serve eight people.[186]

There are various ways to make covered tarts with cream tops or other ingredients, and indeed the possible ingredients are varied as well. In my opinion, the following method is most noble and apt for any great banquet.

Take three pounds of the finest flour and mix it with water and salt. Prepare eight or ten sheets of dough, as you prefer, and layer half of them, each greased with butter or lard. Then prepare the following concoction: place two pounds of cream tops in the mortar with three ounces of candied quinces, half a pound of Genoese-style dough, half a pound of rich grated cheese, three ounces of marzipan paste, three ounces of sugar, four fresh egg yolks, and the juice of one lemon. Mix everything together with a quarter ounce

184 I am not sure of what this word means, but it sounds distinctly Iberian; *alcaparrado* today refers to a variety of olives.

185 Latini calls this Raù, but it has little to do with what one might call ragoût today—or any Naples *ragù*, which is usually a thick tomato and meat sauce.

186 As discussed in the introduction, the distinguishing marks of the crostata in Latini are that it is covered, and that it uses the thin multilayered dough he describes here (I will generally use covered tart for crostata). *Pizze alla reale* are also included here: as noted above, pizza in Latini's time referred fairly generally to tarts (whatever the ingredients, and covered or not).

of cinnamon and place it over the layered sheets of dough. Cover this with the remaining sheets, always well greased with butter, bake it, and serve it with sugar on top.

With peaches.

Take twelve peeled peaches, sliced, and boil them in good wine with sugar; grind them in the mortar with three ounces of candied pistachios, two ounces of candied citron, half a pound of provatura or fresh mozzarella, grated, or rich cheese, two ounces of sugar, half an ounce of ground cinnamon, four ounces of butter, and two fresh egg yolks; grind it all together to make the filling, covering it below and above with layers of the dough described above; serve it hot, sprinkled with sugar.

With domestic pigeons.

Take four fat pigeons, spit-roasted, with salt as needed; remove the bones and pound the meat with a knife. Marinate it in lemon juice, a bit of cooked must, pepper, and cinnamon. Remove it from the marinade, and give it a quick turn in a pan with fresh butter. Prepare the sheets of dough and fill them with the meat together with its juice; dust it with mostacciolo crumbs, and add three ounces of sliced candied citron, a bit of pepper, half a pound of ox marrow in bits, thin slices of rich cheese, three egg yolks beaten with sugar, and lemon juice. Cover it with the other sheets, bake it, and serve it hot with sugar on top.

With pink apples.

Take two pounds of sliced pink apples, cooked in embers, and grind them in the mortar with half a pound of cooked pine nuts, two ounces of grated candied citron, the candied peel of a sweet orange, two ounces of sugar, two ounces of rosewater, two grains of musk, half a pound of butter, and four fresh egg yolks. Once everything is ground together, form the filling above sheets of dough made with flour, sugar, butter, rosewater, and pine nut milk. Grease the pan very well with fresh butter and dust the sheets with sugar and cinnamon. Bake the tart, and then make a sugar crust over it. You can serve this hot or cold, as you wish.

With quinces.

Take at least six ripe quinces, cooked in embers, pit them and grind the pulp in the mortar with two ounces of mostacciolo crumbs, three ounces of fine sugar, half an ounce of cinnamon and half of nutmeg, half a pound of butter, four fresh egg yolks, and half a pound of sponge cake crumbled in good wine; once everything is mixed together, form the filling, with below and above sheets of the same dough, always well greased with butter; bake it in the oven, and serve it with much sugar on top, cold or hot, as you wish.

With medlars.

Take two pounds of pitted ripe medlars, or of medlar jam, add four ounces of marzipan paste, two ounces of grated peel of candied citron, one and a half ounce of mostacciolo crumbs, and one quarter ounce of fine cinnamon; grind everything together, adding three ounces of butter, four fresh egg yolks, with only one egg white, half an ounce of rosewater; form the filling on the sheets of dough in the pan, greased well with butter, and bake it; when it is nearly cooked, make a glaze for it like marzipan, and serve it hot or cold, as you wish.

With medlars, in another way.

Take two pounds of pitted medlars, half a pound of grated cheese, half an ounce of fine ground cinnamon, an eighth of an ounce of crushed pepper, two ounces of mostacciolo crumbs, three ounces of candied peel of sweet orange peel, well ground, three ounces of powdered sugar, four of butter, three fresh egg yolks, and mix everything to form the filling, on the sheets of the usual dough, and covered with more sheets, bake it in the oven, and serve it hot with sugar on top.

With asparagus.

Take three pounds of asparagus, in bunches, especially the most tender parts. Boil it in lightly salted water; remove it once aptly cooked and place it in fresh water, so that it loses that vegetable odour it has. Pound it lightly with a knife and grind it in the mortar together with two pounds of rich sheep ricotta, half a pound of parmesan cheese, half a pound of marzipan paste, three ounces of grated peel of candied citron, two ounces of mostacciolo crumbs, four fresh egg yolks and only one egg white, a bit of salt and pepper, and one ounce of rosewater. Prepare the pan, greasing it well with good butter, and place the dough sheets, form the filling and cover it with the usual sheets, bake it in the oven, and serve it hot, with sugar on top.

With wether gigot.

Spit-roast the gigot, then finely grind part of it (about two pounds), and add a pound of cream tops, four ounces of candied citron, three ounces of ground cooked pine nuts, four ounces of sponge cake soaked in lemon juice and sugar, half a pound of fresh butter, one ounce of rosewater in which you have diluted a little bit of ambergris, four fresh egg yolks, one ounce of mostacciolo crumbs, one ounce of fine powdered sugar, and lemon juice; mix everything well together and form the filling, over the sheets of the usual dough, and cover it with the same sheets, bake it in the oven, greasing it well with butter first, and serve it hot with sugar.

With capon skin.

Take four or more fat capons, as you need, well cleaned and boiled, remove their skin and cut them in the shape of vermicelli; mix them, without grinding them, with two pounds of cream tops, half a pound of fine sugar, three ounces of grated peel of candied citron, one quarter ounce of cinnamon, a bit of pepper, four fresh egg yolks, four ounces of grated parmesan cheese, four ounces of butter, and a bit of ambergris diluted in rosewater; form the filling, use the sheets of dough, grease it well and bake it, and serve it hot with sugar on top.

With pumpkins and onions.

Take four onions and remove their superfluous skins, cut them finely, and boil them with cream tops and sugar in a glass pot, with enough cream tops to cover the onions; prepare also two pounds of tender pumpkins, boiled in milk and passed through a cloth sieve;[187] add the pumpkins to the pot with mostacciolo crumbs, one ounce of fine cinnamon, salt and pepper as needed, four fresh eggs, eight ounces of grated parmesan cheese, one pound of rich ricotta; mix everything together well and form the filling, with the usual sheets under and over it, put it in the oven with a lot of butter, serve it hot, with sugar on top.

With wheat, called pastiera in Naples.

Take the best wheat you can find and clean it diligently; boil it in rich milk, and, once it is cooked to suitable thickness, sift it; then take two pounds of the sifted wheat, and add eight ounces of grated parmesan cheese, one pound of rich sheep ricotta, two ounces of sponge cake flour, pepper, salt, and cinnamon as needed, two ounces of powdered sugar, half a pound of crushed pistachios, marinated in rosewater with musk, four ounces of marzipan paste, carefully diluted in pistachio milk, and a bit of ambergris. Mix all these ingredients and form the pastiera in a pan, over sheets of the usual dough, and cover it with the same; grease it very well with butter and bake it; it should stay soft, and is served hot, with sugar on top.[188]

With strawberries.

Prepare the sheets of dough as usual, well greased with butter or lard, one by one, up to five or six as you prefer, in the pan, then take two fresh eggs and beat them, yolks and whites, and use them to grease the top sheet, then add four ounces of crumbs of Savoy cookies or mostaccere; then take three pounds of strawberries, or more or less, as you deem best, well cleaned, and mix them with two or three small candied lemons, finely minced, a bit of sugar, and a quarter ounce of fine ground cinnamon. Then take as many layers of the dough, grease them as above, and cover the filling; cut it across with a hot knife; bake it in the oven and serve it with sugar on top, hot or cold as you prefer.

With sour cherries.

Take three pounds of sour cherries and boil them in sugar for a little while, then take them out of the sugar carefully and place them on the sheets of dough, adding mostaccere or sponge cake crumbs, as you prefer, and also small candied lemons or candied citron, and a bit of cinnamon at your discretion; cover it as above and serve as you prefer, and it will be tasty.

---

187 The ordinary sieve (made then usually with horsehair) was—and is still—called *setaccio*; Latini here refers to a *stamigna*, which usually indicates a cloth sieve; see examples in Scappi, *Opera*.

188 This is still recognizable as a version of the main Easter dessert in Naples today: I would not use pepper (nor musk or ambergris!), and I am doubtful about the parmesan or the marzipan, but a pastiera is still basically a sweet covered tart (today typically in lattice pattern) with ricotta and wheat as the main ingredients.

TREATISE XIV: *Of various sauces and condiments.*[189]

Sauce or condiment made with pork ham.

The condiment made from this ham is very good to dress roasts, and very effectively restores the appetite. Take the raw ham, cleaned of its nerves and fat, and cut it finely; after grinding it thoroughly in the mortar, dissolve it in a bit of malmsey wine and rose-flavoured vinegar, and then pass it through a cloth sieve; add pepper, cloves, and cinnamon, mostacciolo crumbs, and a bit of powdered basil. Boil it, and then use it to dress roasts of all types.

Ham opens the stomach, but is highly nourishing. The least harmful way to use it is sliced and grilled, with powdered basil on top.

An anchovy condiment.

Anchovies are very tasty and help the appetite. To make a condiment of them, take the salted Genoa ones, and after washing them well in vinegar and removing their bones, grind them in the mortar with a bit of pepper, cinnamon, cloves, candied orange peel, and mostacciolo crumbs; having ground everything, dissolve it in rose-flavoured vinegar, then pass it through a sieve, and boil it briefly in a pot. You can use this to dress any sort of fish; in the same way you can make a condiment with salted tuna belly, mullet roe, or caviar, though the caviar condiment must be dissolved in lemon juice. These condiments are truly tasty and restore the appetite; it is best however not to use them often; the best among them is that made with anchovies.

Another way.

Take the clean anchovies, as above, washed in vinegar; remove their bones; boil a bit of sour orange juice in a pot on embers, and add the anchovies to it, and let them dissolve in it; add the usual spices, but make sure you do not boil it for too long; you can use this to dress all boiled fish, and it will be very tasty.

A condiment made with damaschine or Marseille plums.

Take the plums and pit them; place them in a glass pot to boil together with cooked must and a glass of malmsey wine. When they are breaking apart, pass them through a cloth sieve; pay heed that while they boil you always add cooked must, so that the flavour remains strong. After straining them, put them back in the same pot, add cinnamon, cloves, pepper, and nutmeg, and boil it briefly. This condiment is good to dress birds, game, and all land animals, and it will be good at all times and in all forms; in the same way you can make a condiment with cherries, sweet grapes, or sour cherries, which all will be quite good in their season.

---

189 What Latini labels sauces (*salse*) are thicker and usually added in the kitchen, condiments (*sapori*) are thinner and often used for dipping at the table, though Latini, as usual, is not entirely consistent.

A condiment made with muscat grapes or mustard.

To make a muscatel condiment, make sure the grapes are fully ripe; take twenty pounds, remove the seeds, and put the grapes in a good tinned pot. Boil on a low fire, stirring with a wooden spatula; add four ripe quinces, thinly sliced, peeled, and pitted, and four sliced appie apples, well cleaned. Stir everything with the spatula, always reaching the bottom of the pot; pay heed to when the quinces and apples are cooked; if you wish to know whether they are, put a little piece in the palm of your hand and press it with your other hand; if you feel that it sticks, you will know for sure that they have cooked to perfection. Remove from the fire. If you wish to skim this, you can pour the thinner liquid in a large pot, and then give it flavour with cloves, nutmeg, pepper, and cinnamon, which you will slowly boil in it, to reduce it a bit, also by putting in it a few mostacciolo crumbs; you can keep this to serve with roasts or boiled meats, and it will be most tasty. The thicker part of the condiment can be passed through a loose cloth sieve, and then given flavour as described above, and kept in pots for various occasions. In the same way one can make all condiments of dark and clear grapes. This most delicate of fruits was created by God to nourish man with its precious liquor, and to make many condiments.

Another condiment, of pomegranate.

To make a pomegranate condiment, place its seeds in a clay pot; press them with your hands to draw their juice, and let it settle; then pour it and place it in a tinned pot; if you have three pounds of juice, add two pounds of fine sugar, and boil it until it reaches the consistency of syrup, making sure the fire is not too strong, because it burns easily; you can serve it also without sugar on top. Pomegranates are very useful to the body, especially to strong ones; they benefit the liver and help fight strong fevers, make the mouth less dry, mitigate a heated stomach, and diminish choler; in winter, you can take their seeds and in the evening place them in water outdoors; if you eat them in the morning, on an empty stomach, they will extinguish your thirst and moisten your body; their syrup prevents superfluous liquids from running through the bowels, and prevent vapours from rising to the head.

Another condiment, of strawberries.

Take the strawberries and squeeze them very well in a tin pot, to make three pounds; add a pound and a half of fine powdered sugar, half a glass of malmsey wine, and boil it on coals, always stirring with a wooden stick; when it starts to thicken, pass it through a sieve; if it seems too light and not entirely cooked, you can put it back on the fire, and flavour it with citron flower water; this condiment does not keep, so you only need make a small quantity of it.

Another condiment, of myrtle.

Take myrtle seeds and grind them well; set aside the little juice they produce, and put the solid parts to boil in a bit of water; when it separates from its little bones, then you pass it through a sieve; take two pounds of what you have passed through the sieve and add a pound and a half of Madeira sugar, diluted in the myrtle juice above, and boil it on a low fire, stirring often with a spatula; once it is near cooked, add three ounces of lemon juice and one ounce of powdered cinnamon, and stir everything together well, add flavour with a bit of ambergris diluted in citron flower water; you will see that it is cooked when it starts turning dark and when in boiling it forms little bumps; instead of lemon juice you can use light verjuice, and it will be most sweet; this condiment keeps a long time and can be served in many ways, especially with roasts of game meat, like wild pig, wild goat, and others.

Another condiment, of lemons and sour oranges.

The condiment from these two fruits is made simply with their own juice and fine sugar; take therefore two pounds of lemon juice and one and a half pound of fine sugar and in a good tin or clay pot put them together to boil, on an apt fire, until it gains the thickness of syrup; you can flavour it with musk and ambergris; these condiments are most beneficial; some people prefer them to be more solid, which you obtain by taking four pounds of this condiment and three pounds of candied lemons, which you first must grind finely, then you boil the condiment and add the ground lemons, and let it thicken; you can flavour it with musk, as above.

Another condiment, of sour cherries.

Take ten pounds of sour cherries and remove the pits and stems, put them in a tin pot on the fire; when they start to break apart pass them through a sieve; first take their juice, of which you can also make a most perfect condiment, adding, if you have two pounds of it, one and a half of sugar, and putting it on the fire and letting it cook well; you can flavour it with ambergris and use it any way you wish. Be aware that all condiments that are wholly liquid are to be served without sugar on top.

Another condiment, of peaches.

Take ten pounds of pitted peaches, very well cleaned, and boil them in enough water to cover them; remove them from the fire once they are cooked; remove the foaming syrup, add to it four pounds of sugar, and boil it until it is almost cooked. Then you grind the peaches in the mortar and pass them through a sieve, and then add them to the sugar and syrup, and cook them very slowly; flavour it with ambergris diluted in jasmine water; you can use this in any occasion.

Another condiment, of medlars.

Take six pounds of ripe medlars, pass them through a copper sieve, or a loose cloth one, as you prefer; prepare three pounds of sugar, cleaned and slowly cooked; add the medlar pulp and boil it to perfection, which will be when it sticks a bit to the spoon with which you will constantly be stirring the pot from the bottom, because the medlars burn easily. Flavour the condiment with a quarter ounce of cloves, half an ounce of fine cinnamon, and three ounces of perfumed water. Do not overboil this, because it may toughen; serve it in plates with sugar; if you prefer this to be a touch sour, when you place it in the little serving dishes you can add a bit of perfumed vinegar, or sour orange juice.

Spanish-style tomato sauce.

Take half a dozen ripe tomatoes; place them over the embers to roast them, and when they are darkened peel them carefully, and finely mince them with a knife; add finely chopped onions, at your discretion, chili peppers also finely chopped, and a little bit of thyme or pepperwort; mix everything together, and dress it with a bit of salt, oil, and vinegar; it will be a very tasty sauce, to use over boiled meat and other dishes.[190]

A condiment of currants, in Naples called the cardinal's sauce.

Pick the currants when they are ripe, when the berries are almost black (since they are usually red, they can seem always ripe); wash them well in water, and drain them in a colander; prepare the sugar ahead of time, well cleaned and almost cooked; once the currants are dry add them to the sugar and boil them briefly, because they easily break apart; stir them constantly with a wooden spatula. Once they are cooked, pass them through a sieve or cloth sieve. This condiment keeps for a long time, and even though it is uncommon here in Naples, because there are no currants here, it is used in Rome and elsewhere and much esteemed by great lords; it is served in small round plates, with fine sugar and cinnamon on top, and it needs no other flavouring. This sauce is good for roasted chicken or any other birds, and for boiled meats. The most perfect currants ripen in September and October, and in some mountains one can find them even in November; the best ones are cultivated in gardens, which are good for the stomach and of great quality; you can give this sauce also to the convalescent, but in small quantity.

Royal sauce.

Take the best vinegar you can find and put it in a small pan, with sugar (more sugar than vinegar), and boil it on a low fire for a quarter of an hour; then add whole bits of cinnamon, cloves, as you prefer, a bit of ground pepper, a bit of ground or grated nutmeg, a few peels of fragrant small lemon, finely cut, or tips of green citron or sour orange, ground in the mortar, but in small quantity; once it is cooked, you can use it for roasts, both fat and lean, and it will be a very appetizing sauce.

Another sauce, another way.

Take as much vinegar as you see fit, depending on how much sauce you want to make, and set it to boil in a small pan, adding sugar, as in the royal sauce; take one or more pomegranate, as you prefer, remove their seeds, and boil them with the sugar and vinegar for a little while, adding bits of cinnamon, whole cloves, and a bit of ground pepper; use it, together with the seeds, for roasts or fried dishes, as you prefer; you can serve this hot or cold, and will be a most tasty sauce.

Sauce of olives and capers that can be used for fat or lean days.

Take the olives and pit them, add capers and pine nuts, and boil them in vinegar and sugar, making sure the sour flavour is stronger than the sweet one. Add also whole bits of cinnamon and cloves. Once cooked, this can be used hot or cold, as you prefer.

---

190 Here (on page 444 of the original) is the recipe Latini is best known for, the first ever printed recipe for a tomato-based sauce: it is, suitably to the tomato's American origins, more of a salsa (in the modern sense) than a sauce.

Sauce for roasted partridges.

Take a bit of white wine, two cloves of crushed garlic, at your discretion, a bit of oil, ground pepper, cloves, and cinnamon, and sour orange juice. Boil all these together in a pot; you can serve this as you wish, in small round plates or on the aforementioned roasted partridges.

Mostacciolo sauce.

Take sugar and vinegar and boil them in a pot; once they boil, add mostacciolo crumbs, making sure this ends up fairly thick, with the usual ground spices.

Sauce, of woodcocks.

Take the innards of the woodcocks and cook them in a pot or pan with a bit of sliced ham and a bit of good broth, lemon juice, pepper, cinnamon, and ground cloves; once it is cooked pass it through a sieve and use it as you wish.

Sauce to cover roasted hare.

Take amibivera or powdered sugar, perfumed vinegar, raisins, pine nuts, bits of candied citron, bits of cinnamon, whole cloves, and boil everything together; once it is cooked you can use it like the others, and it will be a tasty sauce.

Green parsley sauce.

Take the cleaned parsley and grind it in the mortar with a bit of crustless white bread, soaked in vinegar; if you want the sauce to be sweet, add a bit of sugar. Make sure to prepare this just when you need it, because it quickly loses its colour; served as soon as it is ready, it will be most perfect for boiled meats.

Sauce of sour grapes.

Peel the sour grapes, halve them, and remove their seeds; set them to boil in a small pan with a bit of sugar syrup, as you prefer, adding ground cloves and cinnamon; once it is cooked, put it on small round plates, and use it for any roast, as it will be a most tasty sauce.

Sauce of Cornelian cherry.[191]

Set the ripe Cornelian cherries to boil in a small pan with powdered sugar or sugar syrup, and add ground cloves and cinnamon; once it is cooked, pass it through a cloth sieve or another way as you prefer, making sure that it is fairly thick; serve it in small round plates, and it will be perfect.

These cherries are very beneficial to human bodies, because they are an effective remedy for all stomach movements; when they are green, they are prepared like olives; when they are ripe they can be used for jams, with sugar and honey; this helps against dysentery and it strengthens the stomach; they can be given also to those who have a fever.

---

191 This (*crugnali* in Latini) is a plant of the dogwood family.

White condiment of almond paste.

Grind cleaned, shelled ambrosine almonds in the mortar, and while you grind them always sprinkle them with water, so that they not turn too oily. Once they are well ground, use four ounces of the almonds and two of sugar and dissolve them in lemon juice, making sure the paste is dense and not too thin; serve it as you wish, it will be a tasty sauce, and apt for fat or lean days.

Sauce of capon livers.

Take six livers and fry them in butter or lard, then grind them in the mortar, then flavour them with a bit of cinnamon and cloves, nutmeg, and one ounce of sugar; dilute it all with half a glass of white wine, plus a bit of lemon or sour orange juice, at your discretion. Then pass it through a sieve, and cook it on a low fire in a pot or small pan, for a short time, as it needs just a brief cooking. You can use it on roasted game, or other roasts; it will be a noble and very tasty sauce.

Sauce made with the kidney of a suckling calf.

Take the kidney and spit-roast it carefully, then grind it finely and put in a small pot adding the usual apt ground spices, a bit of roast juice, lemon juice at your discretion, a bit of ground candied citron; dissolve everything together and cook it on a low fire; you can use this sauce on veal roasts and all sorts of bird roasts; it will be perfect.

TREATISE XV: *To make perfumes in various ways.*

If you wish to prepare a fragrant perfume, to use in silver censers, take half an ounce of storax, three eighths of an ounce of benzoin, one quarter ounce of aloe wood, one eighth of an ounce of cinnamon, another of cloves, and another of citron peels, two eighths of an ounce of rose petals, three of Levant paste, and grind everything for a while, then put it in a pot with rosewater as needed, over a low fire, so that it will emit more mist and a sweeter smell.[192]

Another way.

Fill the bottom of the censer with citron flowers or rosewater, and add two eighths of an ounce of Levant paste, one of aloe wood, one of storax [here another variety of storax named *calamita*], one of benzoin, six grains of musk, and boil it; it will produce much mist, and a great fragrance.

---

192 These are among the most exotic ingredients that appear in Latini; I am not sure what *pastella di Levante* is. The preparations described in this chapter were part of a passion for scents and smells that swept early modern European culture, see Evelyn Welch, "Scented Buttons and Perfumed Gloves: Smelling Things in Renaissance Italy," in *Ornamentalism: The Art of Renaissance Accessories*, ed. Bella Mirabella (Ann Arbor: University of Michigan Press, 2011), 13–39.

Another perfume.

Take eight grains of ambergris, six of musk, one eighth of an ounce of aloe wood, the same quantity of Indian sandalwood, and place everything in a small pot filled with Catalan jasmine water; heat it on a low fire, and it will give a most precious scent.

Another way.

Take three eighths of an ounce of whole cloves, one eighth of an ounce of benzoin, one of aloe wood, one of whole cinnamon, one of orange peels, and one of Indian sandalwood, with one nutmeg; grind everything together coarsely and then boil it slowly in a small pot with orange flower and lavender water, and you will smell a most pleasant scent.

Another way.

Take a whole grated lemon and put it in a glass pot with citron flower water; add half an ounce of aloe wood, two eighths of an ounce of camphor, fifteen grains of musk, ten grains of ambergris, three eighths of an ounce of Indian sandalwood, another three musk glands cut into small pieces, six grains of civet musk diluted in the same water; close the pot well and let it stand in the sun for eight days; then, put ordinary water in the censer, set it on a fire, and pour in it three eighths of an ounce of the liquid from the pot, and the sweetest fragrance will emanate from this.[193]

Another fragrant perfume.

Take two glands that used to contain musk and cut them most finely, place them in Catalan jasmine water, add eighteen grains of civet musk, six small lemons grated or thinly sliced, the peels of four appie apples, and place all these things in a lidded pot; keep it in the sun for eight days. When you place just a bit of this mixture in the censer, you will smell a scent most sweet.

---

[193] Civet musk is the glandular secretion of an Ethiopian feline, which supposedly was among the gifts the Queen of Sheba gave to King Solomon, see Andrew Dalby, *Dangerous Tastes: The Story of Spices* (Berkeley: University of California Press, 2000). A 1715 anonymous Neapolitan short poem about the land of Cockaygne, the utopian place of abundance and pleasure, mentioned that the beds there are covered "with musk, ambergris, and even civet: this is a life for lords" ("La piacevole historia di Cuccagna," *Giambattista Basile. Archivio di letteratura popolare* 2, 11 (November 1884): 84–85 at 85). Lest modern readers scoff at some of these ingredients, I note that in 2010 coffee beans eaten and excreted by Southeast Asian civets (and thus allegedly endowed with superb taste) fetched over $200 a pound, *The New York Times*, April 18, 2010, 5.

TREATISE XVI: *In which we teach how to prepare various sorts of perfumed vinegars, very nourishing and of great usefulness to human bodies.*[194]

Rose vinegar.

Take as many flasks as you need and fill them a bit more than half way with a strong and clear vinegar; pick the roses when they are half open in the morning, when the sun rises, because this way they have a stronger fragrance, and let them wilt for half a day; remove their leaves and all their seeds, and fill the flasks with them. Close the flasks and place them in the sunlight for two days, but keep them indoors overnight. After two days, strain the vinegar and place it back in the flasks with new roses; do this five times. Leave the last roses in the flasks, because they help keep the vinegar and maintain its clarity; this way, you can use it whenever necessary. In the month of May, you can refresh it with new roses and vinegar, and this way you can continue to keep it, and it will be improved.[195]

With elder tree flowers.

Take little sprigs with elder flowers, when the sun rises and the dew has dried; shake them over a white cloth, so that the flowers fall on it; prepare the flasks ahead of time, a bit more than half filled with vinegar; add the flowers, filling the flasks completely. Close the flasks and place them in the sun light for four days; then strain the vinegar and replace the flowers, and do this six times. The last time, place the flasks back in the sun light for the entire month of August, always well closed, but keeping them indoors overnight. Then strain the vinegar very carefully through a felt cloth and replace it in the flasks, adding two handfuls of the same flowers, dried in the shade; close them carefully and store them in a dry place; be careful never to leave the flasks open, lest they lose much of their smell. This vinegar is very effective against migraines, and it must be used by those suffering from dropsy.

With cloves.

Take a flask holding about two *boccali* [about 2.7 litres] of vinegar; take three quarter ounces of good cloves which have never been in salted water, and put them in a mortar, and smash them two or three times with the pestle, then add them to the flask and close it well, with sugar and parchment, and cover it for ten days with straw and manure, making sure the flask does not break; after ten days, remove the flask and wash it very well, then place it in the sun for twenty days, leaving it outdoors also overnight; then you

---

194 These vinegars served medicinal and gastronomical goals, and the steward needed to make sure they were prepared at the right time of year and stored carefully. Latini as usual enjoyed the opportunity to show off some erudition.

195 The mention of the steward picking flowers and placing flasks in the sun, and the assumption (which comes up in the next preparations) that he will have easy access to straw and manure (*stabbio*), indicate that Latini imagines a steward who, for all his careful management of an urban household, has easy and frequent access to a farm.

will strain the vinegar through a felt sock; wash the pot diligently and close it with a new lid, to use as you need. True cloves come from the Moluccas; they are very useful in both foods and medicines.

With Catalan jasmine flowers.

Pick the jasmine flowers at sunrise, and prepare the flasks, about half-filled with filtered vinegar, so that it be clear; put the flowers in the flasks and place them in the sun, well lidded, and leave them there for two days; then remove the flowers and place fresh ones in the flasks, and do this for eight days; then filter the vinegar and place it back in the flasks with new flowers, close the flasks well and put them back in the sun, and leave them there for the whole month of August, moving them indoors overnight; this will be perfect and useful; you can use this vinegar in the most delicate things, for instance for sauces, which will have a miraculous fragrance.

With citron flowers.

Pick the flowers at sunrise and let them wilt in the shade for half a day; prepare the flasks more than half-filled with very good, clear vinegar, fill them with the flowers and place them under straw and manure for eight days, then remove them, wash them, and filter the vinegar and put it back in the flasks with new flowers, but not many; close the flasks well and put them in the sun for twenty days, which will make it perfect; this vinegar goes well with many dishes; if you give it to drink to someone who ate poisonous mushrooms, it will soon heal him; similarly, if you heat it and give it to someone who has ingested arsenic or monkshood extract, it will certainly cure him.[196]

With rosemary flowers.

Pick the flowers in midday, and prepare the flasks, filling them as I said of the others; after filling them with the flowers, stir them with a wood rod, and then close them well and place them under straw and manure for eight days; then remove them, filter the vinegar, and fill them again up to the rim; you will find in the flasks a sort of oil produced by these flowers, which you will diligently collect, as it is precious; add to the flasks new flowers, lid them, and place them in the sun for eight days; then keep the flasks, without pouring the vinegar, as it will work fine to pour it when you need it. The above-mentioned oil is beneficial to those who suffer from headaches, if you grease their forehead and temples; if you grease someone's head, it will kill his worms; it also helps those who suffer from cold stomachs and those who cannot retain food.

With sage flowers.

Pick these flowers like the rosemary flowers and put them in the vinegar, changing them three times, which is enough, since this flower is intense; you can keep it for when you

---

196 The poisons are *solimato* (which I think is related to arsenic) and *sugo di nappello*: the latter played a role in Neapolitan history, as it was allegedly used to kill King Ladislaus (ruled 1386–1414), having been delivered to him unwittingly by a young woman during sexual intercourse, as chroniclers greatly enjoyed relating.

need it and it is very beneficial to those who suffer in the spleen and to those who spit blood; with these flowers, you can also make jams with sugar, and they are very good for the stomach.

With sweet orange flowers.

Pick these flowers like citron flowers and put them in the flasks with the vinegar, as I said of the others, changing them eight times, because this is a flower which does not willingly release its fragrance; the flasks must also stay for eight days under straw and manure; then filter the vinegar through a felt cloth, put it back in the flasks, add new flowers, and put them in the sun for twenty days, always very well lidded; this is a most fragrant vinegar which kills worms; if you warm it and keep it in your mouth, it removes the bad smell of your teeth.

With fine cinnamon.

Take two flasks, each holding two boccali, and fill them with vinegar; divide between these two flasks one ounce of fine cinnamon, not ground, but broken into small pieces, which you will have placed in the sun for three days. Add to each flask one quarter ounce of the cinnamon, and close them well; place them under straw and manure for twenty days. Then remove the flasks, strain the vinegar, and put it back in the flasks, after cleaning them well, and add another quarter ounce of the same cinnamon to each flask. Close them very well and keep the vinegar for any need or occasion. One can find cinnamon of all sorts, but the true one is breakable, clean between the knots, thin, biting to the taste, sweet, with a pleasing smell, prickly to the tongue, and of a reddish colour, but not too fiery. It grows in the East Indies, and the best comes from Ceylon, where the land is most fertile and the most delightful in the world; the Indians say that the Elysian Fields are there, such is the abundance and sweetness of that land.

With musk.

Take flasks holding about one and a half boccale each and fill them with vinegar, well filtered, strong, and passed through a felt cloth; put in each flask eight grains of Levant musk, ground in a porphyry mortar; close the flasks very well and put them in the sun for twenty-five days, and then remove them; keep this for any occasion, and make sure you never leave the flasks open. Musk is hot in the second degree and dry in the third; it strengthens the heart and gives vigour to the intestine.

With ambergris.

Ambergris vinegar is made the same way as musk vinegar, with the same quantity of vinegar and the same eight grains per flask, placing them in the sun, the same way. Ambergris comes from the East Indies, and it is generally believed to be bitumen emerging from springs at the bottom of the sea. It has great virtues and is useful for many things. There are three types: the first and best is coloured; the second is white, and less good; the third is black and of no value. Ambergris is hot and dry in the second degree; its smell strengthens the heart; it relieves weakened limbs; it is helpful to those suffering from colic; it also assists those who suffer from epilepsy, and those who are frigid or paralytic.

With juniper seeds.

Pick these seeds when they are red and ripe; smash them gently and put them in the flasks with the vinegar, as with the others; for each flask holding two boccali you need half a pound of these seeds; close them well and put them under straw and manure for eight days; then remove them, and keep the vinegar carefully, putting it back in the same flasks after washing them and adding new seeds, without crushing them; place them for six days in the sun, and then keep the vinegar for whenever you need it. I have chosen to write about this vinegar too, because I have found it most helpful for those who are thought to suffer from the plague, and very healthy, both if you spray it in rooms and if you use it in food; it also helps those who were bitten by poisonous animals and produces many good effects in human bodies, to preserve health.

TREATISE XVII: *Of various ways to keep different types of fruit for the whole year.*

To keep fresh grapes.

Pick the grapes when they are ripe, in good weather, in the early afternoon, after at least eight days without rain. Then leave them in the sun over four days, watching that they do not wilt. Keep a pot on the fire with hot rain water; take the grapes and, bunch by bunch, tie them upside down and dip them quickly in the very hot water; then hang them in an airy place exposed to a northerly wind. This way you will protect them from humidity and they will keep for a long time; when you want to use them, place them first for a short while in warm water and then in cool water, and you will see that they stay most beautiful, green, and fresh, as if they were just picked from the vine. You can also keep them, after picking them when they are ripe, by leaving them in the sun for three or four days, but when the sun is not too hot and in an airy, windy place; then place them on barley straw in a small enclosed room, where no air passes; check on them every now and then, and if you find any rotting grape remove it with small scissors; this way the grapes will keep long. There are many other ways to do this, which I will not mention, as these are easier, proven, and safe. Grapes three days after they are picked produce less windiness, and white ones are tastier. I wrote this essay for those regions where it is not easy to keep grapes; here in Naples one can find beautiful grapes at all times, almost as if they were just picked from the vine.

To keep peaches or apricots for a long time.

Pliny states that peaches have to be picked somewhat unripe, as the sun sets, and when it is not too hot. When these fruits have had two days of sun, cover them very well with thinned fresh wax and place them in new pans, well covered with sawdust, then close the pots with chalk and keep them in a cold and dry place. Palladius and Columella say the same thing as Pliny, and I tried this, and for the most part the peaches remained intact, with the flavour, smell, and colour as if they had just been picked from the tree. They can also be kept if you pick them not too ripe, in midday, then place them in the sun for four days, then with a spoon add a bit of thinned pitch in the little hole of their pit and set them in layers in a box with ilex sawdust, making sure the peaches do not touch each other. Close the box and keep it in a cool and dry place, and this is the safest way to keep them. Peaches rot very easily, and it is marvellous to see them in February or March.[197]

To keep plums.

In order to keep plums, they must be solid and not watery; various types of plums, especially if they have much pulp, can be very well kept in this way: take a new barrel and remove one of its two lids, nail many little nails to the sides of the barrel, mixed with some small pieces of wood in the shape of crosses; pick the plums in midday, with their little stems and leaves, and place them for six days in the sun, when it is not too strong; then tie them to the little nails, so that they do not touch each other; then place the lid back and close the barrel well, and wrap it in straw; put it, thus closed, in a mound of sand, in a fairly cold but not humid room; leave them there until you need them, and you will undoubtedly find them very beautiful.[198]

To keep quinces.

Pick the quinces at the hottest point in the day, with their little stems, and hang them in the sun for eight days; then take the clay one uses for pots or vases and dilute it with water, but making sure it remains fairly dense; with a large brush, cover the quinces with it, and then place them in the shade, in a place where the sun light enters; when the clay dries up, add another layer of it; do this four times; if by chance the clay should tend to fall off, you may add some hare fur to it; make sure the quinces are not exposed to the air; once the clay is dry, hang the quinces in a room in which there is some dry straw, and the room should not be humid, but it should be cool; when you wish to use them clean them well; make sure they all hang from a beam. You can also keep them in barley, but they should not touch each other, in a dry and dark place. You can also keep them by placing them in raw honey; the quinces though must be the round ones, with a bit of fuzz on them, which are the true quinces, and more fragrant than others; Galen in his treatise on plants reports that this is indeed the true quince, since not only it is more fragrant, but it is also sweet to the taste, and more helpful than the others for one's health; though there are other ways to keep them, I want you to follow these rules, which are infallible.

To keep various types of pears.

You can keep pears in various ways, as long as they are of these four varieties: *sementine*, bergamot, Florentine, and good Christian, picked when they are slightly unripe at the hottest time of day, and placed in the sun four times; then, wet their flowers with hot

---

197 Pliny and Columella were both first-century AD Roman authors of natural history texts; Palladius wrote on these subjects in the fourth century. These pages offer further evidence of Latini's admiration for the climate of Naples, and of his concern for the steward's ability to astonish his master's guests.

198 Latini lists three specific types of plums: damaschina (purple plums, mentioned before), *marabolana*, and *pernigona* (a purple-green variety), plus "round big plums."

thinned pitch and hang them to the ceiling, each by itself, in a room where there is a fire, and they will keep very well.[199] You can also keep them, placing them in the sun as above, and then in a dark room over dried seaweeds, always making sure they do not touch each other, and closing the room very well so that air does not enter it, and this way they stay green and beautiful; another way to keep them is to boil some sea water, and, holding the pears by little strings attached to their stems, dip them quickly twice in the water, then hang them to dry in the air, and after six days remove them and hang them in the room with the fire, a room which is used every day, and you will see them always green and beautiful.

To keep hazelnuts, called *nocelle* in Naples.

Pick the hazelnuts, shell them, and set them aside for two days; then scatter them on sand in a cool and not humid room where no air circulates, and they will keep for a long time. Some bury them under the sand, unshelled; but I believe this is wrong, as this helps them rot. Others place the hazelnuts in pots closed with pitch, under water, and that way keep them for the whole year, very beautiful. This fruit is not that good for human bodies, as it produces headaches, and often it causes vomiting, because its nature is to remain separate from other foods, and it is difficult to digest.

To keep lazzarole.

Pick the lazzarole in midday and put them under sand, in a dry place, as with hazelnuts, and then put them in the sun for two days, and they will be very beautiful. You can also keep them by covering them with fresh wax, as with peaches, and they keep similarly. But be careful as to how you remove the wax: take the lazzarole, still covered with wax, place them in a basin, and cover them entirely with shaved ice, so that one cannot see them, and leave them like this until they get quite cold, then uncover them and you will see that the wax falls off by itself, bit by bit, and that the lazzarole are beautiful, and covered in droplets as if with dew; you can do this also to clean peaches, which will also be beautiful. Lazzarole rot easily, so you must make sure, when you pick them, that they are not fully ripe, and that it has not rained for at least six days.[200]

To keep pomegranates.

You must pick pomegranate only when they are fully ripe, and you must first twist their stem while they are still on the tree and then wait eight days to pick them; then pick them one by one and tie them with a string, making sure they do not touch each other, because otherwise they rot easily; when you want to pick them, make sure that it be in a new moon, and in the hottest season; keep them in the sun for about fifteen days, then hang them from the ceiling in a room where there is a fire. You can keep them in another

---

199 The names Latini gives are old names for seasonal varieties; today, good Christian pears (*buone Christiane*) are Bartlett, but that variety dates to the late 1700s, and thus the name must have referred to another variety in Latini's time; bergamot pears are usually yellow.

200 *Neve*, literally snow, usually refers to shaved ice, which was widely used in Naples in summer to cool foods and drinks.

way: pick them and place them under the same clay as I wrote of quinces; once they are quite dried, hang them in an airy and dry room, always making sure they do not touch each other. You can also dip them in boiling sea water, as I said of pears, then put them in the sun for ten days, and then hang them in a dry room that is used regularly, and they will keep for the whole year. I say no more about this fruit, because I have discussed it when describing condiments; make sure however that they not be opened, because if so they would rot.

To keep citrons.

You can keep citrons for a long time in barley; the best are those that are beautiful and large, and in this kingdom of Naples you can find very beautiful ones, and though there are other ways to keep them, this is truly the most perfect and proven.

Citron peel, if eaten or used for a tisane, gives good breath and helps in the digestion; citron seed is a remedy against all poisons, especially that of the scorpion; if drunk, it provokes menstruation and kills stomach worms, if taken with citron juice on an empty stomach; if eaten, it helps against the plague, corrupt air, and poison; water distilled from a whole citron is very sweet to the taste and greatly aids the heart and the brain, and if taken together with citron jams it is admirable against pestilential fevers; it extinguishes thirst and fever, resists putrefaction and the corruption of the humours, and the water distilled from citron flowers is helpful against the plague, corrupt air, pestilential fevers, and petechiae; since it is very helpful to the heart, it causes sweating, and lightly provokes vomiting; we read that two people, because of their evil nature, were condemned to be devoured by snakes, and when they passed by an innkeeper who was eating citron, he, moved by compassion for those miserable people, gave them his citron to eat, to comfort them; when they reached the place designated for their death, they were bitten by the snakes, but not harmed at all, and it was believed that this was thanks to the citron they had eaten; the next morning, one of them was fed citron, and not the other, and, when they were attacked by those fierce venomous animals, the one who had eaten citron lived and the other one died; this demonstrated how powerful citron is against poisons; the candied peel is very useful for all the above-mentioned things, and the oil extracted from the peel or seed of the citron is helpful to the heart, if used to anoint one's wrists and the area of the heart.

TREATISE XVIII: Of various triumphs to be placed on tables when there are house guests, weddings, or other occasions that might occur.[201]

I must warn that triumphs should not be placed too near each other on the table, but rather at some distance, so that the guests may see and examine them; they must be displayed in good order, so that each triumph should match its well garnished cold display dishes [rifreddi], and that the table be all filled; those who lack sufficient experience may draw guidance from the attached image, which I placed here to assist in the ordering of triumphs; if you use this guide, you will be certain not to err; although the image is here attractively presented, each steward may arrange triumphs as he sees fit, according also to the circumstances.[202]

It is also customary to prepare dish-holders, about one and a half palmo high, to hold well garnished cold dishes; one can place these between each place setting, in order to have three rows, including the middle one, and this will create a beautiful and elegant sight. Keep in mind that, when the guests sit down to eat, it is necessary to remove these dish-holders, lest they inconvenience the guests. They are not used here in Naples; but I have used and prepared them on many occasions, not without winning praise and esteem from those who saw them. The first requirement a banquet must fulfill is to please the eyes with its variety, to nourish the intellect with rich and sumptuous decorations, and to satisfy the palate with good preparation of the food; one cannot call a banquet royal unless it is accomplished in all these elements, namely: triumphs, cold display dishes, statues, original creations, garnishes, five kitchen services, all distinct and well ordered, with fruits, confections, and candied things, in royal dishes; these are

---

201 This section introduces the final 100 or so pages of Volume I, in which Latini describes several banquets he arranged for his masters. He starts by describing the elaborate table decorations (many made of edible materials) that were at least as important as the food to the éclat of a Baroque banquet. Triumphs (*trionfi*) was the term used for these sculpted and ornate decorations. In the opening paragraphs Latini offers his general philosophy of banquets. He probably first learned this grand approach when in service in the Barberini household in Rome in his youth (for Barberini banquets that Latini might have heard about in his youth, see e.g. Peter Rietberger, *Power and Religion in Baroque Rome: Barberini Cultural Politics* (Leiden: Brill, 2006), chap. 4; see also Jennifer Montagu, *Roman Baroque Sculpture: The History of Art* (New Haven: Yale University Press, 1989), chap. 8, on all the ephemera that characterized the grand life of Italian aristocrats in the seventeenth century).

202 The rifreddi, as mentioned before, were decorative dishes holding food prepared in advance for display, and also as appetizers as the guests sat down and the banquet started. Here the book includes a foldout print depicting elaborate table decorations (see Figure 2 in this volume): on this image, titled *Chiarezza* [Fame], see di Schino, "Il potere della dolcezza, ovvero *Saccharum Triumphans*," in *I fasti del banchetto barocco*, ed. di Schino (Rome: Diomeda, 2005), 35–56 at 41; Maurizio Fagiolo dell'Arco, *La festa barocca* (Rome: De Luca, 1997), 18; and Alba Cappellieri, "Filippo e Cristoforo Schor, 'Regi architetti e ingegneri' alla corte di Napoli," in *Capolavori in festa: Effimero barocco a Largo di Palazzo (1683–1759)*, ed. Giuseppe Zampino (Naples: Electa, 1997), 73–89, plus the catalogue entry for the image in the same volume. Cappellieri suggests that the image illustrates a specific banquet described by Latini, though the print appears almost 100 pages before that banquet's description (see below). This is the largest of the images inserted in Latini's two volumes.

so called not because they are served to kings or monarchs, but because they can be garnished and decorated so as to strengthen and amplify the majesty of banquets; they are therefore properly called royal services and banquets, even when there is no royalty present.[203] He who wishes to organize a banquet well must therefore take principal care of the order, display, preparation, and good dressing of the dishes, and give them the garnishes they require and the most apt and remarkable accompaniments. The folding of table cloths and napkins must be organized by good masters and sculptors, who should use proper wooden bases, and these statues must be covered with folded cloths in various ways;[204] if you wish to make them of cardboard or other materials, they can be covered with a paste made with starch flour, candy, and fine powdered sugar. Here in Naples in many places I have seen the use of paper figures and cardboard galleys, but these are not very apt, and unsuited to the dignity of banquets. There are many ways to speak of triumphs: I have written this short essay to assist beginners in organizing them; I trust that those more skilled than I will operate whichever way they prefer, and according to the circumstances they will encounter; and although in this essay there are sets of triumphs already arranged for various banquets, nonetheless everybody can use these examples as they wish and can.

First triumphs.

1. You can make on one end of the table a triumph of the subtlest cloth, to represent a garden filled with flowers, in which one can see Armida who, in sorrowful countenance, tears her hair, as Rinaldo and his companions are about to depart.

2. On the other end a triumph representing a green meadow surrounded by various trees and groves, and in the middle a larger tree which, in the horror of its bark, displays the appearance of Briareo with numerous arms brandishing swords and shields, and at its feet Rinaldo, with his sword, about to strike.

3. In the middle of the table you can make a triumph entirely of sugar, gilded, to represent Justice, Piety, and Valour, in such a posture that, each with one hand, they hold aloft a large silver eagle, and in the pedestal of this triumph you can impress in golden letters these words:

   May thus the imperial eagle cross the paths of the sun.

These sorts of inscriptions for triumphs can be made depending on the circumstances of the principal guests, and according to the judgement of whoever organizes the banquet.[205]

---

203 The word play here is between *reali*, royal, and *regali*, here meaning garnishes.

204 The artistic folding of table cloths and especially napkins (Latini used the term *Cambraje*, the Neapolitan version of the name of the French city of Cambrai, famous for its fine cloths) was a highly developed tradition in the seventeenth century.

205 Rinaldo and Armida are characters in the epic-chivalric poem *Jerusalem Delivered* (1575) by Torquato Tasso, one of the most famous Renaissance literary works and extremely influential on Baroque art: the enchantress Armida keeps the knight Rinaldo in her magical palace until his companions rescue him by unveiling to him the hidden ugliness of both Armida and her surroundings. Briareo was a Greek mythological monster with a hundred arms: Armida turns into

Other triumphs for other banquets.

1. Love on one end of the table, bow and arrow at the ready, pressing his feet on weapons, sceptres, and crowns, everything made in gilded sugar.

2. Then you can use Hymen, placed at the other end of the table, also made of sugar, with a lit torch in his hand, from which a fragrant mist may emanate.

3. For the triumph for the middle of the table you may use the same Hymen in the act of caressing a lion, and the three Graces adorning Hymen with flowers, all contoured in gold and made with the utmost perfection.[206]

Other triumphs for other banquets.

1. In the first plate, two lions fighting with each other, neatly and beautifully made, placed on royal plates at the end of the table, and covered with butter.

2. The second triumph can be a ballet of nymphs and shepherds, made of butter, placed in a royal plate, with a tree before them heavy with fruits made of sugar, and at its root a sitting shepherd, also made of butter, who plays the panpipes.

3. The third plate can display a triumph of a horse and lion in fight.

Other triumphs for other banquets.

1. First triumph: a quantity of silver and gold vessels, surrounded by the most elegant cloth folds, the most imaginative fronds, and ingenious crystals, to adorn the credenze and bottle sideboards.

2. Another triumph placed in the middle of the table, representing two flowering arches, made of fine cloth, and below the first one Jupiter raised aloft by an eagle while he strikes the giants with lightning, all done with the most marvellous folding; and below the other arch [Hercules (?)] dismembering a lion, and near them a small landscape with varied trees, that hold tomatoes, again all done by folds.[207]

Other triumphs for other banquets.

1. A triumphal chariot drawn by two peacocks, and on it Juno with a sceptre in her hand, and with a rainbow over the goddess with the three Graces, embracing each other, in the act of offering little bunches of flowers made of sugar and painted in their natural colours to two Germans, one of whom places the bunches on one side of the chariot, and the other German does the same on the other side, these little

---

him while fighting to retain Rinaldo. This first set of triumphs seems to be intended for political references, as shown by the imperial eagle and the inscription.

206 This set would be most suitable, of course, for a wedding banquet.

207 The fact that the tomatoes appear in this decorative context reminds us that they were first regarded primarily as an ornamental plant. The *bottiglieria* was a sideboard displaying bottles, glasses, and all beverages, and in particularly sumptuous banquets a rich credenza da mostra and a bottiglieria might be prominently arrayed opposite each other. A word appears to be missing in the description of who or what is fighting with the lion.

Germans should be adorned with corals and pearls around their necks, and with a halberd in their hand; at the other sides of the chariot, two little Moorish girls, with pearls around their necks and corals in their hands, and in the middle of them all one will admire the Graces.

2. Atlas with the sphere of the world on his shoulders, and in the middle of the sphere the arms and emblem of the banquet host, with two young ladies on Atlas's sides who hold other arms and emblems, as you wish.

3. In the middle of the table, two statues, one representing Prudence and the other Justice, holding up high an emblem or something else, as the steward prefers; everything made in marzipan paste contoured in gold.

Other triumphs for other banquets.

1. Four shepherds made of marzipan paste, gilded, holding up high a small basket in which is a lamb made of sugar, garnished with several flowers, also made of sugar.

2. Four nymphs holding cymbals, in the act of dancing around a lamb, also made of sugar; the nymphs should wear flower garlands around their necks.

3. Four small baskets made of sugar, contoured in gold, filled with various fruits, made of sugar and gilded.[208]

Other triumphs for other banquets.

1. Andromeda tied to her rock, the monster, Perseus, and other figures related to that story.

2. The Centaur who stole Hercules' divinity, the hydra, and the lion.

3. A peacock, standing with its tail open, made with diligence and skill.

Oher triumphs for other banquets.

1. Four sirens in sea waves, holding up high a shell with a Venus made in sugar.

2. Mars armed with a sword, in the act of striking, on a chariot, enriched with warlike and martial triumphs made of sugar.[209]

Other triumphs for other banquets.

1. Three statues in sugar depicting Venus, Bacchus, and Ceres.

2. Hercules holding Antaeus to his chest.

3. Orpheus with his lyre and various animals around him, listening to the music.

---

208 Pastoral themes and images were extremely popular in Italy at the turn of the eighteenth century; the Italian literary academy of Arcadia—devoted to pastoral poetry—was founded in Rome in 1690.

209 Both the sea waves and the chariot (and possibly the sirens and Mars—the text is ambiguous) are described as made with *riccio*, the word for both the sea urchin and the hedgehog, neither of which makes much sense here; since the word (as an adjective) also means curly, I suspect that here it indicates a frilly kind of cloth.

4. Diana at the bath, with Actaeon transformed into a stag, everything done in folded cloth, and decorated with flowers in fine cloth.

Other triumphs for other banquets.

1. An arch in the middle of the table done in folded cloth, with columns and capitals, with their bases, also made in folded cloth, in a fishbone pattern, with garlands decorated with flowers in fine cloth, and ribbons of various colours, all retouched in gold, and two similar arches for the two ends of the table.
2. Juno on a chariot drawn by two peacocks.
3. Pallas armed, a spear in her hand, and a helmet on her head, surrounded by a circle of hunters.
4. Venus with Cupid on a chariot, drawn by two doves, all made diligently in folded cloth.

Other triumphs for other banquets.

1. Two giants in fight.
2. Alexander the Great riding his horse Bucephalus.
3. Nereids dancing with Tritons in the sea waves.
4. Neptune standing, holding his trident, surrounded by four rivers, namely the Po, the Reno, the Arno, and the Tiber.
5. A whale with four knights on its back, armed with silver scales, riding sea horses, and aiming their spears at each other; all done with sugar paste.[210]

Other triumphs for other banquets.

1. Charon in his boat, an oar in his hand.
2. Cerberus, tied up in chains, and the three Furies, horrible to contemplate, made with marzipan paste.[211]

Other triumphs, to be used in various occasions.

1. You can make Juno, Cybele, Vulcan, and Neptune on chariots; Vulcan with his arm raised, a hammer in one hand and pincers in the other, with various extravagant things, and leaves around the chariot and in the basin.
2. Neptune in a chariot, his arm raised, the trident in his hand, drawn by two sea horses, with a horn in front.

---

210 Marine themes were also quite popular in Baroque decorative art; Nereids were marine nymphs; since the other three rivers are Italian ones, I assume the *Reno* here refers to the river in Emilia, and not to the Rhine (also *Reno* in Italian).

211 After this rather grim final pre-arranged set with a thematic unity, Latini lists 167 other individual triumphs with various themes and made with a variety of materials. In some cases, the wording is ambiguous, so that it is not clear which element of a description is made with which material.

3. The transformation of Daphne, along the banks of the river Peneus, at the moment when she is reached by her young lover; by true allegory and moral intelligence, this represents to our understanding the penalty God imposes on those who follow the senses.[212]

4. Four nymphs in four basins, with a palm tree, one nymph in each basin, the first with weapons and raised spears, the second with a sceptre in her hand, the third with a cornucopia, the fourth one with a mirror or something else in her hand, as you wish, depending on the occasion.

5. Justice and Peace in a basin, Victory and Royal Valour in the other, over a great bunch of weapons and trophies.

6. A turkey, skinned and cleaned, its innards removed from above or in some other way, diligently, so that the hole from which the innards have been removed not be visible, or cut and re-sewn and fixed with wire, with a small table, as large as the bottom of the plate, covered with various leaves, made in dough or confections, as you wish. This turkey should be shown with one leg raised, with a halberd attached to its foot; place it in the oven enough to give it a quick cooking, and garnish the breast with confected cinnamon sticks or with candied oranges and citrons all along; add arms made with sugar paste, tied to the hole with a little flesh-coloured ribbon; the head and neck can be made with dough; you can do the same with chickens and cockerels, dressed as pilgrims, with their staff at their foot; these will be honourable triumphs, and inexpensive, and can be arranged in various ways.

7. A pelican made with sugar paste, with its young drawing its blood.

8. A white peacock with its tail open, decorated with silver ribbons, with a crown, and with perfumes in its mouth, with several long cinnamon sticks, half retouched in silver, and varied fragrant flowers.

9. A pheasant made in almond paste carrying a cart filled with little cookies or mostaccere made in sugar and decorated.

10. an arch made of napkins, with fluted columns and capitals with the coat of arms of the banquet host in the mid-point, and under these four sugar statues representing Justice, Temperance, Charity, and Fortitude.

11. A galley with oars, sails, artillery, and other apt things, made above folded cloth, and almond paste.

12. A stork with a snake around it, made of the same material.

13. A dragon with fire in its mouth, made of the same material.

14. A child holding a little basket above his head with both hands.

15. A crane with a ball at its foot.

16. Two white peacocks decorated with flesh-coloured ribbons, with pearls and white jewels.

17. A rooster on a column.

---

212 Daphne, pursued by Apollo, asked her father, the river god Peneus, to save her, and he turned her into a laurel tree; the scene was popular in Renaissance and Baroque art: Latini probably knew Bernini's famous statue.

18. A statue shaped like a bride.

19. A rabbit dressed like a monkey, with a belt on its neck, pushing with two hands a wheelbarrow filled with little cookies.

20. Six satyrs made of butter, dancing, holding hands one with the other, forming a circle, with another satyr in the middle.

21. A chariot made with almond paste with Cupid on it, drawn by two white doves, and comfits in the chariot.

22. A Centaur with an arrow in its hand.

23. A pie shaped like a dragon, with fire in its mouth.

24. A unicorn, dipping its horn in a river.

25. An eagle, standing, black, and large.

26. Two little baskets, made of almond paste, holding glazed ham made of sugar inside, with a gilded lid.

27. Two figures made with blancmange representing Venus holding Cupid's hand.

28. A pie shaped like a dragon, gilded, emitting a fragrant fire from its mouth.

29. A decorated peacock over columns made with folded napkins.

30. Pheasants in the guise of eagles.

31. Various stars made of flaky pastry, filled with almond paste, candied citron, and mostacciolo crumbs diluted in rosewater and musk.

Here follow triumphs and cold display dishes made of butter.

32. A young man with a dog on a leash.

33. A bull fighting a lion.

34. A labyrinth filled with an egg-based soup of various colours, and in the middle of the labyrinth the coat of arms of the prince.[213]

35. A statue decorated in various places with silver aniseeds.

36. Cream tops shaped into various figures, with a triumph of confections that may serve at the beginning or end of the banquet.

37. A chariot carrying an emperor, drawn by two pheasants, dressed and decorated with ribbons, pearls, and corals, and in the chariot various preserves.

38. Various cups with Neapolitan mostaccioli, with a sugar glaze on top, and a cover over the glaze.

39. A chariot drawn by two white turkey pullets, made of almond paste, which should seem alive; the coachman, also made of almond paste, with the reins in hand, made of silver ribbons; the chariot should be filled with *cialdoncini* [wafers], small ciambelle, and taralli, made of almond paste, and some chunky quince jam in an open box.

---

213 The soup is *ginestrata*, which I presume refers to a traditional egg- and wine-based Tuscan soup.

40. A tower filled with fragrant flowers, and a bunch of them in the middle retouched in musk.

41. A chariot drawn by four white pigeons, which should seem alive, made in almond paste, with a driver in the same material, and the chariot filled with various types of comfits, most of them decorated with silver.

42. A chariot drawn by two white capons, as above, and inside it various Genoa candied things.

43. Another chariot, drawn by two rabbits, as above, with inside confections decorated in silver.

44. "Lady's mouth" [usually an almond cake] in Neapolitan style, half decorated in silver.

45. An Actaeon in almond paste.

46. A palace of delights, in perspective, made of sugar.

47. A statue of Liberality, beautifully and variously decorated.

48. A gilded turkey in a small box of almond paste, made with jelly, with a lid.

49. Mount Parnassus with the nine Muses and various putti in different poses.

50. Angelica on a sea rock, freed by Ruggiero riding the Hippogriff, made of biscuit paste.[214]

51. A horse running, of the same material, with a lion also running and biting its left leg, with underneath a motto in golden letters: *Dura Patientia* [with patience (one achieves) hard things].

52. A hedgehog with the imperial crown.

53. A tower in almond paste, and inside it several live little animals.

54. Three fountains on a mountain, spouting perfumed waters.

55. A chariot drawn by two dolphins, and on it Neptune with two sea nymphs.

56. Mucius Scaevola holding his hand on the fire, with a dagger in his other hand, in a pensive posture, as if thinking that he has killed the emperor.[215]

57. A mountain made of dough, with grass and flowers, with a sauce of various colours, and above a fire of distilled wine, and inside live rabbits.[216]

58. A cage made with fine dough with two rabbits that are exiting the cage, which is filled with small birds.

---

214 This refers to a famous episode from Ludovico Ariosto's *Orlando Furioso*, one of the most influential masterpieces of Renaissance chivalric-epic poetry.

215 In this famous episode from Roman history, the soldier Mucius sneaks into the enemy camp, and kills a man he mistook for the enemy king, Porsena; when caught, he places his hand on the fire, to show the enemy that Romans do not fear death or pain.

216 Latini calls this an *acquavita*; acquavite is defined as distilled wine (often with an added flavour) and as typical of France and Italy in a 1747 Naples translation of a celebrated English encyclopedia, Giuseppe Maria Secondo, *Ciclopedia ovvero dizionario universale delle arti e delle scienze*, translation of Ephraim Chambers' *Cyclopaedia* of 1728, 8 vols. (Naples: De Bonis, 1747–1754), 1:48–49.

59. A sugar castle, surrounded by artillery, cannons, and soldiers.

60. A ship with Ulysses tied to the mast, and the sirens on the rocks, and his followers around him.

61. Various little baskets, decorated in silver, filled with various sorts of fruits made of sugar, with small animals around them also made with sugar, such as frogs, locusts, and similar ones, with a bunch of flowers in the middle.

62. A chariot drawn by four lions, each in its own pose, where usually the driver sits one can place an eagle with the wings almost open, which looks upon a figure entitled Fame, which holds a sun in her raised right hand, while her other hand is placed on the chariot, with rays made of the thinnest of veils and wires, placed upon a mountain all made with folded cloth or sugar, as you prefer, and about five palmi in height.[217]

63. An ostrich made of folded cloth or of sugar paste, as preferred.

64. A standing eagle made of sugar paste.

65. A unicorn made of sugar, in a basin, surrounded by standing eaglets.

66. A lion in a basin, crowned with an imperial crown, in the act of drinking from a fountain, made in sugar.

67. A few sea horses, standing, with two eagles, in the pose of observing the above-mentioned lion, without fear.

68. The fountain of Piazza Mattei in Rome, with its statues and turtles made of sugar.

69. The fountain of Piazza Navona in Rome, with its statues and obelisk and with the four rivers that surround it.

70. The Column of Trajan in Rome, made of sugar paste.[218]

71. Various vases of flowers, surrounded by eagles and other animals, made of folded cloth or sugar paste.

72. A crow and Moors, with tin chains on their necks, made of caviar.

73. Royal salads, four palmi high, with their accompaniments, with four or five crowns, all on top of each other.

74. Little fruit trees of various types, three palmi tall, with on them fruits made of sugar and painted their natural colour.

75. Phaeton's chariot, with other figures, according to your whim.

76. Various citrus fruits in little baskets, five palmi high, with various other things, and in each a citrus fruit, well arranged, with various bunches of flowers and leaves; this triumph can be placed in the middle of the table or at either end of it.

77. Little baskets of strawberries and other fruits, mixed with flowers.

78. The four seasons, made of folded cloth or sugar, as preferred.

---

217 The image mentioned at the start of this section might in fact depict this very chariot.

218 Latini's references to these Roman sites indicate the development of cultural tourism by his time.

79. A sturgeon made of dough, with the interior structure made of wire and stubble, retouched in gold and silver.

80. Ice obelisks, very high, filled with fruits of all sorts.[219]

81. Large ice vases filled with various fruits.

82. Little baskets containing flower pots with flowers, and a variety of fruits, dewy with shaved ice.

83. Small boxes of almond paste wrapped all around, divided into several compartments filled with fruits in syrup, very cold.

84. The three Graces holding a crown, over a turquoise lily, held aloft by a gilded pedestal.

85. Three little Erotes holding a crown, atop an eagle, standing on a pedestal.

86. Large basins, each depicting a clearly arranged different little garden, made with gilded marzipan paste, in which one can see various little trees and a variety of fruits.

87. Basins filled with various candied things and fruits in syrup, retouched in gold, and over them a large standing eagle made of sugar and crowned, holding in its beak a turquoise lily, and around the basins one will admire various gilded sugar crowns.

88. A few towers made of candied things, with quartered escutcheons, and in their midst the coat of arms of the prince in relief.

89. A small box made of dough twisted in bands, divided into the shape of a rose, covering the bottom of a plate, filled with compartments with various things; the rim of the box should be gilded and surrounded with figures made of blancmange, and over the box in the middle an eagle made of marzipan paste, wrapped in ribbons, with a cover made to look as if made of twisted cord, which on two sides should display the coat of arms of the groom, and on the other two that of the bride.[220]

90. Four standing lions, made of marzipan paste, retouched in gold, holding a crown, and on the lions on one side the coat of arms of the groom and on the other that of the bride.

91. A very tall pyramid made of ice.

92. Vases made of ice, with various fruits inside.

93. Four sea shells made of sugar, as large as a royal plate, all filled with various candied things.

---

219 The word Latini uses is *aguglie*, the same he used in item 69 (in the list) for the Piazza Navona fountain (and that one is certainly an obelisk); in Naples, however, *guglie* were also high, carved, and decorated monuments, a few of which were erected in the city in the early modern period, all with a religious statue on top.

220 This is a good example of the challenges of Latini's prose: between the strange words (twice he writes *rapportata in banda*, to speak of the dough box and of the eagle, but it seems unlikely that the meaning is the same in both cases) and the generous and casual use of commas, which makes it hard to know which clause refers to which antecedent, this description is quite hard to decipher. I assume that the rose's compartments might be shaped like petals, and that the plate is quite large so that the box does not occupy all of it, and it almost makes sense to me until the cover; at that point, I confess that I lost sight of what this decoration would actually look like.

94. Big gilded cups made of sugar with inside white confections, smooth and musk-fragranced.

95. Little gilded boats made of sugar, filled with candied quinces and other candied things.

96. Two very high arches, made with thin folded cloths, with garlands of fruits and flowers hanging from them, made of sugar, and in between two gilded statues made of sugar, representing Justice and Piety, each holding with their right hands the coat of arms of the groom or of others, also gilded and made of sugar.

97. Galleys made of sugar, retouched in gold, filled with all sorts of candied things, with twelve ships, also made of sugar, filled with various jams, candied quince, and things made by nuns.

98. Two plates with on them two fishermen, made of dough, with a net made of candied things and silk strings, in which there are several small sturgeons, cooked in water, with other fish garnishes.

99. A statue made in sugar representing Abundance, with a cornucopia and ears of wheat in her hands.

100. A statue made of sugar, representing Peace, with an olive branch in her hand.

101. Small Tritons made of marzipan paste riding dolphins made of dough, with a small fish on their shoulders and another under their arm.[221]

102. A few pies shaped like a cornucopia and gilded.

103. Blancmange shaped like various figures retouched in gold.

104. Harpies made of sugar, holding little gilded baskets filled with various candied things; two trees made of delicately folded fine cloth, which come to show the coat of arms of the prince, and natural fruits on them.

105. An arch decorated with flowers, made of folded cloth, with garlands in the middle, and another arch made of sugar, and displaying on one side the coat of arms of the groom and on the other that of the bride, all rimmed in gold, and underneath the arches Cupid with his bow, arrows, and quiver, and Hymen with a torch, all made of sugar and gilded.

106. Tritons made of silver-touched dough, with scales, and at their mouths they hold the shells of sea snails, made of sugar, as if they were making a sound, seated around a sea shell made of almond paste, marked in gold.

107. Camels made of sugar and starch flour, their load all sorts of candied things, reclining on the plate, also made of sugar, and filled with flowers also made of sugar, painted in natural colours and retouched in gold.

108. Standing peacocks over gilded myrtle, their tails open, and with their natural wings, decorated with coloured ribbons [tremolanti] and various gold and silver strips.

109. Hunters made of almond paste in the middle of the plate, with a hare made of sugar, painted its natural colour, with hunting tools on their shoulders, and two greyhounds on the leash, made of the same material, with gilded strings.

---

221 I am hypothesizing that *govio*, the word Latini uses, refers to a small fish (*gobio* in Spanish).

110. Europa made of sugar, seated on a bull, adorned of a sumptuous dress, with flowing golden hair, and a kingdom in her bosom, with two different crowns, various gold necklaces, and a sword.

111. Asia made of sugar, seated upon a crocodile, dressed in a habit of various colours, with an azure turban on her head.

112. Africa seated upon a lion, half-naked, with various gold bracelets and jewels around her neck, with a turret on her head, her hair tied with yellow or cerulean ribbons, and a sceptre in her right hand, and various crowns, sceptres, and jewels in her lap; on the other side, a Turk with arrows, bow, and scimitar, and at his feet various open caskets filled with gold coins.

113. America, in the shape of a beautiful naked young woman, but decently covered by bands, with golden hair, jewels on her arms, thighs, and breasts, encrusted with gems, and a necklace on her neck made of large pearls and corals; she holds a fan of peacock feathers in her right hand, and a rich fur in her left hand; she sits on an elephant, over a delightful carpet, with several gold and silver vases filled with gold coins, some vases standing and some overthrown, and nearby a few parrots.[222]

Other triumphs apt for occasions when some great personage begins his governance of a province or kingdom.

114. Piety, her hands joined at her breast, and kneeling, with the coat of arms of the prince on one side of this figure.

115. A standing figure with in one hand a raised sheaf of wheat and in the other a dove, its wings open, that looks at her breast.

116. A figure wearing on her head a morion helmet and feathers, in her left hand a scale and in the other the coat of arms of the city or kingdom.

117. A double-headed eagle holding a royal plate, crowned with various crowns.

118. A slave, with a plate on his head and his hands raised to support the plate, half naked and half dressed, with his quiver and arrow.

119. A siren with a plate on her head, and in one hand a palm and in the other a crown.

Cold display dishes that can be interspersed with the triumphs.[223]

120. A few tarts filled with various candied things, with a statue on top made of sugar and retouched in gold.

121. A capon pie, shaped like an eagle, retouched in gold and silver.

---

222 This representation of America throws everything together in a rather jumbled manner, even more than for the other continents; there were numerous attempts to create standard iconographies for all continents, and especially for the New World, but variety prevailed.

223 Most of these rifreddi, though also primarily decorative, certainly could be eaten (at least parts of them could).

122. A whole pork ham, cooked in wine, then baked, with a glaze made of sugar, egg whites, and lemon juice, garnished with various flowers made of sugar, and raised by four porters, made of marzipan paste, painted to look natural.

123. Jelly shaped like a pork belly, in various colours, served surrounded by masks made of blancmange.

124. Strawberries washed in good wine, then glazed, with sugar.

125. Blancmange sculpted in bas-relief, with little domes of jelly around it in various colours.

126. Glazed cream tops with sugar on top.

127. A cold capon covered with strained eggs, with a crown around it retouched in gold.

128. Five camels, made of marzipan paste, retouched in gold, burdened with pheasants in which are stuck little gilded sticks of cinnamon; also a young Moor made of marzipan with in his hand a silk leash tied to the necks of the camels, which he is guiding.

129. Stars, made with flaky pastry, with appie apples in syrup and almond paste, and decorated above with the coat of arms of the prince, made of sugar, and outlined in gold.

130. A pie shaped like a piglet, retouched in gold on its hair, with a chain at its neck made of gilded sugar, reclining over strained eggs, and surrounded by the same.

131. A glazed ham, made of sugar, with stars and square waves in flaky pastry, encrusted with aniseeds of various colours, with a lid made of dough encrusted with red aniseeds, placed over little columns made of dough, on the sides of which should appear the coats of arms of the groom and bride.[224]

132. A soup made with lemon juice, perfumed water, and sugar, in a gilded crystal cup, very cold.

133. A covered tart filled with various things in syrup; above it a tiger and around it a crown, both made of marzipan paste and retouched in gold.

134. A capon cooked in broth, served with a soup of sponge cake, with a little dove on top made of marzipan paste, retouched in gold.

135. A spit-roasted capon, larded with large pieces of candied citron, served with a ribbon of almond paste around it.

136. A pie made of marzipan paste and uncovered, with various fruits inside it, and four lions around it made in ice and dewy with shaved ice, and also around it various flowers made of sugar.

137. A ham made with marzipan paste, painted its natural colour, sliced, garnished with various flowers over it, and in the middle a lion, of the same paste, retouched in gold.

138. A veal pie, shaped like the mouth of a lion, retouched in gold and silver.

139. A marzipan tart retouched in gold, with the coat of arms of the groom and bride on top.

140. A turkey in the guise of a phoenix with nimbus and flames made of cinnamon that burn under the rays of the sun, retouched in gold and silver.

---

224 The square waves are *rastelli*, a heraldic term for square wave or embattlement lines.

141. A pie in the shape of a lion, gilded, and various flowers on top.

142. A glazed ham in a basket made of sugar paste, and over it a statue of the same paste, retouched in silver.

143. A very cold soup made with lemon juice, cream tops, and strawberries, with sugar, placed in a silver vase.

144. An obelisk made of jelly with little fish inside it of various colours, and a crown made of sugar around it, retouched in gold.

145. Various decorations made of dough, retouched in gold and wrapped all around, divided into compartments filled with fruits in syrup.

146. A bull fighting with a lion, both made of butter.

147. A pie shaped like a sea monster, with its scales in silver.

148. A hunter with dogs on leashes, made of butter.

149. A soused carp, with lemons around it.

150. A turkey pullet covered with jelly, with stars around it made of blancmange, outlined in gold.

151. A soused sole, garnished with decorations in citron and laurel branches, retouched in gold and silver.

152. Blancmange made in a mould, surrounded with little obelisks made of jelly, mixed with stars made of marzipan paste, outlined in gold.

153. A capon seasoned with salt and pepper, with its wings, neck, and tail made of sugar, and a cover also made of sugar, in lattice pattern, placed over stars forming a triangle, made of marzipan paste, retouched in gold.

154. A pistachio tart, and under it gilded laurel branches.

155. Salami cut in half and spiced, covered in stars made of candied quinces, with above them a city made of sugar and retouched in gold, held by four small putti made of marzipan paste.

156. Leaves made of Genoa dough mixed with candied lettuce stems, and over them two bears made of marzipan paste.

157. A roasted turkey larded with pieces of candied citron, the tips retouched one of gold and one of silver, with wings, neck, and tail made of sugar, everything retouched in gold.

158. A covered tart of *caravelle* pears garnished with sliced candied quinces.[225]

159. Candied citrons studded with confected cinnamon sticks, and on them strained eggs, over white fragrant little napkins, with various fruits in syrup all around, retouched in gold, surrounded with various gilded decorative borders made of sugar, and in

---

225 Carovelle pears (Latini writes "caravelle") were a prized (large, round, summer) variety, but now are very rare.

the middle a small statue raising a spear, in the act of inflicting a wound, everything made of sugar, outlined in gold and silver.[226]

160. Nefs filled with *giuncata*, displayed naturally, over wheat stalks, surrounded by various flowers, and mixed with small masks made of marzipan paste, retouched in gold and silver.[227]

161. A royal pie of flaky pastry, with a glaze like marzipan, and around it eaglets made of marzipan paste filled with things in syrup, retouched in gold.

162. A royal pastry twist filled with various things in syrup, with a glaze on top like marzipan.

163. Strained eggs and in the middle a small statue made of sugar, garnished with mostaccere.

164. A covered tart with all sorts of jams, with a glaze, studded with cinnamon sticks retouched in gold and silver, with a small crown in the middle outlined in gold.

165. A large pie with veal inside, made with soppressata and thin slices of ham, apt spices, with the coat of arms of the prince on top, outlined in gold.

166. The mouths of two lions, one facing the other, with a syruped pizza in them, glazed with sugar, with a crown also made of sugar around it, retouched in gold.

167. A royal double-headed eagle, made with flaky pastry, filled with marzipan paste and Genoa paste.

Here are described several banquets and sumptuous meals prepared on various occasions by the author, who was employed by princes and titled nobles in the correct organization and preparation of these events.

There is no doubt that he who arranges a banquet should decide the seat assignments at the table, depending on the location. It is a general rule that those who sit at the head of the table should face the door through which the food is carried in the hall; for marriage banquets, one must make sure that the closest relatives of the bride and groom sit nearest to them. If there are ladies and gentlemen, the gentlemen usually serve the ladies, and eat after them; if they should wish to eat together, one can place the ladies on both sides in good order, and next to them place the gentlemen who are their closest relatives, and then the others. One must also remember that, if there is some great personage attending, one must offer him some special distinction, by giving him for instance differ-

---

226 Here and several times in the following descriptions of banquets I am translating as decorative borders what Latini calls *coroncine*, literally small crowns: this can mean a rosary crown, i.e., a circular string of beads or other things, here used as garnishes for the plates; a later example of one made with pomegranate seeds seems to suggest the nature of these decorations, made of varied materials.

227 Giuncata is a soft cheese, similar to ricotta, named from the rush (*giunco*) containers in which it used to be kept. The word near the end is *mascaroncini*, which recurs a few other times in Latini's descriptions of decorations; it suggests carved grotesque masks, in solid and/or edible materials (of course, this might also be a misspelling of "maccaroncini," or small maccheroni, and I have tried to be guided by what seems likelier given the context). In item 123 above the term is *mascheroni*, or larger masks (unless, again, a somewhat perverse typographical error occurred).

ent chairs or place settings, in the best places, and when he is served to drink one must use small carafes with their own lids.[228] If Lord Cardinals attend, one must use the bread holders as place settings, complete with their own toothpicks and flower bouquets, depending on the season, and gilded forks and spoons. One must also have at the ready the *bavarola*, as it is commonly called: this is a very light cloth, bordered in lace, shaped like what is called *mantesino* in Naples and *zinale* in Rome [i.e., an apron], long enough to cover from the neck to the waist. This cloth is elegantly folded, and has two little strings attached to its higher ends, which each wine waiter will tie together behind the cardinal's neck once the cardinal is seated at the table. Above the place settings one must place two well folded napkins. Whoever serves the Lord Cardinals must carefully, at the end of the meal, untie the bavarola from behind, where it was first tied, and it will fall by itself in the lords' laps. This cloth is only granted to Cardinals and royal personages.[229] Once the meal has ended, the settings should be removed, a plate over them, with a modest curtsy. The steward must watch out that those who serve at the table not remove the plates until the gentlemen indicate that they have finished; I have seen many times some gluttonous servants, as soon as they see a gentleman just a little distracted, deprive him of a dish of which a moment before the gentleman was partaking with great pleasure. The steward must watch for this, by constantly touring the table, so that his eyes and legs work harder than anything else; on these occasions, the steward should not also serve as carver, if at all possible, so that he can be always vigilant that all things keep in good order and without confusion. Once the first table has finished, one must make sure everybody was satisfied, and that those who will eat in the second or third table be treated with abundance, and thus the steward will be greatly praised to the great lords. The steward must also make sure, in these banquets, that two cloths be placed on the table, so that when one is removed the other should remain, for the moment of the washing of hands; once that is done, then the second cloth should immediately be removed as well, starting from the lesser seats, in order not to inconvenience the greater guests, with the usual curtsy, and the table-clearer; the silk sheet should remain on the table. Finally, the steward should never allow anyone else to rule the table, if he wants things to go well, and decorously.[230]

---

228 Place setting is here *posata*, which in Italian today is the generic name for tableware but in Latini's time referred to the setting every diner would find in front of him or her, usually including some sort of board or plate, bread, a salt cellar, spoons and forks, toothpicks, a napkin (usually elaborately folded), and perhaps some decorative elements; the term was typical of Spain and Naples, see Benporat, *Storia*, 157.

229 This was clearly an important matter of protocol—and also meant presumably to protect the cardinals' ample and very bright robes from staining.

230 In large banquets diners ate in shifts, so to speak, with the main guests eating first, followed by lesser gentlemen and eventually by the guests' own servants (the second and third "table"); before the main guests rose from the table, water would be brought to them to wash their hands. The *sfratta tavola* (literally, the table-clearer) was a basket (of silver, or of lesser materials) employed to remove plates and other objects from the table; in later periods, it became one of the names for a dining-room side table.

Figure 2. Table set with examples of "triumphs," illustration from between pages 468 and 469 of Volume I of *Lo Scalco alla Moderna*.

BANQUET

held in Torre del Greco in the farm of the Most Illustrious Lord Regent,
my lord and master, DON STEFANO CARRILLO Y SALCEDO,
Dean of the Supreme Collateral Council of His Catholic Majesty
in the Kingdom of Naples, and First Minister,
on the occasion when the Lord Marquis del Carpio,
DON GASPAR DE HARO GUSMAN, then Viceroy and Captain General
of the Kingdom of Naples, came to stay there
together with the Lords Marquis of Cocolludo, at that time General
of the Galleys of the said Kingdom, today Duke of Medina-Celi and
Catholic [i.e., Spanish] Ambassador in Rome to His Holiness Our Lord
POPE INNOCENT XII, the Lord Duke of Maddaloni, and other gentlemen,
in the number of twelve, with a large number of servants.[231]

This banquet was ordered and held in the month of May, with the service for the invited lords set at one royal plate, and one service per plate.[232]

Before I describe this rich and sumptuous banquet, offered by the above-named my Lord Regent to the above-mentioned Lord Viceroy and his noble company, I thought it would enrich my work to describe the beauty of this farm and its location, where the banquet was held. It is situated about a league to the east of Torre del Greco, and spreads

---

231 *Reggente* was the title of all Collateral Council members, of whom Carrillo was by this point the dean in seniority; "first minister" was thus simply an honorific (the Collateral Council was the supreme administrative and governing organ of the kingdom, and included the viceroy's main collaborators); for Carpio's role as a patron of the arts see Zampino, *Capolavori in festa*. The duke of Medina-Celi himself served as viceroy in Naples in 1696–1702 (many Spanish ambassadors to Rome were promoted to the viceroyalty of Naples).

232 This refers to the structure of the banquet, with only one set of "kitchen" (i.e., hot) dishes, served with one main serving plate per dish; this banquet comes with Latini's most extensive description of the overall entertainment, fully demonstrating how the food was only one component of a Baroque feast.

from the royal road to the sea line to the south; by Neapolitan measurements, it covers about 800 *moggia* [about 2.5 square kilometres], or 800 *stadii*. It includes large arable lands, trees, vineyards that produce the most precious grapes, and orchards, gardens, groves, and some uncultivated land; this makes it rich also in birds, rabbits, and hares, which are raised there for the amusement of a good hunt.

In its midst, as in a majestic centre, rises a noble mansion, enlarged by the good spirit and delicate taste of the same Lord Regent, with modern buildings, noble and elegant, prettily finished in stucco; its sight pleases, so that it is held the first among the many that Nature has placed in the delightful Riviera of Naples, down to Torre Annunziata; it has been embellished and ennobled by the Lord Regent as a place for his own pleasure, to which he retreats a few times a year.[233]

Thus, knowing the fame of this noblest villa, and used to have constant and intimate meetings with the Lord Regent, His Excellency [the viceroy] was induced to visit there, to show the confidence he had in the Regent, and somewhat to lighten his burdensome, though most happy, government; he therefore brought with him, aside from the above-mentioned gentlemen, also some robe ministers [i.e., members of the administrative elite].

The Lord Regent, in order to convey the impression rather of a simple country diver-sion than of a planned feast indoors, had the idea—as noble as it was original—to pre-pare the table under no other roof than the serene sky, given the season, and to use a large opening in front of the villa. Therefore, the previous night, he ordered numerous workers to build with clever industry a spacious hall, about forty palmi on each side, attached to a great white mulberry tree; the structure was in wood, with four doors and as many oval windows, and it was then all covered with pretty and sweet-smell-ing greenery, well decorated on each side, with garlands of branches and bouquets of diverse and beautiful flowers; in its midst was placed the table. In one corner the cre-denza and in the other the bottle sideboard, both adorned with the noblest plates, bowls, and faience vases, ingeniously decorated in the most lively colours, and all retouched in gold, the most famous work seen in our time; a work not less celebrated than the paint-ings by Raphael of Urbino, though not painted by his marvellous brush; I can state truly that, though I have seen and toured many places, I have never seen in any court a nobler and richer service, since the table was moreover always served with dishes of the same material and decoration.

To add to such recreation another delight, the Regent arranged for the same mulberry tree and its leafy branches to spout copious waters in the guise of a most beautiful spring, which seemed produced by Nature, and not made by art, Nature's imitator. The water fell perfectly over a great apparatus of varied delicate and tasty fruits which had been placed at the foot of the tree, in front of the table; similarly from all the tree branches hung vari-

---

233 Latini calls the farm a *massaria*, which traditionally defined a large farmhouse surrounded by an agricultural enterprise; here it seems to be primarily a villa (a term Latini also uses in this account), but the farmland was probably quite valuable as well, as the volcanic soil at the base of Vesuvius formed one of the most fertile areas in the kingdom. "Riviera of Naples" refers to the fertile coast along the slopes of Vesuvius: the distance between Naples and Torre del Greco is about twelve kilometres, and from there to Torre Annunziata about eight kilometres.

ous and most noble fruits. Thus in one single tree one could see, as if in a compendium, an infinite number of fruit-bearing trees, interspersed with varied flowers, both the fruits and the flowers frequently refreshed by little water spouts, so that the fantastical garden of Armida was here made real in a spring so delightful and admirable. If the palate tasted the dishes, the eyes were nourished by the beauty of the fruits and flowers, and while still desiring the former, they also wished to taste the latter. This apparatus turned out so noble and beautiful that, in order to make it even more unforgettable, and to end the day with greater joy, His Excellency ordered his own servants and those of the other guests to sack it, as was immediately done, not just with benefit and enjoyment of the sackers, but also with great amusement and satisfaction of the prince.[234]

The table was set with the lightest Flanders table cloths, with the noblest folds, under which was a lower table cloth of crimson damask, covered with a very light veil. The settings were equally most beautiful for their folds and the leaves that covered them, which all admired; it seemed that air itself wished to favour this day by its blandishments, with stronger winds blowing at the hour of the feast, which were initially regarded as a disturbance but in the end brought relief and joy. In fact, to avoid these winds, which went beyond what one might call zephyrs, the Regent ordered that at each door be placed a drape of crimson damask; these drapes, gently moved and turned by the winds, formed a sort of reverent and harmonious accompaniment to the beautiful and sumptuous banquet. The guests were served at one royal plate, and the table was filled with the following cold dishes.

A small round plate with very cold strawberries, with clear sugar, and sprinkled with a generous wine.

Another with cream tops, and one with sliced soppressata, garnished with aniseeds of various colours, and over laurel branches retouched in gold and silver.[235]

Another with pieces of Giugliano fillet, finely pulled, garnished with strained eggs, and small lemon slices, all retouched in gold and silver, with decorative borders.

A royal salad, placed in the middle of the table, surrounded by various small putti and decorative borders carved in citron pulp.

A plate of whipped butter passed through a pastry tube in a mould with a bas-relief, surrounded by decorative borders, arabesques, and whimsical fronds.

A ham cooked in wine, placed in a stand box made of dough and moulded in bas-relief, with a sugar glaze on top, all encrusted with aniseeds of various colours, placed over laurel branches and retouched in gold and silver, and garnished with confected cinnamon sticks and bits of cinnamon.

---

234 Such ritualized festive sackings were common features of early modern life, from Carnival chariots to maypoles and so on, and were seen as expressions of princely magnificence.

235 Gold and silver were often used to decorate dishes, as we have seen many times above; if properly prepared, they could be edible, though they are both without taste, aroma, or nutritional value; those wishing to follow this model may consult Carole Bloom, "Decorating Pastries and Confections with Gold," in *Look and Feel. Studies in Texture, Appearance, and Incidental Characteristics of Food*, Proceedings of the Oxford Symposium on Food and Cookery 1993, ed. Harlan Walker (Totnes: Prospect Books, 1994), 36–40.

Another plate filled with large slices of sponge cake dipped in good malmsey wine, with cinnamon above and arabesques around the sides of the dish, and placed over shaved ice, so that they were most cold.

A pie with arms stuffed with turkey pullets, veal slices, and other ingredients, retouched in gold and silver, and under it some greenery.

A covered tart with glaze above it, decorated to look like marble, surrounded by various candied fruits, and garnished by flowers and greenery.

First kitchen service.

A bowl of broth for each guest, with slices of toasted bread in it, and covered with its lid, quite hot.

1. Roasted young pullets, garnished with toasted crostini with ham slices, surrounded by pastries filled with blancmange and lemon slices.

2. Fried veal sweetbreads, with slices of veal liver, first soaked in milk, lamb testicles, and chicken livers, surrounded by thin ham slices sautéed in a pan, with a pomegranate sauce; the plate was garnished with lemon slices and fried beignets.

3. A suckling veal thigh, voided and then re-filled with its flesh, together with ground chicken breasts, ham slices, bits of pork throat, truffle slices, pine nuts, pitted sour cherries, slices of candied citron, egg yolks, fresh butter, marrow, whole kid sweetbreads, and small birds, with the usual spices and other noble ingredients, all garnished with cloves and little bits of cinnamon, wrapped in veal caul, and inside also thin slices of ham; this was then spit-roasted to a half-cooking, then placed in a pot to be sautéed in good butter and a bit of malmsey wine, so that it gained a good flavouring, also with other apt ingredients; then it was placed in a large plate garnished with little spit-roasted larded tarts with a royal sauce; mixed with bits of lamprey, also spit-roasted, decorated with laurel leaves, and a crust above made of mostacciolo crumbs, surrounded with sour orange slices, and various short crust pastries, and with a cover in lattice pattern, retouched in gold and silver.

4. A veal head, deboned and stuffed and mixed with four small heads of kid, also stuffed with ground veal, kid eyes, sliced truffles, St. George's mushrooms, pine nuts, bits of candied citron, mostacciolo crumbs, egg yolks, cream tops, sweetbread bits, bone marrow, aromatic herbs, apt spices, and other noble ingredients; covered with a baked custard, and the dish garnished with udder slices dipped in egg and fried, mixed with little tarts filled with sour grapes in syrup, and lemon slices.

5. A pie foe each guest, made with short crust pastry, filled with finely ground chicken breasts, kid sweetbreads, chicken testicles and livers, a little mixture of garlic, pine nuts, and whole green pistachios, with a little broth made with egg yolks and lemon juice, and a sugar glaze.

6. A gigot of turkey breast, flavoured in the same plate with juice of roasted wether, covered with kid sweetbreads, first sautéed, thin ham slices, cockscombs and chicken testicles, everything sautéed, with the usual spices; the plate garnished with various types of seafood, and its sides garnished with short crust pastries surrounded by lemon slices and pomegranate seeds, and inside a lemon juice and over it a cover.

7. An English-style pie filled with chops of Sorrento veal, bits of tender pigeons, udder slices, small birds, sweetbreads, bits of bone marrow, thin ham slices, lamb testicles, bits of veal tongue, artichoke quarters, St. George's mushrooms, truffles, pistachios, sour grapes, the usual spices, and other noble ingredients.

8. Tender cockerels in a scapece, first boiled and cut in half, dredged in flour, dipped in egg, and fried, the plate garnished with pears in syrup wrapped in pastry strips rolled in ambivera and encrusted with aniseeds of various colours, surrounded with lemon slices, and over the plate we scattered confected pistachios.

9. A Spanish oglia, with two capons, beef and wether meat, Giugliano fillet, ham, pork belly, the usual spices, white chickpeas, soppressata, pork tongue, aromatic herbs, turnips, cabbages, a bit of saffron, whole garlic heads, the whole thing in a stand pie.

10. A plate of quinces, first cooked under embers, then boiled in wine and cooked in syrup, filled with pitted sour cherries, candied pumpkin and citron, bits of ground candied pistachios, hard egg yolks, and ground cinnamon; all placed in a small stand pie moulded in bas-relief, but first dipped in ambivera and all encrusted with aniseeds of various colours; above it a glaze made with egg whites, sugar, and lemon juice; then placed in the oven to gain colour; surrounded by fried Genoa-style pastries covered with sugar, and the plate garnished with short crust pastries.

11. A plate of blancmange, moulded in bas-relief, retouched in gold and silver, surrounded by strained eggs.

12. A sweet covered tart filled with things in syrup and other noble ingredients, with a glaze around it made like marzipan.

Second credenza service.

Each guest received a small salad with various ingredients and country greens.
The first cold dishes were quickly removed, and the following were placed on the table.

1. A plate of parmesan cheese, over a napkin, with laurel leaves, moulded in various ways, and retouched in gold and silver.

2. A plate of bergamot pears, surrounded by myrtle and flowers, retouched in gold and silver.

3. A plate of plums of various types.

4. A plate of cold cherries and sour cherries, surrounded by various flowers.

5. A plate of tender almonds.

6. A plate of fennel.

7. A plate of fresh grapes, surrounded by flower bouquets.

8. A plate of large Spanish olives with lemon slices and other things, all cold, with shaved ice on top.

9. A small round plate for each guest with truffles over a little soup.

10. A small round plate of St. George's mushrooms, as above.

Once these dishes were eaten, we placed on the table boxes of various jams and candied things, and of these boxes the Lord Viceroy generously gave to his servants. This noble meal lasted over two hours, with great amusement and joy of the guests, as in this banquet all the senses were fully satisfied. Toasts were made with the most faithful and obsequious reverence, to the health of His Majesty the Catholic King, whom Our Lord protect, and then many other toasts to the health of several most serene princes and great personages, and of various prominent relatives and friends.

At the merest of signs from my Lord the Regent, the settings were removed, with rich table-clearers, and then perfumed water was offered for the hands, with a bouquet of flowers for each guest. Once the guests rose, the fruit on the tree was sacked, and, with spirits relieved, the guests retired to rest.

After a sweet rest, towards evening, His Excellency with the entire noble group went to the above-mentioned place with the rabbits and hares, which were most abundant, and thus a good and agreeable hunt was held. After they returned from this, the guests were served with various types of *sorbetti* and sweets with diverse spices, in quantity and quality apt to such personages.[236]

With the same order of the first table, the second table of gentlemen was served, who ate at the same time as the first one. After this service, we did not neglect to serve the hunters, sailors, coachmen, footmen, and lackeys, those attached both to the lords and to the lords' gentlemen; these, after they had richly eaten to their satisfaction, by an order of my Lord the Regent also received the [leftover] pies and pastries to take home, together with other foods, as was done, to their great pleasure.

This was not the only time His Excellency was pleased to visit this villa, because indeed many times my Lord the Regent had the good fortune of serving His Excellency with the same order and even greater splendour. It was noted that this great personage always ate there with good appetite, though he was weak of complexion and often indisposed; this was probably the effect of that healthy air and of that site, which produces the most delicate wines of various types from the grapes of this farm, so that I might say that not even the choicest lands on this Riviera, nor even better ones, may produce such good wines.

When the cruel Fates cut short the thread of the life of the above-mentioned prince, in the shade of whose justice and integrity the Kingdom of Naples had rested secure and quiet, his successor was the Most Excellent Lord the Count of Santo Stefano, who, with his innate goodness, makes us feel how great are the knowledge, wisdom, and munificence of Spanish princes. He too has heard the fame of the unparalleled delights of this noble farm, and he has had the kindness of imitating the good taste of his predecessor, so that my Lord the Regent has twice had the honour to serve him with his usual splendour, fit to oblige the greatest personages; the second time, he visited with his Most Excellent Lady the Countess his wife and with the Most Excellent Lady the Marquise of Aytona his daughter and the Most Excellent Lord the Marquis her husband, with twelve of her ladies in waiting; I will describe later the banquet that was arranged for them in this villa by the incomparable munificence of my Lord the Regent, ever full of that generous spirit that results from the nobility of his birth.

---

236 Sorbetto is another complicated term: in Latini, it usually indicates a water ice, though it could also include dairy or egg. I have left it in Italian to avoid the confusions attached to sherbet or sorbet; see also a specific section below.

BANQUET

Held by the Most Eminent Lord
THE CARDINAL DEL GIUDICE
Then Cleric of the Chamber, on the occasion of his *villeggiatura* in Albano,
with the attendance of the Most Excellent Lord Prince
DON LIVIO ODESCALCHI
*Nephew of His Holiness Pope Innocent XI, of holiest memory,
and of other prelates, numbering twelve in all.*[237]

The Lord Don Livio Odescalchi had gone hunting in the fields of Rocca Priora, and the hunt was rich in every animal; he was then invited by that Most Eminent Lord to enjoy a sumptuous banquet, arranged with all splendour and magnificence, in the palace of the Royal Chamber, where the guests were served at one royal plate.

The table was set with all the settings, with the noblest folds, worthy of admiration; each setting had four small round plates, one filled with a condiment of currants, with a little ribbon around it, dusted with fine sugar; one held Bologna mortadella with confected aniseeds on top, and underneath laurel branches; the third held a little royal salad with decorative borders for each guest; the fourth held lemon slices with sugar on top.

The table was filled with these cold display dishes:

First cold service.

1. A covered tart with pink apples and other candied things, with a sugar glaze on top, of the colour of cinnamon.

2. A large apple covered in strained eggs, garnished all around with eaglets made of marzipan paste.[238]

3. Naples melons, sliced, over laurel branches.

4. Pie with the coat of arms of the Lord Prince Don Livio, stuffed with pieces of pigeons, veal sweetbreads, veal chops, sliced ham, salami, and udder, and other noble ingredients.

---

237 Innocent XI (ruled 1676–1689, beatified in 1956) famously opposed nepotism and did not promote his relatives within the church hierarchy, but his family still of course gained great status among Italian aristocrats (their palace in Rome is one of the grandest from this era). The pope's nephew Livio (1652–1713) became duke of Bracciano and Ceri, fought with distinction against the Ottomans, and served as Captain General of the Church. Francesco del Giudice (1647–1725) came from a prominent Naples aristocratic family, and served in various clerical posts before being made a cardinal in 1690 by Pope Alexander VIII (ruled 1689–1691); at various times he served as viceroy of Sicily, archbishop of Monreale in Sicily, and as Grand Inquisitor in Spain; by the time of his death he was the dean of the College of Cardinals. Villeggiatura was the vacation (usually in late summer or fall) Italian elites traditionally spent on their country estates; Albano, on a pretty lake in the hills near Rome, was one of the most popular destinations, in an area filled with villas belonging to prominent ecclesiastics.

238 Latini calls this fruit a large *pomo d'Adamo* (literally, Adam's apple); I assume the term refers to a variety of apple (or possibly to another fruit), but I have not been able to identify which, so I will simply translate it as "large apple." Ridolfi, *Rinascimento*, 219, claims that this means medlars, but elsewhere Latini uses the standard word *nespolo* for medlars.

5. Blancmange garnished all around with eaglets made of candied quinces, and strained eggs.

6. Butter shaped in various figures, with decorative borders around them made with a pastry bag.

First hot service.

1. Each guest was served a thin stew with the finely sliced flesh of grey partridges, with cream tops and sugar, and a bit of lemon juice.

2. Spit-roasted ortolans mixed with veal sweetbreads wrapped in caul, and whole chicken livers with small lemons around them.

3. Meatloaves made with pounded veal, and also fresh eggs, candied citron, grated parmesan cheese, pistachios, truffles, and other noble ingredients, and around them small birds, stewed, mixed with sliced lemons and sour oranges.

4. A whole veal liver, finely larded and spit-roasted, and on it royal sauce, and around it whole lamb testicles mixed with fine flaky pastries stuffed with various things in syrup.

5. Grey partridges, finely larded, spit-roasted but not to a full cooking, then boiled in a fat broth, with cauliflowers, thin slices of ham, veal chops, stuffed truffles, and other noble ingredients, the plate garnished with halved tender pigeons, stuffed, and cooked in a pan, with the usual ingredients and rolls made with veal liver.

6. Deboned capons, well hanged, stuffed with their own flesh, ox marrow, grated parmesan cheese, fresh eggs, grated candied citron, pine nuts, sliced truffles, aromatic herbs, and the usual spices, cooked in good broth, garnished with sausages in Milanese style mixed with stuffed lettuces and thin slices of ham, boiled.

7. Capirottate made with capon flesh, mixed with slices of rich cheese, mostacciolo crumbs, cow marrow, bits of candied quinces, fresh egg yolks, and cream tops, with a fat broth.

8. Small cockerels, cooked in milk, served with a soup underneath with sliced white bread, toasted and dipped in capon broth, and fresh eggs on top poached in the same milk, with parmesan cheese and cinnamon on top.

9. English-style pies shaped like eagles, filled with veal chops, veal meatballs, thin slices of ham, quartered artichokes, first boiled and sautéed, chicken livers, quartered tender pigeons, pine nuts, pistachios, and other noble ingredients, with the usual spices and lemon juice, and around it a gilded sugar crown.

10. Larded grey partridges in Maltese style, spit-roasted, mixed with flaky pastries in French style, and sliced lemons.

11. Spit-roasted woodcocks, with a slice of cured back fat in their breasts, and cloves, garnished with fine sausage, also spit-roasted, and meat rolls made with veal liver and a sauce made with the innards of the woodcocks, with lemon and sour orange slices on the sides of the plate.

12. A tart of short crust pastry filled with blancmange, covered with sliced candied citron and pumpkin, with a glaze on top made with egg whites and lemon juice, to look like marble.

13. Roasted turtledoves, with a covered tart made of mostacciolo crumbs, mixed with halved sour oranges and lemons, the sides of the plate garnished with flaky pastries filled with blancmange, dusted with sugar.

14. Tender pigeons, spit-roasted, then halved and fried in good lard with on them a bastard sauce made with olives, capers, the usual spices, and other noble ingredients, mixed with halved sour oranges and roasted quails.

15. Suckling piglets, spit-roasted, stuffed with various ingredients, placed on the plate with their sauce inside, and garnished with decorative borders made with lemon pulp, and lemon slices.

16. A covered tart of things in syrup, candied pears, cinnamon, perfumed water, and sugar on top.

Second credenza service.

The settings were quickly removed, and the next ones were set, which were already prepared, with the following.[239]

1. Pears of various sorts.
2. Sliced parmesan cheese.
3. Cleaned fennels.
4. Sliced marzolino cheese from Florence.
5. Fresh grapes with flowers.
6. Apples of various sorts.
7. Chestnuts with sugar and pepper.
8. Cardoons with salt and pepper.
9. Celery, as above.
10. Large olives with sliced citron.
11. Stewed cauliflowers, with good oil, and sliced truffles.
12. Truffles with sliced oranges.
13. Oysters with lemons.
14. St. George's Mushrooms with a soup under them.
15. Tails of large shrimp.
16. Blancmange made with sugar and capon flesh.

These were taken away and four large boxes of confections were set on the table, in silver basins, with various other candied things, which was truly splendid, and gave just grounds for loud applause, with acclamations, and repeated "Hail!," and warm wishes of greater honours addressed to that most worthy prelate, who deserves the sacred purple

---

239 Here and in several other places Latini calls the following foods "fruits," though they include cheese and other things we would not call fruits today; the word fruits in this context meant, in a way, dessert, in the sense of things served at the end of the meal.

[i.e., the cardinalate] due to his marked talents and to his prominent services rendered to the Holy Apostolic See; because of these, he was indeed awarded the sacred purple by the happy memory of Pope Alexander VIII, who was most worthy of his Triregnum;[240] and nobody should think that I should speak out of passion, because I had the good fortune of serving him for three years, because I simply conform the praise I give him to that of the Roman people, who have always celebrated his glorious acts.

Once the banquet had ended, which was truly royal, with great splendour more than two hundred people were served from the staff of the above-mentioned Lord don Livio Odescalchi and of others in his company, so that the applause for such a generous prelate resonated from everyone's mouth.

LUNCH

Offered in Rome, in the month of December
By the Most Excellent Lord
THE PRINCE OF FEROLETO
On the occasion of his passage through Rome, on his return to Naples,
with the Most Excellent Lady
DONNA FULVIA PICA
Daughter of the Most Excellent Lord the Duke of Mirandola,
And with the Most Excellent Lord
THE PRINCE GIOVANNI,
Brother of the said Lady.[241]

The Most Excellent Lord Prince of Castiglione, father of the groom, to enjoy the delights of that magnificent city, spent eight days there together with the said bride, with a following of one hundred people, and on every day of that stay he received great honour from the Most Eminent Lord Cardinal Cybo, uncle of the bride, who had the prince served every day with his coach, and often also honoured him with his presence. The lunch was most sumptuous and lavish, and was thus arranged.

---

240 The Triregnum is the three-crowned tiara indicating the pope's supremacy in the temporal and spiritual realms.

241 The 1687 marriage of Tommaso, prince of Feroleto (1669–1721), son of Luigi d'Aquino, prince of Castiglione, to Fulvia Pica (1666–1731) was one of the grandest of the age in Naples. The Aquino were a very wealthy family of recent nobility; the bride was the daughter of Alessandro II Pico, duke of Mirandola and as such the lord of an actual independent principality—albeit a tiny one—in north-central Italy; the bride's mother was the sister of the duke of Modena, a somewhat greater Italian independent prince (Latini had worked in Mirandola and knew the duke and duchess, as appears in his story about the duke's pheasants earlier in his work). This marriage greatly increased the groom's family's status, and in 1699 Tommaso was granted a hereditary Spanish grandeeship, not without causing some scandal among grander families in Naples who did not receive that honour, see Giuseppe Galasso, *Napoli spagnola dopo Masaniello*, 2 vols. (Florence: Sansoni, 1982), 1:271 and 2:501. Cardinal Alderano Cybo (1613–1700) was the brother-in-law of the bride's paternal great-aunt.

First credenza service.

The table was covered with a very rich cloth of green eastern silk, outlined in gold, with a table cloth over it, very beautiful and most delicately folded, with the settings decorated with leaves, shaped in the figure of birds and peacocks, all made with the craft of the noblest folds; the guests were served at one royal plate.[242]

Each setting had three small round plates, filled with the following.

1. A small round plate with butter passed through a pastry bag to form various figures, with decorative borders around it, and sugar on top.

2. Another one filled with mortadella from Bologna, over laurel branches, with various aniseeds of various colours, everything retouched in gold and silver.

3. Another with a little royal salad with various little figures and decorative borders around it, everything in gold.

The table was filled with these cold dishes.

1. A pie with the coats of arms of the spouses, filled with meat of young wild pig, sliced cured back fat and ham, the usual spices, and other noble ingredients, with arabesques retouched in gold and silver.

2. Blancmange moulded in bas-relief retouched in gold and silver, mixed with *cuppelletti* made of short crust pastry, filled with strained eggs.[243]

3. A covered tart filled with various things candied and in syrup, retouched in gold and silver.

4. Amber-coloured jelly.

First hot kitchen service.

1. A thin stew for each of the noble guests, made with bits of sweetbreads, thin slices of ham, tender peas, quartered artichokes, veal meatballs, as large as a button, cooked in good broth, the usual spices, and aromatic herbs, served over slices of toasted bread, with a lattice pattern cover retouched in gold and silver.

2. Boiled capons, with around them pulled ham, mixed with little tarts made with short crust pastry and filled with green sauce, with their little covers.

3. Pigeons stuffed, between their skin and flesh, with their own livers, bits of sweetbreads, veal brains, everything pounded together, with marrow, grated cheese, pistachios, the usual spices, and other ingredients, well sautéed in a pan, with good broth, placed on the table and covered with a baked custard made of milk, cream tops, sugar, eggs, cinnamon, ground candied citron, and sponge cake crumbs, with a cover on it made in lattice pattern, retouched in gold and silver.

---

242 The silk is *ormesino*, named after the city of Ormuz, whence it came.

243 I have not been able to identify cuppelletti specifically, but they are clearly small pastries; the name must be related to their shape, possibly little hats (they recur in a couple of other banquets in Latini, and are possibly the same as the gubbelletti of an earlier example).

4. A small pie for each guest, made with short crust pastry, filled with ground turkey breast, bits of sweetbreads, thin slices of ham, pine nuts, whole pistachios, first soaked in rosewater, and on top a good little broth of egg yolks and lemon juice.

5. Small cockerels wrapped in pork caul, spit-roasted to a half-cooking, then stewed in a pot with a bastard condiment, mixed with little pies made of chicken livers cooked on embers, marzipan paste, pine nuts, pistachios, candied citron ground in the mortar, everything kneaded together with egg yolks and a few spices, then braised, first greased with lard or butter, and the plate garnished with slices of bread dipped in egg, and lemon slices.

6. A fillet or kidney of roasted veal, garnished with flaky pastries filled with blancmange, mixed with lemon and sour orange slices.

7. A covered tart made with pears in syrup, candied citron, cinnamon, and other noble ingredients, with sugar on top.

Second credenza service.

1. Parmesan cheese, on a napkin, retouched in gold and silver.

2. Bergamot pears on napkins, with laurel branches, retouched in gold and silver.

3. Pink apples with greenery and flowers around the plate.

4. Cardoons and celery with salt and pepper.

5. Fresh artichokes, brought from Naples.

6. Green fennel.

7. A little truffle soup, and one of St. George's mushrooms, for each guest.

During the eight days that these noble people stayed in Rome they were always served most splendidly, with great magnanimity, and no expense was spared, even for the lower servants.

BANQUET

Held in Naples, in the month of June
Hosted by the Most Excellent Lord
MARQUIS OF LA GRANCIA
Then General of the galleys of that Kingdom
For all the lord commanders of the Royal Fleet, who were served,
in three royal plates, for a number of twenty gentlemen.[244]

The table was filled with these cold dishes.

First cold service.

1. Three large pies with the coat of arms of His Majesty, stuffed with suckling veal chops, bits of tender cockerels, veal sweetbreads, chicken livers, artichoke stems, pine nuts, sliced ham and truffles, the usual spices, and other noble ingredients.

2. Blancmange made with milk, capon flesh, and perfumed water, the plates garnished with small pastries [cuppelletti] made with marzipan paste stuffed with strained eggs.

3. White and red melons, sliced, over laurel branches and shaved ice, very cold.

4. Peeled figs over laurel branches and shaved ice.

5. Tarts made with moscarelle pears, with a glaze made like marzipan, and studded with sticks of confected oranges.

6. Soups made with sponge cake slices, dipped in cold malmsey wine, with sugar and cinnamon on top, garnished with arabesques made of fine sugar and ground cinnamon.

7. Large Spanish olives, the plates garnished with decorative borders made of lemon pulp.

8. Nola soppressata sliced thinly, over laurel branches, encrusted with confected aniseeds of various colours.

9. Ham cooked in wine, with the usual spices, in a box made of dough, with arabesques around it, studded with cinnamon sticks and other confected sticks, with a glaze on top of sugar, in two colours.

10. Damaschine and pernigone plums over laurel branches, with shaved ice on top, which Spanish lords tend to like.

First kitchen service.

1. Slices of veal liver, first soaked in milk, and fried in good lard, mixed with veal sweetbreads and fried lamb testicles, the plates garnished with slices of blancmange dipped in egg and fried and lemon slices, with a royal sauce on top.

---

244 Nicolás Fernández de Cordoba (1626–1693) became in 1679 the first marquis of La Granja, and served as general of the Naples galleys as well as leading Spanish military and naval forces in New Spain.

2. Turtledoves, spit-roasted until they are more than half-cooked, then placed in a pan with a good fat broth, covered with white fennel cooked in good broth, mixed with fine sausages and thin slices of ham, with the usual spices.

3. Capons stuffed with a mixture of veal flesh, marrow, fresh eggs, grated parmesan cheese, bits of ground ham, pine nuts, aromatic herbs, the usual spices, and other noble ingredients; the plates garnished with stuffed onions mixed with cauliflowers, first boiled and sautéed, and pulled ham; we served two capons in each plate, on an apt soup.

4. Tender pigeons, eight in each plate, wrapped in paper with thin slices of cured back fat and ham, a bit of salt, mixed with veal sweetbreads wrapped in caul, the plates garnished with German pastries, fried, and mixed with lemon slices.

5. Round small boxes made of almond paste, filled with oysters, truffles, St. George's mushrooms, small birds from Cyprus, and other noble ingredients, with arabesques made of dough all around; we gave one box to each guest.

6. Small pies made with bits of hare and other noble ingredients, shaped like hares, and garnished with other things in dough that joined the pies, mixed with rolls made with veal liver and other apt ingredients, and we gave one pie to each guest.

7. Bits of sturgeon larded with pork cured back fat, and on them a bastard sauce, the plates garnished with Genoa-style pastries and lemon slices.

8. Meatloaves in the shape of stars, stewed, and in each ray of the star they held small birds, artichoke stems, and other noble ingredients, the plates garnished with roasted turtledoves, wrapped in caul, mixed with lemon slices.

9. Fried trout, and on it a little condiment made with olives and capers and other noble ingredients, the plates surrounded with lemon slices and fried beignets.

10. Turkey pullets, three in each plate, wrapped and spit-roasted, the plates garnished with ribbons made of Barbary dates, slices of candied citron, boiled first in a good white wine, and on the plates also various white comfits and pomegranate seeds, with fine sugar inside, and lemon slices around.

11. Small pies filled with capon flesh, cockscombs and chicken testicles, pine nuts, pistachios, with an apt little broth inside, and sugar on top; we gave one to each guest.

12. Suckling piglets stuffed with various ingredients, covered with young swallows and other small birds, bits of chicken livers, and an apt little condiment; the plates were garnished with small pastries stuffed with blancmange, and lemon slices.

13. Young grey partridges, seven in each plate, minutely larded in Maltese style, the plates garnished with small boxes made of dough stuffed with things in syrup, and mixed with slices of lemon and sour orange.

14. An oglia, in a box made of dough, with two capons, cabbages, Catalan turnips, garlic, onions, chickpeas, halved soppressata, bits of ham, beef, and wether, the usual spices, a bit of cumin and saffron, and other noble ingredients.[245]

---

245 The saffron, onions, and garlic mark this dish—and a few of the others in this event—as suited to the particular taste of Spanish lords.

Second credenza service.

1. Covered tarts or pizze made with things in syrup, with several candied fruits on top, with a glaze made like marzipan, with flowers around it.

2. Parmesan cheese.

3. Pears and apples.

4. Grapes and fennel.

5. Cherries and sour cherries.

6. Cold strawberries.

7. Plums and apricots.

8. Almonds and lazzarole, everything with leaves underneath and retouched with gold and silver, with shaved ice on top.

LUNCH

Held in Posillipo, in the month of September,
in the palace of the Most Excellent Lord
THE PRINCE OF ISCHITELLA
Attending was also the Most Excellent Lord
THE DUKE OF PARETE
Most Worthy Regent of the Supreme Council of His Catholic Majesty
And also the Most Excellent Lady
DONNA MADDALENA TRIVULZI
Bride of the son of the above-mentioned Lord Duke
AND THE MOST ILLUSTRIOUS LORD MAESTRO DI CAMPO
Brother of the same
And other lords, in the number of six, who were served at one royal plate.[246]

The table was set in the middle of a room that looked out on the sea, delightfully, and it was covered with a cloth of crimson damask, outlined in gold, and over it the lightest of table cloths, and napkins, all beautifully folded, so that they represented various figures. The table was filled with the following cold dishes.

---

246 Emanuel Pinto (1639–1690), of a Portuguese (possibly originally Jewish) family, rose to high office in the Spanish financial administration, became very rich, and in 1681 prince of Ischitella. Francesco Moles (d. 1713), of a Spanish family that had moved to Naples in the sixteenth century, duke of Parete in 1675, had a career at the very top of Spanish government ranks, serving as a high official, ambassador, or chancellor in Naples, Madrid, Milan, Venice, and Vienna; this gathering probably took place in 1682, when the duke of Parete served on the *Consejo de Italia* (the Spanish monarchy's supreme administrative body for all its Italian dominions) and as chancellor (the highest judicial position) of Milan, where his son Giovanni's marriage to Maddalena Trivulzio, of one of the grandest Milan aristocratic families, caused some scandal with other noble families (the marriage was not happy, and by 1694 the spouses lived separately, see Galasso, *Napoli spagnola*, 1:287 and 1:386); Francesco's brother Annibale had a distinguished military career, serving in Milan, Sicily, and Greece ("maestro di campo" was a military office).

1. Blancmange made with milk, sugar, and capon breast, and on the plate also small masks, made with the same blancmange, the colour of cinnamon.

2. Strained eggs arranged in the shape of fountains, in two orders, with small figures made of marzipan paste, a pretty and noble sight.

3. A covered tart or pizza made with marzipan paste, pigeon breast, candied citron, bone marrow, cinnamon, candied pistachios, cooked in the oven, with a glaze on top made to look like marble, made with egg whites, sugar, and lemon juice, garnished with various fruits in syrup.

4. A ham cooked in water and wine with whole cloves and cinnamon; after cooking it, we placed it in a box made of dough with varied arabesques, shaped like a small boat, with inside a few sailors made with marzipan paste, with oars in their hands; the ham was all studded with large confected sticks, mixed with bits of cinnamon, and with the skin of the ham we made a sail; the empty spaces in the boat were filled with candied things.

5. Nola soppressata, sliced, and on it aniseeds of various colours, and below it laurel branches, retouched in gold and silver.

6. A royal salad shaped like a pyramid with inside, in neat compartments, filled with candied citron, raisins, pine nuts, pitted olives, white and black grapes, pomegranate seeds, capers, and other noble ingredients, surrounded with a crown.

All the plates were served with greenery under them, and retouched in gold and silver.

First kitchen service.

1. Bits of veal liver, larded, spit-roasted, with royal sauce on top, garnished with fried blancmange all around, mixed with lamb testicles or glands, and slices of veal sweetbreads, spit-roasted, with various other pastries and lemon slices.

2. Turtledoves, spit-roasted but not to a full cooking, the cooking finished in good broth, with white fennel, soppressata or Giugliano fillet, placed in the plate with stuffed lettuce, cooked in good ox broth, and around them ground salami.

3. Deboned capons, stuffed, and garnished with stuffed onions, cauliflowers, and pulled ham.

4. Rabbits from Nisida [small island near Naples], stuffed with olives, capers, and other noble ingredients, stewed, garnished with fruits in syrup and confected aniseeds on top, mixed with various small birds, spit-roasted, and lemon slices.

5. Small pies made with short crust pastry, filled with ground veal, marrow, pine nuts, bits of sweetbreads, sautéed, with a little broth made with egg yolks and lemon juice, with a sugar glaze on top.

6. Small cockerels, first boiled, then halved, dredged in flour, dipped in egg, and fried in good lard, mixed with slices of udder, first boiled, dipped in egg, and fried, placed on the plate with a royal sauce on top, and various white confected aniseeds, the plate garnished with flaky pastries filled with ground candied citron, marrow, egg yolks, cinnamon, and perfumed water.

Second credenza service.

The pizza that was already on the table was divided up, and also the royal salad, and a small round plate of it was given to each guest, and the following were placed on the table.

1. An iced pyramid with figs and other fruits.
2. Spanish olives with lemon slices around them.
3. Grapes with flowers around them.
4. Bergamot pears with flowers and greenery.
5. Parmesan cheese, over napkins and with laurel branches on top, retouched in gold and silver.
6. Very cold melons.

These were removed, and we placed on the table four large basins with candied things; then we removed those and brought water to wash hands, and the guests returned to their apartments to rest.

For the afternoon, we prepared sorbetti of all kinds, cold and hot chocolate, and pyramids of iced fruits; many ladies and gentlemen arrived around 8 p.m., and they all partook of these things.

In the evening, the table was again prepared, and twelve guests dined, served at one enhanced royal plate, in the same order as at lunch, and in the same way.

The table was set and filled with four large basins holding things in marzipan paste and other convent pastries, a noble and pretty sight.

1. Each setting has a small salad, made with various ingredients, with decorative borders made of lemon pulp.
2. Sliced soppressata, over laurel branches, and aniseeds of various colours on top, mixed with lemon slices.
3. Very cold strawberries, washed in wine, with sugar on top, and arabesques on the sides of the plate, also made of sugar.

First hot service.

1. Roasted cockerels, mixed with crostini with slices of roasted ham, dipped in a vinegar condiment, mixed with flaky pastries and lemon slices; the pastries were under the cockerels, and on top the *cassoliglia* [a casserole].
2. Cassoliglia made with bits of pigeons, bits of sweetbreads, veal chops, thin slices of ham, chicken livers, small birds, bits of boiled kid tongue, thin slices of cow udder, marrow, sliced truffles, St. George's mushrooms, various seafood, the usual spices, with lemon juice, and other noble ingredients, the plate garnished with little pastries filled with marrow, candied citron, marzipan paste, and cinnamon, and fried in good butter, with sugar on top, mixed with lemon slices.
3. A plate of halved pigeons, cooked in scapece, first boiled, halved, dredged in flour, soaked in beaten eggs, and fried in good lard, with a sauce on top made with mostacciolo crumbs, perfumed vinegar, bits of cinnamon, whole cloves, and other ground

spices, [all to make] a little condiment first boiled and then poured on the pigeons, with confected aniseeds on top, the plate garnished with halved quinces in syrup, covered with aniseeds of various colours.

4. A plate of lasagne made by nuns, which were exquisite.

5. Roasted veal fillet mixed with flaky pastries filled with blancmange, with sugar on top, mixed with small lemons.

6. A pizza or covered tart made with short crust pastry, filled with apples in syrup, candied pumpkin, mostacciolo crumbs, perfumed water, and other noble ingredients.

7. Various seafood, cooked on embers, with their shells, sea urchins, opened oysters, in a small round plate for each guest, with the necessary spoons.

Second credenza service.

1. Parmesan cheese.

2. Bergamot pears.

3. Fennel.

4. Sweet apples.

5. Tender artichokes.

These were removed, and we placed back on the table the usual four basins with various convent pastries and other candied things.

This noble gathering ended around 4 a.m., and by that point the boats were ready, so all the guests went back to their own homes.[247]

---

247 Though roads existed, it was elegant (and no doubt very pleasant) to travel to and from Posillipo by boat.

BANQUET

Held in the city of Loreto, at the Holy House, in the month of December
On the occasion when the Most Excellent Lord
THE PRINCE OF FEROLETO
Went to meet the Most Excellent Lady his bride
DONNA FULVIA PICA
Daughter of His Most Serene Highness
THE LORD DUKE
OF MIRANDOLA.[248]

The prince left Naples together with the Most Excellent Lord his father the prince of Castiglione, with a retinue of twelve gentlemen, eight pages, four room servants, five coaches, a litter, six smaller coaches, twelve carriages for the luggage, all covered with beautiful drapes, all embroidered in silk, and other baggage, which all produced a beautiful sight.[249] The pages and gentlemen were all richly clothed, with suits outlined in gold, of the finest cloth, with two excellent buglers, footmen, gentlemen's attendants, and other low servants, numbering one hundred. When we had arrived in Valcimara, in travelling to meet the above-mentioned Lady Princess, we were met with a courier, sent by the Lord Prince Galiotto, her brother, with the news that the bride was staying in Ancona. The Lord Prince had the complaisance of sending me ahead by post, with the order, and the money, to get to the Holy House in Loreto and there obtain a palace, the best possible, well adorned, without regard to the cost, and I promptly executed the orders of His Excellency, and rented a palace situated in the area known as Monte Reale, in the city of Loreto, very well decorated and convenient to receive such distinguished guests. The next day the Lord Prince of Castiglione and the Prince of Feroleto, his son the groom, arrived, in the evening; another courier arrived shortly thereafter for my lords the Princes with the news that the above-mentioned Lady Princess the bride was eight miles from the Holy House, with a retinue of over one hundred and fifty people. My lord the prince, with another gentleman, immediately rode his horse to meet his Lady bride, and he found her travelling, in between two coaches, accompanied by the Lady Marquise Tassoni, from Este; the Prince gestured to the coachman to stop, and the Prince the groom approached her in the most galant manner, and explained to the ladies that he had been sent by the Lord Prince of Feroleto to acquire news of his Lady bride, of whether her health was good, and of whether she was enjoying her travels, adding that the groom was just a few miles away; the ladies, from the way in which he spoke and behaved, were in some doubt, but the Lady bride, who had his portrait on her chest, immediately recognized him, and the Marquise Tassoni called the Prince Galiotto, brother of the bride,

---

248 This is the same couple for whose marriage the lunch in Rome was held, described a few pages earlier. Loreto, in the Marches (Latini's birth region), was (and is) a major pilgrimage site because of its miraculous relic of the Holy House: this home, in which the Virgin Mary lived, was transported by angels to Loreto in the Middle Ages; the Virgin of Loreto is, appropriately enough, the patron saint of air travellers.

249 The smaller coaches are *calessi*, which today refers to a two-wheel coach.

and told him that the Duchess their mother had entrusted his sister to the marquise's care, that she was right then being attacked on the road, and that she did not know what to do; many of the gentlemen who accompanied the bride were already dismounting, out of curiosity to know what was happening, and to see the prince, the groom; the Lady Marquise surrendered her own place to the Prince; in the meantime I ordered a beautiful refreshment prepared, with iced and hot chocolate, various other iced waters, and candied things, and mostaccioli, and, reflecting that these Lords and Ladies might arrive during the night, I thought it expedient to take forty torches, of Venice wax, and another twenty; I brought them together with the refreshment, and with enough people to carry everything; I met the group three miles [from Loreto]; they all dismounted and partook of the refreshment with the greatest satisfaction, and since the sky was already darkened by the sunset and the night imminent, we lit the torches, about one and a half mile from the Holy House, and this beautiful lit procession made for an admirable sight, so that the local inhabitants all lined the streets to witness such a noble entrance, with the sound of trumpets and the splendour of the lights, and to the astonishment of the viewers; the whole company reached the palace, which I had already arranged, and since it was not large enough for so many people, a large number of the servants was sent to the inn, and only ladies, damsels, and knights remained in the palace, where the tables were already nobly set and prepared, filled with the following cold dishes.[250]

On the first table, at which the bride, groom, and princes were to eat, was set with a cloth of crimson damask, richly outlined in gold, with a carefully folded table cloth on it, with one and a half palmi of Flanders lace all around it, and the settings were decorated with various birds, rocks, little boats with oars, and whimsical leaves, all proportionate, with various flowers around them, and in their natural colours.[251] At the end of the table were:

1. A large pie bearing the coats of arms of the bride and groom, stuffed with halved small pullets, veal chops, sliced ham, veal sweetbreads, and other noble ingredients, with arabesques all around it, retouched in gold and silver, and with gilded bay leaves.

2. Blancmange shaped in moulds in bas-relief, mixed with little mounds of jelly of various colours, retouched in gold and silver.

3. Slices of mortadella from Bologna over laurel branches on a napkin, retouched in gold and silver, and on top aniseeds of various colours.

4. A covered tart made with appie apples in syrup, with bits of ground candied citron and pumpkin, cinnamon, and perfumed water, with a glaze on top made like marzipan; in the middle an eagle of the same paste, artfully made, and retouched in gold and silver, with bay leaves around it.

5. Sliced red melons, brought on purpose from Naples, with bay leaves in top, retouched in gold and silver.

6. Large Spanish olives, well and neatly arranged, with decorative borders around them.

---

250 This whole set of scenes, with the groom pretending to be someone else, and the guardian lady pretending to be frightened, sounds of course remarkably like a theatre performance.

251 All these decorations were presumably made with folded cloth.

7. A turkey, with its tail and wings open and made of marzipan paste, the turkey seasoned with salt and pepper, covered with a jelly made [to look] like pork belly, the plate garnished with small pastries [cuppelletti] filled with strained eggs, everything retouched in gold and silver.

8. A turkey, standing, with a halberd in its left foot, raised so as to seem as if the bird were holding it in its hand, the breast larded with long confected citrons, half covered with marzipan paste, with the coat of arms of the bride and groom in its beak, made of sugar paste; with a retinue of four cockerels, dressed like pilgrims, with their little mantles, made of marzipan paste, around their necks, and the pilgrim staff, similar to the turkey.

Each setting had three small round plates, one with a condiment of currants, with a little ribbon around it, made of marzipan paste, retouched in gold and silver.

The second held a little royal salad, with its decorative borders.

The third was filled with cauliflowers, first cooked, mixed with sliced truffles, first sautéed in good oil, garnished with a little border, and we dressed them with oil and vinegar when the guests sat down.

The groom and bride dined, attended, this first evening, by two titled young ladies; the lady marquise Tassoni, with the lord marquis Tassoni from Este, her husband, the Lord Prince Galiotto, the Lord Prince Giovanni, brother of the lady bride, the Lady Baroness Orsini, who arrived for the occasion, to welcome the bride, the Lord Prince of Castiglione, father of the groom, and other titled lords, numbering twelve, and they were served at one enhanced royal plate.

First kitchen service.

1. A tender boiled pigeon for each guest, in a small plate, with slices of toasted bread under it, bits of sweetbreads, first sautéed, sliced truffles, asparagus tips, green pistachios, with a little broth on top made with fresh egg yolks and lemon juice, with a cover on top made with marzipan paste, in lattice pattern, retouched in gold and silver.

2. Thrushes, spit-roasted, mixed with veal sweetbreads, wrapped in caul, fine sausage, with chicken livers, wrapped in pork caul, the plate garnished with flaky pastries filled with various noble ingredients, mixed with slices of sour orange and lemon.

3. Pigeons, filled with pounded veal, thin slices of ham, egg yolks, pitted sour cherries, the usual spices, aromatic herbs, and other noble ingredients, with a baked custard on top made with eggs, milk, and sugar, green pistachios on top, and an apt cover retouched in gold and silver.

4. A small pie for each guest, made with ground capon breast, bits of sweetbreads, cockscombs and chicken livers, clean pine nuts, with a little broth of egg yolks and lemon juice, and sugar on top.

5. Two hare haunches, spit-roasted, mixed with grey partridges, larded in the English style, with inside a royal sauce made with vinegar, sugar, raisins, pine nuts, bits of candied citron, the plate garnished with pears in syrup, with white aniseeds around them, mixed with small pies of short crust pastry filled with various things in syrup.

6. A casserole with bits of pigeons, bits of sweetbreads, veal chops, veal meatballs, with the usual ingredients, small birds, peas, artichokes, asparagus tips, chicken livers, the usual spices, St. George's mushrooms, thin slices of truffles, and other noble ingredients, the plate garnished with flaky pastries filled with blancmange and sliced candied pumpkin, with sugar on top, and the usual cover in lattice pattern, retouched in gold and silver.

7. Spit-roasted quails, wrapped in pork caul, mixed with pork fillet, one slice for each guest, also spit-roasted, with salt and ground wild fennel, the plate garnished with various short crust pastries, shaped like mostaccioli and other whimsical shapes, mixed with sour orange slices.

8. Maccheroni made with fine flour, milk, eggs, and sugar, cooked in capon broth, mixed with slices of provatura, first fried in butter, and good grated parmesan cheese, the plate garnished with faldicchere eggs, placed over a nest of strained eggs.

9. Wild pig, cooked in a lard broth, with the usual ingredients and fruits in it; enhanced with wild pigeons, the plate garnished with quinces in syrup filled with various candied things, and placed in small boxes, with a glaze of sugar paste made with egg whites, an apt cover on top, then browned in the oven.

10. A veal fillet, spit-roasted, well larded with cloves, mixed with small meatloaves, their crust removed, and stuffed with capon flesh, bits of sweetbreads, the crustless bread from the loaves, egg yolks, sliced candied citron, sugar, and cream tops, everything dipped in milk, and cooked in the oven, with butter, and with a sugar glaze on top, the loaves mixed with royal cookies, and around them also shells made of dough outlined in gold on the outside, and filled with grilled oysters mixed with truffles and lemon juice, first cooked in a pan, with pepper as needed on top, and sliced lemons around.

11. Slices of sturgeon, each weighing about ten ounces, grilled, with salt, wild fennel, and a little condiment on top made of olives, capers, pine nuts, raisins, bits of candied citron, cinnamon, cloves, cooked in a perfumed vinegar, with sugar, so that it was sweet and sour, the plate garnished with small pies filled with oysters, truffles, sturgeon soft roe, St. George's mushrooms, first soaked in malmsey wine, pine nuts, raisins, and shrimp tails, the usual spices, and aromatic herbs, with an apt little broth made with ambrosine almonds, with a proper glaze on top; of this one small round plate for each guest.[252]

12. Spit-roasted woodcocks, finely larded, mixed with turtledoves, the plate garnished with halved sour oranges and fried German pastries, and on top the usual sauce made with the birds' innards.

13. Large roasted red mullets, two for each guest, mixed with small squid, fried, in small boxes made of dough, the plate garnished with lemon slices.

---

252 Soft roe in Italian is *latte di pesce* (literally, fish milk; in fact, seminal fluid).

Second credenza service.

1. Blancmange retouched in gold and silver.
2. A covered tart made with caravelle pears, in syrup, mixed with Florentine citron jams, with thin slices of candied citron under it, retouched in gold and silver.

Then these were quickly placed on the table.

1. Bergamot pears.
2. Parmesan cheese.
3. Pink and appie apples mixed.
4. White cardoons with pepper and salt.
5. Celery with pepper and salt.
6. White fennel.
7. White and black grapes.
8. Artichokes.
9. Tender peas, brought from Naples.
10. Fresh pine nuts, sprinkled with rosewater.
11. Confected aniseeds.
12. Boxes of candied quince.

Everything was on a napkin, with laurel branches, decorated in various ways, retouched in gold and silver.

Everything was removed, and four basins were placed on the table, two with white confections and two with candied things of all sorts.

We gave water for the hands, and toothpicks, with lemon slices, on napkins.

A most beautiful ball began, and a sumptuous musical concert, with various instruments, which lasted for the greater part of the night.

While the dinner was taking place, we arranged the second, third, fourth, and fifth tables, where ate the attending ladies and young ladies of the Lady bride, and other attending women, with other servants; thirty gentlemen were served at the second table, with the same arrangement, since the Lord Prince had commanded me to treat these gentlemen lavishly; this noble recreation lasted for eight days, and that whole time we kept the tables set, and since, given the multitude of guests, I did not have sufficient silverware, Monsignor Ferretti, then Governor of the Holy House, lent some to me with the greatest courtesy, giving to my credenziero four hundred plates of various sorts; after eight days, we left Loreto, early in the morning, and Monsignor the Governor had the complaisance of letting us enjoy a beautiful hunt, about two miles from the Holy House; the whole trip was joyful and pleasant, and brought great earnings to innkeepers, because of the large company, which could not fit in a single establishment; after five days, we arrived in Rome, after a happy travel, and at Ponte Mollo we were met with a most splendid honour coach sent by the Lord Cardinal Cybo, then the pre-eminent cardinal, to serve the bride and groom, with twenty-two other coaches, belonging to several others; we alighted at the palace of Monsignor Carafa, at the Ciambella, where we stayed eight days, entertaining always with the most lavish care, filled with generous splendour; after eight days, we left for Naples, reaching Velletri the first evening, where we were welcomed in the palace of the Lord Cardinal Ginetti, with a sumptuous and splendid dinner; after a few more days, we happily reached Naples, where we found a most splendid banquet, which I had arranged and organized before our departure.[253]

BANQUET

Held in the villa of the Most Illustrious Lord
THE REGENT CARRILLO,
MY LORD AND MASTER
In Torre del Greco, for the Most Excellent Lord
THE COUNT OF SANTO STEFANO
And the Most Excellent Lady
THE COUNTESS HIS WIFE
With the Most Excellent Lady
THE MARQUISE OF AYTONA
Their daughter
AND THE MOST EXCELLENT LORD MARQUIS
Husband of the same lady
With others, numbering six, who were served at the first table,
at one royal plate, in the month of April.[254]

The table was set in a large room in the villa, from which through a large window one could see Capri on one side, and the famous Mount Vesuvius through another, while from a balcony opposite the table came to view a large street filled with trees on all sides, such that the eye could not have enough of such an enticing view, and such a varied one, of sea, of land, of mountains; the table was covered with a cloth of crimson damask, with the finest table cloths on it, all laced around, and the settings displayed beautiful folds, with leaves and whimsical arabesques, worthy of admiration; this was the banquet's arrangement.

---

253 Monsignor Ferretti is possibly Raimondo Ferretti (1650–1719), bishop of Loreto and Recanati in 1690–1692 (the Pico-Aquino wedding took place in 1687, but perhaps Ferretti was governor of the Holy House before being appointed bishop); Latini calls Cardinal Cybo "cardinal master," the term usually used for the cardinal-nephew, which Cybo was not; he was however secretary of state and then dean of the college of cardinals beginning in the late 1670s. The Ciambella is an area in the old centre of Rome, near the ruins of the baths of Agrippa. Giovanni Francesco Ginetti received the red hat in 1681 and died in 1691.

254 We have already been in this villa with a prior banquet; Francisco Benavides, Count of Santo Stefano, succeeded the marquis del Carpio and served as viceroy of Naples in 1687–1696; his son-in-law, Guillén de Moncada (d. 1727), was the sixth marquis of Aytona.

First credenza service.

1. A veal pie, shaped like a shield, with the coat of arms of His Excellency on it, made with sugar paste outlined in gold, with myrtle and laurel branches under it, and roses around it.

2. Roasted turkeys, larded with candied pumpkin strips, their wings, tails, and necks made of marzipan paste retouched in gold and silver, the plate garnished with little mounds of jelly in various colours.

3. Covered tarts of moscarelle pears, mostacciolo crumbs, sugar, and cinnamon, over laurel branches, retouched in gold and silver, and around roses and flowers.

4. Blancmange the colour of cinnamon, in royal slices, the plate garnished with strained eggs.

5. Ham glazed with sugar, with a cover on it in lattice pattern, placed over four little statues of marzipan paste, which held it up by their hands.

6. Strained eggs served over a pyramid made of almond paste, and around the plate a crown covered with the same eggs, and at the bottom of the plate slices of sponge cake.

7. A soup made with large slices of sponge cake, soaked in good muscatel wine, kept cold by shaved ice, the sides of the plate garnished with various arabesques made of sugar and cinnamon.

8. Butter shaped like a fortress, with its artillery, also made of butter, with an artificer and soldiers all around, the outside of the plate garnished with various flowers and roses; each guest's setting included three small round plates, one with a little salad with its decorations and other noble ingredients; another with pulled ham all encrusted with aniseeds of various colours, with a little ribbon around it, in bas-relief; and the third with a pomegranate sauce with arabesques around it made in fine sugar; the table was covered with the lightest veils, with gilded lace.

First hot service.

1. A bowl of broth for each guest, with inside slices of toasted bread, the broth made with beef, two wild doves, a chicken, bits of ham, soppressata, the wings of several chickens, and wether meat, everything cooked together with a whole garlic head, a bit of saffron, chickpeas, apt spices, and the usual aromatic herbs.

2. Spit-roasted Sorrento veal, mixed with thrushes, also roasted, the plate garnished with small pastries filled with blancmange, mixed with lemon slices.

3. A fried dish made with sweetbreads, lamb glands or testicles, bits of veal liver, soaked for several hours in milk, bits of brains dipped in egg, quartered artichokes, whole chicken livers, slices of udder dipped in egg, bread slices also soaked in milk, everything dipped in egg, with a royal sauce on top, and the plate garnished with short crust pastries and lemon slices, with a cover on top.

4. Small pies in Spanish style, made with a bit of turkey cockerel, ground Sorrento veal, bits of sweetbreads, bits of ham, cockscombs and chicken testicles, a garlic condiment, clean pistachios over it, dipped in rosewater, and an apt little broth made with egg yolks, one pie for each guest.

5. A casserole made with bits of pigeons, veal chops, sliced ham, sweetbreads, lamb testicles or glands, saveloy, peas, artichokes, razor shells, wedge shells, limpets, and other seafood, truffles, St. George's mushrooms, and other noble ingredients; with an apt meat juice, the plate garnished with small tarts and fruits, with compartments filled with sour cherries in syrup, green and white sauce, mixed with rolls made with the usual ingredients; the usual cover on top, in lattice pattern, retouched in gold and silver.

6. Grey partridges wrapped in paper and roasted, mixed with small Spanish-style pies, lemon slices, and halved sour oranges, one bird for each guest.

7. A Spanish-style casserole, with tomatoes, pigeons, veal breast, stuffed chicken necks, cockscombs and chicken testicles, ham, then thickened with eggs, the plate garnished with small boxes made of dough filled with a stuffing of pounded veal and other noble ingredients, mixed with lemon slices, with an apt cover on top.[255]

8. Tender pigeons, first boiled and then halved, dredged in flour, and fried in good lard, with a sauce on top, the plate garnished with pears in syrup and little stars made of candied quinces, all covered with aniseeds of various colours; with its cover.

9. An impanata made with rabbits, minced veal chops, ham slices, mixed with halved quails, with the usual spices, and other noble ingredients.

10. Small cockerels, filled with pounded veal, bits of ham, marrow, bits of soppressata, pine nuts, pitted sour cherries, crustless bread soaked in broth, fresh egg yolks, whole pistachios, with the usual spices and aromatic herbs, all cooked first in a pan, with a good meat juice; over it we placed a baked custard made with milk, eggs, sugar, and bits of candied citron, the plate garnished with slices of quinces in syrup, and a cover, all encrusted with poppies of various colours.[256]

11. Oglia made with capon, wether back, beef, soppressata, a piece of Giugliano fillet, whole heads of garlic, slices of ham, chickpeas, saffron, Catalan turnips, cabbages, aromatic herbs, and other noble ingredients, everything in a box made of dough, with arabesques around it and a cover on top.

12. A pizza of quinces in syrup, decorated with a glaze on top.

13. Ravioli made with fine flour mixed with eggs, milk, sugar, and crustless bread, with sugar and cinnamon on top.

14. Blancmange moulded with various figures in bas-relief.

---

255 Here Latini calls the stuffing *salpicone*, an Italianized Spanish term, which might be in tribute to the guests, as with impanata just below, and the presence of saffron, chickpeas, garlic, and other "Spanish" ingredients throughout this banquet.

256 The poppies are *papagnini*, an uncommon Neapolitan word (I am not absolutely sure of this translation, but it seems likely in the context).

Second credenza service.

1. Bergamot pears.
2. Parmesan cheese over a napkin and laurel branches, retouched in silver.
3. Grapes with flowers around it.
4. Pink apples with flowers and a napkin underneath.
5. Curly celery, arranged to look like a mountain, and decorated with flowers around.
6. Halved fava beans with flowers.
7. Early almonds with flowers.
8. Artichokes mixed with flowers.
9. Fennel, also with flowers.

These were removed, as was the first table cloth, and we placed in the middle of the table various boxes with confections, candied things, and preserves, and then we offered perfumed water to the guests to wash their hands.

At the same time, the young ladies were served who had come in the retinue of the Lady Vicereine, with the same folded settings, and the same order and service as the Lord Viceroy, Lady Vicereine, and their companions, with the same confections, fruits, and other cold dishes, all perfect.

After these tables had finished, we started another one, with twelve gentlemen, who had come to serve the Lord Viceroy and Lady Vicereine; once all the tables had finished, the guests went to rest in the various rooms in the villa, all adorned in royal style, thanks to the splendour of my Lord Regent, who in all his actions always displays incomparable magnanimity.

After a brief rest, they went to the usual hunt of rabbits, hares, goats, and other wild animals, which greatly abound, since this hunt is reserved for the villa, while the ladies who accompanied the Lady Vicereine spent time dancing and singing along the pleasant roads of this place.

During this time, we prepared various refreshments, including iced chocolate, sorbetti of various sorts, pyramids of fruits, also iced, and all this was served to the guests, and then what was left over was distributed to all their servants, including the lowest ones, numbering over three hundreds, between hunters, coachmen, grooms, sailors, and others, so that everybody was quite satisfied, and they all shouted with joy and jubilation long live the Lord Viceroy, and hurrah for the generosity of my Lord Regent.

When the time came to return to Naples, all ladies, before they entered their coaches, were presented with a fan of the finest workmanship, and Rome-style gloves of rare leather.

Everything was done with decorum and satisfaction, even though the Lord Regent was unable to attend, as he had to stay home because of an indisposition that did not allow him to leave his bed.

BANQUET

held on the arrival of the married couple in Naples,
for the nuptials of the Most Excellent Lord
THE PRINCE OF FEROLETO
and the Most Excellent Lady
DONNA FULVIA PICA,
daughter of His Most Serene Highness
THE LORD DUKE
OF MIRANDOLA,
*in the month of January, attended by twenty-four ladies
and thirty gentlemen, served from two royal basins.*[257]

When this most noble lady arrived, the Lady Donna Giovanna d'Aquino, princess of Castiglione, mother of the groom, a lady filled with generous spirit, wished to display her magnanimity in the preparation of her palace, at Santa Lucia, in a location most elegant and delightful by its view of the sea.[258] The said Lady ordered the apartments of this palace adorned richly and superbly, so that all who saw them admired them, in particular the pomp of certain draperies embroidered by needlepoint, which showed the life of the Angelic Doctor Saint Thomas Aquinas, ancestor to this most noble family. In one of these decorated rooms one marvelled at a magnificent bed of incomparable worth, the most exquisite that art could produce, ready for the bride and groom to enjoy its rich feathers; this filled everybody's eyes with admiration. Equally admirable were the credenze richly covered with silverware, both white and gilded. It was remarkable how all the functions of this nuptial solemnity took place with perfect punctuality and without any disorder, thanks to the diligence, hard work, and vigilance of those in charge of them.

First the table was set, with a green cloth all embroidered in gold, and above it a very light table cloth, with all its folds, bordered in Flemish lace one and a half palmi long; the table settings also with beautiful folds showing various figures, and covered in the finest cloth, also folded in the shape of leaves, with a beautiful and creative design.

The table was filled with the following cold dishes and triumphs, all retouched in gold.

The first triumph, in the middle of the table, was a chariot above a small hill, filled with flowers, all made with the subtlest folds of white cloth, with four lions drawing this chariot, and an eagle, its wings open, where the coachman would be. The eagle looked at a figure entitled *Fame*, which sat above this chariot, surrounded by rays made with the lightest of veils, retouched in gold and silver; the figure had its arm raised, holding in its right hand the sun, as an allusion to the symbol of Saint Thomas and to the coat of arms of the House of Aquino; the chariot was five palmi high.[259]

---

257 Yet again we meet this couple, now finally arrived in Naples.

258 The d'Aquino couple continued to rise in prominence, and indeed the last Spanish viceroy of Naples, the duke of Villena, stayed for a long time in their palace in Santa Lucia after his arrival in the city in 1702 (Galasso, *Napoli spagnola*, 2:634); the Santa Lucia area is right along the sea coast, just west of the old city centre.

259 The sun was part of the iconography of St. Thomas Aquinas (Tommaso d'Aquino in Italian), the great Dominican theologian of the thirteenth century, to whose family the Aquino of seventeenth-

There were also six other triumphs, three palmi high, namely standing eagles, ostriches, and sirens, all made of the subtlest folds.

First cold service.

1. Two pies in the shape of the sun, filled with bits of veal, cockerels, ham slices, and other noble ingredients, retouched in gold, placed over laurel branches, also gilded.

2. Tarts with candied things, with marzipan on the bottom, showing the coats of arms of the bride and groom, retouched in gold and silver.

3. Strained eggs shaped like sea rocks, with small pastries on top [cuppelletti] and around the plate a large number of bees, made of sugar paste, in the act of making honey.

4. Pigeons, first boiled and then fried, with a sauce on top, and confected white pistachios; the basins garnished with pears in syrup in small pastry boxes made of marzipan and retouched in gold and silver, encrusted with aniseeds of various colours.

5. Capons seasoned in salt and pepper, with their heads made of marzipan paste, displayed as in the act of pecking each other on the chest, covered in an amber-coloured jelly, and garnished with pine nut cores, the sides of the plate decorated with jelly slices made to look like pork belly, surrounded by small pastries filled with pitted sour cherries, retouched in gold and silver.

6. Small boxes of Portugal candied quinces, with napkins underneath, retouched in gold and silver.

7. Blancmange moulded in a bas-relief, retouched in gold and silver.

8. Two hams in a stand pie, wrapped all around with arabesques, and around it little weathervanes made of sugar paste, and two lions on top made of marzipan paste, retouched in gold and silver.[260]

9. Two plates of butter in the shape of various figurines, in natural colour, and around it decorative borders, retouched in gold and silver.

10. A mountain of *struffoli* covered in sugar, around them small taffeta weathervanes, and the coats of arms of the bride and groom made in sugar paste, retouched in gold and silver.[261]

Each setting had three small round plates.

1. One filled with pulled ham, with on top aniseeds of various colours, carved small slices of lemon, and around it decorative borders also made with lemon.

2. Another filled with a salad, made with olives, capers, pine nuts, and other noble ingredients, with the usual decorative borders around it, and in the middle figurines made of chard roots.

---

century Naples claimed—somewhat improbably—to belong. This chariot is probably the one depicted in the print in Latini's volume, by Filippo Schor, discussed above.

260 *Banderola* is literally weathervane, though here and nearby below it might simply be a small flag.

261 Struffoli are today one of Naples' classic Christmas desserts: small fried balls of dough, covered with honey and sugared treats.

3. Another with a sauce made with a pomegranate wine, with a little garland around it, and cinnamon on top.

First kitchen service.

1. Four boiled capons in each basin, with underneath a soup made with slices of toasted bread covered with cardoon stems, first boiled in a good broth, celery stems, bits of pork belly, cut sausages, and other noble ingredients; the basins garnished with soppressata slices, and little tarts stuffed with green sauce, and on top a lid retouched in gold and silver.

2. A fried dish of veal liver, first soaked in milk, quartered tender pigeons, Sorrento veal sweetbreads, udder slices, first boiled, dredged in flour, dipped in egg, and fried, whole chicken livers, lamb testicles, ham slices, first sautéed in a pan, and brains first dipped in egg and fried, the dish garnished with various fried pastries, lemon slices, artichoke quarters, and fried asparagus, a lid on top encrusted with varied aniseeds, retouched in gold and silver.

3. Roasted partridges, larded in the French style, with the birds' own heads, the basins garnished with small pastries with things in syrup, surrounded with slices of lemon and sour orange, with the little sauce customary for partridges, and in the middle a small hawk, one palmo high, made of marzipan paste, in the act of pecking a partridge.

4. Large English-style pies, stuffed with veal chops, small birds, cockscombs, chicken testicles and livers, veal meatballs, made with the usual ingredients, bone marrow, ground veal kidney fat, peas, truffles, St. George's mushrooms, pine nuts, pistachios, thin ham slices, artichoke quarters, first sautéed, and other noble ingredients, with sugar on top.

5. Tender boiled pigeons, cut in half, dredged in flour and fried, with a sauce on top made with *merausto*, the basins garnished with little pastry boxes.[262]

6. Roasted woodcocks surrounding a boar thigh, spit-roasted, lightly larded, with cloves, over bread slices, and covered by their innards with lemon juice and pepper; the basins garnished with flaky pastries filled with blancmange, surrounded by sliced lemons and sour oranges.

7. Veal heads stuffed with veal flesh, cream tops, bits of candied citron, small birds, diced ham, bits of pork belly, bone marrow, wedge shells, truffles, St. George's mushrooms, whole pistachios, the usual spices, veal brains, and other noble ingredients, surrounded with halved cockerels stuffed with a spicy mixture. Along the rim of the basins a pastry twist stuffed with things in syrup, retouched in gold and silver, with an apt baked custard over it made with milk, cream tops, and eggs, with a lid.

8. Small pies stuffed with finely minced capon flesh, cockscombs, chicken livers and testicles, bits of sweetbreads, with the usual little broth made of egg yolks and lemon juice, and served with sugar on top.

---

262 Merausto is the Italianization of the Catalan *miraus,* a traditional sauce made with almonds, broth, sugar, verjuice, and various spices, which was typically used for fowl, see Scappi, *Opera,* 263.

9. A Genoa-style gigot, made with several turkey breasts, well seasoned in a meat juice, garnished with sautéed sweetbreads and various types of seafood, with a border of pomegranate seeds, the basins garnished by little twisted pastries [ciambellette], with a lid on top, and lemon juice inside.

10. A casserole with veal chops, veal meatballs, cockscombs and chicken testicles, quartered tender pigeons, small birds, thin slices of ham, bits of pork belly, bits of sweetbreads, udder slices, first boiled, lamb testicles, truffles, St. George's mushrooms, pine nuts, tender peas, artichoke quarters, first boiled and then sautéed, razor shells, morels, wedge shells, and clams, with their juice, and other noble ingredients and the usual spices; on top clean pistachios, first soaked in rosewater, fried asparagus tips, and lemon juice, the basins garnished with clams made of paste, filled with oysters, first cooked in a pan, with lemon juice and pepper, and around it lemon slices, and an apt lid retouched in gold and silver.

11. Roasted young pullets surrounded by ham slices over toasted crostini sprinkled with fat from the dripping pan, the basins garnished with lemon slices surrounded by beignets.

12. Covered tarts filled with candied things, retouched in gold and silver, with the coats of arms on top; these were already on the table among the cold dishes.

Second credenza service.

1. Parmesan cheese, retouched in gold and silver, over a napkin and laurel branches.

2. Bergamot pears, above gilded laurel branches, and myrtle tips, retouched in gold and silver.

3. White and black grapes, over napkins, with gilded laurel branches, everything retouched in gold and silver.

4. Appie and pink apples.

5. Fennel with salt and pepper.

6. Cardoons and celery with salt and pepper.

7. Cantaloupe.

8. Artichokes.

9. Tender peas.

10. Boxes of candied quince, with aniseeds.

11. Chestnuts roasted under embers, on a napkin, with wild fennel, salt, and pepper.

These things were quickly removed and confections were placed on the table, and after that we gave the guests water for hand-washing, at which point the confections were removed. Since the settings were ready, the tables were immediately set to serve the gentlemen, in the same order. Some of the ladies stayed behind cheerfully, and served their husbands and relatives. Once the gentlemen had eaten, a beautiful ball began, which lasted a good part of the night, with excellent instruments and musicians of all perfection, and thus it was done every evening for fifteen or twenty days, with the same balls, and music, and abundant refreshments, and with the greatest satisfaction of all those who took part.

LUNCH

Held in Miradoja, by the Most Illustrious Lord
DON SEBASTIANO COTES
Regent of His Majesty's Collateral Council,
and Lieutenant of the Royal Chamber for the same Catholic Majesty
Attending was also the Most Excellent Lord
DON FERDINANDO VALDESI
General Maestro di Campo of this Kingdom
And the Most Excellent Lord
THE MARQUIS OF AYTONA, GRANDEE OF SPAIN,
and other gentlemen, numbering ten, who were served
at one enhanced royal plate, in the month of September.[263]

First cold dishes.

1. A pie with the coats of arms of the guests, stuffed with pieces of Sorrento veal, quartered cockerels, sliced udder and ham, pine nuts, sour grapes, apt spices, and other ingredients.

2. A covered tart made with quinces in syrup, ground candied citron, cinnamon, and perfumed water.

3. A plate of cockerels, first boiled, halved, then marinated in strong vinegar, crushed garlic, and oregano, then taken from the marinade, dredged in flour, and fried in good lard, with a sauce on top made with a bit of vinegar, from the same marinade, sugar, mostacciolo crumbs, and the usual spices; the plate garnished with small pastries [gubelletti] filled with things in syrup, with a sugar glaze on top, mixed with lemon slices and comfits on top.

4. A ham cooked in wine, with cinnamon and whole cloves, in a box made of dough, garnished with greenery and flowers around it.

Each setting had four small round plates, one with soppressata and sliced ham, one with figs, one with melons, and one with peeled plums, all decorated with greenery and flowers, and everything very cold.

---

263 The Royal Chamber (*Real Camera*) of the Sommaria was the main organ of financial administration in the kingdom; Cotes became its lieutenant (or leading member) in 1689; Valdes served as maestro di campo (or high commander) of the kingdom's armed forces from 1687 to 1695, when he was transferred to Milan. Miradoja was on the hill of Capodimonte, just outside Naples.

First hot kitchen service.

1. A bowl of broth for each guest, with in it slices of toasted bread, the broth made with pieces of beef, ham, soppressata, Giugliano fillet, wild doves, capons, chickpeas, garlic heads, aromatic herbs, and the usual spices.

2. A turkey cockerel for each guest, wrapped in dough, larded in Maltese style, studded with cloves, spit-roasted, the plate garnished with small pastries filled with things in syrup, lemon slices, and small tarts filled with a sauce of pomegranate.

3. A fried dish with veal sweetbreads, whole chicken livers, slices of udder, warblers, first put in a marinade, then dredged in flour, and fried, veal liver, first soaked in milk, veal brains and feet, thin ham slices, sautéed in a pan, mixed with spit-roasted warblers, with thin slices of cured back fat, inside an onion peel, first browned on embers, mixed with small pies made of short crust pastry, filled with chicken breast, cockscombs, and sour grapes, with an apt little broth made with meat juice and lemon juice, the plate garnished with sliced lemons and short crust pastries.

4. A pie for each guest, made with short crust pastries, stuffed with chicken breasts, pounded veal, bits of mammary glands, ground pork belly, marrow, pine nuts, clean pistachios, with an apt little broth made with egg yolks and lemon juice, dusted with sugar.

5. A fillet of Sorrento veal, roasted, garnished with beignets and lemon slices.

6. Sorrento veal breast, stuffed with pounded veal flesh, pigeon breast, first roasted and then ground, cream tops, butter, bits of ham, thin slices of pork belly, crustless bread, first soaked in milk, fresh egg yolks, bits of sweetbreads, chicken livers, pitted sour cherries, ground citron, thin slices of truffles, dried St. George's mushrooms, pine nuts, clean pistachios, the usual spices, and other noble ingredients; this was then spit-roasted, and turned over a low fire for a short while, then placed in a pan, with thin slices of cured back fat and ham, a glass of Greco wine, whole cloves and cinnamon, and it was sautéed well, then the cured back fat was removed, and instead meat juice and good broth were added; once it was cooked, it was covered with a sauce made with razor shells, morels, clams, wedge shells, shrimp tails, sea urchins, cockscombs, chicken testicles, asparagus tips, and other noble ingredients, the plate garnished with various short crust pastries mixed with small pies filled with various condiments, lemon slices, and the usual spices.

7. A gigot made with cream tops, milk, ground candied citron, chicken breasts, first roasted and then ground, fresh eggs, little Savoy cookies, perfumed water, cinnamon, cooked in a silver plate, with a pastry twist around it made with short crust pastry, the plate garnished of small pastry in Genoese style, and other short crust pastries.

8. Quinces, first cooked under the embers, then boiled in wine, placed in syrup, and then stuffed with pitted sour cherries, marzipan paste, ground candied citron, bone marrow, fresh egg yolks, cinnamon, and other noble ingredients, then cooked and placed in a small box made with sugar paste, with a glaze on top made with egg whites, sugar, and lemon juice.

9. An obelisk made with wether tail, beef, wild doves, capons, ham, Giugliano fillet, Nola soppressata, Catalan turnips, garlic, onions, chickpeas, cabbages, and other usual herbs, with saffron as needed inside.

10. A large dentex, grilled, with a sauce on top made with vinegar, sugar, pine nuts, raisins, pitted olives, capers, bits of cinnamon, whole cloves, the plate garnished with pears in syrup and sliced lemons.

11. Large rock red mullets, one for each gentleman, grilled, with a little condiment of vinegar, garlic, and oil.

12. A covered tart of apricots in syrup, cinnamon, and sugar on top.

Second credenza service.

1. Parmesan cheese with a napkin and greenery under it.

2. *Spina* pears [small summer variety from the Naples region].

3. Large peaches and apricots.

4. Lazzarole and plums.

5. Muscat and Catalan grapes, everything with shaved ice.

These were removed and we served abundant boxes of confections, and various jams. Then everybody went to rest, and afterwards we prepared a large quantity of sorbetti of all sorts, very cold waters, and precious wines, cold melons of all sorts, and displays of candied things.

The second table was served in the same order as the first; all the servants, of whom there were very many, also received an abundant and lavish meal.

When night came, everybody went home highly satisfied with the amusements and pleasures of the day, and with great praise and hurrahs for the generosity of the Lord Lieutenant, who with his magnanimity had known how to satisfy the taste of such great personages.

BANQUET

Held in the month of December in the Castle of Sant'Eramo
by the Most Illustrious Lord
DON GIOVANNI ALONSO
DE SALCEDO
Member of the Collateral Council, maestro di campo, and perpetual
Governor of this Castle for His Catholic Majesty, Whom God preserve,
For the wedding of the Most Illustrious Lady
DONNA CHIARA SALCEDO,
HIS DAUGHTER,
With the Most Illustrious Lord
THE MARQUIS DEL TUFO
With twenty-four ladies and gentlemen who were served at two royal basins,
with twelve hot dishes, attended by two stewards and two carvers.[264]

The credenze and bottle sideboards were set with the most sumptuous silverware and crystals, which created a beautiful and noble sight, and the table was covered with a cloth of green damask, with over it a table cloth of the lightest Flanders cloth, all with folds; the lords' settings were shaped like leaves and arabesques, and each represented a different figure; the table was filled with these cold dishes.

First credenza service.

1. Two large basins with inside them pies with the coat of arms of the groom and bride, filled with pieces of rabbits, veal chops, ham slices, halved cockerels, sliced udder, apt spices, and other noble ingredients, placed over laurel branches retouched in gold and silver.

2. Two large basins with jellies of various colours, and in the middle a pyramid covered with the same jelly, which reflected like a mirror, with various arabesques around it, worked to seem like a mosaic, with various pretty colours, which made an admirable sight, the sides of the basins garnished with little mounds of amber-coloured jelly mixed with lemon slices, retouched in gold and silver.

3. Two large basins of blancmange, garnished with sliced candied citron, retouched in gold and silver.

4. Two turkey cockerels, standing like eagles, with heads and crowns on top, all covered in marzipan paste, except their wings and tails, retouched in gold and silver, placed over two large basins with four little pyramids in each basin made of the same paste, retouched in gold and silver, and the bottoms of these basins covered with various confections.

---

264 Salcedo (a Spaniard) became a member of the Collateral Council in 1691; the del Tufo were an old aristocratic family from Naples. Sant'Eramo (today usually Sant'Elmo), founded by King Robert of Anjou in the early fourteenth century, is one of the four major castles in Naples, and is located high on a hill overlooking the city.

5. Two large basins with pizze of bocca di dama, made with marzipan paste, pigeon breasts, first roasted, candied things, cinnamon, and other noble ingredients, with a glaze on top, mixed with various candied things.

6. Two large basins of quinces, first cooked under embers, then cooked in syrup and stuffed with ground candied citron, hard egg yolks, marzipan paste, marrow, butter, pitted sour cherries, ground cinnamon, perfumed water; once they were stuffed, we put them in small boxes made of marzipan paste, with a glaze on top, like shaved ice.

7. Two large basins with two turkeys, seasoned with salt and pepper, mixed with jellies, over laurel branches, retouched in gold and silver.

8. Two large basins of strained eggs on top of mostaccere and cookies, the basins garnished with pears in syrup, garnished with aniseeds of various colours.

9. Two large basins of soppressata, sliced, mixed with ham slices, and on it small white comfits, then covered with a cover made of marzipan paste in lattice pattern, garnished with little ribbons of various colours, retouched in gold and silver.

10. A large royal salad, placed in the middle of the table, made with various ingredients, with a column in the middle, two palmi high, surrounded by various columns made with citron pulp, with nice decorations, filled with various flowers, everything retouched in gold and silver; every gentleman received a little salad made with noble ingredients, and garnished with apt decorative borders, and in the middle were beautiful flowers which were very agreeable to look at.

First hot service.

1. Two large basins with soup made with slices of toasted bread, tender pigeons, first half-cooked on the spit, and then quartered and finished cooking in a pan with a good meat juice, apt spices, arranged neatly in the basins, mixed with sautéed sweetbreads, bits of ham and *verrinea*, cardoon stems first sautéed, with other ingredients, good parmesan cheese, soaked with good broth and meat juice, and then placed to gain flavour in the oven, and these were served hot.[265]

2. Two large basins with a fried mixture made of veal liver, first soaked in milk, sweetbreads, bits of veal mammary glands, small birds, first marinated, quartered artichokes, cardoon stems, first boiled, veal brains, slices of udder, first boiled, whole chicken livers, thin slices of ham, the plate garnished with flaky pastries filled with blancmange, and lemon slices.

3. A French-style pottage, made with veal chops, small birds, thin slices of ham, asparagus tips, cauliflowers tips, first boiled and fried, tender peas, quartered artichokes, also fried, rolls made with veal liver wrapped in pork caul, St. George's mushrooms, truffles, pine nuts, bits of mammary glands, and other noble ingredients, the plate garnished with small pies filled with veal flesh, pine nuts, and pistachios.

---

265 Verrinea is a pork product, used to make a type of salami; its main component, according to a guide for farmers published in 1843, is the udder of a sow that has been nursing her newborns, Giuseppe Cestoni, *Elementi di agricoltura pratica* (Naples: Zambrano, 1843), 125.

4. Bread loaves, first soaked in milk, then stuffed with bits of candied citron and pumpkin, marzipan paste, hard fresh egg yolks, butter, pitted sour cherries, candied pears, ground cinnamon, perfumed water, and other suitable ingredients, surrounded with a baked custard made with milk, eggs, sugar, and candied citron.

5. Turkey cockerels, made in Swiss style, with ham slices, a bit of white wine, onions, and other ingredients, the basins garnished with quinces in syrup, placed in small boxes of short crust pastry, all encrusted with small white comfits, mixed with short crust pastries, and lemon slices.

6. Tender pigeons cooked in a pan with ham slices and meat juice, covered with a sauce made with razor shells, morels, wedge shells, oysters, sliced truffles, St. George's mushrooms first soaked in wine, bits of mammary glands, cooked separately, the basins garnished with flaky pastries and carved halved lemons.

7. Fillet or loin of suckling veal, carefully roasted, the basins garnished with small boxes filled with a ham sauce, and lemon juice.

8. Small pies made of short crust pastry, filled with pounded veal, bone marrow, kid sweetbreads, clean pistachios, pine nuts, sliced truffles, with a little broth made of egg yolks, and the usual spices, with sugar on top.

9. Cockerels, first boiled, and marinated in vinegar, garlic, oregano, and chili pepper, then dredged in flour and fried, and covered with a sauce made with vinegar, sugar, olives, capers, pine nuts, thin slices of candied citron, bits of cinnamon, and whole cloves; the basins garnished with pears in syrup, garnished with aniseeds of various colours.

10. Genoa-style small pastries, filled with ground candied citron, marrow, cinnamon, and other noble ingredients, mixed with baskets made of fried blancmange, dusted with sugar, the sides of the basins garnished with strained eggs.

11. Deboned pigeons, filled with pounded veal flesh, bits of marrow, ham, and verrinea, pitted sour cherries, thin slices of truffles, pine nuts, and other suitable ingredients, the basins garnished with small pastries of flaky pastry, filled with things in syrup.

12. Roasted grey partridges, minutely larded with their usual sauce, made with capon livers, cooked on embers, ground in the mortar, with two garlic cloves, and chili pepper, diluted in white wine, sour orange juice, and a bit of oil, then quickly boiled in a pan, the basins garnished with various fried beignets and lemon slices.

13. Pizze and covered tarts of bocca di dama.

14. Quinces in syrup, which were already on the table.

Second credenza service.

1. Two large basins with parmesan cheese, provola, and caciocavallo.

2. Two others with bergamot pears.

3. Two with large appie apples from Spain.

4. Two with fennels.

5. Two with cardoons and celery.

6. Two with white and black grapes.

There were also wines of great quality, and toasts were given to the health of His Majesty and other personages, and at each toast cups and crystal glasses were broken, so that, of a great number we had, none remained.

Once the fruits and cold dishes were removed from the table, six large basins of confections were brought; we gave water for hand-washing, and once the guests left the table, a most lavish music began, and when that ended, we gave many sorbetti, iced and hot chocolate, and all sorts of cookies.

SNACK AND SUPPER
TOGETHER
Offered in Pozzuoli, in the month of June, by the Most Illustrious Lord
DON SEBASTIANO
VILLA REALE
Knight of Calatrava, and Maestro di Camera of the Most Excellent Lord
THE COUNT OF SANTO STEFANO
VICEROY OF NAPLES
To the Most Excellent Lord Viceroy, the Lady Vicereine, their daughter the
Lady Marquise of Aytona, her children, and young ladies and gentlemen
who attended to Their Excellencies, and they were all richly served.[266]

Don Sebastiano, who was then governor of the city of Pozzuoli, to entertain splendidly these Most Excellent Lords and Ladies, had two tables set with a damask cloth, and table cloths of the finest Flanders cloth, all folded, and the tables were filled with these cold dishes.

First cold service.

1. A pie bearing the coat of arms of the Lord Viceroy, filled with pieces of veal, halved cockerels, veal sweetbreads, ham slices, marrow, sliced udder, the usual spices, and other noble ingredients.

2. Capons seasoned in salt and pepper, over a glaze, served with a cover in openwork on top, made of sugar, placed on six large apples [pomi d'Adamo] mixed with four candied citrons and strained eggs, with the coat of arms of His Excellency.

---

266 This is described as *merenda e cena*; merenda today means a mid-afternoon (or mid-morning) light meal or snack. The meal in fact is rather informal and simple, by Latini's standards, though, especially in June, it must have lasted quite a while to end well into the night. The maestro di camera was one of the top administrators of a princely household; the Naples viceroys, in their roles as stand-ins for the King, kept a large and sumptuous household and court. Pozzuoli, on the bay and just to the west of Naples, was a popular location for noble villas.

3. Eaglets made of flaky pastry, filled with candied pumpkin, citron, and pears, mixed with small masks made of blancmange the colour of cinnamon, with a cover on top in lattice pattern, all garnished with little ribbons of various colours.

4. Two pyramids made of ice, surrounded by various iced fruits.

5. A covered tart made with sour grapes in syrup, candied citron, sugar, cinnamon, and other noble ingredients.

6. A royal salad decorated with various small putti and crowns, which made for an admirable sight.

The setting for each Lord had a small salad made with various country greens, Spanish olives, capers, slices of salted tuna belly, salted anchovies, garnished around with small radishes, shaped like stars, and other noble ingredients.

A small round plate of very cold strawberries, washed in a strong wine, with sugar on top.

Another small round plate with soppressata mixed with thin slices of ham, cooked in wine, over laurel branches, with confected aniseeds on top, and lemon slices around it.

First hot service.

1. A big plate of mixed fried things, made with veal liver, bits of sweetbreads, chicken livers, pieces of veal brains, ham slices, cooked in a pan, slices of udder, with fried asparagus on top, the plate garnished with various short crust pastries and lemon slices.

2. Pigeons cooked in a pan, with ham, sautéed thoroughly, with the usual spices and aromatic herbs, a glass of malmsey wine, and all well seasoned; once cooked, they were covered with bits of sweetbreads, cockscombs and chicken testicles, artichoke stems, first boiled and sautéed, sliced truffles, pistachios, and other noble ingredients; everything cooked separately, with a little broth made of egg yolks and lemon juice, the plate garnished with little tarts filled with sour cherries and sour grapes in syrup, with aniseeds on top.

3. Small pies in Spanish style, made with short crust pastry, prepared with butter, egg yolks, and sugar, stuffed with capon breast ground and then sautéed, bits of kid sweetbreads, bits of lamb testicles, cockscombs and chicken testicles, pistachios, pine nuts, sour grapes, with a little garlic condiment, and a little broth made with egg yolks and lemon juice; these were quickly placed in the oven, and when they were perfectly cooked we made a sugar glaze for them.

4. A veal fillet, spit-roasted very carefully, and mixed with various beignets, well greased with ambivera, and lemon slices around.

Second credenza service.

1. Parmesan cheese, over napkins and laurel branches.

2. Moscarelle and royal pears, the same way.

3. Fresh sliced almonds.

4. Apricots.

5. Cherries and sour cherries.

6. Tender artichokes.

7. Various plums.

8. Fennels, everything with shaved ice, mixed with bouquets of carnations and other flowers.

The second table was served just like the first, and at the same time; when we served the fruit, we brought lamps, since it was already night, and we gave water for hand-washing, with little bunches of flowers, and a wonderful comedy was prepared in another room, and played in front of the Lord Viceroy and Lady Vicereine and their company, and gave everybody great satisfaction.

They returned to Naples, late into the night, accompanied by artillery fire, and in great spirits.

Before they left, they were served abundant chocolate and sorbetti; we also gave to eat to the grooms, coachmen, servants of the various gentlemen, and sailors, numbering two hundreds.

LUNCH

Held in Barra, by the Most Excellent Lady
THE PRINCESS OF TARSIA
For the Most Excellent Lord
THE MARQUIS OF LAINO
AND COUNT OF ACERRA
WITH THE EXCELLENT LADY MARQUISE
His wife
AND THE EXCELLENT LORD THE YOUNG MARQUIS
His eldest son,
Numbering six guests, served at one royal plate, at the end of July.[267]

In this noble gathering, each setting had four small round plates, one with figs, another with ham slices, one with cream tops, and the fourth with Acerra melons, everything with shaved ice, very cold.

---

[267] Barra is just east of Naples, on the sea; both families held land in and around it. The Spinelli (one of the many branches of which were the princes of Tarsia) intermarried frequently in the seventeenth century with the Cardenas, marquis of Laino and counts of Acerra, a family of Spanish origin settled in Naples since the time of Charles V (Acerra is also near Naples, and perhaps Latini chose melons from there for the first dishes in honour of the guests); given the dates of Latini's work in Naples and of his book, the hostess in this case was probably Angela Spinelli, princess of Tarsia, widow of Prince Giovanni Vincenzo (d. 1668) and mother of Prince Carlo Francesco (who did not marry until 1688), whose own mother was Maria de Cardenas; her guests were probably Carlo de Cardenas, marquis of Laino and count of Acerra since 1664, his wife Francesca Spinelli, and their son Alfonso, born in 1680; Carlo de Cardenas, as we saw at the start, was the dedicatee of Latini's first volume.

First cold dishes.

1. Sliced soppressata with laurel branches under it and confected aniseeds on top, and lemon slices around.

2. A plate of butter, squeezed through a pastry bag to form various figurines, all decorated and with sugar on top.

3. Covered tarts with bits of candied citron, candied pears, sour cherries, cream tops, cinnamon, perfumed water, and other noble ingredients.

4. A soup made with whole sour cherries boiled in good wine, sugar, and cinnamon, then after they were cooked we poured them, together with the wine, over slices of toasted bread, placed on the plate, and the soup was covered with a glaze made with egg whites, sugar, and lemon juice, and browned in the oven; it was served cold, the sides of the dish garnished with various convent pastries.

First kitchen hot service.

1. An appetizer made with bits of tender pigeons, sweetbreads, lettuce stems, asparagus tips, bits of ham, bits of chicken livers, everything first sautéed, then boiled in good broth, and when it was cooked we thickened it with egg yolks and lemon juice.[268]

2. A boiled goose, with a piece of beef, Giugliano fillet, and ham, placed on the plate with herbs on top, and garnished with slices of boiled soppressata and small tarts filled with green sauce.

3. Small cockerels, first spit-roasted to a half-cooking, then finished cooking in a pan with meat juice, thin slices of ham, whole cockerel livers, quartered artichokes, sour grapes, aromatic herbs, apt spices, and other noble ingredients, the sides of the plate garnished with Genoa-style small pastries and lemon slices.

4. Small pies made with short crust pastry, stuffed with ground veal, bits of pork belly and ham, kid sweetbreads, first sautéed, bits of marrow, pine nuts, sour grapes, apt spices, and the usual little broth, and after they were cooked an apt glaze of sugar [was added], and they were served hot.

5. Fillet of Sorrento veal, spit-roasted, the plate garnished with thin toasted crostini, soaked in the juice of the roast, and over it thin ham slices, grilled, mixed with lemon slices.

    Salads made with country greens and other noble ingredients, one for each guest.

6. The covered tarts that were already on the table.

Second credenza service.

1. Caciocavallo and provola, on napkins.

2. Spina and *cremesina* pears [the latter presumably a crimson variety].

---

268 This is the only occurrence of the word *antipasto* in Latini (today appetizer, literally what is served before the meal, though in this case obviously it came after the cold dishes).

3. Cherries and sour cherries.

4. Fennels with salt and pepper.

5. Apricots and peaches.

6. Muscatel grapes, everything with shaved ice.

7. Sliced peaches in little cups of porcelain, with cold wine and sugar on top, one for each guest.[269]

BANQUET

Held in the month of May, on the occasion of the wedding of the Most Excellent Lord
DON MARTIO ORIGLIA
DUKE OF ASCIGLIANO
And general of the artillery in this Kingdom of Naples
for His Majesty (Whom God preserve)
With the Most Excellent Lady
DONNA FRANCESCA
SPINELLI
Marquise of the Holy Roman Empire.[270]

Twenty most noble ladies attended this banquet, who were served by as many gentlemen, who ate after them, and the same banquet was served to both, in two royal basins, with two stewards and two carvers, with an extraordinary sumptuousness.

First cold dishes.

1. Pies in the shape of shields, filled with bits of veal, halved cockerels, thin slices of ham and soppressata, slices of cured back fat, veal sweetbreads, sliced truffles, pine nuts, pistachios, the usual spices, with a glaze on top made like marzipan, garnished with bay leaves, roses, and other flowers.

2. A royal salad, shaped like a temple decorated in mosaic, with various vegetable roots, citron pulp, garnished with crowns around it, with various small putti also made of citron pulp, which looked real.

3. Two turkey cockerels, seasoned in salt and pepper, all covered with feathers made with candied citron and pumpkin, their beaks pointing to their breasts, with a twig in their mouths, garnished all around with small boxes made of dough filled with various condiments, mixed with carved lemon slices.

---

269 This mention of porcelain (one of only two in Latini) marks an early appearance of what became the dominant material for serving vessels at eighteenth-century banquets.

270 Origlia had a prominent career in the armed forces over forty-plus years; he was very close to Viceroy Santo Stefano, and died in 1696; his wife Francesca Spinelli (b. 1678) was far younger, married again the year after Origlia's death, and died in 1728 (her Holy Roman Empire title meant little in this period).

4. Two covered tarts or pizze, filled with cream tops, egg yolks, slices of sponge cake, and Savoy cookies, with sugar and cinnamon inside; the first layer was covered with strawberries, then a layer of cookies, covered with a sugar glaze; they were cooked in the oven and then we made another glaze of ambivera, made like marzipan; the plate was garnished all around with carnations, flowers, and laurel branches.

5. Two hams, cooked in wine, then placed in a box of dough with various leaves around them, retouched in ambivera, all encrusted with aniseeds of various colours, garnished with myrtle leaves, laurel branches, roses, and other flowers around it, with a sugar glaze on top, the colour of flesh, all studded with little sticks and cinnamon.

6. Blancmange mixed with little mounds of strained eggs.

Each setting had three small round plates, one filled with sour cherries, cooked in wine and sugar, with a little soup under them and cinnamon on top, garnished with a sugar glaze and decorative borders around.

The second plate was filled with Spanish olives, capers, thin slices of fish eggs, with a little condiment, the plate garnished with lemon slices, and little borders of candied things.[271]

The third plate was filled with a little condiment of sour cherries, the plate garnished with various decorations in marzipan paste, with a little ribbon around made of mashed candied citron and pumpkin.

First hot service.

1. A little soup in Spanish style, with ground chicken breast, first roasted, then set to cool, mixed with slices of toasted bread, soaked in good broth, and bits of tender pigeons, first boiled, with a little broth of egg yolks and lemon juice, browned in the oven, with the usual spices.

2. A fried dish with sweetbreads, veal liver, veal brains, sliced udder, first boiled, then dipped in egg, whole chicken livers, lamb testicles, with a bastard sauce on top, the sides of the plate garnished with flaky pastries filled with blancmange, mixed with lemon slices.

3. A small pie for each guest, made with short crust pastry, filled with pounded veal, bits of sweetbreads, cockscombs and chicken testicles, pine nuts, and pistachios, with a little broth inside made with egg yolks and lemon juice, with the usual spices, and an apt glaze on top.

4. Two large fillets of suckling veal, spit-roasted, mixed with various fried beignets, garnished with lemon slices and little tarts filled with various condiments.

5. A bisque made with tender pigeons cooked in a pan, first half-cooked on the spit, and with ham slices, veal chops, rolls made with veal liver, parmesan cheese, egg yolks, raisins, pine nuts, mostacciolo crumbs, the usual spices, and other noble ingredients, wrapped in caul; also bits of veal sweetbreads, spit-roasted, wrapped in paper, with

271 The eggs here are *targhe*, which, from the context of the description of the province of Capitanata at the very end of this volume, appears to refer to the eggs of some freshwater fish.

inside slices of ham; chicken livers, cooked in a pan; then everything was placed in the basins, over slices of toasted bread, and a sauce on top made with meat juice, pistachios, lemon juice, the usual spices, and other suitable ingredients; the sides of the basins decorated with short crust pastries mixed with lemon slices.

6. Small boxes filled with various ingredients made by the lady nuns.

7. A roast of turtledoves and tender cockerels, the basins garnished with Genoa-style small pastries filled with candied pumpkin and citron, bone marrow, egg yolks, mostacciolo crumbs, and fried in butter, mixed with lemon slices.

8. Swiss-style turkey cockerels, cooked with bits of sweetbreads, thin slices of ham and truffles, St. George's mushrooms, and other suitable ingredients, the basins garnished with Spanish-style small pies filled with ground capon and pine nuts, with the usual spices, with sugar on top.

9. A Genoa-style gigot made with veal flesh, roasted turkey cockerel breast, with an apt roast juice and lemon, and garnished with various seafood and other noble ingredients.

10. Quails, mixed with thin slices of ham and of small lemons, the basin garnished with various short crust pastries.[272]

11. Lasagne with sugar and cinnamon on top.

12. Pizze with strawberries, which were already on the table.

Second credenza service.

1. Cherries and sour cherries.

2. Tender almonds.

3. Moscarelle pears.

4. Fennels.

5. Apples.

6. Parmesan cheese.

7. Plums.

8. Apricots.

9. A large basin with radishes, everything with shaved ice.

We served four large basins of various confections, and gave water for hand-washing; after the ladies had eaten, the gentlemen sat down and were served in the same order; after the gentlemen had eaten, a beautiful feast began which lasted into the night, and many sorbetti and cold and hot chocolate were served.

---

272 The quails are *sguazzariate*, a Neapolitan term that means shaken in a liquid; I am not sure what cooking this suggests, probably something like a quick cooking in broth. The term does not appear in other cookbooks I have seen. Latini was in a Neapolitan mode here—the cherries and apricots below are also listed with their Naples dialect nouns (which he uses frequently for cherries, but not for apricots).

BANQUET

Held in the month of November, by the Most Eminent Lord
CARDINAL ROSSETTI
Then bishop of Faenza, and vice-dean of the Sacred College
On the occasion when the Most Eminent Lord
CARDINAL D'ETRE'
Came to Italy, with the Lord Duke of Villarsi, and other princes, numbering nine.[273]

My Lord the Cardinal had learned that these Lords were coming to Rome since they were in Turin, and so he called me, who then was in his service, and ordered me to provide for everything necessary to receive such guests and to treat them magnificently. Since there was plenty of time, I executed what His Eminence wished for, albeit little was lacking already in the house, because this Lord Cardinal always kept it well provided of all that was needed, since, out of his natural nobility, he enjoyed keeping an open house for whoever should pass through, so that, if any foreigners should come, and if he had not been informed of it, he immediately ordered that the innkeepers who had failed to notify him be jailed. The said Lord Cardinal and his company arrived in Faenza on a Sunday in November, they were served, ten of them at the table with my Lord Cardinal Rossetti, at two royal plates, and the table was filled with the following triumphs and cold dishes.[274]

By order of my Lord Cardinal, the said Most Eminent d'Estrées was served in large plates, to manifest the esteem in which Cardinal Rossetti held such a great prelate.[275]

First triumphs.

1. A chariot drawn by four white swans, made of sugar paste, outlined in gold and silver, with a coachman holding in his hands the reins, made with strips of gold and silver.

2. The pontifical Triregnum, held high by three small putti, one of whom held in one hand the keys of Saint Peter, everything in sugar paste, outlined as above.

3. Another chariot drawn by two Hydras, in which sat a king and queen, with a sceptre in their hand, and a baldaquin over them, all in sugar paste, retouched in gold.

---

273 Latini already referred to Rossetti, bishop of Faenza and cardinal since 1643, whom Latini had served in his youth; Faenza (famous for its majolica, known as faience) is near the Adriatic coast, about fifty kilometres southeast of Bologna. The French guest is likely Cardinal César d'Estrées (1628–1714), bishop of Laon, cardinal in 1671; the occasion for the cardinal's visit to Italy is likely the conclave of 1676 that elected Pope Innocent XI; the duke travelling with him is probably Claude Louis, duke of Villars (1653–1734).

274 If Latini is serious here, one wonders how the innkeepers of Faenza felt about the Cardinal's hospitality! In the text, Latini says November in the banquet's title, but January here; this is one of the six errata he corrects on the last page of this volume.

275 Latini calls these special plates *piatti da cappone* (or, fit to serve capon), an expression that clearly indicated large, elegant plates.

First cold dishes.

1. Pies with the coat of arms of Cardinal d'Estrées, in bas-relief, with a cornucopia around it, made of sugar paste, filled with bits of veal, quartered capons, ham, and other ingredients, retouched in gold and silver.

2. Blancmange in royal plates, moulded in half-relief, and garnished around with little obelisks of jelly, and in between other decorations in sugar retouched in gold.

3. Capons covered with jelly, with a glaze under them, mixed with little statues made of jelly of various colours, everything retouched in gold and silver.

4. Covered tarts made with caravelle apples, candied citron and pumpkin, with a white glaze on top, mixed with candied lazzarole and pears, retouched in gold and silver.

5. Pheasants, spit-roasted, larded with strips of candied pumpkin, with their natural heads and necks, and wings and tails made of sugar paste.

6. Pelicans with their young, made of sugar paste, in the act of suckling their mothers' blood, with the blood, which was pomegranate juice, flowing naturally.[276]

7. Candied large apples [pomi d'Adamo], mixed with little mounds of strained eggs, on which were little weathervanes made of taffeta, retouched in gold and silver.

8. Struffoli arranged to form a mountain, with weathervanes on top, and some grottos in which were visible little wild animals made of sugar paste.[277]

9. Royal salads shaped like a fortress, with bulwarks, cannons, and soldiers, all made of mashed citron and carrots, in natural colours.

10. Large trout seasoned in salt and pepper, garnished with herbs and pomegranate seeds, and lemon slices around them.

Each setting had three small round plates, one filled with a currant condiment decorated with aniseeds of various colours; one had local mustard; and the third had a little salad made with olives, capers, wild herbs, dried tuna salami [*muscimano*], fish eggs [targhe], raisins, pine nuts, and other ingredients.

Hot kitchen dishes.

1. A little stew for each guest, made with chicken livers, veal meatballs, lettuce stems, St. George's mushrooms, truffles, bits of sweetbreads, sliced bread underneath, and clean pistachios on top, with a little lid in lattice pattern made of sugar paste.

2. Boiled capons mixed with pulled ham, sliced salami, garnished with various little boxes made of dough filled with condiments.

---

276 The pelican, who supposedly gave its blood to nourish its young, was often used as a symbol of Christ's love for mankind, though this particular display, with its combination of religious kitsch and creepiness, appears to me, at least, as rather excessive even within a Baroque aesthetic.

277 The struffoli and the weathervane were combined also in an earlier example; again, banderole might simply be little flags, and the struffoli are small bits of fried dough, today mainly a Christmas dessert.

3. A fried dish made with veal sweetbreads and brains, whole chicken livers, quartered artichokes, thin slices of ham and bread, sliced cow udder, first boiled, all mixed with spit-roasted thrushes, the plate garnished with fried pastries and lemon slices.

4. A French-style dish made with bits of tender pigeons and veal tongue, veal chops and meatballs, bits of sweetbreads and ham, tender peas, ortolans, other ingredients, and apt spices, with a twist made of short crust pastry filled with various candied things, and a cover on top in lattice pattern.

5. Small pies filled with ground capon flesh, bits of sweetbreads, pistachios, and pine nuts; after cooking them, we added to them a little broth made with egg yolks and lemon juice, with a glaze on top.

6. Spit-roasted pheasants, finely larded, with their natural [i.e., uncooked] wings, tails, and heads, the plate garnished with various short crust pastries and small boxes filled with ham sauce, mixed with lemon slices.

7. Spit-roasted sturgeon, finely larded with ham, both fat and lean, over a royal sauce, the plate garnished with small pastries filled with blancmange, with a cover.

8. Turtledoves, spit-roasted but not to a complete cooking, then placed in a pan with good broth and ham slices, then set in the plate and covered with white fennel, slices of fine sausage, bits of pork belly, the plate garnished with bits of kid heads, deboned and stuffed, and pomegranate seeds, with an apt cover on top.

9. Tender deboned pigeons, stuffed with pounded veal flesh, bits of sweetbreads, egg yolks, marrow, parmesan cheese, pitted sour cherries, pine nuts, apt spices, and other noble ingredients; after cooking them, we covered them with a baked custard made with milk, eggs, sponge cake crumbs, candied citron, sugar, and powdered cinnamon, the plate garnished with various short crust pastries, and a cover on top.

10. Spit-roasted veal, mixed with slices of bread soaked in the roast juice, and on top slices of ham, the plate garnished with little tarts filled with a pomegranate sauce, and lemon slices.

11. Deboned cockerels, lightly stuffed, stewed, garnished with onions filled with cheese, egg yolks, candied citron, and mostacciolo crumbs; in the middle of the plate, roasted fat ortolans, mixed with pastries made with German dough, shaped like mushrooms, filled with grated candied citron, and fried, with their stems dipped in chocolate.[278]

12. Boiled capons with herbs on top, covered with a sauce of anchovies and sliced truffles, cooked in good oil, the plate garnished with spit-roasted lampreys, mixed with lemon juice.

13. English-style pies, filled with ground veal flesh, veal chops, small birds, ham and truffle slices, St. George's mushrooms, pistachios, pine nuts, and other noble ingredients.

14. Large flaky pastries, fried in good lard, garnished with fried cauliflowers, and around them lemons and sour oranges.

---

278 This looks like a case of Baroque imagination gone awry: fake fried mushrooms filled with citron and stuck in a layer of chocolate must have been quite a sight, and rather amusing for the guests.

15. Roasted partridges, wrapped in paper, with their heads, with ham slices; we removed the paper and garnished them on the plate with various fried beignets, mixed with small boxes made of dough filled with condiments apt for the roast.

16. Blancmange, the colour of cinnamon, mixed with strained eggs.

17. Covered tarts filled with things in syrup, with marzipan on top.

Second credenza service.

The first table cloth was removed, and another one uncovered, made with the lightest folds, with other settings, sprinkled with perfumed waters, and we set the following on the table.

1. Truffles in a truffle sauce, over slices of toasted bread, with sour orange juice, one plate for each guest.
2. Cardoons in a truffle sauce.
3. St. George's mushrooms over a soup.
4. Bergamot pears.
5. Florentine pears.
6. Parmesan cheese.
7. Chestnuts on a napkin, with salt and pepper.
8. Small quince pies.
9. Fresh fennels.
10. Sorbus fruits and medlars.[279]
11. Grapes.
12. Candied quince from Portugal and Bologna.

We removed the second table cloth and immediately placed on the table twelve basins with confections, and gave water for hand-washing, then we removed the third table cloth, which uncovered a cloth of crimson damask.

The Lord Cardinal and his company stayed in Faenza for four meals, and they were all always served lavishly, to their great satisfaction and enjoyment, and in the same order, except that we varied the specific dishes.

I have esteemed it useful and helpful, after showing how to set tables and prepare banquets for great lords, to alert all professionals that, if one is arranging a banquet for a royal personage, or for princes of the highest sphere and the greatest authority, the table must be proportionate to the guest, with a single setting for this personage; one must hold the other settings ready, but out of sight, so that, if the prince should ask other gentlemen to join him at the table, his orders may immediately be executed; the stewards must obey these commands at the merest hint.[280]

---

279 Sorbus fruits (*sorbe*) come from the service tree, and are small round fruits, similar in fact to medlars.

280 This final advice follows directly after the last banquet description, with simply a straight line across the page to separate it. On the next page, Latini starts "Brief Description" which concludes the first volume.

BRIEF DESCRIPTION
OF THE KINGDOM OF NAPLES,

*with a list of the edible fruits and other things that are produced and
are of rare quality in particular places of this Kingdom, according to the
testimony of various authors, and as is confirmed by usage and experience.*

The heavens were never, in any time, as prodigal of their beneficent influence to
any kingdom as they were to this Neapolitan one, which many call Sicily before the
Lighthouse, because some, who ruled over both the island of Sicily and this continental
territory, styled themselves Kings of the Sicilies. This kingdom is bathed by three seas,
the Adriatic, the Ionian, and the Tyrrhenian, and watered by many rivers; it is fertile in
all that is necessary for human life, except a few spices of which it is abundantly provided from the Indies. The air is almost everywhere most clement, so that it seems that
Nature has gone to every effort to manifest here its kindnesses, while at the same time
the skills cultivated to all perfection by the kingdom's natives demonstrate that nowhere
but here can one's eyebrows reasonably rise to form arches in astonishment. The capital
of such a beautiful and noble dominion is the delightful City of Naples, which offers its
name to the kingdom as a whole, a city so noble and well peopled that it easily surpasses
all the other cities in Italy; it sits on the sea coast, in a bay that resembles a majestic
theatre; it is surrounded by delightful hills and beautiful plains, so that it seems that
here indeed all the delights of the whole world are collected. Near this city, the river
Sebeto, so celebrated by poets, flows to bring its tribute to the sea; the poets tell that this
city was built by a siren, named Parthenope, though the truth is that she was not truly a
siren, but a young lady of high worth and extraordinary prudence, daughter of Eumelus,
King of Pherae in Thessaly. After a long time, the city was rebuilt by the Cumans, who
called it *Neapolis*, which in Greek simply means new city, and from this then came the
name that now defines the entire territory forming the kingdom, which is currently
divided into twelve provinces, namely:[281]

> Campania Felix, today called Terra di Lavoro.
> Principato Citra.
> Principato Ulra.
> Basilicata.
> Calabria Ultra.
> Camabria Citra.
> Terra d'Otranto.

---

281 This description reports both facts (like the two foundations of the city by different Greeks or
that Naples was then by far the largest city in Italy) and longstanding myths (the story of Eumelus'
daughter), and repeats old, but alas erroneous, commonplaces about the fertility of the kingdom,
which in fact, aside from a few areas near Naples, was overall quite poor in terms of land and water
resources. The most common tradition about Eumelus identified him as the son of Admetus and
Alcestis, and king of Pherae (Fera in Latini) in Thessaly. The text gives his name as Gumelo, which
the errata page corrects to Eumelo. The Lighthouse is the one at Messina, which was the border
between the "two Sicilies."

Terra di Bari.
Abruzzo Citra.
Abruzzo Ultra.
Contado di Molise.
Capitanata.

All these provinces provide the great City of Naples of all things; the first of them was rightly called Campania Felix, and today Terra di Lavoro, since I do not believe that there could be another province more fertile in producing the fruits of the earth, and therefore worthier of being diligently cultivated. In this province sits Naples, and in the plains near the city one can admire an innumerable number of fruit-bearing trees, and beautiful springs; this area is named Poggio Reale, because in old times it was the delight and garden of the kings who ruled here; aside from the most exquisite fruits, famous fennels are born here, and in a nearby place called Le Padule all sorts of greens and vegetables are produced that can serve for human food. In the fertile beach of Chiaia one can harvest celebrated peas, cardoons, artichokes, radishes, and roots, besides all sorts of new greens, and especially the most beautiful cauliflowers; the same is true of the most delightful hills of Posillipo, which produce the most exquisite lettuces one could taste and all sorts of fruits that any land can produce. I do not believe that any place could ever be found more fertile or more delightful, located as it is on the pleasant and audacious coast of Mergellina, of which it kisses the ever smiling shores, which have such natural placidity, where the sea, never troubled but by the sweetest zephyrs, enjoys this place so dear to the Muses, which deserved indeed first to hear the harmonious song, and then to collect the immortal ashes, of the great Maro [Virgil], and of the incomparable Sannazzaro.[282]

A bit further one finds the most ancient City of Pozzuoli, which, besides being prodigal in all that can be found on earth, abounds in beautiful asparagus, artichokes, peas, and zucchini even out of season, and produces also new sour grapes in the month of March, which greatly astonishes the city.

Procida offers Naples all sorts of fruits.

Ischia produces wonderful white and red lazzarole, very good Greco wines, a quantity of pheasants, and other animals to hunt.

Capri beautiful calves and wonderful quails, and all sorts of hunting options; these three are islands.

Sorrento [yields] suckling calves of the greatest tenderness and goodness, and good pigs.

Vico splendid quails and other birds.

Castellammare di Stabia the sweetest onions, and other things.

At Torre del Greco one can fish exquisite grey mullets.

---

282 It is difficult to do justice to Latini's flights of fancy and convoluted metaphors. It was indeed traditionally believed that Virgil was buried in Naples (his alleged tomb is still to be visited in Mergellina, west of the old city); Jacopo Sannazzaro (or Sannazaro, 1457–1530) was a famous Humanist and poet who spent most of his life in Naples.

At a place on the sea called Granatiello one can catch celebrated red mullets, though I only mention this as a curiosity, since Naples at all times abounds in all sorts of fish, and at convenient prices.

The land at the feet of Vesuvius, today called Mount Somma, on all sides is most prolific in exquisite fruits, and its Lachryma wines are so desirable that they suffice to produce joy and laughter everywhere.

Orta [produces] watermelons and good soppressata.

Nola celebrated soppressata and perfect Vernotico wine.

Aversa exquisite nougat.

Cardito melons that can be kept for winter.

Arienzo delightful and extraordinarily large apricots.

Acerra, fiefdom of the Most Excellent Lord Count de Cardenas, flavourful melons and the best provola.

Giugliano is very well known for its pork fillets and cardoons.

Capua in its river has celebrated lampreys.

Gaeta [offers] good olives, and perfect salted meats are produced there.

Venafro abounds in oils, olives, and exquisite legumes.

Campagna di Sora is irrigated by two small rivers which bring a large number of trout, and its territory is most copious in animals for the hunt, and produces much wine and oil; and in the island where resides the Most Excellent Lord the Duke Boncompagni, there are water delights which also yield beautiful trout.

Principato Citra.

All sorts of things are found in this province.

Salerno produces the most celebrated rice, in great abundance.

Agropoli dried figs and the most exquisite tiny fish.

Sanseverino is famous for its flavourful wines, produced in its delightful vineyards, and exquisite trout, and cherries also out of season.

Nocera the tenderest capons, very tasty.

Principato Ultra.

It contains many cities, all rich, among them Benevento with very good saveloy, very large and sweet onions, and very good nougat.

Avellino many hazelnuts, and abundance of the most delicate freshwater fish, called *bianchine*.

Basilicata.

This is a most fertile province, and it has some beautiful territories, all abundant.

Laterza good caciocavallo and very good game, and they make there the noblest majolica in the kingdom, such as those [in the fiefdoms of] the Lord Marquis Perez Navarrese.

Calabria Citra.

Across this province they make good cheese, ricotta, *rasche*, sugar, apples, and many other things.[283]

Cosenza has in its territory mines of gold and iron.

Rossano perfect oils, capers, oleander, and wild saffron.

Belvedere the sweetest raisins, which travel across the world, and famous muscatel wines.

In the territory of Cassano they make caciocavallo of various types, equal to the marzolino of Florence in its goodness, and [grow] peaches of extreme size, beautiful cauliflowers, and other very beautiful fruits.

Calabria Ultra, once called Magna Graecia.

This is one of the most fertile provinces.

Seminara offers a large quantity of the most perfect oils.

Terra d'Otranto.

This province abounds everywhere of meat and dried figs, and many other things.

Gallipoli produces quantities of perfect oils, wines, and cheeses.

Taranto, oysters preserved in small wood barrels, and all sorts of seafood.

Ostuni abounds in wine, oil, almonds, and wild game.

Terra di Bari.

This province feeds a large number of animals, and very good wethers are raised there, and they make exquisite cheeses.

Molfetta almonds, oil, oranges, and lemons.

Bitonto kids nursed by two goats, of extraordinary goodness and taste.

Abruzzo citra.

This province is not inferior to the others in any way.

Sulmona is admirable for the making of sweet confections.

Abruzzo Ultra.

This province holds everything the others do.

Aquila is most abundant in saffron.

Cicoli in very good hams.

Contado di Molise.

It is inferior in little to the other provinces.

Campobasso produces very beautiful hams, and abundant St. George's mushrooms and truffles.

---

283 Rasche are a cheese made with bovine milk, similar to ricotta.

Capitanata.

This province is celebrated for the building of that famous temple, which angels carved over a dangerous rock, and dedicated to the Archangel Saint Michael, and there a large quantity of manna is produced; at the foot of that mountain there is a lake, called Varano, which yields a large number of eels, tench, and grey mullets, from which one can get eggs [targhe] that are used across the kingdom.[284]

It is not to be marvelled at, if I write so briefly in discussing the abundance of these provinces, because I do this lest I be prolix, since it is clear that each of these provinces holds in itself everything good that is in the world's beautiful treasury.[285]

284 Manna today refers to the edible secretions of some trees, and within Italy it is produced primarily in Sicily; Monte Sant'Angelo has been a centre of worship since the early Middle Ages and it still houses a famous sanctuary to the Archangel Michael.

285 This is on p. 606 of Latini's first volume; the volume ends with an eight-page "table of all the most notable matters and subjects contained in this book" and one page with six errata (which corrections I have integrated in their proper spots in the text).

Figure 3. Portrait of Antonio Latini, from
Volume II of *Lo Scalco alla Moderna* (Naples, 1694)

THE MODERN
S T E W A R D ,

Or
the Art of Preparing Banquets Well,
BY THE KNIGHT
ANTONIO LATINI
FROM COLLE AMATO DI FABRIANO
IN THE MARCH OF ANCONA,
Experienced in the service of various prelates
and great princes.
In which we teach the easy and thorough way to prepare all sorts of fish, with
descriptions of their quality and season; to prepare various pies, pizze,
or tarts, various composite dishes, and to make blancmange
exquisitely, as well as various salads, and fish jellies,
how to clarify sugar, and to prepare many things
in syrup, to make sorbetti with the proper
dosage, and flavoured waters and
perfumed vinegars; with a
new method of cooking
without spices;
How to arrange meals in noble fashions, how to prepare sumptuous banquets,
and delightful tables, with fish-based dishes, how to prepare various types of
wines, together with the discoverers of all these, various healthful artificial
waters, as well as many exquisite natural ones, known to few, with a
medicinal formula for how to well nourish the convalescent,
through thirty days of convalescence.

PART THE SECOND.

In which we discuss specifically lean dishes.
IN NAPLES 1694. In the new print shop of the partners
Domenico Antonio Parrino and Michele Luigi Mutii
With licence and privilege of the authorities.[1]

---

1 Latini's second volume appeared in 1694, two years after the first, but was clearly planned since the start. It is leaner not just in subject matter, but also physically: though the same height and width, it comprises 256 pages versus the 606 of the first volume; there are fewer illustrations, and more lines of text per page, so the typographical look is also simpler. On the other hand, between the two volumes Latini had been knighted by the pope (the Neapolitan Innocent XII Pignatelli), and therefore the second volume not only included a new print portrait of Latini (see Figure 3 on the opposite page), adorned with a magnificent wig, a lace neckerchief, and a knightly cross on his sleeve, and holding a copy of his own work, but the header "by the knight Antonio Latini" appears at the top of each right page throughout the volume.

TO THE MOST ILLUSTRIOUS AND EXCELLENT LORD, MY MOST RESPECTED LORD AND MASTER THE LORD

DON ANTONIO GRUTHER,

DUKE OF SANTA SEVERINA.

My respects are obliged by the multiplicity of favours that Your Excellency has bestowed upon me with a generous hand, so that this dedication to your glorious name is nothing but a pure act of correct retribution, all the more because in you concur such qualities that can give subject matter to the most elevated pen. I, as all the wisest esteemers of merit, admire in you mature counsel, even in your tenderest years, refined prudence, sagacious ability, ready nonchalance, sweet affability, munificent benignity, discreet zeal, and an incredible propensity to all virtuous actions; you may be called the Maecenas of all the virtuous, the protector of good disciplines, indeed, among the most conspicuous literary men, the most conspicuous; you manifest yourself by your actions the worthy offspring of two celebrated families, GRUTHER, and CARRARA: the first, originally from Germany, from Colonia Agrippina [the Latin name of Cologne], has settled in all those places where it has brandished its valiant sword, and has crowned itself of triumphal laurels in all those military actions in which it demonstrated its valour, as happened most recently in the wars of 1662 when that glorious PIER MATTIA GRUTHER, your paternal uncle, a strenuous warrior, in the courageous defence of an important pass, entrusted his name to fame among posterity; the second family, the CARRARA, from which most noble origin descends the Lady Duchess your mother, a true mother of the poor, adorned with incomparable gifts, to say everything in few words, is the same family which independently ruled the famous City of Padua, and which gave birth to the light of the world, and to the glory of heaven, that famous prelate, splendour of the purple, the Blessed Bonaventura Carrara, great Patriarch of Constantinople. I would have to write a long catalogue, to enumerate all the heroes of these two families, which I will not do, in order not to offend the rare and particular modesty of Your Excellency, whose hands, in dedicating with this book all of myself, I kiss most reverently.

Of Your Excellency
the most humble, most devoted, and most obedient servant,
The knight Antonio Latini.[2]

---

2 This fulsome dedication is followed, as in the first volume, by the usual mediocre poems and anagrams in praise of the work, and by the approvals of the secular and ecclesiastic censor. Cecilia Carrara, mother of the dedicatee, purchased the fiefdom of Santa Severina in Calabria for her son. The rest of the information in the dedication is somewhat dubious: I cannot find any evidence of a Blessed Bonaventura da Carrara who was patriarch of Constantinople (or indeed of any figure by that name). I also cannot find information about this Pier Mattia Gruther (though a later man by that name served in the kingdom's armed forces in the early eighteenth century).

OF THE MODERN STEWARD

BY THE KNIGHT
ANTONIO LATINI
FROM COLLAMATO.
SECOND PART.
PRELUDE TO THE WORK.

In my first book, I set myself the goal of presenting to the world a rich arrangement of birds and quadrupeds, to satisfy good taste; now in this second book I offer for public utility, in an agreeable arrangement of scaly dishes, the tasty products that what is born in seas and rivers suggests to us. Fish is indeed not inferior to the choicest meat in satisfying our palate, and it is rather the tastiest and most delightful food that Nature produces, and the most welcome nourishment that water might suggest to satisfy the variety and gluttony of our appetite. Many great individuals grew tired of the delights of ruling because of their desire for fish. Fish was the most welcome food at Cleopatra's celebrated meals; many great lords enjoyed divine banquets thanks to fish. Often the most esteemed banquets arranged for kings were those based on fish. The tables of ancient emperors often drew from scaly inhabitants of the sea their most exquisite and sweet delights. Lucius Lucullus, Quintus Hortensius, and other Roman consuls and senators took so much pleasure in fish that they wanted their tables always filled with it; the emperors Vitellius [ruled 69 AD] and Tiberius [ruled 14–37 AD] never enjoyed any more welcome bait. In our own days no banquet is truly sumptuous without the fruits of fishing, as we observe the sentence of Columella, "*Triumphant dinners are ennobled by the use of fish.*" It comes to further glory of fish to have often been chosen for their food by Christ Our Lord and the Apostles, and to have been multiplied to sate the hungry crowds. Because it is the child of water, fish extinguishes the flame of concupiscence and combats the pride of sensual instincts. Thus it was allowed and used by the great Saint Francis of Paola and by the Holy Mother Theresa as part of religious mortification for the best ordered cloisters; ancient hermits ate fish too, for instance Saint Bruno, as part of penitence; and Holy Church destined it for Lenten food, because it knew fish to be apt to repress the boiling desires of human fragility. It suffices to remember the daily example of the Queen of Heaven worshipped at Monte Vergine, who is pleased to endorse the holy food of waters, so that if anyone, in that holy place sacred to her, by error should eat meat or dairy, She displays her indignation by sudden lightning, thunder, tempest, and wind. One of the greatest punishments ever inflicted by God on the world was the Flood, and fish did not suffer from that, since in that time fish alone, happy and festive, danced through men's homes and ate the most prized food, which men—now drowned—had kept with such care. I conclude therefore that fish is a noble food, healthy for body and soul; it offers beneficial nourishment in cloisters, and a rare pleasure to the most majestic palates in royal palaces. Thus it is sensible to give fish the praises that are briefly encapsulated in the words composed by the letters of its name, thus:

PISCIS:

nourishment of the innocent, food of health, sweetness of fasting.[3]

---

3 Latini here writes in Latin: "Pabulum Innocentiae, Salutaris Cibum, Iejunii Suavitas," the

If the reader should meet in this work and in its style with some coldness, he should be lenient, and reflect that, when the sun is in Pisces, it shines through the icy rigours of winter. And if critics will condemn me, I will not be aggrieved, because in handling fish it seems impossible not to be pricked by a bone.[4]

TREATISE I: *Of the nature of fish, its seasons, quality, and cooking.*

Of sturgeon.

Cleops king of Egypt was the first to eat sturgeon. He was very rich and built the superb pyramids of Egypt.

Sturgeon, though it is a seawater fish, grows in freshwater; when it is young it is called *porcelletta*, and when it is grown sturgeon, and there are different varieties of it. Good ones are caught in rivers, especially in the Po and Tiber, and they are exquisite. The season to catch it is from April through the summer, when it spawns; in Rome one can find it all year long. This fish is hot in the first degree and moist in the second. Those caught in rivers are best because they are fatter and tastier than the sea ones; those from the river at Capua are also celebrated. It is a nourishing fish, it refreshes the arteries and stimulates coition; it is highly esteemed at the table, where indeed it occupies first place among water creatures. From its eggs one makes caviar, which is eaten raw or cooked: it tingles the palate, stimulates the appetite, and gives one thirst. The sturgeon's best parts are the head and the belly, especially when hanged and then boiled in water and vinegar; the best preparation is then with a white condiment, vinegar, and cinnamon inside.

One can also boil sturgeon, whole or in pieces, in water, vinegar, and salt; it can be used for pies, ground, in fish-balls or fish loaves, in various ways; as chops, in various small pies; also roasted or fried; with its flesh and soft roe one can make various tarts, also covered ones; one can also fry the liver, eggs, and soft roe; the eggs can be made into Ferrara-style caviar; and it can be garnished with different condiments.

The same applies to the young sturgeon, boiled, roasted, in pies, with the usual ingredients. I conclude that sturgeon can be served, garnished, or dressed in the same ways as the suckling calf, because it is an exquisite and most noble fish, and highly nourishing, as I mentioned above, and it can be used in many preparations, as I will say in its place.

---

initials of which words form the word PISCIS, fish. St. Francis of Paola (d. 1519) was a southern Italian hermit and founder of the Minim friars; St. Theresa of Avila (d. 1582) was a great Spanish mystic and reformer of the Carmelites; St. Bruno (d. 1101) founded the rigourous Carthusian monks. The sanctuary dedicated to the Virgin Mary at Monte Vergine, near Avellino, inland from Naples, is still quite popular, though I am unaware of frequent sudden storms in its vicinity.

4 Throughout these opening pages, Latini revels in Baroque metaphors, puns, and allegories, all fish-related. In particular, I fear I am unable to do any better to render Latini's rather awful puns in the final paragraph: *freddura* (coldness) also means pun, and the Italian word for fish bones (*spine*) also means thorns.

This fish is eaten only at the tables of great lords, as it is not fit for everybody, as Francesco Bossueto reports, speaking of fish, in these verses:

> Sturgeon only suits the tables of heroes, nothing in Rome was ever
> of greater price, it is a rare gift that adorns royal banquets.

And Martial, in speaking of the same:

> Sturgeons are fit for imperial tables, a rare gift to adorn immortal banquets.[5]

Of corb.

Asmondo Beriado was the first to eat this fish, which the Greeks called *sciena*, which means shadow, because it can swim away so fast that it seems more a shadow than a fish; it is born and lives in the sea, next to mossy reefs, and it does not enter freshwater.

Corb is good all year long, but the best is caught in spring, because it is fatter and tastier; it has good taste, provides perfect nourishment, and is easy to digest; it tempers hot blood, and aside from sturgeon no other species equals it; it is moderately hot, and moist in the first degree.

This noble and exquisite fish can be cooked and prepared in all the ways I mentioned for sturgeon. I must alert you though that corb is whiter and more tender than sturgeon. Thus, every intelligent cook will know to cook it for less time than sturgeon; with its eggs, salted and smoked, one can make very good *bottarga*; its soft roe, liver, and eggs can be served and prepared in all the ways I mentioned for sturgeon, and its flesh can be used for blancmange, and to make various jellies.[6]

Small corb can be prepared in all the same ways as large corb, and since it is more agreeable it can be boiled in white wine, and with the condiments I will mention later; after parboiling it in wine, it can be prepared in a pottage with apt ingredients; it can also be soused, with the usual condiments and sauce; it can also be marinated or cooked in a scapece, or cooked in milk, dressed with good butter.

Of swordfish.

Thareso Storico was the first to eat swordfish, which is a flat fish, and some writers claim that he was the discoverer of *sparolo*, which is a small and humble fish, similar to gilthead bream, and it lives along mossy coasts.[7]

Swordfish is cold in the first degree and moist in the second; many are caught here in Naples, and also near the Lighthouse at Messina, where they are especially large; this fishing starts in spring and lasts through August.

---

5 Bossueto is likely François Boussuet (1520–1572), a French doctor, author of a learned poem about fish; the Martial poem is *Epigrams* 13.91 (Latini cites both poems in Latin). Sturgeon's first rank among fish and its status as most suited for elite diners was commonplace in early modern European cookbooks and continued after Latini: Corrado wrote that sturgeon was "greatly esteemed on the tables of the great," *Il cuoco galante* (1786 edit; repr., Bologna: Forni, 1990), 72.

6 Bottarga is cured roe, still a typical Mediterranean delicacy.

7 It is rather odd to call swordfish a flat (*piano*) fish, a term Latini also uses more suitably for sole and turbot.

This fish must be beheaded as soon as it is caught, and the head boiled, because it easily rots.

Its flesh can serve for marinades, or in ground dishes, or fish loaves, or in pottages, as I said about sturgeon.

Of meagre.

Masconico from Torsi was the first to cook meagre, which feeds on algae and gives birth twice a year. In the sea, it is yellow, in lakes it is black.

This fish is caught from the start of spring through July; it is highly nourishing; best is that caught in the sea, near the mouth of rivers; it is hot in the first degree, dry in the second.

Its flesh bears great resemblance to dentex flesh, though it is harder; thus it is easy to make jellies from it, and it can be prepared in all the same ways as grey mullet, both large and small.

Of dentex.

Diogenes Fabro was the first to eat dentex, and he reports that it was very nourishing.

The best is caught from the start of winter to spring.

The fattest is caught in the Slavonic sea, and Slavonians often take it to sell it in nearby countries, with great profit, especially at the market in Senigallia; it can be prepared with a yellow jelly, thus tinted with a bit of saffron; it is hot in the first degree and dry in the second.[8]

This fish is very nourishing, but when it is too fat it is less beneficial, though in fact easier to digest.

It aids those suffering from dysentery, because by its nature it is astringent; it can be used in ground dishes, as I said of sturgeon, or in stews, and can be used in all other dishes. It is better than any other fish to make jellies.

It can be cooked and prepared in all the same ways as salmon, both large and small.

Of trout.

Carebbo from Marseille was the first to eat trout, and he reports that it is has a very good taste and is nourishing.

Carebbo lived a long time and was a capital enemy of women.

The Greeks did not know trout. Among the Latins, Columella, Aelian, and the poet Ausonius call it by various names; if it dies, it is best to eat it immediately. Gluttons say that it should be cooked in the broth of a very fat capon; if caught in lakes it is harmful to the infirm, but not if caught in rivers; it can help against strong fevers, and it augments one's sperm.[9]

---

8 Slavonia today is the name of an inner region of Croatia, but in early modern Italy the term usually referred more broadly to the northeastern areas of the Adriatic coast; Senigallia is a port town in Latini's native Marches, on the coast opposite what Latini probably meant by Slavonia.

9 As in the first volume, Latini uses these sections to show off his erudition, most of it copied from various other writers: the "discoverers" of each animal, the medical information, the classical references, the odd details. Columella and Aelian both wrote on nature or animals, and both appear

Of grouper.

Its season is May through October, it is difficult to digest, but very nourishing, though if large less so.

It is hot in the first degree and dry in the second; its meat is tough and can be prepared in many ways. It is caught in great quantity near Messina and in the sea around Calabria, especially large groupers. It feeds on the grass found on reefs, and especially where corals develop.

Its head can be boiled with water, vinegar, and salt, and also its flesh.

It can be cooked in a pan with apt ingredients, and it is quite tasty, and can be served to a lordly table.

Its flesh, sliced, can be marinated, or cooked in a scapece, or fried, and if eaten hot it will be quite good.

It can be grilled, first soaked in vinegar, oil, salt, and powdered fennel.

It can also be prepared in a Venetian-style pottage, with onions, saffron, and other ingredients, as I will say in the chapter on dishes.

It can be used in impanate and pies, to be eaten cold, and they will be quite tasty.

Its tripe, cleaned, can be boiled in water and salt, and when it is nearly cooked you can prepare it just like veal tripe, and it will not be inferior to it, as I will say below, so much so that many will be deceived by it, and think that it is not in fact fish.

Of sole.[10]

Alcinenone of Athens was the first to eat sole, which is a flat fish, and very tasty; if applied to the spleen, it heals it.

It is fished in winter and spring; it is harmful to the decrepit and to those of weak complexion, because it is difficult to digest, since it is a very viscous fish. It is quite nourishing for hardy young people, who have a hot stomach.

Its quality is cold in the first degree and moist in the second.

It can be fried or roasted; it is also good boiled in water and vinegar, or in a scapece, or marinated with apt ingredients; it can be stuffed, and it is also quite good, as I will say in the chapter on dishes.

Of sea bass.

Cabreno Dorico was the first to place the sea bass on the table, and he esteemed it as a most delicate food.

This fish holds a powerful enmity with grey mullet, and when they meet it bites the mullet's tail, except in the months of June, July, and August, when they are the best of friends. Exquisite sea bass is caught in Rome in the ponds near the sea; it is fished from

---

also earlier in Latini's text; Ausonius (d. 395 AD) wrote poetry on various subjects and in various genres.

10 Latini gives three names for this fish (*linguattola*, *palaja*, or *sfoglia*), all of which in Italy today are regional names for the common sole; linguattola, though, is also the proper Italian name for the spotted flounder. I have translated all these terms as sole.

the start of January through March; it is a nourishing and beneficial food; in its head we find a stone that is healthful for those who suffer from kidney or ground stones.

It can also bring coolness to those who are too heated, because this fish has a cold humour; it is highly esteemed at the table of great people.

Best is that caught near Castel Sant'Angelo, between the two Tiber bridges.

Its quality is cold and moist in the second degree.

With its eggs one can make bottarga; its innards, flesh, and head can be prepared in the same ways as sturgeon.

Of salmon carp.[11]

Vatino Maleno was the first to eat this, and he never ate it hot; it is a sweet fish; it is caught in many places in Italy, especially in Lake Garda, though it is also found in Slavonia and in some places in France, in some rivers, and in a place called La Pesca [Fishing] belonging to the Lord Duke of Alvito, but only small ones.

This fish used to be called *Pione*, but because it is so highly esteemed, *Car* was added, and now it is called *Carpione*.[12]

It can be called the head of all fish, due to the great nourishment it brings, and it is exquisite in all preparations; since in its intestines we find nothing but golden sand, everybody believes that it eats gold.

It is fished especially in July and August; if caught in winter, it is very good, but it must be cooked fresh, in order to be tasty and useful.

Its quality is moderately hot, and moist in the start of the first degree.

After boiling it with water and salt, it can be prepared in all the same ways as sturgeon, and it can be given to the convalescent, since it is a temperate fish.

Of the gilthead bream.

Aurelio Ceste was the first to eat this fish, and it is very tasty and healthful; it gives birth near the coast, and, when the summer heat is at its peak, it stays hidden under the sand for sixty days.

It is caught from October through February; best is that caught in deep sea, especially in the Turkish seas, as that is the most nourishing.

Its quality is moderately hot, and dry in the first degree.

It can be prepared in all the same ways as sturgeon and salmon; it is tastiest if fried or roasted.

---

11 The precise identification of *carpione* is difficult: Scappi, *Opera*, tends to call this carp, while Riley, *The Oxford Companion*, calls it a type of salmon; Latini himself (early in his work) mentions that carpione is a type of trout of the Naples area. Since both carp (*pesce reina*) and salmon appear below, I will use salmon carp for this one.

12 This rather silly statement is based, I presume, on the notion that *Car* refers to *caro* (or dear, in both senses).

Of lamprey.

Sinesio of Cyrene was the first to eat lamprey, which Alberto calls small moray eels, and they have this name because they are always licking stones; the Latins call it *Mustella*, the Greeks *Galessia*, and the Germans *Nine-Eyes*.[13]

The best ones are caught in spring, in the river in Rome; in Spain one finds very big ones, and at the beginning of spring they come into freshwater, and at the start of summer they return to the sea.

The decrepit should avoid this fish, and also those suffering from gout, because it is hard and difficult to digest.

Those who are young and have a good complexion can eat it because it brings them strength and vigour; they are well regarded at the table of great people.

Its quality is moderately hot and moist in the first degree.

It can be spit-roasted, or grilled, like eel, and it is good boiled with butter or whipped butter, or with good-quality oil.

It can also be fried, and eaten cold, and it will be very good; or used in pies, with the usual ingredients and condiments; it will be good to kill it in white wine or milk, and then you can use this wine or milk in cooking it.

Of red mullet.

Calimaco of Granopoli was the first to eat red mullet, called *Mallas*, and *Barbone* by the Venetians, because it has a beard on its lower lip, and in the Marches it is called *Rossoli*; this fish feeds on algae and sea hares, and it is sacred to Diana; it enjoyed great fame among the ancient Romans; it gives birth three times a year, which is attributed to the Three-Form goddess [Diana]; it is a sea fish; Calimaco was the first to grill it, moistening it with oil and vinegar, with salt, sage, and rosemary.

Red mullet, among its virtues, includes the fact that whoever drinks wine in which this fish has been drowned, forever will hate wine; it is tasty and nourishing.

It suppresses erotic appetites, and heals poisonous bites, if placed over the injured part.

It is better small than large; it is tastier when caught on reefs and in clear waters; our seas produce very good ones, especially in a place called Granatello, near Naples.

It is fished from May through August.

Its quality is moderately hot, and dry in the first degree.

It can be marinated, soused, or used for fish-balls.

It can be used in various pottages, it is good boiled with vinegar and salt, fried, and roasted with apt ingredients, and very good cooked in paper on the grill with raisins and pine nuts; with its liver one can make exquisite small pies.

---

13 I am not sure who Alberto is (it may be Albertus Magnus, author of an essay on animals), or why Latini included all these alternative names.

Of gurnard.

Democritus the Tyrant was the first to eat gurnard, and its liver is highly praised.

It is a healthy fish, nourishing, and easy to digest.

It suits every complexion, because it is quite delicate; large ones are better.

It is fished in winter and spring; the best ones are caught in the Adriatic Sea.

Its quality is moderately cold and moist.

It can be used to make blancmange, and is useful in various pottages.

With its flesh one can make fish-balls, it can be boiled with water and salt, or grilled.

It can be used to prepare good and healthy dishes for the convalescent.

Of tuna.

Orlio the Norman was the first to eat tuna, a fish that is good salted; it is also called *Palamide*.

The best tuna is young, caught in September and October; the lean one is better than the fat one; it aids against the bites of rabid dogs.

Its belly is quite tasty, and coveted at the tables of the great; it is very good marinated; when salted, it is called *Tarantello*, lean salted belly is called *Tonnina*.

Its eggs are also salted, to make bottarga, similarly to those of grey mullet.

Its quality is cold in the first degree and moist in the second.

From its flesh one can prepare various pottages and ground dishes; it is good roasted and marinated, with garlic cloves, vinegar, sage, rosemary, and spices; it can be prepared in all the ways in which one prepares swordfish.

Of pandora bream, in Naples called *Luvaro*.

This fish is red in colour, the Greeks called it *Erythicinos*, in Venice it is called *Arbore*, the Latins called it *Rubelli*; it is a sea fish and is not found in freshwater; because it is always found full of eggs, it is believed that it is always female; it is better eaten in winter than in summer.

It is often used in cooking; it is healthy and nourishing, easy to digest, since it is tender and delicate.

It is fished from October through spring, its quality is moist in the first degree and moderately cold.

Its flesh can be used for fish-balls or fish loaves, it can be soused, or marinated, and it will be very good grilled; it is also good boiled, with an apt little sauce.

In preparing it, you can use the same approach as with sturgeon.

Of grey mullet.

Anchise Menocchio was the first to eat this fish, and to discern that the one from the sea is better than the one that lives in rivers; this fish is sordid by nature, and therefore can be seen dipping in the high sea to wash itself, and it is quite lustful, and thus easily prey of fishermen.

There are four types of this fish, the first called *Cefalo*, the second *Cestreo*, which is smaller and has a small head, the third *Labeone*, and the fourth *Moccone*, because it feeds on tiny newborn fish [*mucco*], which name in Italian becomes *Mosella*.[14]

The best is caught in the sea, in clear, not turbid, water, and in rocky areas; that caught in Torre del Greco is praised, called *Bocche Grassolle*, and in Rome that caught in the ponds of the Lords Mattei.

Here in Naples, it is also caught in Lake Patria, though it is not that well known, but if it is big it can be very good in impanate or pies, both cold and hot, but better in the cold season.

This fish is good against constipation, but if it is too large, fat, and heavy, it can be insipid.

It is fished from October through April; its quality is cold in the first degree and moist in the second.

Large or small, it can be prepared in various ways, for instance whole or in pieces in pies or impanate, grilled, spit-roasted, or fried, or boiled with water, vinegar, and salt; after cooking it, you can season it in salt and pepper, dredge it in flour, and fry it, it can be soused and marinated like sturgeon, it can be smoked and salted, and if then you desalinate it you can use it in various stews with legumes.

With the innards, called in Naples *Mazzoni*, you can make various pottages, and with the eggs you can make bottarga.

Of scorpion fish.

This is a sea fish, and best is the one that looks almost red.

It is fished in fall and spring; its flesh is hard, and thus difficult to digest.

It is beneficial to those of any complexion, and can be given to the convalescent.

Its quality is cold in the first degree and moist in the second.

It is good boiled with water, vinegar, salt, and wine.

It can be cooked in a pan with various fresh and dried fruits; it can be prepared in all the same ways as gurnard.

It must be well cooked, because its flesh is hard; its flesh, deboned, can be used in blancmange.

Of John Dory.

The best is caught in winter and spring.

Its quality is cold in the first degree and moist in the second.

It can be used in various dishes, except for jellies and blancmange, because it is not fleshy.

It can be boiled with an anchovy sauce on top, in pottage, braised, or fried, in the same ways as turbot.

---

14 This odd information, like much else in this chapter, is copied often word for word from previous books, including Frugoli, *Pratica*.

Of turbot.

Archelao of Lisbon was the first to eat turbot, which is a flat fish, and was once highly praised; the best one is caught near Ravenna; it is similar in colour to sole, and of a similar shape, though a bit rounder.

This fish is nourishing and easy to digest.

It is good at all times of the year, its quality is hot in the first degree and moist in the second.

It can be prepared in various ways, stuffed, braised, or grilled.

It can be used in pies, small pies, and pottages; it is good boiled, with water, vinegar, and salt, with an anchovy sauce.

It can be fried, marinated, or soused; its eggs can be used to make bottarga.

The innards, well washed, can be fried and dressed with various condiments.

Of carp.

Cardemo Panniccio was the first to eat the fish called *Ciprino*, called *Carpa* and *Reina* in Lombardy, and also *Reina* in Rome; it is celebrated by many gluttons.

Those caught in Lake Bracciano near Rome are exquisite, and also in other freshwater ponds.

It is helpful to those who do not suffer from phlegmatic humours.

It is fished in the month of January and through summer.

Its quality is cold in the first degree and moist in the second.

It can be prepared in various ways, it is good boiled in white wine, water, vinegar, and salt.

It can be used in pottages, and in pies, whole or in pieces.

It can be fried, or grilled; its eggs can be used in various pottages; its soft roe and liver must be fried.

Of shad.

Quirino of Capua was the first to eat shad, which the Greeks call *Thrissa*, the Venetians *Chieppa*, and here in Naples is called *Alosa*; if it did not have so many bones, it would be the tastiest fish.

Best is that caught in freshwater, and with eggs.

Those caught in the sea are dry and hard. Here in Naples very good ones are caught in the river of Capua.

As soon as this fish enters a river, it becomes fat; at the beginning of June it returns to the sea to give birth.

Those caught in the Tiber in May and April are the best; they are found filled with eggs, and are delicate to the taste.

This fish is nourishing, it provokes sleep, and it has a stone in its head that can heal quartan fever.

It is caught from March through July. Its quality is cold in the first degree and moist in the second.

It can be boiled in water and vinegar; it is good roasted, braised, or fried.

It can be marinated or soused, used for chops, and prepared in all the same ways as grey mullet; if it is big, it can be used to make pies, and it is good hot or cold; it is full of bones, so one must eat it with caution.

Of large pike.

Tito Valgio was the first to eat pike, which is beneficial to sight, and maybe it was called *Luccio* because it is beneficial to light [*luce*]; large ones can be caught in Lake Vico; they abound in Lombardy, and a few can be caught in the Tiber in Rome, and they are exquisite; the largest pikes are best.

It is caught in lakes and rivers in clear, not turbid, water.

It is nourishing, and very good in all seasons, though less so in spring, because it is then in heat.

It is fished from fall through March.

Its quality is cold and moist in the second degree.

The flesh of this fish can be prepared in various ways, and especially in blancmange.

It can be boiled with water, salt, and vinegar, or in Lombard white wine.

Ground, it can be given to the convalescent, with melon seeds.

It can be used for chops, or in ground dishes, or grilled, or spit-roasted, with vinegar, oil, and fennel.

With its flesh you can make sausages with various ingredients.

Its liver, eggs, and soft roe can be used in various soups or pottages, to be served hot or cold.

Of lobster.

Lobster is greatly esteemed at the table, and it consists of three flavours: one in the neck, one in the body, and one near the tail. It is caught in abundance everywhere, among other places in the island of Ponza, from where it is brought to Naples.

This fish is good at all times, especially if caught in fall or spring; the female is far better.

It is nourishing, but hard to digest; it is hot in the first degree, and cold in the second.[15]

It can be boiled with water, vinegar, and salt.

It can be used in pies, whole or in bits, but cleaned of its shell.

It can be prepared in fish loaves, after parboiling it, and it can be prepared in various dishes; it is good cold and hot.

One can grind its flesh in the mortar and make a juice for various composite dishes, which are very tasty, diluting the juice in almond milk, and then draining it through a cloth sieve.

---

15 Ponza is a small island off the coast between Naples and Rome; Latini uses *pesce* (fish) as his general word for water creatures of all sorts. I assume that he meant to write that lobster is moist (or dry) in the second degree, not cold, as no creature could be both hot and cold—there is a similar error a bit below regarding salted salmon.

Of squid.

Termilius of Provence was the first to eat squid and cuttlefish, and they are of the same species; Atheneus holds that it is beneficial to the stomach, though hard to digest, and that it generates raw humours, because it is highly nourishing.

This fish holds a black humour with which it darkens water when it is seen by fishermen, and so it escapes capture.

It is not worth much when it is pregnant, or caught in stagnant waters.

Small squid is better than large, because it is more tender and easier to digest; it is tasty, appetizing, and nourishing; it is cold in the first degree and moist in the second; big ones must be hanged.

It is caught in winter and through spring.

It can be prepared in various dishes; small squid are fried, and we may call them sea sweetbreads.

Of salmon.

Anasarco Capriotto was the first to eat salmon; this fish is perfect in Aquitaine and in the Rhone river, near Seville, and in various parts of Spain.

The Spanish usually salt salmon, and that way it is moist in the first degree and dry in the second.

When fresh, its quality is cold in the first degree and moist in the second.

It is fished from spring through October.

It can be used in pies, cooked in a pan, in chops, fried, in ground dishes, and in small pies.

The liver, eggs, and soft roe can be used in various dishes, and they are quite tasty when fried.

Salted salmon can be prepared like fresh salmon, first boiling it in water, vinegar, and salt, and kept for a short while in fresh water to desalinate it, then garnished with apt ingredients.

Of sardine.

The poet Theseo Bisuntio was the first to eat sardines, which must be eaten as soon as they are caught, to be good and of a delicate flavour. This fish enjoys music, and therefore when it hears music one can see it jump out of the water.

It is nourishing; one can give one or two salted sardines to the convalescent to stimulate their appetite and purify the stomach of superfluities.

The best sardines are those caught in spring, in a sandy but not muddy sea.

They are cold in the first degree and moist to the top of the first.

They can be prepared in various ways, for instance in small pies, roasted on embers, or grilled.

They are good dredged in flour and fried, in pottages, braised, and boiled in water, vinegar, and salt.

From their flesh one can make very tasty fish-balls, as I will show in a later chapter; they can be roasted on embers and served just like that, and they come out very good.

They can be salted or smoked, and after desalinating them they can be prepared just like fresh ones.

This fish is so useful that, if one cannot find any other fish, from this one alone one can make many different things; more than once I found myself without any fish, and with sardines alone I prepared some good meals.

Of eel.

Nicearco was the first to eat eel, which is so called because it resembles a snake;[16] it is the only fish that does not swim, it lives for ten years, and it can live outside of water for eight days, it craves clear water, and in summer it does not like any change; some claim to have seen eels as long as thirty feet in the Ganges river; Aristotle in his *History* says that eels are neither male nor female; Pliny says that they are abundant.

Atheneus says that in Arethusa, near Negroponte, he saw domesticated eels carrying golden rings, and taking food from the hands of people, and he also says that at a dinner there was a most beautiful eel, and that one of the guests said, you will be the Helen of this banquet, and I shall be Paris.

Eel is nourishing and delicate in flavour; the ones caught in a sandy but not muddy sea are better; best are those caught in clear water. Here in Naples beautiful eels are caught in the underground, not turbid, waters below the fountains, which are the best; they must be cooked as soon as they are caught; those of Lake Bolsena are exquisite, and those of Lake Comacchio, when salted.

They keep a long time, and are beneficial for phlegmatic stomachs.

They are fished in spring, and their quality is cold in the first degree and moist in the second.

They can be prepared in various dishes, such as fish-balls, and fish loaves, mixing their flesh with that of other fish.

Eels are also good in ground dishes, and their flesh can be used in ground dishes with the meat of various land animals and birds; they can be mixed in small pies with other fish.

Their skins, well cleaned, can be filled with their own flesh and that of other fish.

When making fish-balls or fish loaves with eels, you can mould them in the shape of various birds and poultry; they can be used in pies or impanate, which, eaten cold, are very tasty.

After skinning eel, you can use it to make a stew, or roast it with crustless bread, or in pies with the usual ingredients, also without skinning it.

Both sea and river eels can be fried, and prepared in all the same ways as lamprey.

Salted and smoked, eel can be braised in the oven, or grilled, or [cooked] under ashes; you can kill it in brine, and then, before cooking it, soak it in white wine, and then give it the usual condiments.

---

16 *Anguilla* is the Italian name for eel, and *angue* (*anguis* in Latin) is an archaic word for snake.

Of cod.

Stafficatro the Roman was the first to eat cod; it has a flat and wide head and many teeth, its scales are small, and its colour close to ashen.

This fish offers limited nourishment, and is difficult to digest.

It is caught in summer and spring, and is hot in the first degree and moist in the second.

It can be fried; it is also good boiled in water, vinegar, and salt; one can make chops from it, and it can be used in various dishes; it can be salted and smoked, or dried in the sun, and then it can be used in the Spanish style.

To desalinate it, soak it in water, and then fry it or dress it with other ingredients as you prefer; when it is salted, it is called *Baccalà*.

Of garfish.

Aaron the Hebrew prophet was the first to eat garfish, and this is why Jews call it Aaron's Green [*Verde di Aronne*]; this fish is much loved by Jews.

The bigger it is, the better; it is not very nourishing, and better fried than in any other preparation.

It is fished in fall and spring; it is cold and moist in the first degree.

It can be cut into pieces and roasted, like eel.

It can be used for pies, and cooked in all the same ways as sardines and anchovies.

It can be salted, and once desalinated it can be boiled in water, vinegar, and salt, dressed with the usual ingredients.

Of mackerel.

Trino of Thebes was the first to eat mackerel; in Spain there is an island called Sgombraria because of its abundance of this fish [*sgombro*]. The best, as Pliny says, are found near Carthage.

It is a sea fish, not very good; it is fished in May and all summer.

It is hot in the first degree and moist in the second.

It can be made into chops, fried, roasted, boiled with water, vinegar, and salt; it can be prepared in all the same ways as cod.

Of saupe.

Solpitio the Persian was the discoverer of saupe, as Pliny says; it must be eaten as soon as it is caught; in the sea, they feed under reefs, as it is a sea fish; it rots quickly; it is fished in summer and winter. It is hot in the first degree and moist in the second.

It can be roasted, or boiled with water, vinegar, and salt; it can be fried, or cooked in a thin broth, Venetian-style.

Whitebait [Naked fish], in Naples called *cecinello*.

Archiselenus was the discoverer of the naked fish; as soon as it sees the fire, this fish is cooked.

It is a nourishing fish, and easy to digest.

It is caught in winter and throughout spring, only at sea; it is temperately cold and moist.

It can be prepared in fritters, or fried by itself; it can be used in covered tarts, boiled in water, vinegar, and salt, or ground and used to make fish-balls with apt ingredients.[17]

Of smooth hound and parrotfish.[18]

This fish is cold and moist; it is fished in November and all spring. It is usually boiled, with water, vinegar, and salt; it is also good in a pan.

Its eggs can be fried, and cooked in various dishes.

Of rayfish, monkfish, and saddled bream.

The best of these three fish is rayfish; they are fished from spring through fall.

They are hot in the first degree and moist in the second.

They can all three be cooked in the same way.

Monkfish and saddled bream are not as good as rayfish.

They can be used in pies, in pottages, boiled with water, vinegar, and salt, in a thin broth, fried, in fish-balls, or braised; but only when you cannot find other fish.

The belly of these is very good, especially of rayfish, and it is usually boiled, as above, with apt ingredients.

Saddled bream can be cooked like mushrooms.

Of barbell, *cavadente*, and roach.[19]

Thelefane was the first to eat barbell, which was called *Barbo* because it had a beard [*barba*] on its lower lip, and is also called *Mulo*, and some call it *Barbatolo Mulo*; it can be found in the river at Rome, and in other rivers.

It is fished in summer and spring.

Cavadente is fished in the same periods, and roach from November through April.

These can all be fried or roasted on embers or grilled, and they can be prepared in all the same was as grey mullet, the goodness and perfection of which none of these can reach. Roach is fished in various lakes.

Of octopus.

It is fished in the month of January, through spring.

It is hot and moist in the first degree.

It is cooked in all the same ways as squid, but for a longer time because its flesh is much harder; it is good fried, and it can be used in various pottages.

---

17 Latini calls it naked fish (*pesce ignudo*), and gives the traditional Neapolitan name; in Italian today it is called *bianchetti*.

18 Latini mentions two names (*pesce palombo* and *pappagallo*), as if they were two different fish, but then only discusses one, though the two are actually quite different. Similarly crowded sections follow.

19 I have not been able to identify cavadente fish (the name literally means toothpuller).

Of *frittura francese* and *bua*.[20]

This fish is caught all year long, and its quality cannot be described because it is a mixture of various tiny sea fish.

The best is caught in the month of March and April, which is quite nourishing.

Bua is caught in spring through July; it is hot in the first degree and cold in the second. This fish is caught with a trawling net.

Both are best fried, but they can also be roasted, and prepared in all the ways mentioned for sardines and anchovies.

Of sea and freshwater smelt.

Smelt is fished in winter through March; those caught in rivers or lakes are nourishing and easy to digest.

Smelt in large quantities is fished in Lake Nepi near Rome, and they are very tasty.

From the smelt caught in the waters at Castel Gandolfo [also near Rome] the largest can be roasted on embers; smaller ones are fried, or prepared in the ways mentioned for sardines and anchovies, with the usual ingredients.

Of conger and moray eel.

These are very nourishing.

They are fished in November through April; they are sea fish, cold in the second degree and moist in the third.

They are prepared in the same ways as lamprey, with the same ingredients and condiments; they make good jellies, which are good cold.

Of small freshwater fish.

Among these, the best are those fished in running waters, clear and neat, especially in the river at Rome.

They are fished all year long; they are moist in the first degree and cold in the second; they are tasty and flavourful.

Many good ones are caught also in the river at Sora.

They can be boiled with water, vinegar, and salt; roasted on embers or grilled; the smallest are fried.

Tortoise and sea turtle.

Herodotus of Cyprus was the first to eat water turtles, the Romans called them *Lateritias Testudines*, and the Greeks called them *Emidas*. They give birth to eggs with a hard shell, and of two colours, like those of birds, and they bury them underground; they often visit and set their eggs; within a year, the eggs hatch.

---

20 I have not been able to find English translations for these two terms (the first one literally means "French fried dish"), and Latini himself suggests that the first at least is a generic name for a variety of tiny fish. It is somewhat odd that he refers to a discussion of anchovies, since this long chapter, which includes dozens of fish, does not actually include a section on anchovies (*alici*).

The best turtles are land tortoises, especially large and oval ones, which taste better.

One must feed them with good food; they are highly nourishing; they are cold in the second degree and moderately moist; water turtles are moist and cold in the first degree.

The season for tortoises is June through October, for water turtles from February to October.

With sea turtles, you remove the head and the blood, and boil them well, and then use them to prepare various dishes.

They can be fried, or used in pottages and pies, with apt ingredients.

The eggs and the liver can be fried or used in frittate.

Tortoises can be prepared the same way as water turtles.

Tortoises require less cooking, as they are gentler and more delicate.

From their blood you can make sanguinacci,[21] which will be similar to those one makes with pig blood, stuffing pig guts with it.

I conclude that with turtles one can make the same dishes as with wether, as I will show in a later chapter.

Of tench.

Nirsia, daughter of Sesostris King of Egypt, who predicted her father's royal future, was the first to eat tench, in Lombard-style, stuffing it with garlic and sweet herbs.

The best tench is caught in rivers and clear lakes, with waters that are not muddy and turbid. In the fish market in Rome I have seen tench as big as twenty-five pounds.

The female one is better than the male, and quite nourishing.

It is fished in spring through fall; its quality is cold and moist in the second degree.

Slicing it open from its back, one can roast it or stuff it.

It can be braised, boiled, with water, vinegar, and salt, or with a good Lombard white wine.

It can also be fried and cooked in all the same ways as trout with the usual ingredients.

Of sea and freshwater shrimp.

Nello Brentio was the first to eat shrimp. One finds them in freshwater in various parts of Italy, and here in the kingdom of Naples in Isernia; they can have a soft or hard shell, and the sea ones also can be of different sorts; they live near beaches and can be so fast that they are hard to catch.

Freshwater ones are better, and highly nourishing.

One catches them in spring; they are cold in the second degree and moist in the first.

Small ones can be fried, as one can do also with the flesh of larger ones; they are good boiled in water, vinegar, and other ingredients. The flesh can be used in ground dishes and pottages; if parboiled, it can be used in pies, or also as a garnish for various dishes. You can use their juice to flavour many fish dishes.

---

21 Turtle blood is thus the lean substitute in this preparation Latini already discussed among pig products.

Of crab and spider crab.

Best are those caught at the full moon; they are nourishing and are caught in the sea in fall and spring.

Their quality is moist in the first degree and cold in the second.

They can be prepared like the tails of river shrimp, parboiled in water, vinegar, and salt.

They can be roasted with their shell, and eaten hot or cold as preferred, with apt ingredients.

Of freshwater crab.

The best are caught in clear water; they are nourishing, stimulate coition and urination, and purge ground stones.

They are caught in fall and spring; their quality is cold in the first degree and moist in the second.

Those with a hard shell are prepared like lobster.

Those with a soft shell can be fried or cooked in a pan, in almond or goat milk, with the usual ingredients; in Rome they are abundant and very good.

Of frog, or musician fish.

Glauco Perricone was the first to eat frogs. They have two livers; they copulate at night; on the islands of Cyrene and Seriso they are mute; Pliny at Book 8, Chapter 29, states that the people of a city in France were forced to abandon their city because a great multitude of frogs grew there.

The best ones live in rivers or lakes, not in swamps.

Very good ones are abundant in Lombardy, and there every noble table includes them.

They help heal various infirmities and they might be called a remedy to all poisons that come from snakes. If eaten with their bones, they help against kidney gravel.

They are caught in June and July, and can be prepared with verjuice.

They are cold in the second degree and moist in the first.

To make them beneficial to health, they must be boiled in water, oil, and salt; they can be fried, and used in pies of all sizes, and the pies will seem to have been made with capon flesh; they can also be used in many tasty and appetizing pottages, as I will show below.

When they are fried, one can detach the legs from the bones, but not entirely, and dip them in a green parsley sauce. They can be boiled with water, oil, and salt, with the usual spices; on lean days one can use the broth they make to cook rice or pasta, and it will seem to have been done with meat broth.[22]

---

22 Frogs (like turtles and tortoises) were regarded as water creatures and thus allowed on lean days; they were prized exactly because of their capacity to resemble meat products. In 8.29 (today usually numbered 8.43) of his *Natural History*, Pliny does indeed refer to a district in Gaul devastated by frogs.

Curious observations about shellfish and seafood.

I have judged it apt not to neglect a few observations which researchers have made on shellfish and seafood, to satisfy the desires of curious readers.

First of all, it has been observed that shellfish and seafood have neither voice nor hearing; they have no mouth, and yet they feed, and Nature has denied them liver, bile, and spleen.

Secondly, it is the prerogative of shells to generate pearls, which, though Tertullian called them the sea's refuse, are nonetheless a precious ornament to the shell.

Thirdly, it is noted that shellfish that are born in the sea, rather than in lakes or rivers, and especially in the seas of East India or the southern oceans, are more fruitful and colourful and, though they are born in water, they have a very hard shell, and many of them live without moving, attached to rocks.

Fourthly, it has been noted that seafood can live longer out of water than other fish, because they partake more of the terrestrial. It has also been observed that sea urchins have five eggs and five teeth; when there is a full moon, they are fatter, because they are filled with more humour; they are lazy and stolid animals, because they partake more of the aqueous and terrestrial than of the aerial or igneous; they do not change their shell, as crustaceans do with theirs, because they cannot easily dry up the humidity which they hold.

Of limpets.

These are harmful for weak or phlegmatic stomachs, because they are hard to digest.

They are caught in fall and spring; they are hot in the first degree and moist in the second.

Once shelled, they can be used in many pottages, pies, and small pies; they can be prepared in all the same ways as oysters, though with a good cooking, because they always come out a bit hard.

Of oysters.

The best oysters are those caught in winter and spring in lakes; they are very tasty if eaten immediately, as is done in Venice.

They are beneficial to those who have trouble digesting, because they move the body, excite the appetite, and stimulate coition.

They are hot in the first degree and moist in the second.

Once shelled, oysters can be used in pies and in various dishes and little pottages; on the half-shell, they can also be roasted on a grill or on embers; without the shells, they may be roasted on paper.

They can be marinated and salted and used in small pies; many of great quality come from Taranto.

Of razor shells [*cappe longhe*].

Polipio from Mogorra was the first to eat all sorts of razor shells, of which Venice is especially abundant.

Best are those caught in fall and spring.

They are cold in the first degree and moist in the second.

They can be prepared in all the same ways as oysters, but, unlike oysters, they cannot be salted.

Of wedge shells [*telline*].

The best are the bigger ones. They are only good when fresh; they are appetizing and lubricate the stomach, and are good all year long.

Their quality is hot in the first degree and dry in the second.

They can be used for soups, and sautéed, once shelled.

They can be used in various pottages and serve as garnishes for many dishes; they are apt for all condiments and ingredients.[23]

Of clams [*gongole* and *peverazze*].

The best are caught in fall and spring; their quality is cold and moist in the first degree.

They are prepared like wedge shells and are suited for the same condiments and ingredients.

Of scallops [*cappe di San Giacomo*].

These are good in all seasons of the year.

Their quality is cold in the first degree and moist in the second.

Washed in white wine, and well cleaned, they can be prepared in their own shell, roasted; they are also used in soups and various dishes.

They are useful for pies, small pies, and ground dishes with other fish, with the usual condiments and ingredients.

Of cockles [*chioccole*].

The best are caught in the sea in October.

They are cold in the first degree and moist in the second.

They can be boiled, and, removed from their shells, washed in white wine and cooked in various dishes, also placed back in their shells, with the usual condiments and ingredients.

They can also be used in various tasty and appetizing pottages.

Of snails.

Cheroso of Melara was the first to eat snails.

The best ones are caught in winter in vineyards or bushes and in mountainous places.

Those found in swamps have little flavour and are not nourishing.

Their quality is cold in the first degree and moist in the second.

---

23 The terms for all these types of seafood are somewhat confusing, so I am providing also the Italian names (Latini often gives both an Italian and a Neapolitan name); most times, Latini calls razor shells *cannolicchi*, not cappe longhe (or lunghe) as here; see Riley, *The Oxford Companion*, on many of these terms.

Very good ones are caught in Norcia [in Umbria] and in other mountains.

One must first cleanse them in a covered pot, where they should be kept for three days.

Once parboiled, they can be used in various dishes with good condiments.

Snails, after having been cleansed for two or three months, can be fed ground talcum for fifteen days; then they can be ground together with their shells and distilled, and this produces a wonderful water that ladies can use to wash their face: it will render the face clear and shiny.

Of mushrooms.[24]

They are cold up to the fourth degree and moist in the second.

Those we here call *spinaroli* are exquisite.

They grow in spring and last through June.

One can dry them in shade or in the sun, and they can be used as garnishes for many composite dishes; when they are fresh, they can be used for light soups with oil, pennyroyal, and lemon juice; they can be used in various pies and small pies in English style; one can use them in little soups with ham; they can be soaked in malmsey wine and then cooked as above.

In Rome they are called *brugnoli*, and are greatly esteemed by the great.

Dried they cost one *dobla* per pound, but they must be small, such as those one finds in the mountains of Camerino and the Marches.

Other mushrooms called *bolledri* resemble egg yolks; they are like the others in their coldness and moistness; one eats them boiled with salt and pepper, and they can be used in pottages; they garnish various composite dishes, both fat and lean.

One must eat them in small quantities, because they can otherwise be harmful.

Other mushrooms called *spugnoli* are of better quality here in Naples than elsewhere. Their season is spring, and brief.

They are used in stews, they can be roasted, and can be stuffed with fish of all sorts They go well in all composite dishes.

They are nourishing, easy to digest, and less harmful than any other type of mushrooms.

Other mushrooms called *chioppetti* are born up and down in poplar trees.[25]

They are very good; they can be boiled, or used in composite dishes, as above, or in pottages, with pennyroyal and a little garlic condiment, and other ingredients

Larger ones can be roasted on embers with oil, garlic, pepper, and ground pennyroyal.

Other mushrooms are born among stones, and the Most Illustrious Lord Regent my master has often received them as gifts; they are healthful and not harmful, and they grow to the size of a large ducat.

---

24 Both Romoli (1560) and Frugoli (1638) included mushrooms among water creatures, though some of the botanical writers of the period included them among vegetables; Corrado (1786) placed mushrooms among vegetarian ("Pythagorean") foods.

25 Brugnoli (or prugnoli) and spinaroli are St. George's mushrooms; spugnoli are morels; bolledri (or boleti) are porcini mushrooms; chioppetti are poplar mushrooms.

One can hang them by the stem in the shade, protected from wind and dust; then crumble them in water with broad bean flowers, with wine or broth.[26]

One can give, four hours before meals, one or two scruples of this, depending on their complexion, to those who suffer from colic or ground stones, because it provokes urination and helps expel stones and gravel. One can then bury the expelled stones and cover them with a bit of soil, water them in the evening, and protect them from the sun in the morning; this way, what is left in the stone from the mushroom hardens and every year it bears fruit, grows, and produces new mushrooms; these mushrooms can be roasted on embers, with garlic, oil, and ground pennyroyal.

Genoa mushrooms are very good both fresh and salted, and they garnish various composite dishes.

One can soak them and then dredge them in flour and fry them in good oil, and serve them with a parsley sauce.

If mixed with Genoa pumpkin and cooked in a good broth, they are very good.

They can serve as sauces for fish dishes, with artichoke and cardoon stems, asparagus tips, slices of salted tuna belly, desalinated, all sautéed together; this comes out very good, with apt spices and other noble ingredients.

They are also good as sauces for chicken, together with Genoa pumpkin, slices of pork throat, good parmesan cheese, and the usual spices.

They are also used in Neapolitan-style oglias, with other ingredients, as I will describe below.

I conclude that mushrooms, cooked and desalinated, on lean days, can be used for many tasty dishes, just keeping in mind that by themselves they do not work so well, but together with other ingredients they will give great satisfaction.

* * *

How to tell if fish is fresh.

Here in Naples we could eat some good fish, but fishermen are malicious and, when it is hot, they place their catch in grottoes to preserve it, in order to sell it at dearer prices in lean times, despite penalties and prohibitions; thus one is well advised to cook fish as soon as one buys it, because otherwise within half an hour it rots and will taste bad. Even experienced purchasers at times can see fish looking so good that they buy it, imagining it to be fresh; but one must look it sharply in the eye, which, if the fish is not fresh, becomes pale, whereas fresh fish has a lively and shining eye. One must also check the scales, which reveal the fish's flaws by their bad smell; though fishermen often squeeze the scales of fresh fish and sprinkle that blood on the scales of older fish, to make it seem fresh, by looking carefully one can easily see the fish's real quality. In Rome sellers keep fish in buckets of salt water, because the sea is farther; thus the cook must remember, in dressing the fish, not to exceed in salt, because there it is already sufficiently salty.[27]

---

26 The broth is *di aronide*, which I have not been able to identify (perhaps a mis-spelling of a word for swallow).

27 These suggestions are typical of Latini's jaundiced attitude towards all food sellers, peasants, and fishermen. They also indicate his own lifetime of experience in the marketplaces of Rome and Naples. Demand for fish, and thus its price, obviously increased during Lent and other lean times.

TREATISE II: *Of boiled fish.*

Even though there are different types of fish, I have here described only a few, just to show beginners how to cook them, since one boils all fish in the same way, although they can be garnished in various ways and served with different sauces and condiments, as I will show below in another chapter.[28]

Sturgeon.

Boil the sturgeon in water, white wine, and vinegar, with good oil, lemon juice, and pepper; once it is cooked, place it on a plate and garnish it with flowers, herbs, and sliced lemons and sour oranges around it.

Tuna.

Boil it well and serve it with good oil and lemon juice, garnishing the plate with herbs, pomegranate seeds, and sliced lemons.

Sea bass.

Boil it with water, salt, and a bit of vinegar; once it is cooked, place it in a plate with a sauce of salted anchovies and good oil, and garnish the plate with sliced lemons, and parsley on top.

Dentex.

Boil it in water, salt, and a bit of wine; once it is cooked, pace it on the plate with good oil, the usual spices, sour orange juice, and its own broth, garnishing the plate with white fennel, first boiled, and oil and pepper on top.

Swordfish.

Cook it in water and salt, with also rosemary and sage and a bit of vinegar; once it is cooked, place it on the plate with a bit of good oil, the usual spices, and a bit of its own broth, adding thin slices of truffles, first sautéed, and garnish the plate with slices of lemons or sour oranges.

Corb.

Boil it as above, and serve it on a plate garnished with slices of desalinated salted tuna belly, herbs, sliced lemons, and good oil.

German-style trout.

You can boil it in white wine, with the usual spices, vinegar, and half a mostacciolo, or sugar and vinegar, so that the sour flavour be stronger than the sweet; serve it hot with good oil or butter, adding a bit of its own broth, and garnish the plate with little bunches

---

28 Truer words were rarely written: this is probably the most repetitive chapter in the whole work, though the increasing use of herbs lends it some interest.

of asparagus, first boiled and sautéed, with oil, lemon juice, sliced lemon around it, and over slices of toasted bread.

Grey mullet.

Cook it in water, vinegar, and salt, with sage and rosemary; once it is cooked, place it on the plate and cover it with thin slices of salted tuna belly, cooked and desalinated, celery stems, first boiled and sautéed, good oil, lemon juice, and the usual spices, mixed with lemon slices.

Salmon carp.

You can boil it as above; once it is cooked, dress it on the plate with butter or good oil, with the usual spices, herbs, and lemon slices over and around it.

Pandora bream, or luvaro.

Cook it in water, salt, and vinegar; once it is cooked, dress it with oil or good butter, the usual spices, and herbs, and garnish the plate with crostini with caviar on them, mixed with sliced lemons or sour oranges.

Lamprey.

Boil it in water and salt, and once it is cooked dress it on the plate with lemon juice and good oil or butter, and crushed pepper, mixing it with slices of salted tuna belly, first cooked and desalinated, and herbs on top, and garnish the plate with sliced lemons and sour oranges.

Carp.

Boil it as above; once it is cooked, dress it on the plate with good oil, a bit of its own broth, apt spices, and herbs on top, and garnish the plate with little bunches of hops, first cooked and sautéed, sour orange juice, pepper, and salt, mixed with lemon slices and borage flowers.

Pike.

Cook it in water, salt, and vinegar; once it is cooked, serve it on a plate with good oil, lemon juice, the usual spices, herbs, and crushed pepper; garnish it with borage flowers and herbs, mixed with lemon slices.

Shad.

Clean it first, remove its innards, and cook it in water, vinegar, and salt; once it is cooked, serve it on the plate with oil, vinegar, and the usual spices, garnishing it with halved sour oranges and herbs around it.

Amberjack.

Cook it in water and salt with two bay leaves, and lemon slices, removing the bay leaves soon so that it does not make it bitter; serve it with a little sauce made with salted anchovies, lemon juice, and the usual spices; garnish the plate with asparagus, boiled and sautéed, and slices of lemon around.

Sea pike.

Clean it of its scales and innards, boil it like shad; once it is cooked, serve it on a plate with a little sauce on top made with lemon juice, a bit of sugar, oil or whipped butter, boiled in a pan; once these ingredients are cooked, pour it over the fish; garnish the plate with herbs and sliced lemons.

Gurnard.

Cook it as above; once it is cooked, serve it on a plate with sour orange juice, a bit of good oil, apt pepper, and herbs on top, garnishing it with sliced lemons and halved sour oranges.

Large cod.

Cook it like amberjack; once it is cooked, place it on the plate and serve it with an anchovy sauce, and garnish the plate with herbs and lemon slices.

Grouper.

When the grouper is large, cut it into pieces and cook it in water and salt, with a bit of vinegar; once it is cooked, dress it with good oil, a bit of vinegar or lemon juice, and garnish the plate with herbs and flowers mixed with slices of sour orange.

Smooth hound.

Cut it into pieces, clean it, and boil it as above; once it is cooked, serve it on the plate with good oil and sour orange juice, herbs, and crushed pepper on top.

Saupe.

Clean it of its innards and scales; boil it in water and salt, with a bit of vinegar. Once it is cooked, serve it with ground pepper, good oil, lemon juice or vinegar, herbs on top, and sour orange slices around.

TREATISE III: *Of various lean stews for all those times when fat eating is forbidden.*[29]

First lean stew.

Take sturgeon flesh, pound it well with a knife, adding aromatic herbs, bread, first soaked, the usual spices, and a bit of garlic.

Make small fish-balls from this mixture, and cook them in good oil, with truffle slices, raisins, pine nuts, shrimp tails, over sliced bread, and with cinnamon on top, and lemon juice.

Another stew, made with artichoke bits.

Boil the artichokes in a fish broth, together with asparagus tips; then place them in a pot to sauté in good oil, adding shrimp tails, pine nuts, the usual spices, lemon juice, and a bit of saffron, with bread slices underneath.

A composite lean stew to be prepared for house guests or for monasteries of monks or friars.

Take a large pan with good oil and sauté a minced onion, then add peas, tender broad beans, Genoa mushrooms, lettuces filled with fish flesh, slices of salted tuna belly, and artichoke stems. All these ingredients must first be boiled; add also small fish-balls, and at the end hot water as needed. Cook everything as long as necessary, with the needed spices; then thicken it with some pine nut milk, and cover it with asparagus tips, boiled and then sautéed; it will be a most tasty dish.

Another stew.

Sauté together bits of cauliflower, truffles, and St. George's mushrooms, with the usual spices and lemon juice, and [serve with] slices of bread underneath.

Another stew.

Take the soft roe of various fish and sauté it in good oil with aromatic herbs, asparagus tips, lemon juice, a bit of shrimp juice, and add hot water, to make sure it is not short on broth, with an apt lemon juice, the usual spices, and slices of bread underneath.

Another stew of clams.

Open the clams on the fire, inside a boiler, with a bit of water and oil; when they open, remove them from their shells, and drop them in the same boiler; then take them and place them in cold water, and wash them a couple of times; then place them in a pan with good oil, aromatic herbs, and a bit of garlic, adding the juice from the boiler, making sure

---

29 I am going to use stew for these minestre, to be consistent with Volume I, but these are usually far lighter concoctions, in several cases fairly simple vegetable dishes with not much of a stew about them.

none of the sand goes into it; garnish them with the usual spices, with little razor shells on top, and sliced bread underneath, and lemon juice.

Another stew.

Take chops from a small fish, with sliced truffles and asparagus tips, sauté everything together in good oil and aromatic herbs, with a little onion condiment, and apt spices; prepare milk made with pine nuts crushed in the mortar, with a bit of verjuice and lemon juice; garnish the plate with slices of toasted bread underneath and clean pistachios on top.

Another stew of fish-balls.

Make fish-balls with the flesh of sardines, pounded with apt aromatic herbs, the usual spices, a bit of soaked bread, raisins, pine nuts, and lemon juice, with slices of toasted bread underneath.

Another stew of rice flour.

Cook it in almond milk; when it is quite dense, remove it from the fire, then add a bit of fine sugar and bring it to a boil; it will be better with salt as needed. Place it in the plates with diced crostini of toasted bread, and serve it with cinnamon on top; it will be a noble stew.

Another stew of semolina.

Cook it in almond milk, with salt as needed, and serve it with sugar and cinnamon on top.

Another stew of semolina, made another way.

Sauté it with a bit of garlic or onion, in good oil, with aromatic herbs, or something else, adding a bit of hot water and salt; boil it in a pan or pot, and when it starts boiling, add the semolina and finish cooking it that way.

Another stew with emmer wheat.

Take the emmer wheat, all cleaned in hot water, and cook it in water and salt; once it is boiled, if it has dried up a bit too much, you can refresh it with some almond milk, and that way you can finish cooking it; serve it on a plate with sugar and cinnamon on top.[30]

Another stew with emmer wheat, made another way, useful for those suffering from stomach pain.

Take the emmer wheat, clean it well, and put it in a clean pot with a bit of sugar in a loaf, up to at least one fourth as much as the emmer wheat. Close the pot well with a lid and a stone over it and place it in the oven, which should not be too hot. Let it dry well over-

---

30 In Italy today menus often render *farro* as spelt (as is the case also in Scappi, *Opera*), but Riley (*The Oxford Companion*, 180) and Harold McGee (*On Food and Cooking: The Science and Lore of the Kitchen* (New York: Scribner, 2004), 466–67) insist it is in fact emmer wheat.

night, and you may use it for fat or lean stews; you can also give this to the convalescent, and you can cook it with almond milk or broth, and serve it with cinnamon on top.

Another stew, of cabbage.

Clean the cabbage well and boil it in water, then drain it and put it in a pan with ground garlic and good oil; sauté it well, adding a bit of pepper, salt as needed, wild fennel (dried or powdered), and a bit of hot water or another liquid.

Another stew, of carrots.

Clean the carrots well, and boil them; when they are almost cooked, sauté them in a pot with a little garlic condiment, good oil, and the usual spices, adding a bit of cooked must and vinegar, and serve them hot.

Another stew, of cauliflower tips.

Sauté them first in oil or good butter, then put them in a pan with sliced truffles, well sautéed, with apt spices and sour orange juice, and pour the sauté stuff on the stew, with little bits of salted tuna belly, cooked and desalinated.

Another stew, of large onions.

Clean them and peel them, and give them two cuts, without opening them entirely, and boil them in water; once they are cooked place them in a pan with a well heated oil or butter, with apt spices, and aromatic herbs, adding a bit of cooked must and a bit of saffron; it will be a tasty stew.

Another stew, of cardoons.

Clean them and cut them into small pieces, put them in cold water with sour orange juice, so that they do not turn dark; after boiling them put them in a pan or pot with good oil, ground garlic, and aromatic herbs; after sautéing them in butter, add almond milk, and boil them for a bit; you can also thicken this with eggs and lemon juice, and it will be a tasty stew.

Another stew, of celery.

Clean the celery and cut it into small pieces, boil it and when it is cooked put it in a pan or pot with good oil or butter, with a little garlic condiment, aromatic herbs, and the usual spices; sauté it well and you may add pine nut milk or something else as you prefer, with lemon juice; serve this hot, with cinnamon on top.

Another stew, of Bibb lettuce stems.

Boil the lettuce, after removing the leaves; then sauté it in oil or butter, with the usual spices; you may also add small fish-balls, bits of fish liver or soft roe, thin slices of truffles, and thicken it with pine nut milk; serve it with cinnamon and lemon juice on top, and it will be a noble and tasty stew.

Another stew of white fennel.

Cook it in water, salt, and good oil, with dried plums, garlic cloves, and pepper; once it is cooked, serve it with sour orange juice.

Another stew of fennel, made another way.

Clean the fennel of the green leaves, leaving only the white parts, and cook it in water, salt, and oil, forming little tied bunches; once these are cooked, place them in small round plates over slices of toasted bread, with a couple of bunches, now untied, in each plate; on top, add a bit of good oil, sour orange juice, and pepper, and serve them like this, dry; it will be a tasty stew.

Another stew of asparagus.

Boil the asparagus, then sauté it with oil or butter with the usual spices; serve them over sliced bread and with sour orange juice; you may also thicken this with almond milk; add cinnamon on top.

Another stew of hops.

Clean them and cook them in water, salt, and oil, with apt spices, dried plums and sour cherries, or raisins, as you prefer; it will be a very healthy stew.

Another stew of tender peas.

Clean the peas and put them in a pan with oil and a bit of finely minced onion, and apt aromatic herbs; sauté them and add quartered Bibb lettuce, with the usual spices; cook everything together.

Another stew of spinach.

Clean the spinach well and sauté them without water; once cooked, mould them into balls and squeeze all water out of them; cut them with a knife and put them in a pan with oil and a bit of ground garlic, and sauté them well with the usual spices, salt, raisins, and pine nuts; if you want them to have some broth, you can add hot water. Serve them hot with lemon juice on top; you can also sauté them in a pan with a bit of finely minced onion, raisins, pine nuts, the usual spices, and a bit of cooked wine; the wine goes well with the first way of cooking them too.

Another stew of artichokes and peas.

Quarter the artichokes and boil them; when they are almost cooked, drain them and put them in a small pan or pot with good oil and finely minced onions, and aromatic herbs; add tender peas, first sautéed with apt spices, and add a bit of hot water and salt as needed.

Another stew of cooked bread.

Mince the bread into small pieces and put it in a pot or pan with water, bits of mozzarella or provola or whipped butter; cook the bread in the same water, and serve it with grated cheese on top.

Another stew of eggs, called *scioscello*.

Beat the eggs well in a pan with water, butter, and a bit of salt, then cook them, turning them often, and let them rest.

Another stew of a thin broth.

Beat the egg yolks and boil them in water, with butter and a bit of salt; dilute the yolks with lemon juice, turning them often with a wooden spoon; you will know that they are well cooked when they stick to the spoon densely; make sure to beat then well in the pan after the water starts boiling; once they are cooked, serve them over sliced bread, with cinnamon inside.

Another stew of almond milk.

Prepare almond milk, pass it through a cloth, and put it in a pan or pot, over a coal fire, and boil it; when it boils, add some rice flour and fine sugar and let it cook; you may use this for an *amandolata*.

Another stew of almond milk, called amandolata.

This is a very nourishing dish, and it must be done carefully. Make and strain almond milk and set it to boil with one third as much fine sugar; boil it until it thickens, then serve it in little bowls with sugar and cinnamon on top.

Another stew of pine nut milk.

Grind the pine nuts and dilute them in a good fish or wedge shell broth, then cook them in a pan on a low fire, and serve them over sliced toasted bread and with sugar and cinnamon on top.

Another stew of Genoa pumpkins.

Cook them in boiling water, and place them in a pan or pot, with aromatic herbs and apt spices, slices of salted tuna belly, first cooked and desalinated, and bits of eel; boil all this with fish broth.[31]

---

31 The eels here are *capitoni*, Neapolitan for larger, female eels, today typical at dinner on Christmas Eve (usually fried or stewed); these are scary creatures, because one buys them alive and they continue to move even when cut into pieces, slithering around on kitchen tables and forever haunting those who witnessed this ritual. In later examples, I will indicate when Latini identifies the eels as capitoni (as opposed to anguille).

Another stew of Genoa mushrooms.

Desalinate the mushrooms in cold water for one day, then boil them in water; remove them, drain them well, and sauté them in a pan with oil; once they are sautéed with apt spices, soak them in a fish broth, and garnish them with fish chops and pieces of salted tuna belly; then boil them in almond milk diluted in fish broth, long enough to give them some of its flavour, and serve them in individual plates.

Another stew of various ingredients.

Take bits of lobster tails, small mushrooms, and bits of cardoons; sauté everything together with aromatic herbs, raisins, and pine nuts; the main part of the lobster, first boiled, ground in the mortar, and diluted with a bit of fish broth, you will strain through a cloth and add to the other ingredients, which also need first to boil for a little bit; serve this with lemon juice.[32]

Another stew of chicory roots.

Take the roots and slice them in the middle, removing the core, and boil them; once they are cooked put them in cold water, then remove them and sauté them in a pan in good oil, with pepper, cooked must, and vinegar, and serve them hot.

Another stew of snails, also called *maruzze*.

Clean the snails well and place them in a boiler, over a low fire, so that they will come out of their shell; when they are all out, increase the fire so that they boil quickly; once they are cooked, place them in cold water and wash them by frequently changing the water. Then place them in a pan or pot with good oil, crushed garlic, pennyroyal, parsley, and apt spices, and sauté them with or without the shells. Add a bit of hot water and then serve them with a bit of lemon juice.

Another stew of eggplant.

Cut them in small pieces, together with finely minced onions, fresh pumpkin, also finely cut, and small bits of tomatoes; sauté everything together with apt aromatic herbs, sour grapes if in season, and the usual spices; it will be a very good Spanish-style stew.[33]

Another stew of gooseberries.

Clean the grapes and boil them in fish broth, with butter and salt as needed, with apt aromatic herbs and the usual spices; then inside this beat some fresh eggs; when it is cooked, serve it over sliced bread, with cinnamon on top.

---

32 Here too the wording is unclear: I gather the main lobster part is ground and strained by itself, and then added to the sautéed ingredients, but the mention of the boiling at the end is rather confusing.

33 Here is another of Latini's few mentions of tomatoes, and here too the dish is identified as Spanish (as shown also by the eggplants, see e.g., Nadeau, *Food Matters*, 9).

Another stew of sour grapes.

Boil the grapes as with gooseberries, in a fish broth or water with butter and salt; add the beaten eggs with aromatic herbs, and serve this over sliced bread and with cinnamon on top.

Another stew of ricotta.

Take chard or other leafy greens and boil it in water with butter, adding bits of ricotta; thicken it with eggs and serve it with pepper on top.

Another stew of fresh chickpeas.

Take them from their pods and sauté them in a pan or pot with good oil and fried onion, aromatic herbs, and the usual spices; serve them over sliced bread, and you may add a bit of hot water.[34]

Another stew of caviar.

Dilute the caviar in clear water, and then add some bread crumbs, with apt spices, then, in a pan with good oil, sauté minced onion and aromatic herbs; when these ingredients are sautéed, add the caviar, with raisins and pine nuts, and when it has thickened and has turned white, you can serve it over thin slices of bread, with a bit of lemon juice.

A stew of truffles and St. George's mushrooms.

Slice the truffles and wash the mushrooms, if they are dried, in warm white wine, leaving them in the wine for three or four hours. Sauté everything in a pan or pot with good oil, and add a bit of the wine in which you soaked the mushrooms. Serve them with sour orange juice and pepper, over bread slices. It is a hot dish, which stimulates Venus and is beneficial to the old.

Another stew of rice with milk.

Clean the rice well, and cook it in water and salt, adding the milk with a bit of butter; after boiling it for a bit, serve it with sugar and cinnamon on top.

Another rice stew, made another way.

Take white rice, that has a good smell, and clean it diligently, with hot water, then place it in a pan or pot with almond milk, making sure it stays dry and not watery; after it is cooked, pass it through a cloth sieve and put it back in the pot, with crushed cooked pine nuts and mostacciolo crumbs; dilute it with cream tops, adding, while it boils, two beaten fresh eggs with a bit of rosewater or another fragrance; turn it often with a spoon and when it starts to thicken you can serve it with sugar and cinnamon on top; this dish can also be prepared in a good broth.

---

34 The onion here is fried (*fritta*), but I wonder if this is not a typographical error for *trita*, minced.

Another rice stew.

Cook the rice and then take frog legs and debone them. Sauté the frog legs in a pan with aromatic herbs, apt spices, a little garlic condiment, and good oil. When they are well sautéed, add a bit of hot water, and when they are fully cooked add everything to the rice. This will be a very tasty stew, which will seem to be made with meat; take heed not to alert the diners as to what it is.[35]

Another stew of Spanish pumpkin.

Clean the pumpkin, slice it in large slices, and boil it in water in a boiler, then grind it well and pass it through a sieve, then place it in a pan to boil with almond milk, and serve it with sugar and cinnamon on top; this will be a good stew. You can prepare this way any other pumpkins.

TREATISE IV: *Of noble and appetizing roasts made with various fish, and of the manner of preparing them so that they be most exquisite.*

Roast sliced sturgeon.

Slice the sturgeon into slices of nine or ten ounces, clean it well of its innards, without removing the skin; it will be better if you do not wash it. Put the slices in a good pot, and add finely minced salt, good oil, ground coriander, a bit of vinegar, and move the slices well around the pot, so that they take the flavour of these ingredients; then grill them, and baste them frequently, with a fennel stem, so that they stay soft. Place them on a plate, and add a bit of the marinade; garnish the plate with lemon slices.

Another roast of sliced sturgeon, made another way.

Grease the slices well with oil, butter, or whipped butter, with salt as needed; grill them, as above, but make sure that the embers are not too hot, so that the slices not burn; put them in a silver plate with a sauce made with vinegar, sugar, pine nuts, raisins, bits of candied citron, and capers; garnish the plate with slices of bread fried in oil or butter, white confected aniseeds, and lemon slices.

Another roast of slices of tuna belly and tuna slices.

Take the tuna belly and put it in a marinade with salt, crushed garlic, minced chili pepper, pepper, and oregano, and turn it well in these ingredients; let it sit for three or four

---

35 Of these three examples of dishes similar to a risotto, only this one is fully "lean," since the other two include milk or butter or cream tops. Latini was always amused by the ability of frogs to mislead guests resigned to a lean meal; Neapolitans long enjoyed these illusionistic preparations: in 1787 Goethe observed that in Naples "during Lent the fish is served in forms which make it look like meat," Johann Wolfgang von Goethe, *Italian Journey* (London: Penguin, 1962), 202.

hours, or even overnight; grill it, greased with good oil, and cook it carefully; garnish the plate as you wish.

Another roast of swordfish.

Clean and slice the swordfish, greased well with oil or butter, with salt and wild fennel flowers; once it is cooked, place it in a pan with a bit of a condiment made with strong vinegar, crushed garlic, a bit of pepper, and oil, which you first boil quickly; it will be quite tasty.

Another roast of sliced corb.

Prepare the slices with oil and salt, a bit of vinegar, coriander, and cook them carefully, then put the slices in a plate with a royal sauce made with vinegar, sugar, cloves, whole bits of cinnamon as well as ground cinnamon, pepper, a bit of the peel of a sour orange or lemon, sliced thinly to add a good smell; garnish the plate with slices of fried sponge cake and lemon slices.

Another roast of stuffed whole corb.

Take the corb, well cleaned, cut it by the back and remove the bones and innards; grease it well with oil, with salt as needed and a bit of vinegar. Stuff it with the eggs and liver of corb or another fish, cut into pieces and sautéed in a pan with apt spices, adding raisins, pine nuts, thin slices of appie apples, pitted olives, little bits of candied citron, bits of Barbary dates, sour cherries, oysters, sliced truffles, the usual spices, and a bit of salt. Sauté everything together and use it to stuff the corb; then re-form the shape of the fish, tying it up with a well-oiled twine; once it is cooked, remove the twine and place the fish on a plate, garnishing the sides of the plate with lemon slices.

Another roast of sea bass.

Clean the sea bass and grease it with good oil, cutting it in two or three places on the back, so that it cook well, and continue greasing it with oil, vinegar, and salt; then serve it in a plate garnished with fried beignets and lemon slices.

Another roast of grey mullet.

Clean the fish and lard it with strips of salted tuna belly, first desalinated; baste the fish as above, and once it is cooked serve it with a sauce made with vinegar, sugar, and spices, and garnish the plate with pears in syrup and lemon slices.

Another roast of grey mullet, made another way.

Clean the fish and cut it open on the back, remove all the innards, and stuff it with bits of liver, eggs, and soft roe from the same fish, all sautéed in good oil or butter, with the usual spices, adding raisins, pine nuts, sliced truffles, halved sour grapes if in season, sautéing everything together with salt; after stuffing the fish, roast it like corb.

Another roast of sole.

Clean the sole, remove its scales, and dry it with a cloth; put it in a pot with on top salt, oil, and wild fennel flowers, or powdered coriander, and grill them carefully on a well oiled grill, so that the sole not stick to it; serve it hot, garnishing the plate with small pies made with ground fish flesh, raisins, pine nuts, and pistachios, and with lemon slices.

Another roast of sole, made another way.

Roast the sole, well cleaned, and garnish them with a sauce made with vinegar, sugar, raisins, pine nuts, oysters, bits of candied sour orange, bits of cinnamon, whole cloves, boiling everything together, and then pouring it on the fish, and serve it with sliced sponge cake, dipped in egg and fried, and lemon slices.

Another roast of large red mullet.

Grill the mullets, well greased with good oil, strong vinegar, crushed garlic, and minced salt, without cleaning them first, just the way they come out of the sea, basting them often with the above-mentioned condiment, and serve them with the same condiment, but remove the garlic.

Another roast of red mullet, made another way.

Take white paper and grease it with oil and salt, put the fish on it one by one, well arranged on the paper, add on top of them raisins, pine nuts, aromatic herbs finely minced, and a bit of oil; if you notice that they do not fully cook, you can take the hot baking peel with fire on it and place it near the fish, but making sure the paper does not burn; once cooked, you serve the fish with the paper, in a plate with halved sour oranges.

Another roast of pieces of sturgeon, made another way.

Lard them with bits of small lamprey and slices of fat salted tuna belly, first desalinated, and then roast them; once they are cooked pour on them a royal sauce, as I will say in its place, and then place them on the plate, garnishing them with flaky pastries filled with things in syrup, with sugar on top, and lemon slices.

Another roast of sliced corb, made another way.

Clean the slices, removing also the scales, and grease them with good oil, a bit of perfumed vinegar, crushed garlic (without removing the peel), and salt; once they are cooked, place them in a pan and add a condiment made with a bit of oil, sliced truffles, St. George's mushrooms or small mushrooms, first sautéed with apt spices, and sour orange juice, and thus you will serve them in a plate, garnishing it with caviar crostini.

Another roast of sliced grey mullet.

Slice the fish, and cook the slices in a pan with good oil or butter, salt, and half a glass of Greco or a strong white wine, adding muscatel or raisins, halved sour grapes if in season, and pine nuts; serve them in a plate with sour orange juice, garnishing it with fried beignets mixed with fried soft roe and lemon slices.

Another roast of stuffed red mullet.

Grill the fish with good oil, stuffed with moscarelle pears in syrup, bits of dates, two or three clean pistachios, four pine nuts soaked in perfumed water, everything ground together except the pistachios and pine nuts, add a bit of oil and salt, serve them on a plate garnished with small pastries made with the flesh of large fish, finely ground, and other usual ingredients.

Another roast of sardines, made another way.

Wash the sardines and throw away the heads and innards, place the fish on white paper spread like a sheet, arrange the sardines so that they barely touch each other, and so that the back of each is turned towards the belly of the next one, with a bit of oil on top, and salt, aromatic herbs finely minced, raisins, pine nuts, and a little condiment of minced garlic; cook them with the hot baking peel over them, and serve them with the paper and sour orange juice.

Another roast of anchovies.

Arrange them like the sardines, with powdered coriander, and grill them, and serve them on a plate garnished with lemon slices and halved sour oranges.

Another roast of anchovies, made another way.

Grill them as I wrote of the sardines, with the paper, after throwing away their heads, and serve them with aromatic herbs, raisins, pine nuts, and crushed garlic, in the same paper, with lemon or sour orange juice.

Another roast of fresh eels [capitoni].

Spit-roast the eels, cut into pieces, with oil and salt, or butter, placing bay leaves (from which first remove the tips) between the pieces; when they are close to being cooked oil them well and garnish them with bread crumbs, salt, and sugar; once cooked, serve them in a plate with the bay leaves, garnishing them with Genoa-style small pastries filled with bits of candied pumpkin and citron, pitted dried sour cherries, and a bit of oil; fry these pastries in good oil and surround them with sliced sour oranges; it will be a noble and tasty dish.

Another roast of eels.

Cook this the same way as with the capitoni.

Another roast of lamprey, shaped like taralli or ciambelle [i.e., ring-shaped].

Spit-roast the lampreys, well greased with good oil, and salt as needed; once cooked, garnish them with a sauce made with vinegar, sugar, raisins, and pine nuts, and serve them with lemon slices around.

Another roast of chops of large fish.

Spit-roast the chops and wrap them in white paper, well greased with oil, with inside also thin slices of fat salted tuna belly, a bit of salt, and crushed pepper; dress this with a sauce made with vinegar, sugar, pitted olives, capers, raisins, pine nuts, bits of candied citron or the peel of candied sour oranges, a bit of salt, and the usual spices; then remove the fish from the paper and pour this sauce over it, after boiling the sauce well; garnish the plate with sliced bread, first soaked and fried with on it a fried egg, mixed with lemon slices, and it will be a tasty roast.

Another roast of corb, made another way.

Grease it with good oil, salt, and ground coriander and cook it well on the grill; prepare a pan or pot with oil, oysters, truffles, St. George's mushrooms, the usual spices, and a bit of wine, and sauté everything together; when the corb is cooked, remove it from the grill and cover it with these ingredients, over sliced bread, with lemon or sour orange juice; garnish the plate with slices of fried bread, and thin slices of salted tuna belly, cooked and desalinated.

Another roast of sturgeon, made another way.

Lard the sturgeon with strips of fat salted tuna belly, first desalinated, and roast it on the spit or grill; prepare a royal plate, preferably, with slices of yellow bread, made with [dipped in?] saffron and fish juice, and a bit of lemon juice and cinnamon on top; place the sturgeon on the plate with on it a little condiment made with pistachios, pine nuts, clean almonds, mostaccioli, cloves, and lemon juice, and a bit of cooked wine, boiling everything first; serve it on a plate garnished with a pastry twist made with short crust pastry, moulded in bas-relief, filled with things in syrup.

Another roast of trout.

Clean the trout and place it in a pot with rose vinegar, a bit of malmsey wine, the usual spices, a bit of cooked must, fennel flowers, salt, and good oil, and leave it for four or five hours in this marinade, then sprinkle it with a bit of fennel flower and ambrosine almonds ground and oiled; cook the trout on the grill, basting it often, and serve it in a plate greased with good oil and dusted with mostacciolo crumbs, with on it a condiment made of salted tuna belly, desalinated, bottarga ground in the mortar, whole ambrosine almonds, candied citron, and apt spices; after boiling this condiment for a bit, add it to the fish, season it for a bit in the oven, and garnish it as you wish.

Another roast of dentex.

Take a clean dentex and grill it, dusted with powdered fennel, oil, and a bit of perfumed vinegar; once it is cooked, prepare a condiment with verjuice or lemon juice, pitted dates, pine nuts, capers, and a bit of sugar, making sure this tastes good, both sweet and sour; garnish the plate with marzipan paste and lemon slices.

Another roast of large tench.

Clean the fish, remove scales and innards, and grease it in good oil, vinegar flavoured with cloves, and powdered fennel, then grill it, stuffed with moscarelle pears, eggs or soft roe from the tench or another fish, pine nuts, dates, small pieces of candied sour orange, sliced truffles, pine nuts, a bit of cinnamon, and a bit of oil; baste the fish often, and garnish the plate with thin tagliolini and halved lemons.[36]

Another roast of large corb, made another way.

Take the clean corb, cut it on its back a few times, grease it in good oil and salt, and grill it carefully; prepare a pan or pot with pomegranate wine, sugar, capers, thin slices of moscarelle pears, pine nuts, and the usual spices; boil these ingredients for a little while, and then pour them on the fish, garnishing the plate with slices of lemon and fried eggs.

Another roast of oysters.

Open them carefully and clean them of their dirt; cook them well in their shells, with a bit of oil and pepper, and when they are done garnish with sour orange juice; serve them on a plate with their shells.

Another roast of oysters, made another way, easier and tastier.

Open the oysters and take them out of the shell, put them in a pot with their juice, making sure no piece of the shell falls in, add good oil with a bit of pepper; cook them adding sour orange or lemon juice; take the shells again, and place one or two oysters in each shell, without putting them on the fire, and add a bit of the juice they will have produced; serve them hot, with their shells, on the plate.

Another roast of spider crab.

Take as many crabs as you need and boil them in water; when they are cooked, take their flesh carefully, and set aside the clean shells; sauté the flesh in a pan with good oil, aromatic herbs, the usual spices, salt, raisins, pine nuts, and crustless bread; once this is cooked, put it back in the shells with sour orange juice, then grill them for a little bit, to show that they have been roasted; serve them in their shells, in a plate garnished with halved sour oranges.

Another roast of lobster.

Cook the lobster in water, as I said of spider crab; once it is cooked, remove its neck; stuff it and serve it as I said of spider crab.

Another roast of freshwater shrimp.

Boil the shrimp and prepare them as I said of lobster, stuffing them with their ground necks; remove their flesh carefully and stuff them as I said of lobster, with sour orange juice.

---

36 The pine nuts are repeated, presumably in error.

Another roast of wedge shells.

Open them carefully and put them in a pot with their juice; wash them well and put them in a pan with good oil and sour orange juice; give them a quick boil, and then put them back in their shells; serve them like that, and you can do this with all seafood.[37]

Another roast of razor shells.

Grill them with a bit of bread crumbs and good oil, and serve them in a plate with their shells, and they will be tasty.

TREATISE V: *Of fried fish.*

Because fish are all fried the same way, I have described here only a few, so that the inexperienced may draw some guidance for all eventualities; one may serve fried fish with all sorts of different sauces and condiments, which will be described later on, so that everybody may choose them depending on what fried dish he is preparing.

Sturgeon.

If the fish is large, you can slice it into slices of half a pound or more each, dredge them in flour, and fry them in good oil or butter; serve them in a plate with or without a sauce, and with lemon slices around.

Tuna.

Slice and fry it like sturgeon; since this fish is drier, of necessity you will prepare a royal sauce, and serve it with maccheroni around it, mixed with sliced sour oranges.[38]

Swordfish.

Clean it well, slice it as above, and after frying it garnish the plate with asparagus tips, first boiled and then fried; on the rim of the plate place lemon slices and pomegranate seeds.

Dentex.

Clean it of its scales, and cut it various ways on its back, then dredge it in flour and fry it, and serve it with bastard sauce, garnishing the plate with fried pastries dipped in ambivera.

---

37 Some of the steps in these seafood "roasts" are somewhat confusing—and in some cases there seems to be no actual roasting involved (or at least mentioned).

38 The maccheroni are *raganelli di pasta*: the tone and context suggest to me a type (shape) of maccheroni, but I have not been able to identify the specific term Latini uses here.

Sea bass.

Cut it like dentex, and fry it like it too, but serve it with a sauce made with vinegar, sugar, raisins, pine nuts, pitted olives, bits of cinnamon, and cloves, so that it taste more sour than sweet, and pour the hot sauce on the fish; serve the fish hot or cold, depending on the circumstances.

Sole.

Fry the fish and place it in the plate; prepare a condiment with slices of salted tuna belly, vinegar, a bit of sugar, sour grapes, bits of cinnamon, and cloves, all sautéed well, then pour it on the fish, and garnish the sides of the plate with small mostaccioli made with marzipan paste and sliced lemons.

Sole, another way.

Clean the soles well, dredge them in fine flour, fry them in good oil, and place them on the plate, with their tails raised to form a pyramid; garnish the sides of the plate with soft roe and eggs from some other fish, also fried, but first boiled, mixed with lemon slices and carved halved sour oranges.

Corb.

Clean it and cut it two or three times on its back, on both sides, dredge it in fine flour, fry it in good oil, which should cover the whole fish; serve it with Genoa mushrooms, first desalinated and boiled, then dredged in flour and fried, and halved artichokes, also fried, and decorate the plate with little tarts made with ordinary dough and filled with green sauce, mixed with decorated halved sour oranges.

Another fried corb.

Cut it into pieces, eight or ten pieces for each corb, wash and drain them well, dredge them in flour, and fry them in oil; place them in the plate, mixing them with hops, first boiled, dredged in flour, and fried, with minced salt and lemon juice, and garnish the plate with lemon slices and halved sour oranges.

Grey mullet.

Clean the grey mullets well, and make three or four cuts on their backs, then dredge them in flour and fry them in good oil, enough to cover them entirely; place them neatly on the plate; prepare a pan with a bit of vinegar, cooked wine, sugar, spices, salt, raisins, pine nuts, and bits of candied citron; boil all these three or four times, and then pour everything on the fish; garnish the plate with slices of quinces in syrup and of lemons.

Lampreys.

Cut off their heads and place them to die in milk, so that all their blood will come out in the milk; then cut them into round pieces, dredge them in flour, and fry them in butter or oil. Then surround them with rice fritters, garnishing the plate with little tarts filled with sour cherries in syrup, and lemon slices.

Taranto oysters.

These are brought from Taranto in small barrels, and you need to drain them well, then dredge them in fine flour, and fry them in good oil; place them neatly on the plate, and on them place small tarts filled with green sauce; garnish the sides of the plate with fried pastries.

Red mullet.

Wash the red mullets well, dredge them in flour, and fry them in good oil or butter; then place them on a silver plate, well greased with butter, and spray lemon juice on them and a bit of malmsey wine, adding sugar and cinnamon; then decorate the plate with a layer of short crust pastry on top, and place it for a short while in the oven; then take it out, remove the cover, and add a little condiment made with small candied walnuts, bits of candied quince, ground in the mortar, the juice of sour cherries in syrup, or pomegranate wine, and lemon juice; then put the plate back in the oven for a short time, with the pastry cover, to which you add a star made of marzipan paste, as large as the plate; between the star's rays place little pieces of sponge cake dough.

Roman-style fried dish in a scapece, that is, marinated.

Take any kind of fish and fry it in good oil, and you can prepare this hot or cold, though hot will be better; put it in a pan or pot, and in another pan prepare a sauce with vinegar, spices, rosemary, sage leaves, raisins, pine nuts, a bit of saffron, and ground garlic; boil this marinade, and pour it on the fish, cover the pot immediately, and leave it well covered for three or four hours; you can use this depending on the occasion, as this marinade will keep, in a cool place, for three or four months.

Another marinated fried fish.

Take pieces of corb and fry them in good oil, then place them on a plate or pot; prepare a marinade with a bit of vinegar, cooked must, a little bit of hot water, a bit of crushed garlic, sugar, and saffron; boil everything together, and after it has risen to a boil four or five times, pour it on the fish, adding leaves of Roman mint, which gives it a good smell; garnish it with lemon slices.

Fried sole, another way.

Fry the soles in good oil or butter, then remove their bones and stuff them with oysters, St. George's mushrooms, bits of soft roe from sturgeon or another fish, with the usual spices; in a pan, cover them with sliced truffles and sautéed herbs; prepare a milk juice made with almond milk, lemon juice, ground cooked pine nuts or pistachios; boil everything together, and pour it on the soles, but make sure not to use too much of this milk juice; garnish them with cinnamon on top, and fried pastries around.[39]

---

39 I am using milk juice for *lattata*, a lean preparation based on a non-dairy milk and other ingredients.

Young sturgeon.

Clean the fish well, and fry it like the other fish; place it in a silver plate and add good oil, lemon juice, mostacciolo crumbs, and a bit of muscatel wine, and let it season well; garnish the plate with sliced lemons and quartered artichokes.

Sar breams in a scapece.

Cut their heads off, place them in cold water for three or four hours; then remove them, dredge them in fine flour, and fry them in good oil; once they are fried, take a bit of cooked must, sugar, and vinegar, with the usual spices, and boil these to make a condiment; when it is hot, pour this condiment over the sar breams and leave them like this for about two hours; you can use these on any occasion, with green mint over them, and they will be appetizing.

All these fried fish dishes can be accompanied or surrounded with other fried things, such as cauliflower, artichoke quarters, Genoa mushrooms, fresh small mushrooms, asparagus tips, and other ingredients, as I will say below; for frying, remember that the oil must always cover the fish, and be sufficiently hot.

TREATISE VI: *In which we teach how to make lean pies of all sorts.*

How to make small pies which will seem fat, but are lean.

Take frog legs and sauté them in good oil, with a bit of garlic, without spices; when they are near cooked, place them to cool in a plate; when they have cooled, debone them carefully and finely mince the flesh. Prepare small pies, with dough of fine flour, sugar, and warm water, and fill them with the frog flesh, together with pine nuts, a few pistachios, and the frog livers, having removed the bile; cover the pies with a dough lid, and bake them in an oven; then take them out of the oven and remove the lid; add pine nut milk and lemon juice and put them back in the oven without the lid, until the little broth thickens, then put the lid back and add a glaze made with egg whites and sugar. If the banquet is on a Friday or Saturday, you can add a little broth of fresh egg yolks and lemon juice. This will be as tasty as if it were made with meat.[40]

To make another similar pie.

Take pieces of fish and grind them, with apt spices, bits of tortoise, first boiled and then sautéed in good oil, with the usual spices and aromatic herbs; use a little broth with egg yolks and lemon juice, and add raisins, pine nuts, and other things as you prefer.

---

40 Again the frogs work their magic; the final comment indicates how the recipe can be adjusted to degrees of lean eating (the egg yolks—not the frogs—being forbidden at times of stricter fasting).

Other small pies.

Take small pieces of various fish, for instance bits of soles, of red mullet flesh, sardine fish-balls, the usual spices, and aromatic herbs; form the small pies and put them in the oven; when they are cooked, add a bit of pine nut milk with lemon juice.

Another pie or impanata.

Take a whole corb, well cleaned, cut it on its back on both sides, and sauté it in a pot with good oil, the usual spices, aromatic herbs, well ground, raisins, pine nuts, pitted olives, and bits of salted tuna belly. Prepare a stand pie, shaping it like the corb, decorated with arabesques around it. Bake the pie and after it is done brown it with a bit of saffron diluted in hot water, using a feather brush; then put it back in the oven for a short while, and serve it as you like.

A pie, or rather a large pie, made another way.

Prepare the dough; then in a pot sauté bits of salmon, first cooked and desalinated, slices of salted tuna belly, also first cooked and desalinated, bits of lobster necks, morels if in season, peas, artichokes, asparagus, first boiled, bits of eel [capitone] and grey mullet, thin fish chops, bits of turtle, turtle eggs, pine nuts, raisins, pistachios, truffles, shelled wedge shells and other seafood, such as razor shells and Taranto oysters, with the usual spices, aromatic herbs, and lemon juice; after everything is sautéed place it in the stand pie, and cover with a dough lid. Once the pie is cooked, remove it from the oven, uncover it, and add some pine nut milk with the juice of ground lobster, strained through a cloth, and a bit of lemon juice, turning it with the tip of your knife, so that the little broth mixes well with the rest; place it back in the oven and serve it hot or cold, as you prefer.

Another pie.

Take clean sea bass and sauté it whole in a pot, with oil, salt, aromatic herbs, raisins, pine nuts, sliced truffles, and a bit of lemon juice; then place everything in the pie and shape it like a sea bass, with arabesques around and other decorations; once it is cooked, serve it as you wish.

Another pie.

Prepare various pieces of fish, well cleaned; put them in a plate or pot, add salt, good oil, aromatic herbs, and apt spices; turn them diligently so that they get well seasoned, and then place the fish in the stand pie; add slices of salted tuna belly, cooked and desalinated, raisins, pine nuts, and a bit of lemon juice; give this pie a round shape, like the sun, and retouch the rays in gold and silver.

To make a large pie or impanata, shaped like a dolphin.

Take a large fish and clean it well, dress it with good oil, salt, aromatic herbs, apt spices, slices of salted tuna belly, olives, raisins, and pine nuts; put everything in the pie, which you will have prepared in advance, shaped like a dolphin.

Another pie.

Clean grey mullets and dress them with spices, aromatic herbs, good oil, and slices of salted tuna belly, olives, raisins, and pine nuts; place the fish in the stand pie, shaped like a shield, with a ribbon around it filled with things in syrup, all done in bas-relief; once it is cooked, take it out of the oven and make a glaze on top with egg whites and fine sugar, like marzipan.

Another pie with marzipan paste.

Prepare the pie, and fill it with bits of candied citron and pumpkin, bits of candied sour oranges, pitted sour cherries, and a bit of citron preserves, and make a pie, with a glaze on top made like marzipan; let it season well in the oven.

Other small pies in Spanish style.

Take the flesh of red mullets, bits of other fish, grilled and carefully deboned, and grind them, dry as they are or greasing them with oil; make sure to remove the scales; once everything is ground, add apt spices, salt, a bit of oil, raisins, and pine nuts; form the small pies and fill them with this mixture, together with eight or ten green pistachios, and a few thin slices of truffles, and cover them with the usual lids; place them in the oven and cook them well, then take them out and uncover them, and add a milk juice made with ground pine nuts, diluted with cold water, and a bit of lemon juice, mixing this well with the tip of the knife; put the pies back in the oven, then when you take them out again add a glaze with egg whites and sugar, and put them in the oven yet again until the glaze thickens; serve them hot or cold as you prefer.

Another pie in English style.

You can make this with chops of a large fish, adding oil, salt, aromatic herbs, the usual slices, bits of cardoons, celery stems, quartered artichokes, first boiled and then sautéed in good oil, fresh peas if in season, slices of salted tuna belly, fish-balls, raisins, pine nuts, sliced truffles, olives, and St. George's mushrooms; after placing these ingredients in the stand pie, cover it with a cover made of flaky pastry, and put it in the oven to cook; once it is cooked, you can add a milk juice made with pine nut milk and lemon juice; put it back in the oven with a glaze of egg whites and sugar until the little broth has thickened.

Another pie, in a silver plate.

Prepare four or five thin layers of dough, well greased with warm butter, and place them on the plate one on top of the other, and arrange on them the flesh of red mullets, thin chops of sole, and fish-balls from some other fish, with apt ingredients and spices; add bits of cardoons, quartered artichokes, asparagus tips, and sliced truffles, everything first sautéed in good oil or butter; you may also add pine nuts, gooseberries, and sour grapes (their seeds removed) if in season, slices of salted tuna belly, cooked and desalinated, and thin slices of eel [capitone]; cover all this with another four or five well greased layers of dough, as above; cut off the excess dough around the plate with the knife, and decorate it all around, then bake it in the oven; serve it with sugar on top, hot or cold as you wish.

Other small pies in Spanish style.

Fill small pies with red mullet flesh, bits of large fish, and bits of fat salted tuna belly, all finely ground, sautéing everything first in a pan with good oil; after sautéing it, let it cool and then grind it again, adding the usual spices, pine nuts, raisins, sliced truffles, five or six pistachios for each pie, first soaked in a perfumed water; stuff the pies, adding good oil, and cover them with the lids; bake them in the oven and when they are almost cooked take them out; prepare almond milk in advance, with the juice of ground lobster, mixed with the milk, and a bit of lemon juice, and add it to the pies, making always sure that the dough rises higher than its content by at least one finger; cook them again in the oven until the milk thickens; when you think they are fully seasoned, serve them with sugar on top, or with the usual glaze.

Another pie, made with a large fish.

Take pieces of large fish, weighing five or six ounces each, clean them, and sauté them in a pot with oil, salt, minced aromatic herbs, slices of salted tuna belly, first cooked and desalinated, olives, raisins, pine nuts, the usual spices, mixing everything well, so that the pie gains its full flavour; prepare a layer of dough and put the ingredients in it, giving it the shape you prefer, making sure the dough is well greased; then put it in the oven and when it is cooked give it some colour with water with saffron, and put it back in the oven, so that it will be coloured nicely; serve it hot or cold as you wish.

Another round pie.

Take small pieces of grey mullet, corb, and eel [capitone] and put them in a pot with good oil, salt, spices, minced herbs, Genoa mushrooms, first cooked and desalinated, quartered artichokes and bits of cardoons, first boiled and sautéed, a bit of oil, lemon juice, pine nuts, capers, and a bit of saffron; after forming the pie, fill it neatly with these things, and then cover it with a lid and bake it in the oven; when it is almost cooked, take it out and uncover it, and add a milk juice made with pine nuts, mixing it well with the tip of the knife to make sure it blends fully, cover it again, and make a glaze for it with egg whites and sugar; serve it hot.

Other small pies, oval-shaped.

You can make these pies with bits of deboned corb, sliced lettuce stems, first boiled and sautéed, wedge shells taken out of their shells and carefully washed to remove the sand, shrimp tails, tender crabs, aromatic herbs, the usual spices, sour grapes, and pine nuts; when they are almost cooked, remove them from the oven and add a milk juice of almonds, diluted with verjuice; make sure the pies are not dry and that they are well flavoured; add a glaze on top and serve them hot.

Another pie in English style.

Take bits of corb, carefully deboned, eel flesh, skinned, lobster necks, and shrimp tails; grind everything and fry it in a pan with good oil; when it is well cooked, let it cool and then grind it again, adding wedge shells, sour grapes, pine nuts, pistachios, and the usual spices; fill the pie with this mixture, with oil as needed, and add tender crabs and slices of lobster necks, first boiled; cover the pie and bake it in the oven; when it is almost cooked, remove it and uncover it, and add a little broth made with almond milk and lemon juice, with bits of candied citron; put it back in the oven until it is fully flavoured, and serve it hot or cold, with the usual glaze on top.

Another pie, of capitone or large eel.

Take the fish, clean it well, and cut it into pieces that are at least four fingers in thickness; put them in a pot and sauté them with salt, good oil, minced aromatic herbs, raisins, pine nuts, slices of salted tuna belly, first cooked and desalinated, the usual spices, sour orange juice, and a pinch of saffron; turn everything together well to flavour it fully; prepare the pie in whatever shape you wish, and fill it neatly with this mixture, adding slices of salted tuna belly; cover it and bake it in the oven, then remove it and add some saffron colour, or the usual glaze.

Small pies.

Take the soft roe and liver of various fish; make fish-balls with well pounded sardines, salt, aromatic herbs, oil, crustless bread, first soaked in warm water, a little garlic condiment, raisins, pine nuts, and lemon juice; once you have made the fish-balls, sauté them in a pan; put five or six of the fish-balls in each pie, adding bits of good deboned fish, the liver and soft roe mentioned above, oysters, truffles, asparagus tips, St. George's mushrooms or bits of morels, a bit of fat from salted tuna belly, pine nuts or clean pistachios, and cover them; bake them in the oven and when they are almost cooked, take them out, remove the lid, and add a milk juice of pine nuts and lemon juice; put them back in the oven until the milk thickens; serve them hot with sugar and a glaze on top; they will be very tasty and noble pies, worthy of the table of any grand personage.

Other pies of fish-balls of sturgeon or another noble fish.

Take sturgeon or another noble fish, and make fish-balls with the usual ingredients; put them in the stand pies adding shrimp tails or bits of lobster, cooked, one tender crab in each pie, sliced truffles, sour grapes or gooseberries depending on the season, two little chops of sole flesh, pine nuts, and the usual spices; after filling the pies, cook them and when they are almost cooked add almond milk and lemon juice, and a glaze on top.

Other small pies shaped like little ships.

Take clean red mullets and put them in a pot with good oil, salt, minced aromatic herbs, pine nuts, raisins, sliced truffles, and the usual spices; arrange neatly this mixture into the little boat-shaped pies, and cover them; cook them, and when they are almost cooked add the usual little broth, and put them back in the oven until they are fully flavoured; serve them with a glaze in top.

Another pie or impanata, like an eagle.

You can make this with any large noble fish, cutting it three of four times on its back; then put it in a pot with good oil, salt, minced aromatic herbs, raisins, pine nuts, slices of salted tuna belly, first cooked and desalinated, Genoa mushrooms, also first cooked and desalinated, bits of cardoons, celery stems, artichoke quarters, first boiled, and sauté everything with the usual spices and lemon juice; place this in the pie, shaped like an eagle, and bake it in the oven; once it is cooked, give it some colour with water and saffron; serve it hot or cold as you prefer.

Other small delicate pies.

Form small pies and fill them with little pieces of a noble deboned fish, small fish-balls, and other ingredients, with the usual spices, aromatic herbs, truffle slices, unborn chicken eggs, little bits of butter, clean pistachios, and lemon juice, with the usual little broth, and a glaze on top; serve it hot.

Another pie, made with short crust pastry.

Take fine flour, butter, sugar, warm water, and salt, and make a pie shaped like a snail; place inside it sliced shrimp tails, little bits of sturgeon, the innards of a good fish, and pine nuts; also add bits of eel [capitone], cooked and desalinated, and other noble ingredients. Once it is cooked, serve it in a royal plate, and around it place many small snails made of marzipan paste, of various shapes, filled with blancmange and finely minced candied citron; garnish the plate with sugar on top.

Another noble pie.

Make the stand pie with marzipan paste, that is with almonds and sugar; fill it with the flesh of roasted red mullets, which you have first set to cool, and liver of red mullet; grind the red mullet heads in the mortar with a shrimp juice and pine nut milk; this mixture you will add to the pies after they are cooked, after removing their lid; put them back in the oven, and serve them hot, with clean pistachios inside.

TREATISE VII: *Of a few lean soups, tasty and nourishing, for use in all occasions.*

Sturgeon soup, mixed with other ingredients.

Boil the sturgeon head in water, salt, good oil, aromatic herbs, and a bit of saffron; carefully take out the flesh and arrange it, together with the fat parts that it holds, on the plate, mixed with slices of toasted bread and seafood, first sautéed, and apt spices; add some of the broth produced by boiling the head; set it to brown on a low fire, and, when it is time to bring it to the table, take the central parts of a lobster, first boiled and ground in the mortar, dilute it with a bit of the same broth, pass it through a cloth, and make it boil twice with spices and aromatic herbs; use this to garnish the soup, and serve it hot, and it will be quite tasty.

Another soup of morels.

Take the morels when in season and fill them with ground fish, pine nuts, raisins, minced aromatic herbs, crustless bread soaked, salted tuna belly, desalinated, and apt spices, and cook them in scorpion fish broth, prepared as usual, and when they are cooked mix them on the plate with slices of toasted bread, fish chops, quartered artichokes, and truffles, first boiled and sautéed, with the usual spices, moistening it with the same broth; it will be most appetizing.

Soup fit for a queen.

Fill squid with pounded sardine flesh, diced truffles, raisins, pine nuts, aromatic herbs, and the usual spices; place them in a pan to boil with clean gurnard, with all the usual ingredients; when they are cooked, place them neatly in the plate mixing them with slices of toasted bread, roasted fish flesh, salted tuna belly, first boiled and desalinated, moistening it all with the same broth, in which you will also have diluted toasted ambrosine almonds, ground in the mortar, and candied citron, nutmeg, cinnamon, and cloves; before you add this broth to the soup, cook it briefly in a pan on the fire; serve with cinnamon on top.

Soup of fish soft roe and eggs.

Sauté in a pan some sturgeon soft roe, eggs of sea bass or of a similar fish, tender peas if in season, first boiled, and apt spices; once it is all cooked, surround it with the usual bread slices, and lobster necks first boiled and cleaned. Then pour over it some fish broth, well prepared, tinted with saffron; first dilute in it some ground pine nuts with a few aromatic herbs. Then give it a short cooking in the oven, and serve it with cinnamon; it will give great satisfaction.

Another soup.

Take clean corb and slice it into slices of about half a pound each, and boil them in a pan with lobster necks, and apt aromatic herbs and spices; when they are cooked place them on the plate over slices of sponge cake, and on them ground salted tuna belly; add the corb, well deboned and skinned, and pour on this the same broth, tinted with saffron, ground toasted almonds, and a bit of verjuice; give it a short cooking on a low fire, and serve it like this, and it will be exquisite.

Turtle soup.

Kill the turtles by cutting their head, and boil them in water with their shell; once cooked, remove them from the shells and clean them of their innards; cut them into bits and sauté them in a pan with good oil, minced onion, aromatic herbs, a bit of white wine, fish broth, and a bit of saffron; when they have taken a good flavour, place them on a plate, surrounded by the usual slices of toasted bread, raisins, pine nuts, sliced truffles, and St. George's mushrooms, sautéed separately; pour over it some of the broth left over in the pan, a bit of lemon juice, and mostacciolo crumbs; give it a quick cooking in the oven. It will seem rather a fat than a lean dish.

Clam soup.

Boil the clams in water and open them; take their flesh, cleaned from all sand, and sauté it with oil, herbs, and spices; once it is sautéed, add some fish broth and a bit of the broth left over from boiling the clams, carefully cleansed. Place the sautéed clams in a plate with the usual slices of bread and quartered artichokes (first boiled and sautéed); add more of the broth, in which you will have diluted five or six ounces of ground candied pistachios and a bit of lemon juice, with the usual quick final cooking; it will be most appetizing.

Another soup.

Grind almonds and make almond milk, put it in a pan to boil, adding fish-balls, made with the usual ingredients, fish chops, apt spices and aromatic herbs; when it is all cooked, place them in the plate with the usual bread slices, cauliflower tips, first boiled and sautéed, and slices of salted tuna belly, cooked and desalinated, and pour over it the almond milk mentioned above, with cinnamon in top; cook it briefly in the oven, like the others, and it will bring great pleasure to those who eat it.

Shrimp soup.

Take the tails of shrimp from Sarno, or from wherever else you are able to find them, and sauté them in a pan with the usual ingredients, adding cardoon stems, first boiled, sliced truffles, St. George's mushrooms, pine nuts, asparagus tips, bits of salted tuna belly, desalinated, with the broth of a good fish; when they are cooked, mix them as usual on the plate, and pour on them the broth, in which you will have diluted the ground shrimp bodies, and ground pine nuts, with clean pistachios on top; cook it quickly as usual, and it is very tasty and appetizing.[41]

Another soup.

Mix on the plate slices of toasted bread, slices of provola or mozzarella, bits of whipped butter, and ground fish, pour over this boiled almond milk, sugar and cinnamon on top, quickly cook it in the oven, and serve it hot.

Another soup.

Take slices of sponge cake, and place them in the plate mixed with cream tops, mostacciolo crumbs, and other ingredients; brown it in the oven, then cover it with strained eggs; it will be a tasty and noble soup.

Another soup.

Boil scorpion fish in a pan with all the usual ingredients, and when it is cooked carefully remove the bones; take the white flesh and mix it in the plate with the usual slices of toasted bread, razor shells, first sautéed, asparagus tips and quartered artichokes, also boiled and sautéed, St. George's mushrooms, first soaked in good wine and then sautéed, and pour on this the same broth, tinted with saffron; a quick cooking in the oven, and it will be quite tasty and elegant.

---

41 Sarno is behind Vesuvius, toward Salerno, and not on the coast.

Another soup.

Take red mullet or another noble fish and grill it, then remove bones and skin and let it cool, then grind it like a gigot, and mix it on the plate with slices of toasted bread, wedge shells cleaned of their sand, cauliflower tips, sliced lobster necks, everything sautéed separately; pour on this a broth made with fish heads, diluted with pine nuts, ground lobster flesh, and lemon juice; cook it quickly in the oven, and serve it like the others.

TREATISE VIII: *In which we show how to make lean tarts and covered tarts, good and exquisite.*

First tart of cream tops.

Make dough with fine flour, butter, sugar, fresh eggs, and a bit of warm water, and form the crust; grease it with butter and inside it place the following mixture, first all ground in the mortar: a pound of cream tops, three ounces of candied quinces, four of candied peaches, and four of marzipan paste, two or three ounces of sugar, four fresh egg yolks, and a bit of rosewater; then cover it with strips of the same dough, greased with butter, in a lattice pattern; cook it well in the oven and serve it hot with sugar and a sprinkling of flower water on top.[42]

Covered tart with appie apples.

Make the layers as above and prepare a baking pan, well oiled and sprinkled with bread crumbs; place the first layer, well greased with a sweet oil; prepare three pounds of apples, cleaned and sliced, and cooked in syrup; when they are cooked, place them in the pan and add bits of candied citron and ground cinnamon; once this layer is well arranged, cover it with another layer of dough, greasing it well like the first one, and cover it with the same things; do this four or five times. Cook it well and serve it hot or cold, with sugar on top; it will be good even if the apples are not cooked in syrup.

Covered tart or pizza with strawberries.

Prepare four or five layers, as above, greasing them well with good oil; before the strawberries, place in the first layer in the pan a beaten egg, seven or eight Savoy cookies or mostaccere, finely ground; then add the strawberries, two pounds for six people, with half a pound of candied small lemons, finely ground, four ounces of sugar, and a quarter ounce of ground cinnamon, mixing the layers as with the apples; once ready, cook it and serve it like the others.

---

42 As in Volume I, these crusts are made with a dough that includes eggs, usually deployed in thin, separate, greased layers. In some of these examples, torta is not entirely covered while crostata is, but Latini does not follow this distinction altogether consistently; he also terms some examples of both types as pizze, which thus again seems to be a less specific term.

Another strawberry pizza, made another way.

Prepare the layers as above; take about two pounds of strawberries and cook them in syrup, then place them in the layers neatly, with a bit of mostacciolo crumbs on top, adding to the mixture also half a pound of candied small lemons, ground, and a quarter ounce of ground cinnamon; when it is ready cook it well and serve it with sugar on top.

Another tart with apricots or peaches.

Take a dozen apricots or peaches and boil them in good wine, with a bit of sugar; let them cool, pit them, and mix them with some cooked pine nuts or pistachios, three ounces of candied citron, five or six ounces of provola or mozzarella or another rich cheese, four ounces of butter, three of sugar, and two fresh egg yolks; pound everything well in the mortar, and then put it on top of the layer of dough, greased with butter; pour over this a bit of rosewater, and sprinkle a quarter ounce of ground cinnamon; cover it with the usual dough strips in lattice pattern; serve it hot with sugar on top.

Another covered tart with quinces.

Take six ripe quinces and cook them under the embers, then slice them thinly; prepare the layers of dough ahead of time, well greased with good oil, and form the tart; fill it with appie apples mixed with the sliced quinces, six ounces of sugar, to spread on the fruit, six of candied citron or candied small lemons, ground, a bit of ground nutmeg, four ounces of mostacciolo crumbs, and a bit of perfumed water; cook it, and serve it hot with sugar on top.

Another pizza.

Take two pounds of almond paste, six egg yolks, and two whites, half a pound of candied pumpkin, one pound of cream tops, a quarter ounce of cinnamon, four ounces of sugar; pound everything together and form the tart with the usual layers, well greased with oil or butter; once cooked, serve it with sugar.

Another pizza with pink apples.

Take three pounds of pink apples and cook them under the embers, then peel and slice them, adding six ounces of cooked pine nuts, two of candied small lemons, three of sugar, four of butter, four fresh egg yolks, and a bit of rosewater; pound everything together with a quarter ounce of cinnamon, and form the pizza with the usual well greased layers; bake it and serve it hot or cold, with sugar on top.

A Bologna-style tart.

Take one pound of ricotta, six ounces of grated cheese, two of butter, and four of sugar, with four fresh eggs; then take chard leaves, give them a boil, drain them, and mince them. Mix the chard with the other mixture; prepare the crust, well greased with butter, and place the filling in it, with ground cinnamon on top; cover it with strips, in lattice pattern, adding, before covering it, a layer of ricotta, so that it will appear all white; serve it like the others.

Another tart, made another way.

Prepare the dough as usual, greasing the pan with good oil, and spreading bread crumbs in it too, so that the tart not stick to the pan; prepare the layer, also well greased, and on it put spinach, first boiled, squeezed of the water, and finely minced, pouring over them some good oil, raisins, pine nuts, a bit of salt, four ounces of sugar, slices of salted tuna belly, cooked and desalinated, halved sardines without their bones, well cleaned, and other bits of fish, and bits of candied sour orange, everything ground and mixed together; cover it with the usual strips of dough or other patterns, and sprinkle on it a perfumed water, with sugar on top; serve it as you prefer.

Another tart with medlar pulp.

Take three pounds of ripe medlars, peeled and pitted, grind them in the mortar and pass them through a sieve, then add five ounces of marzipan paste, three of candied citron, two of mostacciolo crumbs, a quarter ounce of ground fine cinnamon, four ounces of butter, four fresh egg yolks and one egg white, with a bit of rosewater; mix everything together and form the tart with the usual dough, and cook it diligently in the oven; when it is almost cooked, prepare a glaze like marzipan, with egg whites, lemon juice, and fine sugar; serve it hot or cold, as you think best.

Another medlar tart, made another way.

Clean and grind the medlars as above, adding four ounces of grated rich cheese, four of candied small lemons, a quarter ounce of cinnamon, a bit of crushed pepper, four ounces of fine sugar, four of fresh butter, four fresh egg yolks, and sprinkle on it a bit of perfumed water; after mixing everything well, form the tart in the dough, and cover it in lattice pattern; once cooked, serve it as usual.

Another tart with asparagus tips.

Take the tender tips, form little bunches of them, and boil them in water; while they boil, add a little bit of salt, to remove that smell they have; once cooked, put them in cold water for a little while, then drain them well, and grind them in the mortar, adding six ounces of rich ricotta, six of grated parmesan cheese, four of marzipan paste, four of ground candied citron, and three of mostacciolo crumbs, four fresh egg yolks, one egg white, and a bit of perfumed water; prepare the dough, well greased with oil or butter, and form the pizza, cover it with strips; cook and serve it like the others.

Another tart with onions and pumpkin.

Take four onions, well cleaned; mince them finely and put them in a pan with cream tops and four ounces of sugar diluted in water; cover the pan and boil well until the onions are cooked; prepare the pumpkin, cooked in milk, ground in the mortar, and passed through a sieve; mix it with the onions, adding four ounces of mostacciolo crumbs, half an ounce of ground cinnamon, a little bit of salt and crushed pepper, four fresh eggs, six ounces of grated parmesan cheese, eight of rich ricotta, and four of ground candied citron, with a bit of perfumed water. Mix everything together and form the tart, with the usual layers, and cook and serve it as usual.

Another tart with sour cherries.

Take three pounds of pitted sour cherries and put them on the usual layer of dough, well greased with butter, in a pan, and with a bit of crustless bread both under and over the dough (before the cherries); add two or three ounces of Savoy cookies or mostaccere, three of sugar, and a quarter ounce of cinnamon; place the usual strips on top in lattice pattern; cook it well and serve with sugar on top.

Another tart with tender peas.

Clean and shell the peas, and boil them for a short while, then place them in cold water; then drain them and sauté them in a pan or pot with a bit of butter and salt; once they are cooked, remove them and add four ounces of candied pumpkin and four of cooked pistachios, two of candied citron or of candied sour orange flowers; grind everything together with four ounces of butter, a quarter ounce of cinnamon, four egg yolks and one egg white, four ounces of cream tops and four of grated parmesan cheese, and a bit of perfumed water; mix everything together and form the pizza with the usual layers; cook it as usual, and serve it with a glaze on top; it will be very tasty.

Another tart with bocca di dama.

Take six ounces of marzipan paste, half a pound of butter or whipped butter, ten egg yolks (four hard and six fresh), four ounces of cooked pistachios, three of musk-flavoured candied peaches, a quarter ounce of cinnamon, two ounces of candied citron flowers, and a bit of sugar; grind everything together and make a mixture; place it on the layer of dough, greased with butter and sprinkled with mostacciolo crumbs; make the usual strips in lattice pattern; once cooked, serve it with sugar on top.

Another covered tart with sour cherries.

Take five pounds of pitted sour cherries and cook them in syrup, then place them on the layers, well greased with butter or good oil; add a couple of candied small lemons, finely ground, a bit of mostacciolo crumbs, a quarter ounce of ground cinnamon, and cover these ingredients with the layers, always well greased as above; once cooked, serve it with sugar on top, cold or hot as you prefer.

Another covered tart with sour grapes.

Take two pounds of sour grapes, remove the seeds, and cook it in syrup; once it is perfectly cooked, remove it from the sugar and place it on a plate, adding slices of provatura, mozzarella, a quarter ounce of cinnamon, and four ounces of ground candied citron; place this mixture in the layers, well greased on top, and cook it; once it is cooked, sprinkle sugar on it.

Another covered tart with moscarelle pears.

Take four pounds of these pears and clean them well, slice them, and add half a pound of candied pumpkin, thinly sliced, and six ounces of sugar; if the pears are cooked in syrup, then you can use less sugar; add also four candied small lemons, ground, and a bit of rosewater; place the mixture on the layers; cook it as usual, and serve it with a sugar glaze on top.

Another tart with lean blancmange.

Take slices of this blancmange, as much as needed for the number of guests, and add thin slices of candied citron and pumpkin, six egg yolks and two egg whites; prepare the layers as usual, greased well, and place the ingredients on them, after mixing them all together; once cooked, serve it with sugar on top.

Another tart with candied things.

Take four ounces of candied citron, four of candied pumpkin, three of candied lemons, four of cooked pistachios or pine nuts, four of lettuce stems, four of marzipan paste, four of candied moscarelle pears, four of citron flowers, or of citron preserves, and half an ounce of cinnamon; grind everything together with eight egg yolks; once you have this mixture, place it on the layer of dough, and bake it in the oven, but not too hot; when the composition has condensed, make a glaze on top in the shape of a Maltese cross, with egg whites, sugar, and lemon juice; put it back in the oven to brown and serve it cold.[43]

Another covered tart with sour cherries in syrup.

Take a pound of sour cherries in syrup, half a pound of candied lettuce, finely minced, one candied small lemon, ground, a bit of perfumed water, half an ounce of cinnamon, and three ounces of mostacciolo crumbs; mix everything together, prepare the layers, well greased with oil or butter, place the mixture on them, covering it as usual; once cooked, serve it with sugar on top.

Another covered tart with fish.

Take one pound of headless sardines, wash them well, drain them of any water, and place them in a pan with a bit of oil, aromatic herbs, a little garlic condiment, and salt; give them a half-cooking, then place them on a plate to cool; then cut them in half and remove the bones; place them over the dough layers, and add spinach, first sautéed, well dried, and finely minced, plus four ounces of sugar, raisins, pine nuts, spices, and salt as needed, with a bit of good oil; place all these things over the layers, mixing them all with the halved sardines and slices of salted tuna belly, first cooked and desalinated; cover with the usual dough strips, in lattice pattern. Make sure it does not end up being too high; cook it as usual, and serve it hot.

---

43 The lettuce stems seem somewhat odd; Latini does not specify that they too are candied, though it seems to be implied (and the lettuce is candied in the next recipe).

Another covered tart made with marzipan paste.

Take marzipan paste and grind it in the mortar, adding candied pumpkin, egg yolks, a bit of butter, a quarter ounce of cinnamon, pitted sour cherries in syrup, and a bit of perfumed water; grind everything together with a bit of mostacciolo crumbs, and place it on the layer of dough, greased as above; then take whole moscarelle pears and lazzarole, both in syrup, and stick them into the mixture; cover the tart, grease it well with butter, and bake it in the oven; once it is cooked, make the usual glaze on top, brown it again, and serve it cold.

Another covered tart.

Prepare the layers as above, well greased with butter, and put on them this mixture: ground toasted almonds, candied citron and pumpkin, ground with the almonds, fresh egg yolks, mostacciolo crumbs, and the usual cinnamon; once cooked, serve it with sugar on top.

Another covered tart with appie apples.

Take the apples and clean them, slice them thinly, and stew them in a pot with fresh butter or whipped butter, sugar, and a bit of white wine; once they are cooked, remove them from the fire and put them in the layers together with slices of fresh provola, sugar, ground cinnamon, bits of butter, and sponge cake crumbs; cover it with the other layers, bake it, and serve it cold; you can do this with all sorts of apples and pears.

A sweet dish, very delicate, called tartera.

Take one pound of cream tops, three carafes of extremely good milk, ten fresh eggs, well beaten and mixed with the milk, one pound of minced and ground candied citron, one pound of ground Savoy cookies, eight ounces of sugar, a quarter ounce of cinnamon, perfumed water as you see fit; beat everything together and cook it in a baking pan or on a plate, with fire above and under; serve it cold.

After this is cooked you can cut it into pieces, dredge it in flour, and fry it in good oil or whipped butter, and serve it with sugar on top; it will be a very tasty and delicate dish.[44]

Another royal pizza with strawberries.

Take one pound of cream tops, six ounces of ground candied citron, half a carafe of milk, four eggs, four ounces of sugar, six of mostaccere, a quarter ounce of cinnamon, flower water at your discretion; mix everything together, so that it is a bit dense, and place it on the layers; add two pounds of strawberries with a bit of cinnamon and sugar, and cover it with more layers, well greased as above; cook it and serve it with sugar on top.

---

44 This is therefore a crustless tart, basically a baked custard, and it can be also cut and fried, as is still done with custard in many parts of Italy; Latini uses it in many complex dishes.

TREATISE IX: *Of lean composite dishes.*

In making lean composite dishes, one must keep in mind that things are quite different from non-lean times, because ordinarily the steward may order whatever he likes, but he cannot do that on lean days, since he must first consider what fish is available and then order as best he can. It would be hurtful to his reputation if he ordered some dish, only to discover that the necessary fish is not available. Thus he must first consider the available fish and then arrange things as he sees fit. It is true on the other hand that one can have many things prepared in advance, for instance lobster, shrimp, or seafood juice, or broth made with fish heads; best for this is scorpion fish, which will give a very good broth if cooked in a pan, or it can be roasted and then ground and cooked in a pan with broth of other fish or even water, and it will be very good. One can also have ready salted tuna belly, truffles, St. George's mushrooms, pistachios, pine nuts, raisins, Genoa and fresh small mushrooms, cauliflower, asparagus, cardoons, artichokes, celery, good oil, and butter, where the latter is used. As I said in my first volume in discussing banquets, any great feast can be held with twelve hot dishes, and I repeat it here; what is most important is to know how many guests there are, to check that one has enough fish of the same type for all guests, because one could not call it good order to mix various fish in the same serving; namely, if you are serving a roast, you could not give one gentleman grey mullet and another red mullet or some other fish. Rather, if, say, there are ten guests, you should serve with one dish, namely, the cook will have five grey mullets of at least one pound each, and will make the dish from these, giving each gentleman one half; if it is red mullets, then one or two per guest; and so on. All this provided you can have fish at all, because, if this should fail, you will have to remedy as best you can. Make sure not to use black truffles in any dish, unless you first slice them and place them in hot water and then in cool water, so that they lose that sulphurous odour they have; white ones can be used freely, because they are most good, except in Rome, where the white ones have a bad taste while the black ones are good. If you use the juice of lemons or sour oranges, or other acidic flavours, make sure to add them to the dishes only when they are brought to the table, lest they become bitter. Those who are not experienced should know that when frying fish one must check the weight of the fish, and use half as much in oil, and no more; as for other dishes, one should use one's discretion. In making pies or impanate, for each pound of fish use one of flour, two ounces of oil, two of sugar, half an ounce of pine nuts, and a quarter ounce of spices, between pepper, cloves, and cinnamon; if the pie is of short crust pastry, all these quantities should be increased by half.

A dish of fish-balls inside chops.

Take the flesh of the sturgeon's belly or back and chop it in long and broad slices, as you prefer; pound them a bit with the back of a knife; dust them with ground fennel, salt, and pepper, and sprinkle them with a bit of verjuice; take some more of the flesh and grind it like a sausage, adding cinnamon, cloves, nutmeg, a bit of light verjuice, sugar, saffron, raisins, and aromatic herbs finely minced. Make a mixture with all these things and use it to stuff the slices; roll them, and roast them carefully, so that the stuffing not fall out; once cooked, serve them with what sauce you prefer; you can do this with tuna too.[45]

Sardine fish-balls.

Take the flesh of the sardines, first well cleaned of scales, bones, and everything else, and pound it well with a knife; for each pound of sardines add three ounces of salted tuna belly, first soaked, minced aromatic herbs, crustless bread, the usual spices, and raisins; beat everything together and make it into fish-balls, which you can roast, as I said of sturgeon, or cook in a pan; if it is not a day of strict fasting, instead of the tuna you can use cheese and egg yolks; serve them with or without a sauce, as the occasion requires.

Another dish with turbot in pottage.

Take the cleaned turbot and fry it in good oil, with minced aromatic herbs, a little garlic or onion condiment, and spices; add dried fruits, such as sour cherries, plums, pine nuts, raisins, a bit of saffron, and salt as needed, with sour orange juice.

Another dish of trout, made another way.

Take cleaned trouts and cook them in water and salt; when they are ready, place them on a silver plate which you will have greased with good oil or butter, and set them to warm on a low fire; cover them with bits of salted tuna belly, first cooked and desalinated, and fennel, first cooked in water, good oil or butter, with salt as needed, and spices; garnish the plate with fried bread and bits of lemon or sour orange.

Another dish of large fish.

Take a large fish and slice chops of eight or nine ounces each, cook them in a clay pot, well greased with butter or good oil, sprinkling the fish chops with bread crumbs, with embers above and underneath, and apt spices; prepare a sauce made with mostacci-olo crumbs, strong vinegar, a bit of sugar, bits of cinnamon, and whole cloves; boil all these together and pour the sauce on the fish chops with a bit of ground candied citron; encrust the dish with confected white aniseeds.

Another dish of trout, made another way.

Take one or several trouts, boil them in water, vinegar, and salt; then place them on a silver plate or in a pot; prepare a little stew of artichoke stems, tender peas, pine nuts, fish-balls made with another fish, and a milk juice made with almonds and lemon juice, boiled in the same mixture as the other ingredients; pour the sauce on the trouts neatly, and garnish the sides of the plate with little spinach bunches, first boiled and sautéed in good oil, with a bit of sour orange juice.

---

45 As usual, sturgeon comes first; today we might call these *involtini*, though Latini calls them *polpette* (the usual term today for meat- or fish-balls).

Another dish of soles.

Take the cleaned soles and boil them as above; place them in a plate, well greased with butter, and arrange on top of the fish cauliflowers, asparagus tips, first cooked and sautéed, thin slices of white truffles, St. George's mushrooms, and pine nuts; pour over this a milk juice made with pine nuts and juice of lobster and shrimp, boiled, with lemon juice; garnish the sides of the plate with sliced mozzarella or provola, fried in good whipped butter, and lemon slices.

Another dish of stuffed bread loaves.

Put the loaves to soak in almond milk, after greasing them with good oil; take bits of sole, first boiled and sautéed, with oysters, St. George's mushrooms, sliced truffles, wedge shells, bunches of asparagus, first boiled and sautéed, a milk juice made with almond milk and whole pine nuts; once everything is ready, place the loaves on a plate, putting on them a glaze with egg whites, sugar, and lemon juice; place the plate in the oven to brown, and garnish the sides of the plate with toasted bread crumbs, sugar, and cinnamon, with arabesques around and over the plate.[46]

Another dish of anchovies.

Clean the anchovies well and wash them several times in water, removing their heads; sauté them in a pan with oil and minced onion, aromatic herbs, and spices; add a bit of hot water or pine nut milk, raisins, and sweet grapes, and serve them with lemon juice; garnish the plate with sliced lemons.

Another dish of cuttlefish in pottage.

Take the cuttlefish, wash them well, and remove their heads and bladder, where they have their ink, so that they become very white; cut them into pieces, or, if they are small, just halve them; in a pot prepare good oil, aromatic herbs, and a bit of minced onion; add the cuttlefish, with the usual spices, a glass of white wine, pine nuts, raisins, and dried sour cherries, and serve them with lemon juice; it will be a tasty dish, but not a very noble one.

Another dish of octopus.

Clean the octopus well and peel them, remove the tips of their tentacles and the ink they hold inside; prepare them like the cuttlefish, though they need to cook a bit longer, because they are harder; smaller ones that have been hung are better.

Another dish of tender crabs.

This sort of crabs is hard to find, and I have only ever seen them in Rome and Venice. Take them and drown them in almond or pine nut milk; then prepare a pot with good oil, butter, aromatic herbs, spices, and salt as needed, a little garlic or onion condiment,

---

46 Latini never spells out that all the ingredients are to stuff the loaves, but the title of the dish implies it.

and sauté the crabs with these ingredients, stirring carefully; when they are done, place them in the milk in which they died, with a bit of lemon juice, and boil them for a little while. Garnish the plate with fish soft roe and eggs, and lemon slices, and the usual bread slices underneath.

Another dish of lampreys.

Drown the lampreys in milk and cut them into pieces, then place them in a pan or pot and sauté them in good oil or butter with aromatic herbs and the usual spices, with half a glass of malmsey or Greco wine; when they are cooked, add the milk in which they died, together with their blood; cook them some more, and place them on a silver plate, and cover them with cauliflowers, tender artichoke quarters, and asparagus tips, first boiled and sautéed in oil or butter, with salt as needed, spices, and lemon juice; garnish the sides of the plate with slices of salted tuna belly, cooked and desalinated, with herbs on top, and lemon slices.

Another dish of salmon carp.

Clean the fish well and cook it in water, wine, and salt; place it on a plate and cover it with cauliflowers and asparagus tips, first boiled and stewed with the usual spices; add sliced truffles, cooked separately, good oil, crushed pepper, and lemon juice; garnish the plate with lemon slices.

Another dish of salmon carp, made another way.

If the carps are big, you can slice them, if small cook them whole; remove their innards and scales, and sauté them in good oil or butter with a bit of minced onion, aromatic herbs, and the usual spices; when they are cooked, add a milk juice made with pine nuts and a bit of lemon juice, but make sure to use only a little milk; once they are done, pour over it some shrimp juice mixed with milk and a fistful of clean pistachios, soaked in rosewater or another perfumed water; garnish the sides of the dish with sliced lemons and sour oranges.

Another dish of the same fish, made another way.

Slice the fish into slices of eight or nine ounces, and wash them; sauté them in good oil, with spices, and then add half a glass of malmsey or Greco wine, to give them flavour, and a bit of hot water, raisins, pine nuts, sour cherries, dried plums, or similar fruits, saffron at your discretion, and lemon juice, but watch that the dish not become too liquid; if you wish to thicken the broth you can add a bit of bread crumbs or fine flour.

Another dish of mackerel.

Grease a pan well with oil or whipped butter, spread in it ground salt, spices, and bits of mackerel, and dust it with bread crumbs; cook this with fire over and under it; when it is cooked, dress it with a royal sauce, decorating the sides of the dish with fried beignets and sliced lemons.

Another dish of turbot, made another way.

Clean the turbot, remove its innards, and open it with a knife, then stuff it with bits of ground fish, shrimp tails, first cooked, raisins, pine nuts, a bit of salted tuna belly, cooked and desalinated; make a mixture with all these things, with the usual spices, and thinly sliced truffles and St. George's mushrooms; once you have stuffed the turbot, sew it close carefully, and place it in a pan or pot, where you will already have sautéed oil or butter, the usual spices, and aromatic herbs; turn the turbot in the pan to while it cooks, then add a milk juice made with ambrosine almonds diluted in rosewater, and passed through a cloth sieve; add shrimp and lobster juice, and lemon juice, and finish cooking it this way; it will be a tasty and noble dish.

Another dish of John Dory.

Clean the fish, remove the innards and most of its bones; sauté it in good oil with the usual spices and aromatic herbs; when it is well cooked, add a bit of hot water, adding raisins, pine nuts, lemon juice, and saffron.

Another dish of eels [capitoni] in pottage.

Clean the eels and cut them into pieces; sauté them in a bit of good oil, aromatic herbs, the usual spices, half a glass of Greco wine or of another strong white wine, pine nuts, raisins, sour cherries, plums, sour orange juice, and a bit of hot water; serve it in a plate garnished as you please.

Another dish of dentex.

Slice the dentex into chops of eight or nine ounces, and sauté them in good oil or butter with the usual spices and aromatic herbs; once it is cooked, you may add tender peas, cooked in a fish broth, lettuce stems, small mushrooms, a bit of hot water; once they have gained flavour, serve them with lemon juice.

Another dish of mantis shrimp.

Boil the mantis shrimp and then remove their shells; prepare a pan or pot with good oil or butter, aromatic herbs, a little onion or garlic condiment, the usual spices; add oysters, wedge shells, fish-balls, and sliced truffles; sauté everything together in the same pan with a bit of hot water, and pour this on the mantis shrimp, to finish cooking them, with salt as needed, and sour orange juice.

Another dish of garfish in pottage.

If the garfish are large, cut them into small bits; clean them well, and sauté them with good oil, aromatic herbs, apt spices, and a little condiment with crushed garlic; when they are cooked, add a bit of hot water, raisins, pine nuts, and lemon juice.

Another dish of eels.

Cut off the eels' heads, wash them repeatedly in water, and remove their innards; sauté them in good oil, with minced aromatic herbs, apt spices, pine nuts, and raisins, adding a bit of hot water; serve them with lemon juice.

A dish of eels, made like sausages.

Skin the eels, starting with the head, and pulling away the skin; pound the flesh, and add to it some salted tuna belly, first cooked and desalinated, and other pounded fish flesh; make a mixture of this, together with soaked crustless bread, aromatic herbs, apt spices, raisins, pine nuts, lemon juice, a bit of oil, and salt; stuff this mixture in the eel skins and sauté them in good oil, together with oysters, raisins, and pine nuts; then pour over it milk juice made with fresh pine nuts and lemon juice.

Another dish of trout, made another way.

Cook the fish in water, salt, and wine; prepare a pan with truffles, St. George's mushrooms, bits of morels, aromatic herbs, the usual spices, sliced salted tuna belly, first cooked and desalinated, and good oil; sauté everything together, and pour it over the trout; cover with clean pistachios; garnish the plate with lemon slices and halved sour oranges.

Another dish of carp.

Take the carp and clean it well; sauté it whole or in pieces, in good oil or bitter, with a little garlic condiment, minced aromatic herbs, apt spices, and a bit of white wine; once it is done, add a bit of hot water, and finish cooking it adding raisins, pine nuts, and other dried fruits, with lemon juice.

Another dish of stuffed pumpkin.

Take a long fresh pumpkin, cut it into pieces, and remove its seeds and all its interior parts; boil it, and then place it in cold water; stuff it with a mixture made with the flesh of various fish, aromatic herbs, bread crumbs, oil, salt, raisins, pine nuts, and a bit of candied citron, all of which you should first sauté in a pan with good oil or butter, adding also a milk juice of ambrosine almonds and lemon juice; on a Friday, you can also thicken this with eggs.

Another dish of sole, made another way.

Take large soles and cut them length-wise, open them by the breast, and remove the bones; take shrimp tails, pine nuts, raisins, sliced truffles, clean pistachios, bits of ground candied citron, thin slices of lobster, bits of another large fish, aromatic herbs, apt spices, oysters, and wedge shells; sauté all these ingredients, and then stuff the soles with them; place them in a pan or pot and sauté them in good oil or butter; pour over them a milk juice made with ambrosine almonds, shrimp juice, and lemon juice; finish cooking the soles, and serve them in silver plates garnished with carved lemon slices, mixed with fish eggs and soft roe, fried.

A dish of large whole fish.

Take whatever large fish you prefer, clean it and remove the scales, and open it length-wise on its back; remove its bones and innards, without troubling its belly. Prepare a stuffing made with wedge shells, oysters, shrimp tails, quartered artichokes, first boiled and then sautéed, sliced truffles, pine nuts, green pistachios, lettuce stems, first boiled and then sautéed, everything finely minced with salt, spices, oil, and lemon juice as needed. Stuff the fish and place it in a pan where you have sautéed good oil or butter, a bit of minced onion, herbs, salt, and the usual spices, with a bit of hot water; give the fish a half-cooking, and then add a milk juice made from pine nuts, lemon juice, and shrimp juice; finish cooking the fish, and serve it on a silver plate, with on top cauliflower and asparagus tips, first boiled and then sautéed, with lemon juice and pepper; garnish the sides of the plate with sliced lemons and halved sour oranges.

Another dish of large fish, made another way.

Take a large fish as above and stuff it as above, with dried sour cherries, dried plums, pine nuts, raisins, apt spices, shrimp or lobster juice, lemon juice; cook it as above; gar-nish the plate with bunches of wild fennel, first cooked and sautéed, mixed with slices of salted tuna belly and crostini with caviar.

Another dish of swordfish.

Make chops from the swordfish and sauté them in good oil, with aromatic herbs, a bit of garlic and onion, salt and spices as needed; add a bit of hot water and boil them, adding raisins, pine nuts, sour grapes, gooseberries, or lemon juice, as you wish; serve this on the plate with a little sauce of your choice.

Another dish of pike.

Take the whole pike or cut it into pieces, clean it well, and boil it in water, salt, and vin-egar; then place it on the plate and cover it with fennel, cauliflower tips, first cooked and sautéed, with the usual spices and lemon juice; garnish the plate with crostini of toasted bread, soaked in sour orange juice, mixed with slices of salted tuna belly, cooked and desalinated, with pepper and oil on top.

Another dish of sea bass.

Boil the sea bass in water, salt, and vinegar; prepare a sauce with sour orange juice and salted boiled anchovies, with the usual spices; garnish it with artichoke stems stuffed with well pounded fish flesh, and crustless bread, aromatic herbs, raisins, and pine nuts.

Another dish of cod, made another way.

Take the cod, whole or in pieces, as you prefer, and sauté it in a pan with good oil, aro-matic herbs, apt spices, raisins, pine nuts, and a bit of hot water; when it is cooked, add a pinch of saffron and sprinkle sour orange juice over it; garnish the plate with bunches of hops, first cooked and sautéed, with apt pepper and sour orange juice.

A dish of lobster necks.

Take these necks and cut them length-wise or slice them, boil them in water, and then sauté them in good oil, with the usual spices and aromatic herbs; add clams, shelled and well washed of their dirt, and a bit of clam juice. Add sliced truffles, pine nuts, pistachios, and oysters. When it is all well sautéed add a bit of water and dilute in it the juice drawn from the flesh of the lobsters, pounded in the mortar and strained through a cloth or sieve; add also a half glass of pine nut milk with a bit of lemon juice; serve this hot with cinnamon on top.

Another dish of large fish, made another way.

Take a large fish and clean it; cut it into pieces and sauté them in good oil or whipped butter, adding a bit of hot water or a fish broth, with pine nuts, asparagus tips, small halved artichokes, first boiled and sautéed in good oil, with the usual spices, aromatic herbs, a pinch of saffron, and a bit of lemon juice; serve it hot, with sliced lemons around.

Another dish of stuffed turnips.

Take round turnips, all the same in size, clean them, and empty them, cutting their little stems to form a hole, and stuff them with a mixture of deboned fish flesh, finely pounded, aromatic herbs, bits of salted tuna belly, crustless bread, moistened in hot water, a little garlic, raisins, pine nuts, oil, and salt; cook all these things in water; prepare a pan with good oil, minced garlic or onion, and a bit of fish juice, sauté these things, and then pour them over the stuffed turnips; cover them then with fish-balls, fish chops, pine nuts, Genoa mushrooms, desalinated and cooked, bits of sautéed morels, a bit of saffron, and lemon juice; serve them hot, and garnish the sides of the plate with bread slices, fried in oil or butter.

Another dish of pandora bream.

Cook the fish in water, salt, and vinegar, having first removed its innards and scales; when it is cooked, put it in a plate and cover it with asparagus tips, cauliflowers, quartered artichokes, everything first boiled and sautéed in good oil; add the usual spices and sour orange juice; mix it with slices of salted tuna belly, cooked and desalinated, and serve it with lemon juice and herbs on top.

Another dish of meagre.

Cook it whole or in pieces, in water, wine, and salt; once it is cooked, place it in a plate and cover it with cardoon stems and bits, quartered artichokes, asparagus tips, and Genoa mushrooms; mix it with slices of salted tuna belly, sautéed in good oil, spices, and lemon juice; serve it hot with toasted crostini with caviar on top.

Another dish of large red mullets, made another way.

Take the mullets and cook them in a pan, well greased with butter or good oil, with minced salt as needed, and bread crumbs; turn them carefully while they are on the fire; prepare a royal sauce made with strong vinegar, sugar, cinnamon bits, whole cloves, raisins, and pine nuts; place the mullets on a plate and cover them with the sauce, which you will have boiled, adding a bit of ground candied citron; garnish the plate with sliced sponge cake, fried in butter, mixed with lemon slices.

Another dish of the heads of any fish.

Clean the fish heads and cook them in water, vinegar, and salt; prepare a pan with good oil, spices, and sautéed aromatic herbs; add to this a bit of hot water, various fruits, raisins, pine nuts, and a pinch of saffron; pour this concoction, with a bit of lemon juice, on the fish heads; garnish the plate with sliced lemons and halved sour oranges.

Another dish of trout, made another way.

Clean the trout well and sauté it in butter or good oil, with the usual aromatic herbs; once it is cooked, put it in a plate, and cover it with cauliflowers, asparagus tips, and white fennel, first cooked and sautéed in good oil, with sour orange juice, adding pine nuts, first soaked in water, sliced truffles, first sautéed by themselves, and a bit of good broth.

A dish of sea turtle.

Cut the neck of the turtles, make sure all the blood comes out, and set it aside. Before it curdles, add a bit of salt, spices, raisins, pine nuts, a few bread crumbs, perfumed water, minced onion, coriander, and a bit of ground candied citron; prepare and clean the turtle tripe and intestines, and stuff them with these ingredients, and make them into sanguinacci, cooking them in water. Bring the turtle flesh to a boil two or three times, and remove it from the water. In a pan place good oil, minced onion, spices, salt as needed, raisins, pine nuts, and a bit of hot water from the turtle broth, which should not be too fatty; place in the pan what is left of the tripe and intestines, as well as the sanguinacci you have made. Then when they are hot pour all these things on the turtle flesh, together with a few chickpeas, cooked separately. Garnish the plate as you wish, it will be quite tasty.[47]

A dish of grouper tripe.

Clean the grouper tripe well and boil it in water; when it is cooked cut it into pieces; in a pot sauté minced onions in good oil or butter, then remove them and add the tripe to the pot, and then add a fish broth and cook the tripe well. Then thicken the dish with pine nut milk, and if it is not a lean day you can thicken it with eggs, cheese, and other ingredients. I close by remarking that this tripe can be prepared in all the same ways as beef tripe, and it will taste even better; it is also very good sautéed in a pan with aromatic herbs, a bit of saffron, raisins, pine nuts, and the usual spices.

Another dish of turtle, made another way.

Take the turtle and cut it into pieces, sauté it in oil or butter, and add raisins, pine nuts, sour cherries, dried plums, and other fruits as you prefer, and serve it with lemon juice.

---

47 Tasty, and somewhat gruesome to prepare; sanguinacci, as we saw, were usually made with pig blood, but turtle blood was a standard substitute for lean times. Latini calls this a *piatto di montogno*, which I have not been able to clarify.

A fish dish.[48]

Take slices of eel [capitone], corb, dentex, and small squid; fry them in good oil, then place them on a plate and pour on them a sauce made with vinegar, sugar, bits of cinnamon, ground mostacciolo, and the usual spices; first boil the sauce properly; make sure it has both sour and sweet taste; on the plate put slices of candied citron and white small comfits; garnish the sides of the dish with pears in syrup; when you wish to prepare a seviero, you can make it with all other fish as well; it is also good with roasted fish, but it is much better fried.

Another dish, English-style.

Prepare sturgeon chops of four to six ounces each, place them in a pan, in which you will already have sautéed minced onions; sauté the chops with the onions, and turn them well in good oil or butter (the latter will be better), then add aromatic herbs and good spices; in another pan sauté truffles, St. George's mushrooms, sliced lobster, and shrimp tails, first boiled; then grind the heads of the shrimp in a marble mortar, dilute them with pine nut milk, and pass them through a sieve; pour everything on the chops, and season them on the fire; garnish the plate with fried shrimp tails, pitted olives, and sliced lemons.

Another dish of trout.

Having boiled the trout, accompany them with a little pottage with tender peas, artichoke stems, asparagus tips, truffles, white fennel tied in bunches, with a condiment of malmsey wine; dress this well with salt and spices; garnish the plate with stuffed artichokes mixed with slices of salted tuna belly, desalinated, and sliced lemons; boil them simply in water, vinegar, and salt, and serve them dry, dredged in bread crumbs, with a good cooking.[49]

Another dish of sole.

Clean the fish well, and remove the bones; open the fish and stuff it with sardines and cod, well ground, with salted tuna belly, desalinated, aromatic herbs, pine nuts, raisins, salt, and spices; make a mixture of all this, with a bit of bread crumbs, and use it to stuff the sole; close the fish and sauté it in a pan, in which you have already sautéed a bit of onion; turn it, and once it is cooked add shelled wedge shells, sliced truffles, shrimp tails, St. George's mushrooms, sour grapes or gooseberries, a bit of Greco wine, and pistachio milk with shrimp juice; when it has all gained flavour, place it on the plate, well garnished with spices, with little fish loaves around, made with the same stuffing and baked in the oven, bits of pine nut cores, mixed with sliced shrimp and lemon.

---

48 Latini calls this a *seviero*, another term I have not been able to identify; *siviero* appears in nineteenth-century cookbooks as a type of preparation for fish.

49 The syntax here is unclear: it is not clear what is boiled at the end, though my hunch is that it is the trout, before they are united with the pottage.

Another dish of grey mullet.

Take clean mullets and remove their scales, and place them in the oven, first well greased with butter; turn them often lest they burn, and sprinkle them with salt; when they are cooked, remove them and stuff them with a little pottage, prepared separately in a pan, made with lobster slices, slices of salted tuna belly, desalinated, oysters, artichoke stems, pine nuts, raisins, with onion well sautéed in butter, a bit of wine, and pine nut milk, all well seasoned over the fire; garnish the plate with beignets and soft crabs fried in butter, first soaked in milk, and lemon slices.

Another dish of corb.

Prepare round chops from a large corb, cook them in the oven as with the grey mullet, with good oil or butter, and turn them often; sprinkle them with sponge cake crumbs, pepper, salt, ground coriander, and cinnamon; make sure they stay juicy; once they are cooked, place them on a plate and cover them with a sauce made with salted anchovies, shrimp tails, thin slices of candied citron, sugar, cinnamon, vinegar, muscatel wine, and clean pistachios; garnish the plate with little fried pastries stuffed with pine nuts, raisins, moscarelle pears in syrup, and mostacciolo crumbs, diluted with royal sauce, and mixed with lemon slices.

Another dish of swordfish.

Slice the swordfish into chops, with sliced lobster, desalinated Genoa mushrooms, slices of salted tuna belly, artichoke stems, liver and eggs of various fish, truffles, and sour grapes; pour on everything a strong white wine, with a bit of sautéed onion, aromatic herbs, good spices, a bit of saffron, and nutmeg, with good oil; mix everything together in a pan; form a stand pie and stuff it with all these things, cover it well, and bake it in the oven; when it is cooked, raise the cover and pour in a sauce made with almond milk, shrimp juice, and lemon juice; cover it again, and put it back in the oven to season; serve it hot with a glaze over the cover made with egg yolks and cinnamon.

Another dish of sea bass.

Take sea bass weighing six to eight ounces each, sauté them in a pan, with onion, and the chops of another large fish, fish-balls or sardines, as I have said before, with fish eggs and soft roe, truffles, asparagus, cauliflowers, St. George's mushrooms, slices of salted tuna belly, desalinated, artichoke stems, shelled snails, first sautéed; season everything with good oil, and various spices at your discretion; place everything on a plate, over a soup with toasted bread, and with a sauce made with shrimp juice, clean pistachios, lemon juice, and aromatic herbs; add all around stuffed eggplants mixed with small fish chops and lemon slices.

Another dish of tench.

Cook the tench in a pottage, in strong white wine, with good oil and spices; then cover them with a little pottage made with fish-balls, sautéed in butter, slices of clean cardoons, truffles, peas, asparagus tips, seafood, razor shells, and limpets, with verjuice and aromatic herbs; garnish with butter pastries, sliced lemons, and bunches of fried asparagus.

Another dish of asparagus.

Take large eels [capitoni], and cut them into pieces of about half a palmo each, clean them, add salt as needed, grease them well with butter or good oil, and braise them with fire over and under them; sprinkle them with mastic and ground cinnamon; when they are half-cooked, add oysters, sliced artichokes and truffles, pine nuts, capers, half a carafe of rich cow milk and lemon juice; garnish the plate with strips of candied pumpkin, appie apples in syrup, and dust everything with sugar and cinnamon.[50]

Another dish of turbot.

Take a big turbot and prepare it in a pottage, with pine nut milk, the juice of shrimp heads and tails, wedge shells, St. George's mushrooms, truffles, sour grapes, and lemon juice; garnish the plate with stuffed squid, slices of salted tuna belly, desalinated and roasted under embers, and lemon juice, everything seasoned with good spices and aromatic herbs.

Another dish of sea turtle.

Cut the sea turtles into pieces, wash them in wine, then sauté them with onion, and add shelled wedge shells, St. George's mushrooms, flesh of mantis shrimp, with good oil, spices, aromatic herbs, sweet grapes, clean pistachios for the top of the dish, and crushed ones for inside; garnish the plate with little pies of glory made with marzipan paste, and fried turtle liver, marinated in royal sauce, with sliced lemons.

Another dish of stuffed squid.

Stuff them, with a soup under them; clean and stuff the squid with ground fish flesh, salted tuna belly, desalinated, crustless bread soaked in a sweet white wine, aromatic herbs, and good spices; close the squid with their own heads, then sauté them, then add as much water as needed, with apt spices and a bit of wine, with toasted bread underneath, capers, and a little pottage of oysters, razor shells, truffles, St. George's mushrooms, everything sautéed in good oil; garnish the plate with shrimp, fish-balls, clean pistachios, and sliced lemons.

Another dish.

Take a fish gigot in Genoese style, from the flesh of a large amberjack, first roasted in the oven, well greased with oil or vinegar, and with butter it will be better; grind this finely, with salt and pepper and a bit of nutmeg, all mixed together well; place it on a plate, greased with butter, and fill the plate up to the rim; on top add pieces of fish liver, artichoke stems, slices of lobster and of fat salted tuna belly, desalinated, and truffle slices, soft crabs, and shrimp tails; pour on this a sauce made with the broth of wedge shells, the juice of shrimp heads, white wine or good oil, and lemon juice; place the plate in the oven to season, but the oven should not be too hot; garnish the sides of the plate with fried pastries and lemon slices.

---

50 I presume the asparagus of this dish's name is implied.

Another dish of lampreys.

Take clean, large lampreys, cut them into pieces, and place them in a pan, in which you have already sautéed onion with good oil; sauté the lampreys; add a bit of hot water, good spices, salt, slices of salted tuna belly, desalinated, aromatic herbs, raisins, pine nuts, fresh or barrel oysters, marinated in warm white wine, ground cloves, cinnamon, and mostacciolo; garnish the dish with marzipan, candied quince, sugar, cinnamon, butter, with pears in flaky dough, sliced lemons, and fried small lampreys around.

Another dish of amberjack.

Take a large, clean, amberjack, whole or in pieces, boil it in water, vinegar, salt, and halved lemons; serve it with a little pottage of cardoons, celery, cauliflowers, truffles, everything sliced, St. George's mushrooms with good oil, a bit of minced aromatic herbs, a bit of good wine, spices, and pine nut milk; cook it all well, and garnish the plate with flaky pastries, little fritters, or similar things, and lemon slices around.

Another dish of sardines.

Make a mixture with sardines, cod flesh, salted tuna belly, desalinated, crustless bread, minced aromatic herbs, salt, spices, and egg whites as needed, with a bit of garlic; with this mixture, well ground together, form a pie, as you would with dough, and fill it with corb flesh, bits of eel [capitone], bits of lobster, first boiled with oysters, razor shells, limpets, truffles, St. George's mushrooms, cauliflowers, and artichokes; these ingredients you should first sauté and season well in a pan until they are fully cooked; then put everything in the oven to harden; prepare fish broth, lemon juice, a bit of white wine, pine nut or pistachio milk, and a pinch of saffron, and make a glaze for the dish; serve it hot and you may garnish it with flaky pastries and sliced lemons.

Another dish of spider crab.

Boil the whole crabs and when they are cooked open them; take their insides and put them in a pot, where you will already have sautéed minced onions and aromatic herbs in good oil; then put them in a stone mortar with a wooden pestle, and mince them well, adding cleaned pine nuts, raisins, sliced truffles, two salted anchovies, boiled in vinegar, all diluted with a bit of Greco wine, lemon juice, and spices as needed; put everything back in the pot on the fire, to harden; then use this to fill the crab shells, which you first wash well; serve them like these, hot, with lemon slices around.

Another dish of sole.

Take sole flesh, first fried, gurnard flesh, first boiled, the flesh of eels [capitoni], first roasted and deboned; put everything in a pot, in which you have already sautéed a bit of onion and minced aromatic herbs in butter or good oil; when the fish is cooked, add a milk juice made with pistachios, with sliced truffles, St. George's mushrooms, sponge cake crumbs, good spices, and lemon juice; serve this hot with a cover made with the dough for ciambelle, with a sugar glaze on top, and all around small squid filled with marzipan paste, hard egg yolks, with sugar and cinnamon on top.

Another dish of sliced tortoise.

Take large tortoises and place them under the embers to cook until their shells open; remove the insides carefully and sauté them in a pot with good oil and good spices; add hot water, ground roasted almonds, lemon juice, slices of fat salted tuna belly, desalinated, with St. George's mushrooms, truffles, finely minced aromatic herbs, a bit of wine, and mostacciolo crumbs; garnish with little tarts filled with sour cherries in syrup, mixed with stuffed eggs.

Capirottata.

Take red mullets and other noble fish, and fry them in good oil; then remove the bones and let them cool; then grind them, each separately, as you would for gigot, and serve them separately on the plate, with on them a sauce made with clams, fresh oysters, razor shells, and wedge shells; first boil the seafood, take their juice, and sauté it in a small pan, diluting in it a bit of candied citron, clean pistachios, the insides of sea urchins, everything ground together with nutmeg and pepper; add a bit of muscatel wine; garnish the plate with the seafood, neatly arranged, with lemon juice, and garnish the sides of the plate with artichokes and sea urchins filled with various ingredients.

Here follow other dishes that individuals more experienced in our craft may prepare.[51]

1. Sturgeon boiled in wine and vinegar, served in royal plates with oil, lemon juice, and around herbs and flowers.
2. Corb chops, braised, cooked in a pan, with a condiment of roasted almonds, mostacciolo crumbs, a bit of sugar, diluted in wine and lemon juice, nutmeg, and cinnamon.
3. Turbot in pottage with almond milk, raisins, pine nuts, aromatic herbs, and apt spices.
4. Trouts cooked in wine, served by themselves, over a napkin, with herbs and flowers around.
5. Roasted sturgeon, larded with strips of small lampreys and fat salted tuna belly, with royal sauce on top.
6. Plates of locusts, with salt and water, removed from their shells, sliced, dredged in pine nut milk and flour, fried in good oil.[52]
7. Shad cooked in water, with herbs and flowers around.
8. Royal pies made with flesh from sturgeon, grey mullet, and sea bass, with a little broth of pine nuts and almonds diluted with lemon juice.
9. Grilled corb, with St. George's mushrooms on top and asparagus around.
10. Fried sole with on top fried asparagus, lemons, and sour oranges.

---

51 In spite of this statement, some of these recipes seem fairly simple; the section mirrors one in the first volume.

52 Latini calls this *piattigli di locuste*: piattiglio is a Spanishism for a small plate; locuste literally are locusts, but I imagine this is an old or Neapolitan name for a crustacean I have not been able to identify. I presume they are first boiled in salt and water, though boiling is not explicitly mentioned.

11. Sea bass, boiled, then deboned, and fried, sprinkled with sugar and mostacciolo crumbs, with lemon juice.

12. Small pies with oysters, truffles, pistachios, and pine nuts, with lemon juice on top.

13. Ground corb flesh with pine nuts, raisins, ground candied citron, and lemon juice.

14. Fried sole, then stewed with oil, lemon juice, a bit of muscatel wine, and mostacciolo crumbs.

16. Boiled trout, served in royal plates, with various flowers around.[53]

17. Bread loaves, greased with oil, and stuffed with bits of sole and other fried fish, with various types of seafood.

18. Red mullets, marinated with lemon juice, rose vinegar, verjuice, salt, and ground fennel, then dredged in sponge cake flour and mostacciolo crumbs, and fried, with lemon juice on top.

19. Grilled dentex with a little condiment on top made with dates and sour grapes cooked in pomegranate wine, with sugar and cinnamon.

20. Roasted sturgeon served with bastard sauce and other ingredients.

21. Pies made with sturgeon flesh, fat salted tuna belly, shrimp tails, soft crabs, artichoke stems, sliced truffles, and dates, cooked in malmsey wine, and underneath a pine nut milk.

22. Lampreys drowned in malmsey wine, then marinated, and spit-roasted on a low fire, then boiled in a good flavoured juice, and served on a plate with on top a good condiment and mostacciolo crumbs, encrusted with cloves and cinnamon bits.

23. Small sturgeon chops, weighing about half a pound each, well greased with oil and spit-roasted, sprinkled with good ingredients, and served on a plate with a little condiment made with good caviar, roasted almonds, nutmeg, and cloves, all ground in the mortar and diluted with malmsey wine, and lemon juice.

24. Trouts, their innards removed, placed under a weight and well pressed, stuffed with noble ingredients, then cooked in the oven, and served in the plate over bread slices soaked in verjuice, fried, and covered with a little condiment made with dates boiled in malmsey wine, candied quince, mostacciolo crumbs, diluted with lemon juice and verjuice.

25. Sturgeon chops, marinated in lemon juice, fennel crumbs, ground rosemary, and other ingredients, wrapped in paper well greased with butter, and spit-roasted; then removed from the paper, placed back in the marinade, in a plate greased with butter, and dusted with mostacciolo crumbs, with bread slices wrapped in fried eggs, sprinkled with malmsey wine on top, and lemon juice, sugar, and cinnamon; this goes with a little condiment made of capers ground in the mortar, mostaccioli, raisins, pine nuts, little bits of candied citron, diluted in the sturgeon marinade, and spices as needed; then the whole thing is baked with slices of provatura or mozzarella, and on top green pistachios that have soaked in perfumed water. Garnish the plate with appie apples in syrup with aniseeds on top.

---

53 There is no number 15 (and this volume lacks an errata page).

26. Large red mullets, marinated and served like the sturgeon chops.

27. Fried sole, deboned, stuffed with wedge shells, shrimp tails, bits of sturgeon eggs, St. George's mushrooms in malmsey wine, pine nuts, sliced truffles, aromatic herbs, lemon juice, and other suitable ingredients, with on top a sauce made with almond milk and pistachios, diluted with lemon and shrimp juice, with a cover in lattice pattern.

28. Bread loaves stuffed with candied pumpkin, strained eggs, marzipan paste, candied pistachios, sponge cake crumbs; soak the loaves for a bit in milk, then bake them in the oven; add a sugar glaze on top, and serve with a cover in lattice pattern.

29. White ravioli made with provatura, ricotta, parmesan cheese, cream tops, eggs, and cinnamon, with good butter and parmesan cheese on top.

30. Sturgeon head, boiled in wine, rose vinegar, verjuice, and apt spices; then wrapped in a white cloth soaked in wine and placed between two royal plates; then remove the cloth and prepare a little condiment with cooked pine nuts, starch flour, sponge cake flour, slices of candied citron, diluted with the same broth in which you have boiled the head, and lemon juice; boil this condiment a bit before, in a pot, and make sure it is fairly dense.

31. Large boiled trouts with parsley and lemons around, mixed with cut pumpkin filled with shrimp tails, egg yolks, various fruits, grated parmesan cheese, cooked in a pan with butter and verjuice; garnish the plate with fine flaky pastries, fried in butter.

32. Stuffed squid, thickened with pine nut milk and egg yolks, then stewed in the oven and served in a plate with fried pastries, sugar on top, and sliced lemons.

33. Large young sturgeon, cooked, braised, and larded with salted anchovies and salted tuna belly, desalinated, served on a plate with sliced lemons.

34. Tench in a pottage with various fruits, and with sliced salted tuna belly inside; serve this with the fruits on top; garnish the plate with fried Naples-style pastries.

35. Fish loaves made with ground fish of various sorts, cooked in an earthen pot, with various fruits inside, thickened with pine nut milk.

36. Large turbots in a thin Venetian-style broth, with pine nuts, raisins, and other fruits inside, with white wine, saffron, and apt spices, served in a plate with pastries and sliced lemons around.

37. Boiled corb, covered on the plate with cauliflowers, oil, pepper, sliced truffles, and sour orange juice.

38. Fish loaves made with flesh from sardines, red mullets, and other fish, salted tuna belly, desalinated, candied citron, raisins, pine nuts, and other suitable ingredients; garnish the plate with crostini with caviar, and sour orange juice on top.

39. Grouper tripe with its innards, made in a pottage with liver and soft roe of various fish, thickened with eggs, raisins, and pine nuts; garnish the plate with short crust pastries and lemon slices.

40. Tench in a pottage with fresh peas and lettuce, apt spices, and aromatic herbs; garnish the plate with cooked apples wrapped in dough.

41. Large boiled fish loins, with inside an anchovy sauce, herbs, and sour oranges around.[54]

42. Dentex chops, larded with strips of fat salted tuna belly, grilled, and dusted with fennel crumbs; garnish the plate with pieces of quinces in syrup and aniseeds on top, mixed with lemon slices.

43. Six turtles, made into a pottage, placed back in their shells, and covered with dough made with the usual ingredients; the plate garnished with scallops made of dough, filled with various condiments.

44. Chops of a large fish, weighing one pound each, grilled, with a condiment made with roasted almonds and muscatel; garnish the plate with small pies filled with wedge shells, shrimp tails, soft roe, and red mullet liver, mixed with lemon slices.

45. Boiled trout, covered with asparagus and small mushrooms, with herbs on top, and around halved sour oranges.

46. Fish loaves made with sturgeon flesh, shaped like eagles, stuffed with the usual ingredients, encrusted with pine nuts to form various decorations, thickened with pine nut milk; garnish the plate with little tarts filled with sour cherry sauce.

47. A piece of sturgeon weighing fifteen pounds, larded with strips of salted tuna belly, baked in the oven, with bastard sauce on top; garnish the plate with sliced lemons.

TREATISE X: *Of eggs, their quality and cooking, and of how to make various frittate, to be used in any situation.*

Licastus the Chaldean was the first to eat eggs in any style.

Eggs are moderately hot and moist; this is because the white is cold, the yolk is hot, and together they are moist. The white generates the chick, and the yolk the liver and other noble parts.

The best eggs are those laid fresh, by fat hens, fed with wheat and impregnated by roosters; pheasant eggs are also good; those of ducks or geese are bad, because they have a heavy smell and are hard to digest.

Eggs are quite nourishing and they provoke sleep, and thus are good for the elderly and the convalescent. They stimulate coition, increase sperm, are beneficial to the consumptive, clear the chest, and strengthen the voice, especially fresh eggs taken with a pinch of salt.

The best ones are poached, eaten with salt, spices, and verjuice, and they are easy to digest, whereas fried eggs are hard to digest.

First frittata.

Take six eggs, ground candied citron, and mostacciolo crumbs; beat everything together, and prepare a pan with hot butter; cook this diligently; add on top of it pistachios, studded by the long side, hard egg yolks, first cooked in ambivera, or faldicchere eggs, mixed with fried bits of sponge cake, and a bit of perfumed water; serve it hot.

---

54 The word is *lombi*, which means loins, though I suspect here it is a type of fish I have not identified (perhaps a typographical error for *lompo* or lumpfish).

A royal frittata.

Take six eggs, four ounces of cooked pine nuts, well ground, two ounces of sponge cake flour, and two ounces of mostacciolo crumbs; beat everything together with a bit of salt and cold water, and make a frittata, to cover the bottom of a plate, well greased with butter; add thin small slices of sponge cake. Cover with strained eggs and grated candied citron; add on top another frittata, similar to the first one, all covered with cream tops and a lot of butter. Bake it in the oven, and add a glaze made with egg whites, sugar, and lemon juice. Serve it hot, and it will be a frittata worthy of any banquet; you can increase the quantities as you need.

Another white frittata, made of three frittate.

Take as many egg whites as there are guests, and put them in a pot with a bit of milk, six ounces of cooked pine nuts, and cream tops; beat everything together; prepare the pan on the fire, well greased with hot butter; form the first frittata, and then place it on a silver plate, well greased with butter; place on top of it strained eggs, thin slices of sponge cake and blancmange, first fried in butter, and thin slices of candied citron; make the second frittata as above, and place it on the first one; with the same composition, form the third one, stacking them on top of each other; serve it hot.

Another frittata, made with three frittate.

Take as many eggs as you need for the number of guests you have, and put them in a pot with a bit of cold water; add marzipan paste or ground cooked pine nuts, and mostacciolo crumbs; beat everything together and prepare the pan with hot butter and cook the first frittata; place it on a silver plate, well greased with butter, and put on top of it cream tops, crumbled egg yolks, slices of provatura, cooked in butter, and bits of butter, and grated candied pumpkin; form the second frittata, and lay on top of it cream tops, thin slices of sponge cake, crumbled hard egg yolks, with the usual butter; form the third frittata; then take egg whites and lemon juice and make a glaze on top; place it in the oven to brown, and serve it hot when it is needed.[55]

Another frittata *rognosa*.[56]

Take sufficient eggs and beat them well, with water and salt, add bits of fat salted tuna belly, first cooked and desalinated, rich cheese, a bit of pepper, and finely minced Roman mint; beat everything together and put this mixture in the pan with hot butter; form the frittata, well cooked, turning it often, and serve it hot when it is needed.

---

55 Latini mentions *rossi d'uova sgranate*, and only the second time he adds that they are hard-boiled, but the context suggests that these are crumbled, so I presume they are hard-boiled the first time too.

56 *Rognoni* are kidneys, which are not included in this recipe; *rognoso* as an adjective means mangy, and, figuratively, also annoying, troublesome. This unflattering term today refers to a local frittata from Piedmont made with salami; this lean version in Latini uses the tuna belly instead.

Another white frittata.

Take as many egg whites as you deem sufficient for the number of guests, and beat them well with water and salt, sugar at your discretion, ground pine nuts and pistachios; put this mixture in the pan with hot butter, form the frittata, and cook it without turning it; once it is cooked place it in a silver plate, well greased with butter; take the egg yolks, and cook them in ambivera, or use faldicchere eggs, or other fresh egg yolks boiled in milk, but make sure that they are not hard; around these eggs place green pistachios, and riddle the frittata with thin slices or strips of candied pumpkin; serve it hot when it is needed.

Another frittata, in Carthusian style.

Take twenty or twenty-five eggs, more or less, depending on the number of guests, making sure none of them have gone bad; beat them well in a pot, and while beating them add five or six ounces of cold water and a bit of minced white salt; prepare a pan with oil and butter and when it boils add the eggs; touch the frittata with the tip of a knife to mix it well, so that it cooks in all parts; to turn it better, you can keep adding oil and butter, always hot; once it is cooked, serve it hot with sugar and cinnamon on top.

Spit-roasted eggs.

I mention this recipe just as a curiosity, as it is not done: if you wish to employ this, prepare a red-hot spit and diligently skewer the eggs, as many as you wish, and then turn them on the fire; give them a little prick with the tip of the knife before skewering them.

Stuffed eggs.

Boil the eggs, let them cool, and cut them in half; remove the yolks, grind them finely, and mix them with raisins, pine nuts, bits of butter and ricotta, ground candied citron, lemon juice, salt, spices, and aromatic herbs. Stuff the whites with this mixture, and place them in a plate with hot butter and pine nut milk; once this is all boiled, serve it hot, giving a couple of eggs to each guest.

Eggs poached in milk.

Put a small pot on the fire with good milk, and when it boils add the fresh eggs; once they are cooked, serve them in a plate with melted butter, and salt, pepper, and cinnamon on top.

Strained eggs.

Take ten egg yolks, after removing the whites, and beat them well; place them in a cloth and strain them through it carefully. Then take a couple of egg shells and make a small hole at the bottom; after preparing a pan on the fire with hot sugar or ambivera, strain the egg yolks little by little through the shells into the pan; once they are cooked, remove them and use them as you wish.[57]

---

[57] Here is an example of a basic preparation Latini already employed in numerous recipes in both of his volumes; the Italian terms he uses are misside or filate; the term may also refer to strips of custard, strained and dipped in warm sugar (see Maria Attilia Fabbri Dall'Oglio, *Il trionfo*

Eggs Astorga-style.[58]

Take broth or water as you prefer, with salt, oil or butter, a bit of saffron, and a bit of pepper; boil the water with everything else in it and break into it healthy fresh eggs, including the whites, making sure they do not become hard; when they are perfectly cooked, serve them hot with cinnamon on top, giving two to each guest.

Eggs Spanish-style, also called *Acqua Cominos.*

To prepare a couple of them, take a garlic clove, chili pepper, and a bit of cumin, grind everything together, then take sufficient water to cook this; dilute everything by boiling it in a pan; when it boils, add the beaten eggs, and when they have thickened, as in an egg broth [*sciuscello*], serve them in the plates; they are very beneficial to cold stomachs.

Another dish of eggs Spanish-style.

Take a deep large spoon, and put a bit of butter or oil in it, and when it boils break into it healthy eggs, turning them carefully; once they are cooked, serve them with pepper and salt on top, giving two to each guest.

TREATISE XI: *Of milk, its quality and cooking.*[59]

Cambles king of the Ondians was the first to eat milk, butter, ricotta, and other things that come from milk; he was such a big eater that he even ate his wife, as we read in the Greek Musonius Acetius, which I mention here as a fable.[60]

Milk is moist in the second degree and moderately hot; it consists of three substances: a watery one called serum, which is moist and cold, nitric and soluble; a thick one called butter, which is temperate; and another thick one, from which we make cheese, and this one is thick, viscous, and phlegmatic.

The best milk is women's, and, when it is made into butter, it heals the marks of smallpox (here in Naples called *bone*), if one applies it for fifteen days, and it leaves no mark at all; it is also marvellously good for ear pains, if one applies it warm, with rue juice, using two or three drops at a time, and the pain will quickly go away.[61]

---

dell'effimero, lo sfarzo e il lusso dei banchetti visti nella cornice fastosa delle feste della Roma barocca (Rome: Ricciardi, 2002), chap. 5).

58 This preparation seems to have little in common with Latini's earlier dish of veal "Astorga-style."

59 From here and for a while the original book no longer starts each new chapter on a new page.

60 This is one of Latini's most esoteric—and bizarre—erudite references; I have found a mention, in an abridged 1812 edition of Dr. Johnson's *Dictionary* available online, of Cambles, "a gluttonous king of Lydia"; Musonius (Rufus, not Acetius) was a Roman philosopher of the first century AD who also wrote in Greek, but I have found no reference that paired him with Cambles—or the (to me) unknown "Ondians."

61 Women's milk was traditionally regarded as the healthiest, which of course made perfect sense within the prevailing humoural theory, as it was by definition the most suited to humans.

Second best is jenny milk, and after that comes sheep milk, then goat milk, and finally cow or [water] buffalo milk; goat milk is thinner than sheep's, and cow milk more beneficial, if taken fresh from the animal's teats.

One must keep in mind that the best milk is not watery, because those who sell it often make it so that it cannot be used; also, it should be white, and not yellowish.

Milk strengthens the brain, fattens the body, is beneficial for the consumptive, cools the urine, is highly nourishing, gives a beautiful colour to the body, invigorates for coition, removes cough, clears the chest, and heals the convalescent or consumptive, if one drinks three ounces of it with a bit of sugar, and then neither eats nor drinks anything else for three hours, nor engages in any exercise.

One can make many cheeses from milk, and butter, cream tops, giuncata, ricotta, various rich cheeses, milk foam, and custards, which can serve for many composite dishes.

One can also make sweet dishes from milk, adding egg yolks and half as many whites, bits of candied citron, Savoy cookies or mostaccioli or sponge cake crumbs, with perfumed water, cinnamon, and sugar, cooked on the fire; this can serve for sweet dishes, as I wrote in its place.

One can use milk to make blancmange of all sorts.

Also, one can make various sorbetti, with bits of candied citron, and sugar and a bit of perfumed water.

Milk can be eaten curdled, and is served cold, with sugar on top, in the first credenza service.

One can also eat it Spanish-style, giving it simply a quick boil over a low fire, then cooling it in a silver plate or bowl, and adding Roman mint leaves; serve this with Savoy cookies, and it is quite tasty.

The latter can be served in the first credenza service; it develops a thin film on top, and is very tasty and noble, well warmed but not quite boiled.

After boiling it quickly, as above, it can be used for other types of sorbetti, and it too is exquisite.

One can also use milk to make ring-shaped cookies or various sweet breads.[62]

It can also serve for the dough to make many types of maccheroni.

One can use it to make various creams, in a stand pie, with beaten eggs, sugar, cinnamon, and perfumed water, with strips of dough on top.[63]

Of butter, or whipped butter, its quality and cooking.

Butter is hot and moist to the low first degree.

Best is fresh butter, and the most praised is made with sheep milk, and it can be made out of ricotta, well beaten in warm water and then dropped in cold water, so that the butter floats to the top, which one can then put on grape leaves and store in a cellar to congeal, whereas with what is left in the water, after boiling it, one can make ricotta, adding a bit of salt.

---

62 Latini calls the cookies *bracciatelli*, a term still used in some Italian regions for a variety of ciambelle; the sweet breads are *panesigli*, two recipes for which Latini provides later in this volume.

63 Latini calls these creams *lattaroli*, which usually means mammary glands, but in this context he seems to mean creams.

Butter, eaten with sugar and honey, heals catarrh, because it pulls out excess fluids from the chest; it heals asthma and cough, especially if eaten with honey and bitter almonds; it mitigates pains and is highly nourishing.

Butter serves as a condiment for many dishes, both lean and not.

It can also serve in many tarts and covered tarts.

In various pies, with cover or without.

And in many things that use dough with and without cover, and mixed with sugar and rosewater it can be passed through a pastry bag and served as an appetizer, with sugar on top.

You can also make a dough with butter, sugar, rosewater, egg yolks, cooked and then ground with the rest, and use it to mould various statuettes in bas-relief or even full relief.

You can use it to cook frittate and eggs.

Germans always like it with heavy bread, and they eat it at the end of meals, after fruit.

One can eat it on slices of toasted bread, with sugar.

It can serve to make short crust pastries, mixed with egg yolks and sugar.

It is used in various *zeppole* and fritters.[64]

Of ricotta, its quality and cooking.

Ricotta is cold and dry in the first degree.

Best is that made fresh with good milk.

It benefits men of a hot complexion; it aids those who have an overflow of choleric humour; it extinguishes thirst and the ardor of choler, and provokes sleep.

Ricotta can be prepared in all the ways and dishes that I will discuss for cream tops, after diluting it with milk, in dishes, and tarts, and fillings, or little tarts.

With ricotta one can make many sorts of ravioli, both with a casing and without, with eggs, sugar, grated or fresh cheese, all ground in them together, with spices and good aromatic herbs finely minced; then one cooks them in water with enough salt and serves them hot, with grated cheese, sugar, and cinnamon on top.

You can pass it through a pastry bag with rosewater and sugar and use for small plates, as mentioned above.

It can be used for covered and uncovered tarts, with eggs, sugar, and candied citron inside.

It can be used in many stews, both lean and not, together with leaf vegetables.

It can be used for Genoa-style vegetable tarts, with eggs, chard, sugar, and apt spices.

It can be used to make Roman-style *pappardelle*, after grinding it with egg whites and sugar, dredging it in bread crumbs, passed through a sieve, or in fine flour, and they can be fried in good lard; they should be served hot, with sugar on top.[65]

Ricotta can serve as an appetizer, with rosewater and sugar.

Giuncata can be used as above, though I have only seen this done in Rome.

---

64 Zeppole are very airy, fried (or baked) pastries that are very popular in Naples, especially around the feast day of St. Joseph (March 19): today, they are filled with custard and sour cherry jam.

65 In the prior recipe, the dishes are *gattafure*, an old term for tarts with leaf vegetables; pappardelle today in Italy generally are a type of flat, long, usually fresh pasta, but in Latini's time they were a type of fritter (see a recipe for them below).

TREATISE XII: *Of various maccheroni, lasagne, small gnocchi, and of how to make them very well.*

Meluzza of Como was the first to eat maccheroni and all other types of pasta; she died of pleurisy, and because of her nice discoveries she was given a fine burial monument with a beautiful epitaph.[66]

Take two pounds of fine flour and mix it with clear warm water, four eggs, and a bit of salt; mix it strongly, and when you see that it is well mixed make it into small clumps; spread these thinly to six fingers in length and width; and cut them into squares of about four fingers each side. Then place them in sheets of paper, on top of each other, making sure they do not stick together; after a couple of hours, place them in a boiler with boiling water; keep in mind that when they are thin they should cook only a very short time. Once they are cooked, place them in cold water, and then in a plate, well greased with butter, with grated parmesan cheese, caciocavallo, and grated provola, with a bit of Puglia cheese; form a layer of the lasagna mentioned above, mixed with little bits of butter or thin slices of provola; serve them with sugar and cinnamon on top, hot or cold; you can place the plate to warm above a boiler with boiling water.[67]

Another dish of maccheroni.

Take crustless white bread and the best flour, mix it with milk, and make small gnocchi; boil them carefully in a boiler; once cooked add good parmesan cheese, mixing them with butter; garnish the plate with strained eggs, and with cinnamon on top, and cover it with another plate.

Another dish of maccheroni.

Take fine flour and mix it with milk, grind it in the mortar with egg yolks, as with fritters; make it into small gnocchi, cook them in milk, and serve them with good cheese, mixed with bits of butter, and sugar and cinnamon on top, and with boiled egg yolks around the dish.

Another dish of naked ravioli, enough for six people.

Take two pounds of ricotta, four egg yolks and two whole eggs, a bit of grated parmesan cheese, and six ounces of sugar; make the ravioli out of this mixture and cook them in boiling water; be aware that when they float to the top they are cooked; place them in a plate with a bit of butter, and sugar and cinnamon on top.[68]

---

66 This is one of three examples in Latini of women as "discoverers" of food.

67 As was traditional in Latini's time in elite cooking, pasta dishes are usually sweetened, and they all use fresh pasta.

68 As is still the case on Italian menus today, "naked" here means that these ravioli lack an outer dough casing.

Another dish of maccheroni.

Take crustless white bread and mix it as with fritters; grind it in the mortar with enough egg yolks, wrap it in butter and parmesan cheese and cook it in milk; serve it with a little mound in the middle of strained eggs, and with sugar and cinnamon on top.

Twice-cooked maccheroni.

Take fine flour and mix it with milk and crustless bread, first soaked in milk. Make it into a dough and place it in a boiler on the fire, turning it always with a spoon, until you think it is perfectly cooked; make small gnocchi with it, and then cook them in another boiler and serve them with parmesan cheese and melted butter on top.

TREATISE XIII: *In which we teach how to make different types of zeppole and fritters.*

Melibea of Manerbio discovered how to make all sorts of tasty fritters; she was a woman of such daring and strength that with her own hands she killed a bear of enormous size.

To make rice fritters.

Take clean rice, well washed in hot water, and cook it in milk or water as you prefer, with a bit of salt and saffron; grind it in the mortar and pass it through a cloth sieve; cool it and add a bit of fine flour, then place it on the fire in a pan with boiling oil, and with the hook of the spoon handle break it into fritters; serve them with sugar or honey on top as you prefer.

To make fritters in another way.

Take some milk and add to it a glass of good white wine; boil it on the fire, and when it starts to boil add fine flour, turning it often with the spoon or a wood stick; grind this mixture in the mortar, and add six eggs, that is, three whites and three yolks, or more if you prefer; add also sugar at your discretion; cook everything, making sure it does not stick, in good oil or lard, as you prefer; serve the fritters with sugar or honey on top, as you wish.

Fritters made another way.

Take hot water and add a bit of flour, with a little bit of yeast, and make it so it feels like a thick glue; mix it all well and leave it covered, next to the fire, with a bit of flour on top, for four or five hours, or maybe from evening to morning; then knead it again well, and add salt, water, and saffron, to give the fritters colour; you can also add raisins and dried or fresh rosemary leaves; once you have formed the fritters, fry them in good oil and serve them with honey on top, or a sugar ambivera.

Fritters made another way.

Take a pound of fine flour, two ounces of cold melted butter, two ounces of sugar, two ounces of rosewater, a bit of saffron and salt, and add eight eggs and a glass of warm milk; knead it all together so that it feels like a well beaten glue, and let it rest in a pot, in a warm place, for a quarter hour; then knead it very well one more time, make the fritters, and cook them in good oil; serve them hot, with sugar on top. You can also add to the mixture elder tree flowers, mint, or ground marjoram.

To make another type of fritters.

Take a pound of grated cheese and four ounces of crustless bread, also grated, and first soaked in goat milk; mix everything together with ten beaten eggs, two ounces of sugar, and ten ounces of fine flour; make this into a dough, and form the fritters, cook them in good oil, and serve them with sugar or melted honey on top.

To make another type of fritters.

Take two pounds of flour, one pound of milk, and two ounces of yeast diluted in six ounces of milk, and six ounces of parmesan cheese, or of another rich cheese, a quarter ounce of cinnamon, a bit of saffron at your discretion, and eight fresh eggs; pound everything together in the mortar, making a dough that feels like a well beaten glue; set it to rest for one hour in a warm place, well covered; then put it again in the mortar and form the fritters with the handle of an iron spoon; cook them in boiling oil; serve them hot, with sugar or melted honey on top.

Roman-style fritters, called pappardelle.

Take fresh ricotta and pass it through a cloth sieve, and for every pound of ricotta add three eggs, three ounces of sugar, and three ounces of crustless bread, soaked in milk and well squeezed; knead it together, to be fairly hard, make the fritters, and fry them in oil or melted butter; once they are cooked, serve them hot.

Roman-style fritters, called zeppole.

Take a pound of red chickpeas, first soaked, and shell them, then boil them in water with six ounces of shelled chestnuts; take them all out of the water, drain them, and grind them in the mortar with six ounces of shelled walnuts, watching that they not be rotten, and add four ounces of sugar, a quarter ounce of cinnamon, and a quarter ounce between cloves and nutmeg; work everything together with a bit of mint or marjoram, and beat everything with a knife; use this mixture to make balls and fry them in oil or butter; then sprinkle them with rosewater and serve them hot with sugar and cinnamon on top.

To make fritters called *frascate*.

Take eight ounces of flour with ten fresh eggs, three ounces of sugar, a bit of saffron, salt as needed, and one ounce of rosewater; make sure this mixture is well beaten, and place it in a pan with hot oil, inside a holed spoon; use another spoon, without holes, to spread the mixture so that it covers the whole pan; as soon as it starts rising, turn it carefully, so that it not become too hot, and remove it quickly, because this mixture cooks rapidly; then form the fritters and place them one on top of the other, dusting them with sugar; if you wish to keep them, you can place them in the oven at a low temperature, covering them with rag paper.[69]

To make Venetian-style fritters.

Boil six pounds of milk, in a well tinned pan, with six ounces of fresh butter, three of sugar, and four of rosewater, with a bit of saffron, and salt as needed; when it all starts to boil, add two pounds of flour, bit by bit, stirring it with a wooden spoon, until it becomes fairly hard; then remove it from the pan and grind in the mortar for a quarter hour; then place it in a copper pot, turning it with a wooden spoon until it has cooled; then add twenty fresh eggs, one by one, stirring frequently with the wooden spoon, until it becomes rather runny; then beat it for a quarter hour, until it forms bubbles, and then set it to rest for a quarter hour in the pot, well covered, in a warm place; then beat it yet another time; prepare a pan with hot oil; put the mixture on a carving board and, with the knife's tip, well greased, cut the fritters, and fry them in good oil; once they are cooked, remove them with the holed spoon and serve them hot with ground sugar on top.

Other fritters, also called zeppole.

Make fritters with blancmange, dip them in eggs, and sprinkle them with flour; fry them in good lard or butter; once they are cooked, serve them hot with ground sugar on top.

TREATISE XIV: *In which we teach how to make lean blancmange, and similar preparations.*

Causellus of Toledo discovered blancmange, which the Greeks call *Leuphagon*; he was a fine thief. Emperor Galba ate a lot of blancmange, and he added salt and rosewater to it, so that it would not rot so quickly in the stomach.

To make lean blancmange, for a day of stricter fasting.

Take two pounds of ambrosine almonds, shell and peel them in hot water, then place them in cool water, and grind them well in the mortar, often moistening them with clear water, using a little brush. Then pass them through a fairly loose cloth sieve, adding two carafes of cold water. Prepare a boiler, and add a pound of rice flour, but not all at once, and make sure the fire is not too strong; use white salt as needed, with a lump of Venice sugar and a bit of musk or perfumed water; mix everything in the boiler, and then pour it into a bowl or mould, as you prefer.

---

69 An almost identical recipe appears in Scappi, *Opera* (497); Scappi's editor offers no reason for the name of these fritters.

To make another lean blancmange, for an ordinary lean day.

Take a cleaned gurnard and boil it in good water, then let it cool, take its flesh and grind it in the mortar, as you would with capon meat; dilute it in two pounds of milk, a pound of rice flour, six ounces of perfumed water, and a pound of sugar; cook it well and serve it as usual.[70]

To make an almond dish for four people.[71]

Take one pound of ambrosine almonds and shell and peel them in hot water, then immediately place them in cold water, and grind them in the mortar, then dilute them with fresh water and pass them through a fairly loose cloth sieve, adding four ounces of sugar; set them to boil in a little pot, and when they start to thicken, serve them in bowls with sugar and cinnamon on top; this will be tasty and nourishing.

To make another almond dish.

Take half a pound of ambrosine almonds, grind them well, and when you have produced their milk, set it to boil in a pot, adding three ounces of rice flour and four ounces of sugar; when it starts to thicken, it means that it is ready, and you can serve it in bowls with cinnamon on top.

To make a royal dish of blancmange.

Take six ounces of rice, six ounces of well ground almonds, three carafes of milk, eight ounces of fine sugar, four lobster necks, the juice of one lemon, and rosewater at your discretion, and if you should think that the rice flour is not enough you may choose to add some at your discretion, and if you cannot find lobsters, you can use gurnard flesh, well pulled.

TREATISE XV: *Of various fish salads and jellies.*

A sturgeon salad.

Take a piece of roasted sturgeon, from the back; let it cool and debone it; place it on small dishes with good wine, raisins, cloves, and cinnamon; season it with good oil, perfumed vinegar, and salt; first boil everything together; garnish the sides of the dishes with thin slices of sturgeon, and you can also place in any open space a Spanish olive, retouched in gold and silver. You can make the same salad with boiled sturgeon, or another noble fish, and garnish it with thin slices of candied citron and basil flowers.[72]

---

70 Blancmange was a very popular and old dish, in its "fat" version centring on capon meat and milk, and considered noble and elegant because of its dominant whiteness (hence its name, literally "white food"); we have already seen it as part of many of Latini's preparations. The Italian name for gurnard is *pesce cappone*, so its use to replace capon meat easily suggested itself. The first recipe here is for *giorno di vigilia*, i.e., for a strict fasting day, when all (land) animal products would be prohibited; the second is for the more relaxed *giorno di magro*, when milk could be used.

71 Latini calls this and the next dish an amandolata (from *mandorle*, almonds).

72 There is no introduction—or "discoverer"—to this section. Latini's sentence structure is confusing, and the mention of "boiling everything together" comes after the seasoning: I think what is to be boiled is the wine, raisins, cloves, and cinnamon, to be added to the fish before the seasoning.

To make another salad, of large grey mullets.

Roast the fish, greasing them with good oil, salt, nutmeg, fennel, and pepper; once they are cooked and have cooled, skin them and place them in the tondini, dressed with vinegar, oil, and crushed pepper, with a little bit of cooked must and four raisins; garnish the sides of the plates with bits of dates boiled in good wine, and a bit of sugar and cinnamon, mixed with pomegranate seeds retouched in gold and silver.

Another salad of corb, a most noble fish.

Roast the corb as with sturgeon, then take the leanest part and let it cool; then slice it or pull it as you prefer and dress it with good oil and perfumed vinegar, and a little bit of pepper; you may add a sauce with raisins, muscatel, sugar, and cinnamon, boiling everything together with a bit of good wine; garnish the plate with thinly sliced truffles, pomegranate seeds, pitted olives, and thin slices of lemons, everything retouched in gold and silver.

Another salad of gurnard.

Take the largest gurnard you can find and boil it in water, vinegar, and sufficient salt; once it is cooked, set it aside to cool; slice it thinly and place the slices in the tondini, dressed with perfumed vinegar, good oil, pepper, and finely minced parsley; garnish the sides of the plates with slices of sweet oranges, retouched in silver, mixed with pomegranate seeds and raisins boiled in wine; you may also make a sauce for this, with perfumed vinegar, good oil, cinnamon, and muscatel, all first boiled in wine, and garnish the sides of the plates with thin slices of candied quince and candied truffles.

Another salad of salmon carp.

Fry the fish in good oil, then remove it from the pan and put it on a white cloth for the oil to dry; pour on it minced salt, pepper, ground cloves and nutmeg, and cover it with bay leaves; once it has cooled, slice the fish thinly and place the slices in the tondini, dressing them with perfumed vinegar, good oil, and sugar at your discretion; garnish the sides of the tondini with sliced lemons and aniseeds of various colours.

Another salad of chicory roots.

Clean the roots well and boil them in water; then place them in cold water; dress them with oil, salt, vinegar, and raisins, garnishing the plate with sour orange slices and aniseeds of various colours, or with anything else you like.

Another salad of small pumpkins.

Take as many pumpkins as you need and wrap them in their own leaves or in vine leaves; place everything under the embers, and cover them first with hot ashes, with the embers on top; once they are cooked, let them cool and cut them in long or round slices, as you prefer; place them in the plate and prepare a sauce with peeled garlic cloves, vinegar, and chili pepper, grinding everything together, with pepper and salt at your discretion; pour the sauce over the plates, with a bit of powdered oregano on top. It will be a refreshing salad, healthy and tasty.

Another royal salad.

Take endive or escarole and finely mince it; set it aside and prepare a large basin, on the bottom of which place eight or ten cookies or taralli or *friselle*, soaked in water and vinegar, with a bit of white salt;[73] add the minced endive to the basin, mixing it with other lettuces, also minced; raise this salad as high as you see fit, adding roots sliced lengthwise, and filling the spaces in the basin with the ingredients mentioned below, all neatly arranged: four ounces of pine nuts, six of pitted olives, four of capers, one pomegranate, ten ounces of grapes, white and black, twelve anchovies, four ounces of salted tuna belly, three ounces of fish eggs [targhe], six of comfits, twelve of candied citron and pumpkin, four hard-boiled eggs, four ounces of clean pistachios, four of raisins, six of other black olives, four ounces of caviar, six of cinnamon sticks, six of ground white fish flesh, plus small radishes, salt, oil, and vinegar at your discretion; garnish the plate with bands made of citron pulp, and flowers all around; make sure not to add salt or other seasonings until the plate is brought to the table and the meal begins.

Another salad of borage flowers.

Clean them well without washing them, and place them in the plate with a seasoning of good oil, perfumed vinegar, and salt; garnish the plate as you wish.

Another salad of rosemary flowers.

Clean them of their leaves and twigs, and dress them with good oil, vinegar, salt, and a bit of powdered sugar at your discretion; garnish the plate as you wish. These flowers are very healthy, as is asserted by the Salerno school [a famous medical school].

Another salad of elder flowers.

One should pick these flowers at the hottest point of the day; let them drop on a white cloth, wash them, and arrange them in the plates, just a few of them, and dress them with oil, vinegar, and salt as needed; these flowers are healthy and lubricate the body, as stated by Castel Durante.[74]

Another salad of jasmine flowers.

Pick them in the morning, wet with dew; prepare them like the other flowers, and they are of very good quality.

To make a tasty lean jelly.

Take two pounds of skate and two of turbot, clean them, and wash them in good white wine; cut them into pieces and place them in a pot with two carafes of white wine, a quarter ounce of cinnamon, a quarter ounce of pepper, and six whole cloves, all tied in a

---

73 Taralli, as we saw, are ring-shaped, savoury, hard breads; freselle (today's more common spelling) now are slices of savoury, twice-baked bread.

74 Castor (not Castel) Durante (1529–1590) was an Italian botanist, physician, and poet whose work focused on herbs; Latini mentions him again a few pages later (this time with the right name).

little cloth; when the fish is cooked, remove the cloth, because the jelly will already have gained its flavour; when it has reduced by about half, pass it through a cloth sieve, and let it cool; then with a brush remove the oil and fat that is on the top, and add two egg whites and the juice of one lemon; put it back on the fire and when it has boiled once or twice, and you have removed the foam, add the juice of two lemons and a bit of sugar at your discretion; you can colour this as you please.

To make another jelly of freshwater fish.

Take two pounds of large eels and two pounds of trout, all cleaned, and wash them in white wine; put them on the fire with a bit of water and vinegar and a couple of glasses of wine, with salt as needed; boil this on a low fire; when the broth has reduced by about half, remove it from the fire and pass it through a cloth sieve; give it the colour you prefer.

To make another tasty jelly.

Take a weever and a skinned moray eel, and cut them both in pieces; clean them and wash them in white wine, then boil them in water and salt, with a bit of vinegar, a glass of malmsey wine, and the usual spices; when it has reduced by one third carefully take out the fish, so that it does not dissolve; take away the fat and add lemon juice and egg whites; once it is cooked, squeeze on it the juice of four sour oranges, so that the jelly will be golden in colour. In winter, place it to cool outside, in summer place shaved ice above it; garnish the plate as you wish.

TREATISE XVI: In which we teach how to cook and season dishes without spices, and we also speak of the virtues of parsley and thyme.[75]

Parsley, to be good, must not yet have produced seeds, and its leaves must be tender and fragrant; this herb is much used in the kitchen and in dishes; it goes well in sauces, it can be eaten raw or cooked, it softens the kidneys, provokes urine and sweat, purges the liver and the uterus of blockages, and benefits the mammary glands. A parsley infusion is good against cough and poison, and mitigates a hot stomach; its roots are used in many exquisite stews and nourishing broths; it is hot in the second degree and dry in the third.

Thyme is very good for the chest and for anyone who vomits blood; with its pleasant smell it comforts the stomach and cheers the heart; it too can be used in all dishes and sauces, just like parsley; it is hot and dry to the third degree.

You will pick these herbs at the end of the month of May or the start of June, to use them in the kitchen.

Parsley, thyme, wild thyme, basil, marjoram, pennyroyal, mint, chili pepper, wild saffron, ginger.

---

75 From here there are page breaks again, with little drawings separating the sections.

Gather all these herbs in May and June, each separately, as much as you need; set them to dry in the shade, then grind them in the mortar, pass them through a loose sieve, and collect them each in its little sack. Usually one keeps them, well closed in their little sacks, in the kitchen or in another warm suitable place; you can use these for all dishes, also composite ones, as they will be tasty to the palate, healthy to the stomach, and beneficial to the purse; with these seasonings you can save pepper and other spices, and the dishes will actually be tastier, as is practised among others by the Capuchin Fathers.

Now that I have taught you how to season without spices, it seems good to give you the recipe to season composite dishes, or make a Spanish-style marinade, or a Naples-style stew, with the appropriate spices.

Take half an ounce of fine cinnamon, half an ounce of coriander, a quarter ounce of nutmeg, a quarter ounce of cloves, an eighth of an ounce or more of nutmeg flower; grind them one by one, and pass them through a sieve, if you wish; mix everything together, and you can use it in any situation; grind the pepper separately and use your discretion as to in which dishes to use it, keeping in mind that it is not apt for all preparations.

TREATISE XVII: *Of various tasty sauces and condiments, and of how to prepare them perfectly.*

A condiment of fennel stems.

Take the tender fennel stems and grind them in the mortar, adding a bit of crustless bread soaked in broth, a bit of ground candied citron, diluted in broth or vinegar or lemon juice, and the usual spices; if this turns out too liquid, you can add some mostacciolo crumbs. Pass it [through a sieve], and serve it with sugar on top and arabesques around it, giving one tondino to each guest.

To make another condiment.

Take perfumed vinegar and put it in a pot with a bit of sugar at your discretion, raisins, pine nuts, bits of whole cinnamon, and whole cloves; boil everything together, adding a bit of fragrance, as you wish. This sauce you may sue to cover any fish roast.

A condiment of cherries or other fruits.

Take two pounds of fresh cherries, not too ripe, and cook them in a pot with half a pound of white sour grapes, a bit of mostacciolo crumbs, two ounces of crustless bread, six ounces of sugar, the usual spices, and salt at your discretion; once cooked, pass it through a sieve and let it cool; serve it with fried fish. You can make the same condiment with gooseberries or red berries.

Another condiment with carrots or parsnips.

Clean them well and boil them in a pot; once they are half-cooked, remove them from the water and put them in a pan with clear verjuice; for each pound of carrots, add six ounces of sugar, four of quinces, and half an ounce of cinnamon, a quarter ounce of pepper, and a quarter ounce of cloves and nutmeg together; boil everything together with four ounces of rose vinegar; once they are cooked, crush them and pass them through a sieve, making sure they still have a bit of body. It is a very tasty condiment, and it is named after Emperor Maximilian, because he often used it at his table.

Another condiment of pomegranate wine, made another way.

Take a pound and a half of clarified pomegranate wine and a pound of sugar; boil it in a pot on a slow coal fire; taste it to check when it is cooked; keep it in glass or earthen jars. This condiment is often called Cicero's sauce, because that most eloquent senator liked to use it at his table.

To make another quince condiment.

Grate the quince lightly, including the peel, and drop all the juice that comes out through a cloth sieve; when you have enough juice, put it in a pot to rest, then put it in a pan, throwing away the solid remains, and cook it on a low fire, adding sugar at your discretion, a bit of vinegar, half a glass of Greco wine, cloves, cinnamon, and nutmeg at your discretion; cook this like royal sauce, and it will be tasty; this condiment is usually called "Talks little," because its sourness seems to impede talking.

Another condiment with the juice of appie apples, which common people call "the bride's sauce."

Take two pounds of appie apples, grate them, including the peel, as we said of quince, and squeeze the juice onto a cloth sieve or press; take the juice and cook it as I said of quince, with the usual spices; it will be a tasty sauce, which you can use as you please.

To make another condiment with sour grapes, made another way, called the peasant's sauce.

Take two pounds of sour grapes and remove their seeds; cook it with a glass of verjuice, two ounces of mostacciolo crumbs, six ounces of sugar, a bit of dry crustless white bread, one ounce of a strong perfumed vinegar, half a quarter ounce of whole cinnamon, and eight cloves; once it is cooked, pass it [through a sieve], and use it cold, and soon, because it rots easily.

To make another green sauce, which common people call the servant woman's sauce.[76]

Take sufficient verjuice, with crustless bread soaked in verjuice, and add a bit of saffron, sugar, pepper, and salt; pass it [through a sieve] and set it to cook until it thickens a bit; you can use this for fried dishes, roasts, or other dishes as you wish.

---

76 Latini uses the Neapolitan term *vajassa*, which indicates originally a lowly female servant, and by his time also could indicate a vulgar, loud, uncouth woman (the latter is the main meaning of the term today). Latini attributes these nicknames to the *volgo*, or common people.

Another condiment of black grapes, which common people call the slave woman's sauce.

Take the black grapes and set them to boil in a casserole with a bit of must or water, for one hour or more, at your discretion, on a low fire; when they are cooked, squeeze them with a spoon and pass them through a cloth sieve; for each pound of juice, add six ounces of sugar, which you will have boiled in another pot with a bit of salt and whole cinnamon; serve this sauce in glass vases or majolica jars.

To make another condiment, or Moorish-style sauce.

Take half a pound of Levant raisins and grind them in the mortar with three hard egg yolks, two ounces of mostacciolo, one ounce of toasted bread, soaked in rose vinegar; you can dilute everything well with three ounces of good white wine and two of clear verjuice; pass everything through a sieve, adding four ounces of sugar, one of sour orange juice, a quarter ounce of ground cinnamon, half an ounce of cloves, pepper, and nutmeg together, grinding everything together, then pass it [through a sieve] and give it a quick boil; let it cool; you can serve this in tondini, with sugar and cinnamon on top, giving one tondino to each guest; it is quite tasty with roasts and in boiled dishes.

To make another condiment called *peverata* [i.e., pepper-based].

Take half a pound of bread crumbs or of ground toasted bread, and put it in a pot with three ounces of cooked must, a bit of lean fish broth, a bit of water, two ounces of perfumed vinegar, a quarter ounce of cinnamon, a bit of nutmeg, pepper, and cloves at your discretion; cook it, and pass it through a sieve, adding three ounces of sugar and half a glass of malmsey wine, which you will boil in a pan; once it is cooked, serve it with sugar and cinnamon, sprinkling it with perfumed water.

To make another Moorish-style condiment to cover fish.

Take a large quince, sliced, four ounces between muscatel and *schiava* [reddish, typical of northern Italy] grapes, five ounces between dried sour and sweeter cherries, three ounces of toasted bread, one glass of white Greco wine, four ounces of cooked must, half a carafe of red wine, a quarter ounce of pepper, one of cinnamon, and one of nutmeg and cloves, two ounces of mostacciolo crumbs; place everything in a pot to boil over the embers, far from the flame, closing the pot with paper and with its lid; once this is cooked, grind it in the mortar, pass it through a sieve, and add two ounces of sour orange juice; if it should not be sweet enough, add more sugar; if you need this to cover birds, you can make it more liquid than when you need it for soups.

To make another condiment with salted tuna belly.

Take sufficient salted tuna belly, cooked and desalinated; grind it in the mortar with candied lemons as needed, mostacciolo crumbs, pepper, cinnamon, and cloves; then dilute it with perfumed vinegar, and pass everything through a sieve; put it in a pot and boil it on a low fire; once it is cooked, remove it from the fire and you may use this to cover various sorts of fish.

To make another condiment with caviar.

Take sufficient caviar and dilute it with lemon or sour orange juice, adding the usual spices, mostacciolo crumbs, and candied citron, as needed; put everything in a pot on the fire and cook it for a quarter of an hour; you can serve this in tondini with sugar and cinnamon on top; it can also serve to cover various roasts or fried dishes, both fat and lean.

To make another condiment of bottarga, in Naples called targhe eggs.

Take sufficient bottarga and soak it in warm water, adding candied sweet orange peels, pepper, cinnamon, and cloves, with mostacciolo crumbs; grind everything together and dilute it with perfumed vinegar; pass it through a sieve; cook it only to a first boil; you can use this as I said above of the salted tuna belly or caviar.

A condiment with appie apples and onions.

Take half a pound of appie apples, unpeeled, and remove the cores; add two ounces of large onions, first cooked on embers, and two hard egg yolks, two ounces of crustless white bread, first soaked in red wine and perfumed vinegar; grind everything together in the mortar and pass it through a sieve, then place it in a casserole with two ounces of lemon or sour orange juice and a bit of clear verjuice and cooked must, and three ounces of sugar; should you not like the onions, you can use four cloves of cooked garlic. Cook everything on a slow fire with a bit of Greco wine; you can serve this sauce hot or cold as you wish.

To make another condiment called *agliata* [i.e., garlic-based].

Take walnuts, well cleaned and shelled, as many as needed; grind them in the mortar with one or two garlic cloves, a bit of crustless bread, soaked in water or broth, a bit of white salt and a bit of white vinegar, or the juice of two lemons; make sure the sauce is a bit thick; you can use this to cover fish, or fried cod.

To make another tasty condiment.

Take one pound of roasted almonds and grind them in the mortar with musk-flavoured mostacciolo, then dilute them in a pound of malmsey wine with a bit of sour orange juice and clear verjuice, and four ounces of broth; pass everything through a sieve, adding six ounces of sugar, half an ounce of cinnamon, a quarter ounce of pepper, and another quarter ounce of cloves and ground nutmeg; put everything in a casserole on the fire and stir it with a spoon until it gains body, making sure the condiment is both sweet and sour; once it is cooked, let it cool and serve it in tondini with sugar and cinnamon on top; you can also use it to cover birds or game or other meat, and in such cases you may make it a bit more liquid.

To make another anchovy sauce, made another way, called the little sassy one.

Take anchovies as needed, wash them with vinegar, and debone them; put them in a small pan with sour orange juice and boil them quickly, stirring them with the spoon handle so that they do not fall entirely apart; add the usual spices; pour this preparation on any sort of boiled fish.

To make another Spanish-style sauce.

Take two tomatoes and a bit of onion, and finely mince everything together with a bit of minced chili pepper and wild thyme, with salt and oil; mix everything together, and you can serve this in tondini, on both fat and lean days.

To make a sauce of any fish innards, called gara.

Take the innards of fish, that is livers, soft roe, and eggs; heat them, grind them in the mortar, pass them through a sieve, and add sour orange juice, in which you will have boiled some salted anchovies; add a bit of oil and the usual spices, and you can use this for any boiled fish. Lucullus loved to use this sauce, as did other Roman emperors, as Castor Durante mentions.[77]

Spanish-style olive sauce.

Take three ounces of sugar, two fresh chili peppers, a pinch of oregano, one of wild thyme, and one of dried fennel, four garlic cloves, four mint tips; grind everything in the mortar and then dissolve it in vinegar and oil, making sure it is sweet and sour; then pour it over two pounds of olives, first sweetened and crushed, and dress them well; you can use this, as it will be very good, also to drink; you can surround it with small lemon slices.

TREATISE XVIII: *How to make a Milan-style ciambuglione.*[78]

Aristosimus of Cyrene was the first to eat Milan-style ciambuglione; he was such a glutton that in the evening he used to water lettuce with cooked wine or honeyed water, so that it should grow faster and tastier.

To make ciambuglione.

Take four fresh egg yolks, four ounces of malmsey or another strong white wine, three ounces of clear water, two of sugar, cinnamon at your discretion, and a bit of butter, and grind everything together in a mortar, then pass it through a sieve and place it in a boiler of boiling water, with enough water to cover the mixture by three fingers, and boil it until it becomes dense; serve it hot in bowls.

---

77 *Garum* was a celebrated fish sauce used in ancient Rome.

78 This is the shortest of Latini's chapters. Both Riley and Novelli see this as a version of *zabaione* (a frothy mixture of egg yolks, sugar, and wine—the latter only when not served to children), Riley, *The Oxford Companion*, 588; Novelli, *Né pomodoro*, 158.

To make ciambuglione another way.

Take four fresh eggs, four ounces of clean pistachios, ground and diluted with this wine: four ounces of malmsey wine or muscatel, or another strong wine, and three ounces of sugar; beat everything together, as above, with a bit of cinnamon and perfumed water; half a bowl of this can keep a man without eating anything else for a day, and you could use this especially while travelling.

To make ciambuglione another way.

Take four ounces of ground pine nuts, diluted with malmsey or another strong wine, four fresh eggs, four ounces of the same wine, four ounces of sugar, and a bit of cinnamon; cook and serve it as usual.

TREATISE XIX: *In which we teach how to clarify sugar and how to cook various things in syrup.*[79]

Caligula [ruled 37–41 AD], who wasted in banquets and sumptuous dinners the whole treasury left to him by Tiberius, was the first to make all sorts of elegant things out of sugar, as is practised today in Naples, mother of all delights.

To clarify three pounds of sugar, place as much water in a pot as you judge will cover that much sugar; add two fresh egg whites, beating them with the water so that they foam; put the pot on the fire and boil it slowly, far from the flame, until sufficient foam will rise, then boil it with the foam for a quarter of an hour, and then remove the foam carefully with a spoon with holes; you can save the foam you remove, because if you have enough you can use it to make mostaccioli or other things. Make sure always to remove the foam carefully and that nothing but the sugar is in the pot. You will know that it is done when the tip of the spoon you use has a thin layer attached to it. Once it is perfectly cooked, you can use this in all your needs. I have always thought it greatly helpful to be familiar with this preparation. If you prefer not to remove the foam, you can also just drain it once it is cooked.

To cook quinces in syrup, take four of them and cook them in water; make sure that in cooking they do not fall apart, and that they remain solid; let them cool, and then clean them; grate them with the same grater you use for cheese; prepare a casserole on the fire, so that the sugar be well clarified and half-cooked; add the quince pulp, and cook it at your discretion; it will be a good quince preserve.

To cook sour cherries in syrup.

Take three pounds of ripe sour cherries, cut them, pit them, and remove their stem; squeeze them and set the juice aside; place them in the sugar, not yet much cooked; when you have thus prepared them, you can use them for pizze or in other ways as you wish.

---

79 Latini uses the verb *sciroppare* here and throughout the chapter.

To preserve quinces cooked under the embers in syrup.

Take and clean these quinces, slice them lengthwise; cook the sugar sufficiently, and add the sliced quinces; boil them for a bit, and serve them in plates or bowls, as you wish.

To cook pears in syrup.

Have the clarified or drained sugar ready, and just before it is entirely cooked, boil the pears in water, clean them well, and grate them; when you have as much as you need, place them to boil in the sugar, stirring frequently; when the sugar becomes dense, you can tell that they are done; place them in little cases or jars, and use them when you need them.

This way you can prepare other fruits in syrup too: just pay attention to the different times they need to cook.

How to make small Savoy cookies, or mostaccere, mostaccioli in the Naples style, sponge cake, and similar things, with their doses and preparation.[80]

To make small Savoy cookies, in Naples called mostaccere.

Take six fresh eggs and break them into a clean pot, add eight ounces of fine well ground sugar, and beat them for half an hour with a bunch of little wooden sticks; when you want to prepare the cookies, add four ounces of starch flour; form the cookies on the sheets and bake them in a moderate oven; they will be very good.

To make a different kind of cookie, with almond paste and starch flour.

Take a pound of ambrosine almonds, cleaned, and baked at a low fire, so they do not become red; grind them in the mortar, adding two ounces of candied citron flower, half a pound of fine sugar, and one and a half pound of starch flour; grind everything together and add four egg whites; if you like, you may add a grain of musk or ambergris; mix all these ingredients into a dough, and form and bake the cookies, in a large pan, dusting them with flour; make sure the oven is not too hot, and if it should be so, lower its heat. These cookies should be the size of a Roman *piastra* [coin].

To make panesigli with fresh butter, very good and nourishing.[81]

Take twenty-five pounds of the best flour you can find; add yeast and once it has risen take fifty eggs, two pounds of rosewater (watch that it not taste of smoke), four carafes of fresh milk, and one pound of fresh butter; the milk should be warm; make sure the dough is not too hard or dense, but suited to the purpose; mix it with warm water, mixed with milk, carefully, to make sure it gains flavour; in winter, you should make sure to cover the dough; cook this in a moderate fire, and the panesigli will be good.

---

80 This section is introduced by a heading, but has no "treatise" number, and indeed the next treatise is numbered the twentieth; it is not clear why Latini placed these preparations in the sugar section or whether the publisher simply omitted the treatise number.

81 These (the word is probably of Spanish origin) still exist in southern cuisine, usually today as sweet breads with raisins and candied citron and pumpkin.

How to make panesigli in another way.

Take eleven pounds of flour, four ounces of rosewater, four pounds of milk, two pounds of fine sugar, twenty-five eggs, six ounces of butter. Mix everything together with warm water, making sure the dough has risen and is flavoured; form the panesigli and put them in boiling water; when they float to the surface, remove them and place them immediately in cold water; then bake them in a moderate oven.

To make fifty perfect *sosamelli*.[82]

Take two pounds of white flour, three pounds of sugar, one ounce of cinnamon, a bit of ground pepper at your discretion, three fresh egg yolks, two egg whites, a bit of rosewater and salt; make a dough, a bit hard, and knead it well; form the sosamelli; you may add a bit of musk if you wish; then place them in a pan, in the oven, moderately hot.

Dough for Roman-style struffoli [here spelled strufoli].

Take fine flour and mix it with eggs, sugar, and water; make the little struffoli and fry them in oil or butter; then fry them again in melted honey, and serve them with sugar on top; with these little struffoli you can make various nice preparations, such as [shaping them as] grape bunches, little tarts, or loaves, and so on, as you wish.

To make Naples-style mostaccioli.

Take three pounds of red sugar, three of fine flour, one ounce of powdered citron and cloves, a quarter ounce of pepper, one nutmeg, four ounces of minced candied citron, four of ground almonds, a quarter ounce of cinnamon; mix everything with clear water, make the mostaccioli, and cook them in the oven, not too hot; then glaze them with sugar, as you think best.[83]

TREATISE XX: *Of various types of sorbetti or iced waters.*

Marina Briancesca was the first to use the *limonea*, today called *sorbetta*, of which in this city we use a large quantity, given our habit of sugar and shaved ice.

Though I here give dosages to make a few sorbetti and iced waters, I declare that I have no intention of damaging the interests of any professionals, or of any credenzieri. I simply wish to instruct those who have no experience in this profession; I did not devote much space to this subject because here in Naples it seems that everybody is born with the instinct and talent to make sorbetti. I thus protest that this essay of mine

82 Sosamelli (or susamielli) in Naples today are Christmas cookies, with almonds and honey, quite hard, and usually S-shaped.

83 These are the spiced cookies—today popular as Christmas sweets—that Latini uses as an ingredient in many recipes throughout his two volumes; red sugar is unrefined cane sugar.

is not meant to refresh experts, but only for people of little knowledge, who happen to be in the service of prominent individuals, so that they may know how to do their job.[84]

To make twenty jars of lemon sorbetto.

You need three pounds of sugar, three and a half pounds of salt, thirteen pounds of shaved ice, three large lemons; if they are small, gauge the quantity by your own judgement, especially in summer.

To make another twenty-five jars, in a season not too hot.

Take twenty-two pounds of shaved ice, four pounds of salt, and four pounds of sugar.

To make twenty-four jars of strawberry sorbetto, you will need five pounds of strawberries, three of sugar, four of salt, and six rotoli of shaved ice.

To make twenty-four jars of chocolate you will need two pounds of chocolate, two pounds of sugar, and salt and shaved ice as above; if you want to shape it into tablets, you will need more shaved ice and salt, i.e. twelve rotoli of shaved ice and six pounds of salt.[85]

To make twenty-five jars of sour cherry sorbetto, you will need four pounds of sour cherries, four of sugar, four of salt, and twenty-two pounds of shaved ice.

To make twenty-five jars of various candied things, shaped like a pyramid, you will need two pounds of candied things, sixteen rotoli, that is forty-eight pounds, of shaved ice, ten pounds of salt, and six of sugar.

To make ten jars of foamy chocolate, you will need two pounds of chocolate, two pounds of sugar, twelve pounds of shaved ice, and three pounds of salt; mix it all well, so that it foams up, and serve it iced.

To make ten jars of cinnamon water, you will need one and a half ounce of cinnamon, four pounds of sugar, one pound of shelled pine nuts, twelve pounds of shaved ice, and three of salt.

To make another sorbetto with cooked milk, you will need one and a half carafe of milk, half a carafe of water, three pounds of sugar, six ounces of ground candied citron or pumpkin; for the salt and shaved ice, manage as above.

To make half a *barile* [about twenty-two litres] of raisin water, as it is called here in Naples.

Take sixteen pounds of raisins and cut them carefully, then place them in a half barrel; prepare a pot of hot water and when it boils well pour it in the barrel and close it well; roll it around and upside down, so that the raisins mix; leave the barrel near the fire for one day and one night; then place it in a northern exposure, in a spot that does not get direct sun, and after eight or ten days, depending on how cold it is, one can start drinking it, because it will have reached its tartness. This water heals the chest and the heart;

---

84 Nowhere else did Latini exhibit such concern for professional rivalries; here he was clearly entering the credenziero's domain; "to refresh experts" is my attempt to render Latini's awkward pun (*per sorbettar i periti*).

85 Latini uses the word chocolate (*cioccolata*) for both the starting ingredient and the final product.

one can drink it freely, without fearing harm; it is better to make it in winter, for the cold season.[86]

To make lemon water.

Take lemons as needed, squeeze them, take the juice, and mix it with sugar, as much as you need depending on how many jars you wish to have.

To make another strawberry water.

Take ripe strawberries, picked at least one day before; put them in water and squeeze them with your well washed hands or with a spoon, as you prefer; if the water does not gain much colour, you can add a bit of spice; drain this water through a sock or cloth, after it has rested for a while, so that it gain the smell of the strawberries; add sugar as needed, ice it, and use it as you wish.

To make another sour cherry sorbetto.

Take the sour cherries, halve them and put them in the water with their pits too; add sugar as needed, and mix them well with a spoon; then you can drain the water, ice it, and use it as you wish; if you want to make this when the cherries are out of season, you can use dried ones: first boil them, and grind the pits, and put everything in the water, to give it flavour.

To make a syrup with distilled wine, easily.[87]

Take three pounds of sugar and clarify it, and cook it until it is a perfect syrup; take five and a half pounds of distilled wine and put it in a pot or basin; when the syrup is ready, well cleaned and the foam removed, put it, as hot as it is, in the pot with the wine, and stir it with a spoon; then place this in a pitcher, and close it well; let it rest for several days; if you wish to give it a cinnamon flavour, you should add bits of crushed cinnamon to the boiling syrup, and let it stay in the wine for twenty-four hours; then drain this, and you could give it a hint of musk or ambergris or anything else you wish; but make sure to grind the musk with a bit of fine sugar.

To make a distilled wine that will be very useful to all.

Take six pounds of strong distilled wine in a flask or pot of thick glass, and add to it four ounces of well ground cinnamon and two pounds of well ground sugar; close the flask well with its cork and parchment paper; if it is the time of the August heat you will clean it carefully and place it in a basin, so that it should not break. You can give this to those who suffer from stomach ache, colic, and other bodily pains, and for those who suffer

---

86 The raisins are from *orace* grapes, a variety I have not identified.

87 The distilled wine is *acqua vita*, as also in the recipe below (elsewhere Latini wrote acquavita); Latini calls the syrup a *gileppe* (today the word would be *giulebbe*), which is julep or syrup. The pitcher is a *lancella*, a vase with a narrow beak and a wide body.

from indigestion; I received this recipe from a cleric who had seen it prepared at the imperial court; in small quantity it also helps with headaches.

To make three carafes of hippocras, in the style of the court at Madrid.

Take two scruples of cloves, three drams of grana paradisi, one ounce of cinnamon, three scruples of nutmeg, three drams of mace, one dram of ginger, eight ounces of fine sugar, three carafes of sweet wine, and add all these to red wine in a pot or bowl; beat the mixture well with a wooden stick, and let it rest for a quarter hour; pass it through a sock or cloth sieve and pour it into flasks; this is beneficial for those with cold and weak stomachs, and is usually taken in cold seasons. It was invented by Godfrey of Monteleone, as we read in a Greek book.[88]

Here follow some perfumed waters and vinegars, of which, though I discussed them in the first volume, I thought it good to add here too a few examples, so that, if a reader should desire to know only about lean preparations, he could find in this volume everything I have been able to do to please him. Girolamo, a physician from Rhodes, discovered perfumed waters and vinegars.

First perfumed water.

Take a glass carafe, with inside one pound and six ounces of good rosewater, a quarter ounce of storax, half a quarter ounce of benzoin, one quarter ounce of aloe wood, two drams of yellow sandalwood, and two drams of cinnamon; grind everything together, and once it is all ground put it in the carafe to boil on a low fire; when it boils, add two grains of civet, two of musk, and two of ambergris; boil this so that it reduces by three fingers; then remove it from the fire, and keep it well lidded, lest it evaporate; place it in the sun for six days, then drain it and keep it in a vase, to use as you need it.[89]

To make another perfumed water.

Take two pounds of good rosewater, two pounds of sour orange flower water, and two pounds of Tripoli water, a quarter ounce of Venetian benzoin, two drams of storax, two drams of aloe wood; grind everything together and put it in a white thin cloth; fold this into the size of a button, tied with a fairly long string; hang this inside the carafe [where the waters are]; you may add four grains of musk or another fragrance at your discretion.

---

88 Hippocras was a very old preparation, popular in medieval courtly culture. The dram and the scruple still exist as apothecary measures; grana paradisi (also known as Guinea grains or pepper) was a spice hardly ever used by Latini's time.

89 In these preparations Latini again deploys all the exotic arsenal of earlier medical and culinary art; I am rendering as yellow sandalwood Latini's *sannoli citrini*, where sannoli seems to be a Neapolitanized version of *sandali*, and citrini (I think) refers to citrus colouring—"sandali citrini" appears in several sixteenth- and seventeenth-century pharmaceutical texts as an ingredient in various curative waters.

To make angels' water.

Take two pounds of rosewater, one pound of sour orange flower water, one of myrtle water, six ounces of gilded clover, six ounces of laudanum water, one eighth of an ounce of mace, one of cloves, one of aloe wood, one of cinnamon, and half a dram of spikenard; grind all these things together and put them in a glass flask with the above-mentioned waters; close the flask carefully with cork or paste or parchment, so that it not evaporate, and set it to boil on a low fire; after it has boiled for a while, set it to cool, and drain the water in a basin through a sock or cloth sieve; then transfer it to a carafe, adding half a glass of malmsey or another strong white wine, with four grains of musk and four of ambergris; close the carafe well and place it in the sun for eight days; serve it as you wish.[90]

To make a rose vinegar.

Take good vinegar and pour it in a flask, filling it up to more than half; clean the roses and add them to the flask, filling it with more vinegar and roses; place it in the sun for two days, then change the roses, and let it stay in the sun another two or three days; once it has gained the fragrance, you can use it as you wish.

To make another vinegar with elder tree flowers.

Take vinegar as above, and the white flowers of ripe elder trees; wrap the flowers in a cloth and place it in the flask, which should be more than half-filled with vinegar; close it well and put it in the sun for three days; then drain the vinegar, and add fresh flowers three times; the last time, leave it in the sun for fifteen days; drain it again, and add a handful of flowers that you will have picked three or four days before; this vinegar, well kept, will taste like muscatel, and will be beneficial to headaches, if you use it to smear the nostrils and temples.

To make another vinegar with cloves.

Take a flask of vinegar and add one ounce of cloves, smashed with the pestle; close the flask with cork and parchment, and put it under straw and manure for eight days; then remove it, clean it, and place it in the sun for ten days, leaving it outdoors also overnight; pass it through a loose cloth sieve and transfer it to another flask, well lidded; you can use it for whatever you need.

To make another vinegar with rosemary.

Take rosemary flowers as needed, and use them to fill a flask [containing vinegar], well closed; place it under straw and manure for eight days, then drain the vinegar and pour it in another flask with new flowers, and place it in the sun, well closed, for eight days. When you remove the flask from the straw and manure, you will find in the neck of the flask a good finger of oil, produced by those flowers; make sure to gather and keep this carefully, because it is very good and beneficial; it helps with headaches, if you smear it

---

90 I am using gilded clover for *trifoglio dorato*, a species of clover; the laudanum water sounds risky; spikenard is a rare Asian vegetable aromatic oil.

on the forehead and temples; it kills worms in small children, it heats cold stomachs, and it benefits those who cannot retain food.

To make another vinegar with sour orange flowers.

Take these flowers, picked at the right time, and put them in a flask with the vinegar, at your discretion; change the flowers four or five times, place the flask under straw and manure for five days, then drain it and pour it back into the flask; add new flowers, close it well, and place it in the sun for ten days; keep it; this vinegar can kill worms, and, if you warm it up and keep it in your mouth, it will remove the bad smell of teeth.

To make another vinegar with cinnamon.

Fill an ordinary flask with vinegar, add half an ounce of cinnamon broken into bits and crushed; close it well and place it under straw and manure for fifteen days; then drain it and put it in a new flask, adding a quarter ounce of cinnamon, making sure the cinnamon is as good as it can be; keep the flask well closed, and use it when the opportunity arises.

To make a fragrant mist, when there are guests, banquets, or feasts.

Take a quarter ounce of storax, two eighths of an ounce of Venetian benzoin, a bit of aloe wood, an eighth of an ounce of cinnamon, ten cloves, a bit of citron peel, a pinch of dried roses, and half an ounce of Levant paste; grind these things briefly in the mortar, and put them in the censer or in another vessel as you wish, with rosewater; boil it on a low fire, so that it produce more mist, and a sweeter fragrance.

To make another very pleasant fragrance.

Take ten whole cloves, or more or fewer at your discretion, a bit of benzoin, a bit of aloe wood, a little piece of whole cinnamon, a bit of sour orange peel, a bit of white sandalwood, and one nutmeg; grind these together coarsely, and put them in a pot or censer, with sour orange flower water.

To make a liquid that can be given as a gift to ladies or gentlemen, called little balsam.

Take a pound of distilled wine, cooked seven times, which in Naples is called *sflemmata*, add to it one and a half ounce of benzoin, a dram of storax, a quarter ounce of white balsam of Peru, still with its tips, half an ounce of myrrh in grains; grind everything together and put in a carafe; place this in the sun, with a basin underneath it, so that it does not break; leave it there for five days; when you remove it from the sun, it will have become reddish; pour it into another carafe, draining it of anything solid; keep it well lidded; this keeps a long time; it is a water of such strength that if one should use it to wash oneself, the fragrance will last for three days; it is the best liquid one can find; it can be used freely, without fear of any harm, it can be made at all times, and it is very useful.[91]

---

91 The acqua vita (distilled wine) called sflemmata in Naples (literally, it has had its phlegm

The Queen of Hungary's water.

Take three pounds of purified distilled wine, elsewhere called "cooked seven times," and put it in a clean pot; add half a pound of rosemary flowers, close it well, and let it stay for a day; then distill it again, and keep it in flasks; it will be very good for all sorts of aches, swellings, and bruises; it can also be kept in small carafes for its fragrance, and it is a remarkable thing, how it comforts those who suffer from headache and other aches; since it is a well known thing, I will not describe its qualities.

TREATISE XXI: *Of various garnishes for lean dishes, and fish condiments.*

1. Cauliflower, boiled and then sautéed, with lemon and pepper.
2. Sautéed asparagus, with lemon and pepper.
3. Hops in bunches, boiled and then sautéed, with sour orange juice and pepper.
4. Cardoons and cardoon stems, boiled and then sautéed.
5. Celery, as above.
6. White fennels, in bunches, first boiled and sautéed.
7. Artichokes, first boiled, then sautéed in good oil or something else.
8. Red roots of soft greens, cooked and then sliced, which can be used to garnish several dishes.
9. Stuffed cucumbers and fried parsley.
10. Soft greens, with fried fish jelly.[92]
11. Slices of salted tuna belly, first cooked and desalinated.
12. Caviar with crostini of toasted bread, and sour orange juice.
13. Sliced bottarga.
14. Low small dough boxes, filled with salted anchovies, with herbs and a bit of vinegar.
15. Genoa mushrooms, first desalinated and then fried.
16. Fish liver, eggs, and soft roe, fried.
17. Sliced lemons and sour oranges.
18. Carved pieces of citron and lemon.
19. Pears or apples in syrup, surrounded by aniseeds of various colours.
20. Sautéed onions stuffed with various fish-based mixtures.
21. Stuffed turnips, so that their tips stay green.

---

removed, so purified, clarified) is described as *di sette cotte*, which I take to mean that it has been cooked seven times.

92 Latini says *colla fritta* (literally, fried glue), but I presume he means *colla di pesce*, or fish jelly; this recurs a bit further below.

22. Apples or pears, stuffed, surrounded by a band of dough baked in the oven.

23. Artichokes stuffed with various fish-based mixtures.

24. Stuffed truffles, and thin slices of truffles in a small box.

25. Genoese-style small pastries, with candied things and sour cherries, fried.

26. Small pastries filled with various things in syrup.

27. Small pies filled with things in syrup, with sugar on top.

28. Small pies of ground fish, with the usual ingredients.

29. Small boxes of dough, with various sauces and condiments inside.

30. Little tarts filled with green and white sauce.

31. Bread slices, first soaked, then sautéed.

32. Little sticks of candied citron.

33. Small mostaccioli made with marzipan paste.

34. Sliced sponge cake, fried, or prepared another way, and dredged in ambivera.

35. Fried soft crabs, first well washed.

36. Sliced boiled lobster.

37. Shrimp tails in a dough box.

38. Oysters in their shells, cooked with oil, pepper, and sour orange juice.

39. Various seafood, snails made with marzipan paste, with oysters inside.

40. Mushrooms made of marzipan paste, with their stems, cooked with foamy chocolate, so that they should appear as natural as possible.

41. Sliced apple, with the usual fried fish jelly, with sugar on top.

42. Sliced jelly of various colours.

43. Sliced blancmange.

44. Various fried beignets.

45. Dough balls made with yeast, in the shape of onions, fried.

46. Various fritters.

47. Fried eggs, one by one, with pepper on top.

48. Eggs poached in milk.

49. Florentine-style little frittate, thin and rolled.

50. Tagliolini made with frittate.[93]

51. Hard egg yolks, mixed with whites.

52. Egg yolks dredged in ambivera.

53. Faldicchere eggs, and strained eggs.

---

93 Latini writes *tagliolini di frittatini*, which I take to mean the shape of tagliolini (strips) made with frittate (which in his text are usually thin and unrolled, not like modern omelets).

54. Large wafers stuffed with things in syrup.

55. Sliced soppressata made with marzipan paste.

56. Sausages made of marzipan paste, as above.

57. Fresh fava beans, made with marzipan paste.

58. Almonds made of the same paste.

59. Sour cherries in syrup, in little dough boxes.

60. A condiment made with white almonds, in little dough boxes.

61. Mostacciolo sauce, in a small box.

62. Barbary dates and bits of candied citron, in a small box, with other ingredients.

63. Crostini of toasted bread with butter.

64. Small masks made with blancmange.[94]

65. Slices of bread, fried, with butter.

66. Bits of citron, confected.

67. Small white comfits, of various colours.[95]

68. Various candied things, as you wish.

69. Bits of candied quince, in the shape of a star or lily, as you wish.

70. Damaschine plums in dough boxes.

71. Little mounds of jelly, and small maccheroni made of butter.

72. Pastries made with dried bread, fried.

73. Slices of bread, heated on the fire, with oil, sour orange juice, and pepper.

74. Bread sliced in strips and fried.[96]

75. Diced bread, first soaked, then fried in butter.

76. Bread crumbs with sugar and cinnamon, which is used to decorate the sides of plates.

77. Olives, capers, and fruits in vinegar.

78. Cauliflower stems, stewed, and fried cauliflowers.

79. Fritters made with red carrots, fried together with dough.

80. Tagliolini with fried blancmange.

81. Little buns of dough and fried pears.[97]

---

94 The text here has mascaroncini (small masks), though it could be a typographical error for maccaroncini (which appear in item 71).

95 I am not sure how these are both white and of various colours, unless the base is white, with colourful decorations.

96 Here the bread is sliced "as one does lardoons," which I assume means in strips (as would be used in larding).

97 The buns are *rosette*, which today are bread buns; the term literally means small roses, so they might have originally been shaped like roses.

82. Stars, eagles, lions, and flower blossoms made with fried dough.

83. Little buns of dough filled with various things in syrup.

84. Little tarts filled with egg-based soup [ginestrata], and small pies with oysters.

84 [# 84 appears twice]. Halved broccoli, boiled, with green sauce on top.

85. Fritters of naked fish [whitebait].

86. Pike flesh, in jelly.

87. Crostini with appie apples, ground, with muscatel grapes, pine nuts, and sugar.

88. Fritters of German dough.

79 [typo for 89]. An eagle with egg-based soup [ginestrata].

90. Small pies with cauliflower stems, French-style.

91. A pumpkin dish, Spanish-style.[98]

92. Small pies with dates, muscatel grapes, pine nuts, and appie apples in syrup.

93. Marinated shrimp tails.

94. Little tarts with pine nuts, pistachios, and powdered sugar.

95. Bugloss and borage flowers.

96. Little tarts with sour grapes in syrup.

97. Crostini of toasted bread with caviar.

98. Crostini of bread with salted anchovies.

99. Crostini of bread with crustless bread soaked in vinegar, and various herbs.[99]

100. Bits of roasted eel [capitone].

101. Bits of roasted eel, with crustless bread.

TREATISE XXII: *Of some cold display dishes, useful for any occasion.*[100]

1. Strained eggs in a royal plate, placed over six slices of sponge cake arranged in the shape of a star; in the middle a candied large apple [pomo d'Adamo] or a bunch of sugar flowers, surrounded by a decorative border of sugar retouched in gold; in the middle of the apple a little tree which holds the coat of arms of the bride and groom, or of the guests, depending on the banquet's purpose.

---

98 Latini calls this a *carabazzata*, which comes from the Spanish word for pumpkin.

99 This is *cappone di galera* (literally, galley capon), an old dish of crustless bread soaked in vinegar, and accompanied by various fish or seafood, popular especially in Rome.

100 Rifreddi, as mentioned before, were decorative dishes prepared in advance for display and as appetizers as guests arrived and the banquet began. Latini follows them with thirty tondini, or side dishes served in small round plates.

2. Sea bass pies, shaped like the fish, retouched in gold and silver; you can make pies with other fish the same way.

3. Marinated soles, with flowers around them, and other elegant decorations, at your discretion.

4. Large grilled sea bass, with a condiment of pitted olives, capers, raisins, pine nuts, thin slices of candied citron, cloves, cinnamon, and sugar, diluted with strong vinegar; served with a lid made of dough, encrusted with white aniseeds.

5. A pillow glazed with sugar, with a decoration like marzipan, each of the corners decorated with a statuette made of marzipan paste, each of which should hold a coat of arms, as the circumstances require.[101]

6. Jelly shaped like little amber-coloured mounds, encrusted with pine nut cores, around them buns made with sugar paste filled with marzipan paste and retouched in gold, surrounded by decorative borders made of cinnamon-flavoured sugar retouched in silver.

7. Blancmange in half-relief, with the sides of the plate decorated with little stars made of jelly, mixed with statuettes made with Genoa dough.

8. Grilled dentex, with on top a condiment made with pine nuts, capers, sliced dates, and raisins, diluted as usual; garnish the sides of the plate with citron leaves and sliced lemons.

9. A royal plate of strawberries, soaked in strong wine, with sugar and shaved ice on top.

10. Tarts with peaches and the usual ingredients, covered with thin slices of candied citron, sugar, and cinnamon.

11. Cannelloni, pistachios, pine nuts, almonds, and small oranges, all confected, with corianders both smooth and rough, in a royal plate.[102]

12. A royal salad with its [decorative] crowns, and apt ingredients, and shaved ice underneath.

13. Pastry twists filled with moscarelle pears, thin slices of candied things, and other noble things.

14. Large pastries filled with peaches in syrup and marzipan paste, served in a royal plate, with decorative borders of sugar retouched in gold.

15. A large rose made with flaky pastry, filled with provatura, sour grapes, sugar, and cinnamon, first dredged in ambivera.

16. Pappardelle [fritters] made by nuns, served with a lid of sugar in lattice pattern, retouched in gold, placed over turtles made of marzipan paste, retouched in gold and silver.

---

101 I suspect the pillow is made of some edible material, but Latini does not specify this.

102 *Cannelloni confetti* appear in several gastronomical books also before Latini's (clearly, they are not the modern baked pasta dish); the word resembles the word for cinnamon (*cannella*), so it might indicate large sticks of cinnamon.

17. White tarts made with blancmange and cream tops, glazed with sugar, served with a cover also of sugar, placed over eaglets made with Genoa dough, outlined in gold and silver.

18. Small pies with quinces, cooked first under the embers and then in syrup, served in a plate with a crown of marzipan paste retouched in gold, the pies covered with a cover of silvered sugar, encrusted with white aniseeds.

19. A royal plate of candied pumpkin, citron, pears, and peaches, with Siena-style little marzipan buns.

20. An imperial plate with boiled milk, cream tops, and egg whites, all well beaten together, sponge cake crumbs, sugar, thin slices of candied citron and pumpkin, and whole pistachios, everything boiled together; when it has become dense, let it cool, and place it over slices of sponge cake, forming little mounds, surrounded by hard egg yolks, dredged in ambivera, and riddled with green pistachios; place it then in the oven, surrounded by an imperial crown made with sugar, at the top.

21. Columns made of jelly, with live small birds and fish inside them, and capitals on top; under the base and above each column a small statue made of sugar, holding the coats of arms of the guests.

22. A pyramid made of ice, with apricots and lazzarole in syrup.

Here follow a few tondini, to be placed in front of the table settings, as part of the first and last credenza service.

1. Sliced melons with shaved ice, one [tondino] for each guest.

2. Butter or whipped butter with sugar on top, one for each guest.

3. Brogiotti figs, one tondino for each guest.[103]

4. A soup of sour cherries in syrup, one for each guest.

5. Cooked salads with flowers around, one for each guest.

6. Cooked salads with flowers, served in the same way.

7. Asparagus with oil, vinegar, pepper, and salt, one plate for each guest.

8. Strawberries with sugar and shaved ice, served as above.

9. Sour cherries and other cherries, with shaved ice, one tondino for each guest.

10. Little covered tarts with sour cherries in syrup, one for each guest, with mostacciolo crumbs.

11. Artichokes sautéed with garlic and parsley, and fried, one for each guest.[104]

---

103 Latini specifies this (fairly common) variety of fig; in some of these entries, he simply writes "one for each guest," clearly implying a tondino per guest.

104 Here and in item 13 Latini uses the form *tartufolati*, which presumably means cooked like truffles; I think this is the same term as what is today called *trifolare* (sautéing quickly with garlic, oil, and fresh parsley).

12. Cream tops over slices of sponge cake, with sugar on top, glazed with shaved ice, served as above.

13. Truffles sautéed with garlic and parsley, over slices of toasted bread, one for each guest.

14. Peaches in wine with lemon peels glazed with shaved ice, served as usual.

15. Glazed milk with honey, one for each guest.[105]

16. *Cartocetti* served on napkins, one for each guest.[106]

17. Small pies with peaches in syrup, carved on top, one for each guest.

18. Fresh halved almonds, one tondino for each guest.

19. Royal little salads, made with all that is needed, one for each guest.

20. Fresh cardoons served on napkins, one per guest.

21. St. George's mushrooms, dressed as usual, one tondino for each guest.

22. Shrimp with vinegar, salt, and pepper; this will be better served in porcelain, one tondino for each guest.

23. Small pies with oysters and Florentine pears, served the same way.

24. Small ring-shaped biscuits [ciambellette] and Portugal candied quince, served over napkins, one for each guest.

25. Salted tuna belly, well dressed, served with lemon slices, in the usual way.

26. Fish eggs [targhe], sliced, served with the usual ingredients, and flowers, one tondino for each guest.

27. Dried tuna salami [muscimano] mixed with salted anchovies, well cleaned and halved, one for each guest.

28. Caviar adorned with slices of large sausages, and garnished with sour orange juice, served as usual.[107]

29. Sliced sturgeon, garnished with Spanish olives, one for each guest.

30. Blancmange in a cinnamon colour, shaped in various forms in bas-relief, garnished with various little flowers around it, served as usual.

TREATISE XXIII: *Of various wines, and their discoverers.*

The Scriptural verse "Wine cheers the heart of man" [Psalms 103:15] is most true. Wine gladdens our heart, comforts our spirit, strengthens our temper, awakens our mind,

---

105 This is *lattimele*, which today is sometimes used to mean whipped cream, but which in Latini's time probably referred to a mixture of milk beaten with honey.

106 I do not know what this refers to; today, a *cartoccio* is a paper cone holding food or used to cook it.

107 I presume these sausages are either purely decorative, or made with a "lean" material.

sharpens our ingenuity, excites our enthusiasm, grants the Muses their metres, and renders our intellect fit for good studies. It is true, however, that its enjoyment must be moderate: moderation and frugality of life, in the temperate use of earthly things, are like a sacred tribute, a divine right and due, that God, the highest father, in entrusting man with the great vineyard that is the world, has reserved for Himself in its fruits, almost like a homage to, and acknowledgement of, His divinity. Those who live but to eat and drink are unworthy of life; parsimony in feeding ourselves is our lesson not only from Christ's followers, but also from the pagan emperors, as we read that Caesar had his baker punished because he had prepared for Caesar a different sort of bread from what his servants ate, that Augustus never asked for more than two dishes and one type of wine at his table, and that Hannibal was content with as much. I here hold discourse of wine not to excite to inebriation, but to suppress it, and I affirm as have many others that just as wine in moderation is a cordial and elixir of life and health, so, if drunk immoderately, it is a poison to life and virtue.

The first to cultivate vines was Canaam, son of Cam and grandson of Noah; he was the first to produce sweet grapes, and from them to draw wine; Noah his grandfather was the first to drink it, and became drunk for a while, so that his children mocked him. We read in Valerius, Aulus Gellius, and Andrea Fulgoso that the Romans punished women who drank too much wine just as if they had committed adultery, and the Roman Ignatius Metellus killed his wife by beating her with a stick, because he found her drinking wine, and nobody either reprimanded or punished him for this.[108]

Plato in the *Timaeus* holds that man and woman, when they must be together in order to procreate, must abstain from wine, and Lycurgus made a law that no child could drink wine until the age of eighteen and that no army general, governor, judge, or other governing administrator should drink wine; he prohibited wine to the young because, since they are of a hot and ardent nature, they are in danger of enflaming their soul, from which many ills could result to the body. He also said however that wine should be allowed to those who are over forty years of age, who, since they are beginning to join the society of the elderly, need wine, in that they are beginning to lose their natural warmth; [he argued] that wine should be given to women only very moderately, because it may lead them to decline much in virtue and to acquire vices.[109] Wine contributes to good nourishment, it generates good blood, it brings good colouring to the face, and it stimulates urination; it must be [drunk] in such quantity that food should not float in the stomach. Regarding its quality, it should be neither too young nor too old, pure and clear in substance, of a white or half-red colour, and of sweet smell; in tasting it, wine should not seem watery or bitter, but rather sweet, though not excessively so; thus it will be apt for everybody, of all ages, but always more for the elderly, as hold all writers about natural things.

---

108 Valerius Maximus was a first-century AD Roman historian and collector of anecdotes and Aulus Gellius a second-century AD Roman grammarian and erudite; I have not identified Andrea Fulgoso; the anecdote of Egnatius (which Latini Italianizes to Ignatius) Metellus is in Valerius Maximus.

109 Lycurgus was the legendary early Spartan law-giver, a famously stern figure.

Here follows a brief note of wines imported to Europe.

1. Crispo Fabiano brought to Lombardy various types of Vernaccia.
2. Pirro di Ponte brought the wines of Valtellina, Chiavenna, and Prioli.
3. Scipione Bruno brought the wines of Como and Trezza.
4. Filippo Posello brought Trebbiani wines.
5. Lucio Frosello brought to Lombardy the wines of Monferrato.
6. Galen brought those of Salerno and San Severino.
7. Wines were brought to the island of Corsica from Velletri and Piperna.
8. The wine of the Cesena area came from the area near Cosenza.
9. The emperor Julius Caesar very much enjoyed wines from Friuli.
10. Tito da Tiano discovered the wines of Vicenza.
11. Pliny described the Bersamini wines.
12. It is believed that a courtier of the King of France brought the wines of Orléans to Languedoc.
13. A merchant who did business there brought Hungarian wines.
14. A certain Bassiano of Macedon brought the malmsey wines that are harvested in the territory of Ragusa.
15. Papinio Lucessano of Scio, one of the islands of the [Greek] archipelago, brought the Greco wine that is harvested on the slopes of Mount Vesuvius.
16. Sempronio Megillo from Canea, a place on the island of Crete, brought the wines of Mirandola.
17. Pompeo Ponzio brought the vines that make the Lucca wines.
18. Eolo Filo, a noble knight, brought vines from Ephesus and transplanted them in the Maremma near Siena, where today exquisite wines are harvested.[110]

List of the most praised wines that are drunk in Italy.

1. Lachryma of Naples, also called of Galitte or of Torre del Greco, is vermilion and ruddy.
2. Greco of Naples, of a white golden colour.
3. Vernotico of Nola, white colour but not too golden.
4. Gragnano wine, red colour.
5. Moscatello of Trani, white colour.
6. Moscatello of Amalfi, white golden colour.
7. Albano of Rome, white golden colour.
8. Malvasia [malmsey] of Candia, white colour.

---

110 I presume Latini pilfered this information from a prior source; I have adjusted some of his spellings, but otherwise made no attempt to verify any of it.

9. Gensano of Rome, white colour.

10. Strong Spanish wine, white or vermilion in colour.

11. Wine from the Borghese villas in Rome, white golden colour.

12. Wine of Rosina, a delightful place near Frascati belonging to the noble Falconieri, white colour.

13. Pisciarello of Bracciano, white colour.

14. Moscatello of Perugia, clear colour.

15. Verdea of Florence, white colour, leaning to light green.

16. Another Verdea, of Narcetti and Scandicci, white colour.

17. Piccianco of Florence, red colour.

18. Moscatello of Montalcino, clear colour.

19. Montepulciano wine, white and red colour.

20. Orvieto and Raspea wine, colour as above.

21. Montefiascone wine, colour as above.

22. Wine from Languedoc in France, red colour.

23. Wine called Claret of Avignon, reddish colour.

24. Pistoia wine, white and red colour.

25. Trebbiano of Brescia, white and clear colour.

26. Trebbiano of Modena, white colour.

27. Wine called Balsamino of Macerata, red colour.

28. Florence wine, white and red colour.

29. Moscato of Castello, white colour.

30. Claret of Castello, red colour.

31. Carmignano wine, red and white colour.

32. Artimino and Valdarno wine, white and red colour.

32 [# 32 is repeated]. Florence Chianti, white and red colour.

I thought it good to mention these wines, which are commonly drunk in Italy, because often the conversation touches upon wines, and it is good for the steward, or others, to be able to offer a few comments on them and answer questions that might be posed. All these wines are easy to digest and good to drink during meals, and can be freely drunk by men and women, with little water, because they do not give a headache, as long as one drinks them moderately, and not to satiety.

A rule for drinking without harm.

The Lachryma of Naples, which is counted among the stronger wines, must be watered with our good Formale water, or with other infusions, according to the disposition of our own bodies, that is to say, with infusion of mastic, anise, or other, which all will be apt.[111] When a wine is strong, one must add water an hour before drinking it, and when a wine is weak and watery, one should drink it without water, because wine that is over-watered moistens the stomach, generates windiness in the intestine, and more easily makes one drunk, because wateriness makes it more penetrating. Therefore those who have weak stomachs should not drink wine after lunch, until they have finished digesting the food, because at that point wine will contribute to nourishment.

Cold wine kept with shaved ice is beneficial to many and harmful to many. Many of those who suffer from colic, retention of urine, and other stomach ailments will have to deny themselves the delights of iced wine. I have however seen that many, with a good draught of cold iced water, have rid themselves of the most acute fevers; once, while I was serving the Lord Duke of Altemps in Soriano, one of his fiefdoms, fifty miles away from Rome, with about five or six thousand inhabitants, at a time when a grave and dangerous illness was running around, in July and August, the physician of that town told the Lord Duke that the illness could be cured by taking iced drinks. The Lord Duke held a quantity of ice, which had been gathered for his own convenience, so he issued an edict that all should go collect it for free, both the rich and the poor; and thus, in a few days, the illness and deaths ended. It will therefore be good for everybody to act according to their complexion and age, as it is most true that the ancient Greeks drank warm wine in many infirmities, and from that drink drew health. I also advise that nobody should drink wine on an empty stomach, because this can bring many ills and greatly harm the brain and the nerves.

Which grapes make a strong wine, or a middling one, or a light one, and of the nature of young and old wine.

Black grapes produce a strong wine, white grapes a middling one, and well ripened yellow grapes a light one; young wine is most cold, and old wine is most strong, and purified of any bad thing that may have been in it.

To make strong wine.

You must harvest grapes when they are well ripened; press them, and then ferment them in a vat for four days; on the fifth day place the wine in barrels. Do not ferment this for any longer, because otherwise it becomes heavy and loses flavour, it easily turns into vinegar, and becomes black like ink. One should especially watch out for over-fermenting, because such wines cloud the intellect, tie the limbs, drown the liver, remove the appetite, and impede digestion. Wine that ferments for a short time retains very beautiful colour and very good taste, and the French regard this as the best wine. To strengthen it, you can take mistletoe roots, saw them, and add the sawdust to the wine; this can only be drunk when much water is added.[112]

---

111 Formale water came to Naples through streams (many of them underground) from the slopes of Vesuvius.

112 Latini says "boiling" throughout this section, but I assume he is referring to fermentation.

To make an agreeable wine.

Ferment the wine in the vat for eight days, then place it in barrels, with one fourth as much water; it will be most agreeable.

To make a sweet or piquant wine.

Take wine from well ripened grapes, ferment it in the vat for four or five days together with dry oregano and then place it in the barrel, and it will be most sweet; or, place the grapes in the sun for two days, then press them in the vat and ferment them as above; and if you want the wine to be piquant, pour it for eight days from one pot to another and then preserve it, and you will find it sweet and piquant.

To make a wine for servants.

If you want to make this sort of wine, take twenty barili of must and place it in the vat, add ten barili of water; then remove the first twenty and add another ten barili of water, then remove ten barili and add five more barili of water, and that's it: this should be drunk soon, because it does not last long.[113]

To make a similar wine.

Take the best grapes you can find; remove the seeds and fill the wooden pots; then pour over them one barile of good old wine for each four pots, and then fill them with boiling water; when it stops boiling, close the pots carefully, so that the wine be strong; when you think it has cooled off, you may start using the wine; if you need more, you can always add water, and this will keep for seven or eight months.[114]

To make another wine, if needed.

Take fifty pounds of raisins and boil them in a boiler with water and a quarter barile of strong vinegar. After this has boiled for a good time, let it rest for twenty-four hours, and then place it in a vessel that holds ten barili, filling the vessel with boiling water, and closing it tightly. Leave the pot like this for seven or eight days. This will be a perfect wine, tasty and good for the stomach; this is a most rare secret, and can be used during a siege; this wine lasts a long time if it is done by these rules.

To make another sort of wine.[115]

Put in a vat two or three barili of water, and add as many pressed grapes as you deem fit, and must; ferment it for a day or so, and remove two or three barili, and add three or

---

113 This last example is wine *per famiglie* (which in this context means for servants), and Latini's syntax is confusing, but it seems to be a highly watered down must (the juice of ripe grapes), likely of very low quality. In the prior example Latini writes *piccante*, which today means spicy (below he also uses a synonym, *razzente*); he also uses the Naples dialect word for oregano.

114 The pots are *carrarelli*, which today refers to medium-sized wooden barrels used primarily for wine.

115 Latini says that this is done like *evaludia*, a term I have not been able to identify.

four other barili of water, and leave it to ferment for five or six days; remove it and pour it in the barrels, and it will be a perfect wine.

To make another sort of wine.

Fill a well arranged barrel with grapes, and add a barile of old wine; fill the barrel with boiling water, and close it well on all sides; leave it like this for thirty days; then add cinnamon, and drink at your pleasure; if you wish to add water to this, it will still be good for servants.

To make wine as in Mirandola and nearby places.

Put well pressed grapes in a vat, which can hold up to twelve or fifteen barili; add three barili of water to each vat; after it has fermented for nine days, move the wine to barrels; it will be an exquisite wine; if you wish it to be sweeter, let it ferment only five or six days; the longer it ferments, the drier it will be, and the less time it ferments, the sweeter it will be; follow these guidelines.

To make wine with grapes, called where this is practised a seed wine.

Take the best grapes available at the farm, and take out the seeds; place it in a standing barrel, and fill the barrel with must taken from other grapes; make sure to leave at least one palmo of wood free in the barrel; ferment this for thirty days, and remember to place a weight on top of the barrel, so that in fermenting the wine not overflow the barrel.[116]

To make another sort of wine.

Pick the grapes and place them in the sun for three or four days; then press them, adding also some wild grapes, maybe one hundred pounds to a barrel; it will be a most perfect wine.[117]

To make drained wine as they do in Rome.

Press grapes in a vat, then ferment it for just twenty-four hours; then move it to another vat or half-barrel; prepare colanders the size and shape of the hood of a Capuchin friar, made with rough netting; make sure that when there are a lot of dregs in the colander you should wash it in cold water; pour the must through the colanders, and at first it will go through easily, but then the dregs will stop it; drain it bit by bit, into basins or pots placed on a ladder, or whichever way you wish; eventually it will be clear, with a golden colour; place the wine in barrels, and keep it in a cool place; these wines can easily over-ferment, and they spoil easily, and therefore it will be good, as soon as it is done, to add it to a dry wine, which will become sweet; the discoverer of this wine was Cosimo of Mirandola.

---

116 The must is taken from *uva capata*; I am not sure what this refers to; the name of the preparation is *vino di grana* which in this context I believe refers to the seeds (taking out the seeds is *sgranare*).

117 The wild grapes are *ciambrusco*, a term used particularly in the Rome area.

To keep a wine piquant, so that it not change.

If you wish to make sure wine stays piquant, make sure, when you pour it from one to another pot, to stir it first with a piece of wood, without touching the bottom of the pot; thus, the wine will be turbid in the pot, but in three or four days it will become clear again, and it will always stay piquant.

To turn white wine into red, and red wine into white.

To turn red wine into white, add to it the serum that is left over from making ricotta, or the ashes of burned white vines; for the reverse, to turn white wine into red, place in it ashes of red vines, and you shall see the effect. Ground artemisia added to wine prevents it from turning into vinegar, and confers good colour and taste.[118]

To make turbid wine clear.

Ground fennel added to turbid wine makes it clear. Similarly, gypsum powder, added to wine, makes any turbidity move to the bottom. If you add two pounds of honey to a barrel of wine, it will make the wine clear within four days.[119]

To find out whether there is water in the wine.

If you wish to know if there is water in wine, take a wild apple or pear and put it in the wine; if it floats the wine is pure, if it sinks there is water. Wet a cane in oil and place it in the wine: if there is water you will see water droplets sticking to the cane, if there is no water the cane will remain as it was. If you wish to separate the water, place liquid alum in the wine pot and then with a sponge soaked in oil block the opening and let the pot lean down a bit; the water will exit from that opening.

To give wine a nice smell.

Take a sour orange or a citron and stuff it well with whole cloves; place it in the wine pot, but so that it not touch the wine; carefully close the opening of the pot. This will preserve the wine with a very good smell. You can also rub the rim of the barrel with pine or cypress fronds, and the result will be the same. And to avoid bad smells you can place a crown of oregano around the opening of the pot, and this will preserve the wine without risk.

To give wine a muscatel smell.

Gather the flowers of wild vines, that is the vines that grow in woods, also called *Paina*; dry them in the shade; when you wish to give a smell to the wine, take these dried flowers and put them in the pot with the wine, as many flowers as you wish; this will give it an admirable fragrance; if you wish to do this with must, take these flowers and ferment them in a vat with the must. You can do the same with the herb called San Giovanni [St.

---

118 Artemisia is the name of a group of shrubs and herbs which includes wormwood and mugwort.

119 The two pounds are of *mele*, which means apples, but I think here Latini means honey (*miele*, but occasionally spelled without the "i").

John's wort], or *Sclarea*: gather a bunch of it, use it to block the opening of the barrel, and you will certainly find the wine with a good smell; you can also tie this into a small bunch and lower it in the barrel with a string; then block the opening, and you will find the wine as above.

To find out if wine will keep.

Drill a hole in the middle of the barrel and take a bit of wine; boil it for a bit, then let it cool, and taste it; as you find it this time, so it will stay. Or, you can check if the flowers of the wine are red or not; if red, the wine will keep, if yellow or black, it is a bad sign, and if white, it is a sign that the wine is too strong.[120]

When one should rack wines.

Wines produced in rich, humid soil must be racked in November when the moon is new; those produced in dry soil must be racked in March when the moon is new; if one racks them when the moon is growing, they will certainly turn into vinegar; the same times are good to fix wines.

How to keep wine from turning into vinegar.

If you add to the wine ashes of white vine or of pumpkin you will keep it from turning into vinegar; or take a bit of roasted cured back fat, wrapped in cloth, and place it in the wine about halfway down into the pot, and this too will prevent the wine from turning into vinegar; or you can place olive oil in the wine pot, just enough to cover the surface of the wine, and this too has the same effect. These are all proven remedies.

To protect wine from thunder and lightning.

Cover the opening of the pot with an iron lid and laurel branches, and this indubitably protects it from thunder and lightning.

To prevent wine from spoiling.

Take, at your discretion, as much burned salt as needed for the size of the wine pot and throw it into the pot, and this will keep it for a long time; or grind sweet almonds and place them in the wine, and they preserve it; you can have the same effect with raisins, first removing the seeds. Milk and honey mixed together also help keep wine, as above. Black chickpeas, half-roasted and ground and placed in the wine, achieve the same result, and they also provoke urination. Similarly a pound of purified distilled wine placed in a barrel of wine achieves the same result, and these are all proven remedies.

---

120 *Fioretta* (little flower) is a disease of wines (affecting especially young, not very strong wines), called mycoderma in English, and I presume Latini is here referring to this problem; Latini writes that the white flowers are a sign of "hardness," which I take to refer to excessive strength.

To fix wine so that it will not spoil.

For each barrel of wine take four or five sour oranges and slice them in quarts; tie them to a string, with a stone attached to weigh them down, and lower them more than half-way into the barrel; close the barrel carefully, and after five or six days you will without doubt find the wine fixed and good to drink. You can also fix it this way: take spoiled wine and remove it from its pot and pour it into a clean one, add a good quantity of cherries and set it to ferment for three days, then change the pot again, using a perfumed pot, and the wine will be perfect to drink and it will keep well. Quartered radishes placed in wine also remove any bad odour from it. Medlar peels placed in wine will make any wine good, however bad it might be. Also, you can take as much fennel as will fit through the opening of the pot, tie it with string and attach a stone to it, and lower it down to one palmo above the dregs; then close the opening and leave it like this for eight days, after which remove the fennel, and it will draw out any mould and bad odour.

To protect pots from mould.

Remove the wine from barrels and pots, leaving only a bit of wine; open all the openings and the top; leave them like this, and they will not take any bad odour; or, after removing the wine, wash them well with salted water or good wine, leave them open, and they will be safe; or, turn the pots upside down and let them drain, then close them well, and this will protect them from mould or bad odours.

Remedies against getting drunk.

Before drinking wine, eat roasted goat lung, or raw cauliflower, or bitter almonds, and drink half a glass of olive oil, and so you will avoid drunkenness. If you want to restore someone who is drunk, throw a glass of cold water on his head, or feed him cauliflower dressed in honey; he will also be restored by drinking a glass of very strong vinegar.

TREATISE XXIV: *Of banquets.*

Since I gave in the first volume the rule of how to arrange ordinary banquets, I have chosen to describe here some lean ones; even though the rule of service is the same, I thought it best to renew this information, to benefit those who may read this second volume separately from the first.

DINNER

GIVEN IN NAPLES
by the Most Excellent Lord
DON ANTONIO GRUTTER,
DUKE OF SANTA SEVERINA,
on the occasion of his nuptials with the Lady
DONNA MATTIA CATERINA
UBERTI,

*with two royal basins, for twenty guests, ladies and gentlemen, in the
month of December, on a Wednesday, with two stewards and two carvers.*[121]

I will not at length describe the pomp with which the lady bride was brought to the
house, followed by numerous coaches and accompanied by the noblest of ladies and by
high-ranking gentlemen. Nor will I sketch the magnificence of the apartment to which
she was taken; its adornments—I am in doubt as to whether they were more to be prized
for the gildings that enriched them or the embroideries that decorated them—can without trace of flattery be called majestic and royal. I pass under silence the marvels of the
gallery which served as the stage for such a worthy gathering: in it, Painting, displaying
its perfections, led the eyes of those attending to an ecstasy of awe, and the sweetness of
voices, with the harmony of instruments, all placed in nearby rooms, formed the gentlest
of enchantments for the ears, at the same time as the abundance of sorbetti and brewing
chocolate, accompanied by the choicest confections and rarest candied things, and everything else that ingenious Craft has invented to satisfy in such events pomp and whim,
was all generously available and satisfied everybody's taste. So that no sense should be
deprived of its particular desired pleasure, a ball lasting several hours fulfilled also the
itches of the sense of touch, in that modest way which the observance of good manners
prescribes among the well-born. Since it would be impossible to describe all the magnificence that pervaded this event, I set aside such accounts and move on to the actual dinner, which, though it was done impromptu and among family members, was thus set up.[122]

The credenza rose more than superbly, showing off a treasure in the gold and silver that decorated it in rich symmetry; the creativity of the crystals displayed proudly
offered to the curious an object of marvel; at the end of the dinner not one crystal
remained, as they were all broken with ineffable amusement in the whimsical toasts
that on such occasions are usually proffered.

The table was a stage of magnificence: everybody contemplated with awe the table
coverings decorated in gold, which hid almost in embarrassment under the whiteness
of the table cloths, made of the finest silk woven in Flanders. The same table cloths, as
if they could scarcely match such a sumptuous apparatus, came together in the finest
folds, their forms varying in many ingenious figures, protean fantasies of such a majestic
banquet. But I would speak for too long if I tried to describe the liveliness of the settings,
no less beautiful than the table cloths, or the variety of the triumphs that crowned the
great table; I move on therefore to the arrangement of the cold dishes, beginning with
the three tondini prepared for each guest.

Cold dishes.

The first [tondino] held a royal salad, with its decorative borders, filled with various
ingredients.

---

121 The host here is Latini's dedicatee for the second volume.
122 About the dancing, Latini actually wrote *proriti* (itches), today a rather earthy term.

The second with sliced ham and soppressata, garnished with aniseeds of various colours, and lemon slices.[123]

The other one with sliced dried tuna salami, mixed with Spanish olives, slices of salted tuna belly, and fish eggs [targhe], garnished with pomegranate seeds and lemon slices.

1. Pie with the coats of arms of the most excellent bride and groom, filled with bits of Sorrento veal, quartered pigeons, halved cockerels, sliced ham and soppressata, bits of mammary glands, whole chicken livers, slices of udder, first boiled, bits of pork belly, white truffles, pine nuts, apt spices, and other tasty ingredients.

2. Impanata with coats of arms as above, filled with a large fish, sliced of salted tuna belly, bits of cardoons, first boiled, quartered artichokes, capers, olives, asparagus tips, sliced truffles, Genoa mushrooms, raisins and pine nuts, aromatic herbs, and apt spices.

3. Blancmange moulded in bas-relief, made with capon flesh, first roasted, and other ingredients, garnished with strained eggs and sour cherries in syrup.

4. Blancmange made with gurnard flesh and apt ingredients, garnished with little mounds of fish jelly of various colours, and bits of candied citron and pumpkin.

5. Ham cooked in wine, placed in a stand pie in half-relief, garnished with ribbons and aniseeds of various colours.

6. Boiled large fish, with pine nut sauce, lobster juice, bits of cinnamon, cloves, and sliced salted tuna belly, garnished with sliced candied citron and pumpkin.

7. Jelly made with veal feet and other ingredients, in various colours, with a turban made with glaze in the middle, encrusted with flowers, with a crown of sugar around.

8. Marinated soles served with fried asparagus tips, garnished with buns filled with things in syrup, mixed with lemon slices.

9. Uncovered pizza of bocca di dama, made with marzipan paste, garnished with fruits in syrup, with a glaze on top that looked like marble.

10. A similar pizza, but lean, with the same ingredients, and glaze.

Hot kitchen dishes.

1. Fried pastries and lemons, over bread crostini.

2. Roast with large red mullets, with an anchovy sauce, capers, olives, lemon juice, and bits of candied citron.

3. English-style pottage with bits of pigeons, veal chops, mammary glands, thrushes, sliced ham, chicken livers, cardoon bits, artichokes, tender peas, truffles, razor shells,

---

123 Here, and below, this event seems to have included much meat and other non-lean food; Latini offers no explanation for why he included this example among the "lean" banquets; the fact that almost always a "fat" dish is paired with a similar lean dish might suggest that the day was one of not very strict "fasting," so that different guests might have abided by different rules, depending on their personal level of devotion to such practices (this is explicitly the case in the next banquet).

asparagus tips, morels, and other noble ingredients; the sides of the plate garnished with fried German pastries mixed with lemon slices.

4. Pottage with chops of a large fish, stuffed squid, small fish-balls, lobster bits, slices of salted tuna belly, razor shells, morels, tender peas, truffles, asparagus tips, quartered artichokes, and wedge shells, thickened with pistachio sauce and lemon juice; the sides of the plate garnished with quinces in syrup covered with aniseeds of various colours.

5. Genoa-style small pies, filled with pounded veal, bone marrow, sweetbreads, slices of pigeon, razor shells, thickened with the usual little broth; the sides of the plate garnished with a gilded sugar crown.

6. Small pies of ground fish, bits of eel [capitone], razor shells, sliced truffles, small morels, thickened with pine nut sauce, and the sides of the plate garnished as above.

7. Fried dish made with tender quartered pigeons, sweetbreads, chicken livers, quartered artichokes, liver sausages, fine saveloy, thrushes, sliced udder and ham, veal marrow, with pomegranate sauce; the sides of the plate garnished with small pies with cream tops.

8. Fried dish made with soles mixed with small squid, fish livers, quartered artichokes, asparagus tips, fish chops, razor shells, with Genoese sauce; the plate garnished with small pies with syrup mixed with sliced candied citron and pumpkin.

9. Roasted woodcocks garnished with boar ribs and thrushes, the sides of the plate garnished with fried pastries mixed with small pies with things in syrup, and lemon slices.

10. A roast of large fish, with on top a sauce made with olives, raisins, pine nuts, candied citron, bits of cinnamon, whole cloves, and lemon juice; the sides of the plate garnished with halved sour oranges and German pastries.

11. Lasagne such as nuns make, with inside grated parmesan cheese, slices of provola, caciocavallo, mixed with whipped butter and perfumed water.

12. Similar lasagne, with sugar and cinnamon, perfumed water, and other ingredients.

13. Pies filled with small birds, slices of pork belly and soppressata, sliced truffles, and pine nuts, carved and with a glaze on top.

14. Round royal pies filled with sturgeon slices, deboned bits of sea bass, fish-balls made with red mullet, red mullet livers, shrimp tails, thickened with a little broth made with pistachio milk, and lobster and lemon juice, with sugar on top.

Second credenza service.

Parmesan cheese.
Caciocavallo.
Bergamot pears.
Spanish appie apples.
White and black grapes.
Fennels.

Celery.

Cardoons.

Artichokes.

Radishes from Chiaia [a neighbourhood of Naples].

At the end we served abundant confections, and the meal ended with great satisfaction and universal applause; we then served dinner to over eighty attendants, of the second and third table, since that had been the intent of all these lords.

BANQUET

Offered by the Most Illustrious Lord Regent
DON GENNARO
D'ANDREA
On the occasion of his nuptials with the Lady
DONNA FRANCESCA
RECCO
Countess of Rizzanello,
Served at two royal plates, in the month of March with the participation of twenty ladies and gen-tlemen, and since it was during Lent the above-mentioned Lord Regent ordered that the banquet be prepared in both fat and lean manner.[124]

1. Each setting had three tondini, one filled with slices of salted tuna belly, cooked and desalinated, with crostini of toasted bread and caviar, garnished with lemon slices and aniseeds of various colours.

   In the next tondino were bread slices with over them crustless bread soaked in vinegar [cappone di galera] prepared with various aromatic herbs, olives, capers, lemon slices, and pomegranate seeds, with a little ribbon around the rim of the plate.

   The third tondino had fish eggs [targhe] and bits of herrings, garnished with lemon slices, encrusted with confected aniseeds, and a little salad, with decorative borders around.

2. Two pies, one fat and one lean, with the coats of arms of the lord groom and lady bride, shaped like double-headed eagles, the lean one stuffed with bits of eel [capitone], slices of corb, Genoa mushrooms, pine nuts, and raisins, and underneath it bay leaves, everything retouched in gold and silver, and the fat pie stuffed with veal chops, turkey cockerels, ham slices, and apt spices.

---

124 Gennaro d'Andrea (1637–1710) was one of the most prominent members of Neapolitan officialdom, and during his career occupied many of the highest administrative and judicial offices in the kingdom; in 1687 he married Francesca Recco; he became regent (member) of the Council of Italy in Madrid in 1690, where he served until 1695, and later served on the Collateral Council in Naples from 1695 to 1709. I cannot find Rizzanello, but Lizzanello is a small town near Lecce in Puglia.

3. A basin with strained eggs shaped like a mountain, with little lions climbing it and coming out of some grottoes, all decorated with poppies [papagnini] of various colours, with a decorative border around the rim of the plate.

4. A royal salad in a basin, three palmi high, and arranged in three levels, and each level had its crown, with small putti made with turnips and radishes.

5. A plate of salted tuna belly in syrup, with a lid, held high by four lions made of marzipan paste, with the heads of the lions touching the sides of the plate, all encrusted with poppies [papagnini], retouched in gold and silver.

6. A plate with large Spanish olives mixed with carved lemon slices, retouched in gold and silver, with a decorative border around made with citron pulp.

7. Ten large soused soles, arranged neatly in the plate, with a sauce over them made with raisins, pine nuts, bits of candied citron, pitted olives, capers, and bits of cinnamon, with in the middle a flower between the fish tails, which were raised and retouched in gold and silver; the sides of the plate garnished with pears in syrup, and all covered with white confected aniseeds, mixed with lemon slices.

8. A covered tart made with marzipan paste and other candied things, with over it a glaze shaped like a Maltese cross, half white and half the colour of cinnamon, retouched in gold and silver, with laurel branches around, arranged in various ways.

9. A soup made with slices of sponge cake, shaped like mostaccioli, four fingers large, soaked in good malmsey wine, all covered with sugar, with cinnamon on top; the plate garnished with small mostaccioli of two colours, one white and the other the colour of cinnamon, mixed with half-moons made with a paste of candied quince.

Hot kitchen dishes.

1. A small plate of fat appetizers for each guest, with slices of toasted bread, soaked in good broth, with Sorrento veal chops, meatballs also of Sorrento veal, bits of sweetbreads, quartered artichokes, ham, truffles, and St. George's mushrooms, with the usual spices and aromatic herbs, with a little apt cover on top, retouched in gold and silver.

   A lean plate of sturgeon chops, each weighing six ounces, cooked in a pan with aromatic herbs and the usual spices, small mushrooms, and truffles, with a thin broth made with roasted almond milk and lobster juice, with an apt cover on top.

2. A fried dish of soles mixed with small squid, fish livers and soft roe; the plate garnished with fried beignets mixed with small lemons, and with borage flowers around the rim of the plate.

   A dish of fried fat things, such as sweetbreads, brains, slices of veal liver, quartered artichokes, first boiled, chicken livers, asparagus tips, first boiled, slices of bread dipped in egg; the plate garnished with small pastries stuffed with blancmange and sliced candied pumpkin, mixed with lemon slices, with on it lemon juice, the usual spices, and pomegranate seeds around.

3. Small pies filled with bits of corb, fish soft roe, sturgeon eggs, fish-balls made with pounded fish flesh and the usual ingredients, sliced truffles, St. George's mushrooms,

aromatic herbs, raisins, and pine nuts, with a little broth made with ambrosine almonds and lemon juice, with the usual spices; one small pie for each guest.

Small flaky pies filled with veal chops, bits of sweetbreads, small birds, cockscombs and chicken testicles, St. George's mushrooms, truffles, pine nuts, and green pistachios, first soaked in rosewater, with the usual spices and lemon juice; one small pie for each guest.

4. A plate with two large dentex, grilled, with a little condiment on top made with perfumed vinegar, pine nuts, raisins, a bit of sugar, bits of candied citron, bits of cinnamon, and cloves; the plate garnished with quinces in syrup arranged in bands of dough, all encrusted with confected aniseeds of various colours, and the plate also included short crust pastries fried in good oil.

A fillet of Sorrento veal, spit-roasted, mixed with roasted thrushes and ham slices, served with muscatel grapes, as Astidamus of Miletus used to prepare this dish, which he discovered; he was so gluttonous that once, invited by Ariobarzanes the Persian, he alone ate the entire banquet, which had been prepared for many guests.

5. A pie filled with sturgeon chops, bits of salted tuna belly, bits of eel [capitone], St. George's mushrooms, Genoa mushrooms, artichoke stems, first boiled and then sautéed, slices of truffles, cardoon stems, sliced, boiled, and then sautéed, aromatic herbs, raisins, and pine nuts, with the usual spices, and a bit of lemon juice.

Another flaky pie filled with halved cockerels, quartered tender pigeons, veal chops, ham slices, thin slices of soppressata, bits of veal tongue, first boiled, bone marrow, with apt aromatic herbs and spices, and a bit of lemon juice inside, with a sugar glaze on top.

6. Marinated soles, with a sauce made with vinegar and sugar, with a festoon around the sides of the plate, filled with appie apples in syrup and slices of candied pumpkin, and cinnamon and sugar on top.

Cockerels in a scapece, with on top a bastard sauce, and the plate garnished with pears in syrup.

7. A plate with a sturgeon head, boiled in water, with herbs on top and a sauce made with anchovies, the plate garnished with bunches of asparagus mixed with slices of sour oranges and of salted tuna belly.

A plate with two veal breasts, filled with various ingredients, boiled in water, with herbs on top, the plate garnished with slices of boiled soppressata and small tarts with green sauce inside.

[8.] A plate with red mullets, grilled, with a little condiment made with vinegar, oil, and a little garlic flavour, two mullets for each guest.

A plate with veal mammary glands, wrapped in paper, with spit-roasted ham slices, mixed with sausage from Abruzzo and kid livers, wrapped in caul, with a royal sauce on top; the plate garnished with small pies made with chicken breast, with a little garlic flavour, and pine nuts and pistachios on top, mixed with carved lemon slices.

We gave a salad to each guest.

9. A plate with lasagne made with roasted almonds, sugar, cinnamon, and perfumed water.

   A plate of lasagne made by mixing eggs, boiled in water, mixed with slices of mozzarella, parmesan cheese, cheese from Puglia, and butter; this was then stewed over a cauldron of boiling water, and was served with sugar and cinnamon on top.

10. A pizza made with marzipan paste, candied citron and pumpkin, sour cherry pulp, citron preserves, perfumed water, mixed with candied whole fruits, and a glaze made to look like marble.

    A flaky pizza, made with apples in syrup, ground candied citron and pumpkin, and cinnamon, served with sugar on top.

We removed the cold dishes and soon we served the fruits, leaving only the royal salad on the table.

A plate of Spanish appie apples.
One of bergamot pears.
One of grapes.
One of cardoons with pepper and salt.
One of celery with pepper and salt.
One of fresh peas and fava beans.
One of fennels.
One of Spanish olives.
One of small fresh almonds.
One of artichokes.
One of parmesan cheese.
One of chestnuts roasted under the embers, with salt and pepper.

The first to serve cheese with fruit at the table was Vedius Pollio; he was so fond of delicate things that he threw his servants into fish ponds, so that the fish gained a more welcome taste, by eating human flesh, which is most sweet in taste.[125]

We removed the fruits and placed on the table six large basins of confected things, which were distributed to all, and everyone filled their handkerchiefs with them; then everybody retired to their apartments, and in the evening there was a most beautiful ball which lasted well into the night, with excellent music and instruments.

The Lord Regent, with his usual splendour, ordered another banquet on the following Sunday, because not everybody had been ready at the arrival of the lady bride, which had not been widely known, and so little was eaten that all the dishes were given as gifts to friends of the Lord Regent; on that Sunday all the guests promptly came and they were served with the same order as on the first day.

---

125 Vedius Pollio was a supporter of Augustus and died in 15 BC; this horrid anecdote was popular among ancient authors: it is mentioned by Ovid, Seneca, Pliny, Cassius Dio, and Tertullian.

BANQUET

MADE FOR THE NUPTIALS
Of the Most Excellent Lord
THE DUKE OF ASCOLI
MARULLI,
With the Lady
DONNA VITTORIA CAPANO,
The guests were served in silver basins, with four kitchen services, with two basins for each service,
on a lean day, and attending were forty ladies,
each of them served by her husband or relative, in the month of March.[126]

First credenza service.

The table was filled with various cold dishes, in the middle of which were four triumphs made with sugar paste, thus:

1. Love with bow and arrow at the ready, stamping under his feet weapons, sceptres, and crowns, all in gilded sugar.

[2.] Fame with the trumpet in her mouth, surrounded by fronds, and the basin in which this figure stood was filled with candied things sliced and tied with ribbons of various colours, mixed with carnations made with sugar which stood out quite a bit from the basin, everything outlined in gold, with the coats or arms of the most excellent groom and bride, about four palmi high.

3. Another triumph represented Hercules when he dismembered the lion, at the bottom of the basin, all made with arabesques and fronds outlined in gold.

4. Atlas bearing on his back the globe, all coloured in azure, outlined in gold. The basin where this figure stood was all covered with fronds, whimsically made, and arabesques, and other various flowers, all made with sugar, and outlined in gold.

These cold dishes followed.

1. Three pies made with sea bass, with the coats of arms of the most excellent bride and groom, the pies shaped like dolphins, retouched in gold and silver.

2. Blancmange made with fish flesh, moulded in bas-relief, retouched in gold and silver.

3. Large grilled gilthead breams with a little condiment on top made with olives, pine nuts, dates, thin slices of candied citron, vinegar, capers, sugar, and cinnamon; the plate garnished with pomegranate seeds and lemon slices, retouched in gold and silver.

4. Soused soles with borage flowers on top and little festoons around them made of marzipan paste, retouched in gold and silver.

---

126 The Marulli came from Puglia, became dukes of Ascoli in 1679, and joined the ranks of the Naples nobility; this duke is presumably Sebastiano Marulli (1654–1704), who in 1684 married Vittoria Capano of the counts of Celso.

5. Salted tuna belly in syrup, garnished around with sliced lobster and tagliolini made of dough and fried, with a cover on top in lattice pattern, held by four lions in marzipan paste; all encrusted with poppies of various colours, retouched in gold and silver.

6. Jelly made with a whole gurnard, of various colours, the plate garnished with carved lemon slices, retouched in gold and silver, with a cover on it in lattice pattern, all encrusted with aniseeds of various colours, outlined in gold and silver.

7. Pizze or covered tarts of bocca di dama, with a glaze made to look like marble, and various candied fruits, retouched in gold and silver.

First hot dish.

1. A little Roman-style stew, made with asparagus tips, fish eyes, oysters, celery stems, cardoon stems, bits of artichoke, bits of salted tuna belly, thin slices of lobster, small fish-balls; the plate garnished with lemon slices.

Second dish.

2. A fried dish with liver and soft roe from various fish, fish chops, asparagus tips, quartered artichokes, small squid, mixed with little rice and milk fritters, as large as a Spanish olive; the plate garnished with small tarts of marzipan paste filled with condiments of various colours, and with German pastries and lemon slices.

Third dish.

3. One small pie for each guest, filled with ground fish, bits of turtle, white truffles, wedge shells, shrimp tails, small fish-balls, with clean whole pistachios, and with a little broth made with almond milk and lemon juice, with a cover in openwork made with marzipan paste, and sugar on top.

Fourth dish.

Corb chops, of one pound each, cooked in a pan with apt spices and aromatic herbs, with a little condiment on top made with shrimp juice, ground pine nuts, and seafood, with a light broth to thicken it; the plate garnished with small pastries made with things in syrup and sugar on top, and lemon slices around.

Fifth dish.

Braised red mullets filled with a paste made with moscarelle pears and sour cherries, with marzipan paste, braised; the plate garnished with halved quinces in syrup with white aniseeds on top, mixed with lemon slices, and a cover on top.

Sixth dish.

Large boiled corb with a condiment on top made with pine nut milk, lemon juice, and a bit of sugar; covered with bits of celery, cardoon stems, bits of salted tuna belly, pulled salmon, white truffles, asparagus tips, bunches of white fennels, the plate garnished with crostini with caviar and slices of fish eggs [targhe], with small tarts with white, green, and red condiments, with aromatic herbs on top, and the usual spices.

Eighth dish.[127]

Red mullets cooked in paper on the grill, with good oil, salt, raisins, pine nuts, and finely minced herbs, two mullets for each guest, served in the same paper.

Ninth dish.

Sturgeon chops cooked on an earthen base, with a little condiment on top made with perfumed vinegar, sugar, mostacciolo crumbs, and apt spices.

Tenth dish, called Raù.

Chops of fried fish, bits of salmon, roasted red mullets, and soused gilthead breams, all neatly arranged, with a sauce on top made with pine nuts, pistachios, shrimp and lobster juice, with the usual spices and lemon juice; the sides of the plate garnished with small pies filled with marzipan paste and sour cherry pulp, all thickened with milk, sugar, and lemon juice; on the plate also caviar crostini, lemon slices, and pomegranate seeds, scattered on the plate.[128]

Eleventh dish.

A dry oglia, made with boiled scorpion fish, bits of cardoons, Genoa mushrooms, sliced truffles, St. George's mushrooms, bits of salted tuna belly, roasted chestnuts, chickpeas, bits of celery, the usual spices, and lobster juice, all placed in a stand pie with arabesques around, all encrusted with aniseeds of various colours.

Twelfth dish.

Spider crabs filled with various ingredients, one for each guest.

Thirteenth dish.

Large dentex, roasted on the grill, larded with strips of salted tuna belly, stuffed with oysters, wedge shells, shrimp tails, sliced truffles, sour cherry pulp, bits of Barbary dates, bits of candied moscarelle pears; the plate garnished with quinces in syrup, covered with white aniseeds, mixed with lemon slices, and on top an anchovy sauce.

---

127 In yet another example of the greater sloppiness of the second volume, there is no seventh dish; also, the actual numbers appear at the start of only the first three dishes.

128 Nobody today in Naples would call this a ragù, which is a heavy sauce usually made with tomatoes, various meats, and red wine. Latini used the term also for another dish in the first volume—also not having much to do with today's version.

Fourteenth dish.

A Moorish-style dish, made with sliced eel [capitone] and corb, cooked in a pan, but dry, with just a little juice, mixed with bits of lobster necks and morels, with a sauce on top made with Marseille plums and roasted almonds; the sides of the dish garnished with aniseeds and pistachios.

Fifteenth dish.

A pizza of bocca di dama.

Aside from the cloth foldings, made whimsically with various leaves, which produced a lovely effect, each setting had in front of it four tondini, as follows.

A little royal salad made with olives, salted tuna belly, anchovies, capers, raisins, pine nuts, and other noble ingredients, with a decorative border around it with pomegranate seeds.

Another tondino with slices of toasted white bread, with on them crustless bread soaked in vinegar [cappone di galera], with various aromatic herbs, and other ingredients, with arabesques around made with aniseeds of various colours.

Another tondino with bits of salted tuna belly, desalinated, slices of fish eggs [targhe], caviar crostini, and small tarts with various condiments and colours, and pomegranate seeds.

Another tondino with condiments of various colours, shaped like a Maltese cross, with an apt decorative border around.

Second credenza service.

Bergamot pears.
Pink apples.
Large appie apples from Spain.
Cardoons, with salt and pepper.
Celery, with salt and pepper.
Artichokes.
White and black grapes.
Small almonds.
Roasted chestnuts, with pepper on top.

After removing the fruits, we placed on the table twelve basins of confected things; we gave water for hand-washing, and this splendid gathering ended with excellent music, sung by the best voices in Naples, and famous instruments, with universal pleasure and joy.

LUNCH

OFFERED IN POZZUOLI
By the Most Excellent Lord
THE PRINCE OF FEROLETO
To the Lord Prince
GIOAN PICA,
HIS BROTHER-IN-LAW,
Who had come thither to see the local curiosities which are
usually seen by the gentlemen who visit this most noble city of
PARTHENOPE,
*In attendance were four other lords, and they were served
at the table at one royal plate, on a lean day, at the start of April.*[129]

First credenza service.

A pie, shaped like a ship, with inside large red mullets, encrusted on top with white confected aniseeds, and underneath gilded bay leaves.

Dentex cooked in water, with borage flowers on top and around the plate, mixed with stars made in almond paste.

Blancmange made with almond milk, moulded in bas-relief statuettes, with a twist around made with marzipan paste, greased with ambivera, and encrusted with aniseeds of various colours.

A pizza made with almond paste, candied quince, citron, and pumpkin, served with various fruits in syrup on top, with a small crown around it made with sugar.

Grilled sea bass with royal sauce on top; the plate garnished with citron leaves, mixed with lemon slices.

Jelly of various colours with inside it live small fish, mixed with clean pistachios and bay leaves.

A royal salad, with a decorative border around it made with lemon peel, and on it a weathervane made of sugar.

Salami made with gurnard flesh, salted tuna belly, salmon, and other noble ingredients, everything pounded together, mixed with slices of fat salted tuna belly and apt spices; served at the table over a napkin, with bay leaves around.

First hot dish.

An almond dish made with almond milk and sugar, served with cinnamon on top, the sides of the plate garnished with fine sugar, with a lid on top in lattice pattern.

Second dish.

Soles, fried and then grilled, with a crust on top made with bread crumbs, salt, and pepper, served with royal sauce on top; the plate garnished with slices of fried bread mixed with lemon slices.

---

129 We have met these people before: the prince of Feroleto married Fulvia Pica, from the ruling family of Mirandola, a marriage which was one of the great social events in late seventeenth-century Naples.

Third dish.

One pie for each guest made with whole red mullets, oysters, first sautéed in a pan, razor shells, clams, limpets, and other seafood, the flesh of various fish, cut into bits, St. George's mushrooms, pine nuts, raisins, slices of salted tuna belly, first cooked and desalinated, the usual spices, and an apt little broth made with almond milk and lemon juice, with an apt cover, and sugar on top; the plate garnished with whimsical fronds.

Fourth dish.

A fried dish made with small squid, mixed with slices of eel [capitone], small anchovies, small soles, Genoa mushrooms, first cooked, desalinated, and fried, all served on slices of fried bread, the plate garnished with carved citron slices, mixed with halved sour oranges.

Fifth dish.

Bread loaves stuffed with a mixture of fish flesh, chops of tuna belly, bits of various fish, sliced truffles, stuffed small squid, oysters, cut razor shells, St. George's mushrooms, pine nuts, raisins, artichoke stems, first boiled and sautéed, the usual spices, everything mixed together, and put inside the bread loaves, which were soaked in almond milk, then baked in the oven, greased with ambivera, and encrusted with aniseeds of various colours; the plate garnished with lobster slices mixed with halved lemons.

Sixth dish.

Bits of tuna belly, marinated and then spit-roasted, larded with fat salted tuna belly, with bay leaves, and a crust made with mostacciolo crumbs and pepper, served with royal sauce on top; the plate garnished with small tarts with a condiment of sour cherries mixed with German pastries.

Seventh dish.

Maccheroni made with almond milk and crustless bread, cooked in pine nut milk, mixed with bits of soft roe from various fish, fried, pine nuts, and sugar and cinnamon on top; the plate garnished with slices of counterfeit ricotta mixed with green pistachios.[130]

Eighth dish.

Chops made with swordfish flesh, stewed, with St. George's mushrooms, pine nuts, raisins, truffles, shrimp tails, artichoke stems, and the usual spices, with a thin broth made with pine nut milk and lemon juice; the plate garnished with slices of counterfeit salami, mixed with lemon slices, with a cover on top in a threaded pattern.

---

130 By counterfeit I assume Latini means something lean made to look like ricotta (cheese being also prohibited on strict lean days); see also the next dish.

Ninth dish.

Halved lobsters, first cooked, served with salt, pepper, and lemon juice, with thin slices of sautéed truffles; the plate garnished with empty flaky pastries, mixed with carved lemon slices and parsley.

Tenth dish.

A pizza made with various candied things and fruits in syrup.

Each setting had three tondini, one with a royal salad with decorative borders, another with a white condiment diluted in lemon juice and with sugar on top, and the third held fat salted tuna belly, with borage flowers on top.

Second credenza service, fruits.

Bergamot pears.
White and black grapes.
Large appie apples from Spain mixed with other types of apples.
Tender almonds.
Fresh peas.
Fresh fava beans.
Fennels.
Celery.
Halved cardoons, with salt and pepper.
Artichokes.

Once the gathering had ended, everybody returned to Naples, all being satisfied with the beautiful amenities they had seen in that ancient city.

LUNCH

offered by the Most Excellent Lords
THE MARQUIS SERRA
in their palace in Pizzo Falcone,
to the Lady
COUNTESS MARESCOTTI,
the Lady
DONNA ISABELLA DI GENNARO,
the Lords
PRINCE AND PRINCESS
OF SATRIANO,
and others, in the number of ten, served from one royal basin, on a Friday.[131]

The table was set with most beautiful table cloths and settings made with diverse folds and fronds; it was then covered with the following cold dishes.

A pie, or impanata, of corb, in the shape of a dolphin, with inside it small bits of eel [capitone] and lobster, the usual spices, and other apt ingredients.

A royal dish of blancmange, in the shape of stars, garnished with mostaccioli made with candied pistachio paste.

A large grey mullet, grilled, served with a sauce of dates, pitted olives, capers, pine nuts, cinnamon, cloves, and sugar, diluted in vinegar.

A dish of fresh egg yolks, dipped in other eggs beaten with sugar, starch flour, and pistachio milk, then fried in butter like fritters, and arranged in the plate in the shape of a sea rock, surrounded by small sponge cake cookies, with sugar and mostacciolo crumbs on top.

A royal basin of soused soles, served with borage flowers on top and lemon slices around.

A pizza made with candied citron, candied pumpkin, candied small lemons, egg yolks, cream tops, sugar, cinnamon, and perfumed water.

There followed for each setting three tondini.

One with whipped butter beaten with sugar, and arabesques around it.

One with melons over shaved ice.

And the other with a little salad, over small taralli, served with slices of salted tuna belly, pitted olives, capers, anchovies, and other apt things, with bands around it.

---

131 The Serra, later dukes of Cassano, were a family of Genoese origin, long settled in the Kingdom of Naples; their palace in Pizzofalcone (one of Naples' oldest neighbourhoods), which they acquired in 1679, is one of the finest examples of eighteenth-century architecture in the city (the appearance of the palace today dates to a few decades after the meal Latini describes), see Gérard Labrot, "Naissance et croissance d'un quartier de Naples, Pizzofalcone 1530–1689," *Urbi* 1 (1979): 47–66.

Hot dishes from the kitchen.

A plate of trout boiled with white wine, vinegar, and verjuice, served with an anchovy sauce on top, and around it aromatic herbs and lemon slices.

Fresh eggs with napkins, one tondino per guest.

A little stew for each guest, with artichoke stems, clams, wedge shells, thin slices of salted tuna belly and truffles, bits of lobster, aromatic herbs, apt spices, and lemon juice, over bread slices.

One small pie for each guest, made with short crust pastry, filled with sturgeon chops, shrimp tails, St. George's mushrooms, truffle slices, sour grapes, pistachios, the usual spices, all diluted in a milk juice made with pine nuts, shrimp juice, and lemon juice.

Sliced sturgeon, grilled and then dressed with good oil, salt, powdered fennel, ground nutmeg and cloves, and perfumed vinegar, served with a little condiment made with fish soft roe, salted anchovies, and lemon juice.

A white frittata in a royal plate, made with egg whites, sugar, ground candied pistachios, confected pistachios, salt, and a little bit of water, then fried in butter, and served with faldicchere eggs above, encrusted with green pistachios.

Fried soles, without their bones and filled with various seafood, truffle slices, pine nuts, and bits of candied lemons, served with a milk juice made with almonds, oil, and lemon juice.

A fried dish of large red mullets and slices of corb, with fried herbs on top and lemon slices around.

A sweet pizza in a royal basin.

Second credenza service.

Parmesan cheese.

Caciocavallo.

Fennels.

Celery.

Appie apples and large appie apples from Spain.

White and black grapes.

Bergamot pears, and other fruits, with celebrated and choice confections, which I omit in order not to appear verbose.

LUNCH

HELD AT PIETRABIANCA
for a gathering of ten ladies and gentlemen,
the guests served from one royal basin, on Saturday, April 17, 1694, on the occasion when they all went to see the prodigious eruption of Mount Vesuvius.[132]

The table was set in the country style and these lords and ladies were served as follows: each setting had four tondini.

The first of strawberries washed in a strong wine, with sugar on top and shaved ice below.

The second with a little royal salad made with rustic greens, olives, capers, salted tuna belly, salted anchovies, and other usual ingredients.

The other with whipped butter.

And the fourth with slices of boiled lobster, well garnished.

The following cold dishes followed.

A large impanata made with bits of swordfish, slices of salted tuna belly, first desalinated, artichoke quarters, sliced truffles, first heated and sautéed, pitted olives, and the usual spices.

A royal dish of soles in a scapece, the sides of the plate garnished with small pastries filled with things in syrup.

Another plate with a large boiled dentex, served with the usual spices; the plate garnished with herbs and flowers.

A sweet pizza, made with ricotta, candied citron, candied pumpkin, sugar, cinnamon, perfumed water, and other apt things.

Hot dishes from the kitchen.

A casserole made with tender peas and fava beans, artichoke quarters, asparagus tips, seafood, fish chops, fish-balls, St. George's mushrooms, morels, bits of eel [capitone], and bits of cauliflower, with a sauce of ground lobster diluted with pine nut milk and lemon juice.

Roasted red mullets from Granatiello, dressed with good oil, vinegar, and fennel flowers.

One small pie for each guest, made with short crust pastry, filled with ground corb, seafood, and fish soft roe, thickened with pistachio milk, and also whole pistachios inside.

---

132 Pietrabianca (literally, white stone) was a small town near the coast of the Bay of Naples; because of its destruction in one of this period's eruptions, it was later renamed Pietrarsa (burned stone); it today houses an interesting museum of railroads. Latini oddly passed up the chance of telling us about his patrons on this occasion; perhaps the eruption was more memorable than any social distinction of the guests. Easter in 1694 fell on April 11, but this Saturday after it was still a lean day (though apparently allowing for ricotta, which Latini does not this time mark as counterfeit). This is the only social event Latini dates so precisely.

Fried small squid mixed with fritters of naked fish, artichoke quarters, asparagus tips, and cauliflower tips, all garnished with lemon slices.

A beautiful roasted dentex, served with a bastard sauce on top.

A sweet pizza.

Second credenza service.

Caciocavallo.

Parmesan cheese.

Fennel.

White and black grapes.

Apples.

Bergamot pears.

Fresh almonds.

After this lunch and a brief rest, this noble company started towards Vesuvius to observe those curious horrors it vomited. I however, to investigate more closely its peculiarities, chose not to go with them, but took another route I liked better through those precipitous heights; by walking from the start to the peak I gathered what I describe here below. So that my reader be better satisfied, before describing what happened this week, I have decided to mention what this mountain has done in the recent past.

Mount Vesuvius, called by locals Mount Somma, rises isolated about seven miles East of Naples and spreads its slopes to a circuit of twenty-six miles; halfway up its slopes it is cultivated with vineyards which produce very strong Lacrhyma and Greco wines and the tastiest fruits; the upper half, on the side that looks down on the city, is covered with woods or cleared for cultivation, on the other side it is almost entirely uncultivated, because of the ashes and rocks. The summit is divided into two peaks: in the left one, which is less high than the right one, there is a deep abyss, from which, as indubitable histories attest, since 1283 BC, at the time of Septimius King of the Assyrians, [the mountain] spewed flames and ashes most copiously. Even greater was however the event of the year 81 AD [in fact, 79 AD], during the reign of Emperor Titus Vespasian, because that time it sent forth not only ashes but also so much fire that, falling down those steep valleys like the fastest torrent, destroyed and annihilated two most famous cities, one called Pompeii and the other Herculaneum, just at the time when the people sat in the public theatre; the strong earthquakes on that occasion struck down the famous Naples Gymnasium. The most learned Pliny the Elder, a researcher in natural history, quickly came to the harbour at Baiae with a galley to investigate more closely the causes [of the eruption], but he was surprised by a sudden cloud of ashes and he saw with his eyes and touched with his hands their strength, but was not able to write an account of them, because he choked to death [in fact, Pliny sailed from Baiae to Stabiae, much closer to the eruption, where he died]. The winds pushed the ashes of that fire all the way to Egypt, Syria, and other eastern coasts and places; Plutarch heard the noise of the eruption in Rome, saw the sky darkened in the middle of the day by frightening blackness, and strongly feared that the sibyls' prophecies of a universal death by fire were coming true.

Many more [eruptions] are recounted after this one, as in the reign of Emperor Leo, of Theoderic [King of the Ostrogoths, d. 526 AD], and of [Pope] Boniface II [ruled 530–532]; one of the most frightening occurred in December of the year 1631. For many days the abyss poured out fiery lava, threw in the air enormous rocks, filled the air with particles and with winds dense with ashes; it inundated the nearby country and villages with floods of fire and absorbed water copiously from the nearby sea shore, so that all the ships anchored in the Naples harbour were grounded until that open abyss regurgitated the water. This terrible fright was augmented by the continuous earthquakes which shook all buildings in Naples and even in farther towns; nor would this terrible evil have stopped if the warmest of prayers had not placated God's wrath, through the powerful intercession of the glorious patron San Gennaro, who with his usual holy protection extinguished that great fire.[133]

From that year forward the great monster of fright seemed tamed, and the peasants and locals, trusting in its quiet and rest and drawn by the fertility of the land and the beauty of the site, competed with each other to cultivate and plant it, nor were their hopes in vain, because they quickly reaped abundantly from their labours, more than making up for their costs, and rather gaining so much that today not a bit of land in the mountain's circuit is unused and abandoned.

The rapacious beast has, yes, slumbered, but it has not ceased to give rise to suspicions, and it has been heard to grumble every now and then, and indeed more frequently in the past four years, and to roar with exhalations of ashes and fire and with the burst of frightful thunders; eventually, on the night of Monday the 12th of the current month of April, 1694, the abyss on the peak appeared more than usually surrounded by flames and darkened by ashes; both flames and ashes, strengthened by copious lava, sulfur, saltpeter, and alum, began to rush downwards, overwhelming any structure that they met on their descent and causing the most frightening noises to resound through the slopes and tremors through the nearby country.[134] Though this happened at the darkest hour of the night, the locals did not fail to flee, and at a rapid pace, carrying their most precious possessions, came towards Naples. Here, as soon as daybreak came, the people were horrified [to realize] that, even though the mountain was far, the brightness of the flames allowed them clearly to see the path of the fire, which ran down a deep valley (caused in the mountain a long time before by rain waters), filling it with rocks and fiery lava, to the point that no trace remains of its old condition except that the lava, now turned to rock, is even harder than the natural stone of the mountain. The lava passed through those slopes (which are named "of the Saviour") through the days of Tuesday, Wednesday, Thursday, and Friday, and by Saturday reached the plain, which is about three miles from the peak and the abyss; there it slowly snaked forward to the greatest peril of the most fertile towns of San Giorgio a Cremano (also known as Sant'Ivorio) and Barra, to protect

---

133 Latini wrote *bitumen* (bitumen, tar), but I think in the context of this description he means lava. Gennaro is still Naples' main heavenly patron, and the 1631 eruption remains his moment of greatest glory.

134 On this eruption, see Sean Cocco, *Watching Vesuvius: A History of Science and Culture in Early Modern Italy* (Chicago: University of Chicago Press, 2013), 182–91.

which many workers of the Royal Fortifications laboured together with innumerable locals; all together, they formed a spacious bed to push the lava to slide down towards the closest sea shore, by raising dams and barriers to control the lava flow.

The course of this fiery lava greatly astonished all because one could see a river of fire which at times was 200 palmi deep [an unlikely estimate] and 100 palmi broad advance for forty-eight hours over a length of three miles, bringing to the surface innumerable fiery rocks. Unlike the sea, which when agitated by winds forms waves, but never loses its basic equality of surface, this fiery river even when it met no obstacle always stayed higher in its middle part, as if it wished to form awesome pyramids at each step. I must note that the surface level tended to harden, whereas the bottom remained liquid and burning.

The erupted rocks consisted of a mosaic of minerals: iron, lead, copper, vitriol, tin, talc, troilite, sulfur, salt, lapis, orpiment, rock crystal, and abundant sulfur oil and salt-peter.[135] Professors of chemistry have conducted experiments and by melting some of these rocks they have extracted pure antimony and a bit of perfect gold; these rocks smell like sea rocks and they taste very salty. The lava finally stopped when the Most Eminent Cardinal Archbishop Cantelmi [of Naples], who had gone there, threw in it with the greatest faith an *Agnus Dei* prayer of Pope Innocent XI. It has also been observed that, a lot of rain having fallen on the mountain on May 11, which soaked the hardened torrent of lava, the lava exhaled such a great smoke, which led people to believe that the fire still burns under that great river of rocks; this is what has been reported thus far.[136]

Since I am writing about banquets, I think it good to offer a brief description of the proto-col used in the papal palace when His Holiness invites Ambassadors of Crowned Monarchs to banquet with him; I have personally observed this ritual on several occasions.

When a royal ambassador is invited to dine with His Holiness, the ambassador is led by Monsignor the Majordomo to the chambers destined to him, and from those to Our Lord's apartment, from which they progress to the banquet chamber. Here the ambassador kneels and offers a towel to the pope after the latter has washed his hands; he remains on his knees until the table is blessed. Then the ambassador, hatless, washes his own hands near his table, and sits down when the Pope gestures for him to do so; he now wears his hat, and unfolds his own napkin. Once His Holiness has begun eating the ambassador also does so, as the Prince of Butera also reports in the second book of his *Political and Christian Ambassador*.[137]

---

135 Troilite (*marchesita* in Latini) is an iron mineral now named after the Jesuit Domenico Troili who found it in a meteorite that fell in central Italy in 1766; orpiment is a mineral frequent in volcanic areas.

136 This account suggests that Latini had nearly completed his book and added these parts in late spring of 1694.

137 *L'ambasciatore politico e cristiano* by the Sicilian aristocrat Carlo Carafa Branciforte prince of Butera was published in 1690 in Mazzarino, Sicily.

The table of Our Lord is placed on a raised surface, with steps, under a baldaquin, and his food enters through a door to the baldaquin's left; he is served by Monsignor the Master of the Chamber, Monsignor the Steward, and other Private Waiters. The ambassador's table is five or six steps distant from His Holiness', towards the right wall, and not on an elevated platform, with triumphs and cold dishes; his food comes through a private stair and enters the room through a door to the right of his table. The two stewards work together, so that the dishes proceed in parallel: there usually are twelve hot dishes and as many cold ones afterwards, presented as usual with the Lord Ambassadors. When Our Lord drinks, the ambassador removes his hat and stands and waits for His Holiness, after he has finished drinking, to signal for him to replace his hat and sit down; when Our Lord may send the ambassador any food from his own table, the ambassador, in receiving it, stands and removes his hat. When he drinks, his own cupbearer serves him with a glass filled with wine and a little water carafe, without a cup.

During the meal, there is music; the players are on the wall opposite His Holiness' baldaquin.

The meal ended, the ambassador, kneeling, offers Our Lord the towel after [the pope] has washed his hands; he remains on his knees through the thanksgiving prayer, then he sits, hatless, to the left of Our Lord's table; after a brief speech, he attends His Beatitude through the antechamber; once they have reached the entrance to the private chambers, the ambassador kneels, kisses His Holiness' foot, and thanks him for the honour he has received.

REFRESHMENT

Offered by the Most Excellent
DUKE OF PARETE,
THE REGGENTE MOLES,
Of the Supreme Collateral Council of His Majesty
ON THE OCCASION OF THE NUPTIALS
Of the Most Excellent Lady
DONNA CATERINA MOLES,
HIS DAUGHTER,
With the Most Excellent Lord
DON FULVIO COSTANZO
PRINCE OF COLLE D'ANCHISE,
in the month of May.[138]

Since our intent in this second volume is exclusively to discuss lean foods, having already in the first volume sufficiently treated non-lean ones, we shall remain silent about the most opulent dinner, and the copiousness of the dishes, which were served in the grand style to the table of the most excellent bride and groom; it suffices to state that the banquet resulted from the splendid generosity of such a noble lord and most benevolent

---

138 We met Francesco Moles, duke of Parete in 1675, at one of Latini's earlier banquets; his daughter married Fulvio di Costanzo, of another prominent family, in 1693.

father; he, although his household is most flourishing in individuals capable of any domestic and civil task, nonetheless was pleased to honour my activities, [by charging me] not only with arranging the meal, the tables, and everything that came together in the banquet, but also with the distribution of confected things and refreshments. Thus, what we shall not do, as mentioned above, in describing the food, we shall instead deploy to depict the lavishness with which all the noble ladies and lords who attended the feast were served. Beforehand, however, to satisfy my own inclination, I shall allow myself to describe the manner in which the attention of this Lord decorated the apartment of the lord groom and lady bride. The hall had an apparatus of crimson brocade, with a gold background, and all the necessary decorations. The first antechamber with hangings in crimson damask, with the richest gold outline, and door hangings of the same materials, with chairs in crimson velvet all around, and at the room's head the baldaquin which is the privilege due to titled lords. The second antechamber, covered in green, crimson, and golden brocade, with similar door hangings, decorated with crimson velvet with the richest gold fringe, and desks which appeared unique in their materials and crafts-manship. The third antechamber had hangings of crimson damask, with large golden fringes, and chairs and door hangings of the same material. These three chambers were nobly furnished with sideboards and desks, decorated with the most excellent silver statues, and large vases filled with silver flowers. After these rooms, there followed the chamber where the nuptial bed was ready, in which most admirable was the pavilion with its varied craftsmanship and gilding, covered with curtains of turquoise marbled taffeta decorated with the richest gilded laces and fringes; the door hangings, window curtains, and chairs were covered in the same materials, with the same richness; in this room one could admire the most elegant objects, and sideboards of the finest ebony, on which where triumphal chariots in silver with gilded statues, the craftsmanship of which matched their lavishness.

Music was not lacking, with various voices, the choicest in Naples, with the sweetest symphonies of many and the best instruments; while these delighted the hearing, the palate tasted hot and iced chocolates, and all the great variety of sorbetti and perfumed waters which art knew to create and craft; we also distributed copiously all sorts of can-died and confected things, as varied as the most refined art could invent. Thus not only the noble guests were satisfied, but also all the servants, which were abundantly pro-vided for and satiated, just as that Lord clearly charged me and all his household; thus, without any care for the expense, the magnanimity of his great spirit was fulfilled, as we precisely obeyed him.[139]

---

139 This unusual section concludes Latini's tales of the glorious events he arranged; I imagine that the prominence of the host and guests, and the fact that the host hired Latini even though the latter was not in his regular employment, made this event appear to Latini as a fitting last account to give his readers.

Here follows a brief essay on several meals I arranged for the convalescent.

I have thus far discussed those foods that can without any trouble be offered to healthy people; now it seems to me that it would be welcome if I also discussed a few meals apt for convalescents. This may seem a matter more fit for physicians, and I do not wish to get involved in that part of medicine physicians themselves call dietetics, but I decided nonetheless to consider how to benefit those infirm people who, because of nausea or an inactive stomach, have no appetite and eat almost nothing, to the great detriment of their strength, which physicians themselves wish to see reinvigorated. It even happens at times that, by the patients' lack of appetite or by negligence on the part of inexperienced physicians, the patients' strength never recovers, or they become so extenuated that they may even perish, when they may have seemed on the verge of recovering health. That is why, to benefit such people, and also to instruct those physicians inexperienced in their craft, I have thought, in this second volume, to propose various dishes no less pleasing to the palate and the stomach than beneficial to restore the strength which one may have lost by infirmity. So that in this work one may not lack for anything that may please or benefit both healthy and ill people, I will here discuss various broths and extracts and cooked waters, with apt ingredients, so that the meals that follow be provided of all that is necessary to convalescence, for as much as my limited experience may suggest. Even though I spoke at some length of such matters in the first volume, in order to lessen the reader's effort, I thought it convenient to offer this brief specific essay, starting from the first day of convalescence, as follows.[140]

On the first day you will give the convalescent the following meal, in the manner indicated, beginning with an extract thus prepared.

Take a well cleaned chicken, stuff it with a dozen pitted sour cherries and two bits of cinnamon, place it on a spit, and roast it, but not too much. Then place it in a bag of white linen, and squeeze it under a press; boil the resulting juice on a low flame for a short while; serve it in a bowl with thin slices of bread, and it will be most nourishing.

Afterwards, you can serve him a thin stew of convent tagliolini, cooked in a good broth, with spices apt for convalescents, then up to six mostaccere, a cooked apple, and, to drink, one of the decoctions described in this essay, or maybe a bit of wine with water, depending on the patient's constitution.

In the evening, do according to the circumstances, keeping in mind that proper diet is always the principal medication; make sure the convalescent is not fatigued.

On the second day give him first a bowl of this broth.

Take a piece of veal thigh, boil it for two hours, then add one quarter of a hen or a wild dove, with two ounces of ham, a few white chickpeas, and two garlic cloves, if the convalescent likes it, the usual spices and aromatic herbs, and cook everything together very well; serve him this broth, with bread slices, and it is a very good thing; you can also use this broth in making stews, soups, thin broths, or other dishes.[141]

---

140 Latini thus shows far less respect for the professional prerogatives of physicians than he did for those of sorbetti-makers.

141 Latini says "two white chickpeas"; in Naples today (and I believe in his time already) "two"

Then give him a thin stew of bread crumbs cooked in the same broth, thickened with egg yolks; a boiled chicken wing, a cooked pear with sugar on top, and the usual to drink.

On the third day you will serve him as follows, and to start four ounces of this extract.

Take two pullets that died that day, halve one of them and cut one half of it into small bits, use the bits to stuff the other, whole, one, adding damaschine plums; roast it, and prepare and serve it in the same way as I said for the first day.

Then give him a thin stew of white chicory with two roasted small birds, a cooked pear, four mostaccere, and adequate drink.

Fourth day.

First, you can give him half a cup of chocolate, three hours before the meal.[142]

A gigot made of roasted chicken breast; a thin stew of parsley roots cooked in a good broth, half a dozen small mostaccere soaked in wine, and a cooked apple.

On the fifth day give him first a bowl of juice, made as here described.

Cut a chicken into small pieces, and sauté it in a pan; then place it in a stand pie, prepared in advance, with two thin slices of ham, a bit of ground cinnamon, a bit of verjuice, and salt; bake it in the oven, then remove it, open it, and press all the ingredients; give the juice from this pie to the convalescent with two thin slices of bread, and it will be quite substantive.

Afterwards a thin stew of borage, cooked in good broth, six pairs of chicken testicles, a cooked apple, and four mostaccere, with the usual drink.

On the sixth day prepare this meal, starting with a ground dish, as follows.

Roast a good piece of gurnard, then clean it of its scales and bones; in a mortar, prepare ground melon seeds; add the fish, and grind them together well, with sugar; then dilute it with a broth made with the gurnard's head, and cinnamon; boil this for a bit, with a few drops of rosewater, and serve it hot, and this will be most pleasant to the stomach; if you do not have melon seeds, you can serve this with crustless bread, or ambrosine almonds.

Then a soup made with slices of toasted bread, soaked in good broth, one quarter of a boiled hen, with a little green sauce, a roasted chicken liver, and a cooked pear.

On the seventh day you can amuse him thus, starting with six ounces of this extract.

Take a cutlet of wether thigh, spit-roast it, and keep the juice that drips from it; once it is half-cooked, debone and press it. Boil the pressed juice together with the juice you collected from the roast, with lemon juice, until it is cooked right, when it has acquired the

---

often means "just a few" (as in, "please just give me two spaghetti," which is definitely not to be taken literally); I have let context guide me, therefore, as to when "two" really means two in these prescriptions.

142 The chocolate cup (as later the coffee cup) is a *chicchera*, another of the Neapolitan terms Latini uses more frequently in his second volume.

colour of a lion's mane; serve it with bread slices and it will taste good; you can also use this in gigots and stews, and they will be very good.

Then a pottage with a young chicken, thickened with eggs, with the usual spices, a bit of sponge cake, and two cooked apples.

In all these broths and extracts you may always dissolve chicken livers or testicles, first roasted and then ground, or pistachio milk, and they will be most nourishing.

On the eighth day, do this, starting with this jelly.

Take two capons, with their necks and feet, clean them well, and cut them into small pieces; boil them in a pot with fresh water rising to four fingers above the capons; after boiling them until the water has reduced by one third, drain them through a sieve; remove the fat from the broth, and boil it again with a stick of cinnamon and one egg white; drain it again, then set it to cool in a cold place (use shaved ice if the season is hot); if you wish to give it colour, you may use pomegranate seeds, ground almonds, lemons, or other things.

Then give him a thin broth in Roman style, with fresh eggs, parsley, and the usual spices; then a bit of boiled Sorrento veal, with pomegranate seeds on top, two cooked pears, a bit of sponge cake, and the usual drink.

On the ninth day you will give him

A thin stew of bread crumbs, cooked in good broth, two small meatballs made with chicken breast and the usual ingredients, two roasted small birds, two apples with sugar on top, and then a concoction made this way.

In the mortar, grind a roasted chicken breast with a bit of cinnamon; prepare a vase with ambivera, at the right cooking point; add the chicken to the pot and boil it for a bit; then use it to make small fritters; keep them in a cold place, and this will be a most pleasing concoction, and also quite nourishing.[143]

On the tenth day do as follows.

Give him a thin stew of lettuce stuffed with apt ingredients, cooked in a good broth; a boiled half chicken with a little green sauce on top; a bit of brain, dipped in egg and fried; two pears in syrup with a couple of small cookies; and abundantly to drink.

On the eleventh day you will give him

A thin stew of small gnocchi cooked with breast of Sorrento veal, a bit more veal, two small chops, a small salad of hops, a bit of beef, and wine and water to drink.

---

143 The concoction is an *elettuario*, which usually means a combination of various agreeable ingredients with curative substances of more dubious appeal, the former being intended to make the latter more welcome to a patient; Latini calls the fritters *pizzette*; in Naples today this term can refer to small pizze, but also to (usually) round fried balls made with dough and various ingredients.

On the twelfth day you will give him

A boiled pigeon, covered with artichokes stems, bits of sweetbreads, thin slices of soppressata, all sautéed with its own thin broth, and lemon juice.

Then a small pie filled with ground chicken breast, chicken meatballs, first sautéed, two roasted apples with sugar on top, and the usual to drink.

On the thirteenth day you can give him

A thin stew of convent tagliolini, cooked in broth, and the fried head of a kid, a roasted Sorrento [veal] rib, with slices of lemon around.

A bit of sponge cake, two cooked pears, and abundantly to drink.

On the fourteenth day you may give him

Gigot of Sorrento veal, two roasted warblers, and a little salad of cauliflower.

Then a bit of almond paste, two apples, and the usual to drink.

On the fifteenth day one may give him

A thin stew of eggs cooked at bainmarie, with cinnamon, two boiled small birds, with fennel on top.

Two chicken livers, wrapped in caul and roasted, served with sour orange juice, four mostaccere, and a few fruits.

On the sixteenth day one may give him

Two segments of sour orange, with sugar on top, to prepare the stomach.

Then a thin stew of white escarole, cooked in the usual broth.

A little impanata stuffed with veal, four sour cherries, a bit of candied citron, and one quartered artichoke; a roasted thrush, and two apples.

On the seventeenth day one may give him

A cup of coffee, and four hours later a thin stew of hops, cooked in a good broth, with half a chicken and a bit of boiled veal with aromatic herbs on top.

Then a few sweetbreads and fried cauliflower with royal sauce on top; two roasted small birds, and a few grapes.

On the eighteenth day you may prepare

A stuffed pigeon with the usual ingredients, baked in the oven.

A roasted fish, with two small veal chops, a small asparagus salad, and two bergamot pears.

On the nineteenth day you may prepare

A soup made with slices of toasted bread mixed with sautéed razor shells, sweetbreads, and asparagus, soaked with a good broth, and cinnamon on top; fried brains and testicles, with mostacciolo sauce.

A roasted thrush, served with pomegranate seeds, four mostaccere, and a few grapes.

On the twentieth day one may prepare

A borage stew, thickened with eggs; a boiled quarter of a chicken with herbs on top.

A cockerel in a scapece; a little asparagus frittata; eggs; and two pears.

On the twenty-first day you will prepare

A wether gigot, with chicken broth and apt spices.

A thin stew of chicory with a small boiled pigeon, and a little green sauce; a small pie, of glory, and two roasted warblers.

On the twenty-second day one should prepare.

Two fresh eggs to drink; then a Portuguese-style chicken, with olives and capers.

Four fried kid feet, with royal sauce on top; a roasted red mullet, and a few fruits.

On the twenty-third day you will prepare

A thin stew of bread crumbs, a bit of boiled veal, and an apt parsley sauce.

Then a little pottage of kid sweetbreads with lemon juice; two veal chops; a few grapes; and four Savoy cookies.

On the twenty-fourth day you may give him

A bit of sponge cake, dipped in wine, two poached eggs, four chicken meatballs, cooked in good broth.

A roasted pigeon with lemon slices and sour grapes, a few fruits, and abundantly to drink.

On the twenty-fifth day you will give him

A stew of emmer wheat with a wild dove, cooked with the emmer wheat, a little frittata made with eggs, brains, and asparagus; a roasted thrush.

Four sea urchins and two bergamot pears.

On the twenty-sixth day one will give him

A Roman-style thin broth, with egg yolks and spices; a boiled chicken with herbs on top.

A fried kid head with royal sauce on top, a roasted red mullet, and a few fruits.

On the twenty-seventh day one will prepare for him

A stew of bread crumbs with two boiled chicken wings, a ground dish with Sorrento veal, over sliced bread, all covered with hard egg yolks, and soaked with good broth.

Two roasted chicken livers; two cooked apples, and water and wine to drink.

On the twenty-eighth day it will be proper [to prepare]

A soup with bread slices interspersed with pigeon breast and kid sweetbreads, soaked with a good broth, and cinnamon on top.

Then a sweet small pie, two veal chops, with two roasted warblers, a few fruits, and the usual to drink.

On the twenty-ninth day, it will be suitable [to prepare]

A thin stew with hops, cooked with a chicken, [and a] roasted kid liver, served with lemon slices.

A little salad of kid feet, some seafood, and a few grapes.

On the thirtieth day you may prepare

Tongue of Sorrento veal, cooked in a pottage; two roasted warblers; a thin soup of millefanti cooked in a good broth.

Lamb testicles and artichoke quarters, all fried, with a sauce on top; a bit of sponge cake, two bergamot pears, and drink as the convalescent wishes.

Here follow a few cooked waters, to be used in the above-mentioned meals.

Cinnamon water.

Take a good quarter ounce of cinnamon in bits and soak it overnight in four carafes of water, then boil it in a different pot, well lidded; after it has boiled long enough, drain it and set it to cool; it will be very good to quiet the stomach, and for the head.

Aniseeds water with cinnamon.

Take one ounce of aniseeds and boil them in four carafes of water; after they have boiled for a quarter of an hour add a quarter ounce of whole cinnamon, and a bit of sugar as you wish; boil this for the same length of time, and drain it; it will be a most perfect water.

Mastic water.

Take bits of mastic and soak them in water for five or six hours; for each carafe of water use one-third of an ounce of mastic. Boil for half an hour and then serve it; this will be very apt for the elderly and for those with a cold stomach, as it is quite hot; if the mastic is dry, it will be even better.

Whoever wishes to drink a most perfect water should get it in Pozzuoli at a well that is in front of the palace of the Lord Prince of Santo Buono; in that palace and also on the marina there one also finds a little fountain which at times in summer dries up; not very far, in the farm of the Lords Mascambruni, there is another well of the same goodness and perfection, with water similar to what one finds in Umbria, which in Rome is called water of Nocera; I have often experienced this water, and my Lord Regent uses it a lot, and knows it to be perfect.

I conclude that one can make many types of cooked waters, according to one's judgement; since they are not rare I will expand no more on this, since anybody can make them as he wishes. All cooked waters are good, and, if one does not have any, one can freely use plain water; in several hospitals and other pious institutions in Rome there are fountains for this purpose, where anybody can take water as he pleases.

If the convalescent desires to drink wine, he should make sure to add water to the wine one hour before, so that they mix better, and it becomes easier to pass the wine; above all, he should not drink the wine when it is too cold, because it may be harmful.

TREATISE: *of a few good rules for the kitchen.*[144]

So that cooks succeed and gain honour and praise in their preparation of dishes, I have thought it good to offer them the advice that follows.

They must first of all have a spacious fireplace, with wall shelves near it, in the most convenient spot to place pans and pots once [their contents] have started boiling; this way the food will be cleaner and more flavourful, and roasts will be better, without inconveniences. Often in winter it happens that the lower servants go to the kitchen to warm up, and it is not good if the pots and pans are in the fireplace, lest some dirt fall into them.[145]

Cooks should not allow too many people in the kitchen, especially near the food.

They should have in the kitchen tables and other necessary things to put everything in proper places.

They should make sure that apprentices and kitchen hands keep the kitchen clean.

They must ensure that kitchen towels be always kept clean, and that every Friday the kitchen hands wash pots and spoons, and scrub and clean the tables.

They should make sure to have a room nearby where one can store coals and other things useful to the kitchen.

I also thought it good to list all the utensils necessary for the cooks' good management of the kitchen: the list below is intended for a kitchen with four cooks, and to prepare meals for various tables.[146]

1. an iron chafing dish, about five palmi long.

2. a large pitcher for hot water, tinned inside, with its ladle.[147]

3. twenty-five tripods, between large, small, and middling.

4. four boilers, between large, small, and middling.

5. eight baking dishes to make pizze and tarts, between large, small, and middling.

6. ten copper chafing dishes, tinned inside, which can all be stacked one into the other, and fit into the portable oven for the country, on the occasion when that may be needed.

7. a large tub of tinned copper, with holes, to drain various things.

8. a small colander, tinned inside and outside, to drain broth.

9. six copper tubs, between large, small, and middling, tinned inside.

10. a copper portable oven for the country, with tiles inside as needed.

11. thirty moulds.

12. thirty small moulds, in different shapes, tinned inside, to prepare garnishes.

13. twelve iron spoons, between holed, concave, and flat.

---

144 This final treatise has no number and does not start on a new page.

145 Latini writes *moriccioli*, or short walls, i.e., stone surfaces where one may easily place boiling pots.

146 In translating this list I have relied on the notes and indices of Scappi, *Opera*.

147 Copper could easily oxidize or flake, so it was usually tinned, Scappi, *Opera*, 126, note 44.1.

14. eight spits, between large, small, and middling.

15. a pastry tube with its parts.

16. six copper round plates, and two oval ones, without rims, to cook various types of pies.

17. a shovel for the oven, and another for the kitchen.

18. two iron lids to close the oven, of the right dimensions for the oven.

19. a small shovel to take fire.

20. four frying pans, between large and small.

21. a long and large baking dish, to boil fish.

22. a dripping pan, to collect the roast juice, called in Naples *cannaruta*.[148]

23. a holed ladle, tinned inside and out, to get the roast juice, with a long handle.

24. two mortars, one large and one small.

25. two wooden blocks to beat meat; they should be of a hard wood, like pear or sorb.

26. a long and large boiler to cook fish.

27. three grills, one large, one small, and one middling.

28. a pan to cook eggs, with its twelve little compartments.

29. a small press to make meat juices or other juices.

30. two oval baking pans, to cook pies when in the country.

31. a boiler of cedar copper, to make syrups and clarify sugar.

32. six small copper kettles, each fitting inside the other, with a single lid for all of them together, and handles, which may serve for the country.

23 [typographical error for 33]. two pairs of spit-holders, to turn the spits.

THE END.[149]

---

148 The Neapolitan term Latini mentions actually means a gluttonous person, so it too implies a pan that is difficult to resist (as does liccarda, the more usual name for the dripping—or "licking"—pan).

149 A "table of all the matters contained in this book" occupying four pages follows (in this case, it is an actual index, in alphabetical order, instead of the table of contents of the first volume, which listed matters in the order in which they appeared in the book); there is no errata page in this volume. With the index, the volume consists of 260 pages.

MEASUREMENTS AND GLOSSARY

Measurements

barile: unit of capacity; for liquids, equivalent to about 43.6 litres, or 11.5 US gallons (or 9.6 UK gallons, being 25 percent larger than the US equivalent)

boccale: unit of liquid capacity; there are 32 boccali in a barile, so a boccale is about 1.35 litres, or 0.36 US gallons

carafe: unit of liquid capacity, about 0.73 litres, or 0.19 US gallons

dramma (dram): unit of weight, used for small quantities, one-sixteenth of a modern ounce (or about 1.8 grams)

libra (pound): unit of weight; the Naples pound in Latini's time was about 320 grams (i.e., a tad under three-fourths of a modern US pound, which is 453.5 grams); it was divided into 12 ounces, so each ounce was just under 27 grams (only a little less than the modern ounce, which is 28.3 grams).

moggio: unit of land surface, about 3.2 square metres, or about 34.4 square feet

palmo: unit of length, about 26 centimetres, or about 10 inches

rotolo: unit of weight, about 0.9 kilos, or about two modern US pounds

scrupolo (scruple): unit of weight, used for small quantities, one twenty-fourth of a modern ounce (or about 1.3 grams)

tomolo: unit of capacity, mostly for solids, about 55.5 litres, or about 14.6 US gallons

Glossary

acquavita/e: distilled and often flavoured wine

agresta: unripe grapes, or their juice (verjuice)

ambivera: possibly a mixture of ambergris and sugar; Latini uses it as an essence and powder, though the specifics remain unclear to me

ambrosina: prized variety of almonds

annoglia: spiced pork sausage (andouille)

annolini: stuffed pasta, usually ring-shaped (Latini also mentions agnoline, which is likely either the same or another type of fresh pasta)

appie apples: small, red variety, typical of Naples

bacile: large serving basin, shallow bowl

baiocco: a low-value coin, in use especially in Rome

barchiglia: boat-shaped pie (or pie mould)

bocca di dama: literally, lady's mouth; today used for sweet almond cookies and cakes; Latini uses the term for several almond dishes (and at least once for a dish without almonds)

bocconotti: small pastries

bottarga: cured fish roe

bottigliero: wine steward; bottiglieria was the bottle sideboard

brodetto: thin or light broth; here translated as "little broth" when referring to a liquid concoction used to thicken ingredients and mixtures inside a pie; see introduction

brodo: broth

brodo lardiero: lard broth (usually from meat cooked with cured back fat, herbs, and other ingredients)

caciocavallo: a hard cheese similar to an aged provolone

candire/candito: to candy/candied; see introduction

cannelloni: today, stuffed pasta tubes; Latini refers to sweet confected ones, so presumably in his case this refers to something I have not identified

capirottata (or capirotada): traditional Iberian composite dish

capitone/i: Naples term for large eels

cappone di galera: literally galley capon (i.e., what would be fancy food on a galley), an old preparation of crustless bread soaked in vinegar and possibly accompanied by some fish or seafood

caravella: a large, round variety of pear, now rare (once, Latini also refers to caravelle apples)

cassoliglia: casserole

cervellata: saveloy sausage (dried sausage, usually made from brains)

cialde (or cialdoncini): wafers (or small wafers)

ciambelle: ring-shaped cookies or breads, today usually sweet

ciambuglione (today, zabaione): a heavy concoction based on eggs and sugar

coderone: fleshy part of an animal, nearest the tail, considered a delicacy

confetti (noun): comfits, i.e., seeds or spices coated in hard sugar

confetti (adjective): confected, when applied to other foods (e.g., *fusticelli confetti* were confected sticks of cinnamon)

confetture: preserves; also thick fruit paste; at times, "confections"; see introduction

conserva: jam, preserves

coroncine: literally, small crows; in Latini, probably decorative borders made with various materials

credenza: sideboard, buffet; station where cold dishes were kept and displayed; credenza da mostra was used to display silver, gold, or other precious objects

credenziero (or ripostiero): household official in charge of cold dishes, sweets, lines, silver, plates, etc.; see introduction

crostata: in Latini, usually covered tart, made with flaky, often multilayered, dough, with a sweet or savoury content, and usually shallower than a pie

crostini (in Latini's spelling, sometimes crostine): slices of toasted or grilled bread, today served with various toppings

cuppelletti: small pastries, possibly shaped like hats (possibly also the same as *gubbelletti*)

damaschina: variety of purple plums

dispensiero: stock manager

folgore: a type of bird I have not identified

foresteria: literally, a place to house foreigners; Latini uses the term to refer to guests staying in the household

freselle (or friselle): savoury, twice-baked bread slices

frittata: in Latini, a flat, unrolled omelet, used as a cover or bottom for various dishes, a sort of large pancake in shape and consistency

gileppe (today, *giulebbe): julep,* syrup

ginestrata: egg soup

giuncata: a soft cheese

gnocchi: today, mostly potato dumplings; Latini uses this term for any mixture of ingredients beaten into a paste, cut into small shapes, and cooked in water or broth

impanata: Spanish term Latini uses as synonym of pasticcio, pie

impasticciare/ato: to use/used in a pie, or to prepare/prepared as a pie filling

lasagna: fresh pasta, usually in thin sheets layered with stuffing

lattata: a milk juice, usually consisting of a non-dairy milk (like almond milk), lemon juice, and other ingredients

latte di pesce: literally, fish milk; in fact, seminal fluid; here rendered as soft roe

lattimele: today usually a whipped cream, but in Latini's time probably a mixture of milk and honey

lazzarole: unusual fruit, between a large cherry and a very small apple; well regarded in Latini's time

liccarda: dripping pan

marzolino: semi-hard cheese, typical of Tuscany

mascaroncini: usually, small masks, made of various materials and used as decorations in dishes and banquets; occasionally, I suspect the word appears as a typo for mac-caroncini (small maccheroni)

merausto (from the Catalan *miraus):* traditional sauce with almonds, broth, sugar, verjuice, and spices

mille infanti (or *millefanti):* literally, a thousand children; tiny grains used in various dishes (a sort of couscous)

minestra: stew, or pottage; see introduction

morselletto: morsel (a concentrated food, in Latini usually pastry-like)

mortadella: today, a type of salami, made with ground pork, marbled with pork fat and flavoured with spices; Latini uses the term more broadly for various pork salami

moscarelle (or *moscatelle) pears:* a sweet variety

moscarole: rare variety of pears (possibly, musk-pears)

mostaccere: a kind of cookie similar to "Savoy cookies" (or ladyfingers), not much used in Italy today

mostaccioli: hard, sweet, spiced cookies, often used by Latini as ingredients, especially ground; today in Naples this is primarily a hard cookie typical of Christmas

mosto cotto (at times also called *sapa): cooked* must, i.e., the boiled juice of ripe grapes

muscimano: dried tuna salami

neve: literally, snow, but usually in Latini it refers to shaved ice

offelle: small pastries, usually flat and sweeter than bocconotti

oglia (from the Spanish *olla):* thick, composite stew

padiata: Neapolitan term for the end part of the intestine

pan di Spagna: literally, Spanish bread; light sponge cake, used by Latini as an ingredient in both sweet and savoury dishes; if cooked twice, it became hard, like a biscuit

panesigli: sweet breads

papagnini: poppies, used in decorations for banquets

pappardelle: today, a type of fresh pasta (flat, wide strips); in Latini's time, a type of fritter, typical of Rome

pasta di siringa: literally, dough passed through a pastry bag (here, beignets)

psta frolla: short crust pastry

pasta reale: almond paste

pasticcio: pie, sweet or savoury, usually with a hard crust and a lid (often not to be eaten)

pernigona (or pernicona): variety of purple-green plums

piattini: small plates

peparolo: Neapolitan term for chili pepper

piccatiglio: term of Spanish origins for a ground dish, usually mixing meat and vegetables, often with broth or eggs

pignatta: general name for a cooking pot

pignoccata: cooked pine nuts

pizza: tart, usually uncovered (but not made with flaky, multilayered dough; see *crostata*)

polpa: animal flesh (i.e., meat cleaned of bones, fat, and nerves)

polsonetto (or polzonetto): boiler with a concave bottom, usually made of copper

posata: table setting (today the word refers to tableware)

potaggio (or pottaggio): pottage

provatura: cheese similar to mozzarella

provola: a kind of smoked mozzarella

quadrupedi: quadrupeds (land animals)

ravioli: fresh pasta, often stuffed; when described as "naked," they had no pasta casing (in which sense they were similar to what Latini calls gnocchi)

reggente: Regent, the title of members of the Collateral Council, the main administrative organ in Naples (and also of members of other administrative bodies in the Spanish government)

rifreddi: cold dishes, usually displayed on the table at the start of a banquet, or part of the first credenza service

rosetta: bun (probably initially shaped like a rose)

salsa: sauce, usually thick and added to dishes in the kitchen (vs *sapore*, condiment)

sanguinaccio: in Latini, a sausage-like preparation based on pig (or turtle) blood; today in Italy this is a chocolate-based, very sweet pudding, typical of the Carnival season

sapore: condiment, usually lighter than a sauce, and available for dipping or adding at the table

saporiglia: a casserole or stew, usually including organ meat

savoy cookies (today there is a type of cookie called *savoiardi*, which are ladyfingers): Latini refers to *biscotti/biscottini di Savoia*, although I am not entirely sure that he means ladyfingers

scalco: steward

scapece: Spanish-style preparation (*escabeche*), vinegar marinade

scigotto: gigot, cooked leg; Latini also uses this term for complex preparations (often with ground meat), usually in the shape of an animal leg

sciroppare/to: to cook (or preserve) in sugar syrup/cooked (or preserved) in sugar syrup; see introduction

sciuscello (or scioscello): an egg broth

sflemmata: purified or clarified, specifically said of distilled wine

soffriggere: to sauté (a lighter, quicker process than *friggere*, or to fry)

soppressata: a dry salami

sorbetto: a water-based ice, though at times it could also include dairy or egg

sorsico: extract or juice

sosamelli (or susamielli): hard cookies, in Naples today typical of Christmas

sottestare: to braise (to cook in an earthenware lidded vessel, a *testo*)

spenditore: purchaser

stagnara: cooking vessel made of tin

stamigna: a cloth sieve

struffoli: small balls of dough, covered with honey and sugared treats, today a typical Naples Christmas dessert

tagliolini: long, thin pasta

taralli: circular, braided, or twisted breads, usually hard and savoury

tartara: usually a crustless tart, or baked custard; tartaretta could also be a pastry

tondini: small round plates; also a category of small side dishes

torta: tart, usually uncovered

tortelli (or tortellini or tortelletti): stuffed pasta, today typically with a folded shape

tramontana apple: variety typical of the island of Ischia in the Bay of Naples

tremolanti: decorative cloth strips or ribbons, creating a "trembling," feathery effect

trionfi: grand table decorations (triumphs)

uova faldicchere: egg yolks mixed with sugar, re-formed in the shape of eggs, and baked until they acquire some solidity (from Spanish *faltriquera*, pocket)

uova filate (or misside): eggs dropped into hot sugar from a hole through the egg shell (here rendered as strained eggs)

uova nonnate (or non nate): unborn eggs, the unlaid eggs found inside dead chicken

uova targhe: fish eggs

vermicelli: today, a somewhat thicker type of spaghetti; Latini uses the term for various things in that shape

verrinea: pork product, primarily from sow udder

vivanda: a prepared dish or food

zeppole: airy, fried or baked pastries, today typical in Naples in mid-March

zuppa: soup; see introduction

WORKS CITED

Primary Sources

Altamiras, Juan. *New Art of Cookery: A Spanish Friar's Kitchen Notebook*. Edited and translated by Vicky Hayward. London: Rowman and Littlefield, 2017.

The Annals of Horticulture. London: Cox, 1848.

Anonymous. "La piacevole historia di Cuccagna." *Giambattista Basile: Archivio di letteratura popolare* 2, 11 (November 1884): 84–85.

Capaccio, Giulio Cesare. *Il forastiero*. Naples: Roncagliolo, 1634.

Cestoni, Giuseppe Domenico. *Elementi di agricoltura pratica*. Naples: Zambrano, 1843.

Corrado, Vincenzo. *Il credenziere di buon gusto*. 1778. Repr., Bologna: Forni, 1991.

Corrado, Vincenzo. *Il cuoco galante*. 1786. Repr., Bologna: Forni, 1990.

Crisci, Giovanni Battista. *Lucerna de corteggiani*. Naples: Roncagliolo, 1634.

Cuoco Napoletano: The Neapolitan Recipe Collection. Edited and translated by Terence Scully. Ann Arbor: University of Michigan Press, 2000.

Evitascandalo, Cesare. *Libro dello scalco*. Rome: Vullietti, 1609.

Felici, Costanzo. *Scritti naturalistici: Dell'insalata*. Urbino: Quattroventi, 1986.

Frugoli, Antonio. *Pratica e scalcaria*. 1638. Repr., Bologna: Forni, 2005.

Goethe, Johann Wolfgang von. *Italian Journey*. London: Penguin, 1962.

Latini, Antonio. *Autobiografia (1642–1696), La vita di uno scalco*. Edited by Furio Luccichenti. Rome: Leberit, 1992.

Latini, Antonio. *Lo scalco alla moderna*. 2 vols. Naples: Parrino and Mutii, 1692–94.

Latini, Antonio. *Lo scalco alla moderna*. 2 vols. Facsimile. Lodi: Bibliotheca Culinaria, and Milan: Appunti di Gastronomia, 1993.

Latini, Antonio. *Lo scalco alla moderna*. 2 vols. plus a volume of commentary. Facsimile. Florence: Polistampa, 2004.

Maestro Martino. *The Art of Cooking: The First Modern Cookery Book*. Edited by Luigi Ballerini. Translated by Jeremy Parzen. Berkeley: University of California Press, 2005.

Martínez Montiño, Francisco. *Arte de cocina, pasteleria, vizcocheria, y conserveria*. 1611. Barcelona: Maria Angela Martí, 1763.

Messisbugo, Cristoforo di. *Libro novo*. 1557. Repr., Bologna: Forni, 1980.

Platina, Bartolomeo. *On Right Pleasure and Good Health: A Critical Edition and Translation of De Honesta Voluptate et Valetudine*. Translated by Mary Ella Milham. Tempe: Arizona Center for Medieval and Renaissance Studies, Medieval and Renaissance Texts and Studies, 1998.

Rabasco, Ottaviano. *Il convito*. Florence: Giunti, 1615.

Ray, John. *Travels through the Low-Countries, Germany, Italy, and France*. 1673. London: J. Walthoe, 1738.

Romoli, Domenico (Panunto). *La singolare dottrina*. Venice: Tramezzino, 1560.

Rossetti, Giovan Battista. *Dello scalco*. 1584. Repr., Bologna: Forni, 1991.

Scappi, Bartolomeo. *The Opera (1570)*. Edited and translated by Terence Scully. Toronto: University of Toronto Press, 2008.

Secondo, Giuseppe Maria. *Ciclopedia ovvero dizionario universale delle arti e delle scienze*. Translation of Ephraim Chambers, *Cyclopaedia* of 1728. 8 vols. Naples: De Bonis, 1747–54.

Stefani, Bartolomeo. *L'arte di ben cucinare*. 1662. Repr., Bologna: Forni, 2000.

Secondary Sources

Albala, Ken. *The Banquet, Dining in the Great Courts of Late Renaissance Europe*. Urbana-Champaign: University of Illinois Press, 2007.

——. *Cooking in Europe, 1250–1650*. Westport: Greenwood Press, 2006.

——. *Eating Right in the Renaissance*. Berkeley: University of California Press, 2002.

——. "Insensible Perspiration and Oily Humor: An Eighteenth-Century Controversy over Vegetarianism." *Gastronomica* 2, 3 (summer 2002): 29–36.

——. "Introduction." In *A Cultural History of Food in the Renaissance*, edited by Ken Albala, 1–28. London: Berg, 2012.

Astarita, Tommaso. *Between Salt Water and Holy Water: A History of Southern Italy*. New York: W.W. Norton, 2005.

——. ed. *A Companion to Early Modern Naples*. Leiden: Brill, 2013.

——. *The Italian Baroque Table: Cooking and Entertaining from the Golden Age of Naples*. Tempe: Arizona Center for Medieval and Renaissance Studies, 2014.

Benporat, Claudio. *Storia della gastronomia italiana*. Milan: Mursia, 1990.

Bloom, Carole. "Decorating Pastries and Confections with Gold." In *Look and Feel: Studies in Texture, Appearance, and Incidental Characteristics of Food*. Proceedings of the Oxford Symposium on Food and Cookery 1993. Edited by Harlan Walker, 36–40. Totnes: Prospect, 1994.

Capatti, Alberto and Massimo Montanari. *Italian Cuisine, a Cultural History*. Italian edition 1999. New York: Columbia University Press, 2003.

Cappellieri, Alba. "Filippo e Cristoforo Schor, 'Regi Architetti e ingegneri' alla corte di Napoli." In *Capolavori in festa. Effimero barocco a Largo di Palazzo (1683–1759)*, edited by Giuseppe Zampino, 73–89. Naples: Electa, 1997.

Carrió-Invernizzi, Diana. *El gobierno del las imágenes: Ceremonial y mecenazgo en la Italia española de la segunda mitad del siglo XVII*. Madrid: IberoAmericana, 2008.

Claflin, Kyri W. "Food among the Historians: Early Modern Europe." In *Writing Food History: A Global Perspective*, edited by Claflin and Peter Scholliers, 38–58. London: Berg, 2012.

Cocco, Sean. *Watching Vesuvius: A History of Science and Culture in Early Modern Italy*. Chicago: University of Chicago Press, 2013.

Cogotti, Marina and June di Schino, eds. *Magnificenze a tavola: Le arti del banchetto rinascimentale*. Rome: De Luca, 2012.

Dalby, Andrew. *Dangerous Tastes: The Story of Spices*. Berkeley: University of California Press, 2000.

David, Elizabeth. *Harvest of the Cold Months: The Social History of Ice and Ices*. New York: Viking, 1995.

Davidson, Alan. "Europeans' Wary Encounters with Tomatoes, Potatoes, and Other New World Foods." In *Chilies to Chocolate: Food the Americas Gave the World*, edited by Nelson Foster and Linda S. Cordell, 1–14. Tucson: University of Arizona Press, 1992.

Day, Ivan. *Cooking in Europe, 1650–1850*. Westport: Greenwood Press, 2009.

Debus, Allen G. *The Chemical Philosophy: Paracelsian Science and Medicine in the Sixteenth and Seventeenth Centuries*. 2 vols. New York: Science History Publications, 1977.

Dickie, John. *Delizia! The Epic History of the Italians and Their Food*. New York: The Free Press, 2008.

Di Schino, June. "Il potere della dolcezza, ovvero *Saccharum Triumphans*." In *I fasti del banchetto barocco*, edited by June di Schino, 35–56. Rome: Diomeda, 2005.

Di Schino, June and Furio Luccichenti. *Il cuoco segreto dei papi, Bartolomeo Scappi e la confraternita dei cuochi e dei pasticcieri*. Rome: Gangemi, 2008.

Eiche, Sabine. *Presenting the Turkey*. Florence: Centro Di, 2004.

Estes, J. "Food as Medicine." In *The Cambridge World History of Food*, edited by Kenneth F. Kiple and Kriemhild Coneè Ornelas, 2:1534–53. 2 vols. Cambridge: Cambridge University Press, 2000.

Fabbri Dall'Oglio, Maria Attilia. *Il trionfo dell'effimero, lo sfarzo e il lusso dei banchetti visti nella cornice fastosa delle feste della Roma barocca*. Rome: Ricciardi, 2002.

Faccioli, Emilio, ed. *L'arte della cucina in Italia*. Turin: Einaudi, 1987.

Fagiolo dell'Arco, Maurizio. *La festa barocca*. Rome: De Luca, 1997.

Flandrin, Jean-Louis. "Diététique et gastronomie, XIV–XVIII siècles." In *Voeding en geeneskunde/Alimentation et médecine*, edited by Ria Jansen-Sieben and Frank Daelemans, 177–92. Brussels: Archives et Bibliothèques de Belgique, 1993.

Freedman, Paul. "Food Histories of the Middle Ages." In *Writing Food History: A Global Perspective*, edited by Kyri W. Claflin and Peter Scholliers, 24–37. London: Berg, 2012.

——. *Out of the East: Spices and the Medieval Imagination*. New Haven: Yale University Press, 2008.

Galasso, Giuseppe. *Napoli spagnola dopo Masaniello*. 2 vols. Florence: Sansoni, 1982.

Gentilcore, David. "Body and Soul, or Living Physically in the Kitchen." In *A Cultural History of Food in the Early Modern Age*, edited by Beat Kümin, 143–63. London: Berg, 2012.

——. *Food and Health in Early Modern Europe: Diet, Medicine and Society, 1450–1800*. London: Bloomsbury, 2016.

——. "The Impact of New World Plants, 1500–1800: The Americas in Italy." In *The New World in Early Modern Italy, 1492–1750*, edited by Elizabeth Horodowich and Lia Markey, 190–206. Cambridge: Cambridge University Press, 2017.

——. *Pomodoro! A History of the Tomato in Italy*. New York: Columbia University Press, 2010.

Grewe, Rudolf. "The Arrival of the Tomato in Spain and Italy: Early Recipes." *The Journal of Gastronomy* 3 (1987): 67–82.

Hanson, Kate H. "Visualizing Culinary Culture at the Medici and Farnese Courts." Unpublished PhD diss., University of Southern California, 2010.

Kümin, Beat. "Eating Out in Early Modern Europe." In *A Cultural History of Food in the Early Modern Age*, edited by Beat Kümin, 87–101. London: Berg, 2012.

Labrot, Gérard. "Naissance et croissance d'un quartier de Naples, Pizzofalcone 1530–1689." *Urbi* 1 (1979): 47–66.

Laurioux, Bruno. *Une histoire culinaire du Moyen Age*. Paris: Champion, 2005.

Mancusi Sorrentino, Lejla. *Maccheronea: Storia, aneddoti, proverbi, letteratura, e tante ricette*. Naples: Grimaldi, 2000.

Marino, John A. *Pastoral Economics in the Kingdom of Naples*. Baltimore: Johns Hopkins University Press, 1988.

Mattozzi, Antonio. *Inventing the Pizzeria: A History of Pizza Making in Naples*. Italian edition 2009. London: Bloomsbury Academic, 2015.

McGee, Harold. *On Food and Cooking: The Science and Lore of the Kitchen*. 1984; New York: Scribner, 2004.

McIver, Katherine. *Cooking and Eating in Renaissance Italy: From Kitchen to Table*. London: Rowman and Littlefield, 2015.

Montagu, Jennifer. *Roman Baroque Sculpture: The History of Art*. New Haven: Yale University Press, 1989.

Montanari, Massimo. *Nuovo convivio: Storia e cultura dei piaceri della tavola nell'età moderna*. Bari: Laterza, 1991.

Muto, Giovanni. "Le tante città di una capitale: Napoli nella prima età moderna." *Storia urbana* 32, 123 (April–June 2009): 19–54.

Naddeo, Barbara Ann. "Urban Arcadia: Representations of the 'Dialect' of Naples in Linguistic Theory and Comic Theater, 1696–1780." *Eighteenth-Century Studies* 35 (2001): 41–65.

Nadeau, Carolyn A. *Food Matters: Alonso Quijano's Diet and the Discourse on Food in Early Modern Spain*. Toronto: University of Toronto Press, 2016.

Notaker, Henry. *A History of Cookbooks: From Kitchen to Page Over Seven Centuries*. Berkeley: University of California Press, 2017.

Novelli, Claudio. *Né pomodoro né pasta*. Naples: Grimaldi, 2003.

Parasecoli, Fabio. *Food Culture in Italy*. Westport: Greenwood Press, 2004.

Pennell, Sara. "'Pots and Pans History': The Material Culture of the Kitchen in Early Modern England." *Journal of Design History* 11 (1998): 201–16.

——. "Professional Cooking, Kitchens, and Service Work: *Accomplisht* Cookery." In *A Cultural History of Food in the Early Modern Age*, edited by Beat Kümin, 103–121. London: Berg, 2012.

Peterson, T. Sarah. *Acquired Taste: The French Origins of Modern Cooking*. Ithaca: Cornell University Press, 1994.

Pinkard, Susan. *A Revolution in Taste: The Rise of French Cuisine, 1650–1800*. Cambridge: Cambridge University Press, 2008.

Portincasa, Agnese. *Scrivere di gusto: Una storia della cucina italiana attraverso i ricettari*. Bologna: Pendragon, 2016.

Ricciardi, Emilio. "Il 'Poggio delle Mortelle' nella storia dell'architettura napoletana." Unpublished PhD diss., University of Naples, 2005.

Ridolfi, Pierluigi. *Rinascimento a tavola: La cucina e il banchetto nelle corti italiane*. Rome: Donzelli, 2015.

Rietberger, Peter. *Power and Religion in Baroque Rome: Barberini Cultural Politics*. Leiden: Brill, 2006.

Riley, Gillian. *The Oxford Companion to Italian Food*. Oxford: Oxford University Press, 2007.

Sentieri, Maurizio. "Un'indagine sulle ragioni della persistenza della dietetica galenica lungo l'età preindustriale." In *Alimentazione e nutrizione secoli XIII–XVIII*. Acts of the 28th Settimana di Studi dell'Istituto Francesco Datini di Prato. Edited by Simonetta Cavaciocchi, 787–95. Florence: Le Monnier, 1996.

Sereni, Emilio. "Note di storia dell'alimentazione nel Mezzogiorno: i napoletani da 'mangiafoglia' a 'mangiamaccheroni'." Originally published in the journal *Cronache meridionali* in 1958. Now in Sereni, Emilio. *Terra nuova e buoi rossi*. Turin: Einaudi, 1981.

Serventi, Silvano and Françoise Sabban. *La pasta, storia e cultura di un cibo universale*. Bari: Laterza, 2000.

Siraisi, Nancy. *Medieval and Early Renaissance Medicine: An Introduction to Knowledge and Practice*. Chicago: University of Chicago Press, 1990.

Smith, Pamela H. "Why Write a Book? From Lived Experience to the Written Word in Early Modern Europe." *Bulletin of the German Historical Institute* 47 (fall 2010): 25–50.

Strong, Roy. *Feast: A History of Grand Eating*. New York: Harcourt, 2003.

Takats, Sean. *The Expert Cook in Enlightenment France*. Baltimore: Johns Hopkins University Press, 2011.

Trémolières, J. "A History of Dietetics." *Progress in Food and Nutrition Science* 1, 2 (February 1975): 65–114.

Watts, Sydney. "Enlightened Fasting: Religious Conviction, Scientific Inquiry, and Medical Knowledge in Early Modern France." In *Food and Faith in Christian Culture*, edited by Ken Albala and Trudy Eden, 105–23. New York: Columbia University Press, 2011.

Welch, Evelyn. "Scented Buttons and Perfumed Gloves: Smelling Things in Renaissance Italy." In *Ornamentalism: The Art of Renaissance Accessories*, edited by Bella Mirabella, 13–39. Ann Arbor: University of Michigan Press, 2011.

Zampino, Giuseppe, ed. *Capolavori in festa: Effimero barocco a Largo di Palazzo (1683–1759)*. Naples: Electa, 1997.